So Simple : So Advanced

Insight into
INCOME TAX

Based on Memory Retention Techniques

CONTAINING MOST TYPICAL PRACTICAL QUESTIONS

So Simple : So Advanced

Insight into INCOME TAX

Based on Memory Retention Techniques

CONTAINING MOST TYPICAL PRACTICAL QUESTIONS

Very useful for students pursuing following courses

CA(PE II / PCC) May / Nov. 2007
CS (Inter) or ICWA (Inter) June / Dec. 2007
B.COM. (H.) Delhi University - 2008
B.COM. Students of all other Indian Universities

C.F.A. Students / B.B.A. Students
M.B.A Students / M.COM. Students / IAS Students

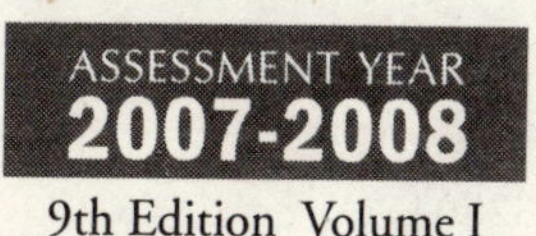

9th Edition Volume I

Kaushal Kumar Agrawal
B.Com. (H); CWA (Inter); ACS
Company Secretary

Insight into Income Tax: Based on Memory Retention Techniques
First Edition, 1999
Second Edition, 2000
Third Edition, 2001
Fourth Edition, 2002
Fifth Edition, 2003
Sixth Edition, 2004
Seventh Edition, 2005
Eighth Edition, 2006
Ninth Edition, 2007

APPLICABLE FOR ASSESSMENT YEAR 2007-08
INCORPORATES AMENDMENT MADE BY FINANCE ACT, 2007. Law in updated upto 1-6-2007.
PRACTICAL PROBLEMS ARE SOLVED AS PER ASSESSMENT YEAR 2007-08

Published by

ATLANTIC

PUBLISHERS & DISTRIBUTORS (P) LTD
B-2, Vishal Enclave, Opp. Rajouri Garden,
New Delhi-110027
Phones : 25413460, 25429987, 25466842

Sales Office
7/22, Ansari Road, Darya Ganj,
New Delhi-110002
Phones : 23273880, 23275880, 23280451
Fax : 91-11-23285873
web : www.atlanticbooks.com
e-mail : info@atlanticbooks.com

Printed in India
at Nice Printing Press

With the Blessings of

Lord Shri Krishna

Hare Krishna Hare Krishna
Krishna Krishna Hare Hare

Hare Ram Hare Ram
Ram Ram Hare Hare

Dedicated to
My dearest son
Anirudh Agrawal

READY REFERENCE

TABLE OF RATES OF TAXATION

	Firm or Domestic Company	Foreign company	Ind/HUF AOP or BOI	Artificial Juridical person
Tax on Long Term Capital gain	20% flat	20% flat	20% flat	20% flat
Tax on Short term Capital Gain (STT paid)	10% flat	10% flat	10% flat	10% flat
Tax on Lottery income etc. (Casual Income)	30% flat	30% flat	30% flat	30% flat
Tax on Normal income	30% flat	40% flat	slab rate	slab rate
Surcharge	10% at all levels of income	2.5% at all levels of income	10% if TI exceeds 10,00,000	10% at all levels of income
Education cess	2% at all levels of income	2% at all levels of income	2% at all levels of income	2% at all levels of income

SLAB RATE (AS PER ANNUAL FINANCE ACT)

Normal Income (NI)	Rate of tax method	Tax Liability method
Upto Rs. 1,00,000	Nil	Nil
Rs. 1,00,001 to 1,50,000	10% of (NI-1,00,000)	10% of NI - 10,000
Rs. 1,50,001 to 2,50,000	20% of (NI - 1,50,000) + 10,000	20% of NI - 25,000
Exceeds Rs. 2,50,000	30% of (NI - 2,50,000) + 25,000	30% of NI - 50,000

COST INFLATION INDEX (CII) OF EACH PY

1981-82	**100**	1988-89	**161**	1995-96	**281**	2002-03	**447**
1982-83	**109**	1989-90	**172**	1996-97	**305**	2003-04	**463**
1983-84	**116**	1990-91	**182**	1997-98	**331**	2004-05	**480**
1984-85	**125**	1991-92	**199**	1998-99	**351**	2005-06	**497**
1985-86	**133**	1992-93	**223**	1999-00	**389**	2006-07	**519**
1986-87	**140**	1993-94	**244**	2000-01	**406**		
1987-88	**150**	1994-95	**259**	2001-02	**426**		

Preface

Income tax is the dynamic, challenging and practical subject concerned with the fiscal implications inherent in the conduct of one's affairs. It is essentially statute based and has, to a large extent, been interpreted by the Court in a number of cases. The tax provisions have been branded by experts as too long and at times too complicated. Many students are filled with trepidation in reading the subject at undergraduate and even professional levels.

The present book *Insight into Income Tax: Based on Memory Retention Techniques,* like its earlier editions, has been designed for both the beginners and the advanced learners of Income Tax, introducing them to the full range of concepts of Income Tax. From the book's inception, three goals have been paramount; first to present the basics of Income Tax in their entirety so that they may be understood in depth; second, to provide user-friendly approach to the subject so as to make it interesting and easily accessible to the average reader; and third, to incorporate the latest tax provisions. The book has been structured into two Volumes, each catering the academic needs of students persuing B.Com. (H/P), CA (PE II), CS (Inter), ICWA (Inter), BBA, MBA, M.Com. or other professional and specialised courses. It is relatively more practical oriented and contains numerous illustrations. In addition, the key points have been particularly demarcated and discussed. In combined form, the book is a complete treatise on Income Tax, covering the syllabi of graduate and professional courses prescribed in several universities across India.

The present work has not been the product of my solo efforts. The active participation of the community of readers, particularly my students, has been of great importance. The remarkable flow of voluntary corrections and suggestions proposed by the readers has improved the standard of the book. Further constructive suggestions are always welcome.

I take this opportunity to thank all those who have directly or indirectly assisted me in completing this work. I particularly acknowledge the cooperation and support rendered by Sh. D.S. Rawat, FCA; Sh. R.K. Mehta, ACA; Sh. S.K. Mittal, FCA; Sh. J.K. Bareja, FCS; Sh. Bibhu Prasad Sahoo, M.Com., M.Phil.; Sh. Sanjay Goel, FCA; Sh. Mahesh K. Gopalika, B.Sc. (Stats), M.Com.; Sh. Atul Mittal, FCS; Sh. Mukesh Gupta, B.Com. (H); Sh. S.K. Monga, M.Com., FICW; Sh. Saurabh Bansal, Faculty in Income Tax; Sh. Vishal Kumar Kejriwal, B.Com. (H), CA (Inter); Sh. Saroj Kumar, B.Sc. (H), CA (Inter); Sh. Sudhir Jain, ACS;

Smt. Suman Agrawal, B.E. (Computer Technology); Sh. Anup Agrawal, FCA; Sh. Ajay Agrawal, FCA; and Sh. Pinaki Banerjee, ACS.

Last but not least, I express my gratitude to Mr. Manish Gupta, Managing Director and Mr. Ashish Gupta, Executive Director, Atlantic Publishers and Distributors (P) Ltd., for publishing my book in short time span.

Kaushal Kumar Agrawal

Residential Address	170, Nimri Colony, Ashok Vihar, Delhi 110 052 Ph. No. 011-27304460 (R); 011-98186-71320 (M)
Office Address	Matrix, 2576, Hudson Lane, Delhi 110 007. Tel. 011-27414532
E. Mail	kaushalagrawal@yahoo.com

CONTENTS

A Few Words to Students of Income Tax

Income tax is the most difficult subject to understand
— Albert Einstein

Income Tax has all along been projected to be the most difficult subject. And it is correct also. One has always wanted to get behind this curtain to experience the subject. All along, you find the complexities of tax laws hard to digest. Though there are innumerable books on tax available but none which projects the tax in a simplified manner — manner in which income tax can be thoroughly understood. Therefore, just to fill this gap and create an interest and confidence among students, this book helps in providing a complete base on tax. The book also makes an attempt to simplify and structure the otherwise complex Income Tax by applying simple Memory Retention Techniques.

At this point I can say with a firm belief that it is a complete treatise which will not only help you understand and memorise Income Tax but also be your proud possession for ever. It is not my opinion only, rather such has been endorsed by many of the students who have referred to this book. A few of the students' opinions provided on the inside page of the book only confirm this fact.

IMPORTANCE OF INCOME TAX

Income Tax is the single most important subject in CA (PE II/PCC) after Accounts. After becoming CA you may either practice accounts or tax or both. Every individual as well as company, be it a multinational or small firm, seeks advice on tax from the Chartered Accountants. A thorough understanding of this book may open ways to earn dollars and reputation and thereby lead a comfortable life.

PATH TOWARDS INCOME TAX

We seriously believe that Income Tax can never be wholly understood at one go. There is a very popular and time tested idea that if you want to understand something which is detailed and complicated, you must structure it in a point-wise fashion. In this way even the bulky looks simple and concise.

Following this idea we have structured Income Tax in two parts. Volume 1 aims at providing a proper understanding of the basics of Income Tax while Volume 2 serves the purpose of an ideal reference source as it makes an in-depth study of all the concepts related to Income Tax. Complementary to each other, the two Volumes are indispensable for all CA (PE II/PCC) students [For detail see about the book].

TECHNIQUES OF UNDERSTANDING & MEMORISING INCOME TAX

Every subject has its own techniques of understanding. Like Accounts needs practice and Income Tax needs memory. There are five steps towards understanding Income Tax.

First step : Knowing and understanding the provisions.

Second step : Knowing and understanding the logic behind every provision.

Third step : Applying the provisions and practising the questions based on provisions.

Fourth step : Memorising the provisions with sections.

Fifth step : Revising and again memorising the provisions with sections.

If you follow the above steps seriously you shall one day become master of Income Tax. Take my word.

MY STUDENTS - THROUGH BOOK, CLASSES OR E-MAIL

I am grateful to my students who are my most precious assets. I hope to be blessed with many more. Thank you very much for pointing out my errors and suggesting the improvements. I am a cogent learner but have certain limitations. Please accept my gratitude.

And, all my dear students, this collection of finest quotations is for you. This has been aptly titled — FOR YOUR MIND. I hope you will certainly understand its meaning in letter and in spirit.

Also, the question — WHO BURDENED YOU WITH INCOME TAX? is of great concern. You know I can never ever attempt to do this.

FOR YOUR MIND

If step by step you can keep your mind clear then nothing will confuse you.

The brighter you are more you have to learn.

Tell me and I will forget,
Show me and I may not remember,
Involve me and I will understand.

Without understanding we cannot see even if we look,
we cannot hear even if we listen, and
we cannot taste even if we eat.

The big do not eat small, it is the fast who eats the slow.

Speed is also the essence; forget slow and steady. You have to learn to move fast. What you give up in terms of perfection, you will gain in terms of speed. And if you fail, again your test will be how fast you can learn, how fast you pick yourself up, dust yourself off, and get on with it.

A price has to be paid for scoring the highest marks or passing a professional exam or for success. Almost invariably those who have reached summits worked harder and longer, studied and planned more assiduously, practised more self-denial, overcame more difficulties than those of us who have not risen so far.

Success is how high you jump when you hit the bottom.

The skill of memory requires that you store things properly so you can later on retrieve them properly.

WHO BURDENED YOU WITH INCOME TAX?

Income tax was introduced for the first time to the world in Britain by Pitt, the younger, in the year 1799 . Tax on income was accepted without enthusiasm as a temporary means to raise money for the Napoleanic wars and was allowed to lapse in 1815, after Waterloo. In the USA also, it came as a temporary measure to bolster flagging revenues during the Civil War in 1861 and was repealed in 1871. In Britain it was revived (again as a temporary measure) by Sir Robert Peel in 1842, to avoid budget deficits while carrying on major tariff reforms. It was only by 1910 that Income Tax was made permanent in Germany, France, Italy, Norway and Sweden and of course in India in 1921.

FOR YOUR SUCCESS
Kaushal Kumar Agrawal

Earn Income : Pay Taxes

1

Basic Concepts

START

TOPIC 1.00 *SECTION 4.* WHAT ARE THE CONDITIONS TO BE SATISFIED TO LEVY INCOME TAX (BASIS OF CHARGE)

Section 4 is the charging section. It is the backbone of the law of Income Tax. In its absence, the other provisions of the Income Tax Act are not applicable. The provisions of section 4 are:

(1) It says that income tax shall be charged for any assessment year at the rates specified for the relevant assessment year in respect of the total income of the previous year of every person.

(2) In respect of income chargeable under section 4(1), income tax shall be deducted at the source or paid in advance, where it is so deductible or payable under any provision of this Act.

From the above following statements are concluded that

1. There must be an *income* and that income must be taxable, *i.e.* it should not be exempted income on which tax is not levied.
2. The total income should be computed for each financial year, which is also known as *Previous Year*. The tax on income of the previous year is levied in the *Assessment Year* at the rates specified in the Annual Finance Act.
3. The total income should be computed by the *method of accounting* employed by the taxpayer or any specific method specified under the Income Tax Act.
4. The tax shall be levied on every *person* who earns the income. The person may be Indian citizen or Foreign citizen or may be resident in India or Non-resident in India.
5. The *person* is an *assessee* as defined under the Income Tax Act.

If all the above said conditions are satisfied, a charge (tax) is levied on income. In the following topics we shall define the above-noted italicised words.

TOPIC 1.01 CONCEPT OF INCOME

Income tax is the tax levied on *income*. The taxpayer has to pay the tax on what he gets or he earns or he receives. It is not necessary that every receipt be treated as income. In this connection income is divided into two categories:

1. Revenue receipt; and
2. Capital receipt.

It is first essential to distinguish these two concepts. Let us see how.

You get something	*from*	*a source of income*
Fruits	from	trees
Crops	from	fields
Cloths	from	machinery
Salary	from rendering of	services
Rent	from	House Property
Profit	by undertaking	business activities
Interest	from	investments
Royalty	from	knowledge

Meaning of revenue receipt	*Meaning of capital receipt*
Fruits, Crops, Cloths, Salary, Rent, Profit, Interest & Royalty are treated as revenue receipt. For every revenue receipt there exists a source of income. That source of income may be a tangible asset or an intangible asset. As you can see that fruits are generated from trees. Therefore tree acts as a *source of income for* fruits. Similarly, rent is generated by letting out a house property *(source of income),* and therefore same can be said for cloths, salary, interest etc. All these receipts have source of income.	Trees, fields, machinery, services, house property, business activities, loans & knowledge are treated as source of income. Receipts for which there does not exist a source of income is a capital receipt. Also receipts arising by sale of source of income can be said to be capital receipt. e.g. sale of trees along with its roots or sale of property. They are all termed as capital receipt.

NOW THE RULES OF TAXABILITY OF REVENUE RECEIPT AND CAPITAL RECEIPT

(i) Rule 1 Is revenue receipt always taxable?

A. Every revenue receipt is taxable, unless otherwise expressly exempted under the Act. There are certain revenue receipts which are taxable but have been made exempted from tax under section 10. Do note that section 10 specifies certain incomes which are exempt from tax.

E.g. 1 Agricultural income though revenue receipt has been made specifically exempt from tax under section 10(1).

E.g. 2 Interest from Gold deposit bonds is a revenue receipt since source of income is Bond. As you know every revenue receipt is taxable but interest from Gold deposit bonds has been made specifically exempt from tax under section 10(15).

E.g. 3 Dividend received from domestic company is a revenue receipt since source of income is shares. As you know every revenue receipt is taxable but dividend from domestic company has been made specifically exempt from tax under section 10(34).

(ii) Rule 2 Is capital receipt always taxable?

Every capital receipt is exempted from tax unless otherwise expressly taxable. Certain capital receipts which are not taxable but have been made taxable under section 45.

E.g. 1 Transfer of a capital asset is treated as capital receipt since source of income itself is being sold but still chargeable to tax under section 45.

ANOTHER QUESTION

Is accident compensation taxable? The answer shall depend whether the accident compensation is a revenue receipt or a capital receipt. For accident compensation receipt, there does not exists any source of income, therefore such receipt is treated as capital receipt. Further such receipt is not from transfer of a capital asset, therefore not taxable.

Are personal gifts taxable? No, since personal gifts are treated as capital receipt for which there does not exists source of income and therefore not taxable. However, gifts from non-relatives are specifically made taxable.

However following gifts are treated as revenue receipt and hence taxable.

1. Gifts received by employee from employer taxable under the head 'Salary'.
2. Professional gifts are taxable under the head 'Business'. *E.g.* Gifts received by lawyer, doctor etc., from his client.

MEANING OF REVENUE EXPENDITURE AND CAPITAL EXPENDITURE

Meaning of revenue expenditure It can be said that any expenditure incurred for maintenance of source of income is termed as revenue expenditure.

Meaning of capital expenditure It can be said that any expenditure incurred for acquisition of source of income is termed as capital expenditure.

TWO MORE QUESTIONS

What is taxable? 'Receipt' or 'Income'; 'Sale' or 'Sale minus purchase'.

Yes, you are right, 'income' is taxable, 'sale minus purchase' is taxable. But how do you compute income? One way is that you subtract purchase from sale. But why are you subtracting purchase? Since there is a sale only due to purchase. No purchase No sale. Therefore you can say that any expenditure incurred in earning income should be allowed as deduction, *i.e.* revenue expenditure should be subtracted from revenue receipts if such revenue expenditure is incurred in earning such revenue receipts. Similarly capital expenditure should be allowed as deduction from capital receipts, if such capital expenditure is incurred for generating such capital receipts.

For the purpose of simplification income is classified into five heads on the basis of source of income. Let us see how.

1. Revenue receipt – Revenue expenditure = Income. This income is divided into 4 heads. They are Income from Salary, Income from House Property, Profits and Gains from Business or Profession and Income from Other Sources.
2. Capital receipt – Capital expenditure = Income. This income is known as Capital Gain.

Now you know that there are five heads of income. It means you are required to compute five sets of profit and loss account unlike in accountancy where you prepare only one profit and loss account.

The concept of classification of income into each of the heads is very important. Since if any income is charged into a particular head, that income cannot further be charged under any other head. Moreover, specific deductions are permissible under a particular head of income. Wrong classification shall lead to wrong computation of income.

All the 5 heads are added to get the Gross Total Income. From this Gross Total Income deductions u/s 80C to 80U are allowed and we get Total Income. On this total income tax is levied at the rate mentioned in the Income Tax Act and Annual Finance Act. Let us see this mathematically.

Computation of total income

Revenue receipt – Revenue expenditure = Income *(4 heads)*	51,000
Capital receipt – Capital expenditure = Income *(Capital Gain)*	9,000
Gross Total Income	60,000
Less Deduction u/s 80C to 80U	5,000
Total income	55,000

Illustration 1.01-P1 (Simple)

Mr. Taxcrazy participated for the first time in a music conference as an amateur and entertained the audience. A listener was so moved that he gave a cash prize of Rs. 5,00,000 to Mr. Taxcrazy. Is the income taxable in the hands of Mr. Taxcrazy?

Solution

No since it is capital receipt. But if a professional musician and singer like Kailash Kher entertains the audience, then it shall be treated as revenue receipt since such receipt is in exercise of a profession and therefore is taxable.

Problem 1.01-P2 [DU (H.) 1995] [Q.5b(i)] [M4]

Miss K suffered multiple injuries in a road accident while travelling in Delhi Transport Corporation bus. She was paid compensation of Rs. 1,50,000. She spent about Rs. 65,000 on her medical treatment. The Assessing Officer wants to assess her on the balance amount of Rs. 85,000. He is of the view that the definition of the "Income" under section 2(24) is inclusive and not exhaustive. Anything which can be properly described as 'income is taxable unless exempted under the Act.' Do you agree with the contention of the Assessing Officer? Give reasons in support of your answer.

Ans: No, Accident compensation is a capital receipt therefore not taxable.

TOPIC 1.02 FEATURES OF INCOME

1. A person cannot earn income from himself. The income must come from outside.
2. Income Tax Act does not differentiate between legal income and illegal income, and therefore income from illegal activity is also taxable.
3. Income may be received in cash or in kind.
4. Application of income is not deductible in computing total income. Like incurring personal expenses is treated as application of income since it is an expenditure out of income.
5. *Basis of recognition of income* Income can be taxed either on accrual basis or on receipt basis or as per the specific method provided in Income Tax Act.
6. As per section 14 all incomes for the purpose of computation of total income are classified into five heads.
7. Income includes loss also.

Problem 1.02-P1

1. Explain concept of income in brief?

2. When you should file your return of income for the AY 2007-08?
3. In which year income is computed and taxable?
4. Who earns income?
5. Who pays taxes?

Solution

1. Income is either revenue in nature or capital in nature. Income may be taxable or exempted depending upon the specific provisions of the Income Tax Act.
2. It is either on or before 31-7-2007 or on or before 31-10-2007 depending upon case to case basis.
3. Income is computed for the financial year and tax is paid in year immediately succeeding financial year known as assessment year.
4. Person.
5. An assessee.

DEFINITIONS

Meaning of inclusive definition When the definition clause uses the word 'include' it signifies that the legislature wants to enlarge the natural meaning of a word. It is an open door definition.

Meaning of exhaustive definition When the definition clause uses the word 'means' it signifies that the legislature wants to exhaust or limit the significance of a word. It is a closed door definition.

TOPIC 1.03 DEFINE ASSESSMENT YEAR AND PREVIOUS YEAR

(A) SECTION 2(9). ASSESSMENT YEAR

Assessment Year means the period of 12 months commencing on the 1st day of April every year. It means the date of commencement of assessment year shall be 1st of April and ending on 31st of March.

For example, assessment year 2007-08 shall commence from 1-4-2007 and shall end on 31-3-2008.

(B) SECTION 2(34) & 3. PREVIOUS YEAR

Section 2(34) Previous Year means the previous year as defined in section 3.

Section 3 Previous year means the financial year immediately preceding the assessment year. For example, for the assessment year 2007-08 previous year shall be 2006-07 and for AY 2006-07, previous year shall be financial year 2005-06.

Determination of first previous year In the case of a source of income newly comes into existence, in the said financial year, the previous year shall be the period beginning with the date on which the source of income newly comes into existence and ending with the said financial year. For example, Mr. X starts a new business on 1-7-2006, its first previous year for the assessment year 2007-08 shall commence from 1-7-2006 and shall end on 31-3-2007. However, subsequent previous year shall start from 1st of April 2007 and shall end on 31st of March 2008.

Note: As many source of income as many previous year but one assessment year.

Illustration 1.03-P1

Mr. Taxcrazy starts a new concern on 2-2-2007. Determine its previous year in relation to assessment year 2007-08 and 2008-09. He has no other source of income.

Solution

Previous year	*Assessment year*
2-2-2007 to 31-3-2007 (2006-7)	1-4-2007 to 31-3-2008 (2007-08)
1-4-2007 to 31-3-2008 (2007-08)	1-4-2008 to 31-3-2009 (2008-09)

Illustration 1.03-P2

Mr. Taxcrazy has regular income from salary and business since 1998. On 13-12-2006 he opens a fixed deposit account to earn interest. Determine its previous year for assessment year 2007-08.

Solution

For salary and business, the previous year is 1-4-2006 to 31-3-2007

For interest on fixed deposits, the previous year is 13-12-2006 to 31-3-2007

Illustration 1.03-P3

A Firm has set up its business on 24-11-2005, though it commenced its operations from 10-1-2007. Determine its first previous year and its assessment year.

Solution

Previous year depends upon the existence of source of income. Its source of income came into existence on 24-11-2005. Therefore its first previous year shall be from 24-11-2005 to 31-3-2006 and its assessment year shall be from 1-4-2006 to 31-3-2007.

Problem 1.03-P4

Mention in which previous year these dates fall and also their assessment year (1) 15-5-2006 (2) 1-1-1999 (3) 11-2-2007 (4) 1-4-2001.

Ans: (1) PY 2006-07 & AY 2007-08; (2) PY 1998-99 & AY 99-2000; (3) PY 2006-07 & AY 2007-08; (4) PY 2001-02 & AY 2002-03.

Problem 1.03-P5

Determine which period is treated as previous year for assessment year 2007-08.

1. Mr. X bought a house on 1-12-2006 and let it out at Rs. 5,000 p.m.
2. X (P) Ltd. a company registered in England keeps his account on calendar year basis.
3. X Ltd. started its business since 1956 but has prepared his final accounts on 30-9-2007.

Ans: (1) 1-12-2006 to 31-3-2007; (2) 1-4-2006 to 31-3-2007; (3) 1-4-2006 to 31-3-2007.

DISTINGUISH BETWEEN ASSESSMENT YEAR AND PREVIOUS YEAR

Assessment year	*Previous year*
Assessment year is the year in which tax is paid.	Previous year is the year in which income is earned.
Assessment year succeeds previous year.	Previous year precedes assessment year.
Assessment year always starts from 1st of April and ends on 31st of March.	All previous year whether first or subsequent shall always end on 31st of March. However start of first previous year shall depend upon the existence of source of income.
The period of assessment year is fixed 12 months.	The period of previous year is of maximum of 12 months. It can exist even for a day if the source of income newly coming into existence, in the said financial year, *i.e.* on 31st March.

(C) EXCEPTIONS WHEN INCOME OF PREVIOUS YEAR IS NOT TAXABLE IN THE IMMEDIATELY FOLLOWING ASSESSMENT YEAR, *i.e.* INCOME OF PREVIOUS YEAR IS ASSESSED IN THE SAME PREVIOUS YEAR ITSELF

Generally income of the previous year is assessed in the assessment year. It means that income of the previous year 2006-07 shall become taxable in the assessment year 2007-08. But in following 5 exceptions, income of the previous year 2006-07 gets taxable in the previous year 2006-07 itself.

1. *Section 172* Income of *a Non Resident* shipping companies who may or may not be having representative or agent in India.
2. *Section 174* Income of persons leaving India either *permanently* or for a *long* period of time.
3. *Section 174A* Assessment of association of persons or body of individuals or artificial juridical persons formed for a particular purpose and for a short duration (*i.e. likely to be dissolved in the same year of formation*).
4. *Section 175* Income of a person trying to *alienate* his assets with a view to *avoid* tax (*There is a mala fide intention*).
5. *Section 176* Income of a *discontinued* business or profession.

Problem 1.03-P6

Mr. Sumantra Ghosal made arrangement for leaving India without Income-tax clearance on 31-7-2006 to join as a lecturer in the University of Italy. He had earned salary income @ Rs. 30,000 p.m. upto 31-7-2006. On receiving the information Assessing Officer proposes to assess his income on 31-7-2006. But Mr. Sumantra Ghosal objected to it with the argument that the previous year is not yet completed. Is the argument valid?

Solution

In view of section 174 of the Income Tax Act, the argument of the assessee is not tenable. Under that section the previous year and the assessment year is same year in respect of income of a person intending to leave India with no immediate intention to return. Accordingly, income tax proceeding initiated by the Assessing Officer for the assessment of his income during the previous year is valid in law.

Problem 1.03-P7 [DU (H) 2006] [M2]

Explain "Income tax is assessed on the income of the previous year in the next assessment year". State the exceptions to this rule.

Hint: Section 2(9), 3 and Section 172 to 176

Problem 1.03-P8 [DU (P) 2006C] [M2]

Choose the correct answer in the following cases : X 'leaves' India permanently on 1st Sept. 2005, The assessment year in this case shall be : (i) 2005-06 (ii) 2006-07 (iii) 2007-08

Ans: AY 2005-06

Problem 1.03-P9

1 What is the general rule of taxation?
2. What will be the period of the previous year for the AY 2007-08?
3. Can a calendar year be treated as previous year?
4. In general, financial year is the previous year and not assessment year, but in certain situations financial year also acts as the assessment year. When?
5. When income of the financial year is taxed in the previous year?
6. What is the meaning of return of income and when the return of income should be filed?

Solution

1. Income of the previous year is assessed or taxed in the assessment year.
2. 12 months.
3. No, previous year shall always be financial year and not calendar year.
4. When the assessee falls in exception to the previous year in such case financial year is previous year and assessment year both.
5. When the assessee falls in exception to the previous year.
6. Return of income is statement of total income and statement of tax liability. The return of income should be filed either on:

   a. 31st July of the relevant assessment year; or

   b. 31st October of the relevant assessment year.

   The due dates of filing of return vary from assessee to assessee. For the time being just memorise these two dates (Details are discussed in Chapter 'Filing of return').

TOPIC 1.04 *SECTION 2(31).* DEFINITION OF PERSON

There are 7 categories of persons on whom tax is levied. All taxes are collected through persons. It is a single unit of taxation and it includes:

	Person	Definition	Who has Control and Management of business
(i)	Individual	Natural person, living person[1]	Individual
(ii)	Hindu Undivided Family (HUF)	Lineally descended from a common ancestor (family *means a group of persons related by blood or marriage)*[2]	Karta or its Co-Parceners
(iii)	Company	Artificial person	Board of Directors
(iv)	Firm	A separate legal entity	Partners
(v)	Association of persons or body of individuals	Refer note below[3] *E.g.* Society	Principal Officer
(vi)	Local Authority	Meaning[4] *E.g.* Municipal Authority	Principal Officer/ District Board
(vii)	Every artificial juridical person not falling within any of the preceding categories. *E.g.* Deities, Mandir, Gurudwara, Mosque, Bar Council, Universities. Such persons are not natural person and has separate legal entity in the eyes of law and may not be directly sued in a court of law but they can be sued through persons managing it. Such person has been provided exemption from payment of tax under section 10.		

Note:

1. Individual includes male, female, minor or a person of unsound mind. In case of minor or a person of unsound mind assessment in such case is made u/s 161 on the guardian or manger of the minor or lunatic. In case of deceased person assessment is made on legal representative.
2. A HUF consists of all person and includes their wives and unmarried daughters. HUF do not includes Christians and Muslims.
3. It is a joint venture between two or more persons which is not a HUF, which is not firm and which is not company. The association may or may not be formed for profit motive. The AOP or BOI may or may not be incorporated. Where a BOI is incorporated under Society Registration Act, then it is referred to as a society. Co-heirs, co-legatees or co-donees joining together for a common purpose or action is assessed as an AOP. Executors or trustees who merely receive the income jointly shall be assessed as BOI.
4. Section 3(31) of the General Clauses Act 'Local Authority' shall mean a municipal committee, district board, body of port commissioners or other authority legally entitled to, or entrusted by the Government with, the control and management of a municipal or local fund. Local authority is taxable in respect of that part of its total income which arises from any business carried on by it in so far as that income does not arise from the supply of commodity or service within its own jurisdictional area. However, income arising from the supply of water and electricity even outside the local authority's own jurisdictional areas is exempt from tax.

Problem 1.04-P1

Determine the status of the following:

1. Mr. Taxcrazy, a sole proprietor of the business.

2. Mr. Taxcrazy, practising Company Secretary.
3. Mr. Taxcrazy, a Chartered Accountant in employment.
4. A joint family of Mr. Taxcrazy, Mrs. Taxcrazy and his son.
5. Balaji Ltd.
6. A joint venture of Mr. X and SS Ltd.
7. Mysore Municipal Corporation.
8. Delhi University.
9. E and F who are legal heirs of G (G died in 2002 and E and F are carrying on a business without entering into a partnership).
10. X and Y get itself registered under the Society Registration Act, 1860.

Ans: Ind; Ind; Ind; HUF; Company or corporate assessee; AOP; Local Authority; Artificial juridical person; Unincorporated BOI; Incorporated BOI.

TOPIC 1.05 *SECTION 2(7)*. MEANING OF AN ASSESSEE

Assessee means a *person* by whom any tax or any other sum of money *(interest, penalty etc.)* is payable under this Act and includes the following:

1. Every person in respect of whom any proceeding under the Income Tax Act has been taken for the assessment of

   his income or assessment of fringe benefit tax, or

   the income of any other person in respect of whom he is assessable, or

   the loss sustained by him or by such other person, or

   the amount of refund due to him or to such other person.

   E.g. The guardian of a minor is assessed on the income of minor.
2. A deemed assessee (In this case a person is treated as an assessee only in the eyes of law), *e.g.*
   a. *Section 159* A legal representative who is deemed to be the assessee in respect of the assessment of the person who is dead.
   b. *Section 160* A representative of a non-resident person.
   c. A representative of a minor child.
   d. A trustee of a trust.
3. Every person who is deemed to be an assessee in default. Where a person does not comply with his statutory duties, *e.g.*
   a. A person failing to deduct tax at source under the Act; or
   b. Has deducted but failed to deposit it with the Govt. *Section 201(1)*

Note

- To be liable to pay tax every assessee should be a "person", but every person need not be an assessee.

Problem 1.05-P1 (CA - N98) Marks 3

Q.2a(ii) A single letter of enquiry was issued by the Income Tax Department to X of Pune. In this letter there was no specific mention of any provision of the Income Tax Act. Can X be treated as an 'assessee'?

Ans: No, since specific provision of income tax act has not been mentioned.

Problem 1.05-P2

1. Who are assessee?
2. Mr. X earns an income of Rs. 1,00,000 during the FY 2006-07 and Rs. 1,80,000 during the FY 2007-08. Determine whether he is an assessee for FY 2006-07 and FY 2007-08?
3. X agrees to pay income tax of Y. Can X be treated as an assessee?
4. When is a company treated as an assessee?

Solution

1. A person who is liable to pay tax or any other sum of money; or
   A person against whom any income tax proceedings have been initiated; or
   A deemed assessee; or
   An assessee in default.
2. Mr. X is a person but not an assessee during the FY 2006-07. However, in the FY 2007-08 Mr. X is a person and an assessee both.
3. No, since department is not a party to the contract.
4. Always, whether the company earns an income or generates loss it is always treated as an assessee, since the company is required to file its return of income even if there is a loss.

RATES OF TAX

TOPIC 1.06 RATES OF TAX LEVIED ON DIFFERENT TYPES OF INCOME ON FOLLOWING PERSONS

(A) SPECIAL INCOMES SUBJECTED TO SPECIAL RATES OF TAX

Special incomes are those incomes which are subjected to special rates of tax. Special rates of tax can also be called concessional rates of tax since here tax is lower than normal rates of tax of 30% or 40%. Special incomes are of 2 types which are:

a. Short term capital gain (STCG). It is where securities transaction tax (STT) is paid. It is subjected to 10% flat rate. But where securities transaction tax is not applicable then such short term capital gain is subjected to normal rates of tax.
b. Long term capital gain (LTCG). It is subjected to two types of rates either 10% or 20% depending upon case to case but never at normal rates. We shall discuss this later. Right now just know that long term capital gain is subjected to 20%. However, Long term capital gain subjected to securities transaction tax is fully exempt from tax u/s 10(38).

Do remember special rates of tax are same on all kinds of assessee whether corporate assessee or non-corporate assessee.

(B) CASUAL INCOME SUBJECTED TO HIGH RATE OF TAX

Casual Income are windfall gains, like income from gambling, races, lotteries, TV game show etc. It is subjected to 30% flat rate on all kinds of assessee whether corporate assessee or non-corporate assessee, whether resident or non-resident.

(C) NORMAL INCOMES SUBJECTED TO NORMAL RATES OF TAX

Any income other than special income and casual income is normal income. Normal income is subjected to normal rates of tax which differ from assessee to assessee unlike in special income or casual income which is same from assessee to assessee. Individual, HUF etc., earning normal income are subjected to slab rate whereas normal income of firm and company are subjected to flat rate.

(D) TABLE OF RATES OF TAXATION

	Firm or Domestic Company	Foreign Company	Ind/HUF AOP or BOI	Artificial Juridical Person
Tax on Long-term Capital Gain	20% flat	20% flat	20% flat	20% flat
Tax on Short-term Capital Gain (STT paid)	10% flat	10% flat	10% flat	10% flat
Tax on Lottery income etc. (Casual Income)	30% flat	30% flat	30% flat	30% flat
Tax on Normal income	30% flat	40% flat	slab rate	slab rate
Rebate u/s 88E	Available	Available	Available	Available
Surcharge	10% at all levels of income	2.5% at all levels of income	10% if TI exceeds 10,00,000	10% at all levels of income
Whether marginal relief available	No	No	Yes	No
Education cess	2% at all levels of income	2% at all levels of income	2% at all levels of income	2% at all levels of income

(E) SLAB RATE (AS PER ANNUAL FINANCE ACT)

Normal Income (NI)	Rate of tax method	Tax liability method
Upto Rs. 1,00,000	Nil	Nil
Rs. 1,00,001 to 1,50,000	10% of the amount by which normal income exceeds Rs. 1,00,000 *i.e.* 10% of (NI-1,00,000)	by solving we get 10% of NI - 10,000
Rs. 1,50,001 to 2,50,000	20% of the amount by which NI exceeds 1,50,000 + 5,000 *i.e.* 20% of (NI - 1,50,000) + 5,000	by solving we get 20% of NI - 25,000
Exceeds Rs. 2,50,000	30% of the amount by which NI exceeds 2,50,000 + 25,000 *i.e.* 30% of (NI - 2,50,000) + 25,000	by solving we get 30% of NI - 50,000

E.g. Suppose your income is Rs. 3,00,000. If you follow rate of tax method, then tax = 30% of 50,000 + 25,000 = 40,000. In case of tax liability method 30% of 3,00,000 – 50,000 = 40,000. You may follow any one of the methods for computation of tax. Both the

methods shall give you the same result of tax computation. We recommend tax liability method since it is simpler and fast way to compute the tax.
However, following assessee can claim concession on account of tax on normal income at following rates:

CONCESSION IN TAX ALLOWED TO RESIDENT WOMAN AND SENIOR CITIZEN

Resident woman	*Resident senior citizen*
In case of a resident woman assessee who is below the age of 65 years at any time during the relevant previous year is not liable for payment of tax upto a normal income of Rs. 1,35,000. If the above income of Rs. 1,35,000 is put in individual slab rate, a resident woman is entitled to a maximum of Rs. 3,500 concession in tax.	In case of a resident individual who has attained the age of 65 years at any time during the relevant previous year is not liable for payment of tax upto a normal income of Rs. 1,85,000. If the above income of Rs. 1,85,000 is put in individual slab rate, a resident senior citizen is entitled to a maximum of Rs. 12,000 concession in tax.

Note : Concession in tax is allowed only from tax on normal income and not from tax on special income and tax on casual income.

ENUMERATE THE BASIC EXEMPTIONS ALLOWED TO VARIOUS ASSESSEES AND TAX CONCESSIONS IF ANY

Assessees	*Basic exemption*	*Tax concession*
1. Firm and company	nil	nil
2. HUF, AOP, BOI and AJP	1,00,000	nil
3. Individual	1,00,000	nil
4. Resident woman	1,35,000	max Rs. 3,500
5. Resident senior citizen	1,85,000	max Rs. 12,000

Illustration 1.06-P1

Compute tax liability of (i) individual (ii) resident woman and (iii) resident senior citizen for the assessment year 2007-08.

	Case 1	*Case 2*	*Case 3*	*Case 4*	*Case 5*
Normal Income	1,30,000	1,40,000	1,80,000	1,90,000	5,00,000

Solution

	Individual *Tax (no concession)*	*Resident woman* *Tax – Rs.3,500*	*Resident senior citizen* *Tax – Rs. 12,000*
Case 1	3,000	nil	nil
Case 2	4,000	500	nil
Case 3	11,000	7,500	nil
Case 4	13,000	9,500	1,000
Case 5	1,00,000	96,500	88,000

Illustration and Problems 1.06-P2

(A) Compute total income and tax liability of (i) firm or domestic company (ii) foreign company (iii) individual, HUF, AOP, BOI and (iv) AJP from the following information for the assessment year 2007-08.

	Case 1	*Case 2*	*Case 3*	*Case 4*
Long Term Capital Gain	10,000	1,00,000	54,000	nil
Long Term Capital Gain (STT paid)	1,50,000	5,40,000	6,000	45,000
Short Term Capital Gain (STT paid)	40,000	5,41,200	14,500	1,20,000
Short Term Capital Gain	5,000	3,10,000	87,000	10,000
Income from TV game show	5,000	2,50,000	60,000	nil
Dividend from Indian Company	5,000	30,000	8,000	12,000
Other Income	1,54,000	4,09,000	58,000	1,45,000
Deduction u/s 80G	4,000	9,000	8,000	5,000

(B) Also compute tax for (i) resident woman and (ii) resident senior citizen.

Ans: (A) (1) 60,588; 72,662; 13,770; 15,147 (2) 4,06,299; 4,52,827; 3,50,199; 3,50,199 (3) 80,055; 88,920; 34,629; 38,092 (4) 63,954; 75,276; 17,340; 19,074 (B) (1) 10,200; 7,650 (2) 3,46,272; 3,36,735 (3) 31,059; 30,855 (4) 13,770; 12,240

Solution: Case 1

Computation of total income

Long Term Capital Gain	10,000
Long Term Capital Gain (STT paid) exempt u/s 10(38)	Nil
Short Term Capital Gain (STT paid)	40,000
Short Term Capital Gain	5,000
Income from TV game show	5,000
Dividend from Indian Company exempt u/s10(34)	Nil
Other Income	1,54,000
Gross Total Income	2,14,000
Less: Deduction u/s 80G	4,000
Total Income	2,10,000

Computation of tax liability

	Firm or Domestic Company	*Foreign Company*	*Ind/HUF AOP/BOI*	*A.J.P.*
Tax on L.T.C.G @ 20% on Rs. 10,000.	2,000	2,000	2,000	2,000
Tax on S.T.C.G. (STT paid) @ 10% on Rs. 40,000	4,000	4,000	4,000	4,000
Tax on casual income @ 30% on Rs. 5,000	1,500	1,500	1,500	1,500
Tax on normal income at normal rates on Rs. 1,55,000	46,500	62,000	6,000	6,000

Tax liability	54,000	69,500	13,500	13,500
Less Rebate	Nil	Nil	Nil	Nil
Tax liability	54,000	69,500	13,500	13,500
Add Surcharge	5,400	1,738	N.A.	1,350
Tax Payable	59,400	71,238	13,500	14,850
Add Education cess @ 2%	1,188	1,425	270	297
Tax Payable	60,588	72,622	13,770	15,147

TOPIC 1.07 COMPUTATION OF TOTAL INCOME (ASSUMED FIGURES)

1. Income from Salaries (*Sections 15 to 17*)		40,013
2. Income from House Property (*Sections 22 to 27*)		21,000
3. Profits and Gains of Business or Profession (*Sections 28 to 44D*)		53,212
4. Capital Gains (*Sections 45 to 55A*)		
• Long Term Capital Gain	6,000	
• Short Term Capital Gain (STT paid)	1,500	
• Short Term Capital Gain	2,500	10,000
5. Income from Other Sources (*Sections 56 to 59*)		
• Dividend, Interest, Royalty etc.	5,000	
• Casual Income like Lottery income, Income from Card Game etc.	15,000	20,000

Following adjustment shall also have to be made in their respective heads.

a. Clubbing of income (*Sections 60 to 64*)

b. Set off and carry forward of losses (*Sections 70 to 80*)

Gross Total Income (GTI) *1+2+3+4+5* *(Computed after adjustment of losses and clubbing of income)*	1,44,225
Less Deduction u/s 80C to 80U *(cannot exceed GTI)*	10,000
Total Income (TI)	1,34,225
Section 288 Rounding it off to nearest tens, less than 5 should be brought down	1,34,230

Note

- Exempted income do not form part of gross total income therefore it shall never be a part of total income. It should always be shown separately as a part of note. *(Sections 10 to 13A)*.
- Do remember until and unless residential status is known total income cannot be computed. Therefore the first step in computing total income is determining the residential status of an assessee. (Discussed in Chapter 2)

TOPIC 1.08 COMPUTATION OF TAX LIABILITY (ASSUMED FIGURES)

1. Tax on Long Term Capital Gain (LTCG) @ 20% flat		400
2. Tax on Short Term Capital Gain. (STT paid) @ 10%		150
3. Tax on Casual Income (CI) @ 30% flat		4,500
4. Tax on Normal Income at normal rates		11,346
Total Tax		16,396
Less Rebate u/s 88E (cannot exceed tax liability)		2,396
Tax after rebate		14,000
Add Surcharge if applicable		Nil
Tax and surcharge		14,000
Add Education cess @ 2%		280
Tax liability		14,280
Less Pre-paid taxes		
• Tax Deducted at Source or Tax Collected at Source *(TDS/TCS)*	4,000	
• Advance Tax paid	5,000	9,000
Tax payable / (Refundable) *(Round it off to nearest rupee)*		1,000

Both the above formats of total income and tax liability should be memorised.

Illustration and Problems 1.08-P1

Compute total income and tax payable for the AY 2007-08 from the following information.

	Case 1	*Case 2*	*Case 3*	*Case 4*
Status	Individual	HUF	Firm	Foreign Co.
Income from Salary	54,000	N.A.	N.A.	N.A.
Income from House Property	44,000	8,50,000	1,40,200	Nil
Profit from Business	22,015	2,54,000	(10,000)	1,25,000
Long Term Capital Gain	10,000	5,000	4,000	1,00,000
Short Term Capital Gain (STT paid)	20,000	12,000	11,300	2,50,000
Short Term Capital Gain	1,45,000	68,500	5,000	1,50,000
Lottery Income	15,000	1,000	2,500	Nil
Other Income	1,65,000	19,000	1,24,800	1,50,110
Dividend from domestic company	10,00,000	(1,000)	15,000	1,24,500
Deduction u/s 80G	10,000	15,496	10,000	41,000
Rebate u/s 88E	6,000	2,000	1,000	4,500
Tax Deducted at Source and advance tax	12,000	2,00,000	52,000	2,60,000

Ans: (1) 68,076; (2) 1,40,303; (3) 34,035; (4) –57,022

Solution Case 1

Computation of Total Income of Individual

Income from Salary	54,000
Income from House Property	44,000
Profit from Business	22,015
Capital Gain	
Long Term Capital Gain	10,000
Short Term Capital Gain (STT paid)	20,000
Short Term Capital Gain	1,45,000
Income from Other Sources	
Lottery Income etc.	15,000
Other income	1,65,000
Dividend from domestic company fully exempt from tax u/s 10(34)	Nil
Gross Total Income	4,75,015
Less Deduction u/s 80G	10,000
Total Income *(rounding off figure)*	4,65,015
Rounded off to nearest tens	4,65,020

Computation of Tax Liability

Tax on Long Term Capital Gain @ 20% on Rs. 10,000	2,000
Tax on Short Term Capital Gain (STT paid) @ 10% on Rs. 20,000	2,000
Tax on Casual Income @ 30% on Rs. 15,000	4,500
Tax on Normal Income at Slab Rate on Rs. 4,20,020 *(4,65,020 –10,000 – 20,000 – 15,000 = 4,20,020)*	76,006
Total Tax	84,506
Less: Rebate u/s 88E	6,000
Tax after rebate	78,506
Add: Surcharge	N.A.
Tax and surcharge	78,506
Add: Education cess @ 2%	1,570
Tax liability	80,076
Less: Tax Deducted at Source	12,000
Tax payable	68,076

Problem 1.08-P2 [Hons 2006]

M has computed his total income for the Assessment year 2007-08, which amounted to Rs. 6,20,000. It includes Rs. 30,000 on account of long term capital gains and Rs. 20,000 on account of winning of horse races. He deposited Rs. 50,000 in a public provident fund during the previous year which is eligible for deduction u/s 80C. Compute the tax payable by M, assuming that;

(1) He is less than 65 years of age.

(2) more than 65 years of age.

Ans: 1,20,360; 1,08,210

Problem 1.08-P3

Find out the tax liability of Shri X for the Assesment year 2007-08:

Long-term capital gain on sale of shares on which Securities Transaction Tax has been paid	1,00,000
Short-term capital gain on sale of shares on which Securities Transaction Tax has been paid	20,000
Long-term capital gain on Gold	5,000
Short-term capital gain on other Assets	12,000
Income from Business	1,38,000
Deposit in PPF [Eligible for deduction u/s 80C]	10,000
Spent on dependent mother's cancer treatment [Eligible for deduction u/s 80DDB]	40,000

Ans: 3,060

Problem 1.08-P4

Compute his taxable income and tax liability for AY 2007-08 from the following information.

1. Income of Mrs. T who has attained the age of 65 years during the PY 2006-07, shows his income of Rs. 14,00,000 after claiming deduction u/s 80C of Rs. 1,00,000. You are required to tax liability for the AY 2007-08 if she is (a) Resident in India (b) Non Resident in India.
2. In the case of an artificial juridical person, no surcharge is payable where the total income exceeds Rs. 10,00,000. (True or False) [CA N06]

Ans: 4,01,676; 4,15,140; False

TOPIC 1.09 * MARGINAL RELIEF

Meaning of marginal relief. It means relaxation in amount of surcharge.

Marginal relief is available in following range of income

Individual, HUF, AOP, BOI	10,00,001 to 10,37,310
Resident woman	10,00,001 to 10,36,790
Resident senior citizen	10,00,001 to 10,35,520

Why marginal relief? As you know in case of ind / HUF etc., surcharge @ 10% is levied if total income exceeds Rs. 10,00,000. Let us examine this point.

Total Income	*Tax Liability*
10,00,000	2,50,000
10,10,000	2,78,300
10,000	28,300

If your total income is Rs. 10,00,000, your tax liability is Rs. 2,50,000; now if your total income is Rs. 10,10,000 your tax liability is Rs. 2,78,300 including surcharge @ 10%. If you examine closely your income increases by Rs. 10,000 however your tax liability increase by Rs. 28,300. Therefore to offset this precarious situation marginal relief is provided which is computed by using following formula:

Marginal relief (MR) = Increase in income minus increase in tax liability. Therefore MR = 10,000–28,300=18,300.

Tax on normal income at slab rate on Rs. 10,10,000	2,78,300
Less: Marginal Relief	18,300
Tax	2,60,000

Similarly tax liability can be computed for all other incomes.

For Individual/HUF

Income	Tax on Income	Income	Tax on Income +Surcharge	Increase in Income	Increase in tax	Marginal Relief	Tax
10,00,000	2,50,000	10,05,000	2,76,650	5,000	26,650	(21,650)	2,55,000
10,00,000	2,50,000	10,10,000	2,78,300	10,000	28,300	(18,300)	2,60,000
10,00,000	2,50,000	10,20,000	2,81,600	20,000	31,600	(11,600)	2,70,000
10,00,000	2,50,000	10,30,000	2,84,900	30,000	34,900	(4,900)	2,80,000
10,00,000	2,50,000	10,32,000	2,82,000	32,000	35,560	(3,560)	2,82,000
10,00,000	2,50,000	10,34,000	2,86,220	34,000	36,220	(2,220)	2,84,000
10,00,000	2,50,000	10,37,310	2,87,312	37,310	37,312	(2)	2,87,310

For resident woman

Income	Tax on Income	Income	Tax on Income +Surcharge	Increase in Income	Increase in tax	Marginal Relief	Tax
10,00,000	2,46,500	10,10,000	2,74,450	10,000	27,950	(17,950)	2,56,500
10,00,000	2,46,500	10,30,000	2,81,050	30,000	34,550	(4,550)	2,76,500
10,00,000	2,50,000	10,36,790	2,83,291	36,790	36,791	(1)	2,83,290

For resident senior citizen

Income	Tax on Income	Income	Tax on Income +Surcharge	Increase in Income	Increase in tax	Marginal Relief	Tax
10,00,000	2,38,000	10,10,000	2,61,800	10,000	23,800	(23,800)	2,48,000
10,00,000	2,38,000	10,30,000	2,71,700	30,000	33,700	(3,700)	2,68,000
10,00,000	2,50,000	10,35,520	2,73,522	35,520	35,522	(2)	2,73,520

TOPIC 1.10 *SECTION 2(29C)*. MAXIMUM MARGINAL RATE OF TAX

As per section 2(29C) maximum marginal rate of tax (MMR) is the highest tax incidence levied on different persons including surcharge and education cess.

- Firm or Domestic Company (30% + 10% surcharge + 2% education cess) 33.66%
- Foreign Company (40% + 2.5% surcharge + 2% education cess) 41.82%
- Individual/HUF/AOP/BOI/AJP (30% + 10% surcharge + 2% education cess) 33.66%

STRATEGY MAKER

The most important chapter as far as theory is concerned. Make sure you memorise all the definitions. In the first reading put in 3 hours and discuss the provisions with your teachers and friends so that you are able to understand the intracacies.

The types of problems which are asked are simple. No practical questions as such are asked. Practical questions are simple and are associated with slab rate and flat rate. As you progress your study step by step you tend to easily memorise these and also learn its application. As far as theory is concern its chances are always bright.

A very common question asked by the students is whether they should memorise the sections. It can definitely be said, you must. Now the question how you shall memorise the sections. Make a chart of sections in one page, it shall lay a roadmap, revise it every day and you shall achieve the impossible of memorising the sections. However do remember more than memorising of sections, the provisions are of the utmost important.

Excellent

You have completed the most important step. The above topics have created a foundation in Income-tax. Now you know what is total income, how you compute tax on total income, etc. But do not stop here and do not forget to revise otherwise you may forget everything. Go to next step. It is waiting for you. Now Run

Keep Running

Where do you live? In India

2

RESIDENTIAL STATUS

TOPIC 2.00 INTRODUCTION

1. *Why there is a need to determine the residential status:* The residential status of an assessee determines the extent of his global income taxable in India. Suppose Mr. X earns an income of Rs. 6 Lakhs from a business in India and Rs. 15 Lakhs from a business in USA. Rs. 6 Lakhs, being an Indian Income, is taxable in India but what about income earned from USA. This Rs. 15 Lakhs shall be taxable in India or not, shall depend upon the residential status of the assessee.
2. The residential status of a person is determined for every previous year since income is computed for each previous year. His residential status in assessment year is immaterial.
3. A person may be resident for one previous year and Non-resident in the next year. Like a person may be resident for the previous year 2006-07 and may be Non-resident in the previous year 2007-08.
4. An assessee may be resident of more than one country in the same previous year.
5. As per section 6, on the basis of residence, assessees are classified into following categories:

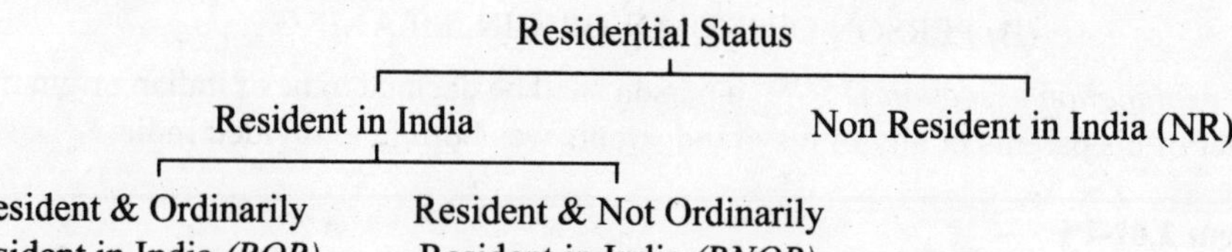

6. ROR and RNOR status is applicable only to Individual and HUF. Other persons are either Resident or Non-resident.

TOPIC 2.01 *SECTION 6(1), 6(6).* HOW TO DETERMINE RESIDENTIAL STATUS OF AN INDIVIDUAL

(A) INTRODUCTION

1. The residential status of an individual do not depend upon the citizenship but is determined solely on the basis of physical presence of the assessee in India *i.e.* for the number of days he stays in India. Below are some of the illustrations shown.

You are required to compute total stay of Mr. X in India for the different previous years from the following information. Periods of less than a day are computed in hours. However for academic purpose do remember the day he comes to India and the day he leaves India both the days are counted as stay in India.

a. Mr. X comes to India on 6-6-2006 and leaves India on 7-9-2006.

   During the previous year 2006-07, Mr. X was in India for 94 days (25 + 31 + 31 +7).

b. Mr. X leaves India for the first time on 8-8-2006.

   During the previous year 2006-07, Mr. X was in India for 130 days (30 + 31 + 30 + 31 + 8) and before the previous year 2003-04 he was always present in India for whole PY.

c. Mr. X comes to India for the first time on 1-10-2006 for 200 days.

   During the previous year 2006-07, Mr. X was in India for 182 days (31 + 30 + 31 + 31 + 28 + 31) and during the previous year 2007-08, he was in India for 18 days (200 - 182).

d. Mr. X comes to India for the first time on 1-3-2006 for 100 days.

   During the previous year 2005-06, Mr. X was in India for 31 days and during the previous year 2006-07, he was in India for 69 days (100 - 31).

2. It is not essential that the stay should be at the same place and also that the stay should be continuous. Purpose of stay and place of stay is immaterial for determining the residential status. Also stay within the territorial waters of India is treated as stay in India.

3. An individual may be an Indian citizen or a foreign citizen or a person of Indian Origin and based on stay in India their residential status may be treated as resident in India or non-resident in India.

   a. Indian Citizen. (He may be resident in India or Non-Resident in India)

   b. Foreign Citizen. (He may be resident in India or Non-Resident in India)

   c. Person of Indian origin or popularly as Non Resident Indians. (He may be resident in India or Non-Resident in India)

(B) PERSON OF INDIAN ORIGIN, MEANING ?

As per *explanation to section 115C(e)* a person shall be deemed to be of Indian origin if he or either of his parents or any of his grandparents was born in undivided India.

Problem 2.01-P1

Determine whether Mr. Taxcrazy a citizen of Sri Lanka is a person of Indian origin in the following cases:

1. Mr. Taxcrazy was born in Karachi on 1-6-1944.
2. Mr. Taxcrazy was born in Karachi on 1-6-1948 and his father was born in India in the year 1930.
3. Mr. Taxcrazy was born in Delhi on 1-6-1970 and leaves his Indian citizenship. His father was born in Karachi in the year 1950. His grandfather was born in the year 1930 in England. His grandmother was born in Bangladesh in the year 1931.

Ans: (1) Yes; (2) Yes; (3) Yes.

(C) RULES FOR DETERMINATION OF RESIDENTIAL STATUS OF AN INDIVIDUAL

To determine the residential status of an Individual following two conditions are checked.

1. *6(1) Basic Condition*. This condition checks whether an individual is a resident in India or Non-resident in India.
2. *6(6) Additional Condition*. This condition checks whether an individual who is a resident in India is an ordinarily resident in India or not ordinarily resident in India.

Let us see how it works

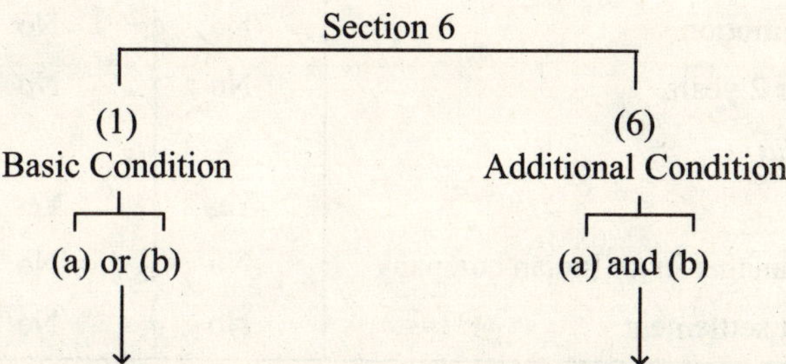

if any one of the basic conditions is satisfied then his residential status is Resident in India.

if none of the basic conditions are satisfied, then his residential status is Non-resident in India.

However if an individual falls in exception to the basic condition only one basic condition exists which is the first basic condition. (Refer point D below)

Now, if *both* the additional conditions are satisfied (besides basic condition), then his residential status is treated as Resident and Ordinarily Resident in India (ROR), otherwise he is treated as Resident and not Ordinarily Resident in India (RNOR).

Do remember Additional condition is required to be checked only when basic condition is satisfied. It means basic condition is a tunnel through which you have to go to Additional Condition.

↓

(D) IF ANY OF THE FOLLOWING CONDITIONS IS SATISFIED AN INDIVIDUAL SHALL FALL IN EXCEPTIONS TO THE BASIC CONDITION (LET US CALL IT A SPECIAL CASE).

a. If an *Indian citizen* who leaves India for the purpose of
   (i) *Employment*. Employment means taking a job outside India, shifting his place of business or profession outside India. Employment does not mean going outside India for training or going for a business trip or going for export promotion; or
   (ii) As a crew member of an Indian ship. Even if a person joins as a crew member of a foreign ship he shall fall in exception since he is going outside India for employment purpose; or
   (iii) Comes on a visit to India. Visit means such person shall return back.

b. If a *person of Indian origin* being outside India comes on a *visit* to India.

Analysis whether following individual falls in exception to the basic condition or not			
	Indian Citizen	*Person of Indian Origin*	*Foreign Citizen*
A. Leaves India			
1. for taking up job in USA	Yes	No	No
2. to join as a crew member of an Indian ship	Yes	No	No
3. to join as a crew member of foreign ship	Yes	No	No
4. for export promotion	No	No	No
5. as a tourist for 2 years	No	No	No
B. Comes to India			
1. on a visit	Yes	Yes	No
2. to join as a manager in an Indian company	No	No	No
3. for permanent settlement	No	No	No

Problem 2.01-P2

1. When only first condition of basic condition is required to be checked *i.e.* 182 days condition?
2. Who are the individuals who can fall in exception to the basic condition?
3. Which individual can never fall in exception to the basic condition?

Solution

1. When an individual falls in exception to the basic condition.
2. It is either Indian citizen or a person of Indian Origin.
3. A foreign citizen.

Section 6(1) and 6(6). Analysis

	Basic Condition	*Addititonal Condition*	*Resi. Status*
Case 1	Satisfieds	Satisfies	Resident-OR
Case 2	Satisfieds	Not satisfied	Resident-NOR
Case 3	Not satisfied	Satisfies	Non-Resident
Case 4	Not satisfied	Not satisfied	Non-Resident

Tips to solve residential status of an individual

1. First determine whether he is an Indian Citizen or a person of Indian Origin.
2. Then check if he falls in exception to the basic condition or not. If he falls in exception to the basic condition then check only the first basic condition. *(Do remember a foreign citizen can never fall in exception category.)*
3. Then check whether he satisfies the applicable basic condition or not.
4. If he satisfies the basic condition, then check both the additional conditions.

(E) SECTION 6(1). BASIC CONDITION

If an individual is in India for

a. 182 days or more during the relevant previous year; or

b. 60 days or more during the relevant previous year and 365 days or more during the 4 years immediately preceding the relevant previous year.

Illustration and Problems 2.01-P3 (Simple)

(A) Mr. Taxcrazy, an Irish citizen comes on a visit to India and travels to Mumbai, Tata & Bokaro Steel City. Determine his Residential Status for the AY 2007-08.

PY	*Case 1*	*Case 2*	*Case 3*	*Case 4*	*Case 5*	*Case 6*
2006-07	192	180	59	182	120	140
2005-06	-	360	190	-	20	100
2004-05	-	360	185	-	120	100
2003-04	20	5	182	-	130	100
2002-03	345	5	170	-	40	70
2001-02	100	-	200	-	140	170

(B) What would be your answer if the father of Mr. Taxcrazy was born in India on 13-8-1947?

Ans (A): (1) Resident in India (2) Resident in India (3) Non-Resident in India; (4) Resident in India; (5) Non-Resident in India; (6) Resident in India.

Ans (B): (1) Resident in India (2) Non-Resident in India (3) Non-Resident in India; (4) Resident in India; (5) Non-Resident in India; (6) Non-Resident in India.

Solution

(A) Since Mr. Taxcrazy is a foreign citizen both the basic conditions are applicable.

1. Since his stay in India is for more than 182 days during the PY 2006-07, he satisfies 1st condition of the Basic Condition and therefore his residential status is Resident in India.
2. Since his stay in India is for more than 60 days during the PY 2006-07 and also he is in India for more than 365 days in 4 preceding PY's, (i.e. for 730 days) he satisfies 2nd condition of the basic condition and therefore his residential status is Resident in India.
3. Since his stay in India is for less than 60 days during the PY 2006-07, he satisfies none of the basic condition and therefore his residential status is Non Resident in India.

(B) Since his father was born in India on 13-8-1947, Mr. Taxcrazy is treated as Person of Indian Origin who comes on a visit to India and, therefore, only first basic condition of 182 days is required to be checked.

1. Since his stay in India is for more than 182 days during the PY 2006-07, he satisfies 1st condition of the basic condition and therefore his residential status is Resident in India.
2. Since his stay in India is for less than 182 days during the PY 2006-07, therefore he does not satisfy the basic condition and hence his residential status is Non-Resident in India.

3. Since his stay in India is for less than 182 days during the PY 2006-07, therefore he does not satisfy the basic condition and hence his residential status is Non-Resident in India.

Problem 2.01-P4 (Typical)

X, Y, Z, K, Q being foreign citizens and Mr. M being an Indian citizen, all of them at some point or another come to India for different purpose as shown below. You are required to determine their residential status for the AY 2007-08 assuming that in the PY 2004-05 all were in India for 365 days.

Name of person	*Date and place of birth*	*No. of days present in India in the PY 2005-06*	*Purpose of coming to India*
Mr. X	13-8-1947 (Hyderabad)	arrived in India on 11-10-2006	To join as a Co. Sec in Delhi
Mrs. Y	25-7-1947 (Shanghai)	83 days	To argue a case in Supreme Court
Mr. Z	19-6-1996 (Nagaland)	160 days	For acting in a film
Mr. K	18-8-1972 (his grandfather is Mr. X)	67 days	To attend his daughter's marriage
Mr. Q	24-2-1973 (Japan) (his mother is Mrs. Y)	70 days	On his marriage
Mr. M (X is brother of Mr. M)	19-6-1960 (Italy)	181 days trip	Business

Ans: X, Y, Z, Q are Resident. K & M are Non-Resident.

Problem 2.01-P5 [Hons 2007]

Mr. X, an actor, went to USA on 1st April, 2006 for a film shooting. Due to ill health he had to stay there just after shooting. He came back to India on 25th September, 2006. He had to go again to USA on 8th December, 2006 and returned to India on 15th Feb., 2007. What is his residential status for the assessment year 2007-08?

Ans: Resident assumming 365 days conditions in last 4 years satisfied.

(F) SECTION 6(6). ADDITIONAL CONDITION

a. He has been Resident in India in atleast 2 out of 10 previous years' immediately preceding the relevant previous year *(To find out whether an individual is resident or non-resident in India basic condition is required to be checked)*; and

b. He has been in India for a period of total 730 days or more during 7 years immediately preceding the relevant previous year.

Illustration and Problems 2.01-P6 (Simple)

(A) Mr. Taxcrazy, a citizen of Mauritius, is present in India for different PY's as follows. You are required to determine the residential status for the AY 2007-08.

PY	Case 1 No. of days in India		Case 2 No. of days in India	Case 3 No. of days in India	Case 4 No. of days in India
2006-07	70	–	185	60	60
2005-06	60	Resident	300	91	92
2004-05	70	Resident	300	92	92
2003-04	34	NR	300	91	92
2002-03	365	Resident	300	91	92
2001-02	182	Resident	300	–	92
2000-01	125	NR	120	100	92
99-2000	190	Resident	300	100	92
1998-99	nil	NR	300	50	92
1997-96	nil	NR	300	60	92
1996-95	61	NR	180	182	92
1995-94	200	NA	180	182	92
1994-93	164	NA	184	264	88

(B) What would be your answer in all cases if the father of Mr. Taxcrazy was born in India on 13-8-1947?

Ans (A): (1) ROR; (2) ROR; (3) RNOR; (4) RNOR.

Ans (B): (1) NR; (2) ROR; (3) NR; (4) NR.

Solution: Case 1

Since Mr. Taxcrazy is a foreign citizen, he does not fall in the exception to the Basic Condition, and therefore, both the basic conditions have to be checked.

Basic Condition: Since his stay in India is for more than 60 days during the PY 2006-07 and also he is in India for more than 365 days in 4 preceding PYs, (*i.e.* for 529 days) he satisfies 2nd condition of the basic condition. As he satisfies basic condition we should also check whether he satisfies both the additional conditions or not.

Additional Condition

1. He is resident in India in 5 out of 10 PY.
2. He is in India for more than 730 days *(*i.e. *1026 days)* in 7 years immediately preceding PY.

Since, he satisfies both the additional conditions (besides basic condition) therefore his residential status is ROR.

Problem 2.01-P7 (Difficult)

(A) Mr. Taxcrazy, a citizen of Malaysia, comes to India every year in the month of April for 100 days for the last 8 years. Find his residential status for the AY 2007-08. (B) What would be your answer if he comes to India every year for 105 days instead of 100 days? (C) What would be your answer if he comes to India every year in the month of April for 105 days for 6 years? (D) What would be your answer in the above cases if his grandfather was born on 15-6-1930 in Kanyakumari?

Ans: RNOR; ROR; RNOR; NR.

Problem 2.01-P8 (Typical)

(A) Mr. Taxcrazy, a citizen of Russia, has been visiting India from the previous year 1997-98 for 160 days every year in the month of June to meet his parents. However on 1-1-2007 he shifted his whole of the business from Russia to India and started living with his parents who were born in Pakistan in the year 1946. Determine his residential status for the AY 2007-08. (B) Suppose in the above question Mr. Taxcrazy comes to India on 15-3-2007 instead of 7-6-2006.

Ans: RNOR; NR.

Problem 2.01-P9 [CA M 91]

Q is an Indian national. He is a marine engineer and is employed with a foreign shipping company. Under the terms of his employment, he is entitled to a leave of 4 months for every 8 months of service rendered on board a ship. Q joined the company's vessel at Bombay on December 10, 2004 and has been sailing with one or the other of the ships of the company not touching Indian shores till October 15, 2006. One of the ships arrived at Madras Harbor on that day for discharge of cargo when Q signed off the company's articles entering leave. The employment with the company is Q's first employment and before joining the company he was residing in India. What is the residential status of Q for the AY 2007-08?

Ans: Non-Resident.

Problem 2.01-P10 (Difficult)

Mr. Perkash, a citizen of India left India on 12-10-1998 for employment abroad. He did not come to India upto previous year 2003-04. During 2004-05 and 2005-06 he visited India for 145 and 205 days respectively. In the previous year 2006-07 he came to India on 17-06-06 and left on 15-01-07. Determine his residential status for the previous year 2006-07.

Solution

PY 2006-07	213 days [17-06-06 to 15-01-07]	on a visit	Resident
PY 2005-06	205 days [as per the question]	on a visit	Resident
PY 2004-05	145 days [as per the question]	on a visit	Non-Resident
PY 2003-04	0 days [as per the question]	on a visit	Non-Resident
PY 2002-03 to PY 99-2000	0 days [as per the question]	on a visit	Non-Resident
PY 1998-99	195 days [1-4-98 to 12-10-98]	for employment	Resident

Mr Perkash satisfies the basic condition of 182 days in the PY 2006-07. His residential status is resident in India. However he does not satisfy the additional condition of 730 days in last 7 years immediately preceding the PY therefore his residential status is Not ordinarily resident.

Problem 2.01-P11 (Difficult)

Mr. K came to India for the first time on 2nd Oct, 2004 and has been staying here since then. What will be his residential status for the previous year ending on 31st March, 2007?

Solution

Computation of Residential Status

PY 2006-07	365	satisfies BC	PY 2000-01	Nil	non-resident
PY 2005-06	365	resident	PY 99-2000	Nil	non-resident
PY 2004-05	181	non-resident	PY 98-1999	Nil	non-resident
PY 2003-04	Nil	non-resident	PY 97-1998	Nil	non-resident
PY 2002-03	Nil	non-resident	PY 1996-97	Nil	non-resident
PY 2001-02	Nil	non-resident			

Basic Condition: He is present in India for more than 182 days in the PY 2005-06, therefore he satisfies 1st condition of Basic Condition.

Additional Condition: He is resident in India in 1 out of 10 years, therefore he does not satisfy 1st condition of Additional condition.

Therefore his residential status is RNOR

Illustration 2.01-P12 (Difficult)

(A) Mr. Taxcrazy, a citizen of Japan, comes to India for the first time on 3-10-2006 for 190 days. Find his Residential Status for the AY 2007-08. (B) What would be your answer if he comes to India on 1-10-2006?

Ans: Non Resident; RNOR.

Solution

(A) During the PY 2006-07 his total stay in India was 180 days. *i.e.* from 3-10-2006 to 31-3-2007. Since he satisfies none of the basic conditions his residential status is Non-resident in India.

Problem 2.01-P13 (Difficult)

X', a citizen of India, left India on 24-9-2005 for employment abroad. During the previous year 2005-06 he comes to India on 25-12-2006 and stayed here for 182 days. Determine his residential status for assessment year 2007-08.

Ans: Non-Resident in India.

Illustration 2.01-P14 (Difficult)

(A) Mr. Taxcrazy, a citizen of Pakistan, comes to India for the second time on 2-3-2006 for 89 days. Find his residential status for the AY 2007-08 assuming that for the first time he was in India for 365 days in the PY 2002-03. (B) What would be your answer if he comes to India on 3-3-2006?

Ans: Non-Resident in India; RNOR.

Solution

(A) During the PY 2006-07 his total stay in India was 59 days, *i.e.* excluding the days from 2-3-2006 to 31-3-2006 which falls in the PY 2005-06. Since he satisfies none of the basic conditions his residential status is NR in India.

Illustration 2.01-P15 (Difficult)

(A) Mr. Taxcrazy, an Indian citizen, goes to Ohio, Japan on 28-9-2006 for the first time for employment purpose alongwith his wife, only to return back permanently on

3-10-2009. Determine the residential status of husband and wife from the AY 2007-08 to AY 2010-2011.

(B) What would be your answer for the assessment year 2010-2011 if they are coming to India on their daughter's marriage.

Ans: (A) Refer soln below (B) Non-resident in India; Non-resident in India.

Solution

PY	No. of days stayed in India		Husband	Wife
2009-10	180	(3-10-2009 to 31-03-2010)	ROR	ROR
2008-09	nil	(in Japan)	NR	NR
2007-08	nil	(in Japan)	NR	NR
2006-07	181	(1-4-2006 to 28-9-2006)	NR[1]	ROR[2]
2005-06	365	(In India)	ROR	ROR

(1) Since he goes out of India for employment purpose, therefore he falls in exception category where only first condition of basic condition is checked.

(2) Since wife is not going out of India for employment purpose, therefore both the basic conditions are required to be checked.

Problem 2.01-P16 (Typical)

Mr. Ajit, an Indian citizen, for the first time leaves India for Singapore for higher studies on July 15, 2003. For celebrating Diwali he came to India on October 12, 2004 and stayed for 49 days. Again he came to India in his Brother's marriage on March 12, 2005 and stayed for 68 days. Finally after completing his studies he came to India on January 1, 2007. Determine the residential status for the AY 2004-05, 2005-06, 2006-07 and 2007-08.

Ans: ROR; NR; NR; ROR.

Problem 2.01-P17 (Difficult)

Mr. Taxcrazy, a foreign citizen and employed in Discovery channel comes to India for the first time on an India exploration.

Case 1 on 1-4-2004 and leaves India on 30-9-2006.

Case 2 on 4-10-2004 and leaves India on 30-9-2006.

Case 3 on 1-4-2004 and leaves India on 15-5-2006.

Determine his residential status in Case 1, 2 and 3 for the AY 2007-08.

Ans: ROR; RNOR; NR.

Problem 2.01-P18 (Difficult)

(A) X, an Indian Citizen after 25 years of stay in India, retires to UK, on July 3, 2003. He returns to India on January 1, 2006 to join a British company in India. Determine his residential status for the AY 2004-05 and 2007-08.

(B) Mr. Acharya is settled in U.K. His parents were born in undivided India. He is employed in U.K. branch of an Indian Company. On 4-10-2002 he joined India Office. On 1-2-2005 he was sent to Bangladesh on deputation. He returned to India and joined his duties on 7-11-2005. On 1-10-2006 he left India to join his duties at his parent U.K. branch. Determine his residential status for the assessment years 2003-04 to 2007-08.

Ans: (A) ROR; ROR; (B) NR in India; RNOR ; RNOR; ROR; ROR.

Problem 2.01-P19 [DU 2006 NEW] [Marks 3]

X, an Indian citizen, is appointed as senior taxation officer by the Government of Libya. He leaves India for the first time on November 3, 2006 for joining duties in Libya. During the previous year 2007-08, he comes to India on December 3, 2007 for 190 days. Determine the residential status of X for assessment years 2007-08 and 2008-09.

Solution

	PY In India		
PY 2006-08	3-12-2007 to 31-3-2008	less than 182 days	comes to India on a visit
PY 2006-07	1-4-2006 to 3-11-2006	less than 182 days	leaves India for employment
PY 2005-06	1-4-2005 to 31-3-2006	365 days	do not leave India

In PY 2007-08 he falls in exception and do not satisfy the first basic condition therefore his residential status for the AY 2008-09 is Non-Resident in India.

In PY 2006-07 he falls in exception and do not satisfy the first basic condition therefore his residential status for the 2007-08 is Non-Resident in India.

Problem 2.01-P20 [DU 2005C] [Marks 2] [Q.1c]

Shri A who was born and brought up in India, went for further studies to United Kingdom on 1-3-2005 and came back to India on 30-9-2006. Find out his residential status for the Assessment year 2007-08.

Ans: R-OR.

Good. Residential status of individual completed.

Keep Running

TOPIC 2.02 *SECTION 6(2), 6(6).* DETERMINATION OF RESIDENTIAL STATUS OF HINDU UNDIVIDED FAMILY

Section 6

(2) Basic Condition	(6) Additional Condition
When resident in India : If 'Control & Management of the affairs of the business' *(not domestic affairs)* of HUF is situated wholly / partially in India then residential *status of HUF is Resident in India.* *When Non-resident in India* : If 'Control & Management of the affairs of the business' is situated wholly outside India then residential status of HUF is *Non-Resident* in India.	*When ROR or RNOR* : If the Karta or manager *(including successive Karta)* of HUF also satisfies both the additional conditions *(as given for Individual* i.e. *2 / 10 and 730, 7)* then residential status of HUF is ROR otherwise RNOR.

Meaning of Control and Management of the affairs of the business

1. 'The Control & Management' means taking policy decisions. The person who takes the policy decisions has the control and management of the business.
2. Policy decisions are like taking decisions concerning finance, marketing, production, advertising, personnel, etc.
3. The Control & Management is situated where vital decision concerning policies of the organisation is taken. In case of a company it can be said that control and management is situated at a place where Board meetings are held. The word '**affairs**' must mean affairs which have some relation to the income.
4. There is a distinction between doing business and controlling business.
5. To quote, it can be said that 'A leader knows what's best to do; a manager knows merely how best to do it.' The leader has the Control & Management of the business.
6. In simple terms it may be said that the person who has power to shut down the business has the Control & Management.
7. The Control & Management of the business can be in two hands. One hand may be located in India and the other hand outside India.

As you know control and management of the affairs of the business of Hindu Undivided Family is with Karta or its Manager.

Illustration 2.02-P1 (Simple)

Tata Sons, HUF whose affairs of the business are completely controlled from India. Determine the residential status of HUF and its Karta for the AY 2007-08 in each of the following cases:

	Basic Condition of Karta	*Additional Condition of Karta*
Case 1	Satisfies	Satisfies
Case 2	Satisfies	Do not satisfy
Case 3	Do not satisfy	Satisfies
Case 4	Do not satisfy	Do not satisfy

Solution

Basic Condition of HUF : Since Control & Management is wholly situated in India, Tata Sons HUF satisfies the basic condition, therefore, residential status of HUF is Resident in India in each of the cases.

Now residential status of HUF shall be ROR if Karta satisfies both the Additional Conditions otherwise residential status of HUF shall be RNOR. Let us check the Additional Condition of Karta.

	Basic Condition of HUF 6(2)	*Basic Condition of Karta 6(1)*	*Additional Condition applicable to both Karta and HUF 6(6)*
Case 1	Satisfies	Satisfies	Satisfies
Case 2	Satisfies	Satisfies	Do not satisfy
Case 3	Satisfies	Do not satisfy	Satisfies
Case 4	Satisfies	Do not satisfy	Do not satisfy

	Residential Status of HUF	*Residential Status of Karta*
Case 1	Resident - ROR	Resident - ROR
Case 2	Resident - RNOR	Resident - RNOR
Case 3	Resident - ROR	Non-Resident
Case 4	Resident - RNOR	Non-Resident

Problem 2.02-P2 (Difficult)

G.D. Birla and Sons is a HUF. Its business is controlled by its Karta from Pilani and by one of his sons Mr. K.M. Birla from USA. Determine Residential Status of HUF for the AY 2007-08 on the assumption that

Case 1 Residential Status of Karta is ROR

Case 2 Residential Status of Karta is RNOR

Case 3 Residential Status of Karta is NR in India

Ans: (1) ROR; (2) RNOR; (3) it can be ROR or RNOR how? Discuss with your friends.

Problem 2.02-P3 (Difficult)

Head Office of Amitabh Sons (HUF) is situated in Hong Kong. The family is managed by A who is resident in India in 2 out of 6 years preceding the PY 2006-07. Determine the residential status of the family for the AY 2007-08 :

1. If the affairs of the family business are wholly controlled from India.
2. If the affairs of the family business are wholly controlled from Hong Kong.

Ans: RNOR; NR.

Problem 2.02-P4 (Difficult)

Taxcrazy & Sons is controlled by Mr. Taxcrazy, a foreign citizen, who was in India on a visit for 150 days in the PY 2006-07. Determine the residential status of HUF and Taxcrazy for the AY 2007-08.

Ans: RNOR; NR

Problem 2.02-P5

1. Whether HUF is resident or non-resident depends upon the residential status of Karta. (True or False)
2. Whether HUF is ROR or RNOR depends upon the residential status of Karta. (True or False)
3. Residential status of an assessee once fixed is fixed for ever. (True or False)

Solution

1. False, since basic condition of HUF and Karta are different.
2. True, since additional conditions of HUF and Karta are same.
3. False. Residential status is determined for each PY therefore residential status can change from year to year.

TOPIC 2.03 *SECTION 6(2).* DETERMINATION OF RESIDENTIAL STATUS OF FIRM, AOP & BOI.

Control & Management of the affairs of the business of a Firm, Association of persons or body of individuals is with partners or its members respectively.

If Control & Management of the affairs of the business of Firm, Association of persons or body of individuals is situated *wholly or partially* in India then its residential status is Resident in India. If Control & Management of the affairs of the business is situated *wholly* outside India then its residential status is Non-Resident in India.

For firm, AOP/BOI there exist only two status either Resident in India or Non-resident in India.

TOPIC 2.04 *SECTION 6(3).* DETERMINATION OF RESIDENTIAL STATUS OF COMPANY

Control and management of the affairs of the business of a company rests with Board of Directors and not with shareholders.

Indian Company : The company registered in India is an Indian company. Indian Company is always treated as Resident in India whether control & management is in India or outside India.

Foreign Company : If Control & Management of Foreign company is situated *wholly* in India then its residential status is Resident in India. If its control & management is situated *wholly / partially* outside India then its residential status is Non-Resident in India.

For company there exist only two status either Resident in India or Non-resident in India.

TOPIC 2.05 *SECTION 6(4).* DETERMINATION OF RESIDENTIAL STATUS OF OTHERS

It is similar to section 6(2). If Control & Management of the affairs of the business of others is situated wholly or partially in India then its residential status is Resident in India. If Control & Management of the affairs of the business is situated wholly outside India then its residential status is Non-Resident in India.

In this case also there exist only two status either Resident in India or Non-resident in India.

Determination of residential status of HUF, Firm, AOP, BOI, Company and others in tabular form

	Control & Management of the business	
	is in India	is outside India
HUF, Firm, AOP, BOI and others	Wholly or Partially	Wholly
Foreign Company	Wholly	Wholly or Partially
Residential Status	Resident in India	Non-Resident in India
Indian company is always treated as resident in India even if the whole of the Control & Management of the affairs of the business is situated outside India.		

Problem 2.05-P1

1. Under what circumstances the residential status of an Indian company be treated as Non-resident.
2. Can a residential status of a company be ROR or RNOR.
3. When a company treated as a non-resident.
4. When a company treated as resident in India.
5. A Non-Indian company is treated as resident, only if the control and management of its affairs is situated wholly in India during the previous year. (True or False) [CA N06]

Solution

1. Under no circumstances.
2. No, the residential status of a company can be either resident or non-resident.
3. Two conditions should be satisfied. First it should be a foreign company and any part or whole of control and management of the business is located outside India.
4. If it is an Indian Company or if it is a foreign company then whole of control and management of the business is located in India.
5. True.

Problem 2.05-P2 (Simple)

(A) Rising Ltd. is registered in India. Its entire share capital is held by a Brazilian citizen and board meetings are generally held in Brazil. Determine its Residential Status.

(B) What would be your answer if the company is registered in New Zealand and board meetings are held in Brazil.

(C) What would be your answer if the company is registered in New Zealand and all the board meetings of the relevant previous year were held in India except one which was held in Australia.

(D) What would be your answer if the company is registered in Australia and all the board meetings of the relevant previous year were held in India.

Ans: Resident in India; Non-resident in India; Non-resident in India; Resident in India.

Problem 2.05-P3 (Typical)

Compute the residential status of XT and Co. in following three cases:

1. The partners of XT and Co. keeps their dwelling place in China. The business is wholly controlled by Mr. X. Mr T being a sleeping partner.
2. The partners of XT and Co. keeps their dwelling place in China. The business is controlled by Mr. B, the manager of the firm who lives in India. The partners however keep tab of Mr. B's decision.
3. The partners of XT and Co. keeps their dwelling place in India. The business is controlled by both the partners. However both the partners were in Norway for 360 days in the PY 2006-07.

Ans: Non-Resident in India; Resident in India; Resident in India.

TOPIC 2.06 **SECTION 6(5).* DETERMINATION OF RESIDENTIAL STATUS ON THE BASIS OF SOURCE OF INCOME

If a person is resident in India in a previous year in respect of any source of income, he shall deemed to be resident in India in the previous year in respect of each of his other sources of income.

TOPIC 2.07 *SECTION 5.* INCIDENCE OF TAX (SCOPE OF TOTAL INCOME)

(A) SECTION 2(45). TOTAL INCOME

As you know until and unless residential status of a person is known total income cannot be determined and as per section 2(45) total income means the total amount of income referred to in section 5, computed in the manner led down in the Income Tax Act.

(B) SECTION 5(1) : TOTAL INCOME OF ROR SHALL INCLUDE FOLLOWING INCOMES

1. *Income which accrues in India.* If the source of income is located in India, income is said to be accrue in India. Where source of income is located outside India, income is said to accrue outside India. Source of income is said to be located in India if

   Business is done in India,

   the income is generated from an **A**sset which is located in India,

   there is a **T**ransfer of asset which is located in India; or

   Services are rendered in India.

   In all such cases the income is said to accrue or arise in India. Therefore if BATS are located in India, income accrues in India.
2. *Income which accrues outside India.* Where source of income is located outside India and income is received outside India, income is said to accrue outside India *i.e.* if BATS are located outside India and income is received outside India, income accrues outside India.

(C) PROVISO TO SECTION 5(1) : TOTAL INCOME OF RNOR SHALL INCLUDE FOLLOWING INCOMES

1. Income which accrues in India.
2. Income which accrues outside India from a business which is controlled from India or from a profession which is set up in India.
3. Income which accrues outside India but is received in India. Do remember income should be received in India. The income should not be brought or remitted or transferred

to India. So how do you differentiate between these two words 'received' and 'remit or brought'?

What is the meaning of 'Income received in India': First receipt of income determines its year and place of receipt. Suppose Mr. X is working in Malaysia and his salary is deposited in a Bank in India. It means the salary income is received in India. But suppose it happened that salary is deposited in a Bank in Malaysia and then Mr. X sends his money to India. In this case he is simply remitting the money in India which he has already earned and received in Malaysia. Do remember we are concerned with first receipt of income and not its subsequent transactions.

(D) SECTION 5(2) : TOTAL INCOME OF NON-RESIDENT SHALL INCLUDE FOLLOWING INCOMES

1. Income which accrues in India.
2. Income which accrues outside India but is received in India.

(E) *Incidence of tax in tabular form*

	ROR	*RNOR*	*NR*
1. If income accrues in India *(source of income is in India)*	Yes	Yes	Yes
2. If income accrues outside India *(if source of income is outside India)*	Yes	*Yes* if C & M of business in India or profession is set up in India *otherwise No*	No
3. If income is *received* in India *(even if income accrues outside India)*	Yes	Yes	Yes
4. Dividend from an Indian company not taxable since exempt u/s 10(34)	No	No	No
5. Past untaxed profit not taxable since assessed in earlier PY	No	No	No
6. Gifts received from relatives not taxable since capital receipts	No	No	No

Problem 2.07-P1

1. If income accrues in India then such income is always taxable in India whether the person is ROR or RNOR or NR. (True or False)
2. If income accrues outside India then such income is taxable only in case of an assessee who is ROR.
3. When the income is *received* in India from a source outside India then such income is taxable in India whether a person is ROR, RNOR or NR.
4. Which income of NR is not taxable in India.
5. On which income a non-resident assessee do not pay tax in India.
6. On which income a ROR pays tax in India.

7. When income which accrues outside India is taxable in India in all cases whether ROR, RNOR or NR.

Solution

1. True.
2. True.
3. True. In case of ROR all incomes are taxable in India whether received in India or outside India.
4. The income which accrues outside India. However if such income is received in India then it is taxable in India.
5. The income which accrues to him outside India and also received outside India.
6. On all such income irrespective of its place of accrual or receipt.
7. If income is received in India.

(F) TIPS TO SOLVE INCIDENCE OF TAX

1. Always check source of income. If source of income is in India, then such income is always taxable in India whether income is received in India or outside India and also whether control and management is located in India or outside India.
2. If source of income is located outside India, then you must check two further requirements. a. The control and management of the business or professional. b. Whether income is being received in India.

Illustration 2.07-P2 (Simple)

Explain the taxability of following transactions with reasons:

1. Profit from a business in Khetri (India) and managed from outside India. Income is received outside India.
2. Profit from a business in Italy & managed from India. Income is received outside India.
3. Salary from services rendered in India. Salary is paid by a foreign company.
4. Salary from services rendered outside India. Salary is paid by an Indian company.

Solution

Incidence of tax

	ROR	*RNOR*	*NR*
1. Profit from a business in Khetri (India)	Yes	Yes	Yes
2. Profit from a business in Italy and managed from India	Yes	Yes	No
3. Salary from services rendered in India.	Yes	Yes	Yes
4. Salary from services rendered outside India.	Yes	No	No

Discuss the reasons with your friends.

Illustration 2.07-P3 (Difficult)

Compute total income of Mr. Taxcrazy if he is ROR, RNOR and NR in India from the following information :

Profit from business in Sharjah, controlled from USA, 75% received in India	10,000
Income from house property in Delhi received in Bhutan	40,000
Profit from business in Gaya controlled from Ghana	50,000

Profit from business in Kochi controlled from Sikkim	70,000
Profit from business in Shimla received in Africa	55,000
Profit from business in Ghana controlled from Gaya	25,000
Profit from agricultural land in Zurich	5,000
Remuneration from services rendered in Rio paid by an Indian company *(50% remuneration remitted to India)*	12,000
Remuneration from services rendered in Chandigarh paid by a foreign company	18,000
Interest from Bonds of U.S.A. *(75% of interest brought to India)*	26,000
Dividend from an Indian Company	8,000
Past untaxed profit remitted to India	80,12,513

Solution

	ROR	*RNOR*	*NR*
Profit from a business in Sharjah *(75% received in India)*	10,000	7,500	7,500
Income from house property in Delhi	40,000	40,000	40,000
Profit from business in Gaya	50,000	50,000	50,000
Profit from business in Kochi	70,000	70,000	70,000
Profit from business in Shimla	55,000	55,000	55,000
Profit from business in Ghana	25,000	25,000	Nil
Profit from agricultural land	5,000	Nil	Nil
Remuneration from services	12,000	Nil	Nil
Remuneration from services rendered	18,000	18,000	18,000
Interest from Bonds of U.S.A	26,000	Nil	Nil
Dividend from an Indian Company exempt u/s 10(34)	Nil	Nil	Nil
Past untaxed profit not taxable	Nil	Nil	Nil
Total	3,11,000	2,65,500	2,40,500

Problem 2.07. P4 [Pass 2005]

Calculate taxable income of an individual if he is : (a) Ordinary Resident; (b) Not Ordinary Resident; and (c) Non - Resident.

(i)	Profit from business in Japan received in India.	10,000
(ii)	Income from agriculture in Pakistan - it is all spent on the education of children there	5,000
(iii)	Income accrue in India but received in England	10,000
(iv)	Income from house property in Pakistan deposited in a bank there	2,000
(v)	Profits from business in America deposited in a bank there. This business is controlled in India.	50,000
(vi)	Profits earned from business in Meerut	12,000
(vii)	Past untaxed foreign income brought into India during the previous year	10,000

Ans: 89,000; 82,000; 32,000.

Illustration 2.07-P5 (Difficult)

Mr. Taxcrazy furnishes the following particulars of his income earned during the previous year relevant to the assessment year 2005-06 :

1.	Interest on German Development Bonds (one-third is received in India)	51,000
2.	Income from agriculture in Bangladesh, remitted to India.	31,000
3.	Income from property in Canada received in U.S.A.	1,10,000
4.	Income earned from business in Kuwait, business being controlled from Mumbai (Rs. 25,000 is received in India)	65,000
5.	Dividend from an Indian company	15,000
6.	Royalty received in Singapore from Mr. David, a resident in India, for technical services provided for a business carried on in Singapore.	25,000
7.	Profit from a business in Chennai; this business in controlled from Singapore	1,25,000
8.	Profit on sale of a building in India, but received in Nepal	2,50,000
9.	Income from agriculture in Punjab, received in Mumbai	30,000
10.	Profit from business in Paris controlled from Delhi (60% of the profit deposited in a bank there and 40% is remitted to India)	40,000
11.	Interest received from Mr. Dayal, a non-resident, on the loan provided to him for a business in India.	28,000

Compute his gross total income if he is : (i) Resident (ii) Not ordinarily Resident, (iii) Non-Resident.

Ans: 7,25,000; 5,25,000; 4,45,000.

Problem 2.07-P6 [CS J00]

X. a foreign citizen (not being a person of Indian origin) came to India for the first time on December 2, 2006 for a visit of 210 days. X had the following incoming during the previous year ended March 31, 2007 :

(i)	Salary before standard deduction received in India for three months	90,000
(ii)	Income from house property in London (received there)	2,69,200
(iii)	Interest on saving bank deposit in Standard Chartered Bank, New Delhi	40,000
(iv)	Amount brought into India out of the past untaxed profits earned in Germany	80,000
(v)	Income from agriculture in Sri Lanka being invested there	12,234
(vi)	Income from business in Nepal, being controlled from India	30,240
(vii)	Gift in foreign currency from a relative received in India	80,000
(viii)	Income from house property in USA received in USA (Rs. 76,000 is used in Canada for meeting the educational expenses of X's daughter and Rs. 10,000 is later on remitted in India)	86,000

You are required to compute his total income for the assessment year 2007-08.

Ans: 2,10,000.

Problem 2.07-P7 [CS J01]

X has following income during the previous year ended March 31, 2007 :

Salary received in India for three months	9,000
Income from house property in India	13,470
Interest on savings bank deposit in SBI	1,000
Amount brought into India out of the past untaxed profits earned in Germany	20,000
Income from agriculture in Indonesia (agriculture operation controlled from Indonesia) being invested there	12,350
Income from business in Bangladesh, being controlled from India	10,150
Dividends received in Belgium from French companies out of which Rs. 2,500 were remitted to India	23,000

You are required to compute his total income for the assessment year 2007-08, if he is a (a) resident and ordinarily resident (ii) resident but not only ordinarily resident; and (c) non - resident.

Ans: 68,970; 33,620; 23,470.

Problem 2.07-P8 [CS D03]

Raman has furnished the following particulars from the previous year 2007-08. Calculate his total income if he is a non - residence.

Salary for 3 months received in India (Computed)	9,000
Dividend received in Germany from British Companies out of which Rs. 3,000 were remitted to India	22,000
Income from business in Pakistan being controlled from India	10,000
Interest on saving bank deposits in State Bank of India	1,000
Amount brought to India out of past untaxed profit earned in Japan	20,000
Income from house property in India (computed)	3,400

Ans: 13,400.

Problem 2.07. P9 (Difficult)

A consultancy firm furnishes following information. Compute total income if Firm is a (1) Resident in India (2) Non-Resident in India.

1.	Income from consultancy services rendered in India to a foreign client	5,00,000
2.	Income from consultancy services rendered outside India to an Indian client	2,60,000
3.	Interest from debentures of Microsoft Inc. Income is received in England	85,000

Ans: 8,45,000; 5,00,000.

Problem 2.07. P10 [Hons 1998]

Mr. X is a foreign citizen. His grandmother was born in Dhaka on August 12, 1929. He comes to India on October 26, 2006 for a visit of 210 days. His income for the PY 2006-07 is as follows:

1. Income earned and received in India: Rs. 3,40,000
2. Income earned and received outside India: Rs. 7,86,000
3. Income from a house property situated in Mumbai but rent is paid outside India in foreign currency Rs. 92,000

Determine the residential status and compute the taxable income of Mr. X for the AY 2007-08.

Solution

Determination of residential status for the AY 2007-08

Since PY 2006-07 ends on 31st March, 2007 his stay in India is computed from 26-10-2006 to 31-3-2007. His stay in India for PY 2006-07 is 158 days. He satisfies none of the basic condition. His Residential Status is Non-Resident in India.

Computation of total income for the AY 2007-08

Income earned and received in India.	3,40,000
Income earned and received outside India.	Nil
Income from a house property situated in Mumbai but rent is paid outside India. *(Income accrues in India as property is situated in India)*	92,000
Total Income	4,32,000

Problem 2.07. P11 [Hons 2004; 2006C]

A, foreign national (not being a person of Indian origin) came to India for the first time on 15-11-2006 for a visit of 200 days. A had the following incomes during the previous year ended 31-3-2007 :

(i) Salary before standard deduction received in India for three months 87,000
(ii) Interest on saving bank deposit in American Express Bank, New Delhi 50,000
(iii) Income from business in Bhutan being controlled from India 1,00,000
(iv) Income from agricultural in Indonesia being invested there 50,000
(v) Income from house property in Paris received there 1,00,000

You are required to compute his total income for the assessment year 2007-08.
Ans: 1,37,000

Problem 2.07. P12 [Pass 2004]

Computing taxable income of Mr. X, if he is (i) Ordinary Resident, (ii) Not-ordinary Resident, (iii) Non-Resident :

(a) Interest on securities paid by Govt. of India 20,000
(b) Pension from former employer in India, received in Nepal 30,000
(c) Profits from business in Africa, but controlled from India 1,60,000
(d) Income from house property in England, received there 40,000
(e) Income from house property in Iran, received in India. 10,000

Ans: 2,60,000; 2,20,000; 60,000.

Problem 2.07. P13 [Pass 2003]

Compute Taxable Income of an individual if he is ordinary resident, not-ordinary resident and non-resident.

(i)	Profit from business in India, but controlled from England	50,000
(ii)	Salary for services rendered in Pakistan, but received in India	60,000
(iii)	Pension from Indian Govt. against services rendered in India, but received in Nepal	20,000
(iv)	Interest on foreign Govt. securities, received in foreign	10,000
(v)	Profit from business in Africa, controlled from India	15,000

Ans: 1,55,000; 1,45,000; 1,30,000

Problem 2.07. P14 [Pass 2002]

'X' is a non-resident in India for the PY 2006-07. Compute his total income, on the basis of the following information :

(i)	Salary (before standard deduction) received in India for 3 months.	90,000
(ii)	Income from house property in London (received there)	2,60,000
(iii)	Interest on saving bank deposit in a bank in New Delhi	20,000
(iv)	Income from a business in Nepal, being controlled in India, half of the Income received in India	40,000
(v)	Income from Agricultural land situated in India	20,000
(vi)	Gift in foreign currency from a relative received in India	80,000
(vii)	Past untaxed foreign income brought to India in the PY	30,000

Ans: 1,30,000

Problem 2.07. P15 [Pass 1998]

Mr. X has received the following amounts during the previous year ending on March 31, 2007:

1. Income from salary in India from SPG Ltd. Rs 80,000
2. Interest on Gold deposits Scheme, 1999 received in U.S.A. and spent there Rs 10,000 (Gross)
3. Income from house property in Pakistan and received there Rs 15,000
4. Income from business in Calcutta, controlled from U.S.A. Rs 25,000
5. $7,000 earned in U.S.A. during the previous year 2001-02 was brought to India.
6. Received $1,000 draft from his uncle in U.S.A. for his daughter's marriage.

Assume 1$ = Rs 45/-

Compute the Gross Total Income of Mr. X if he is

1. Resident, 2. Not ordinary Resident, and 3. Non-Resident.

Ans: 1,20,000; 1,05,000; 1,05,000

TOPIC 2.08 SECTION 9(1). WHEN INCOME IS DEEMED TO ACCRUE OR ARISE IN INDIA

(A) SECTION 9(1)(i). INCOME FROM BUSINESS CONNECTION

Meaning: A business connection involves a relation between a business carried on by a Non-resident and some activity in India (manufacturing, distributing, selling, etc.) which contributes to the earnings of those profits or gains.

A business connection can be established in following ways:

(i) A Non-resident opens a branch office in India.

(ii) A Non-resident appoints an agent in India.

(iii) A Non-resident forms an association in India.

Taxability: Any income which accrues due to business connection in India such income is deemed to accrue or arise in India and, therefore taxable in all cases whether resident or non-resident.

Explanation 1. Cases where income is not deemed to accrue or arise from business connection

(a) *Apportionment of profit.* In case of a business where all its operations are not carried out in India only that part of income which is reasonably attributable to the operation carried out in India is deemed to accrue or arise in India. Suppose manufacturing work is done in India and sales are effected outside India, only a part of whole profit attributable to manufacturing process shall accrue in India.

(b) Income of a Non-resident from operations consisting only of purchase of goods in India for export.

(c) Income of a Non-resident engaged in the business of running a news agency or publishing newspapers, magazines or journals, or activities confined to collection of news and views in India for transmission out of India.

(d) Income of a Non-resident *(who is not a citizen of India)* from operations confined to shooting of any cinematographic film in India.

Problem 2.08-P1 (CS-J98) - M 5

Q.2b : X Ltd. is a non-resident foreign company. It is engaged in the business of shooting a cinematography film in India. The film after completion is sold to another non-resident outside India. None of the shareholders of X Ltd. is an Indian citizen or resident in India. Discuss the tax implication of this transaction.

Ans: Not taxable.

**Business Connection as defined in Income Tax Act*

"Business connection" shall include any business activity carried out through a person who, acting on behalf of the Non-resident,

(a) has and habitually exercises in India, an authority to conclude contracts on behalf of the Non-resident, unless his activities are limited to the purchase of goods or merchandise for the Non-resident; or

(b) has no such authority, but habitually maintains in India a stock of goods or merchandise from which he regularly delivers goods or merchandise on behalf of the Non-resident; or

(c) habitually secures orders in India, mainly or wholly for the Non-resident or for that Non-resident and other non-residents controlling, controlled by, or subject to the same common control, as that non-resident:

Note

- *Provided* that such business connection shall not include any business activity carried out through a broker, general commission agent or any other agent having an independent status, if such broker, general commission agent or any other agent having an independent status is acting in the ordinary course of his business.
- *Provided* further that where such broker, general commission agent or any other agent works mainly or wholly on behalf of a non-resident (hereafter in this proviso referred to as the principal non-resident) or on behalf of such non-resident and other non residents which are controlled by the principal non-resident or have a controlling interest in the principal non-resident or are subject to the same common control as the principal non-resident, he shall not be deemed to be a broker, general commission agent or an agent of an independent status.

Problem 2.08-P2 (CA - M91) - M 6

X Ltd. is Indian subsidiary of an American company manufacturing and selling copier machines. The Indian company among other things purchases and sells these copier machines also. Does any part of the profits of the sales of American company to the Indian company accrue or arise in India? Discuss.

Ans: No if transactions are undertaken on principal to principal basis.

(B) SECTION 9(1)(i). INCOME FROM ASSETS

Any asset (land, building, plant, etc.) from which income is derived is located in India or any gain or loss arising from transfer of that asset.

(C) SECTION 9(1)(ii) & (iii). WHERE SERVICES ARE RENDERED IN INDIA

Section 9(1)(ii). If services are rendered in India income is deemed to accrue or arise in India and also for the rest period or leave period which is preceded and succeeded by services rendered in India and forms part of the service contract of employment shall be regarded as income earned in India. *e.g.* Pension, Gratuity and Leave Salary.

Section 9(1)(iii). Income chargeable under the head "Salaries" payable by the Government to a citizen of India for services rendered outside India shall be deemed to be income earned in India. However under s*ection 10(7)* any allowances or perquisites paid or allowed by Government of India to Indian citizen *(not foreign citizen)* for rendering services outside India is fully exempt from tax.

Problem 2.08-P3 (Simple)

(A) Mr. Taxcrazy, an Indian Citizen, is an IFS officer. For the last 3 years he has been working in Indian Embassy in France. From 5-1-2007 to 31-1-2007 he was in India for some official work. His emoluments for the PY 2006-07 is

Basic Salary	25,000 p.m.
Special Allowance	10,000 p.m.
Perquisites	1,00,000 p.a.

Compute his gross salary for the AY 2007-08.

(B) What if Mr. Taxcrazy is a foreign citizen. (C) What if Mr. Taxcrazy is working in a private concern.

Ans: 3,00,000; nil; nil.

Problem 2.08-P4 [Hons 1998]

'X' is an employee of an Indian Co. and posted in its branch in America. He gets Rs. 20,000 p.m. as basic pay and Rs. 50,000 p.m. as foreign allowance. State what part of the remuneration will be taxable in India if 'X' is a non-resident for tax purposes and is:

(i) an Indian citizen; or

(ii) a non - Indian citizen.

What if he is an employee of Government of India.

Solution

Incidence of Tax : Since Mr. X renders services outside India his remuneration is taxable in following manner.

Services is rendered outside India	Non-Resident in India
Section 9(1)(iii) - Govt. of India pays salary to Indian citizen who are posted abroad.	Taxable however u/s 10(7) allowances and perquisits are exempt from tax
Section 9(1)(ii) - Any other case i.e. if section 9(1)(iii) is not applicable	Not taxable

Problem 2.08-P5 [CA N98] [M 6]

X, an Indian citizen, is posted in the Indian High commission at London during the previous year 2006-07. His emoluments consists of basic pay of Rs. 17,000 per month and overseas allowance of Rs. 12,000 per month. Besides, he is entitled to air fare for going from and coming to India and also to free use of Government's car at London. He has no taxable income except salary income stated above. His employer did not deduct tax at source. X argues that (i) he is not liable to pay tax on salary earned and received outside India since he is a non-resident during the previous year 2006-07, and (ii) even if any tax is due, it is the duty of his employer to deduct tax at source and as such he has no responsibility to pay the tax. Discuss whether his contention is correct. Will it make any difference if X is foreign citizen ? Give reasons.

Ans: His income from salaries is taxable in India because of section 9(1)(iii). However he can claim exemption u/s 10(7) of the Income Tax Act. Therefore only basic salary of Rs. 17,000 p.m. is taxable.

(D) SECTION 9(1)(iv). DIVIDEND

Dividend from Indian company accrues in India whereas dividend from foreign company accrues outside India. However section 10(34) and Section 10(35) provides exemption to dividend from indian company and mutual fund respectively.

(E) SECTION 9(1)(v). INCOME BY WAY OF INTEREST

Source of earning interest is the amount of money borrowed (i.e. *loan*). If loan is utilised in India then such interest is deemed to accrue or arise in India whether interest is payable by resident or Non-resident. But however loan is used in India by Non-resident for purpose *other than the business*, then such interest is *not deemed to accrue or arise in India.* It means that for the income to accrue in India, the NR should utilised the loan for business purpose in India.

E.g. If a non-resident A borrows moneys from a non-resident B and invests the same in shares of an Indian company, interest earned by B will not be deemed to accrue or arise in

India. However if money is used for the purpose of business in India the interest shall be deemed to accrue or arise in India.

E.g. If Reliance Ltd. borrows Rs. 1,00,000 from World Bank and uses the money in India for business purposes or for any other purpose. The interest earned by World Bank shall accrue in India.

Note

- However if interest is payable by Govt. of India then such interest is deemed to accrue or arise in India whether loan is used in India or outside India.

Problem 2.08-P6 (CA - N92) - M 6

X, a non-resident, lent Rs. 5 lakhs to Y, a resident in India. Y used the money borrowed by him for the purposes of business in India. Y paid an interest of Rs. 75,000 during the year ended March 31, 2007 to X in the United Kingdom. Discuss the tax liability of such interest in the hands of X in India.

Ans: Interest income is taxable in India, since source of income is utilised in India.

Problem 2.08-P7 [Hons 2004-2006C, 2002]

True or false give reason in not more than 20 words.

1. "Interest on loan payable by the Government of India to a non-resident outside India invariably deemed to accrue or arise in India (i.e., irrespective of place where money borrowed is utilised.)"
2. X, a non-resident, lent Rs. 5,00,000 to Y a resident in India. Y used the money for business in India and paid Rs. 75,000 interest to X in London for the year ended on 31-3-2007. Rs. 75,000 shall not be deemed to accrue or arise to X in India, therefore it is not taxable.

Ans: (1) True; As per section 9(1)(v) interest payable by Govt. of India is always deemed to accrue or arise in India whether the loan is used in India or outside India. (2) False; Since source of interest income is loan which is used in India, therefore income is deemed to accrue or arise in India & therefore taxable.

Problem 2.08-P8 (CS-J98) - M 5

Q.2c : A Ltd., a non-resident, gets interest from B Ltd. an Indian company outside India. The capital was borrowed by B Ltd. for the purpose of a business carried on by it outside India. Discuss whether the interest is chargeable to tax in India.

Ans: Not taxable in India.

Problem 2.08-P9 [CA M06]

Mr. A, a citizen of India, left for USA for the purposes of employment on 1-05-2006. He has not visited India thereafter, Mr. A borrows money from his friend Mr. B who left India one week before Mr. A's departure, to the extent of Rs. 10 lakhs and buys shares in X Ltd., an Indian company. Discuss the taxability of the interest charged @ 10% in B's hands where the same has been received in New York.

Ans: Taxable in India

(F) SECTION 9(1)(vi). INCOME BY WAY OF ROYALTY

Source of earning royalty is the right / information / property. If such right /information/ property is used in India then such royalty is deemed to accrue or arise in India whether royalty is payable by resident or Non-resident.

Note

- However if royalty is payable by Govt. of India then such royalty is deemed to accrue or arise in India whether such right / information / property is used in India or outside India.

(G) SECTION 9(1)(vii). INCOME BY WAY OF FEES FOR TECHNICAL SERVICES

Source for fees for technical services is implementation of technical agreement. Where technical agreement is implemented in India for purpose of income earning in India, then such fees for technical services is deemed to accrue or arise in India even where training of employees or any other work is done outside India.

Note

- However if fees for technical services is payable by Govt. of India then such fees is deemed to accrue or arise in India whether such implementation is for Business which shall be carried in India or outside India.

Problem 2.08-P10 [Hons 2001]

Discuss the taxability or otherwise of the following receipts by Mr. X, who is a non - resident

(i) Interest paid by Govt. of India.

(ii) Interest paid by Mr. A, a resident in India for money borrowed for earning capital gains outside India.

(iii) Royalty paid by Mr. B, a non resident. Royalty is payable in respect of an information used for the purpose of a business carried on by Mr. B in India.

Solution

	Particulars	*Non-Resident in India*
1.	Interest paid by Govt. of India [As per section 9(1)(v) interest income paid by Govt. of India is always deemed to accrue or arise in India whether source of income is used in India or outside India.]	Taxable
2.	Interest paid by Mr. A, a resident in India. [As per section 9(1)(v) since debt is used outside India to earn capital gain and therefore interest accrues outside India.]	Non-Taxable
3.	Royalty paid by Mr. B, a Non - resident. [As per section 9(1)(vi) since information is used for the purpose of business in India royalty income accrues in India.]	Taxable

Problem 2.08-P11 (Typical)

Suzuki Motors, had the following receipts of income in FY 2006-07. Indicate whether income will be taxable in India, if it is a, (i) Resident company and (ii) Non-Resident Company. Give reasons for your answer.

(a) Rs. 1,55,000 as royalty from the Government of India under an agreement approved by the Government of Japan and India.

(b) Rs. 3,19,000 from Aryan Ltd. for import of technical know-how for use in a business in India.

(c) Rs. 14,75,000 from Matrix Ltd. for import of drawing for use in its business in Indonesia and China;

(d) Rs. 9,50,000 from Crabtree, for use of a formula for a business in India; and

(e) Rs. 6,11,000 from X, an Indian citizen, for use of drawings and technical know-how for a business in the Sweden.

Compute income if recipient of income is (i) Resident; and (ii) Non-resident.

Ans: 35,10,000; 14,24,000.

Problem 2.08-P12 (Typical)

Compute total income of Mr. X if he is ROR, RNOR and NR in India from the following information :

a.	Salary paid by Govt. of India to a foreign citizen for services rendered outside India	40,000
b.	Mr. X who has head office in Delhi and branch office in London.	
	Profit from head office	1,40,000
	Profit from branch office *(50% income is received in India)*	85,000
c.	Legal Consultancy fees received from a Company for infringement of copyright in Norway. Profession is set up in India	35,000
d.	Legal Consultancy fees received from a Foreign Company for infringement of copyright in India. Profession is set up outside India	90,000
e.	Income by way interest paid by Mr J (RNOR). Loan is used outside India.	1,05,000
f.	Fees for technical services for setting up a manufacturing unit of digital equipment.	
	- Unit to be set in Mizoram	1,54,000
	- Unit to be set up in Nepal	3,50,000
g.	Income from units of foreign mutual fund. *(Investment is done out of income earned in India)*	6,000
h.	Profit from sale of land situated in India. *(Land is sold to a Non-Resident, agreement for sale is done in USA and sale consideration is payable outside India)*	3,00,000
i.	Loss from house property situated outside India	1,00,000

Ans: 12,05,000; 8,04,000; 7,26,500.

Problem 2.08-P13 [CS J06]

Arun, a citizen of India residing in Germany for the past 10 years, came back to India for the first time during January, 2007. During the financial year 2006-07, he received the following income :

— He works in a company in Germany and earns a salary of Euro 1,000 per month;

— He owns agricultural land near Bangalore and a residential house in Delhi which has been let-out. While the agricultural income is being remitted to his account in Germany every year, the rental income of Rs.84,000 is being deposited in his bank account at Delhi; and

— He also owns shares in various Indian companies and receives dividend every year, which has been regularly deposited in his bank account at Delhi.

He seeks your advice as to taxability of the above income under the provisions of the Income-tax Act, 1961 as he is an Indian citizen and earning income in India.

Ans: Salary not taxable; Agricultural income not taxable; rental income taxable; dividend not taxable.

Problem 2.08-P14 [Hons 1994]

For the AY 2007-08 X, an Indian citizen, having business interest in India and Hong Kong, is a "resident but not ordinarily resident" in India. How would you find out the tax incidence in his case? Does it make any difference if he is a "Non-resident"?

Solution

Income from Business in India accrues in India and Income from Business in Hong Kong accrues outside India except where control and management is in India. Therefore following conclusion arrives

	R-NOR	*NR in India*
1. Income from Business in India.	Taxable	Taxable
2. Income from Business in Hong Kong and control and management is in India.	Taxable	Not Taxable
3. Income from Business in Hong Kong and control and management is outside India.	Not Taxable	Not Taxable

2.09 COMPREHENSIVE PROBLEMS

Simple & Difficult

Problem 2.09-P1

1. On 1-6-2004, Bigie, a Malaysian citizen, leaves India after a period of 10 years stay. During the financial year 2005-06, he comes to India for a period of 46 days. Later, he returns to India for 1 year on 10-10-2006. Determine his residential status for the AY 2007-08.
2. Mr. M a foreign citizen, a scientist from U.S.A. was appointed as Senior Scientist in India on 1-4-2003. On 31-1-2005, he went to Pakistan but left his family in India. On 1-5-2006, he came to India and took his family in 31-10-2006. Determine his residential status for the Assessment years 2004-05 to 2007-08.

Ans: (1) ROR; (2) RNOR; RNOR; NR in India; RNOR

Problem 2.09-P2

Ascertain the residential status of the assessees in the following cases for the assessment year 2007-08.

(a) Ajay is citizen of India. He left for Iran on 18th April 2006 and did not return to India till the end of the financial year 2006-07.

(b) Preetam left for U.S.A. on 10th March 1998 after having lived in India for 20 years. He returned to India on 10th September 2006.

Ans: NR in India; RNOR

Problem 2.09-P3 (CA - M93) - M 5

Y was sponsored by his employer in India for some training in U.S.A. He left India on June 3, 2006. He came back to India on April 5, 2007. Determine Y's residential status for the AY 2007-08, assuming that he did not go out of India previously.

Ans: R-OR

Problem 2.09.P4 (CA - N91) - M 5

X, after 25 years of stay in India, retires to UK, on February 3, 2004. He returns to India on July 1, 2006 to join a British company in India. Determine his residential status for the AY 2007-08.

Ans: R-OR

Problem 2.09-P5

X and Mrs X came to India on October 15, 2005 for a visit of 7 months. Both of them are Indian citizens. In the earlier years they were in India as follows :

Year	X	Mrs. X
2005-06	240 days	365 days
2004-05	340 days	20 days
2003-04	nil	15 days
2002-03	118 days	120 days

Determine their residential status for the AY 2007-08.

Ans: NR in India.

Problem 2.09-P6

Mr. Srinivasan, an Indian citizen, is appointed as a senior executive by a company in Canada. He left India, for the first time, on September 15, 2006 to join his duty in Canada. During the PY 2007-08, he comes to India for 94 days. State the residential status of Mr. Srinivasan for the AY 2007-08 and 2008-09.

Ans: NR in India; NR in India.

Problem 2.09-P7 (CA - N02) - M 6

Q.1b : In the leap year 2003-04 (previous year) A, a sailor, has remained on ship for a private company owning ocean going ships as follows :

a. outside the territorial waters of India for 183 days

b. inside the territorial waters of India for 183 days.

Is he considered to be resident or not for the assessment year 2004-05 (previous year 2003-04). Comment.

Ans: Resident in India.

Problem 2.09-P8 [Hons 1997]

Determine the residential status of Mr. X for the PY 2006-07, assuming that he did not go out of India before this and came back to India on April 10, 2007 in the following cases:

1. Sponsored by his employer in India for training in U.K. and he leaves India (a) on June 15, 2006 or (b) on May 10, 2006.
2. He goes for employment purposes to U.K. and leaves India on September 15, 2006.

Ans: R-0R; NR in India; NR in India.

Problem 2.09-P9 [Hons 1996]

X is a citizen of Bangladesh. His grandmother was born in a village near Dhaka in 1940. He comes to India for the first time since 1981 on October 4, 2006 for a visit of 190 days. Find out the residential status of X for the AY 2007-08 on the assumption that Mrs. X is a resident but not ordinarily resident in India for the same year.

Ans: NR in India.

Problem 2.09-P10 [Hons 1994]

During the PY 2006-07, X, a foreign citizen, stays in India for just 69 days. Determine his residential status for the AY 2007-08 on the basis of the following information:

(i) During 2003-04, X is present in India for 365 days.

(ii) During 2000-01 and 1999-2000, X is in Japan for 359 and 348 days respectively.

Ans: R-NOR

Problem 2.09-P11 (CS-NEW - J03) - M 3

Q.1d : Z was working as an employee on an Indian ship lying in foreign waters. During the year under assessment, the ship did not touch the Indian coast, except for 80 days. State his residential status for the assessment and taxability of his salary.

Ans: NR in India.

Problem 2.09-P12

X Ltd. and Y Ltd. companies are registered in Nepal and India respectively. All meetings of Board of Directors of X Ltd. were held in India, whereas all Board meetings of Y Ltd. were held in Nepal during the PY 2006-07. Determine their residential status for the AY 2007-08.

Ans: Resident in India in both the cases.

Typical

Problem 2.09-P13 (CA - M98) - M 9

Q.1a : X, an American citizen, is appointed by a multinational company to its branch in New Delhi in 2003. X has never been to India before this appointment. He arrives in Mumbai on April 15, 2003 and joins the New Delhi office on April 20, 2003. His wife and children join him in India on October 20, 2003. The company allotted him a leased residence for purposes of his stay. This residence is occupied by him from the beginning of October, 2003.

On February 10, 2004, he is transferred by his employer, on deputation basis, to be the regional chief of his employer's operations in South East Asia having headquarters in Hong-Kong. He leaves New Delhi on February 11 and arrives in Hong Kong on February 12, 2004. X leaves behind his wife and children in India till August 14, 2005, when they leave along with him for Hong Kong. X had come to India earlier on June 15, 2005 on two months' leave. The members of the family occupied the residence till date of departure to Hong Kong.

At the end of the period of deputation, X is reported to India and joins the New Delhi office of his employer as chief of Indian operations on February 2, 2007.

In what residential status X will be assessable, for the various years, to income tax in India ?

Ans: RNOR; NR; NR; NR.

Problem 2.09-P14

X comes to India for the first time on September 1, 2006. On October 15, 2006, he joins a company on monthly salary of Rs. 6,000, as a part - time production consultant (duty hours 6.30 p.m. to 9.30 p.m.). He does not have any source of income up to October 14, 2006. On October 19, 2006, he starts a trading business in computer hardware after obtaining the approval of his employer. For the previous year ending March 31, 2007, he has the following income:

Salary from the part-time employment : Rs. 90,000; income earned in India from the business of trading in computer hardware : Rs. 1,00,000; and foreign income from the same business : 4,40,000. Find out the residential status of X for the assessment year 2007-08 and income chargeable to tax in India.

Ans: Non-resident; Rs. 1,90,000.

Problem 2.09-P15 (ICWAI - D98) - M 6

Mr. Tik, an Indian citizen, joined Oxford as a Professor on a monthly salary of $ 1,000 on October 1, 2003 on a 6 year contract. He had never been out of India in the past. His wife and two children live in a rented house, which is maintained by him in Delhi. He wants to proceed to India on leave for a period of 10 months to get his own house constructed in Delhi. But at the same time, he wants to be treated as a non-resident during his stay here so that his salary earned in the UK may remain totally exempt from tax in India. He does not propose to make any other visit to India during the period of his contract of service in the UK. Suggest the dates as to how he should plan his 10 months' visit to India.

Hint : Plan his stay in India in two previous years.

Problem 2.09-P16

Mr. Mayank, a Chief Executive Officer of a company, had undertaken foreign tour on various occasions for company's work and was out of India for a total number of 225 days during the PY ending March 31, 2007. Determine the residential status for the AY 2007-08 assuming that during the last 7 years immediately preceding the PY 2006-07 he was in India for 720 days. *(take suitable assumption)*

Ans: RNOR or NR depending upon your assumption.

Problem 2.09-P17

Mr. Taxcrazy, an Indian citizen, is a frequent visitor of foreign countries. His details of foreign visit and purpose of visit is given below.

Period of stay outside India	*Purpose of visit*
11-6-2002 to 17-12-2002	Official tour
5-3-2003 to 7-8-2004	Personal tour
1-1-2005 to 31-12-2006	Employment

On 1-1-2007 he returned to India and before 11-6-2002 he was never out of India. You are requested to determine his Residential Status for the various assessment years.

Ans: ROR (PY 2002-03); NR (PY 2003-04); NR (PY 2004-05); NR (PY 2005-06); NR (PY 2006-07).

STRATEGY MAKER

Points in 1 to 10	Overall Points 5; Practical 2; Theory 7.
Type of problem	Difficult. Theory as well as practical both are important. Each year there is a question either theory or practical. The difficult part is incidence of tax.
What to expect (DU)	Residential status of individual and incidence of tax. Do revise all typical problems of professional exam. Also write a short note on Business Connection.
CA (PE II)	Everything.

Remarkable

You are going to achieve your target if don't stop here. The next step 'Income from Salary' is considered to be very lengthy chapter. But let me assure you we have made this chapter very easy to understand with lots of illustration and problems. Take this chapter very seriously and keep on memorising every topic. Simply understanding the concept shall not fetch you marks.

Keep Running

The first head dealing with servants alongwith masters

3

Income from Salaries

TOPIC 3.01 MEANING OF SALARY

1. Salary signifies remuneration for services rendered. Services may be rendered as a consultant or as an employee.
2. If services are rendered as a consultant, then income earned is taxable either under the head 'Profit from Business' or under the head 'Income from Other Sources' whereas if services are rendered as an employee, then income is taxable under the head 'Income from Salary'.
3. Salary comprises of remuneration in any form (*bonus, commission, etc.*) whether in cash or in kind. It also includes perquisites due for personal service under an express or implied contract of employment.
4. This section assumes a very impressive number of benefits arising from employment - *some of them in nature of income and some not, some of them convertible into money and some not* — which fall to be assessed as salary.

TOPIC 3.02 *SECTION 15.* CHARGEABILITY

(A) WHICH INCOME IS CHARGED UNDER THE HEAD SALARY

Where there exists a relationship of master and servant *(i.e. employer and employee relationship)* then only income is taxable under the head "Salaries". Where such relationship does not exist, income is taxable either under the head "Profit from Business" or under the head "Income from Other Sources". Besides, only those payments which have nexus with the employment are taxable under the head "Salaries".

(i) What is the test to determine relationship of employer and employee ?

Test is degree of control. In case of relationship of consultant, the consultant has the power to take independent decisions. Whereas in case of relationship of employer and employee, employee do not have the liberty to take independent decisions. Their decisions are guided by the decisions of employer. However this is not an absolute test.

(ii) What is the difference between relationship of 'principal and agent' and 'master and servant'?

Principal and Agent relationship or Contract for Service	*Master and Servant relationship or Contract of Service*
Principal has the right to direct what work the agent should do.	However master has the further right to direct how the work should be done.
Here a person offers his services to any person for a price. He conduct his work at his own discretion. He is independent and provides consultancy services. He is entitled to profits and bears the losses.	Here a person offers his services to his master for a monthly or annual remuneration. He conduct his work at the will of his master. He is not independent. He is entitled to fixed remuneration.
Here a person does work for his client.	Here a person does work of his master.
E.g. Statutory Auditor	E.g. Internal Auditor
The income is charged either under the head 'Business' or under the head 'Other Sources'.	The income is charged either under the head Income from Salaries.

Problem 3.02-P1

1. Under which head remuneration received by director is taxable?
2. Under which head salary received by M.P. and M.L.A. are taxable?
3. A lecturer receiving examinership remuneration is taxable under which head?
4. A doctor an employee of AIIMS also does private practice. Explain its tax treatment.
5. Only salary from present employer is taxable. (True or False)
6. What is the place of accrual of salary?
7. Explain meaning of salary?

Solution

1. Income from Other Sources, since generally directors are not the employees of the company. But if the directors are given additional responsibility and appointed as an employee then salary received by director is chargeable under the head salary.
2. Income from Other Sources since M.P. and M.L.A. are not employees of the government.
3. If examinership remuneration is received from the employer then under the head Income from Salary otherwise under the head Income from Other Sources.
4. Salary received from AIIMS is taxable under the head Income from Salary and income from private practice taxable under the head Profit from Business.
5. False. Salary from all employers whether past or present is taxable under the head salary. Even in certain cases as per section 17(3) salary from prospective employer is also taxable under the head salary.
6. As per section 9(1)(ii) if services are rendered in India salary accrues in India. If services are rendered outside India salary accrues outside India. But as per section 9(1)(iii) "Salaries" payable by the Government of India to a citizen of India for services rendered outside India shall be deemed to be income earned in India.
7. Salary denotes consideration for the services rendered by employee under the contract of service from the employer. Remuneration is normally paid in cash. However there are several instances where salary is paid by way of non-monetary benefits, which is normally treated as perquisites and sometimes fringe benefits.

(B) IN WHICH PREVIOUS YEAR SALARY INCOME IS CHARGED TO TAX

Salary is chargeable to tax either on 'due' basis or on 'receipt' basis whichever matures earlier. Thus salary is assessed at an earliest possible time.

Salary may fall due either on the last day of each month or on the first day of next month. If salary falls due on last day of each month then salary of April shall falls due on 30th April and salary of May shall fall due on 31st May and so on. Whereas if salary falls due on the first day of next month salary of April shall fall due on 1st May and salary of May shall fall due on 1st June and so on. Let us see its tax treatment.

Illustration 3.02-P2 (Simple)

Find out from the following cases in which previous year salary is chargeable to tax.

	Due date	*Date of receipt*	*Taxable PY*
Case 1	*31-3-2007*	04-4-2007	2006-07
Case 2	30-4-2007	*24-3-2007*	2006-07
Case 3	*31-3-2006*	04-4-2006	2005-06
Case 4	30-4-2006	*31-3-2006*	2005-06

Solution

In *Case 1* the earlier date is 31-3-2006, which falls in PY 2006-07, therefore salary is chargeable in the PY 2006-07. As you can see the salary which was due on 31-3-2007, is being received on 4-4-2007, therefore it is in arrears of salary. Now, if arrears of salary which has already been taxed on due basis shall not again be taxed on receipt basis.

Arrears of salary : It means the salary which has fallen due but not yet received. Arrears of salary is taxable on due basis even if salary is not received.

In *Case 2* the earlier date is 24-3-2007, which falls in PY 2006-07, therefore salary is chargeable in the PY 2006-07. As you can see the salary which was due on 30-4-2007, is being received before 30-4-2007 *i.e.* on 24-3-2007, therefore it is an advance salary. Now, if advance salary which has already been taxed on receipt basis it shall not again be taxed on due basis.

Advance salary : It means salary which has been received but not yet fallen due. Advance salary is taxable on receipt basis even if salary has not fallen due.

(iii) Enumerate salaries which are chargeable to tax only on receipt basis

1. Advance salary. *(However advance against salary is not a salary but it is treated as loan therefore not taxable.)*
2. Arrears of salary, if not taxed earlier on due basis, is chargeable on receipt basis. This can happen when salary is increased with retrospective effect.
3. Salary in lieu of notice period.
4. Bonus is chargeable only on receipt basis.

TOPIC 3.03 COMPUTATION OF SALARY, ETC.

(A) COMPUTATION OF INCOME FROM SALARY *(assumed figures)*

Basic Salary allowed for basic qualities like qualification experience, etc.	45,000
Dearness Allowance allowed to compensate for inflation	12,000
Commission (*Fixed or variable*)	2,000

Entertainment Allowance fully taxable whether Govt. employee or Pvt. employee		6,000
House Rent Allowance [2,000 × 12]	24,000	
Less: Exempt [500 × 10]	5,000	19,000
All other taxable allowances		7,000
Bonus received		15,000
Arrears of salary if not taxed earlier		2,000
Advance salary		5,600
Fees		4,000
Perquisites if taxable		1,200
Leave encashed during the PY 2006-07		800
Annuity from employer also known as annual payment		8,000
Retirement benefits:		
Gratuity if taxable		12,000
Uncommuted or commuted pension if taxable		9,000
Leave Salary if taxable		18,000
Annual accretion to provident fund if taxable		6,000
Lumpsum withdrawal from provident fund if taxable		52,000
Gross Salary		2,36,000
Less : Deduction u/s 16:		
(i) Standard Deduction (ommitted)	nil	
(ii) Entertainment Allowance allowed only to Govt. employee	5,000	
(iii) Professional or Employment tax	1,000	6,000
Income from Salary		2,30,000

(B) TAX TREATMENT OF SURRENDER OF SALARY

If any salary has accrued it is taxable even if it has been foregone. Foregoing or waiver or surrender of salary would be treated as application of income and therefore chargeable to tax. However if any employee surrenders his salary to the Central Govt. under the Voluntary Surrender of Salaries (Exemption from taxation) Act, 1961, the surrendered salary shall not be taxable whether Govt employee or private employee.

(C) MEANING OF BASIC SALARY AND ITS COMPUTATION

(1) Basic salary also known as basic pay is allowed for basic qualities of employee like qualification, experience, etc.

(2) Where employer before paying the salary deducts certain personal expenditure of employee it is not allowed as deduction and shall be added back for computation of basic salary. *Example*

Salary after deduction of following		4,50,000
Tax deducted at source	25,000	
Employee's contribution towards provident fund	5,000	
Rent of an accommodation provided by employer	15,000	45,000
Basic Salary		4,95,000

(D) PAY SCALE

Generally in a Govt. department pay-scale is fixed which shows initial pay increment and maximum pay of an employee. Increment is provided once in every year. It is provided on first day of joining month. Suppose Mr. X joins on 15-5-2001. He will get an increment from the month of joining *i.e.* from 1-5-2002 and not from 15-5-2002.

E.g. Mr. X is appointed on 11-8-2001 on a pay scale of 20,000-1,000-25,000-2,000-47,000. It means that Mr. X will get initially Rs. 20,000 p.m. as basic salary from the date of joining (11-8-2001) and every year (1-8-2002 and thereafter) he will get an increment of Rs. 1,000 p.m. till he reaches 25,000 p.m., thereafter he will get an increment of Rs. 2,000 p.m. till it reaches 47,000 p.m. In another situation the employer may provide an advance increment. In such case only the initial pay changes and the remaining part of pay scale remains same. Suppose Mr. X gets an 3 advance increments. His initial salary shall be Rs. 23,000 thereafter an increment of Rs. 1,000 p.m. every year.

Problem 3.03-P1 (Simple)

Mr. Taxcrazy is employed in Free Ltd. since 1-9-2003 in the grade of 25,000-2,000-29,000-3000-41,000. He is also entitled to dearness allowance @ 10% of basic salary. You are required to compute his gross salary for the AY 2007-08.

Solution

1-9-2003	25,000	[PY 2003-04]
1-9-2004	27,000	[PY 2004-05]
1-9-2005	29,000	[PY 2005-06]
1-9-2006	32,000	[PY 2006-07]
1-9-2007	35,000	[PY 2007-08]
1-9-2008	38,000	[PY 2008-09]
1-9-2009	41,000	[PY 2009-10]

Since we have to compute for PY 2006-07 therefore

Basic salary is [April to August 29,000 × 5] + [Sept to March 32,000 × 7]	3,69,000
Dearness Allowance [10% of basic salary]	36,900
Gross Salary	4,05,900

Problem 3.03-P2 (Simple)

Mr. Taxcrazy is employed in Orkut Ltd. since 1-1-2002 in the grade of 15,000-5,000-30,000-7000-51,000. He is also entitled to profit bonus @ 1% of basic salary. Commission on sales @ 2% of sales. Sales achieved by employee Rs. 30 lakhs per annum. You are required to compute his gross salary for the AY 2007-08.

Ans: 5,29,650.

Problem 3.03-P3 (Simple)

Mr. Taxcrazy is employed in Google Ltd. since 1-1-2000 in the grade of 4,000-400-8,000-500-16,000 on a initial salary of Rs. 6,400. You are required to compute his gross salary for the AY 2007-08.

Ans: 1,09,500.

Problem 3.03-P4 (Simple)

Mr. Taxcrazy is a Speaker in a Company since 1-10-2004 in the grade of 10,000-500-20,000. He took a advance salary of 3 months on 1-2-2007. You are required to compute his gross salary for the AY 2007-08.

Ans: 1,18,500.

Problem 3.03-P5 (Simple)

Compute Gross Salary from following information for the AY 2007-08.

Salary after tax deduction of Rs. 2,000	1,44,000
Advance salary due for April 2007 received in March 2007	8,000
Arrears of salary already taxed in the PY 2006-07	5,000
Arrears of salary not taxed earlier	7,000
Bonus not yet received	16,000

Ans: 1,61,000.

Problem 3.03-P6 (Simple)

Compute Gross Salary from following information for the AY 2007-08.

Salary Rs. 98,000 after following deduction.

Contribution to provident fund Rs. 5,000. Life insurance premium Rs. 3,000. Recovery of loan Rs. 600 p.m. and income tax Rs. 100 p.m.

In addition he has voluntarily surrendered salary of Rs. 2,000 in public interest.

Ans: 1,16,400.

Problem 3.03-P7 (Difficult)

Mr. X has been drawing basic salary of Rs. 23,000 p.m. for last 2 years. His annual increment falls due on 1-2-2007 of Rs. 6,000 p.m. He is entitled to fixed commission of Rs. 4,000 p.m. which was discontinued from 1-2-2007. His other incomes are long term capital gain from sale of land Rs. 2,00,000. Winning from lotteries Rs. 35,000. He is eligible for deduction under section 80C in respect of contribution towards recognised provident fund Rs. 10,000. Compute Total Income and Tax liability from the following informations.

Ans: 5,53,000; 97,818.

Problem 3.03-P8 (Difficult)

(A) Mr. X a senior Indian citizen lives India for the first time for employment purpose on 1-5-2006 on a salary of Rs. 35,000 p.m. Earlier he was employed in India on a salary of Rs. 18,000 p.m. His other incomes are Income from house property situated in India Rs. 12,00,000 and short term capital gain from sale of shares of an Indian company Rs. 40,000 subjected to securities transaction tax. He is eligible for deduction under section 80C in respect of contribution towards recognised provident fund Rs. 1,00,000. Compute his Total Income and Tax liability for the AY 2007-08.

(B) What shall be your answer if he leaves India on 1-7-2006.

Ans: (A) 11,58,000; 3,24,707; (B) 15,09,000; 4,42,853.

(E) COMPUTATION OF SUPERANNUATION SALARY (SAS)

Superannuation salary (SAS) =

1. Basic Salary +
2. Dearness Allowance if terms of employment so provide. It means dearness allowance should form part of basic salary for computation of retirement benefits. Retirement benefits are Gratuity, Pension, Leave Salary and Annual accretion to the Provident Fund. Where the question is silent whether dearness allowance forms part of salary or not, it means that dearness allowance do not form part of salary.

3. As per Supreme Court Judgement, Commission shall also form part of salary if based on turnover and turnover is achieved by employee. *E.g.* Suppose it is given that Mr. X shall receive 1% of commission on turnover. Turnover achieved by employee is Rs. 1,00,000. In this case commission of Rs. 1,000 shall be included in Superannuation salary. If however fixed commission is given then commission is not included in Superannuation salary. Do remember any other commission like commission based on purchases or profits or fixed commission shall not form part of Superannuation salary.

In short, let us say superannuation salary (SAS) = Basic Salary + Dearness allowance ( ) + commission (if). Do remember always compute superannuation salary on monthly basis. If the question uses the word 'Salary' it means it is superannuation salary.

Problem 3.03-P9 (Simple)

Compute superannuation salary in following three cases:

(1) Basic Salary	8,000 p.m.
Dearness Allowance (30% forms part of salary)	2,000 p.m.
Fixed commission	3,000 p.m.
(2) Basic Salary	3,000 p.m.
Dearness Allowance	20% of Basic salary
Commission	1% of profits
Profits achieved by employee	6,00,000 p.m.
(3) Basic Salary	9,000 p.m.
Dearness Allowance	10% of basic salary
Commission based on sales	1%
Sales achieved by employee	1,00,000 p.m.

Annual accretion to provident fund is 12% of basic salary and dearness allowance.

Ans: 8,600; 3,000; 10,900.

(F) COMPUTATION OF SALARY IF SALARY FALLS DUE ON LAST DAY OF EACH MONTH AND FIRST DAY OF NEXT MONTH.

Computation of salary if salary falls due on last day of each month. In this case salary of April 2006 falls due 30-4-2006, salary of May 2006 shall fall due on 31-5-2006, salary of March 2007 shall fall due on 31-3-2007. It means respective month salary falls due in respective month. Therefore to compute salary for PY 2006-07 salary of April 2006 to salary of March 2007 is taken.

Computation of salary if salary falls due on first day of nect month. In this case salary of March 2006 shall fall due on 1-4-2006, salary of April 2006 falls due 1-5-2006, salary of February 2007 shall fall due on 1-3-2007. It means one month salary of PY 2005-06 salary is taxable in PY 2006-07 and one month salary of PY 2006-07 is taxable in the PY 2007-08. Therefore to compute salary for PY 2006-07 March 2006 to February 2007 is taken.

Illustration 3.03-P10 [Simple]

Mr. Taxcrazy joins TQM Ltd. on 1-5-2004 on a monthly salary of Rs. 10,000 p.m. From July 1, 2006 his salary is increased to Rs. 12,000 p.m. Compute salary chargeable to tax for the PY 2006-07 if (a) salary falls due on last day of each month (b) Salary falls due on first day of next month.

Solution

	Respective months salary	*(a) last day of each month*	*(b) first day of next month*
March 2006	10,000	10,000	10,000
April 2006	10,000	10,000	10,000
May 2006	10,000	10,000	10,000
June 2006	10,000	10,000	10,000
July 2006	12,000	12,000	10,000
Aug. 2006	12,000	12,000	12,000
Sept. 2006	12,000	12,000	12,000
Oct. 2006	12,000	12,000	12,000
Nov. 2006	12,000	12,000	12,000
Dec. 2006	12,000	12,000	12,000
Jan. 2007	12,000	12,000	12,000
Feb. 2007	12,000	12,000	12,000
March 2007	12,000	12,000	12,000
April 2007	12,000	12,000	12,000

Computation of basic salary

If salary falls due on the last day of each month		*If salary falls due on the first day of next month*	
April 2006 to March 2007		March 2006 to February 2007	
April to June (3 × 10,000)	30,000	March to June (4 × 10,000)	40,000
July to March (9 × 12,000)	1,08,000	July to Feb. (8 × 12,000)	96,000
Total salary of PY 2006-07	1,38,000	Total salary of PY 2006-07	1,36,000

Illustration 3.03-P11 [Difficult]

(A) Mr. X joins a company on 1-6-2002 on a salary of Rs. 10,000 p.m. from 1-12-2006 his salary is increased to Rs. 15,000 p.m. Compute his basic salary for the AY 2007-08 assuming that (a) salary falls due on last day of each month (b) Salary falls due on first day of next month.

(B) What would be your answer if he joins the company on 1-6-2006.

(C) What would be your answer if he resigns from the company on 31-1-2007.

Solution : (A)

Computation of basic salary

last day of each month		*first day of next month*	
April 2006 to March 2007		*March 2006 to February 2007*	
April to Nov. (8 × 10,000)	80,000	March to Nov. (9 × 10,000)	90,000
Dec. to March (4 × 15,000)	60,000	Dec. to Feb. (3 × 15,000)	45,000
Total salary of PY 2006-07	1,40,000	Total salary of PY 2006-07	1,35,000

Solution : (B)

Computation of basic salary

last day of each month		*first day of next month*	
June 2006 to March 2007		*June 2006 to February 2007*	
June to Nov. (6 × 10,000)	60,000	June to Nov. (6 × 10,000)	60,000
Dec. to March (4 × 15,000)	60,000	Dec. to Feb. (3 × 15,000)	45,000
Total salary of PY 2006-07	1,20,000	Total salary of PY 2006-07	1,05,000

Solution : (C)

Computation of basic salary

last day of each month April 2006 to Jan. 2007		*first day of next month March 2006 to Jan. 2007*	
April to Nov. (8 × 10,000)	80,000	March to Nov. (9 × 10,000)	90,000
Dec. to Jan. (2 × 15,000)	30,000	Dec. to Jan. (2 × 15,000)	30,000
Total salary of PY 2006-07	1,10,000	Total salary of PY 2006-07	1,20,000

Problem 3.03-P12 [Difficult]

Mr. T. Rao joins as an education officer in ICSI in the grade of 10,000-500-15,000 from 1-7-2005. Compute his basic salary for the AY 2007-08 assuming that (a) salary falls due on last day of each month (b) Salary falls due on first day of next month.

Ans: 1,24,500; 1,24,000.

Problem 3.03-P13 [Typical]

Mr. Taxcrazy joins Star India Ltd. as a Senior Editor on a pay scale of 30,000-3,000-1,02,000 from 11-8-2004. His employer provided 2 advance increments. Compute his basic salary for the AY 2007-08 assuming that (a) salary falls due on last day of each month (b) Salary falls due on first day of next month.

Ans: 4,92,000; 4,89,000. *Hint :* His joining salary shall be Rs. 36,000.

Problem 3.03-P14 [Simple]

Compute basic salary for the AY 2007-08 from the following information if (a) salary falls due on last day of each month (b) Salary falls due on first day of next month.

1. Mr. X joins a company on 1-11-2004 on a grade of 12,000-1,000-20,000.
2. Mr. X joins the Co. on 1-7-2006 on a salary of Rs. 6,000 p.m.
3. Mr. X joins the Co., on 1-6-2002 on a grade of 16,000 - 2,000 - 20,000 - 4,000 - 32,000. He retires on 31-1-2007.
4. Mr. X joins the Co., on 1-5-2006 on a salary of Rs. 15,000 p.m. He retires at the end of February.
5. Mr. X is working with two Companies. A Ltd. pays him Rs. 8,000 p.m. and B. Ltd. pays Rs. 9,000 p.m.
6. Mr. X has been drawing basic salary of Rs. 12,000 p.m. for last 3 years. His annual increment falls due on 1-8-2006 of Rs. 3,000 p.m.
7. Mr. X retires on 31-12-2006. Basic salary at the time of retirement Rs. 8,000 p.m. His annual increment falls due on 1-9-2006 Rs. 2,000 p.m.

Ans: (1) 1,61,000; 1,60,000; (2) 54,000; 48,000; (3) 2,72,000; 2,96,000; (4) 1,50,000; 1,50,000; (5) 2,04,000; 2,04,000; (6) 1,68,000; 1,65,000; (7) 62,000; 68,000.

Problem 3.03-P15 (Typical)

(A) Compute Basic Salary from the following information for the AY 2007-08:

	Case 1	*Case 2*	*Case 3*
Date of joining	1-10-2000	1-5-2003	1-6-2006
Date of resignation	Not applicable	31-12-2006	31-1-2007
Basic Salary from the date of joining	8,000 p.m.	9,000 p.m.	10,000 p.m.
Basic Salary from 1-8-2006	10,000 p.m.	11,000 p.m.	13,000 p.m.

Compute his Gross salary for the AY 2007-08 assuming that (a) salary falls due on last day of each month (b) Salary falls due on first day of next month.

(B) What would be your answer in Case 1 if he joins the company on 1-5-2007.

Ans (A) : (1) 1,12,000; 1,10,000; (2) 91,000; 1,00,000; (3) 98,000; 98,000; (B): 1,04,000; 94,000

ALLOWANCES

1. It is a fixed amount of money payable to employee for particular requirement connected with the service rendered.
2. Allowances may be given for personal purpose or for official purpose.
3. Where the allowances are given for personal purpose it is generally fully taxable. But where allowances are given for official purpose it is generally exempt from tax. Treatment of taxability of allowance does not depend upon the name of the allowance but for the purpose for which it is provided.
4. Allowances are divided into four categories (i) Fully exempted allowances (ii) Fully taxable allowances (iii) Partially exempted allowances and (iv) Special allowance.

TOPIC 3.04 FULLY EXEMPTED ALLOWANCES

Following allowances are fully exempted from tax:

1. Allowances paid to Supreme Court and High Court Judges.
2. Any salary or allowance or perquisites paid to the employees of United Nation Organisation.
3. *Section 10(7).* Any allowances or perquisites paid or allowed by Government of India to Indian citizen *(not foreign citizen)* for rendering services outside India. *(Such salary is deemed to accrue or arise in India)*

TOPIC 3.05 FULLY TAXABLE ALLOWANCES

Ignoring the expenditure incurred by employee following allowances provided by employer are fully taxable whether employee spends for specific purposes or not. Generally following allowances are given for personal purpose, therefore it is fully taxable.

(SCOPE DRIFT is a memory technique for remembering fully taxable allowances)

S C O P E D R I F T

Servant; **C**ity Compensatory; **O**vertime; **P**roject; **E**ntertainment
Dearness; **R**ural; **I**nterim Relief; **F**ixed Medical Allowance; **T**iffin Allowance

Other Fully Taxable Allowances

1. Telephone Allowance
2. Refreshment Allowance
3. Non-Practising Allowance
4. Meal Allowance
5. Holiday Allowance
6. Special Qualification Allowance
7. Dinner Allowance
8. Marriage Allowance
9. Wardenship Allowance
10. High Cost of living Allowance

Note

- Entertainment allowance is fully taxable whether received by government employee or private employee. It is fully taxable even if whole of allowance is spent towards official purpose.

Problem 3.05-P1 (Simple)

Mr. X was appointed on 1-6-2000 in blogspot Ltd. in pay scale of 9,000-500-15,000 on initial pay of 12,000. He is paid 40% of pay as dearness allowance and 10% of pay as city compensatory allowance. Compute his Gross salary for the AY 2007-08 assuming that (a) salary falls due on last day of each month (b) Salary falls due on first day of next month.

Ans: 2,68,500; 2,22,750.

Problem 3.05-P2 (Difficult)

Mr. X was appointed in tadpad Ltd. on a basic pay of 16,000. He took 3 months basic salary in advance on 28-2-2007. He was paid dearness allowance Rs. 2,000 p.m. (not forming part of salary). Entertainment allowance for the entertainment of clients of the company. He spend Rs. 3,000 p.m. out of Rs. 5,000 p.m. which he received. He is also allowed high cost of living allowance @ 50,000. Compute his Gross salary for the AY 2007-08.

Ans: 2,94,000.

TOPIC 3.06 *SECTION 10(13A) & RULE 2A.* HOUSE RENT ALLOWANCE (PARTIALLY EXEMPTED ALLOWANCE)

House rent allowance (HRA) is given to employee for payment of rent. If no rent is paid exemption is not available. But if rent is paid over 10% of salary then exemption is allowed under section 10(13A). The exemption is computed as per Rule 2A. *(Let us call it FAF rule)*

Computation of taxable HRA (assumed figures)

House rent allowance received	5,000 × 12	60,000
Less : Exempt *(Computation is done as per rule 2A)*	3,000 × 12	36,000
Taxable House rent allowance *(this amount is added to gross salary)*		24,000

Computation of exemption as per Rule 2A

(FAF is a memory technique for remembering Rule 2A)

Formula 1	50% of salary (SAS) if place of residence *(not service)* is Metro cities (Delhi, Mumbai, Chennai, Kolkata) otherwise take 40% of salary (SAS)	Least is exempt from tax
Actual	Actual HRA received.	
Formula 2	Rent paid in excess of 10% of salary (SAS) which is *Rent Paid* - 10% of salary (SAS)	

Note

1. Salary (SAS) is equal to [B.S. + D.A.( ) + Comm. (if)] is computed on due basis for the period when rent is paid and rent is paid only when house is occupied by the employee.
2. Since salary (SAS) is computed on due basis therefore neither arrears of salary nor advance salary is included for computing Superannuation salary.
3. If place of stay is not given in the question take 40% of salary (SAS).
4. Actual HRA received minus least is taxable.

Problem 3.06-P1 [CS D05]

Kajol, working in a software company at Bangalore, is drawing a remuneration of Rs. 23,000 per month. She is paid D.A. of Rs. 7,000 per month as provided in the terms of employment. In addition, she is also paid HRA of Rs. 5,000 per month and is entitled to 3% commission on turnover of Rs. 18,00,000 achieved by her during 2006-07. She pays a rent of Rs. 7,200 per month. Further, she received advance salary of Rs. 46,000 in March, 2007 relating to the period April-May, 2007. Determine the taxable income under the head 'salaries'

Ans: 4,75,000.

Solution

Computation of Income from Salary

Basic Salary (23,000 × 12)		2,76,000
D.A. (7,000 × 12)		84,000
Commission on sales (3% of 18 lakhs)		54,000
HRA (5,000 × 12)	60,000	
Less: exempt (3,750 × 12) (Note 1)	45,000	15,000
Advance salary		46,000
Income from Salary		4,75,000

Note 1 : Computation of exemption from HRA

Superannuation salary (SAS) (23,000 + 7,000 + 4,500) Rs. 34,500 p.m.

F_1	50% of SAS	13,800 p.m.	Rs. 3,750 is
A	Actual HRA received	7,000 p.m.	exempt
F_2	Rent paid — 10% of SAS (7,200 – 3,450)	3,750 p.m.	since least

Problem 3.06-P2 [Simple]

X is an employee of private sector company in Mumabi. His salary and allowance are :

Basic Salary Rs. 6,000 p.m, Dearness Allowance Rs. 500 p.m, Entertainment Allowance Rs. 1,000 p.m, Medical Allowance Rs. 500 p.m, Servant Allowance Rs. 300 p.m and House Rent Allowance Rs. 4,000 p.m.

He occupies a flat at a monthly rent of Rs. 3,800 p.m. Compute his income chargeable under the head 'Salaries' for the AY 2007-08.

Ans: 1,11,600. [72,000+6,000+12,000+6,000+3,600+12,000=1,11,600]

Problems 3.06-P3 [CS J99]

X, a resident of Ajmer, received Rs. 48,000 as basic salary during the previous year 2006-07. In addition he gets Rs. 4,800 p.m. as dearness allowance forming part of basic salary, 7 per cent commission on sales made by him (sale made by X during the relevant previous year is Rs. 86,000) and Rs. 6,000 p.m. as house rent allowance. He however, pays Rs. 5,800 at house rent. Determine the quantum of house rent allowance exempts from tax and income from salary.

Ans: Nil; 64,820. [48,000+4,800+6,020+6,000=64,820]

Illustration 3.06-P4 (Conceptual)

	Case 1	*Case 2*	*Case 3*	*Case 4*
Salary (SAS)	4,000 p.m.	3,000 p.m.	11,000 p.m.	7,000 p.m.
Place of stay	Delhi	Agra	Gurgoan	Chennai
Place of service	Noida	Agra	Delhi	Chennai
HRA received	1,500 p.m.	700 p.m.	5,000 p.m.	3,000 p.m.
Rent paid	1,400 p.m.	200 p.m.	7,100 p.m.	5,000 p.m.

Solution

Computation of taxable HRA

	Case 1	*Case 2*	*Case 3*	*Case 4*
F_1	2,000	1,200	*4,400*	3,500
A	1,500	700	5,000	*3,000*
F_2	1,400 – 400 *1,000*	200 – 300 *nil*	7,100 – 1,100 6,000	5,000 – 700 4,300
Taxable HRA (actual minus least)	(1,500 – 1,000) × 12 = 6,000	(700 – 0) × 12 = 8,400	(5,000 – 4,400) × 12 = 7,200	(3,000 – 3,000) × 12 = Nil

Problems 3.06-P5 (Simple)

Mr. Taxcrazy draws following emoluments from Wise Ltd. for the PY 2006-07.

	Case 1	*Case 2*
Basic Salary	2,000 p.m.	3,000 p.m.
D.A. *(60% forms part of salary)*	1,000 p.m.	500 p.m.
Fixed commission	400 p.m.	9,600 p.a.
House rent allowance	1,000 p.m.	1,520 p.m.
Rent paid	700 p.m.	1,650 p.m.
Place of stay	Kolkota	Gurgoan

Compute taxable house rent allowance and Gross Salary for the AY 2007-08.

Ans: (1) 6,720; 47,520; (2) 2,400; 54,000.

Illustration and Problems 3.06-P6 [Difficult]

Mr. Taxcrazy draws following emoluments from Ican Ltd., for the PY 2006-07.

	Case 1	*Case 2*
Place of stay	Gurgoan	Mumbai
Basic Salary p.m.	5,000	3,000
Dearness allowance *(70% forms part of salary)* p.m.	500	400
Commission 1% p.a. based on sales. Sales achieved by the employee p.a.	24 lakhs	1,20,000
Arrears of salary of 98-99 (not *taxed earlier)*	7,000	Nil
House rent allowance	4,000 p.m.	20,304 p.a.
Rent paid p.m.	700	2,030

Compute taxable house rent allowance & Gross Salary for the AY 2007-08.

Ans: (1) 48,000; 1,45,000; (2) 24; 42,024. [SAS (1) 7,350.(2) 4,280.]

Illustration and Problems 3.06-P7 (Typical)

Mr. Taxcrazy draws following emoluments from Iamgenious Ltd., for the PY 2006-07. Compute taxable HRA and Gross Salary for the AY 2007-08

	Case 1	*Case 2*
Basic Salary for first 3 months	4,000 p.m.	7,000 p.m.
Basic Salary for next 9 months	5,000 p.m.	8,000 p.m.
House rent allowance for first 6 months	3,000 p.m.	4,500 p.m.
House rent allowance for next 6 months	4,000 p.m.	5,500 p.m.
Rent paid for first 7 months	500 p.m.	7,000 p.m.
Rent paid for next 5 months	3,700 p.m.	10,000 p.m.
Place of residence for first 10 months	Chennai	Chennai
Place of residence for next 2 months	Pondichery	Chennai

Ans: (1) 30,200; 87,200; (2) 13,500; 1,06,500

Solution : Case 1

Computation of Taxable HRA

	B.S.	*HRA*	*Rent Paid*	*Place of resi*
I Set (3 months)				
April, 2006	4,000	3,000	500	Chennai
May, 2006	4,000	3,000	500	Chennai
June, 2006	4,000	3,000	500	Chennai
II Set (3 months)				
July, 2006	5,000	3,000	500	Chennai
August, 2006	5,000	3,000	500	Chennai
September, 2006	5,000	3,000	500	Chennai
III Set (1 month)				
October, 2006	5,000	4,000	500	Chennai
IV Set (5 months)				
November, 2006	5,000	4,000	3,700	Chennai
December, 2006	5,000	4,000	3,700	Chennai
January, 2007	5,000	4,000	3,700	Chennai
V Set (2 months)				
February, 2007	5,000	4,000	3,700	Pondich.
March, 2007	5,000	4,000	3,700	Pondich.

	I × 3	*II × 3*	*III × 1*	*IV × 3*	*V × 2*
SAS	4,000	5,000	5,000	5,000	5,000
F_1 50% of SAS / 40% of SAS	2,000	2,500	2,500	2,500	2,000
A Actual HRA received	3,000	3,000	4,000	4,000	4,000
F_2 Rent paid — 10% of SAS	100	0	0	3,200	3,200
Least is exempt	100	0	0	2,500	2,000
Taxable HRA	2,900×3 =8,700	3,000×*3* =9,000	4,000×*1* =4,000	1,500×*3* =4,500	2,000×*2* =4,000

Computation of Gross Salary

Basic Salary *(4,000 × 3) + (5,000 × 9)*	57,000
Taxable HRA *(8,700 + 9,000 + 4,000 + 4,500 + 4,000)*	30,200
Gross Salary	87,200

Problem 3.06-P8

An employee posted in Delhi is getting salary @ 5,000 per month. He was given house rent allowance @ Rs. 1,000 per month from 1st October, 2006 by his employer. This employee was living in a rented house since 1st January, 2006 for which he was paying a rent of Rs. 1,500 per month. But on 1st January, 2007 he vacated the rented house as the construction of his own house was completed. Find out the exempted amount of house rent allowance for the previous year 2006-07.

Ans: 3,000.

Problem 3.06-P9 (Difficult)

Compute taxable HRA and Income from salary for the AY 2007-08.

1. Joining date 1-1-2005. Basic salary 10,000-1,000-15,000. Dearness allowance 10% of basic salary. (30% of DA forms part of salary). HRA received Rs. 2,800 p.m. Rent paid Rs. 5,000 p.m.
2. Joining date 1-11-2003. Basic salary 8,000-500-12,000. Dearness allowance 20% of basic salary. (as per terms of employment). HRA received Rs. 3,000 p.m. Rent paid Rs. 4,000 p.m. On 1-3-2007 he shifts in his own house.

Ans: (1) 108; 1,48,608; (2) 505; 1,22,055.

Problem 3.06-P10 (Difficult)

From the following information compute taxable HRA and Gross Salary for AY 2007-08:

	Ace Ltd.	*Sac Ltd.*
Joining date	1-6-1980	1-8-2006
Retiring date	30-6-2006	6-10-2007
Basic Salary	6,000 p.m.	9,000 p.m.
Dearness Allowance	2,000 p.m.	nil
House rent allowance	8,000 p.m.	3,000 p.m.
Rent paid	7,000 p.m. at Noida	54,000 for 9 months at Gurgoan from 1-7-2006
Place of service	Delhi	Faridabad

Ans: 16,800; 1,12,800. [90,000+6,000+16,800=1,12,800]

Problem 3.06-P11 (Typical)

From following information compute taxable HRA and Gross Salary for AY 2007-08:

Basic Salary	10,000 p.m.
Dearness Allowance (20% forms part of salary)	15% of Basic Salary
Commission	7,000 p.a.
Servant Allowance *(The employee engages a servant on 1-4-2007)*	800 p.m.
House Rent Allowance w.e.f 1-7-2006	5,000 p.m.

Rent paid at Gurgoan for 1st 4 months w.e.f. 1-4-2006 — 6,000 p.m.

Rent paid at New Delhi w.e.f. 1-8-2006 for 7 month. — 4,150 p.m.

On 1-3-2007 he shifts in his own house. He also spends Rs. 7,000 on purchase of furniture.

Ans: 19,040; 1,73,640. [1,20,000+18,000+7,000+9,600+19,040=1,73,640.]

Problem 3.06-P12 (Typical)

(A) Mr. Taxcrazy furnishes following information for the financial year 2006-07. You are required to compute taxable HRA and Gross Salary for the AY 2007-08. As per the contract of employment his salary falls due on the last day of each month.

Basic Salary *(His annual increment falls due on 1-1-2007 of Rs. 2,000)*	20,000 p.m.
Dearness Allowance *(forms part of salary)*	5% of Basic Salary
House Rent Allowance	8,000 p.m.
Rent paid at Tata for the period from Feb. 2006 to June 2006	3,000 p.m.
Rent paid at New Delhi from July 2006 onwards	8,400 p.m.

(B) What would be your answer in the above case if salary falls due on the 1st day of next month?

Ans: (A) 37,230; 2,95,530; (B) 37,020; 2,93,220.

TOPIC 3.07 *SECTION 10(14) & RULE 2BB.* SPECIAL ALLOWANCE

Special allowances are generally given for official purposes, therefore amount spent towards official purpose is fully exempt. However it may be given for personal purpose also. Such personal purpose allowance is also exempt to the extent provided in the Act or Rules.

(A) IN FOLLOWING CASES OF SPECIAL ALLOWANCES EXEMPTION DEPENDS UPON THE EXPENDITURE INCURRED

In following cases of special allowance, exemption depends upon the expenditure incurred. If expenditure is incurred for official purpose or for specified purpose then only exemption is allowed. If no expenditure is incurred, exemption is not available.

Type of Allowances *(THAR DUCT)*	Exemption
Transfer Allowance **H**elper Allowance **A**cademic Allowance *(granted to employees for higher studies)* **R**esearch & Development Allowance *(R & D)* **D**aily Allowance *(where employee is sent for official work outside the city limits — fooding, etc.)* **U**niform Allowance **C**onveyance Allowance *(within city limits)* **T**ravelling Allowance *(outside city limits)*	Exemption allowed is amount of expenditure incurred for specified purpose or for official purpose *(It means if expenditure is not incurred or* is *incurred for personal purpose, then such expenditure saved or incurred is taxable)*

(B) IN FOLLOWING CASES OF SPECIAL ALLOWANCES EXEMPTION IS FIXED UPTO A CERTAIN LIMIT IRRESPECTIVE OF THE AMOUNT OF EXPENDITURE INCURRED

In following cases of special allowance, amount of exemption is fixed. It means that whether expenditure is incurred or not exemption is allowed.

(i) Transport Allowance

It is given to commute between residence to office and back. Exemption allowed is upto Rs. 800 p.m. However in case of individual who is blind or orthopaedic handicapped, then exemption allowed is upto Rs. 1,600 p.m.

(ii) Children Education allowance and Hostel Allowance allowed to the children of employee

	Children Education allowance	*Hostel Allowance*
Monthly exemption	upto Rs 100 p.m./child max 2 child is exempt	upto Rs. 300 p.m./child max 2 child is exempt
Lumpsum exemption	Rs. 1,200 per child is exempt max Rs. 2,400 is exempt	Rs. 3,600 per child is exempt Rs. 7,200 is exempt

Problem 3.07-P1 (Difficult)

Mr. Taxcrazy posted at Hyderabad draws the following emoluments from Ishallworkhard unlimited. Compute income from salaries for the PY 2006-07.

Basic Salary Rs. 6,000 p.m. Bonus Rs. 2,000 p.m. Commission Rs. 8,000 p.a. CCA Rs.1,000 p.m. Telephone allowance Rs. 200 p.m. Medical Allowance Rs. 300 p.m. Entertainment allowance Rs. 4,800 (Rs. 6,000 spend on entertainment of clients of companies). Academic allowance Rs. 16,000 (Rs. 9,000 spend on his education). Conveyance allowance Rs. 6,000 (Rs. 7,000 is spend on conveyance for official purpose). Travelling allowance Rs. 18,000 (Rs. 17,000 is spend on conveyance for official purpose). Transport allowance Rs. 2,000 p.m. (Expenses incurred on commutting between residence to office and back Rs. 2,500 p.m.) Children education allowance for 4 child Rs. 160 p.m. per child. Hostel allowance for 3 child Rs. 280 per month per child (expenditure incurred on child education and their hostel Rs. 1,100 per month per child).

Solution

Computation of Income from Salary

Basic Salary (6,000 × 12)		72,000
Bonus (2,000 × 12)		24,000
Commission		8,000
CCA (1,000 × 12)		12,000
Telephone allowance (200 × 12)		2,400
Medical allowance (300 × 12)		3,600
Entertainment allowance (fully taxable)		4,800
Academic allowance	16,000	
Less: Exempt u/s 10(14)	9,000	7,000
Conveyance allowance	6,000	
Less: Exempt u/s 10(14)	6,000	Nil

Travelling allowance	18,000	
Less: Exempt u/s 10(14)	17,000	1,000
Transport Allowance	30,000	
Less: exempt	9,600	20,400
Children Education Allowance (160 × 4 × 12)	7,680	
Less : exempt (100 × 2 × 12)	2,400	5,280
Hostel Allowance (280× 3 × 12)	10,080	
Less: exempt (280 × 2 × 12)	6,720	3,360
Gross Salary		1,63,840

Problems 3.07-P2 [Difficult]

Compute Income from Salary for the AY 2007-08 from the following information.

	Case 1	*Case 2*
Basic Salary p.m.	3,000	5,000
House Rent Allowance	800 p.m.	9,280 p.a.
Entertainment Allowance p.m. *(30% is used for official purpose)*	300	550
Uniform Allowance p.m. *(40% is spent towards personal purpose)*	3,000	700
Transport Allowance p.m.	1,000	600
Children Education Allowance for 3 children	120 p.m./each	5,000
Hostel Allowance for 4 children	140 p.m./each	320 p.m./each

Compute Income from Salary for the AY 2007-08 on the assumption that he lives in his own house.

Ans: (1) 71,280 [36,000+9,600+3,600+14,400+2,400+1,920+3,360]; (2) 90,000. [60,000+9280+6,600+3,360+0+2,600+8,160=90,000]

Problem 3.07-P3 (Difficult)

Mr. X is working with a Smile unlimited. He furnishes following data. You are required to compute Income from Salary and Total Income for the AY 2007-08.

Basic Salary p.m.	4,500
Dearness Allowance p.m.	1,500
House Rent Allowance p.m.	2,500
Rent paid in Delhi for 1st 6 months p.m.	3,000
Rent paid in Gurgoan for next 6 months p.m.	3,500
Research and development allowance *(Rs. 1,000 is spend wholly towards official purpose)*	4,000
Meal Allowance *(Expenditure on meal is Rs. 1,000)*	700
Helper Allowance *(Rs. 900 is spent wholly towards official purpose)*	1,500
Conveyance Allowance p.m. *(whole of allowance is spent towards official purpose)*	500
Hostel Allowance for 2 children *(actual expenditure incurred is Rs. 150 p.m./child)*	250 p.m./child

Entertainment Allowance 800
(whole of allowance is spent towards official purpose)

He also receives dividend on securities from a foreign company Rs. 7,000.

Ans: 82,800; 89,800. [54,000+18,000+5,700+3,000+700+600+0+0+800=82,800+7,000 =89,800]

Problem 3.07-P4 (Difficult)

Compute the Gross Salary of Mr. S. employed in third year from the following details furnished by him.

(a) Basic Salary 96,000

(b) Dearness Allowance 1,92,000

(c) City Compensatory Allowance 18,000

(d) Children's Education Allowance 12,000

(e) Clothing Allowance (given every third year) 24,000

(f) He has received fixed allowance of Rs. 2,500 p.m. for medical treatment for the entire family; had incurred an expenditure of Rs. 12,500 actually.

Ans: 3,45,600. [96,000+1,92,000+18,000+9,600+0+30,000=3,45,600]

(C) * OUTSTATION ALLOWANCES GRANTED TO EMPLOYEES WORKING IN A TRANSPORT SYSTEM)

It is an allowance paid to employee working in a transport system, to meet his personal expenditure during the course of his duty. It is a similar to daily allowance. Exemption allowed is

Maximum Formula	1. 6,000 p.m. 2. 70% of allowance	Least is exempt from tax

Note

- Double benefit of daily allowance and this allowance is not allowed.

Problem 3.07-P5 (Difficult)

Mr. Abhay Jain, Pilot in Jet Airways, furnishes following information. Compute Income from Salary for the AY 2007-08.

Basic Salary 30,000 p.m.
Uniform Allowance *(90% is utilised towards pilot uniform)* 15,000 p.m.
Hostel Allowance for his grandchild 7,400
Flight Allowance 10,000 p.m.

Ans: 4,33,400. [3,60,000+18,000+7,400+48,000=4,33,400]

Problem 3.07-P6 [CS J99]

X is employed as a driver in transport company. During the previous year 2006-07, he has been paid Rs. 24,000 being allowance to meet his personal expenses in course of running trucks from one place to another. He is not in receipt of daily allowance. The expenditure incurred is, however, Rs. 30,000. Find out the amount chargeable to tax.

Ans: 7,200.

Problem 3.07-P7 [Difficult]

X is employed as a caretaker in a transport company at Chennai. He gets a salary of Rs. 9,000 p.m., dearness allowance Rs. 1,800 p.m., entertainment allowance Rs. 250 p.m., house rent allowance Rs. 1,500 p.m., city compensatory allowance Rs. 40 p.m., medical allowance Rs. 200 p.m., children education allowance Rs. 150 p.m. for one child, project allowance Rs. 100 p.m. and transport duty allowance Rs. 3,600 p.m. He spent Rs. 900 in entertaining the visitors of the company and paid Rs. 1,000 p.m. as rent of the house occupied by him for his residence. He has a son who goes to school. Compute his gross salaries for the AY 2007-08.

Ans: 1,67,040. [1,08,000+21,600+3,000+16,800+480+2,400+600+1,200+12,960=1,67,040]

(D) *OTHER NOTIFIED ALLOWANCES

	Particulars	*Exemption*
1.	Tribal area allowance	upto Rs. 200 p.m.
2.	Underground allowance	upto Rs. 800 p.m.
3.	Compensatory modified field area allowance	upto Rs. 1,000 p.m.
4.	Composite field area allowance	upto Rs. 2,600 p.m.
5.	Compensatory field area allowance	upto Rs. 2,600 p.m.
6.	Island Duty allowance	upto Rs. 3,250 p.m.
7.	Counter insurgency allowance	upto Rs. 3,900 p.m.
8.	Special Compensatory highly active field area allowance	upto Rs. 4,200 p.m.

Problem 3.07-P8 [Simple]

On the basis of following information, compute gross salary for the 2007-08. Basic salary Rs. 8,000 p.m. Dearness allowance 50% of basic pay. Tribal area allowance in Madhya Pradesh Rs. 300 p.m. Daily allowance Rs. 6,000. (spent fully on official duties). Medical allowance Rs. 800 p.m.

Ans: 1,54,800. [96,000+48,000+1,200+0+9,600=1,54,800]

DEDUCTIONS ALLOWED UNDER SECTION 16

TOPIC 3.08 *SECTION 16(i).* STANDARD DEDUCTION

Ommitted by the Finance Act, 2005. From the AY 2006-07 no deduction u/s 16(i) is allowed.

TOPIC 3.09 *SECTION 16(ii).* ENTERTAINMENT ALLOWANCE

Entertainment Allowance is fully taxable : Entertainment allowance is fully taxable whether received by Government employee or private employee. It is fully taxable even if whole of allowance is spent towards official purpose.

Deduction of Entertainment Allowance : Deduction on account of entertainment allowance is allowed only to Central and State Govt. employees. It is first included in Gross Salary then deduction is allowed u/s 16(ii).

(MAF is a memory technique for remembering EA)

Maximum Actual Formula	• 5,000 *(Lumpsum)* • Actual EA received in PY • 20% of Basic Salary	Least is deductible from Gross Salary

Note

- Entertainment Allowance even if incurred for official purpose is not deductible *i.e.* any entertainment allowance received must pass through the MAF rule.

Illustration 3.09-P1 (Difficult)

Mr. X a State Govt. employee furnishes following information. You are required to compute Income from Salary for the AY 2007-08.

Case 1

Basic salary	3,000 p.m.
Entertainment allowance	400 p.m.
Tiffin allowance	100 p.m.

Case 2

Basic salary	8,000 p.m.
Entertainment allowance	2,000 p.m.
Transport allowance	600 p.m.

Solution

Case 1 : Computation of Income from Salary

Basic salary (3,000 × 12)		36,000
Entertainment allowance (400 × 12)		4,800
Tiffin allowance (100 × 12)		1,200
Gross Salary		42,000
Less: Deduction u/s 16(ii) in respect of entertainment allowance		
Maximum	5,000	
Actual	*4,800*	
Formula 20% of basic salary (20% of 36,000)	7,200	4,800
Income from salaries		37,200

Case 2 : Computation of Income from Salary

Basic salary (8,000 × 12)		96,000
Entertainment allowance (2,000 × 12)		24,000
Transport allowance (600 -600)		Nil
Gross Salary		1,20,000
Less: Deduction u/s 16(ii) in respect of entertainment allowance		
Maximum	5,000	
Actual	24,000	
Formula 20% of basic salary (20% of 96,000)	19,200	5,000
Income from salaries		1,15,000

Illustration 3.09-P2 (Difficult)

Compute his Income from Salary for the AY 2007-08 from the following information on the assumption that (a) he is a Govt. employee (b) a private employee.

Basic salary up to 31-7-2006	6,000 p.m.
Basic salary from 1-8-2006	8,000 p.m.
Dearness allowance	10% of Basic salary
Commission on sales	12,000 p.a.
Entertainment allowance for official purpose	15,000

Bonus disputed in court	20,000
House rent allowance	66,000
Rent paid	9% of salary

For the purpose of computation of Gratuity 75% of dearness allowance forms part of salary.

Ans: 1,84,800; 1,89,800.

Illustration and Problem 3.09-P3 (Difficult)

(A) Mr. Taxcrazy joins Punjab Govt. as a Finance (manager) on 1-5-2006 and draws following salary for the PY 2006-07. Compute his Income from Salary for the AY 2007-08.

	Case 1	*Case 2*
Basic Salary p.m.	2,500	3,000
Dearness Allowance *(forming part of salary)* p.m.	600	500
Entertainment Allowance for the PY 2006-07 p.m.	500	800
HRA p.m.	1,200	Nil
Rent paid from 1-6-2006 to 31-5-2007 p.m. *(in the month of May 2006 he lives in his own house)*	800	200
Advance Salary	7,000	Nil

(B) What would be your answer in Case 1 if he retires on 30-11-2006.

(C) What would be your answer in Case 2 if he is working in a Semi Govt. Organisation.

Ans: (A) (i) 49,900;(ii) 42,300; (B) 34,160; (C) 47,300.

Problem 3.09-P4 (Difficult)

Mr. Taxcrazy employed with Haryana Govt. furnishes following information for the financial year 2005-07. You are required to compute Income from Salary for the AY 2007-08.

Basic Salary	9,500 p.m.
Dearness Allowance *(10% forms part of salary)*	1,500 p.m.
Fees	15,750 p.a.
Entertainment Allowance	9,000 p.a.
Bonus due for PY 2006-07 *(received on 1-4-2007)*	2,00,000
Commission @ 1% based on purchase. Purchases made by the employee	6,00,000 p.a.
House Rent Allowance	45% (Basic salary + Dearness Allowance)
Rent paid in Delhi upto 31-5-2006 *(On 1-6-2006, his landlord increases the rent to Rs. 6,000 p.m.)*	70% of HRA p.m.

Ans: 1,63,900. [1,14,000+18,000+15,750+9,000+6,000+6,150=1,68,900–5,000=1,63,900]

TOPIC 3.10 *SECTION 16(iii)*. EMPLOYMENT OR PROFESSIONAL TAX

1. It is a tax levied by State Govt. on the person who is in service or is self-employed. Its deduction is allowed whether tax is paid by employee or by the employer on behalf of employee.

2. Deduction of such tax is allowed only if it is actually paid during the relevant previous year.
3. But if such tax is paid by employer on behalf of employee then it is treated as income (perquisite) in the hands of employee and therefore it is first added to Gross Salary and then deduction is allowed u/s 16(iii).

Illustration 3.10-P1 (Difficult)

Basic Salary 11,000 p.m. Dearness Allowance 20% of basic salary. Professional tax re-imbursed by employer Rs. 2,000. Professional tax paid Rs. 3,000 out of which Rs. 500 paid on 1-4-2007.

Solution

Computation of Income from Salary

Basic Salary (11,000 × 12)	1,32,000
Dearness allowance (20% of 1,32,000)	26,400
Re-imbursement of professional tax	2,000
Gross Salary	1,60,400
Less : Deduction u/s 16(iii) in respect profession tax paid during the PY 2006-07.	2,500
Income from Salary	1,57,900

Problem 3.10-P2 (Difficult)

Mr. Taxcrazy posted in Darjeeling with West Bengal Govt. draws the following emoluments for the AY 2007-08.

	Case 1	*Case 2*
Basic Salary	4,84,000	5,43,300
Entertainment Allowance *(30% is used for official purpose)*	16,000	15,000
Hostel allowance for 3 child for 5 months	500 p.m.	8,000
Professional tax paid by employer on behalf of employee		
- on 31-3-2007	4,000	1,700
- on 1-4-2007	500	650
Professional tax paid by employee		
- on 31-3-2007	1,000	1,000
- on 1-4-2007	2,000	800

Ans : (1) 4,94,000. [4,84,000+16,000+4,000=5,04,000–5,000–5,000=4,94,000]; (2) 5,57,300. [5,43,300+15,000+1,700=5,60,000–5,000–2,700=5,52,300]

Problem 3.10-P3 [CA M90]

Compute Income from Salaries from the following informations. Salary Rs. 4,000 p.m. HRA Rs. 1,500 p.m. Commission Rs. 8,000 p.a. Bonus Rs. 6,000 p.a. Income tax deducted Rs. 200 p.m. P.F. deducted Rs. 350 p.m. Profession tax deducted Rs. 40 p.m. He pay house rent of Rs. 1,200 p.m. at Coimbator.

Ans: 69,920. [48,000+8,400+8,000+6,000=70,400–480=69,920]

Problem 3.10-P4 (Typical)

Mr. Taxcrazy is employed as a Revenue Officer in Delhi Govt. on following emoluments :

Basic Salary from 1-1-2006 Rs. 9,000 p.m.; Basic Salary from 1-1-2007 Rs. 12,000 p.m.; Dearness Allowance forming part of salary.

As per the service rule if Basic Salary is upto Rs. 10,000 p.m. then DA = 20% of Basic Salary if Basic Salary exceeds Rs. 10,000 p.m. then DA = 10% of Basic Salary.

Commission @ 1% on the sales effected by him. From 1-12-2006 his term of employment were amended. Accordingly the payment of commission to him was discontinued. But on account of this change, he was paid a sum of Rs. 5,400 as compensation. The sales effected by him during the financial year 2006-07 were Rs. 6,00,000.

He lives in a rented accommodation in Noida where he pays a rent of Rs. 3,300 p.m. The employer pays rent allowance of Rs. 4,000 p.m.

He is given allowance to commute between office and residence (he commutes in his own car) Rs. 800 p.m.

He also receives entertainment allowance of Rs. 3,000.

He was sent to Europe and the salary including DA for 1 month was received by him in Europe.

He is also employed in Right and Left institute on a part time basis as a Tax faculty on an honorarium of Rs. 14,000 p.m including Rs. 20,000 as entertainment allowance.

You are required to compute Income from Salary for the AY 2007-08 on the assumption that salary and allowances fall due on the last day of each month.

Ans: 3,36,680. [1,17,000+19,800+9,400+22,480+0+3,000=1,71,680+1,68,000=3,39,680–3,000=3,36,680.]

Problem 3.10-P5 (Typical)

Mr. Taxcrazy employed on 1-1-2002 on following emoluments.

Basic Salary	11,000-1,000-15,000-3,000-24,000
Dearness Allowance	5% of Basic Salary
City Compensatory allowance	8% of basic Salary and dearness allowance
Tribal area allowance	300 p.m.
Allowance to meet education and hostel expenditure of a child	Rs. 9,000

Metro pass allowance to commute daily between residence to office and back.1,200 p.m.

He has also been given travelling allowance to travel to Orissa for official purpose where he has incurred a personal expenditure of Rs. 17,000.

Compute income from salaries for the assessment year 2007-08 if

(a) salary falls due on the last day of each month.

(b) salary falls due on the first day of next month.

Ans: (a) 2,24,526. [1,89,000+9,450+15,876+1,200+4,200+4,800+0=2,24,526] (b) 2,21,124.

Now, go, revise and memorise everything from the beginning. Start it. Don't be lazy, and did you know we have completed 10% of syllabus.

Keep Running

PERQUISITES [FACILITIES] IN SHORT KNOWN AS PERKS

TOPIC 3.11 MEANING OF PERQUISITE

It is the gain or profit incidentally made from employment in addition to regular salary or wages. It is a kind of tip, given by employer, whether present or past. It is like reimbursing personal expenditure of employee. It denotes something that benefits the man by going into his own pocket. If the perquisite is spent for official purpose then it is not a benefit which goes into the employee's pocket. A perquisite is attached to the office of employment. Perquiste may be provided in cash or in kind.

TOPIC 3.12 WHO ARRANGES AND PAYS PERQUISITES

TAX TREATMENT IF PERQUISITES ARE ARRANGED BY EMPLOYER

Where perquisites are owned or hired by employer and is provided to employee then it is simply a faciltiy which is used by employee. The value of facility valued as per rule 3 is added to gross salary.

Perquisite may be provided from employer's own source or by hiring from outside agency. Where the employer provides own accommodation to the employee it means that accommodation is provided from its own source but where employer takes the accommodation on rent from a third party and then it provides to the employee, it means that accommodation is provided from outside agency.

TAX TREATMENT IF PERQUISITES ARE ARRANGED BY EMPLOYEE

Where perquisites are arranged or owned by employee and employer makes the payment of such perquisites it is said that employer has discharged the obligation of employee. In other words any expenditure which employee should have incurred but is incurred by employer, then it is said that employer has discharged the obligation of employee.

E.g. 1 : Where employee engages a servant, it is the duty of employee to pay salary to the servant. But if employer pays the salary of servant then it means that employer has discharged the obligation of employee. Such sum shall be treated as perquisites and shall be added to gross salary of employee.

E.g. 2 : Where the gas bill is in the name of employee in such a case it is the responsibility of employee to pay the gas bill but if employer pays gas bill, it means that employer has discharged the obligation of employee. Such sum shall be treated as perquisites and shall be added to gross salary of employee.

E.g. 3 : Where income tax, employement tax or any other tax of emplyee is paid by employer, then it is said that employer has discharged the obligation of employee. Such payment made by employer shall be treated as perquisites and shall be added to gross salary of employee.

TOPIC 3.13 MANNER OF PAYMENT

1. Where the word used is 'facility' it means perquisite is owned or hired by employer and is provided in kind.
2. Where the question uses the word 'reimbursement' it means it is an obligation of employee discharged by employer in cash.
3. Where perquiste is owned by employee and payment is not made to employee but directly to the service provider, it means employer has discharged the obligation of employee in kind.

TOPIC 3.14 VALUATION OF PERQUISITE

Perquisites are valued on the basis of cost to the employer. Rule 3 of the Income Tax Rules, 1962 has provided specific methods of valuation of perquisites to be charged to tax.

Where the facility is sold by employer to the employee then it is called recovery which is allowed as deduction from the value of perquisites so arrived.

Meaning of recovery. Where the employer provides any facilities, he recovers some amount from the employee in respect of those facilities. Such recovery is deductible perquisite. Recovery is recovered by the employer by deducting it from basic salary.

TOPIC 3.15 IN WHOSE HANDS PERQUISITES ARE TAXABLE ?

Concept : Going by the strict rule of employer and employee relationship, any perquisites enjoyed by the employee is taxable in the hands of employee. But what about perquisite enjoyed by his or her spouse, children of employee or employee's daughter in law, employee's parents, employee's servant or employee's dependants?

Taxability : In such case, as per the new provisions of the Income Tax Act, 1961, the value of perquisite provided by the employer *(directly or indirectly)* whether to the employee or to any member of his household *(by reason of his employment)* shall always be taxable in the hands of employee.

Meaning of 'Member of household' : It shall include spouse, children and their spouses, parents, servants and dependants.

Problem 3.15-P1

1. When perquisites are not taxable ?
2. When recovery is not allowed as deduction ?
3. Are payments like Income tax, Income tax penalty, employment tax or professional tax treated as obligation of employee ?
4. Are all perquisites provided by the employer taxable in the hands of employee ?

Solution

1. When benefit of perquisite does not go into employee's own pocket. That is when perquisite is spent for official purpose then value of perquisite is not taxable.
2. When recovery is done in respect of that perquisite which is not taxable.
3. Yes and such payment should be made by employee. But if payment is made by the employer it means that employer has discharged the obligation of employee and such payment shall be treated as employee's income.
4. No. There are certain perquisites which are fully exempt in the hands of all employees. Even there are certain perquisites which are taxable only in case of specified employee.

TOPIC 3.16 *SECTION 17(2)(iii).* MEANING OF SPECIFIED EMPLOYEE & NON-SPECIFIED EMPLOYEE

It is essential to distinguish between specified employee and non-specified employee, since there are certain perquisites which are taxable only in case of specified employee.

1. Non-specified Employee : They are those employees who are not specified employee. So who are specified employee?
2. Specified Employee : An employee satisfying any one of the following conditions is treated as a specified employee.

(a) An employee who is appointed as a director of a company in the relevant previous year. It is immaterial whether he is full time or part time or continuing for whole year or part of the year as a director; or

(b) An employee who is a shareholder having substantial interest in a company during the relevant previous year.

As per section 2(32) person who has a substantial interest in the company, in relation to a company, means a person who is the beneficial owner of shares, not being shares entitled to a fixed rate of dividend whether with or without a right to participate in profits, carrying not less than 20% of the voting power.

(c) An employee drawing Income from Salary (whether due from, or paid or allowed by, one or more employers) excluding non-monetary benefits exceeding Rs. 50,000, then such employee is treated as specified employee)

It means you are required to compute *cash taxable salary* after providing all exemptions and deductions u/s 16 *(Standard deduction-ommitted, Entertainment allowance and Professional or employment tax)*. This cash taxable salary if it exceeds Rs. 50,000 then such employee is treated as specified employee. Do remember *cash taxable salary* includes basic salary, advance salary, arrears of salary, bonus, all taxable allowances, perquisites received in cash, gratuity, leave salary, pension, etc. received from all employers whether present or former in the relevant previous year.

Example 3.16-P1 (Difficult)

Examine in the following cases whether Mr. Taxcrazy who is working in two companies in the same previous year is specified employee or non-specified employee with respect to both the companies :

X Ltd	Y Ltd
Employee-Director *(Specified employee)*	Employee *(Non-Specified employee)*
Employee & holds 19% voting power *(Non Specified employee)*	Employee & holds 20% voting power *(Specified employee)*
Basic Salary Rs. 30,000 *(Specified employee)* [1]	Basic Salary Rs. 20,001 *(Specified employee)* [1]

Note 1

Total salary from X Ltd. & Y Ltd	50,001
Less : Deduction u/s 16	nil
Cash Taxable Salary from all employers exceeds Rs. 50,000	50,001

Problem 3.16-P2

1. When can employee of a company be treated as specified employee ?
2. When can employee of a firm be treated as specified employee ?

Solution

1. If any of the abovesaid 3 conditions are satisfied.
2. Only if his cash taxable salary exceeds Rs. 50,000. The first two conditions are applicable only to employer company.

Illustration and Problems 3.16-P3 (Difficult)

From the following information find out whether Mr. Taxcrazy is a specified employee or non-specified employee for the PY 2006-07.

	Case 1	*Case 2*	*Case 3*
Category of employee	Private	Private	Govt.
Basic salary p.m.	3,000	5,000	4,000
DA *(10% forms part of salary)* p.m.	500	500	Nil
Advance salary for the month of April 2008	1,500	200	500
Research Allowance p.m. *(75% spends for official purpose)*	2,000	Nil	Nil
Entertainment Allowance p.a.	500	Nil	5,500
Reimbursement of gas bills p.a.	Nil	1,200	1,000
Bonus due for PY 2006-07 not yet received	800	200	300
Water facility	20,000	6,000	7,000
Cook engaged by employee. Salary of cook is paid by employer directly to the cook.	4,000	2,000	4,500
Reimbursement of professional tax by employer on behalf of employee p.a.	2,100	2,500	4,100

Ans: (1) 50,000 (NSE); (2) 67,400 (SE); (3) 50,000 (NSE)

Solution : Case 1

Computation of Cash Taxable Salary

Basic salary *(3,000 × 12)*		36,000
Dearness Allowance *(500 x 12)*		6,000
Advance salary		1,500
Research Allowance *(2,000 × 12)*	24,000	
Less : exempt *(1500 × 12)*	18,000	6,000
Entertainment Allowance		500
Reimbursement of professional tax by employer		2,100
Total		52,100
Less : Deduction u/s 16		
(i) Standard Deduction (omitted)	nil	
(ii) Professional tax paid during the relevant PY	2,100	2,100
Cash taxable Salary		50,000

Note

- Water facility is not a cash salary, hence ignored.
- Since salary of cook is paid directly to the cook, it is not included in computing Cash taxable Salary.
- Since his Cash taxable Salary is not more than Rs. 50,000 therefore he is treated as non-specified employee. Hence perquisites as specified u/s 17(2)(iii) are not taxable in the hands of non-specified employee.

TOPIC 3.17 *SECTION 17(2).* DEFINITION AND TAX TREATMENT OF PERQUISITES

Perquisites include:

1. *Section 17(2)(i) & (ii)* : The value of rent free accommodation *provided* to the assessee by his employer. The accommodation may be given free of rent or at concessional rent.

   Year of taxability : The value of accommodation is included in salary income only if it is actually *provided* to the employee whether it is enjoyed by the employee or not.

   Taxability in whose hands : Value of accommodation is taxable in *both* the cases of employees whether specified employee or non-specified employee.

2. *Section 17(2)(iii).* The value of any benefit or amenity granted or provided free of cost or at concessional rate. Such amenities are valued under Rule 3.

   (4) **G**as, electricity or water facility; (5) **E**ducation facility; [17(2)(iii)] **M**edical facility; (3) **S**ervant facility; *(Let us call it GEMS).*

   Taxability in whose hands : Value of such benefit *(GEMS)* is taxable only in case of specified employee.

3. *Section 17(2)(iv).* Any *monetary* sum *paid* by the employer in respect of any *obligation* which, but for such payment, would have been payable by the employee.

   Year of taxability : The obligation is taxable on *paid* basis *i.e.* not on accrual basis.

   Suppose electricity bill dated 15-3-2007 of Rs. 6,000 is reimbursed by employer on 1-4-2007. Then such reimbursement is taxable in the PY 2007-08 and not in PY 2006-07.

   Taxability in whose hands : The obligation is taxable in *both* the cases of employees whether specified employee or non-specified employee.

   Every types of obligation is taxable in the hands of employee if employer pays such sum wholly for personal purpose. E.g. Reimbursement of club bills, telephone bills etc.

4. *Section 17(2)(v).* Any life insurance premium *payable* by the employer or to effect a contract for an annuity.

   Year of taxability : Life insurance premium is chargeable to tax on *payable* basis, even if it is not actually paid during the year.

   Suppose life insurance premium of Rs. 6,000 due on 15-3-2007 is paid by employer on 1-4-2007. Then premium is taxable in PY 2006-07 and not in PY 2007-08.

   Taxability in whose hands : It is taxable in both the cases of employees whether specified employee or non-specified employee. Deduction u/s 80C can also be claimed on the amount of premium paid during the relevant PY.

5. *Section 17(2)(vi).* The value of any other fringe benefit or amenity as may be prescribed. It is valued under the Rule 3(7). **S**ale of Assets; **U**se of assets and **L**oan facility (SUL)

   Taxability in whose hands : This perquisite is taxable in both the cases of employees whether specified employee or non-specified employee.

Problem 3.17-P1 (Difficult)

Compute income from salary from the following information for the AY 2007-08.

	Case 1	*Case 2*
Basic Salary	40,000	5,00,000
Re-imbursement of water bill on 31-3-2007.	9,000	18,000
Re-imbursement of electricty bill dated 31-3-2007 paid on 1-4-2007.	12,000	25,000

Life insurance premium of employee paid by employer on 1-4-2007.		
Due date of premium 31-3-2007.	6,000	19,000
Gas facility	5,000	15,000

Ans: 54,000; 5,77,000.

Problem 3.17-P2

1. How are perquisites classified?
2. Which are the perquisites taxable in both the cases of employees?
3. Which are the perquisites taxable only in case of specified employees?
4. When GEMS is taxable in all cases of employees.
5. What is the difference between section 17(2)(iv) and section 17(2)(v)?
6. Salary, allowances, pension, etc. are chargeable to tax on due basis. What about taxability of perquisites?
7. Why there is a need to tax non-monetary benefits?

Solution

1. Perquisites are classified into 3 categories on the basis of taxability.
   a. Perquisites taxable in all cases.
   b. Perquisites taxable only in case of specified employee.
   c. Tax free perquisites *i.e.* perquisites exempt under all cases of employees.

   In other words it can be said that all perquisites are taxable in case of specified employee except exempted perquisites.

   In case of non-specified employee all perquisites are taxable except in case of exempted perquisites and GEMS.
2. Perquisites specified u/s 17(2)(i), (ii), (iv), (v), (vi). They are accommodation, obligation, life insurance premium and SUL
3. Perquisites specified u/s 17(2)(iii) which are GEMS.
4. When it becomes an obligation.
5. Taxability on paid basis and payable basis.
6. Perquisites becomes taxable in the same year in which they are provided except where valuation is based on salary. Suppose X retires on 31-7-2006 and salary falls due on the first day of next month. In this case salary shall be computed for 5 months however value of perquisite shall be computed only for 4 months.
7. The need to tax non-monetary benefits is essential otherwise such non-taxation would create discrimination between person receiving remuneration in cash and those who receive remuneration in kind.

TOPIC 3.18 LIST THE PERQUISITES WHICH ARE FULLY EXEMPT FROM TAX

All perquisites other than those discussed above (i.e. AFLO, SUL, GEMS) are fully exempt from tax. All such other perquisites from the AY 2006-07 shall be subjected to fringe benefit tax (FBT). The perquisites which are exempt in the hands of employees are taxable in the hands of employer. So without putting any restrictions or conditions following facilities shall be fully exempt from tax in the hands of employees.

1. Use of computer, laptop and telephone.
2. Use of car facility.
3. Use of credit card facility.

4. Use of club facility. Similarly use of health club, sports and similar facilities are also fully exempt from tax in the hands of employees.
5. The value of gifts in kind. Gifts in cash is fully taxable.
6. The value of holiday home facility.
7. Transport facility.
8. The value of meals.
9. Where the shares, debentures or warrants are by employer to the employee for free or at concessional rate.
10. Travelling
    (a) Actual travelling expenses paid or reimbursed by an employer for journeys undertaken by employees for business purposes is fully exempt.
    (b) *Explanation to 17(2)(iii)*. Conveyance facility provided to an employee to cover the journey between office and residence is fully exempt.
11. Periodicals or journals required for discharge of work are fully exempt.
12. *Section 10(10CC)*. Tax paid by the employer in respect of non monetary perquisites of the employee, shall be fully exempt from tax.
13. *Section 10(5)*. Amount of Leave Travel Concession (LTC) or actual expenditure incurred whichever is less is exempt.
14. Insurance
    (a) Employer's contribution towards staff group insurance scheme is fully exempt.
    (b) Payment of annual premium by employer on personal accident policy effected by him in respect of his employee is fully exempt.
    (c) Mediclaim insurance premium is fully exempt in the following cases:
        i. Any portion of the premium paid by an employer in relation to an employee, to effect or to keep in force an insurance on the health of such employee under any scheme approved by the Central Government is fully exempt.
        ii. Any sum paid by the employer in respect of any premium paid by the employee to effect or to keep in force an insurance on his health or the health of any member of his family under any scheme approved by the Central Government for the purposes of section 80D is fully exempt.

TOPIC 3.19 DIFFERENCE BETWEEN ALLOWANCE AND PERQUISITES

Allowance	Perquisite
Allowance is always given in cash.	Perquisite is given in cash or in kind.
Allowance generally increase the tax liability.	Perquisite generally reduces the tax liability.

Problem 3.19-P1 (Difficult)

Explain tax treatment of following perquisites in the hands of employee. Mr. X and members of his household enjoys following facilities provided by the employer :

(1) The company sends X to official tour of 10 days to Maldives. X takes his wife also. The expenditure incurred by the company on both were of Rs. 60,000 for 12 days. The scenic beauty of Maldives kept them there for two more days. The company maintains its guest house in Maldives.

(2) Employer gave gift of TV of Rs. 25,000 to son of Mr. X. His son got admission in IIM Ahmedabad.

(3) Mr. X uses company's credit card both for official purpose and personal purpose. On one occasion he is sent to Cochin to buy spices for the company. He purchases spices for Rs. 60,000 and spent Rs. 10,000 on his personal cloths.

(4) The company employed a yoga teacher on a salary of Rs. 1,00,000 p.a. The yoga teacher provides yoga training in company premises. All employees are eligible for training.

(5) The company maintains a guest house at Kodaikanal *(Near Madurai)* exclusively for Key Man employee of the company. Mr. X was in Kodaikanal for personal and official purpose for 5 days. The company incurred an expenditure of Rs. 1,000 per day. However market rent of such facility is Rs. 1,500 per day.

(6) He is also provided with refreshment during office hours. Company incurred the expenditure of Rs. 60 per day.

(7) The value of lunch provided during office hours at business premises Rs. 15,000.

(8) Telephone facility at his residence wholly for personal purpose. Expenditure incurred by employer Rs. 9,000.

(9) Employer pays accident insurance premium of Rs. 1,000.

(10) The employer presents a Swatch watch to X on his birthday. Cost of watch Rs. 17,000.

(11) X joins a health club in his neighbourhood. The annual fees of Rs. 7,000 is paid by the company on behalf of X.

(12) X enjoys meal @ Rs. 20 per meal. Expenditure incurred by the company is Rs. 68 per meal for 200 days. The meal is provided during office hours at the business premises of the company.

(13) The company maintains a holiday home at Puri. The employer gave a discount of 70% for staying and charged Rs. 1,400 where X went to Puri with his family on vacation and also for official purpose.

(14) X, has taken a Citi Bank gold card. Out of initial fees Rs. 2,500, the employer pays Rs. 1,800 on behalf of X.

Ans: All perquisites are exempt from tax except (8) Rs. 9,000 (11) Rs. 7,000 (14) Rs. 1,800.

Problem 3.19-P2

Mr. Taxcrazy employed on 1-4-2006 on following emoluments has following two options. Compute Income from Salary from the both the options.

	Option 1	*Option 2*
Basic Salary	5,00,000	5,00,000
Telephone allowance / Telephone facility	12,000	12,000
Meal allowance / Meal facility	16,000	16,000
Entertainment Allowance / Club facility	25,000	25,000
Conveyance allowance for personal purpose / Car facility	50,000	50,000

Solution

Computation of Income from Salary for the AY 2006-07.

	Option 1	*Option 2*
Basic Salary	5,00,000	5,00,000
Telephone allowance / Telephone facility	12,000	-
Meal allowance / Meal facility	16,000	-
Entertainment Allowance / Club facility	25,000	-

Conveyance allowance / Car facility	50,000	–
Income from salary	6,03,000	5,00,000

Option 2 is better for employee since salary is less therefore tax liability shall also be less.

RULE 3 : VALUATION OF PERQUISITES

TOPIC 3.20 *RULE 3(1)*. VALUATION OF RENT FREE ACCOMMODATION

(A) INTRODUCTION

1. The accommodation may be provided either to Govt. employee or to a private employee.
2. The accomodation may be furnished accomodation (furniture is provided) or unfurnished accomodation (furniture is not provided)
3. The employer may provide accommodation to the employee either for rent free *(no rent is paid by employee)* or at concessional rent *(employee pays certain amount of rent to the employer on account of accommodation).*
4. *Computation* : Where the furnished accommodation is provided, first treat the accommodation as if it is unfurnished and compute the value of unfurnished accommodation. To the value of unfurnished accommodation add the value of furniture to compute value of furnished accommodation. Let us see this mathematically.

Computation of value of accommodation (assumed figures)

Value of unfurnished accommodation	8,500
Add : Value of furniture	1,500
Value of furnished accommodation	10,000
Less : Recovery by the employer from the employee on account of accommodation *(concession in respect of rent)*	1,000
Value of accommodation *(Taxable perquisite)*	9,000

Now let us see how the valuation is done.

(B) ACCOMMODATION PROVIDED TO CENTRAL GOVT. OR STATE GOVT. EMPLOYEES

Where unfurnished accommodation is provided to Central Govt. or State Govt. employees the value of unfurnished accommodation is determined as per Govt. Rules. Value of furniture and recovery is applicable.

E.g. Suppose the fair rent of accommodation is Rs. 5,000 p.m. Rent as per Govt. Rule is Rs. 2,000 p.m. In this case value of unfurnished accommodation is Rs. 24,000.

(C) ACCOMMODATION PROVIDED TO PRIVATE EMPLOYEES OR SEMI GOVT. EMPLOYEES

Following are the new rules for valuation of accommodation which are yet to be notified. We are giving new rules on the assumption that it shall be notified shortly. However for old rules of valuation of accommodation please please refer last page of this book.

1. Where the accommodation is owned by employer and
   — provided in a city having a population of more than 25 lakhs as per 2001 census then value of accommodation is 15% of accommodation's salary.

— provided in a city having a population of exceeding 10 lakhs but upto 25 lakhs as per 2001 census then value of accommodation is 10% of accommodation's salary.

— provided in a city having a population of 10 lakhs or less as per 2001 census then value of accommodation is 7.5% of accommodation's salary.

2. Where the accommodation is hired from third party then value of accommodation is 15% of accommodation's salary or actual rent paid or payable whichever is less.

	Cities having a population of		
	more than 25 lakhs	*more than 10 lakhs less than 25 lakhs*	*less than 10 lakhs*
Accommodation is owned by employer	*15 % of RFA salary is taxable*	*10 % of RFA salary is taxable*	*7.5 % of RFA salary is taxable*
Accommodation is leased or rented by employer	Amount of lease rent paid or payable or 15% of salary whichever is less is taxable		

Illustrations and Problems 3.20-P1 (Simple)

Compute value of accommodation from the following information :

	Case 1	*Case 2*	*Case 3*	*Case 4*
Accommodation is	owned	owned	owned	leased
City Population (2001 census)	130 lakhs	25 lakhs	10 lakhs	–
Lease rental	–	–	–	12,000
Accommodation's Salary	2,00,000	5,00,000	1,30,000	1,60,000

Ans: (1) 30,000; (2) 50,000; (3) 9,750; (4) 12,000

Solution

Case 1 : Since city population exceeds 25 lakhs, 15% of salary (15% of 2,00,000) is taxable which is Rs. 30,000.

Case 2 : Since city population is upto 25 lakhs, 10% of salary (10% of 5,00,000) is taxable which is Rs. 50,000.

Case 3 : Since city population is upto 10 lakhs, 7.5% of salary (7.5% of 1,30,000) is taxable which is Rs. 9,750.

Case 4 : In case of leased accommodation city population does not play any role. What is chargeable is amount of rent or 15% of salary whichever is less is taxable. 12,000 or 15% of 1,60,000 whichever is less = Rs. 12,000 is taxable.

(D) SALARY FOR THE PURPOSE OF ACCOMMODATION

1. Accommodation's salary is computed on *due* basis for the period during which accommodation is *occupied* by the employee.

   E.g. Suppose employer provides accommodation on 15-6-2006, but accommodation is occupied by employee from 1-8-2006. In this case salary shall be computed from 1-8-2006 upto the date of occupation *i.e.* upto 31-3-2007.

   Since accommodation's salary is computed on due basis therefore it shall not include advance salary and arrears of salary.

2. *Accommodation's salary* : It includes all salary except perquisites which are Basic Salary + Dearness Allowance (*should form part of salary for computation of retirement benefit*) + Commission (fixed or otherwise) + Bonus due for relevant previous year + Fees + all taxable allowances + encashed leave + any monetary payment by whatever name called.

   It excludes

   (a) Perquisites as defined u/s 17(2) whether payable in terms of money or not; and

   (b) Employers' contribution towards provident fund.

   As you know, bonus is taxable on receipt basis but for computation of accommodation's salary bonus is taken on due basis, therefore bonus due for the PY 2006-07 is included in accommodation's salary, even where the bonus is not received during the PY 2006-07.

Problem 3.20-P2 (Conceptual)

Accommodation is provided during the PY 2006-07. You are required to say whether following shall be included in computing accommodation salary.

1. Basic Salary.
2. Dearness Allowance forming part of salary.
3. Dearness Allowance not forming part of salary.
4. Dearness Allowance (30% forming part of salary)
5. Commission based on sales.
6. Fixed commission.
7. Servant allowance.
8. Meal allowance.
9. Conveyance allowance for official purpose.
10. Travelling allowance for personal purpose.
11. Uniform allowance (60% spend for official purpose)
12. Children education allowance for 3 child. Rs. 150 p.m./child
13. Hostel allowance for 2 child Rs 6,000.
14. Bonus due for the PY 2006-07 not yet received.
15. Bonus due for PY 2005-06 received in PY 2006-07.
16. Arrears of salary for the PY 2005-06 received in PY 2006-07.
17. Arrears of salary for the PY 2006-07 received in PY 2007-08.
18. Leave encashment.
19. Fees
20. Water facility.
21. Re-imbursement of gas bills.

Ans: (1) Yes (2) Yes (3) No (4) 30% of DA forms part of accommodation salary (5) Yes (6) Yes (7) Yes (8) Yes (9) No (10) Yes (11) 40% of uniform shall form part of accommodation salary (12) Rs. 3,000 (13) Nil (14) Yes (15) No (16) No (17) Yes (18) Yes (19) Yes (20) No (21) No.

Problem 3.20-P3 (Conceptual)

Following is the salary structure of Mr. Taxcrazy. You are required to compute value of accommodation for AY 2007-08.

Basic Salary	7,000 p.m.
Dearness Allowance	1,000 p.m.
Transport Allowance	1,200 p.m.

Compute Income from salary for the AY 2007-08 if

1. He is provided with accommodation at Delhi.
2. He is provided with accommodation at Gangtok. (population as per 2001 census 5 lakh).
3. He is provided with accommodation at Delhi w.e.f. 1-01-2007.
4. He is provided with accommodation at Delhi. Accommodation is taken on rent by employer. Lease rent Rs. 25,000 p.a. However employer could not pay rent of Rs. 5,000 for the relevant year.
5. He is provided with accommodation at Kohima. (population as per 2001 census 4 lakh). Accommodation is taken on rent by employer. Lease rent Rs. 13,000 p.a. However employer paid Rs. 12,000 as lease rent for the relevant year.
6. He is provided with accommodation at Delhi @ Rs. 400 p.m.

Ans: (1) 13,320; (2) 6,660; (3) 3,330; (4) 13,320; (5) 13,000; (6) 8,520

Illustrations 3.20-P4 (Difficult)

Compute Income from salary for the AY 2007-08 from the following information.

	Case 1	*Case 2*	*Case 3*
Basic salary p.m.	5,000	8,000	9,000
DA *(80% forms part of salary)* p.m.	1,000	10% of BS	2,500
Transport allowance p.m.	800	1,500	900
Conveyance allowance for official purpose	18,000	19,000	25,000
Travelling allowance (20% spend for official purpose)	15,000	16,000	40,000
Entertainment Allowance p.a.	500	900	5,500
Advance salary	10,000	12,000	6,000
Bonus due for PY 2006-07 not yet received	1,800	1,200	1,300
Water facility	20,000	6,000	7,000
He is provided with accommodation.	owned	rented	leased
Population	35 lakhs	6 lakhs	4 lakhs
Rent paid by employer for a year	N.A.	50,000	20,000

Solution

Computation of Income from salary.

	Case 1	*Case 2*	*Case 3*
Basic salary	60,000	96,000	1,08,000
DA *(80% forms part of salary)* p.m.	12,000	9,600	30,000
Transport allowance	Nil	8,400	1,200
Conveyance allowance for official purpose	Nil	Nil	Nil
Travelling allowance (80% taxable)	12,000	12,800	32,000
Entertainment Allowance p.a.	500	900	5,500

Advance salary	10,000	12,000	6,000
Bonus not taxable since not received	Nil	Nil	Nil
Water facility	20,000	6,000	7,000
Value of accommodation [see note]	12,585	19,047	20,000
Income from Salaries	1,27,085	1,64,747	2,09,700

Note : Computation of accommodation salary.

	Case 1	*Case 2*	*Case 3*
Basic salary	60,000	96,000	1,08,000
DA *(80% forms part of salary)* p.m.	9,600	7,680	24,000
Transport allowance	Nil	8,400	1,200
Conveyance allowance for official purpose	Nil	Nil	Nil
Travelling allowance (80% taxable)	12,000	12,800	32,000
Entertainment Allowance p.a.	500	900	5,500
Bonus due for PY 2006-07 not yet received	1,800	1,200	1,300
Accommodation salary	83,900	1,26,980	1,72,000
15% of accommodation salary	12,585	19,047	25,800
Rent paid by employer	N.A.	50,000	20,000
Taxable value of accommodation	12,585	19,047	20,000

Problem 3.20-P5 [Simple]

X, who is working with LM Ltd. draws following emoluments. Compute Income from Salary for the AY 2007-08.

Basic Salary	14,000 p.m.
Dearness Allowance *(25% forms part of salary)*	2,000 p.m.
Helper Allowance *(75% is spent towards official purpose)*	1,000 p.m.
Lunch Allowance *(Expenditure on lunch is Rs. 1,000 p.m.)*	900 p.m.
Children education allowance for 3 children	90 p.m./child

He has been provided unfurnished accommodation at Surat. Population 15 lakhs.

Ans: 2,25,768. [1,68,000+24,000+3,000+10,800+1,080+18,888=2,25,768]

Problem 3.20-P6 (Difficult)

Mr. 'X' worked in a company from April to August, 2006 on a salary of Rs. 8,000 p.m. He joined another company from September, 2006 to March, 2007 on a salary of Rs. 10,000 p.m. plus a rent free accommodation at Agra. (Population 11 lakhs). Determine the value of the rent fee accommodation.

Ans: 7,000.

Problem 3.20-P7 [Difficult]

Mr. Taxcrazy employed in Elevate Ltd. furnishes following monthly information of his salary for your perusal.

Basic Salary	18,000
Children education allowance for single child	500
Disc allowance	3,000

The company provides him an accommodation w.e.f. 1-11-2006. The company pays a annual rent of Rs. 24,000 in respect of the accommodation.

Ans: 2,66,800. [2,16,000+4,800+36,000+10,000=2,66,800]

Problem 3.20-P8 (Difficult)

Mr. X who joins TQM Ltd. on 1-5-2006 furnishes the following data. Compute Income from Salary for the AY 2007-08.

Basic Salary	16,000 p.m.
Dearness Allowance *(25% forms part of salary)*	5,000 p.m.
Fixed commission	25,000

He has been provided accommodation for Rs. 500 p.m. at Mumbai.

Ans: 2,82,713. [1,76,000+55,000+25,000+26,713=2,82,713]

Problem 3.20-P9 [CS J06]

Manish is the general manager of a transport company drawing a salary of Rs. 15,000 per month. The company has provided him with accommodation in City (Population 25 lakhs) for which 10% of his basic salary is deducted. Actual rent paid by the company for accommodation is Rs. 1,20,000 per annum. He is also receiving entertainment allowance of Rs. 500 per month. He is in receipt of bonus equivalent to 2 months' salary. Compute his taxable income under the head 'salary' for the assessment year 2007-08.

Ans: 2,30,400. [1,80,000+14,400+6,000+0+30,000=2,30,400]

Problem 3.20-P10 [Typical]

Miss Himani, who is working with SaReGaMa, draws following emoluments. Compute Income from Salary for the AY 2007-08.

Basic Salary (Her annual increment falls due on 1-9-2006 of Rs. 4,000 p.m.)	28,000 p.m.
Dearness Allowance *(as per terms of employment)* (from 1-9-2006 dearness allowance was discontinued.)	1,500 p.m.
Transport Allowance (she uses monthly pass of Metro for which she pays Rs. 600)	1,700 p.m.
Make-up allowance w.e.f. 1-5-2006	4,000 p.m.
Her employer also pays life insurance premium. Premium was due on 16-3-2007 but was paid on 17-4-2007.	62,000
Her electricity and water bill dated 15-3-2007 was paid by employer on the date of payment of life insurance premium.	53,000

On 1-7-2006 she has been provided with unfurnished accommodation worth Rs. 1 crore at Mumbai. She owns a music system worth Rs. 2,00,000 besides furniture worth Rs. 6,00,000.

On 15-3-2006 she was paid four months advance basic salary of the month of April 2006, May 2006, June 2006 and July 2006.

Ans: 4,25,365. [2,52,000+7,500+10,800+44,000+62,000+49,065=4,25,365] [AS=2,80,000+3,000+8,100+36,000=3,27,100]

Problem 3.20-P11 [CS J03] [M 6]

Compute the taxable income of X for the assessment year 2007-08. He is residing in a city where population is less than 10 lakh as per 2001 census and the employer has provided an unfurnished house with effect from October 1, 2006 :

Salary	10,000 p.m.
Dearness allowance (not forming part of salary)	1,000 p.m.
Production bonus	11,000 p.m.
Bonus	7,000 p.a.
Professional tax (paid by employer)	2,400 p.a.
Medical allowance	600 p.m.
Children educational allowance (for 2 children)	400 p.m.

Ans: 2,90,673. [1,20,000+12,000+1,32,000+7,000+2,400+7,200+2,400+10,073=2,93,073–2,400=2,90,673]

Problem 3.20-P12

Mr. X who is working as improvement manager in Kaizen Ltd furnishes following information for the year ended March 31, 2007 :

Basic Salary	23,500 p.m.
Children education allowance–	
• First child	70 p.m.
• Second child	90 p.m.
• Third child	4,800

He has been provided accommodation for Rs. 500 p.m. at Nainital (population as per 2001 census 6 lakhs). Compute Income from Salary for the AY 2007-08. He pays professional tax paid Rs. 2,500.

Ans: 3,00,423. [2,82,000+4,440+15,483+1000=3,02,923–2,500=3,00,423]

Problem 3.20-P13 [Difficult]

Mr. Batman employed in OMYG Ltd. furnishes following monthly information of his salary for your perusal.

Basic Salary	3,500
Hostel Allowance for single child	500
Holiday Home Allowance	50
His annual gas bills were re-imbursed by the company in the PY 2006-07	3,900
He is also provided with following facilities.	
Gas, Electricity and Water facility	4,000
Education facility	5,400
Medical facility	8,000
Servant facility	200

The company provides him an accommodation w.e.f. 1-11-2006. The company pays a annual rent of Rs. 5,000 in respect of the accommodation.

Ans: 50,983. [42,000+2,400+600+3,900+2,083=50,983]

TOPIC 3.21 VALUATION OF USE OF ASSET INCLUDING FURNITURE

1. If asset including other asset is owned by employer then 10% p.a. of the original cost of the furniture is taxable. (not W.D.V of furniture)
2. If asset including other asset is rented by employer then actual hire charges payable is taxable.

E.g. 1 : Mr. Taxcrazy has been provided with an air-conditioner costing Rs. 1,00,000 on 1-1-2007. The use of furniture during the PY 2006-07 is for 3 months. Taxable value shall be 10% of 1,00,000 × 3 ÷ 12 = Rs. 2,500. Suppose the furniture is provided on 12-3-2007. In this case furniture is used by employee for only 20 days. Value of furniture = 10% of 1,00,000 × 20 ÷ 365 = Rs. 548.

Note:

1. Furniture includes radio sets, TV, AC, refrigerator and other household appliances.
2. Other assets includes home theater system, scanner, CD Rom, etc.
3. Use of laptop, computer, telephone and car or its re-imbursement is fully exempt from tax.

Illustration 3.21-P1 [Difficult]

1. Air-Conditioner costing Rs. 50,000. WDV as on 1-4-2006 Rs. 30,000.
2. Television on 1-1-2006 (Cost of television 19,000)
3. Fridge on 1-1-2007 (Cost of fridge 10,000)
4. Microwave oven worth Rs. 8,000 on 1-12-2006 (Actual hire charges Rs. 50 p.m.)
5. Geyser on 3-3-2007 @ Rs. 15 p.m. *(Cost of geyser Rs. 5,000)*
6. Use of computer (Cost of computer Rs. 50,000)

Solution

1. Air-Conditioner [10% of 50,000]	5,000
2. Television [10% of 19,000]	1,900
3. Fridge on 1-1-2007 [10% of 10,000 ÷ 12 × 3]	250
4. Microwave oven [50 × 4]	200
5. Geyser on 3-3-2007 [10% of 5,000 ÷ 365 × 29] – [15 ÷ 31 × 29]	26
6. Use of computer	nil
Value of furniture	7,376

Problem 3.21-P2 [CS D01]

From the following information, find out the value of the rent - free furnished accommodation at Mumbai provided to X, a private sector employee :

	Rs. per annum
Basic salary	54,000
Dearness allowance (50% forming part of salary)	30,000
Uniform allowance (60% spent on purchase and maintenance of uniform)	6,000
Income-tax paid by the employer on behalf of X	2,000
Rent-free accommodation (rent paid by employer)	50,000
Cost of furniture provided	20,000

Ans: 10,710; 1,01,110. [54,000+30,000+2,400+2,000+10,710=1,01,110]

Problem 3.21-P3 [Difficult]

A is a General Manager of ABC Co. Ltd., Bangalore. He has furnished the following particulars of his salary for the Assessment Year 2007-2008. Compute his Income from Salary :

(i) Basic salary	6,000 p.m.
(ii) Dearness Allowance (forming part of salary but not entering into benefits of retirement)	1,000 p.m.
(iii) Bonus	10,000
(iv) Other taxable allowances	20,000
(v) Entertainment allowance	6,000

He is also provided a free furnished accommodation at Bangalore. (Population 30 lakhs.) The original cost of the furniture is Rs. 20,000. Hire charges of air-conditioners are Rs. 8,000.

Ans: 1,46,200. [72,000+12,000+10,000+20,000+6,000+16,200+10,000=1,46,200]

Problem 3.21-P4 [Difficult]

Mr. Y is working in a Private Limited Company in Mumbai. Following information is given in order to calculate his Gross Total Income for Assessment Year 2007-2008.

(i) Salary of Y is Rs. 20,000 per month. He also received a bonus of Rs. 30,000 in the year.

(ii) Y has been provided with a furnished accommodation. The company pays rent at Rs. 25,000 p.m. and recovers Rs. 1,500 p.m. from Mr. Y.

(iii) The actual cost and W.D.V. of the movable assets provided by the company as on 1.4.2006 are as under :

	Actual Cost	*W.D.V. as on 1.4.2006*
(a) T.V.	24,000	19,200
(b) Refrigerator	30,000	24,000
(c) Appliances	15,000	12,000

(iv) Received Rs. 25,000 from Banks as interest.

Ans: 2,99,400. [2,40,000+30,000+22,500+6,900=3,12,900+25,000=2,99,400]

Problem 3.21-P5 [ICWA D2000]

During the previous year 2006-07 X, posted at Ajmer (Population 8 lakhs), receives the emoluments consisting of basic pay Rs. 60,100 (i.e.) Rs. 4,300 per months upto October 31, 2006 and Rs. 6,000 per month thereafter; Dearness pay Rs. 3,000 (forming part of basic salary); project allowance Rs. 3,000 (allowed with effect from January 1, 2007 @ Rs. 1,000 per month) and commission Rs. 3,600. On September 1, 2006 the employer provides a rent free furnished house. Besides, he provides furniture costing Rs. 60,000. Some of the furniture items are however taken on rent @ Rs. 9,000 p.a. Rent of the furniture of the previous year is paid by employer on May 10, 2007 (employer keeps books of account on cash system. consquently expenditure on rent is debited in previous year 2007-08.)

Determine the taxable value of furnished accommodation for the AY 2007-08. As rent of furniture is paid by the employer on May 10, 2007. X insists that the same is not includible in the taxable value of the perquisite for 2006-07. Is the claim of X tenable.

Ans: 3,409; 81.859. [60,100+3,000+3,000+3,600+3,409+8,750=81,859 [AS: 45,450]

Problem 3.21-P6 [Difficult]

Compute Income from Salary for the AY 2007-08 from the following remuneration package of Mr. Taxcrazy working in a HHH Ltd.

Basic Salary	9,000 p.m.
Dearness Allowance	1,000 pm.
Entertainment Allowance	6,000
Special allowance to meet education and hostel expenditure of his child	5,800
Overtime allowance	11,000
Holiday Home Allowance	1,600
Medical Allowance	8,500
Re-imbursement of gas bills	1,500
Conveyance allowance for official purpose	12,000
Travelling allowance *(10% not spend)*	7,500

He has been provided with furnished accommodation at Purulia (Population as per 2001 census 9 Lakhs) @ Rs. 100 p.m. He has also been provided with following asset for its use.

(a) Rented furniture. Rent of furniture paid by employer Rs. 60,000.

(b) Telephone at residence. Expenditure incurred by employer Rs. 15,000.

(c) Home theater owned by employer costing Rs. 20,000.

Ans: 2,21,414. [1,08,000+12,000+6,000+1,000+11,000+1,600+8,500+1,500+0+750+9,064+62,000=2,21,414]

Problem 3.21-P7 [Typical]

Mr. Taxcrazy, a resident in India, furnishes the undernoted particulars of his income. Compute Income from Salary for the AY 2007-08.

Basic Salary Rs. 18,000 p.m.

He encashed 15 days earned leave and received Rs. 24,000. The amount was utilised for a grand and beautiful trip of Kerala.

Bonus due for PY 2005-06 received on 4-5-2006 Rs. 1,100.

Bonus due for PY 2006-07 received on 14-4-2007 Rs. 2,400.

He was provided with a villa at concessional rate in a plush locality of Pondicherry @ Rs. 16,000 p.a. with attached garden and ample parking facility. The employer purchased kitchen furniture for him costing Rs. 2,00,000 and hired a Germany made Sofa Set for his drawing room for Rs. 12,400 p.a. (Population of Pondichery as per 2001 census is more than 10 lakhs)

Ans: 2,93,860. [2,16,000+24,000+1,100+36,360+16,400=2,93,860]

Problem 3.21-P8 [Typical]

Mr. Taxcrazy, joins a company wef 1-6-2006 on following salary structure. Basic Salary Rs. 7,000 p.m. Dearness allowance Rs. 1,000 p.m. Meal allowance Rs. 200 p.m. Transport allowance Rs. 700 p.m. On 1-8-2006 he is provided with furnished accommodation at Mumbai @ Rs. 200 p.m. Cost of furniture Rs. 6,00,000. Compute Income from Salary for the AY 2007-08.

Ans: 1,48,640. [70,000+10,000+2,000+0+6,640+60,000=1,48,640]

Problem 3.21-P9 [Typical]

Mr. Taxcrazy, retires from the company on 28-2-2007. His salary structure is following. Basic Salary Rs. 11,000 p.m. High cost of living allowance Rs. 1,000 p.m. Marriage allowance Rs. 500 p.m. Travelling allowance for official purpose Rs. 80,000. On 1-1-2006 he is provided with furnished accommodation at Delhi @ Rs. 300 p.m. Cost of furniture Rs. 80,000. He is also provided with rented furniture @ Rs. 20,000 p.m. Compute Income from Salary for the AY 2007-08.

Ans: 3,82,158. [1,21,000+11,000+5,500+0+24,200+17,325+2,27,333=3,82,158]

TOPIC 3.22 WHERE ACCOMMODATION IS PROVIDED IN A HOTEL

Meaning of hotel : It includes licensed accommodation in the nature of motel, service apartment or guest house.

Where the accommodation is provided in a hotel, taxable value of perquisite is lower of the following :

1. 24% of salary paid or payable for the period during which such accommodation is provided in the PY; or
2. the actual charges paid or payable to such hotel for the period.

(Recovery is applicable).

However, there will be no perquisite value if :

(a) Such accommodation is provided for a period not exceeding 15 days; and

(b) It has been provided on the transfer of the employee from one place to another.

TOPIC 3.23 OTHER POINTS RELATED TO ACCOMMODATION

(A) MEANING OF ACCOMMODATION

It includes a house, flat, farmhouse or part thereof, or accommodation in a hotel, motel, service apartment, guest house, caravan, mobile home, ship or other floating structure.

(B) ACCOMMODATION PROVIDED IN A REMOTE AREA

Meaning of Remote area : It means an area that is located at least 40 kilometres away from a town having a population not exceeding 20,000 based on latest published all India census.

Accommodation provided in a remote area or at mining site or on an offshore oil exploration site, or a project execution site or an accommodation provided in an offshore site of similar nature is exempt from tax.

(C) *ACCOMMODATION PROVIDED TO SUPREME COURT OR HIGH COURT JUDGES, ETC.

Rent free official residence provided to Judge of Supreme Court or High Court, Officer of parliament, a Union Minister, and a leader of opposition is exempt from tax.

(D) *ACCOMMODATION PROVIDED ON TRANSFER OF EMPLOYEE WHILE RETAINING THE OLD ACCOMMODATION

If an employee on transfer is provided accommodation at new place of posting even while retaining the accommodation at the earlier place, the value of the perquisite will be determined with reference to that which has the lower value for a period not exceeding 90 days. If the employee retains both the accommodations beyond 90 days, he will be charged for both such accommodations.

Problem 3.23-P1 (Typical)

Mr. Taxcrazy is employed by Super Charged Ltd in Bikaner from 1-7-2006. The company pays him a consolidated salary of Rs. 16,000 p.m. alongwith company's own accommodation in Bikaner. On 1-9-2006 he is transferred to Guwahati where his salary is increased by Rs. 4,000 p.m. In Guwahati he is provided with rented accommodation. The rent paid by the company is Rs. 600 p.m. upto 31-1-2007. From 1-2-2007 the rent paid by the company is Rs. 4,300 p.m.

He also occupies the Bikaner accommodation till 31-1-2007. From 1-8-2006 the company deducts Rs. 100 p.m. from his salary as a rent for Bikaner accommodation and Rs. 150 p.m. as a rent for Guwahati accommodation.

Bikaner population as per 2001 census is 10 Lakhs whereas Guwahati population as per 2001 census is 22 Lakhs.

Compute his value of accommodation and Income from Salary for the AY 2007-08.

Ans: 13,050; 1,85,050. [1,200+1,100+450+450+450+1,850+1,850+2,850+2,850=13,050]

(E) *COMPUTATION OF ACCOMMODATION'S SALARY, WHERE SALARY IS PROVIDED BY MORE THAN ONE EMPLOYER

If the employee receives salary from more than one employer (whether present or past), during the period during which accommodation is occupied, then, the aggregate salary received from both the employer is taken, even if accommodation is provided by only one employer.

Problem 3.23-P2 [Typical]

The following particulars relate to income of Shri Ram, an employee of XYZ Ltd. of Patna during financial year 2007-2008 :

(a) Basic Salary Rs. 3,000 p.m.

(b) Dearness Allowance Rs. 300 p.m.

(c) Salary taken in advance for daughter's marriage. Advance for 3 months was taken on 31.3.2007 Rs. 9,000.

(d) Bonus received Rs. 3,000.

(e) Pension from former employer Rs. 4,000 p.m.

(f) A furnished rent-free accommodation has been given by the company. The rent payable for the house is Rs. 2,000 p.m. and furniture costing Rs. 10,000 has been placed in it by the company.

(g) Education allowance of Rs. 50 p.m. for each of his three children is received.

(h) He spent Rs. 1,500 for professional books out of his own pocket.

Compute his income from "Salaries".

Ans: 1,14,340. [36,000+3,600+9,000+3,000+48,000+600+13,140+1,000=1,14,340]

Problem 3.23-P3 [Typical]

Mr. Taxcrazy, a resident in India, employed in two companies furnishes following particulars of his income. Compute value of accommodation and Income from Salary for the AY 2007-08.

	A. Ltd	*B. Ltd*
Basic Salary	20,000 p.m.	4,000 p.m.
Medical allowance from 1-12-2006	—	2,000 p.m.
Lunch allowance upto November 2006	—	1,000 p.m.
House rent allowance	—	4,000 p.m.

A. Ltd also provides accommodation in Noida (Population 24 lakhs) from 1-8-2006 @ Rs. 700 p.m. Before this date he lived in his own house.

Ans: 17,760; 3,67,360.

TOPIC 3.24 *RULE 3(7)(i)*. VALUATION OF LOAN

1. Where the employer provides loan to employee from his own account in excess of Rs. 20,000 in a year
   then Value of loan = (Rate of interest as per the SBI lending rates as on 1-4-2006) x (amount of each loan outstanding as on last day of each month)
2. Where the loans are made available for medical treatment in respect of diseases specified in Rule-3A of the these Rules.

SBI lending rate of interest as on 1-4-2006

Type of loan	*Period or Amount of loan*	*SBI lending rates*
Housing loan	upto 5 years	8.5 % p.a.
	more than 5 years and upto 10 years	8.75 % p.a.
	more than 10 years and upto 15 years	9 % p.a.
	more than 15 years and upto 20 years	9.25 % p.a.
Car loan	upto 3 years (Rs. 7.5 lakh and above)	8 % p.a.
	upto 3 years (below Rs. 7.5 lakh)	8.5 % p.a.
	above 3 years but upto 5 years	8.75 % p.a. (Metro) 9 % (Rural/Semi Urban)
	above 5 years but upto 7 years	8.75 % p.a. (Metro) 9.25% (Rural/Semi Urban)
Three wheeler loan		11% p.a.
Education loan	upto Rs. 4 lakhs	10.5% p.a.
	more than Rs. 4 lakhs	11.5% p.a.
Personal loan		12.75% p.a.

Problem 3.24-P1 (Simple)

Compute the value of loan from the following information :

	Case 1	*Case 2*	*Case 3*	*Case 4*
Purpose of loan	Purch. of House	Air Condt.	Car	Fridge
SBI lending rate of interest	8.5% p.a.	12.75% p.a.	9% p.a.	12.75% p.a.
Amount of loan outstanding	6 lakhs	30,000	9 lakh	20,000
Rate of interest charged by employer	7.5%	nil	2%	nil

Ans: 6,000; 3,825; 49,500; nil.

Illustration 3.24-P2 (Difficult)

Mr. Taxcrazy takes an interest free loan of Rs. 1,50,000 from his employer on 15-6-2006 for purchase of Home Theatre. He repays Rs. 20,000 on the last day of each month every month starting from June month. Compute value of loan for the AY 2007-08. [SBI lending rate of interest 12.75% p.a.]

Ans: 5,206.25

Solution

Month end	*Max outstanding bal.*	*Month end*	*Max outst. bal.*
30-6-2006	1,30,000	31-10-2006	50,000
31-7-2006	1,10,000	30-11-2006	30,000
31-8-2006	90,000	31-12-2006	10,000
30-9-2006	70,000	Total loan	4,90,000

Value of loan = 12.75% of 4,90,000 ÷ 12 = 5,206.25

Problem 3.24-P3 (Difficult)

Mr. Taxcrazy takes an interest free loan of Rs. 3,00,000 from his employer on 10-7-2006 for purchase of Car. The loan is repayable on first day of each month every month starting from the month of August in 10 equal monthly instalment. Compute value of loan for the AY 2007-08. (Assume SBI rate of interest 8.5% p.a.)

Ans: 11,475

Problem 3.24-P4 (Difficult)

Mr. Taxcrazy is provided with a loan of Rs. 2,00,000 on 1-3-2006 for purchasing a house in Kerala. He repays Rs. 60,000 on 2-8-2006 and Rs. 1,00,000 on 15-2-2007. Compute value of loan for the AY 2007-08 on the assumption that employer charges interest @ 6.5% p.a. and period of loan is 3 years. (Assume SBI rate of interest 8.5% p.a.)

Ans: 2,866.67

Problem 3.24-P5 (Difficult)

Mr. X takes a loan of Rs. 2,000 every first day of month we.f 1-4-2006. Compute value of loan for the AY 2007-08 assuming SBI rate of interest 8% p.a.

Ans: 306.67

Problem 3.24-P6 (CA-N02) M 6

X is working as a general manager of A Ltd., on a monthly salary of Rs. 20,000. In the previous year ending March 31, 2007, the company provides him following :

(i) Interest free loan (on October 1, 2006)

(a) For residential flat purchased (repayable in 8 years) [SBI lending rate 9% p.a.] 5,00,000

(b) Education loan for son [SBI lending rate 10.5% p.a.] 15,000

(ii) Loan for purchase of computer on October 1, 2006 (8 percent interest per annum) 30,000

You are required to state the basis of calculation and compute the chargeable perquisite for the assessment year 2007-08.

Ans: 24,000.

Problem 3.24-P7 (CS-J03) M 6

Determine the taxable value of the perquisite in the following transactions for the assessment year 2007-08:

(i) The employer provided an interest-free loan of Rs. 6,00,000 repayable after a period of 5 years to X, an employee, on 1st November, 2006 for construction of new house. (SBI rate of interest 9%).

(ii) An interest-free loan of Rs. 2,50,000 repayable after 3 years has been provided to Y, an employee, on October 1, 2006 for repairs of existing house. (SBI rate of interest 9%).

(iii) Z, an employee, has availed a loan of Rs. 1,00,000 from the employer for purchase of computer, loan bearing interest at 7 per cent per annum on July 1, 2006. (SBI rate of interest 11.85%).

(iv) A company gives two interest-free loan to A, an employee of the company : Rs. 12,000 for children education and Rs. 8,000 for purchasing a washing machine. (SBI rate of interest 12.75%).

Ans: 22,500; 11,250; 2,812.50; nil.

Problem 3.24-P8

Mr. Rajdeep Sardesai is working with NDTV Ltd. Compute Income from Salary for the AY 2007-08.

Salary	4,00,000
Cash reward	25,000
Food and cinema voucher of PVR Cinema for himself and his family members	15,000

He borrowed a loan of Rs. 1,00,000 on 15-3-2006 for repair of house. He repays the loan on 29-4-2006. Again he borrows a loan of Rs. 60,000 on 3-6-2006 for renovation of house. He repays the loan on 28-6-2006. Again he borrowed Rs. 15,800 on 9-7-2006 to purchase an air-conditioner which he has not yet repaid.

Compute Income from Salary for the AY 2007-08.

Ans: 4,25,000.

*RULE 3A. NAME OF SPECIFIED DISEASE

(*a*) cancer; (*b*) tuberculosis; (*c*) acquired immunity deficiency syndrome; (*d*) disease or ailment of the heart, blood, lymph glands, bone marrow, respiratory system, central nervous system, urinary system, liver, gall bladder, digestive system, endocrine glands or the skin or other specified ailment or disease requiring surgical operation.

*REIMBURSEMENT OF MEDICAL INSURANCE

If the employee is reimbursed any amount under any medical insurance scheme, then, the benefit of exemption of interest in respect of that part of loan shall not apply. Amount of medical insurance from the date of receipt of insurance is treated as loan.

Illustration 3.24-P9 (Difficult)

(A) Mr. X takes an interest free loan of Rs. 5,00,000 from his employer on 25-11-2006 for medical treatment of his dependent brother Y who is suffering from cancer. Y who is under a medical insurance cover receives Rs. 2,00,000 on 11-1-2007. As per the terms of loan the loan is to be paid in 10 equal monthly instalments and due date of payment of instalment is 7th of every month. Compute value of loan for the AY 2007-08.

(B) What would be your answer if he get reimbursement of medical insurance on 1-1-2007 instead of 11-1-2007.

Ans: (A) 4,781.25; (B) 3,187.50.

Solution : A

Month end	*Max outstanding bal.*
31-1-2007	2,00,000
29-2-2007	1,50,000
31-3-2007	1,00,000
Total loan	4,50,000

Value of loan = 12.75% of 4,50,000 ÷ 12 = 4,781.25.

TOPIC 3.25 *RULE 3(7)(vii)*. VALUATION FOR USE OF ASSETS

Taxability is same as that of furniture *i.e.* the value of perquisite for use of asset is chargeable @ 10% per annum of the actual cost of such asset or the amount of rent paid by the employer less any amount recovered from the employee for such use. As we have discussed already value of laptop, computer, telephone and car facility or its re-imbursement is fully exempt from tax. However use of other assets like use of home theater, scanner, CD Rom, etc taxable.

TOPIC 3.26 *RULE 3(7)(viii)*. VALUATION OF SALE OF MOVEABLE ASSETS

(A) SALE OF MOVEABLE ASSETS OTHER THAN STOCK IN TRADE

The value of benefit to the employee arising from the transfer of any moveable asset belonging to the employer directly or indirectly to the employee or any member of his household shall be determined as under :

(i) Computation of value of perquisites on sale of asset (assumed figures)

	Computer or electronic items	*Motor Car*	*Other Assets*
Rate of depreciation as per IT rules	50% W.D.V	20% W.D.V	10% S.L.M
Purchase price of the asset	15,000	2,00,000	25,000
Less : Depreciation for completed year for the period the asset is put to use (Let us take 2 years)	11,250	72,000	5,000
Actual cost of the asset to the employer	10,000	1,28,000	20,000
Less : Any amount paid or recovered from the employee	8,000	28,000	2,000
Value of sale of asset	2,000	1,00,000	18,000

(ii) Note

1. Depreciation is computed taking into each completed year during which such asset was put to use by the employer *i.e.* ignore the months or days.

E.g. Suppose the asset is used for 2 years 11 months 4 days. Depreciation is to be charged for 2 years ignoring the months and days.

2. No perquisite value is determined where movable asset *(other than car, computer or electronic items)* is provided by the employer to the employee either free or at concessional rate after using the same by the employer for 10 years or more.
3. If the above assets are given for free it shall be treated as gifts and it shall be fully exempt from tax.

(B) SALE OF STOCK IN TRADE

Goods or services *(manufactured by the employer)* sold by the employer to his employees are fully exempt from tax since such perquisite is now subjected to FBT.

Problem 3.26-P1 [CA N02]

Find out the taxable value of perquiste from the following partiulars in case of an employee to whom the following assets held by the company were sold on June 13, 2006.

Amount in Rs.

	Car	*Laptop*	*Furniture*
Cost of purchase (May 2004)	8,72,000	1,22,500	35,000
Sale Price	5,15,000	25,000	10,000

The assets were put to use by the company from the day these were purchased.

Ans: 66,705.

Problem 3.26-P2 (Difficult)

(A) Mr. Taxcrazy purchases following assets from his company (in a chemical business) on 31-3-2007. You are required to compute value of sold assets.

	Laptop	*Printer*	*Music System*	*Motor Car*	*Two Wheeler*
Date of purchase	20-8-2003	16-7-2004	4-12-2002	15-11-2001	12-2-1997
Purchase cost	45,000	15,000	24,500	4,04,000	65,000
Sale price	6,000	1,000	2,000	54,000	40,000

(B) What would be your answer if the printer is gifted.

Ans: *93,833; nil.*

Problem 3.26-P3 [Difficult]

Miss Shreya Ghosal works as a research engineer in Samsung Electronic India Ltd, manufacturer of computer, white goods and electronic goods. You are required to compute Income from Salary for the AY 2007-08.

Basic Salary	12,000 p.m.
Dearness Allowance	3,000 p.m.

Miss Shreya Ghosal purchases following old and new goods from Samsung :

Particulars	*Purchase value for Shreya*	*Purchase value for Samsung*
1. Furniture *(8 months)*	15,000	22,000
2. Scooter *(2 years 8 months)*	12,000	33,000
3. Printer *(new)*	14,500	not available
4. Air Conditioner *(new)*	nil	28,000
5. Antique clock *(10 years 1 month)*	1,000	39,000

Miss Shreya Ghosal and her family members used following goods provided by Samsung Ltd.:

1. Laptop used by Shreya and her father.
2. Two telephones (cell and landline) used by her and her family members. Expenditure incurred by the company is Rs. 2,500 p.m. (cell) and Rs. 1,500 p.m. (landline).
3. Scanner worth Rs. 18,000 for 98 days in the PY 2006-07.
4. Set-top box worth Rs. 3,500 for 5 months in the PY 2006-07. Hire charges paid by the company is Rs. 150.

Ans: 2,02,033. [1,44,000+36,00+21,400+633=2,02,033]

Problem 3.26-P4 [CS D02]

X is employed with PQR Ltd. on a salary of Rs. 25,000 per month. The company provides him with the following benefits :

A company owned accommodation at Delhi.

A housing loan of Rs. 5,00,000 on July 1, 2006 on which it charges interest @ 6.5% per annum. The entire loan is still outstanding. (SBI lending rate of interest 9% p.a.).

The Company gave him a watch worth Rs. 4,900 as gift on his 50th birthday on October 1, 2006.

He made purchases of Rs. 12,000 on his credit card, This amount along with the annual fee of Rs. 12,000 was paid by the company.

He is allowed to use the video camera belonging to the company. The company had purchased this camera for Rs. 60,000 on May 1, 2003. This camera was sold to him on August 1, 2006 for Rs. 30,000.

The company pays the telephone bills of Rs. 24,000 for the telephone installed at the residence of X.

Compute the gross income from salary of X for the assessment year 2007-08.

Ans: 4,48,375. [3,00,000+45,000+9,375+0+0+2,000+12,000+80,000=4,48,375]

Illustration 3.26-P5 (Typical)

K, whose Basic Salary is Rs. 10,000 p.m.; Arrears of Bonus received for the PY 2001-02 Rs. 30,000. He is provided with rented accommodation from 1-6-2006 whose rent is Rs. 9,000 p.m. He is also provided with following assets from the date of its purchase by the employer.

1. Suitcase. Purchased on 1-6-2004 for Rs. 7,000.
2. Laptop. Purchased on 1-7-2006 for Rs. 55,000.
3. Oven. Purchased on 1-8-2005 for Rs. 8,000.

The Company sold all the three assets to K, at rates shown below :

1. Suitcase. Sold on 10-9-2006 for Rs. 500.
2. Laptop. Sold on 1-1-2007 for Rs. 51,000.
3. Oven. Sold on 31-3-2007 for Rs. 1,200.

Compute Income from Salary for the AY 2007-08.

Ans: 1,81,123.

Solution

Computation of Income from Salary for the AY 2007-08

Basic Salary *(10,000 × 12)*		1,20,000
Arrears of bonus		30,000
Value of accommodation	15,000	
Add : 10% of the cost of oven	800	15,800
Value for use of suitcase *(700 × 163/365)*		313
Value for use of laptop		nil
Sale of laptop		4,000
Perquisite for sale of suitcase - SLM - 10%		
Value at the end of 2 years *(7,000 – 2 × 700)*	5,600	
Less : Amount recovered	500	5,100
Perquisite for sale of oven - SLM – 10%		
Value at the end of 1 year *(8,000 – 1 × 800)*	7,200	
Less : Amount recovered	1,200	6,000
Income from Salary		1,81,123

Note

- Since accommodation is provided from 1-6-2006, perquisite value shall be determined for 10 months. Salary for the purpose of accommodation is Basic Salary for 10 months which is 1,00,000. Therefore taxable value of accommodation is 15% of 1,00,000 = 15,000 or 90,000 whichever is less.
- Suitcase is used for 163 days in the PY 2006-07 (1-4-2006 to 10-9-2006) – and total usage is 2 years and 100 days (1-6-2004 to 10-9-2005). For depreciation purpose ignore 100 days.
- Use of laptop is exempted perquisite. However, sale of laptop is taxable perquisite. No depreciation since there is no completed year. 55,000 – 51,000 = 4,000.
- Oven *(household appliances)* is used for 12 months in the PY 2006-07 (1-4-2006 to 31-3-2007) – and total usage is 1 year and 7 months (1-8-2005 to 31-3-2007).

SECTION 17(2)(iii). FOLLOWING PERQUISITES ARE TAXABLE ONLY IN CASE OF SPECIFIED EMPLOYEE WHICH ARE (GEMS) GAS | EDUCATION | MEDICAL | SERVANT

TOPIC 3.27 *RULE 3(4).* VALUATION OF GAS, ELECTRICITY & WATER FACILITIES

1. Where gas, electricity or water is hired from third party then perquisite chargeable is actual expenditure incurred by the employer less any amount recovered from the employee.
2. Where gas, electricity or water is provided from its *own source (without hiring from outside agency)* then perquisite chargeable is manufacturing cost per unit less any amount recovered from the employee.

Note

- But where *obligation* of the employee, actual expenditure re-imbursed by the employer is fully taxable in all cases of employees whether specified employee or non-specified employee.

Problem 3.27-P1

Compute income from salary for the AY 2007-08.

	Case 1	*Case 2*
Basic Salary	5,00,000	40,000
Re-imbursement of gas bill	15,000	10,000
Water facility	18,000	12,000
Water bill re-imbursed on 1-4-2007	5,000	2,000

Ans: 5,33,000; 50,000.

TOPIC 3.28 *RULE 3(3).* VALUATION OF SERVANT FACILITIES

Any expenditure incurred by employer to provide servant facilities (sweeper, watchman, gardener, any other servant or personal attendant) is fully taxable less any amount recovered from the employee.

Note

- But where *obligation* actual expenditure re-imbursed by the employer is taxable in all the cases of employees.

Illustration 3.28-P1

Analyse the following statements and comment on its treatment.

1. The cook is engaged by employee. Salary of cook is paid by the employer to the employee.

   Firstly to compute cash taxable salary, salary of cook paid by the employer to the employee shall be taken into account *(It is a perquisite in cash)*. Secondly since the cook is engaged by employee it is treated as an obligation and therefore taxable in both the cases of employees whether specified or non-specified employee.

2. The cook is engaged by employee. Salary of cook is paid by the employer directly to the cook.

Firstly to compute Cash taxable salary, salary of cook paid by the employer shall not be taken into account, since salary of cook is paid directly to the cook *(It is a perquisite in kind)*. However since the cook is engaged by employee it is treated as obligation and therefore taxable in both the cases of employees whether specified or non-specified employee.

3. The cook is engaged by the employer. Salary of cook is paid by the employer.

   It is a perquisite in kind and also not an obligation, therefore taxable only in case of specified employee.

Problem 3.28-P2

Compute income from salary for the AY 2007-08.

	Case 1	*Case 2*
Basic Salary	5,00,000	40,000
Re-imbursement of salary of servant	15,000	10,000
Cook facility	18,000	12,000
Servant engaged by employee. Payment is made by employer directly to the servant.	5,000	2,000

Ans: 5,33,000; 50,000.

TOPIC 3.29 *RULE 3(5).* VALUATION OF EDUCATION FACILITIES

1. ON EDUCATION AND TRAINING OF EMPLOYEES : Refresher course & training of employees including boarding and lodging expenses of the employee is fully exempt, since subjected to FBT.
2. EDUCATION FACILITY PROVIDED TO FAMILY MEMBERS OF EMPLOYEE AT INSTITUTION OWNED & MAINTAINED BY EMPLOYER

   a. *Education provided to the children of the employee.*

      Market fee is taxable with exemption : The value of perquisite shall be determined with reference to the cost of such education in a similar institution in or near the locality less Rs. 1,000 p.m. per child less recovery is taxable. (no restriction in number of child)

   b. *Education facility provided to other family members of the employee.*

      Market fee is taxable with no exemption : The value of perquisite shall be determined with reference to the cost of such education in a similar institution in or near the locality — recovery is taxable.

3. OBLIGATION : In following cases education facility is treated as an *obligation* and therefore value of perquisite shall be taxable in both the cases of employees whether specified employee or a non-specified employee :

   1. Payment of school fees of the family members of the employees, by the employer directly to the school is taxable.
   2. Reimbursement of school fees of the family members of employees is taxable.

4. SECTION 10(16). SCHOLARSHIP

   Scholarship granted to meet the cost of education and other incidental expenses is exempt from tax in the hands of employee, since subjected to FBT.

Problem 3.29-P1

Compute income from salary for the AY 2007-08.

	Case 1	*Case 2*
Basic Salary	5,00,000	40,000
Education facility provided in an institution owned and maintained by employer to		
- Child 'A' [Market fees Rs. 1,500 p.m.]	1,200 p.m.	1,200 p.m.
- Child 'B' [Market fees Rs. 300 p.m.]	1,800 p.m.	1,800 p.m.
- Child 'C' [Market fees Rs. 900 p.m.]	1,500 p.m.	1,800 p.m.
- Sister 'A' [Market fees Rs. 2,200 p.m.]	3,500 p.m.	3,500 p.m.
Education facility provided in other institution	15,000	1,000
Re-imbursement of education bill	14,500	6,000

Ans: 5,49,400; 47,000.

TOPIC 3.30 *PROVISO 2 TO SECTION 17(2)*. VALUATION OF MEDICAL FACILITIES PROVIDED TO EMPLOYEE OR HIS FAMILY MEMBERS

(A) MEDICAL FACILITIES IN INDIA

a. *Medical facility in Employer's hospital* : Medical facility provided to employee or his family member in a hospital, clinic, dispensary or nursing home maintained by employer is fully exempt.

b. *Medical facility in Govt. hospital* : Payments or reimbursement made by employer in connection with the medical treatment of employer or his family members in a hospital, clinic, dispensary or nursing home maintained by Govt. or a local authority or a hospital approved by the Govt. for its employees is fully exempt.

c. *Medical treatment of prescribed disease* : Payments or reimbursement made by employer in connection with the medical treatment of employer or his family members for treatment of prescribed disease in an approved hospital, clinic, dispensary or nursing home is fully exempt.

d. *Medical facility in a private hospital* : Medical treatment taken from any doctor for himself or his family members is exempt upto Rs. 15,000. Where there is reimbursement of medical bills then it is taxable in both cases of employees whether specified or non-specified employee and exemption of Rs. 15,000 is also available.

Note

- Do remember exemption is available only if medical treatment is provided to employee or his family.

Meaning of family: It means spouse, child (dependent or non-dependent), and only dependent father, mother, brother and sister.

Problem 3.30-P1 (Difficult)

(A) Compute taxable medical facilities of Mr. X who is a specified employee.

	Case 1	*Case 2*	*Case 3*
	Treatment in Own Hospital or Govt. Hospital	*Treatment of prescribed disease in an approved hospital*	*Treatment in Private Hospital*
For treatment of			
1. X and Mrs. X	16,000	4,000	11,000
2. Married son	500	2,500	4,000
3. Married daughter	800	330	1,200
4. Father (not dependent)	1,000	650	2,400
5. Dependent brother	600	4,200	3,500
6. Married sister	900	1,000	500
7. Dependent grandmother	2,100	6,500	1,200

(B) What would be your answer if Mr. X is a Non-specified employee.

(C) What would be your answer if Mr. X is a Non-specified employee but medicals bills are reimbursed.

Ans (A) : 4,000; 8,150; 8,800; (B) nil in all cases; (C) 4,000; 8,150; 8,800.

Problem 3.30-P2 [CS D2000]

Compute the taxable value of the perquisite in respect of medical facilities availed of by X from his employer during the financial year 2006-07 :

(i) Treatment of X by his family physician : Rs. 4,200.

(ii) Treatment of Mrs. X in a private nursing home : Rs. 7,600.

(iii) Treatment of X's mother (dependent upon him) by a private doctor : Rs. 1,200.

(iv) Treatment of X's brother (not dependent upon him) : 4,000

(v) Treatment of X' grandmother (dependent upon him) : Rs. 1,500.

Ans: 5,500.

Problem 3.30-P3 (Difficult)

X and his family members are treated in the hospital maintained by the employer, the amount of treatment are :

X, Mrs X and their minor child	Rs. 7,000
Major Son of Mr. X (self-dependent)	Rs. 3,200
Parents of Mr. X (Dependent)	5,000
Parents of Mrs. X (Dependent on Mr. X)	11,000
Brother of Mr. X (Dependent on Mr. X)	7,300
Sister of Mr. X (Not dependent on Mr. X)	18,000

Besides, Mr. X took the re-imbursement from employer for the payment made to private medical practioner as follows :

Treatment of Mrs. X and their children	Rs. 3,000
Treatment of mother of Mr. X	4,800
Treatment of Mrs. X's father	2,700

Calculate the value of medical facility which is taxable in the hands of Mr. X

Ans: 31,700

(B) *MEDICAL FACILITIES PROVIDED OUTSIDE INDIA

Expenditure on medical treatment/expenses on stay abroad of the employee or his family member *(with one attendant)* outside India is exempt *to the extent permitted by RBI.*

Note

- Expenses on travelling abroad on the employee or his family members is tax free if his Gross Total Income does not exceed Rs. 2,00,000 *(before including such travelling expenditure).*

Illustration and Problems 3.30-P4 [Difficult]

Compute total income for the AY 2007-08 from the following information :

	Case 1	*Case 2*
Basic Salary	1,70,000	2,00,000
House Rent Allowance *(rent paid is nil)*	8,000	8,000
Medical facilities provided outside India		
-Boarding and medical expenses *(Rs. 15,000 is permitted by RBI)*	20,000	20,000
-Travelling expenses outside India	10,000	10,000
Income from Other Sources	17,000	25,000

Ans: (1) 2,00,000; (2) 2,48,000.

Solution : Case 1

Basic Salary	1,70,000
House Rent Allowance *(rent paid is nil)*	8,000
Medical facilities provided outside India	
-Boarding and medical expenses	5,000
Income from Salary	1,83,000
Income from Salary	1,83,000
Income from Other Sources	17,000
Gross Total Income	2,00,000

Note

- Since Gross Total Income is not more that Rs. 2,00,000 travelling expenses are not taxable as salary.

Problem 3.30-P5 [CS J 05] [M 5]

Himalaya Ltd. reimbursed the following expenditure on medical treatment of the son of an employee Karan. The treatment was done at UK :

(i) Travelling expenses Rs. 1,15,000.

(ii) Stay expenses at UK permitted by RBI Rs. 45,000 (Actual expenses Rs. 70,000)

(iii) Medical expenses permitted by RBI Rs. 50,000 (Actual expenses Rs. 70,000).

Compute the taxable perquisite for the assessment year 2007-08 in the hands of Karan, if his annual income from salary was (i) Rs. 1,70,000; (ii) Rs. 2,00,000 (iii) Rs. 2,10,000.

Ans: 45,000; 45,000; 1,60,000.

COMPREHENSIVE PROBLEMS ON PERQUISITES

Problem 3.30-P6

K, who is working with LM Ltd., draws following emoluments. Compute Income from Salary for the AY 2007-08.

Basic Salary	21,500 p.m.
Hostel Allowance for 1 child	350 p.m.
Entertainment Allowance (wholly spent towards official purpose)	7,000
Income tax paid by employer on behalf of employee	2,000
Re-imbursement of gas bills	10,000
Servant facility (watchman)	150 p.m.

He has been provided with furnished accommodation at Chandigarh. (Population 31 lakhs)

He has also been provided with T.V. whose actual cost is Rs. 7,000. The employer recovers Rs. 50 p.m. on account of accommodation.

Ans: 3,19,340. [2,56,000+600+7,000+2,000+10,000+1,800+39,240+700=3,19,340]

Problem 3.30-P7

Mr. X is working as a legal (manager) with Z Com Ltd. Compute Income from Salary for the AY 2007-08.

Basic Salary	13,000 p.m.
Uniform Allowance *(50% is used for official purpose)*	3,000 p.m.
Re-imbursement of watchman salary	500 p.m.

He is also provided with following facilities :

1. Gardener; Salary Rs. 600 p.m.
2. Furniture. Furniture purchased on 1-4-2005. WDV as on 1-4-2006 Rs. 63,000. *(Rate of depreciation 10%)*
3. The children of employee studies in Chinmaya Vidyalaya. The institution is owned by the company. The expenditure incurred in a similar institute is: first child Rs. 900 p.m. and second child Rs. 1,200 p.m.
4. The employee owns a self-driven Mercedes car which is used partly for official purpose and partly for personal purpose. The employer bears the expenditure of Rs. 18,000.

Ans: 1,96,600. [1,56,000+18,000+6,000+7,200+7,000+2,400+0=1,96,600]

Problem 3.30-P8 [Hons 1996]

Mrs. A is a government employee posted in Delhi. She gets Rs. 47,000 as salary and Rs. 8,000 as entertainment allowance. She has also been provided with following facilities.

1. Gas facility for official and personal use Rs. 100 p.m.
2. A cook. Salary of cook Rs. 300 p.m.
3. Supply of water Rs. 2,000. The employer charges Rs. 500 for the water.

Find out the taxable salary chargeable to tax for AY 2007-08.

Ans: 50,000.

Problem 3.30-P9 [Hons 2003]

X is employed by a firm. During the PY 2006-07 he gets Rs. 40,500 as salary and Rs. 800 p.m. as entertainment allowance. The employer provides a servant facility in his house. All expenses *(Rs. 20,000)* are met by the employer.. Find out the taxable salary for the AY 2007-08. if :

(i) X pays Rs. 1,200 as professional tax on May 10, 2007; or

(ii) X pay Rs. 1,200 as professional tax on March 30, 2007; or

(iii) X pay Rs. 1,200 as professional tax on March 1, 2007; out of which Rs. 1,000 is reimbursed by the employer on March 2, 2007.

Ans: 70,000; 48,800; 49,800.

SALARIES RECEIVED AFTER CESSATION OF OFFICE

As per section 17(1) of the Income Tax Act provident fund, leave salary, gratuity and pension are part of the salary. Leave salary, gratuity and pension are payable by the employer on the retirement or death of employee.

TOPIC 3.31 PROVIDENT FUND

(A) MEANING

1. Provident fund means making provision for the future. It is instrument of saving in the hands of employee where both the employer and employee contribute. The total contributed amount is invested in Bank, Post office or Govt. securities to earn interest.
2. Employer's contribution is treated as income in the hand of employee and therefore taxed under the head Salary.
3. However contribution by employee is out of his own income. It means employee's contribution is a part of income therefore no adjustment required. But if employee's contribution is shown as deduction from salary, then such contribution shall be added back to salary to compute basic salary. Deduction u/s 80C is available on employee's contribution.
4. Interest on employer's and employee's contribution is treated as income and therefore taxed under the head Salary.

(B) TYPES OF PROVIDENT FUND

There are four types of provident fund which are :

1. *Statutory provident fund (SPF)* : This fund is set up under the Provident Fund Act, 1925. It is applicable to Central Govt. employees or State Govt. employees or employees working in Universities.
2. *Recognised provident fund (RPF)* : It is applicable to private employees and is recognised by Commissioner of Income Tax as per the rules given in the fourth schedule of the Income Tax Act.
3. *Unrecognised provident fund (URPF)* : It is also applicable to private employees but not recognised by Commissioner of Income Tax.
4. *Public provident fund (PPF)* : It is applicable to all individuals whether employee or not. In this provident fund employer does not play any role. PPF A/c can be opened at post office or at any branch of State Bank of India.

(C) TAXABILITY OF PROVIDENT FUND

Particluars	SPF	RPF	URPF	PPF
1 Employer's contribution to PF	Exempt	Exempt upto 12% of SAS (Note 1)	Exempt	Does not contribute
2 Interest credited to PF	Exempt	Exempt upto 9.5% on outstanding PF balance (Note 2)	Exempt	Exempt
3 Deduction u/s 80C on employee's contribution	A	Available	NA	A
4 Lumpsum withdrawal from provident fund at the time of retirement or termination of service	Exempt	Exempted provided 5 years of continuous service	Taxable (Note 3)	Exempt

Notes

1. SAS = BS + DA( ) + Commission (if)

   E.g. Basic Salary 25,000. DA (100%) 5,000. Employer's contribution towards RPF 13%. Therefore taxable RPF is 1% of 30,000 = 300.

2. Suppose interest on RPF contribution @ 10.5% is Rs. 10,500. Therefore taxable interest is 1%. But on which amount? Let the amount be x. 10.5% of x = 10,500. X = 1,00,000. Taxable is 1% of 1,00,000 = 1,000. Alternatively taxable amount = 10,500 × 1/10.5 = 1,000.

3. Lumpsum withdrawal from unrecognised provident fund is taxable as under :
   1. Withdrawal of employer's contribution chargeable under the head "Salary"
   2. Interest on employer's contribution chargeable under the head "Salary"
   3. Withdrawal of employee's contribution not taxable since not an income
   4. Interest on employee's contribution chargeable under the head "Other Sources".

Problem 3.31-P1 (Simple)

Compute total income and tax liability for the AY 2007-08.

	Case 1	*Case 2*	*Case 3*
Basic Salary	1,00,000	1,00,000	1,00,000
Dearness allowance *(20% forms part of salary)*	20,000	20,000	20,000
Employer's and employees contribution towards recognised provident fund	14% of salary each	Rs. 20,000 each	15% of BS each
Interest on contribution	@ 11% p.a. Rs. 6,000	@ 11.5% p.a. Rs. 3,000	@ 10% p.a. Rs. 5,000
Other income	1,00,000	2,00,000	2,50,000

Ans: (1) 2,08,338; 17001 (2) 3,08,042; 43,261 (3) 3,57,770; 58,478.

Problem 3.31-P2 (Simple)

Mr. X is working with Almost Completed Ltd. Compute Total Income for the AY 2007-08.

Basic Salary	2,000 p.m.
Dearness Allowance *(50% forms part of salary)*	1,000 p.m.
Gas Facility for personal use. Expenditure incurred by employer	Rs. 1,000
Contribution towards recognised provident fund :	
• Employer's contribution	15% of salary
• Employee's contribution	17% of salary
Interest on contribution @ 10.5%	10,500

Ans: 31,800. [24,000+12,000+0+900=36,900-5,100=31,800]

Problem 3.31-P3 (Difficult)

Mr. Taxcrazy who retires on 31-3-2007 furnishes following information :

Salary after deduction of employee's contribution of Rs. 20,000	76,000
Dearness allowance *(100% forms part of salary)*	24,000

Employer's contribution towards provident fund	15% of salary
Interest @ 10% towards provident fund	20,000

On 31-3-2007 following amounts are withdrawn from provident fund.

1. Withdrawal of employer's contribution Rs. 1,00,000 :
2. Interest on employer's contribution Rs. 50,000.
3. Withdrawal of employee's contribution Rs. 1,00,000.
4. Interest on employee's contribution Rs. 50,000.

You are required to compute Total Income for the AY 2007-08 if type of provident fund is (a) Statutory provident fund (b) recognised provident fund (c) unrecognised provident fund.

Ans: (a) 1,00,000; (b) 1,04,600; (c) 3,20,000.

Problem 3.31-P4

The following are particulars of income of Mrs. 'R' for the PY 2006-07.

(a) Salary Rs. 15,000 p.m.

(b) Contribution to provident fund @ 14% of salary, the employer also contributes a similar amount.

(c) Interest credited to provident fund account @ 13.5% p.a. is Rs. 18,200.

(d) She is provided by her employer with a rent free (unfurnished) house at Ajmer. [Population as per 2001 census 8,00,000]

(e) She paid Rs. 600 as employment tax to the State Government.

Compute her taxable salary for the AY 2007-08 if :

(i) The provident fund is recognised ; and

(ii) It is unrecognised.

Ans: 2,15,393; 2,06,400.

Problem 3.31-P5 (Difficult)

(A) Compute Total Income for the AY 2007-08 if salary falls due on the last day of each month.

Basic Salary upto 30-11-2006	8,000 p.m.
Basic Salary from 1-12-2006	10,000 p.m.
Dearness allowance *(100% forms part of salary)*	2,000 p.m.

Employer's and employee's contribution towards recognised provident fund 20,000 each

Interest credited to provident fund Rs. 3,000 on 1-1-2007 on outstanding balance of Rs. 1,00,000.

(B) What would be your answer if salary falls due on the first day of next month?

Ans: (A) 1,12,640; (B) 1,10,880.

Problem 3.31-P6

Mr. Rohit is a sales manager in Delhi. He furnishes the following particulars regarding his income for previous year 2006-07 :

	Rs.
Basic salary	96,000
Bonus	6,000
Dearness allowance (Rs. 200 p.m. enters into retirement benefit)	1,000 p.m.
Travelling allowance for official duty	25,000

He has been provided a big car for official and personal use. The maintenance and running expenses of the car (including driver) are borne by the company.

He lived in a house belonging to company. Its fair rent is Rs. 2,500 p.m. The company has provided the facility of gardener who is being paid a salary of Rs. 300 p.m.

He has been given cloth worth Rs. 2,600 by the employer free of cost.

Rent recovered from Rohit Rs. 2,600.

The following amount were deposited in his Provident Fund A/c :

(a) Own contribution	Rs. 9,400
(b) Company's contribution	Rs. 13,000
(c) Interest @ 12% p.a.	Rs. 12,000

Compute his taxable income from salary for assessment year 2007-08.

Ans: 1,24,952.

Solution

Computation of Total Income for the AY 2007-08

	Rs.
Basic salary	96,000
Bonus	6,000
Dearness allowance [Rs. 200 per month forms part of salary]	12,000
Travelling allowance for official duty exempt from tax	nil
Car facility	nil
Rent free accommodation [15% of 1,04,400 (96,000 + 6,000 + 2,400)]	13,060
Gardener facility	3,600
Clothes facility	nil
Excess of Employer's contribution towards RPF [13,000 – 12% of 98,400]	1,192
Interest to RPF [12,000 ÷ 12% × 2.5%]	2,500
Income from salary	1,34,352
Gross total income	1,34,352
Less : Deduction u/s 80C [employees contribution towards RPF]	9,400
Total income	1,24,952

Problem 3.31-P7

Compute 'Total Income' of Mr. X for previous year ended on 31st March, 2007.

(i)	Net salary received after deduction of :		1,43,200
	(a) His own contribution in recognised provident fund	18,000	
	(b) Income Tax	14,000	
	(c) House rent	4,800	
(ii)	Employer's contribution to recognised provident fund		18,000
(iii)	Dearness Allowance		20,000
(iv)	Education Allowance for two children		12,000
(v)	Entertainment Allowance		6,000
(vi)	Provided unfurnished house for which rent paid by employer Rs. 36,000, but charged from the employee		Rs. 4,800
(vii)	Free use of gas, electricity and water, costing to employer		4,000
(viii)	Provided 1.6 litre motor car for personal use of employee. All expenses borne by employer.		2,000
(ix)	He earned taxable long-term capital gain		60,000
(x)	Interest earned on fixed deposits in scheduled banks		8,000

Ans: 2,94,140. [1,80,000+0+20,000+9,600+6,000+24,540+4,000+0=2,44,140+60,000+8,000=3,12,140–18,000=2,94,140]

Problem 3.31-P8 [CS J97]

Mrs. X, an employee - director of XYZ Ltd., submits the following information relevant for the assessment year 2007-08.

Salary : Rs. 1,96,000; entertainment allowance; Rs. 8,000; bonus; Rs. 10,200; education allowance; Rs. 4,000 (for her grandchildren); income-tax penalty paid by employer Rs. 2,000; medical expenses reimbursed by employer; Rs. 16,000; leave travel concession Rs. 1,000; free residential telephone: Rs. 4,000; free refreshment during office hours: Rs. 4,000; payment of electricity bills by employer: Rs. 1,060; reimbursement of gas bills: Rs. 1,000; professional tax paid by the employer: Rs. 300; professional tax paid by Mrs. X: Rs. 150. PPF contribution Rs. 2,000. Compute total income.

Ans: 2,22,110.

Problem 3.31-P9 [CS J96]

X received the following emoluments during the previous year ending 31st March, 2007 :

Basic pay	86,000
House rent allowance	38,000
Advance salary for the period April and May, 2007	16,000
Entertainment allowance	10,000

He paid a rent of Rs. 45,000 in Kanpur. He contributed Rs. 5,000 to public provident fund. Determine the taxable income of X for the assessment year 2007-08 and his income from other sources was Rs. 20,000.

Ans: 1,25,600

Problem 3.31-P10

On retirement from service, A received Rs. 60,000 being his dues from unrecognised provident fund. The amount comprised Rs. 25,000 as own contribution, Rs. 5,000 as interest thereon and the balance of Rs. 30,000 being employer's contribution and interest thereon. Discuss A's liability for taxation, if any.

Ans : Rs. 30,000 is chargeable under the head salary and Rs. 5,000 under the head Income from Other Sources.

TOPIC 3.32 SECTION 7. WHEN INCOME IS SAID TO BE RECEIVED OR DEEMED TO BE RECEIVED IN INDIA

The following incomes are deemed to be received in India :

(i) Employer's contribution in excess of 12% of salary towards recognised provident fund.

(ii) Interest credited to the recognised provident fund in excess of 9.5%.

(iii) The transferred balance in a recognised provident fund from unrecognised provident fund.

(iv) the contribution made by the Central Government in the previous year to the account of an employee under a pension scheme referred to in section 80CCD.

This is so where the provident fund is maintained in India, SAS shall be computed for the period during which services are rendered in India and for the period during which services are rendered outside India.

Problem 3.32-P1 (Difficult)

Mr. Taxcrazy a Non- Resident works in an Indian company submits the following particulars of his income. Compute Total Income for the AY 2007-08.

Basic salary for services rendered in India for two month	8,000 p.m.
Basic salary for services rendered outiside India for ten month outside India	10,000 p.m.
Dearness allowance as per terms of employment	3,000 p.m.
Employer's and employees contribution towards recognised provident fund	13% of salary
Interest on recognised provident fund @ 11.5% p.a.	Rs. 12,000

Ans: 5,847.

Problem 3.32-P2 (Typical)

Mr. Taxcrazy, an Indian citizen, is a Manager with Iamdelighted Ltd. at Delhi. From May 1, 2006 he was transferred to South Africa branch of the company for 3 years. He submits the following particulars of his income for the PY 2006-07 :

Basic Salary for 1 month for services rendered in India	28,000 p.m.
Basic Salary for 11 months for services rendered in South Africa	50,000 p.m.
Employer's contribution towards recognised provident fund	12.5% of salary
Interest on recognised provident fund @ 10% p.a.	Rs. 50,000

He was also provided with following facilities in India in the month of April :

1. He lived in a rented accommodation where he was provided with gas and water facility for personal use. Expenditure incurred by the company Rs. 2,500. Electricity bills of Rs. 3,000 was reimbursed on 30-4-2006.

2. Junior Taxcrazy was studying in a school maintained by employer. Market fees of such school was Rs. 1,500. However the company incurs Rs. 3,500.
3. The company incurred an expenditure of Rs. 26,400 on treatment of Mrs. Taxcrazy in a private hospital.
4. The company provided him a domestic servant whose salary of Rs. 1,400 is paid by the company.
5. He was provided with a car wholly for personal purpose. Expenditure incurred by the company Rs. 30,000.

Ans: 36,390. [28,000+2,890+2,500+3,000=36,390]

TOPIC 3.33 *SECTION 10(10).* GRATUITY

(A) MEANING

It denotes a gratuitous (*gift or present*) payment made by the employer to his employee for long services rendered by him. Gratuity may be received by an employee on his retirement or on his becoming incapacitated prior to such retirement or on termination of his employment.

(B) TAX TREATMENT IN CASE OF GOVERNMENT EMPLOYEES

Gratuity received by Central Govt. or State Govt. employees including defence service employees is fully exempt from tax.

(C) TAX TREATMENT IN CASE OF PRIVATE EMPLOYEES

Exemption of gratuity received by private employee depends upon following factors :

Employees covered under the Payment of Gratuity Act, 1972 : This Act becomes applicable in those establishments which employ 10 or more employees.	Other employees **:** It means those employees who are not covered under the Payment of Gratuity Act, 1972. Gratuity is payable to them as per the contract of employment.
Computation of exemption : Least of following is exempt : M. Rs. 3,50,000 A. Actual gratuity received F. 15 working days salary (BS+100% of DA) at the time of retirement for each completed year of service *i.e.* 15 ÷ 26 × salary at the time of retirement × duration of service.	*Computation of exemption :* Least of following is exempt : M. Rs. 3,50,000 A. Actual gratuity received F. Half day average salary (SAS) for each completed year of service *i.e.* 1/2 × average salary × completed year of service.
1. Salary = BS + 100% DA 2. To compute completed year of service a part of month if more than 6 months are regarded 1 year *i.e.* round off the months if more than 6 months. *E.g.* Where duration of service is 18 years 7 months. Completed year of service shall be 19 years. But where duration of service is 18 years 6 months. Completed year of service shall be 18 years.	1. *SAS* = BS + DA ( ) + Commission (if) Average salary is salary of last 10 months immediately preceding the *month* of retirement. *E.g.* Where date of retirement is 15-11-2006, subtracting 10 months from 31-10-2006, we get 1-1-2006, therefore salary of 10 months is computed from 1-1-2006 to 31-10-2006. 2. To compute completed year of service, ignore the months. *E.g.* Where duration of service is 18 years 7 months. Completed year of service shall be 18 years.

Note

- Gratuity received while in service is *not* exempt from tax.

Illustration and Problems 3.33-P1 (Simple)

Compute Mr. Taxcrazy's taxable gratuity for the AY 2007-08 from the following informations by applying following situations :

Situation a : He is covered under the Payment of Gratuity Act, 1972

Situation b : He is paid gratuity under the terms of contract of employment.

	Case 1	*Case 2*
Duration of Service	18 yrs. 7 months	22 yrs. 5 months
Date of retirement	15-9-2006	1-9-2006
Basic Salary	5,000 p.m.	7,500 p.m.
Dearness Allowance *(10% forms part of salary)*	2,000 p.m.	1,800 p.m.
Commission of last 10 months @ 5% based on sales	8,000	15,000
Gratuity received	1,46,731	2,25,000

(B) What is taxable gratuity in Case 1 if you apply Situation 1 on the assumption that 90% of Dearness Allowance forms part of salary.

Ans (A): (1) 70,000; 92,731; (2) 1,06,962; 1,24,020; (B) 70,000.

Solution : Case 1

Situation a : Covered under the Payment of Gratuity Act, 1972

Salary *(for the purpose of gratuity is)* = 5,000 + 2,000 = 7,000

M	Maximum	3,50,000
A	Actual gratuity received	1,46,731
F	7,000 × 19 × 15 ÷ 26	*76,731*

Taxable Gratuity = 1,46,731 – 76,731 = 70,000.

Situation B : In case of other employees

SAS = 5,000 + 200 + (8,000 ÷ 10) = Rs. 6,000

M	Maximum	3,50,000
A	Actual gratuity received	1,46,731
F	6,000 × 18 ÷ 2	*54,000*

Taxable Gratuity = 1,46,731 – 54,000 = 92,731.

Illustration and Problems 3.33-P2 (Difficult)

Compute Mr. Taxcrazy's taxable gratuity for the AY 2007-08 from the following informations by applying following situations :

Situation a : He is covered under the Payment of Gratuity Act, 1972

Situation b : He is paid gratuity under the terms of contract of employment.

	Case 1	*Case 2*
Duration of Service	487 months	786 months
Date of retirement	31-12-2006	15-1-2007
Basic Salary from the month of Dec. 2006	7,500 p.m.	5,500 p.m.
Basic Salary of last 10 months upto Nov. 2006	6,000 p.m.	5,000 p.m.
Dearness Allowance *(do not form part of salary)*	1,000 p.m.	1,800 p.m.
Gratuity received	3,40,000	2,25,000

Ans: (1) 1,38,942; 2,20,000; (2) Nil; 60,875

Solution : Case 1

Situation 1 : Covered under the Payment of Gratuity Act, 1972

Salary *(for the purpose of gratuity is)* = 7,500 + 1,000 = 8,500

M	Maximum	3,50,000
A	Actual gratuity received	3,40,000
F	8,500 × 41 × 15/26	*2,01,058*

Taxable Gratuity = 3,40,000 – 2,01,058 = 1,38,942.

Situation 2 : In case of other employees

Salary *(for the purpose of gratuity is) :*		6,000
M	Maximum	3,50,000
A	Actual gratuity received	3,40,000
F	6,000 × 40 × 1/2	*1,20,000*

Taxable Gratuity = 3,40,000 – 1,20,000 = 2,20,000.

Problem 3.33-P3 (Simple)

X retired as General Manager of DWN Co. Ltd., on 30-4-2006. He received Rs. 92,000 as gratuity after 20 years and 10 months service. Average monthly salary for 10 months ending 31-3-2006 was Rs. 8,500. Calculate the amount of gratuity taxable.

Ans: 7,000.

Problem 3.33-P4 (Difficult)

After serving for 34 years Mr. Taxcrazy retires from service with Philips India Ltd. on 28-2-2007. He received gratuity of Rs. 2,35,000. His monthly basic salary during the calendar year 2004, 2005, 2006 and 2007 has been Rs. 11,500, Rs. 11,600, Rs. 11,700 and Rs. 11,800 respectively. His annual increment fell due on 1st January every year. Determine the amount of taxable gratuity.

Ans: 35,930.

Problem 3.33-P5 [Hons 2006]

X, an employee of PQ Co. Ltd. receives Rs. 78,000 as gratuity. He is covered by payment of Gratuity act, 1972. He retires on December 12, 2007 after rendering service of 38 years and 8 months. At the time of retirement his monthly salary basic and dearness allowance was Rs. 2,400 and Rs. 800 respectively. Is the entire amount of gratuity exempt from tax?

Ans: No, only Rs. 72,000 is exempt from tax.

Problem 3.33-P6 [ICWA]

Mr. Diwakar is the Marketing Manager of Sooraj Ltd. He retired on November 30, 2006 after service of 22 years and 10 months. At the time of retirement he has been paid Rs. 2,80,000 death - cum - retirement gratuity, although Sooraj Ltd. is not covered by the Payment of Gratuity Act, 1972. Find out his salary income chargeable to tax for the assessment year 2007-08.

The following additional information is available :

(a) Salary and Allowances :

Basic Salary at the time of retirement	Rs. 8,000 p.m.
Month from which increment is allowed	July
Amount of last increment	Rs. 1,000
Dearness allowance (fixed since 2003 and only 15% is considered for retirement benefit)	Rs. 2,000 p.m.
Commission (fixed on monthly basis since 2003)	Rs. 500

(b) He gets 0.5 per cent commission on turnover achieved by him. Turnover for different months is as follows :

Period	Rs.
January 2006	70,000
February 2006	80,000
March 2006	85,000
April 2001 to June 2006	2,70,000
July 2001 to October 2006	3,70,000
November 2006	95,000

(c) As per service rules, salary, allowances and commission become due on the first day of the next month and paid on the same day.

(d) Mr. Diwakar retires on November 30, 2006 and hands over the charge on the same day at 5.30 p.m. to the Deputy Marketing Manager.

(e) For the purpose of Section 10(10)(iii) of the Income Tax Act, 1961, average monthly salary is calculated on the basis of average salary for the ten months immediately preceding the months in which an employee retires. Although Mr. Diwakar is not in service after 5.30 p.m. on November 30, 2006, he claims that while calculating "average monthly salary" for this purpose, salary from February 2006 to November 2006 shall be considered as he retires effectively from December 1, 2006.

Ans: 1,90,487.50; 2,85,088.

(D) *GRATUITY RECEIVED FROM SEASONAL ESTABLISHMENT)

15 days for each completed year of service are taken as 7 days for each completed year of service in case employee is working in a seasonal establishment.

(E) *MEANING OF COMPLETED YEAR OF SERVICE

Completed year of service means total service including service under former employer(s) provided he was not paid gratuity by former employer(s).

(F) *WHERE GRATUITY IS RECEIVED FROM ONE OR MORE EMPLOYERS

The maximum amount of exemption shall not exceed the maximum limit which is Rs. 3,50,000. The amount of exemption claimed earlier in the same previous year or earlier previous year shall be reduced from Rs. 3,50,000.

Problem 3.33-P7

Compute taxable gratuity from *illustration 3.33-P2 Case 1* if he had received Rs. 3,00,000 as gratuity from a former employer. Exemption claimed in respect of gratuity is Rs. 3,00,000

Ans: 2,90,000.

TOPIC 3.34 *SECTION 17(1)(ii) & 10(10A).* PENSION

Pension is received after retirement and is taxable just like basic salary.

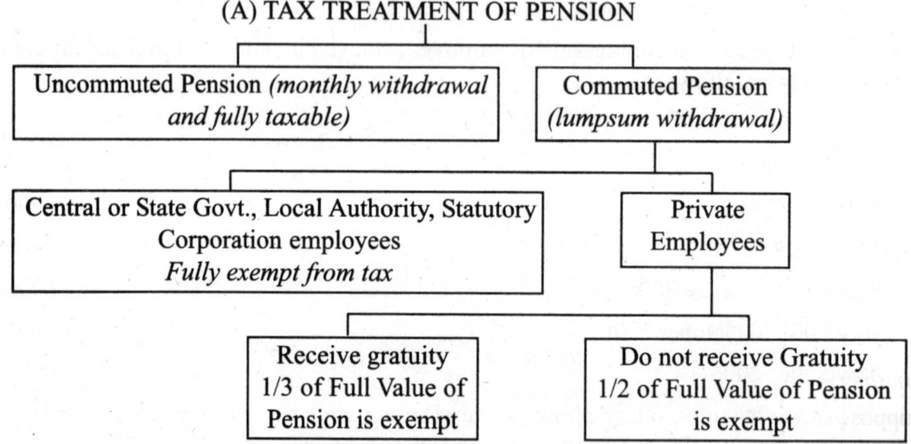

Illustrations and Problems 3.34-P1 (Simple)

Compute his Income from Salary for the AY 2007-08 assuming that (a) Salary or pension falls due on last day of each month. (b) Salary or pension falls due on first day of next month.

	Case 1	*Case 2*	*Case 3*	*Case 4*
Date of retirement	31-1-2007	31-5-2006	28-2-2007	31-3-2008
Basic Salary p.m.	7,000	3,500	24,000	15,000
Pension p.m.	3,000	1,000	10,000	2,000

Ans: (1) 76,000; 80,000; (2) 17,000; 19,500; (3) 2,74,000; 2,88,000; (4) 1,80,000; 1,95,000

Solution : Case 1

Computation of Income from Salary

last day of each month April 2006 to Jan. 2007		*first day of next month March 2006 to Jan. 2007*	
April to Jan. (10 × 7,000)	70,000	March to Jan. (11 × 7,000)	77,000
Feb. to Mar (2 × 3,000)	6,000	Feb. to Feb. (1 × 3,000)	3,000
Total Salary of PY 2006-07	76,000	Total Salary of PY 2007-08	80,000
Less : Deduction u/s 16(i)	nil	*Less* : Deduction u/s 16(i)	nil
Income from Salary	76,000	Income from Salary	80,000

(B) UNCOMMUTED PENSION

Uncommuted pension is a periodical payment received by an employee after his retirement and is taxed under the head salary in all cases of employees whether Govt. employee or private employee.

(C) COMMUTED PENSION

If a pensioner surrenders a part of his monthly pension in exchange of a lumpsum to be paid at a time, he is said to have commuted his pension, and the lumpsum received by him is called the commuted value of pension.

Manner of commutation of pension : Suppose Mr. X who retires on 1-7-2007 is entitled to a pension of Rs. 3,000 p.m. for 10 years. On 1-1-2007 he surrenders 10% of his monthly pension. How much uncommuted pension and commuted pension he is entitled to receive.

a. *Total pension entitlement* = 3,000 × 12 × 10 = 3,60,000.
b. *Entitlement of commuted pension* = 10% of his total pension which is equal to 10% of 3,60,000 = 36,000.
c. *Entitlement of uncommuted pension* during the PY 2006-07 = 18,000 + 8,100 = 26,100
   From 1-7-2006 to 31-12-2006 (6 months) = 100% of 3,000 = 3,000 p.m. × 6 = 18,000
   From 1-1-2007 to 31-3-2007 (3 months) = 90% of 3,000 = 2,700 p.m. × 3 = 8,100.
   Another way of computing uncommuted pension : 90% of 3,60,000 ÷ 10 × 12 =Rs. 2,700 p.m.

Another way of asking the question

Suppose in the question it is given Mr. A commutes 10% of his pension for Rs. 36,000. What is total pension or full value of pension?

Let full value of pension = x. 10% of x = Rs. 36,000. Solving we get x = 3,60,000. Generally questions are framed in this way.

Illustration and Problems 3.34-P2 [Difficult]

(A) Compute taxable pension of Mr. X who is employed in ishallconquertax Ltd. for the AY 2007-08 (a) Salary or pension falls due on the last day of each month. (b) Salary or pension falls due on first day of next month.

	Case 1	*Case 2*	*Case 3*
Date of retirement	31-10-2006	30-11-2006	31-1-2007
Date of commutation of pension	1-1-2007	1-2-2007	28-2-2007
Uncommuted pension received	1,000 p.m.	2,500 p.m.	4,000 p.m.
Amt. of commuted pension received	15,000	25,000	60,000
Percentage of pension commuted	30%	40%	75%
Gratuity received	25,000	60,000	Nil

Ans: (1) 4,100; 3,400; (2) 12,167; 10,667; (3) 25,000; 24,000.

Solution : Case 1

Uncommuted Pension

(a) *Uncommuted pension (Nov. to March)*		(b) *Uncommuted pension (Nov. to Feb.)*	
Nov. to Dec. 1,000 × 2	2,000	Nov. to Dec. 1,000 × 2	2,000
Jan. to March 70% × 1,000 × 3	2,100	Jan. to Feb. 70% × 1,000 × 2	1,400
Taxable Uncommuted pension (1)	4,100	Taxable Uncommuted pension (2)	3,400

Commuted pension

	a	*b*
Full value of pension *(15,000 ÷ 30%)*		50,000
Pension received		15,000
Less : exempt *(50,000 ÷ 3)*		16,667
Taxable commuted pension (1) + (2)		Nil
Total Taxable Pension	4,100	3,400

Problem 3.34-P3 (Difficult)

Miss X a Pvt. employee retires on 31-10-2006. You are required to compute Income from Salary for the AY 2007-08 if (a) Salary falls due on the last day of each month (b) Salary falls due on first day of next month.

Basic Salary	7,000 p.m.
Pension (uncommuted)	1,200 p.m.

On 31-12-2006 she gets her 90% of her pension commuted for Rs. 54,000.

Ans: 75,760; 82,640.

Problem 3.34-P4 [CS D94]

X retires from the service of PQR (P) Ltd. on 31st March, 2006. PQR (P) Ltd. pays Rs. 900 per month as pension but does not pay any gratuity. On the request of X, PQR (P) Ltd. pays Rs. 13,000 in lieu of commutation of 30% of pension with effect from 1st February, 2007. Determine the amount of taxable tension for the assessment year 2007-08 on the assumption that pension becomes due on the last day of the month.

Ans: 29,333.

Problem 3.34-P5 (Typical)

Mohan retired from service of a company on 1st January, 2007. His pension was sanctioned at Rs. 1,600 per month. He received Rs. 60,000 for gratuity also. He got 3/4th of this pension commuted and the commuted value received by him was Rs. 72,000. Compute the exempted amount of commuted value of pension for these assessment year 2007-08.

Ans: 41,200.

TOPIC 3.35 *SECTION 10(10AA)*. LEAVE SALARY

(A) CONCEPT

1. Leave salary is also known as salary in lieu of leave. Employees are entitled to various types of leave while they are in service. They have the option either to avail such leave or not to avail such leave.
2. Where the employee chooses of not availing the leave, the leave may either lapse or the leave which is not availed off can be encashed. If the leave is not encashed leave gets accumulated. Accumulated leave is also known as earned leave. The other name of accumulated leave is leave standing to the credit of employee.
3. Where the leave gets lapsed there is no tax treatment.
4. Where the leave is encashed during the continuity of employment it is fully taxable whether govt. employee or private employee.

5. Accumulated leave can be encashed only on the retirement or death of the employee. Encashment of accumulated leave or earned leave or leave standing to the credit of employee is known as leave salary.

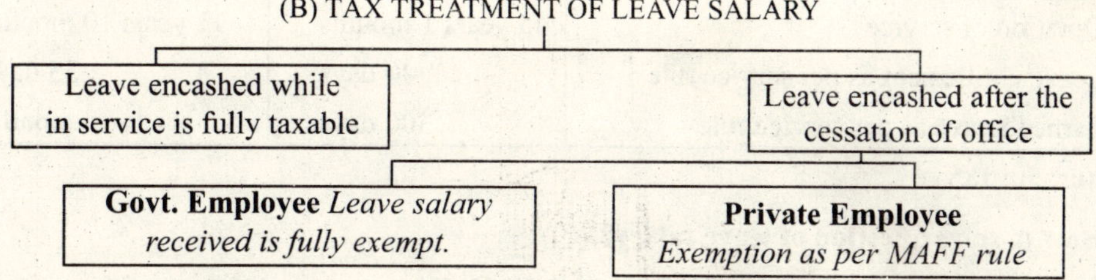

(C) MAFF RULE (APPLICABLE ONLY TO PRIVATE EMPLOYEES)

Maximum	• 3,00,000 *(life time max exemption)*	least
Actual	• Actual Leave Salary received	is
Formula	• 10 × Average salary[2]	exempt
Formula	• Earned Leave (in months) × Average salary[2]	from tax

Notes

1. Salary = SAS = BS + DA ( ) + Commission (if)

2. Average salary is to be computed for last 10 months immediately preceding the *date* of retirement.

E.g. Where date of retirement is 15-11-2006, subtracting 10 months from 15-11-2006, we get 16-1-2006, therefore salary of 10 months is computed from 16-1-2006 to 15-11-2006.

(D) COMPUTATION OF EARNED LEAVE

6. Earned Leave (EL) = Leave Entitlement (LE) – Leave Availed (LA) – Leave encashed while in service.

   Leave entitlement is a max. of 30 days for each completed year of service. *i.e.* if leave entitlement can be less than 30 days if the service rule permits but it can never be more than 30 days.

   In short we can say that 1 Year = 1 month / 30 days *(less than 30 days if service of employment so provides)*

   For computing leave entitlement only completed year of service is taken. *i.e.* ignore the months for duration of service. E.g. Where duration of service is 20 years 7 months. Ignoring the 7 months duration of service = 20 years. Leave entitlement as per Income tax rule shall be = 20 months or 600 days.

Illustration 3.35-P1 (Simple)

Compute earned leave as per Service Rule and as per Income Tax Rule from the following information.

	Case 1	*Case 2*
Duration of service	16 years 8 months	23 years 11 months
Leave entitlement as per service rule	60 days	45 days
Leave availed while in service	305 days	14 months
Leave encashed while in service	3 months	110 days

Ans: (1) 565; 85 (2) 505; 160

Illustration 3.35-P2 (Simple)

Compute earned leave as per Income Tax Rule from the following information.

	Case 1	*Case 2*
Duration of service	25 years 1 months	11 years 10 months
Leave entitlement as per service rule	40 days	35 days
Earned Leave as per service rule	300 days	8 months

Ans: 50; 185

How to solve question of leave salary?

1. First compute salary for the purpose of leave salary
2. Compute average salary
3. Compute earned leave (always in months and do not **round** off its figures)
4. Apply MAFF rule.

Illustration 3.35-P3 (Simple)

Compute taxable leave salary from the following informations.

	Case 1	*Case 2*	*Case 3*	*Case 4*
Duration of service	15 years 11 months	19 years 11 months	25 years 1 month	20 years 11 months
Average salary	35,000	40,000	16,000	45,000
Leave salary received	4,00,000	1,00,000	2,00,000	8,00,000
Leave entitlement as per service rule	60 days	35 days	45 days	20 days
Leave availed while in service	8 months	400 days	26 months	2 month
Leave encashed while in service	2 months	90 days	nil	nil

Solution

Computation of taxable leave salary

Leave entitlement	15 months	570 days	25 months	400 days
Less : Leave availed	8 months	400 days	26 months	60 days
Less : Leave encashed	2 months	90 days	nil	nil
Earned leave	5 months	80 days	nil	340 days
M	3,00,000	3,00,000	3,00,000	*3,00,000*
A	4,00,000	*1,00,000*	2,00,000	8,00,000
F	3,50,000	4,00,000	1,60,000	4,50,000
F	1,75,000	1,06,667	nil	5,10,000
Taxable leave salary (Leave salary received less exempt)	2,25,000	nil	2,00,000	5,00,000

Illustration and Problems 3.35-P4 (Simple)

(A) Compute taxable leave salary from the following informations.

	Case 1	*Case 2*
Duration of Service	27 yrs. 11 months	21 yrs. 8 months
Date of retirement	30-09-2006	31-12-2006
Basic Salary.	9,800 p.m.	13,000 p.m.
DA *(20% forms part of salary)*	1,000 p.m.	500 p.m.
Leave salary received	2,20,000	1,40,000
Leave availed while in service	20 months	660 days
Leave entitlement as per service rule :	1 month	45 days

(B) What if in Case 1 leave availed is 450 days instead of 20 months.

Ans (A): (1) 1,50,000; (2) 1,40,000; (B) 1,20,000.

Solution : Case 1

Computation of exemption of Leave Salary

- SAS = 9,800 + 200 = 10,000
- Average SAS remains Rs. 10,000 since for last 10 months immediately preceding the date of retirement, there is no change in SAS.
- Earned Leave = Leave entitlement – Leave Availed = 27 – 20 = 7 months

M	Maximum	3,00,000
A	Actual Leave Salary received	2,20,000
F	10 × Average of SAS	1,00,000
F	Earned Leave × Average of SAS *(7 × 10,000)*	*70,000*

Taxable leave salary (2,20,000 – 70,000) = Rs. 1,50,000

Illustration and Problems 3.35-P5 (Difficult)

Compute taxable leave salary from the following informations.

	Case 1	*Case 2*
Duration of service	27 yrs. 6 months	14 yrs. 4 months
Date of retirement	15-7-2006	15-09-2006
Basic Salary upto Dec. 31, 2005	6,000 p.m.	6,000 p.m.
Basic Salary from Jan. 1, 2006	7,000 p.m.	8,000 p.m.
Leave Salary received	3,00,000	48,250
Leave availed while in service	20 months	25 months
Encashed leave of earlier years	100 days	126 days
Leave entitlement as per company rule	35 days	31 days

(B) What if in Case 1 Taxcrazy retires on 15-5-2006 instead of 15-7-2006.

Ans (A): (1) 2,75,617; (2) 48,250; (B) 2,76,350.

Solution : Case 1

Since basic salary changes in last 10 months immediately preceding the date of retirement, we are required to compute average salary.

Average Salary of last 10 months immediately preceding the *date* of retirement *i.e.* from 16-9-2005 to 15-7-2006 is Rs. 6,650.

16-9-2004 to 31-12-2006 (3.5 months × 6,000)	21,000
1-1-2006 to 15-7-2006 (6.5 months × 7,000)	45,500
Total salary of last 10 months	66,500

- Average Salary *(for the purpose of L.S. is)* = 66,500/10 = 6,650
- Earned Leave = LE – LA – leave encashed = 810 – 600 – 100 = 110 days

M	Maximum	3,00,000
A	Actual L.S. received	3,00,000
F	10 × average salary	66,500
F	Earned leave × average salary *(6,650 × 110/30)*	*24,383*

Taxable leave salary (3,00,000 – 24,383) = Rs. 2,75,617.

Illustration and Problems 3.35-P6 (Typical)

(A) Compute taxable leave salary from the following informations.

	Case 1	*Case 2*
Duration of service	15 years 6 months & 6 days	26 years 9 months
Date of retirement	10-06-2006	28-02-2007
Basic Salary	2,000 p.m.	3,500 p.m.
Dearness Allowance forming part of salary	500 p.m.	1,000 p.m.
Commission @ 1% based on turnover	Nil	4,400
Leave salary received	90,000	2,00,817
Earned leave as per service rule	540 days	59 days
Leave entitlement as per service rule	60 days	34 days
Total leave encashed upto PY 2005-06	Nil	40 days

(B) What if in Case 1 leave entitlement as per service rule is 45 days?

(C) What is taxable leave salary if Mr. Taxcrazy is employee of Union Territory of Pondicherry?

Ans: (1) 82,500; (2) 2,00,817; (B) 65,000; (C) nil.

Solution : Case 1

- Salary *(for the purpose of L.S. is)* = 2,000 + 500 = 2,500.
- Average Salary remains Rs. 2,500 since for last 10 months immediately preceding the date of retirement, there is no change in Basic Salary + DA( ) + Commission (if).
- For computing earned leave as per income tax rule, we require leave availed which is unavailable. Below is shown computation.
- Leave availed = ? Earned leave as per service rule = 540 days; Leave entitlement as per service rule = 60 days. From the given information we get leave availed = 360 days.

- Leave availed = 360 days; Leave entitlement as per income tax rule = 30 days. Solving get earned leave = 90 days or 3 months.

F	Maximum	3,00,000
A	Actual L.S. received	90,000
F	10 × Average Salary *(10 × 2,500)*	25,000
F	Earned Leave x Average Salary *(2,500 × 90 ÷ 30)*	7,500

Taxable leave salary (90,000 – 7,500) = Rs. 82,500.

Problem 3.35-P7 [CS J 00] [M 3]

X, an employee of the Y Ltd. retired form the service with effect from January 1, 2007, after serving for 16 years and 7 months. At the time of retirement, he received a sum of Rs. 60,000 as leave encashement for unavailed leave of 300 days. He was entitled to 40 days leave for each completed year of service. He was getting a salary of Rs. 6,000 per month at the time of retirement. He had received an increment of Rs. 500 with effect from July 1, 2006. Compute the taxable amount of leave encashement.

Ans: 32,934.

Problem 3.35-P8 [CS J 98] [M 3]

Determine the amount of taxable leave salary for the assessment year 2007-08 from the following information in respect of an employee who retired from a private service on December 31, 2006 :

Salary at the time of retirement (per month)	Rs. 25,000 per month
Average salary received from March 1, 2006 to September 30, 2006	Rs. 24,000 per month
Average salary received from October 1, 2005 to December 31, 2006	Rs. 25,000 per month
Duration of service	26 years
Leave entitlement for each year of service	1.5 months
Leave availed while in service	8 months
Leave at the credit of employee at the time of retirement [26×1.5-8]	31 months
Leave salary paid at the time of retirement (25,000×31)	Rs. 7,75,000

Ans: 5,35,000.

*WHERE LEAVE SALARY IS RECEIVED FROM ONE OR MORE EMPLOYERS

The maximum amount of exemption shall not exceed the maximum limit which is Rs. 3,00,000. The amount of exemption claimed earlier in the same previous year or earlier previous year shall be reduced from Rs. 3,00,000.

Illustration 3.35-P9 (Difficult)

From *Illustration 3.31-P5 Case 1* compute his taxable leave salary for the AY 2007-08 on the assumption that he retires on 15-4-2006 and in PY 2001-02 he had received Rs. 3,10,000 as leave salary from a former employer. Exemption allowed in the PY 2001-02 was of Rs. 2,40,000.

Solution

Average Salary of last 10 months immediately preceding the *date* of retirement *i.e.* from 16-6-2005 to 15-4-2006 is Rs 6,350

16-6-2006 to 31-12-2005 (6.5 months × 6,000)	39,000
1-1-2006 to 15-4-2006 (3.5 months × 7,000)	24,500
Total	63,500
M Maximum *(3,00,000 – 2,40,000)*	60,000
A Actual leave salary received	3,00,000
F 10 × average salary = 10 × 6,350	63,500
F Earned leave x average salary *(6,350 × 110 ÷ 30)*	23,283

Taxable leave salary is Rs. 3,00,000 – 23,283 = Rs. 2,76,717.

TOPIC 3.36 *RETIREMENT BENEFITS RECEIVED BY LEGAL HEIRS OF EMPLOYEE

Gratuity : The gratuity received by the legal heirs of deceased employee is taxable under the head Income from Other Sources. But if gratuity is sanctioned after the death of employee then it is not taxable in the hands of legal heirs of deceased employee.

Pension : It is taxable in the hands of legal heirs under the head Income from Other Sources, since employer and employee relationship does not exist. However deduction is allowed to the extent of 1/3 of pension or Rs. 15,000 whichever is lower. However as per Section 10(19). family pension allowed to armed forces (including para military forces) of the Union has occurred in the course of operational duties, in such circumstances and subject to such conditions as may be prescribed, the family pension received by the widow or children or nominated heirs, shall be exempt from tax.

Leave salary : The leave salary paid to the legal heirs of the deceased employee in respect of privilege leave standing to the credit of such employee at the time of his/her death is not taxable as salary. *i.e.* leave salary is fully exempt in the hands of legal heirs. *(As per the department circular)*

Problem 3.36-P1 (Typical)

Mr. X an employee of Z Ltd dies on 31-1-2007. His salary at the time of death is following. Compute income from salary and total income of X and Mrs. X for the assessment year 2007-08.

Basic Salary	9,000 p.m.
Dearness Allowance *(60% forms part of salary)*	3,000 p.m.
Uniform Allowance *(Rs. 30,000 is spend towards uniform)*	40,000
House Rent Allowance *(Rent paid is Rs. 1,600 p.m.)*	2,800 p.m.
Leave Salary	1,90,000
Gratuity *(sanctioned after the death of employee)*	3,00,000
Pension	3,000 p.m.

Ans: (X) 1,52,800; (Mrs. X) 4,000.

COMPREHENSIVE PROBLEM ON RETIREMENT BENEFITS

Illustration 3.36-P2 [Pass 2004C]

Mr. X, who was an employee of PQ Ltd. Delhi, furnishes the following particulars regarding his income for the financial year 2006-07 :

Basic Salary	5,000 p.m.
D.A.	800 p.m.
Rent paid by X	1,000 p.m.

He retired from service on 1-1-2007 after completing 25 years of service with the company. The company paid him Rs. 84,000 as gratuity, Rs. 2,40,000 (including Rs. 80,000 as interest) from unrecognised provident fund, and pension @ Rs. 1500 p.m. He got half the pension commuted on 1-2-2007 and received Rs. 75,000. The assessee's average monthly salary for the last ten months was Rs. 5,000. One half of the provident fund account balance represents employer's contribution and interest thereon. Salary and pension become due on the last day of each month.

During the year he contributed Rs. 7,500 towards his provident fund. The employer also contributed similar amount.

You are required to calculate Gross Total Income.

Solution

Computation of total income for assessment year 2007-08

Income from Salary :		
Basis salary (5000 × 9)		45,000
Dearness allowance (800 × 9)		7,200
Gratuity	84,000	
Less : Exemption	62,500	21,500
Lumpsum withdrawal of Employer's contribution towards URPF		80,000
Lumpsum withdrawal of Interest on employer's contribution towards URPF		40,000
Uncommuted pension (1500 + 750 × 2)		3,000
Commuted pension	75,000	
Less : Exemption (1/3 of 1,50,000)	50,000	25,000
Income from salary		2,21,700
Income from Other Sources : Interest on contribution to URPF		40,000
Gross Total Income		2,61,700

Note

- Salary for the purpose of HRA is BS = Rs. 45,000

F	22,500 (50% of 45,000)	least
A	9,000 (actual)	is
F	6,300 (10800 – 4500)	exempt

• Salary for the purpose of Gratuity is = Rs. 5,000

M	3,50,000	least
A	84,000	is
F	1/2 × 5,000 × 25 = 62,500	exempt

Problem 3.36-P3 (Typical)

Mr. 'A' is employed with a transport firm in Delhi as member of an unrecognised provident fund. He draws a salary of Rs. 2,000 per month w.e.f. 1st Jan., 2006. Dearness Allowance forming part of pay for super-annuation benefits, is paid @ 10% of his basic pay. He also gets HRA @ Rs. 300 per month. He pays rent of Rs. 500 per month. He contributes 20% of his salary to the fund and the employer also contributes the same. The employer also paid his club bills amounting to Rs. 900. Besides, he is paid Rs. 400 per month as out of station allowance. He retired on 1st January, 2007 after 28 years of service. He gets Rs. 64,000 as accumulated balance from the fund which includes :

(a) employer's contribution Rs. 25,000.

(b) employee's contribution Rs. 15,000.

(c) interest on employer's contribution Rs. 15,000.

(d) interest on employee's contribution Rs. 9,000.

He also receives gratuity of Rs. 40,000.

He is entitled to two months earned leave in a year. He has availed of 40 months earned leave during his service. He is paid Rs. 38,500 for encashment of earned leave.

After retirement he gets pension @ Rs. 600 per month. In January, 2007 he got one half of pension commuted for Rs. 60,000.

Calculate his salary income and gross total income for the Assessment Year 2007-2008.

Ans: 1,16,660. [18,000+1,800+180+0+0+1,080+25,000+15,000+9,200+16,500+900+20,000=1,07,660+9,000=1,16,660]

Problem 3.36-P4 (Typical)

Mr. X, a Govt. employee, retires on 31-12-2006 on following emoluments. Compute Income from Salary for the AY 2007-08.

Basic Salary	2,000 p.m.
Dearness Allowance *(50% forms part of salary)*	400 p.m.
Entertainment Allowance	100 p.m.
Lumpsum withdrawal from provident fund	20,000
Leave Salary	65,000
Gratuity	56,000
Pension	350 p.m.

On 1-2-2007 he gets his 10% of his pension commuted for Rs. 10,000

Ans: 22,580. [18,000+3,600+900+980=23,480–900=22,580]

Problem 3.36-P5 (Difficult)

Compute Income from Salary for the AY 2007-08 from the following data :

Duration of service	17 years 7 months
Date of retirement	31-5-2006
Basic Salary *(He gets an increment of Rs. 1,000 p.m. on 1-5-2006)*	7,000 p.m.
DA *(50% forms part of salary)*	2,000 p.m.
Commission @ 1% on turnover : Turnover achieved by the employee	50,000 p.m.
Leave salary received	3,21,200
Gratuity received *(he is covered under the Payment of Gratuity Act, 1972)*	2,40,000
Leave availed while in service	230 days
Leave encashed in the PY 2006-07 for 110 days	18,900
Lumpsum withdrawal from recognised provident fund	4,00,000

Ans: 4,61,571. [13,000+4,000+1,000+2,78,133+1,46,538+18,900=4,61,571]

Problem 3.36-P6 [Difficult]

Compute Total Income for the AY 2007-08 from the following data :

Duration of service	21 years
Date of retirement	15-2-2007
Basic Salary upto 31-5-2006	5,000 p.m.
Basic Salary from 1-6-2006	6,000 p.m.
Leave salary received	25,000
Gratuity received *(he is not covered under the Payment of Gratuity Act, 1972)*	1,40,000
Earned leave as per Income tax rule	5 months
Earned leave as per service rule	7 months
Lumpsum withdrawal from unrecognised providend fund	
Employer's contribution	40,000
Employee's contribution	40,000
Interest on employer's contribution	5,000
Interest on employee's contribution	5,000

Ans: 1,90,100. [61,000+0+79,100+45,000=1,85,100+5,000=1,90,100]

Problem 3.36-P7 [Difficult]

X was employed in a firm since 1-4-1977. His salary was fixed at Rs. 2,950 in the grade 2,500-150-4,000-200-5,000 with effect from 1-7-2001. As per service rules the firm pays dearness allowance @ 15% of basic salary to those employees whose basic salary does not exceed Rs. 3,500 per month. Employees getting more than Rs. 3,500 per month as basic salary, are paid only 12% of basic salary as dearnes allowance. X retired from service on 1-12-2006. After his retirement he was sanctioned an amount of Rs. 1,200 per month as pension. He opted to get 2/3rd of his pension commuted from 1-1-2007 and received Rs. 32,000 from the firm as commuted amount. X also received house rent allowance @ 20% of his basic salary. He lives in a rented accommodation and pays Rs. 800 per month for the same.

Compute gross income from salary for the AY 2007-08.

Ans: 45,393. [29,150+3,498+2,400+8,000+2,345=45,393]

Problem 3.36-P8 (Typical)

Narad retires from Vaikunth Ltd. Pune on October 31, 2006, after service of 18 years and 8 months. At the time of retirement his employer pays a gratuity of Rs. 60,000 (his average monthly salary of preceding 10 months is Rs. 4,200). He also receives pension of Rs. 1,000 per month but on December 1, 2006 he gets 70 percent of the pension commuted for Rs. 35,000. Besides the aforesaid pension and gratuity, he receives the following emoluments from Vaikunth Ltd. Basic Pay (4,600 × 7); House Rent Allowance (Rs. 600 × 7). [Rent paid by him (Rs. 850 × 7)]. Entertainment Allowance (Rs. 600 × 7); recognised provident fund (contributions of employer and employee; 10% of salary) : Rs. 90,000.

On January 1, 2007 he joins Kailash Ltd., Mumbai. The emoluments relevant to the previous year 2006-07 are : Basic pay (Rs. 8,500 × 3); Medical Allowance (Rs. 600 × 3); High Cost of Living Allowance (Rs. 1,800 × 3); a Rent - Free Furnished House; Cost of Furniture Rs. 90,000; a Free Motor Car for Private and Official Purposes. Expenditure on the car by the Company : maintenance expenditure of 3 months : Rs. 18,000, Salary of cook (Rs. 1,600 × 3) Rs. 4,800; and contribution of the employer and employee towards unrecognised provident fund : 10% of Salary.

Determine the taxable income of Narad for the Assessment year 2007-08.

Ans: 1,21,058. [32,200+1,470+22,200+2,200+18,333+25,500+1,800+5,400+4,905+2,250+4,800=1,21,058]

3.37 COMPREHENSIVE PRACTICAL PROBLEMS

Simple & Difficult

Problem 3.37-P1 [Simple]

Mr. Raghav was employed in a firm as an accountant since 15-7-2003. From 1-4-2006 he was receiving salary @ Rs. 8,000 p.m., dearness allowance @ Rs. 3,000 p.m. and entertainment allowance @ Rs. 1,200 p.m. The firm has provided him a motor car of 1.4 litre (c.c.) for his official and private use. The running and maintenance costs (including driver) are borne by the firm.

He was also given the following amenities by the firm -

(i) Free lunch during office hours for 120 days. The cost of employer is Rs. 75 per meals.

(ii) Facility of sweeper at his residence. The salary of the sweeper is Rs. 250 p.m. which is paid by the employer.

(iii) Facility of cellular phone. Expenditure of employer amounted to Rs. 600 p.m.

(iv) Free use of music system from 1-6-2006 to 30-9-2006. It was purchased on 10-8-2003 for Rs. 30,000 by the employer.

He was employed in this firm upto 30-9-2006 as he submitted his resignation on 31-8-2006 with effect from 1-10-2006 by giving one month's notice in advance.

He was appointed as an accountant in Government of Rajasthan on 1-11-2006 where he received Rs. 12,500 p.m. as basic salary, 150% dearness allowance and 10% city compensatory allowance of basic salary. He was also given house rent allowance @ Rs. 3,500 p.m. and entertainment allowance @ Rs. 300 p.m.

Mr. Raghav has not incurred any expenditure on entertainment for his official duties. He was living in this parental house upto 31-12-2006 and thereafter started living in a rented accommodation for which he paid Rs. 4,000 per month.

Compute taxable income from salary of Mr. Raghav for the assessment year 2007-08.

Ans: 2,47,450. [48,000+18,000+7,200+1,500+1,000+62,500+93,750+6,250+1,500+9,250=2,48,950–1,500=2,47,450]

Problem 3.37-P2 (Difficult)

Miss Taxcrazy, an Indian citizen, has been working as a Public Relation Officer in the German Embassy at Delhi for the last 5 years. She gets salary Rs. 35,000 p.m., house rent allowance Rs. 50,000. She has been provided a motor car facility of 20 h.p. all its expenses including driver's salary of Rs. 5,000 p.m. are borne by the Embassy. The car is used for her public relation work and personal purposes also. She has been provided a free telephone at her residence and all expenses Rs. 25,000 in the previous year were borne by the Embassy. During the previous year, she went to Germany for training for one month, where besides salary she was paid a foreign allowance of Rs. 5,000.

Embassy reimbursed Rs. 25,000 on account of medical treatment of her dependent parents, out of which Rs. 8,000 were incurred for the treatment in a government hospital and the remaining amount was incurred for the treatment in a private hospital. She resides in a rented house in Delhi, the annual rent of which is Rs. 80,000 she has been provided the facility of periodicals and newspapers also on which a sum of Rs. 3,000 was incurred during the previous year.

She gets her house repaired for which the employer reimburses Rs. 4,600.

Compute Miss Taxcrazy's income from salary for the AY 2007-08.

Ans: 4,43,600. [4,20,000+12,000+0+0+5,000+2,000+4,600=4,43,600]

Problem 3.37-P3 (Difficult)

Mr. Aravindam is the Director of M/s Tublai Limited with monthly salary of Rs. 50,000. Being in charge of the latest project of the company he is also entitled to project allowance of Rs. 15,000 p.m. as well as commission @ 1% on Company's turnover. Company agreed to bear income tax burden of Mr. Aravindam to the extent of Rs. 1,00,000 per annum. Company hired a residential accommodation for him in a city with population not exceeding 10 lakhs. Monthly rentals of house and furniture are Rs. 10,000 and Rs. 1,500 respectively. An employee drawing a salary of Rs. 4,500 p.m. has been engaged as cook cum caretaker at Director's residence. An amount of Rs. 300 and another of Rs. 560 are incurred by the company on account of gardening expenses and cooking gas (Company is the registered consumer) every month. Mr. Aravindam deducts Rs. 10,000 p.m. from salaries towards a contributory, recognised Provident Fund of the Company. During the Financial Year 2006-07 Mr. Aravindam received Rs. 63,500 as arrears of project allowance. Compute Mr. Aravindam's income assessable under the head "Salaries" for the Assessment Year 2007-08. Company's turnover for 2006-07 works out to Rs. 70,00,000.

Ans: 11,88,320. [6,00,000+1,80,000+70,000+1,00,000+1,20,000+18,000+54,000+0+6,720+0+39,600=11,88,320]

Problem 3.37-P4 (Simple)

Sri Nihar Ranjan Ray is working as Chief of Group Communications Division, of M/s. Superior Media Services Ltd., Calcutta. His annual emoluments during financial year 2006-2007, were as under :

(i)	Salary	1,48,000
(ii)	Incentive Bonus	1,20,000
(iii)	Dearness/Compensatory Allowances	1,07,000
(iv)	Employer's contribution to a Recognised Provident Fund	1,20,000

(v) Interest credited by the Employer in the above fund on a credit balance of Rs. 2,00,000 @ 14% per annum. 28,000

(vi) He was provided with a Maruti 1000CC car for personal and office use.

(vii) Employer gave him a free furnished bungalow in Brigade grounds, Calcutta which the employer hired on a rent of Rs. 24,000 p.m. for the bungalow and Rs. 400 p.m. for furnishings.

(viii) Sri Ray was also provided services of a watchman at his residence, who was hired by the employer at a salary of Rs. 1,000 p.m.

(ix) During the year Sri Ray entered into a separate professional contract with M/s. Futuristics Ltd., Bangalore for providing expert consultancy services on a project for which he was paid professional consultancy charges of Rs. 1,00,000.

(x) Sri Ray also gave TV interviews and lectures to training groups, for which he was paid honorarium of Rs. 4,500 in aggregate.

Compute the income of Sri Nihar Ranjan Ray under the head 'Salaries' for Assessment Year 2007-2008.

Ans: 5,47,740. [1,48,000+1,20,000+1,07,000+1,02,240+9,000+0+40,200+4,800+12,000= 5,43,240+1,04,500=6,47,740–1,00,000=5,47,740] [Deduction u/s 80C cannot exceed 1,00,000]

Problem 3.37-P5 [Hons 1993]

Mr. X, who is employed with LMN Ltd. upto October 31st, 2006, get the following salary and benefits :

Basic salary Rs. 4,000 per month; bonus Rs. 1,000 per month; club facility (expenditure of the company) Rs. 1,000 per month; house rent allowance Rs. 800 per month; employer's contribution towards unrecognised provident fund Rs. 400 per month (Mr. X also makes a matching contribution) and car facility for personal use (expenditure of the employer Rs. 600 per month.)

On November 1st, 2006 Mr. X joins DEF Ltd. on monthly salary of Rs. 20,000. Besides, he enjoys club facility (expenditure of the company Rs. 400 p.m.) ; car facility for personal use (expenditure of the company Rs. 1,000 p.m.) and employer's contribution towards recognised provident fund Rs. 4,000 per month. (Mr. X also makes a making contribution)

Determine the taxable income of Mr. X for the assessment year 2007-08 on the following assumption :

(i) Salary in both cases, becomes due on the last day of each month.

(ii) He resides in Goa and pays rent of Rs. 400 p.m. throughout the previous year.

Ans: 1,28,600. [28,000+7,000+0+5,600+0+1,00,000+0+0+8,000=1,48,600–20,000= 1,28,600]

Problem 3.37-P6

Compute the Total Income of Mr. S. employed for 4 years in Mumbai for the Assessment Year 2007-2008 from the following details furnished by him, duly supported by a certificate from his employer, a Public Limited Company :

	Rs.
(a) Basic Salary	96,000
(b) Dearness Allowance	1,92,000

(c) City Compensatory Allowance 18,000
(d) Children's Education Allowance 12,000
(e) Clothing Allowance (given every third year) 24,000
(f) Staying in rent free accommodation taken on rent of Rs. 10,000 p.m. by the company.
(g) Furniture worth Rs. 12.5 lakhs provided in the flat by the company.
(h) Has full time use of a Chauffeur driven car provided by the company which had incurred expenditure of Rs. 36,000 on petrol; Rs. 24,000 on repairs and maintenance and Rs. 36,000 as salary to the Driver. The company has also claimed depreciation of Rs. 48,000 on the Ambassador Car.
(i) He has received fixed allowance of Rs. 2,500 p.m. for medical treatment for the entire family; had incurred an expenditure of Rs. 12,500 actually.
(j) Has contributed Rs. 60,000 to the Provident Fund maintained by the employer—which is recognised; employers' contribution is Rs. 24,000 being 8-1/3% of Basic salary and Dearness allowance. (Salary includes dearness allowance as per the terms of employment).

Ans: 5,22,440. [96,000+1,92,000+18,000+9,600+0+51,840+1,25,000+0+30,000+0= 5,22,440]

Problem 3.37-P7

'P' is an employee in a pharmaceutical company. During the Financial Year 2006-2007, he received salary of Rs. 6,000 per month. He is entitled to bonus of 10% of salary. He has been provided a house which the company has hired for a monthly rent of Rs. 4,000. The company is realising a rent of Rs. 500 per month from 'P'. 'P' contributes Rs. 1,000 p.m. to a recognised provident fund. The employer is also paying bills for gas, electricity and water which has been of the order of Rs. 3,000 during the relevant year. 'P' is also provided furniture, free of charge, which cost his employer Rs. 20,000. He has also been provided company's car (self driven) which is also for personal use. There is no information about the expenditure on personal use but all expenses are borne by the employer. Compute 'P's total income for the Assessment Year 2007-2008.

Ans: 87,080. [72,000+7,200+7,880+0+0=87,080]

Problem 3.37-P8

Shri Ashok Kumar is employed in Jaipur Textile Industry Ltd., Jaipur from 1st July, 2003 in the grade Rs. 10,500 - 500 - 12,500. In addition to his basic salary he is given dearness allowance @ Rs. 600 p.m. City Compensatory Allowance @ Rs. 50 p.m., and House Rent Allowance @ Rs. 250 p.m. During the previous year 2006-07 he received following amenities in addition to above mentioned salary and allowances -

(i) He has been provided the facility of a car (with driver) of 2 litre (c.c.) which is used by him for both official and private purposes. The car is sold by the employer to Mr. Ashok Kumar on 20th January, 2007 for Rs. 1,00,000. The expenses of running and maintenance including driver's salary of this car upto 19th January, 2007, was Rs. 40,000 which was fully met by the employer. The employer purchased this car on 31st December, 2004 at a cost of Rs. 2,00,000. The car was put to use on the same date by the employer.

(ii) The electricity and water bills of Shri Ashok are paid by the employer. During the previous year 2006-07 the company spent Rs. 600 on it.

(iii) He is allowed one month leave in January month every year in which he is used to go Darjeeling for a pleasure trip. During the previous year when he went to Darjeeling on leave, his expenses for going and coming back amounted to Rs. 1,200 which were paid to him by the company.

(iv) He has been given the facility of a domestic servant to whom the company pays Rs. 100 p.m.

(v) He is a member of a Recognised provident fund to which he contributes 14% of his salary and dearness allowance. The company also contributes an equal amount.

(vi) Interest amounting to Rs. 2,600 @ 13% has been credited on the balance standing on the credit of his P.F. Account.

(vii) He spent Rs. 17,000 during the previous year on the treatment of his minor child. The whole expenditure was reimbursed by the employer. The treatment was taken in a private hospital.

(viii) The employer gate to Ashok Kumar cloth worth Rs. 4,500 by way of gift on the occassion of Independence day.

Assuming that Shri Ashok lives in ancestral house and he has substantial interest in this company, compute the taxable income from salary of Shri Ashok Kumar for the Assessment Year 2007-08.

Ans: 1,67,836. [1,42,500+7,200+600+3,000+0+28,000+600+0+1,200+2,994+700+ 2,000+0=1,88,794–20,958=1,67,836]

Typical

Problem 3.37-P9

Smt. Renu is an employee of the Ambuja Company Calcutta. She has been fixed in the grade of Rs. 8,000 - 200 - 12,000 since January, 2004. She gets 30% of basic pay as dearness allowance (which is considered as pay for retirement benefits), Rs. 400 p.m. as entertainment allowance and Rs. 1,000 p.m. as travelling allowance. She has also received Rs. 450 p.m. as Education Allowance and Rs. 900 p.m. as Hostel Allowance to meet the cost of education of her three sons.

She has been provided by the Company with rent - free unfurnished accomodation, the fair rent of which is Rs. 25,000 p.a. The company has provided her the amenity of reimbursement of her own medical expenses and during the financial year 2006-07 the Company paid her in this connection Rs. 17,350. The expenses were incurred on treatment by a private doctor. She owns a car which she uses wholly for personal purpose. All the expenses of running and maintenance including driver's salary of car are met by the employer which during the previous year amounted to Rs. 48,000.

The company transferred her to Chittorgarh (population 3 lakhs) on 1st December, 2006. The company has provided her rent free unfurnished accommodation in Chittorgarh also. The fair rental value of this house is Rs. 18,000 per annum. She did not vacate the accommodation at Calcutta upto 31st March, 2007. She uses her car wholly for private work in Chittorgarh also.

She and her employer each contributed @ 12.5% to the Recognised Provident Fund. She paid during the financial year 2006-07 for travel in respect of Employer's work Rs. 10,000 as bus fare to the Roadways Corporation. Determine her taxable income under the head 'Salaries' for the assessment year 2007-08.

Ans: 2,13,955. [1,01,400+30,420+4,800+2,000+3,000+3,600+31,503+2,350+48,000+ 659+700+2,000+0=2,30,432–16,478=2,13,955]

Problem 3.37-P10

Mr. Taxcrazy is the manager of a company at Delhi since 1-1-1989. He is getting a salary of Rs. 10,000 p.m. plus a dearness allowance @ 20% of his basic pay, half of which enters into retirement benefits. He contributes 10% of his salary and one half of dearness allowance to unrecognised provident fund to which his employer contributes an equal amount. On 1-1-2007 he took a loan of Rs. 20,000 from his provident fund for his daughter's marriage. He has been provided with rent-free house owned by the company. He is getting medical allowance of Rs. 200 p.m. and servant allowance of Rs. 200 p.m. His club bills of Rs. 3,000 were also paid by the company.

He has been provided with a facility of a cook who is paid Rs. 300 p.m. by the employer. He is also provided a car of 1.6 litre (c.c) by the employer for official use only. Two children of Mr. Taxcrazy are studying in the institution run by the employer for which no fees is paid. Normal expenditure per student in such institution is Rs. 500 p.m.

He retired on 1-9-2006. He received Rs. 1,30,000 for encashment of leave on 1-9-2006 being 12 months leave not availed of. As per the rule of the company, Mr. Taxcrazy was entitled to 45 days leave for each year of service. He also received Rs. 1,10,000 as gratuity from the employer on the same date. He is not covered under the payment of Gratuity Act. On 1-10-2005 he received Rs. 18,000 being the balance of his provident fund account after deducting the amount of loan.

Compute Mr. Taxcrazy's income from salary for the AY 2007-08 assuming that his salary is due on the first day of next month.

Ans: 2,16,160. [60,000+12,000+1,200+1,200+3,000+10,260+1,500+91,500+16,500+19,000=2,16,160]

Problem 3.37-P11

Shri Sanjay is an engineer in Indian Railways at Chennai at a salary of Rs. 12,000 p.m. His employer has provided him following facilities :

(a) His employer provided him at concessional rate for his residence with furniture of Rs. 50,000. This furniture is taken by employer at a rent of Rs. 600 p.a. Rs. 1,000 was incurred on repairs of this furniture. Employer charges 8% of salary for this house. Employer paid Rs. 7,000 for this house. The value of accommodation according to Govt. rules is 10% of basic salary.

(b) His employer has provided him a car of 1.88 litre cubic capacity without chauffeur which is used for office purpose also.

(c) Employer provided him an interest free loan of Rs. 15,000 as on 1st May, 2006 to purchase domestic items. No instalment paid so far. He also took a loan from his P.F. account of Rs. 50,000. The interest in this P.F. account is credited @ 9% on minimum balance.

(d) Three children and one nephew are getting education free of cost in an educational institute owned and run by employer. The cost of education borne by employer is Rs. 800 p.m. per child while the expenses in similar standard of institution is only 100 p.m.

(e) He is entitled for three free passes to travel anywhere in India. He availed this facility two times and visited to Kolkata, his native place. Every time his employer incurred Rs. 10,000 for the same.

(f) Taxable amount of Rs. 40,000 was due in the previous 2006-07 regarding his leave encashment but it was paid on 10th April, 2007.

Find taxable income from salary for the assessment year 2007-08 if he paid Rs. 2,000 as tax of state government during the previous year.

Ans: 1,86,680. [1,44,000+2,880+600+0+1,200+0+40,000=1,88,680-2,000=1,86,680]

Problem 3.37-P12

Mr. Taxcrazy is placed at a mining site in a company at a salary of Rs. 12,000 p.m. This mining site is 40 k.m. away from a village having a population of 20,000. He received following perquisites during the PY 2006-07 :

1. One furnished house is provided at mining site for which employer paid Rs. 8,000 p.m. and new furniture of Rs. 20,000 is purchased to provide him. A facility of meals is available in a hotel outside office for which employer pays Rs. 60 per meal. He availed this facility for 50 times.
2. He was transferred to Delhi on 1-9-2006 and a rent free house is also provided to him. He holds his old house upto 1-1-2007. This house is taken by employer at a rent of Rs. 6,000 p.m. and different equipment of Rs. 60,000 is provided including a computer of Rs. 38,000 in this house along with all furniture of old house.
3. He is allowed a free meal in a hotel at Delhi along with other employees for which employer paid Rs. 60 per meal. Taxcrazy availed this facility for 100 times in the PY. Facility of breakfast is also available during office hours for which employer spent Rs. 10 per breakfast. He availed this facility also for 100 times.
4. A video camera is sold by the employer at Rs. 8,000 on 1-8-2006 which was purchased by employer for Rs. 80,000 eleven years back. Fair market value of this camera is Rs. 10,000.
5. Company sold a computer to his son on 1-9-2006 for Rs. 15,000 which was purchased for Rs. 80,000 on 1-1-2004. Its fair market price is Rs. 16,000.
6. A car is provided to cover the distance from residence to the place of working at Delhi. Cost of the car is Rs. 3,00,000 and its engine capacity is 1.88 cubic litre.
7. 1,000 shares are allotted to him by the company at Rs. 10 each while the fair market price of the share on that was Rs. 30 per share.
8. His employer sold products of company for Rs. 8,000 while its fair market price was Rs. 38,000.
9. A group insurance scheme is continuing in the company. His employer paid Rs. 5,000 as contribution to include the name of Taxcrazy.
10. His employer spent Rs. 10,000 on entertainment of his family members, which includes Rs. 6,000 as contribution to health club provided at premises.
11. His employer has provided him a facility of credit card which is used for payment of entertainment expenses incurred on customers. Employer maintains full record regarding data and object of use of the card.

Find income from salary of Taxcrazy for the AY 2007-08.

Ans: 1,57,600. [1,44,000+7,200+1,400+0+5,000+0+0=1,57,600]

Problem 3.37-P13

Mr. X furnishes following particulars compute value of accommodation and Income from Salary for the AY 2007-08.

	Govt. Employee	*X Ltd*	*Y Ltd*
Date of joining	1-6-1980	1-6-1998	1-3-2007
Date of retirement	31-3-1998	28-2-2007	—
Pension	Rs. 2,500 p.m.	—	—
Basic Salary	Not applicable	Refer below	Rs. 3,000 p.m.

Salary package from X Ltd.

Basic Salary	8,000 p.m.
Dearness Allowance (20% forms part of salary)	2,000 p.m.
House rent allowance upto 31-7-2006	6,000 p.m.
Rent paid upto 31-7-2006	4,000 p.m.
Lunch Allowance upto 31-7-2006	2,000 p.m.
Leave encashed on 28-2-2007 for every 1 day of leave encashed for each month	11,000
Transport Allowance	1,400 p.m.

He has also been provided with accommodation in Delhi w.e.f. 1-8-2006.

Ans: 13,125; 1,93,085. [30,000+88,000+22,000+11,360+8,000+11,000+6,600+13,125+3,000=1,93,085]

Problem 3.37-P14 (CS-D01) - M 10

Q.2a : X is employed with Y Ltd., an Indian company, having manufacturing unit in South Africa. For the past fifteen years, X has been regularly visiting India for export promotion of company's goods in India. He has stayed in India for 120 days every year. Compute his income under the head 'salaries' from the following particulars for the assessment year 2007-08 :

Salary for 8 months while abroad received there only	Rs. 20,000 p.m.
Salary for 4 months during his stay in India received in India	Rs. 20,000 p.m.

Rent-free accommodation abroad where he and his family members stay for which his employer pays Rs. 15,000 as rent per month.

During his stay in India, he stays in the company's guest house and gets free food. The company incurs an expenditure of Rs. 20,000 for such.facilities.

He has been provided with a motor car of cubic capacity of 1.6 litres in South Africa, which he uses partly for official purposes and partly for private purposes during his stay there. However, the car is used exclusively by family members of X while he is in India. The monthly expenses on car is Rs. 3,000. During his stay in India, he has been given conveyance allowance of Rs. 10,000 out of which he has spent Rs. 8,000. His elder son is studying in India for which his employer spends Rs. 15,000 per year whereas his younger son is studying in U.S.A. and stays in a hostel for which X gets Rs. 700 per month as allowance.

Ans: ROR 2,97,440; NR 97,000. [ROR:2,40,000+36,840+0+2,000+15,000+3,600=2,97,440] [NR: 80,000+0+0+2,000+15,000+0=97,000]

Problem 3.37-P15 (Typical)

Smt Taxcrazy working as CTO of Infosys Ltd., Banglore. Her details salary structure is given below:

a. Basic pay of 10 months @ Rs. 68,000 p.m. (two months basic salary is paid in Sweden where he went on official duty)

b. Salary of 2 months when he was on leave Rs. 1,36,000.

c. Employers contribution to recognised providend fund Rs. 90,000 p.a. Assessee also contribute the same amount. In addition she also earn interest of Rs. 12,000 from public provident fund account in which she deposited Rs. 20,000 during the year.

d. Interest credited to provident fund @ 11% p.a. Rs. 55,000.

e. Entertanment allowance Rs. 10,000.

f. The company provided her with a rent free furnished house taken on rent at Rs. 20,000 p.m. The company furnished the house with furniture etc., at a annual rent of Rs. 60,000. Besides, the following expenses are also met by employer.

i) Pay of watchman and durban Rs. 2,400.
ii) Pay of cook and bearer Rs. 3,000.
iii) Pay of gardener Rs. 2,600.
iv) Pay of sweeper Rs. 800.
v) Electricity, gas and water charges Rs. 1,450.

g. Car facility from a pool of car Rs. 4,000.

h. The company pays a service commission of Rs. 12,420.

i. She is re-imbursed medical bill of her husband Rs. 20,000 including a bill of her mother-in law Rs. 4,500.

j. She is using company's music system of Rs. 24,000 for last 10 years, car of Rs. 5,00,000 for the last 3 years and laptop of Rs. 80,000 for last 8 years. The company sells music system on a token money of Re.1 and car for Rs. 80,000. The company gifts the laptop on 31-3-2007.

k. She took a personal loan of Rs. 20,000 on 1-1-2006 and housing loan of Rs. 12,00,000 @ 3% on 1-1-2007. (SBI lending rate of interest : Personal loan 12.75% p.a. and housing loan 9% p.a.)

l. The company has insured her life and health. Premium paid by the company is Rs. 45,000 including health insurance of Rs. 5,000.

m. Her brother is studying in IIM-A for which the company re-imburses tuition and hostel fees of Rs. 61,000.

n. For a month she was in USA for execution of project where she was paid overseas allowance of Rs. 16,000.

Compute total income and tax liability on the assumption that his other income is Rs. 11,00,000.

Ans: 25,57,040; 8,00,672. [8,16,000+1,36,000+12,420+16,000+10,000+0+7,500+1,48,563+60,000+2,400+3,000+2,600+800+1,450+0+5,000+2,400+0+0+0+0+1,76,000+1,913+54,000+40,000+0+61,000=15,57,046+11,00,000=26,57,046–1,00,000=25,57,040]

STRATEGY MAKER

It is ranked No. 1 chapter in terms of its importance and scoring marks. The types of problems asked range from simple to typical. Make sure you know this chapter to such an extent that you score atleast 9 out of 10. Stand alone question from salary is rare. Following chapters are always attached with salary. Deduction u/s 80C to 80U. Sometimes questions from these chapters are also attached. 1. House property. 2. Capital gain. 3. Agricultural income.

What to expect Everything. Give solid emphasis on perquisite. Also by seeing last 10 years' questions it can be said that questions on gratuity, pension and leave salary are rarely asked. But who knows? Do revise all typical illustrations of perquisites and must do problems.

till here a good work but long way to go

But before you run to next step do revise rate of tax given in chapter 1. Do remember Income from Salaries and Deduction go hand in hand. When you reach at the end of Deduction you will find Deduction attached with questions of salary. You must learn salary chapter.

Keep Running

Welcome EET. Bye Bye EEE

Deduction Under Section 80C and 80CCD

TOPIC 4.01 SECTION 80C: DEDUCTION AVAILABLE FROM SPECIFIED INVESTMENT OR SPECIFIED EXPENDITURES

Deduction under section 80C is available only when investment is done in a specified fund or expenditure is incurred for specified purpose during the relevant PY. The total of investment or expenditure combined is known as Gross Qualifying Amount *(GQA)*.

(A) CONDITIONS FOR CLAIMING DEDUCTION U/S 80C

a. *Section 80C(1).* Deduction under section 80C is available only to *Individual or HUF* whether the assessee is a resident or Non-resident. *(Deduction is not allowed to Firm, Company, etc.)*

b. Deduction u/s 80C is available only from normal income. It is not available from special income and casual income.

c. Deduction is allowed on paid basis system. If the amount is invested or spent during the relevant PY then only deduction u/s 80C is allowed.

   E.g. Suppose where the employee contributes towards RPF on 1-4-2007, then deduction is not available in the PY 2006-07, since contribution is made in the PY 2007-08. However he is entitled to claim deduction in the PY 2007-08.

d. Gross qualifying amount shall be allowed as deduction even if the amount is paid out of exempted income or out of borrowed fund.

(B) SECTION 80C(2). WHAT IS GROSS QUALIFYING AMOUNT (GQA)

Investment in Insurance Companies

1. Contribution made by individual or HUF towards life insurance premium on the life of *self, spouse and any child* or any member of HUF — *Sub limit* to a maximum of 20% of the actual capital sum assured.

2. Contribution made by individual or HUF in Unit Linked Insurance Plan (ULIP) of UTI or Dhanraksha of LIC mutual fund *(self, spouse and any child or any member of HUF).*

3. Contribution made by individual or HUF to annuity plan of LIC or any other insurer approved by Insurance Regulatory Development Authority (IRDA).

Govt. savings and fund

4. Contribution made by individual to Statutory Provident Fund (SPF) or Recognised Provident Fund (RPF).
5. Contribution made by individual or HUF to 15-year Public Provident Fund (PPF) *(self, spouse and any child or any member of HUF)*. [not being repayment of loan]
6. Payment made by individual in respect of non-commutable deferred annuity *(self, spouse and any child)*.
7. Contribution by an individual towards an approved superannuation fund.
8. Subscription by individual or HUF in National Saving Certificate VIII issue *(including interest accrued which is deemed reinvested is also eligible for deduction)*.

   However schemes like NSC VI & VII issue and NSS 1992 have been discontinued w.e.f. 1-11-2002.

Investment in mutual fund or UTI or FI

9. Subscription by individual or HUF to any equity linked saving scheme of UTI or mutual fund.
10. Contribution made by Individual to notified pension fund which is Retirement Benefit Unit Scheme of UTI or Kothari Pioneer Pension Plan of Kothari Mutual Fund.
11. Any contribution made by individual or HUF notified pension fund of National Housing Bank (NHB).
12. As subscription to equity shares or debentures or bonds of an issue made by an Indian public company or a public financial institution including UTI and mutual fund and the entire proceeds of the issue is utilised wholly and exclusively for the purposes of developing, maintaining and operating an infrastructure facility or for generating or / and distributing, power or for providing telecommunication services whether basic or cellular. A lock in period of 3 years is provided in respect of such subscription.
13. As a term deposits for a fixed period of atleast 5 years with a scheduled bank and which is in accordance with a scheme framed and notifed by the Central Govt.

Specified expenditures

14. Subscription made by individual or HUF to any such deposit scheme of—
    (a) a public sector company which is engaged in providing long-term finance for construction or purchase of houses in India for residential purposes; or
    (b) any authority constituted in India by or under any law enacted either for the purpose of dealing with and satisfying the need for housing accommodation or for the purpose of planning, development or improvement of cities, towns and villages, or for both, not being a scheme the interest on deposits where under qualifies for the purposes of computing the deduction under section 80L, as the Central Government may, by notification in the Official Gazette, specify in this behalf.
15. Any payment made by individual or HUF towards the cost of purchase or construction of new residential house property (RHP) the income of which is chargeable under the head 'Income from House Property'. The payments are :
    a. Repayment of loan to Central or State Govt., any Bank including co-operative bank, LIC, NHB, the assessee's employer which is a public company or a public sector company, University, local authority, cooperative society.

b. Repayment of loan to any company in which the public are substantially interested or any co-operative society, where such company or co-operative society is engaged in the business of financing the construction of houses, or

c. Stamp duty, registration fee and other expenses for the purpose of transfer of such house property to the assessee.

d. Any payment made towards self-financing scheme of any development authority engaged in the business of house property.

16. Any contribution made by individual or HUF as subscription to Home Loan Account Scheme of National Housing Bank (NHB).

17. Tuition fees for full time studies *(excluding any payment towards any development fees or donation or payment of similar nature)*, whether at the time of admission or thereafter, to any university, college, school or other educational institution situated within India. [maximum two children]

Illustration and Problems 4.01-P1 (Difficult)

Find out the total income and tax liabilty of Mr. Taxcrazy for the AY 2007-08 from the following informations.

	Case 1	*Case 2*
Gross Total Income	5,00,000	1,50,000
Life insurance premium paid for his married daughter to LIC *(sum assured Rs. 25,000)*	8,000	3,000
Life insurance premium paid for his father to LIC *(sum assured Rs. 1,00,000)*	4,000	3,000
Life insurance premium paid on his self life to LIC on 1-4-2007	6,000	2,000
Purchased equity linked saving scheme of UTI	9,000	11,000
Repayment of loan to LIC for purchase of new residential house property	23,000	21,000
Subscription to equity shares of power company	45,000	18,000
Mr. X is also pursuing M.Com. from Delhi University. Tuition fee paid	13,000	10,000

Solution

	Case 1	*Case 2*
Gross Total Income	5,00,000	1,50,000
Less: Deduction u/s 80C		
- Life insurance premium paid for his married daughter to LIC	(5,000)	(3,000)
- Life insurance premium paid for his father to LIC	N.A.	N.A.
- Life insurance premium paid on his self life to LIC on 1-4-2007	N.A.	N.A.
- Purchased equity linked saving scheme of UTI	(9,000)	(11,000)
- Repayment of loan to LIC for purchase of new residential house property	(23,000)	(21,000)
- Subscription to equity shares of power company	(45,000)	(18,000)
Total Income	4,18,000	97,000
Tax on Total Income	75,400	nil
Add: Education cess @ 2%	1,508	nil
Tax Liability	76,908	nil

Problem 4.01-P2 (Typical)

Mr. Taxcrazy employed in iamtalented Ltd furnishes following particulars of his income and expenditure for the PY 2006-07. You are required to compute tax liability for the AY 2007-08.

	Case 1	*Case 2*
Basic Salary	5,00,000	1,85,000
Long-term capital gain	3,45,000	80,000
STCG (STT paid)	5,10,000	41,200
Dividend from an Indian company	1,00,000	5,00,000
His other expenditure / investment		
Tuition fees of Shiv studying in Harvard, USA *(His employer incurs all educational expenses of Master Shiv)*	10,000	5,000
Tuition fees for her daughter studying in Holy Cross, India	8,200	9,000
Tuition fees of Master Om studying in DPS, India. *(donation of Rs. 5,000 was also given)*	14,400	5,000
Tuition fees of Master Krishna studying in Xaviers, Delhi *(Also purchased books worth Rs. 3,000 for Master Krishna)*	10,000	13,000
Contribution to National relief bond	5,000	3,050
Purchased Kisan Vikas Patra	4,000	1,050
Deposits in Post Office (CTD) Scheme	20,000	20,000

Solution

	Case 1	*Case 2*
Basic Salary	5,00,000	1,85,000
Education facility	10,000	5,000
Income from salary	5,10,000	1,90,000
Long-term capital gain	3,45,000	80,000
STCG (STT paid)	5,10,000	41,200
Gross Total Income	13,65,000	3,11,200
Less: Deduction u/s 80C		
- Tuition fees for her daughter studying in Holy Cross, India	Nil	(9,000)
- Tuition fees of Master Om studying in DPS, India.	(14,400)	Nil
- Tuition fees of Master Krishna studying in Xaviers, Delhi	(10,000)	(13,000)
Total Income	13,40,600	2,89,200
Tax on LTCG @ 20%	2,73,000	16,000
Tax on STCG STT PAID @ 10%	51,000	4,120
Tax on normal Income at slab rate	95,680	8,600
Total Tax	4,19,680	28,720
Add: Surcharge @ 10%	41,968	Nil
Tax and surcharge	4,61,648	28,720
Add: Education cess @ 2%	9,233	574
Tax Liability	4,70,881	29,294

Problem 4.01-P3 (Difficult)

Dr. Prem Usha, a resident, attained the age of 65 years on 23-12-2006. She had following income for the PY 2006-07. Compute tax liability.

1. Long term capital gain 7,00,000
2. Income from Salary 4,00,000

She also invested Rs. 80,000 in ICICI infrastructure bonds specified u/s 80C(2) and made a fixed deposit of Rs. 30,000 in State Bank of India for 6 years.

Ans : 1,71,360.

Problem 4.01-P4 (Typical)

Mrs. Roma, aged 22 years, foreign citizen is employed by Central Govt. furnishes following information. You are required to compute total income and tax liability for the AY 2007-08 if she (a) Resident in India (b) Non Resident in India.

	Case 1	*Case 2*
Salary including dearness allowance for services rendered in India	3,00,000	5,20,000
Employer's contribution towards provident fund	10,000	40,000
Dividend from foreign company deposited in an Indian Bank outside India	80,000	50,000
Own contribution towards the provident fund	20,000	40,000
Life insurance premium paid on self life		
— to LIC of India	60,000	31,000
— to American life insurance company in USA *(1$ = Rs. 45)*	$ 200	$ 500

Ans: (1) 37,230; 19,380; (2) 98,124; 86,394.

Solution: Case 1

	Resident	*NR*
Salary including dearness allowance for services rendered in India	3,00,000	3,00,000
Employer's contribution towards statutory provident fund	nil	nil
Income from salary	3,00,000	3,00,000
Dividend from foreign company	80,000	Nil
Gross Total Income	3,80,000	3,00,000
Less: Deduction u/s 80C		
- Own contribution towards SPF	(20,000)	(20,000)
- Life insurance premium	(60,000)	(60,000)
Total Income	3,00,000	2,20,000
Tax on normal Income at slab rate	36,500	19,000
Add: Education cess @ 2%	730	380
Tax Liability	37,230	19,380

Problem 4.01-P5 (Difficult)

Mahesh Kumar received Rs. 3,20,000 as salary from his employer during financial year 2006-2007. Besides that he was paid bonus of Rs. 24,000 and commission on sales at 1.5%. The sales during the year were Rs. 30,20,000. His employer also contributed Rs. 21,000 towards Provident Fund. He made the following investments and contributions during the year.

	Rs.
1. Premium for the LIC policy of self of Rs. 1,20,000	6,000
2. Own contribution to Provident Fund	48,000
3. National Savings Certificates (VIII Issue)	10,000

He has also interest from banks amounting to Rs. 15,000 and dividend from Indian companies of Rs. 7,500. Compute his total income and tax payable thereon assuming that the Provident Fund is a recognised one.

Ans: 3,40,300; 53,132.

Problems 4.01-P6 (Difficult)

Mr. Z received Rs. 2,44,000 as salary from his employer M/s. ABC Ltd. during financial year 2006-2007. He also received bonus of Rs. 24,000. M/s. ABC Ltd. reimbursed to Mr. Z an amount of Rs. 18,000 for school fees of his son. M/s. ABC Ltd. contributed Rs. 18,000 towards Provident Fund. Mr. Z made following investments and contributions during the year :

	Rs.
(i) Premium for LIC policy in the name of his minor son	9,000
(ii) Fixed deposit in Canara Bank for 5 years.	36,000
(iii) Tuition fess paid of her daughter	10,000

Mr. Z has also received interest of Rs. 13,000 on FDRs with bank and interest of Rs. 7,000 has accrued to him on old National Savings Certificate purchased in past years. Compute his total income and tax payable thereon for A.Y. 2007-2008.

Ans: 2,44,000; 24,276.

Problems 4.01-P7 (Difficult)

Compute the total income and tax payable thereon by Mr. 'A', an employee of a Private Limited Co., posted at Delhi, for assessment year 2007-2008. Particulars of his salary etc. are as under :

Particulars	*(Rs.)*
1. Salary	1,44,000
2. Dearness allowance (qualifies for retirement benefits)	56,000
3. House rent allowance	36,000
4. Special duties allowance	4,000

During the Financial Year 2006-07, he has made following payments, subscriptions, deposits out of taxable income.

(i) Contributory Provident Fund and P.P.F. Rs. 20,000

(ii) L.I.P. Rs. 10,000

(iii) Deposit in NSCs VIII issue Rs. 20,000
(iv) Rent paid for the house hired by him Rs. 48,000
(v) Repayment of house building loan taken from the L.I.C. Rs. 12,000
(vi) Subscription to units of Mutual Fund to be invested in development of infrastructure. Rs. 20,000

Ans: 1,30,000; 11,424.

Problems 4.01-P8 (Difficult)

Compute the total income and tax payable thereon by Mrs. 'A', an employee of a Private Limited Co., posted at Delhi, for assessment year 2007-2008. Particulars of his salary etc. are as under :

1. Salary : Rs.3,00,000/-
2. Dearness Allowance : Rs.1,00,000/-
3. House Rent Allowance : Rs.1,80,000/-
4. Special Duties Allowance : Rs. 12,000/-
5. Un-recognised Provident Fund : Rs. 60,000/-
6. LIP : Rs. 10,000/-
7. Deposit in NSC VIII issue : Rs. 5,000/-
8. Rent Paid by the employee for house hired by her : Rs. 1,20,000/-
9. Repayment of House Building Loan (Principal) : Rs. 60,000/-
10. Tution Fees for three children (Rs.10,000/- per child) : Rs. 30,000/-

Ans: 4,07,000; 73,542.

Problems 4.01-P9 (Difficult)

Compute the total income and tax payable thereon by Mr. 'A', an employee of a Private Limited Co., posted at Delhi, for assessment year 2007-2008. Particulars of his salary etc. are as under :

1. Salary Rs.5,00,000/-
2. Bonus Rs. 76,000/-
3. Free gas, electricity, water etc. (Actual bills paid by company) Rs. 24,000/-
4. Furnished flat provided to the employee for 10 months which actual rent paid by the company per annum Rs.1,20,000/-
5. Hotel rent paid by employer (for two months) Rs. 50,000/-
6. Rent recovered from employee Rs. 10,000/
7. Cost of furniture Rs.1,00,000/-
8. Subscription to infrastructure bonds Rs. 30,000/-
9. Life Insurance Premium Rs. 5,000/-
10. Subscription to NSC (VIII) Issue Rs. 20,000/-
11. Contribution to recognized P.F. : Rs. 36,000/-

Ans: 6,28,040; 1,41,180.

Problems 4.01-P10 (Difficult)

X received Rs. 3,60,000 as basic pay and Rs. 25,000 as bonus during the previous year 2006-2007. He also got Rs. 10,000 as dearness allowance (forming part of basic pay) and 2% commission on sales made by him. The sale during the year is Rs. 15,00,000. His employer contributed during the year Rs. 28,000 towards provident fund. The amount of interest credited to provident fund on Dec. 15, 2006 at the rate of 16% comes to Rs. 2,500. His income from other sources is Rs. 50,000. During the year he makes following contributions and investments :

(i) Own contribution towards provident fund :	Rs. 30,000
(ii) Insurance premium on policy of Rs. 80,000 on own life:	Rs. 8,000
(iii) Contribution towards public provident fund:	Rs. 10,000
(iv) Deposit in National Saving Certificate VIII issue.	Rs. 12,000
(v) Insurance premium on the life of major son :	Rs. 10,000
(vi) Insurance premium on the life of mother dependent on him :	Rs. 5,000

Determine the total income and tax liability of X on the assumption that provident fund is (a) statutory provident fund; (b) unrecognised provident fund.

Ans: (a) 4,05,000; 72,930; (b) 4,35,000; 82,110.

Problems 4.01-P11 (Difficult)

Aditya Nath is an employee of a Ltd. Co. On the basis of the following particulars of his income, compute his taxable income and tax payable for the Assessment year 2007-2008.

(a) Emoluments received from the employer :

Salary	1,80,000
D.A.	30,000
CCA	3,000
HRA	72,000
Bonus	60,000
Employer's Contribution to Provident Fund.	36,000
Reimbursement of Travelling expenses.	24,000
Entertainment allowance.	12,000

(b) He is living in a rented accommodation for which he paid a rent of Rs. 9,000/- per month. He invested Rs. 20,000 in NSCs (VII Issue) and paid life insurance premium of Rs. 12,000 for a policy on his own life.

(c) He is in receipt of Rs. 8,000 as dividend on shares.

(d) He won a lottery of Rs. 50,000 during the year.

Ans: 3,17,400; 46,124.

Problem 4.01-P12 [CS D97]

Mrs. Amrita Joined XYZ Ltd., New Delhi, on 1st April, 1980 as a director. She receives the following emoluments during the previous year ending 31st March, 2007. Determine the taxable income of Mrs. Amrita for the assessment year 2007-08, taking into account the following information :

(i) Salary received	26,000
(ii) Bonus received	2,000
(iii) House rent allowance	5,000
(iv) Salary in lieu of leave	12,000
(v) Entertainment allowance	3,000
(vi) Company provides free gas and electricity (cost)	6,000
(vii) Domestic servant (not being sweeper, watchman or gardener) paid for by the company	12,800
(viii) Free education for her two sons in a school maintained by the company (cost)	52,000
(ix) Free lunch in office	10,000
(x) Salary of cook	12,000

Cook is engaged by Mrs. Amrita. She contributes (a) Rs. 13,500 towards contribution to a recognised provident fund; and (b) insurance premium of Rs. 15,000 on a policy of Rs. 1,40,000 taken on her own life. Her income from other sources is Rs. 26,000.

Ans: 47,500

TOPIC 4.02 **SECTION 80CCD.* DEDUCTION IN RESPECT OF CONTRIBUTION TO PENSION SCHEME OF CENTRAL GOVERNMENT

1. *Who can claim deduction* : Any Individual employed by the Central Government or any other employer on or after the 1-1-2004.
2. *Name of the scheme* : Pension scheme notified or as may be notified by the Central Government.
3. *Amount of deduction allowed* : The deduction allowed is the aggregate of

   — the amount contributed by such individual not exceeding 10% of his salary in the previous year; and

   — the amount contributed by the Central Govt. not exceeding 10% of employee's salary in the previous year.

   For the purposes of this section, "salary" includes dearness allowance, if the terms of employment so provide, but excludes all other allowances and perquisites.

Note

- 80CCD(3). Where any amount standing to the credit of the assessee in his account in respect of which a deduction has been allowed together with the amount accrued thereon, is received by the assessee or his nominee, in whole or in part, in any previous year,

  (a) on account of closure or his opting out of the pension scheme.

  (b) as pension received from the annuity plan purchased or taken on such closure or opting out,

  the whole of the amount referred to in clause (a) or clause (b) shall be deemed to be the income of the assessee or his nominee, as the case may be, in the previous year in which such amount is received, and shall accordingly be charged to tax as income of that previous year.

Illustration and Problem 4.02-P1

Mr. X, a Central Govt. employee, draws following emoluments. Basic Salary Rs. 6,000 p.m. Dearness Allowance as per the terms of employment Rs. 2,000 p.m. Both the employer and employee contribute Rs. 12,000 annually towards pension scheme of the Central Govt. Compute total income for the AY 2007-08.

Ans: 88,800

4.03 COMPREHENSIVE PROBLEMS [SALARY + DEDUCTIONS + TAX LIABILITY]

Simple and difficult

Problem 4.03-P1 [Hons 2006]

X, a director of LMN (P) Ltd., receives the following emoluments during the previous year relevant for the assessment year 2007-08 :

Basic salary : Rs. 1,80,000, dearness allowance : Rs. 24,000 (not forming part of basis pay), commission @ 1% percent of turnover (turnover achieved by X during the previous year 2006-07 : Rs. 10,00,000), arrears of bonus of the previous year 2002-03 : Rs. 6,000 (not taxed earlier), employer's contribution toward recognised provident fund : Rs. 30,000; interest credited in provident fund account @ 13.5 percent on December 3rd, 2006 : Rs. 900; conveyance allowance : Rs. 1,200 (60 per cent of which is unutilised for official purposes) Education allowance for three sons @ Rs. 183.33 per month per child ; Rs. 6,600, rent-free furnished house in Patna (lease rent of unfurnished house paid by the employer : Rs. 90,000, rent of furniture : Rs. 12,000), free services of gardener, cook and watchman (Salary : Rs. 3,000, Rs. 4,000, Rs. 5,000 respectively). On March 10, 2007 LMN (P) Ltd. sells imported furniture to X for Rs. 20,000 (The furniture was purchased by the company on June 30th, 2001 for Rs. 6,10,000 and since then it was used for business purposes). He runs a business during the previous year, income from business is Rs. 3,40,000.

He makes the following payments during 2006-07 :

(a) Own contribution to recognised provident fund : Rs. 32,000.
(b) Deposit in Home loan Account of National Housing Bank : Rs. 4,000 (including advance deposit of Rs. 1,000).
(c) Contribution to N.S.C. VIII issue Rs. 24,000.

Determine the net income and tax liability for assessment year 2007-08.

Solution

Computation of Income from Salaries for the AY 2007-08

Basic Salary	1,80,000
Dearness allowance [not forming part of salary]	24,000
Commission based on sales [1% of 10,00,000]	10,000
Arrears of Bonus	6,000
Excess of employer's contribution towards RPF [30,000 – 12% of (1,80,000 + 10,000)]	7,200
Excess of interest towards RPF [900 ÷ 13.5 × 4]	267
Conveyance allowance [40% of 1,200]	480
Children education allowance [183.33 × 3 × 12]	
Less : Exempt [100 × 2 × 12]	4,200

Value of rent-free accommodation [15% of 1,94,680 (1,80,000 + 10,000 + 480 + 4,200)]		29,202
Value of furniture		12,000
Servant facility [3,000 + 4,000 + 5,000]		12,000
Sale of furniture [6,10,000 – 10% of 6,10,000 × 5 – 20,000]		2,85,000
Income from Salaries		5,70,349

Computation of total income for the AY 2007-08

Income from Salary		5,70,349
Profit from business		3,40,000
Gross total income		9,10,349
Less : Deductions u/s 80C		
- Employees contribution	32,000	
- Deposit in home loan account in NHB	4,000	
- NSC VIII issue	24,000	60,000
Total income (rounded off)		8,50,350

Computation of tax liability

Tax on normal income at slab rate	2,05,105
Add : Education cess @ 2%	4,102
Tax liability	2,09,207

Problem 4.03-P2 (Difficult)

Mr. 'A' is a senior officer of Government of India. Following are the details of his salary for the year ended on 31.3.2006.

(i) Basic Pay Rs. 2,40,000

(ii) DA Rs. 1,02,000

(iii) CCA Rs. 3,600

(iv) Personal Pay (given for following small family norms) Rs. 4,500

There are certain other important information in this case given below—

(i) He occupies a government flat (Type-VI) and the licence fee recovered from him is Rs. 350 per month. The flat would fetch a rent of Rs. 10,000 per month in the open market. License fees charged by the Govt. Rs. 6,000.

(ii) He is provided free Government transport by ambassador car for going to office and return to home for 3 months and for the rest of year he has received transport allowance Rs. 800 p.m.

(iii) He is entitled to free medical facility for himself and family members under the Central Govt. Health Scheme for which a recovery of Rs. 150 is made from his salary every month. The value of such facility availed of during the year is Rs. 15,000.

(iv) He had taken house building advance from the Government. The concession in the matter of interest (the difference between SBI lending rate and the rate charged by the Government) is estimated at Rs. 4,000.

(v) He is reimbursed the expenditure of buying two newspapers for his home. The reimbursement by the employer during the year is Rs. 3,000.

(vi) He has invested Rs. 20,000 in the National Savings Certificate during the year. However, total interest on NSCs purchased in past years accrues to Rs. 7,500.

(vii) He has deposited Rs. 10,000 during the year in a Public Provident Fund A/c in the name of his minor son. However, on subscripts already made to this A/c, interest of Rs. 3,700 has accrued during the year.

(viii) During the year he has received dividends of Rs. 2,500 and interest on FDRs with bank amounting to Rs. 12,000.

Please compute total income of Mr. 'A' for assessment year 2007-2008 and determine the tax payable.

Ans: 3,40,900; 53,315. [2,40,000+1,02,000+3,600+4,500+1,800+0+0+4,000+3,000= 3,58,900–19,500=3,78,400–37,500=3,40,900]

Problem 4.03-P3 (Difficult)

Mr. X, an engineer, working in engineering divisions of L & T Ltd. furnishes following particulars of his income for the year ended March 31, 2007. Compute his taxable income and tax payable for the AY 2007-08.

Basic Salary	3,550 p.m.
Project Allowance	500 p.m.

He has been provided with the following facilities :

1. Own accommodation in Hyderabad (Population as per 2001 census 26 lakhs). The employer charges 10% of Basic Salary on account of accommodation.
2. On 18-1-2007 he has been provided with Air-Conditioner and other household appliances costing Rs. 80,000.
3. The employer takes accident insurance policy of Rs. 15,00,000 on accident of Mr. X. Insurance premium paid Rs. 16,000.
4. The employer takes life insurance policy on life of Mr. X. Insurance premium paid is Rs. 1,500 on 1-4-2007 and Rs. 500 on 17-3-2007. However insurance premium falls due on 15-3-2007.
5. Mr. X has engaged a cook at a salary of Rs. 2,000 p.m. whose salary is paid by employer directly to the cook. Also employer has provided a watchman to Mr. X whose salary is Rs. 600 p.m. The employer charges Rs. 100 p.m. for provision of watchman.
6. Income from Other Sources Rs. 1,50,000.

Ans: 2,23,490; 20,092. [42,600+6,000+2,890+1,000+0+2,000+0+24,000+0=78,490+ 1,50,000=2,28,490–5,000 =2,23,490]

Problem 4.03-P4 [CS J05]

Jolly is an employee of a private limited company at Mumbai. The following particulars of his income for the year ended 31st March, 2007 have been ascertained :

(i)	Basic salary per month	12,000
(ii)	Dearness allowance per annum (ad hoc, i.e., not provided in the terms of employment)	10,000

(iii)	Entertainment allowance per annum	10,000
(iv)	Employer's annual contribution to the provident fund	20,000
(v)	His own annual contribution to the provident fund	20,000
(vi)	Educational allowance per annum for his two sons (for meeting the cost of their higher education)	7,400
(vii)	The company has hired a residential flat (unfurnished) and allotted it to the assessee for his stay (No rent is charged from him). Rent per month	3,500
(viii)	Salary of domestic servant appointed by the employee is paid for the year by the employer.	4,000
(ix)	Gas and electricity bills paid during the year by the company on his behalf	6,000
(x)	The company provided a sweeper at the assessee's residence. Monthly wages paid by the company	200
(xi)	Interest from a nationalised bank received during the year	4,000
(xii)	Jolly also received gross income on units of a mutual fund during the year	10,000

A small motor car belonging to the company has been provided to the assessee both for official and personal use and the company meets the entire expenses on the car's maintenance and running.

Jolly had an insurance policy on his life for Rs. 50,000. He had paid the annual premium of Rs. 6,000 for this policy during the year.

Compute the total income of Jolly for the assessment year 2007-08 giving full reasons for the treatment of each item. Also determine his tax liability.

Ans: 2,95,970; 39,567. [1,44,000+1,20,000+10,000+2,720+5,000+23,850+4,000+6,000+ 2,400+0=3,17,970+4,000=3,21,970–26,000=2,95,270]

Problem 4.03-P5 [CS D99]

X, the general manager of Y Ltd., retired on December 31, 2006 after 30 years of service. The particulars of his income are as follows :

(i) Salary Rs. 8,000 per month from January 1, 2006. House rent allowance Rs. 3,000 per month from January 1, 2006.

(ii) Medical expenses reimbursed by employer : Rs. 21,000 for the period from April 1, 2006 which included Rs. 5,000 paid to a Government hospital.

(iii) The employer provides him a car (cubic capacity of engine exceeds 1.6 litters) for official and personal use. The expenses of running and maintenance of car and salary of a driver for official use was borne by the employer.

(iv) X contributes 22 per cent (12 per cent regular and 10% additional voluntary contribution) to a recognized provident fund and the company matches his regular contribution of 12 per cent.

(v) X has invested Rs. 20,000 in ULIP scheme of UTI and Rs. 10,000 in the public provident fund. He paid Rs. 9,000 towards life insurance premium on policy for a sum assured of Rs. 40,000.

(vi) He lives in a rented house in Delhi and pays Rs. 4,000 per month as rent.

(vii) X received Rs. 1,50,000 as gratuity. He is not covered by the Payment of Gratuity Act, 1972.

(viii) He received Rs. 1,60,000 for encashement of leave, being 16 months leave not availed of.

Compute X's income for the assessment year 2007-08.

Ans: 1,29,160; 2,974. [72,000+1,000+0+0+0+30,000+80,000=1,83,000–53,840=1,29,160]

Problem 4.03-P6 (Difficult)

Mr. Purshottam, a director of Delta India Ltd. receives the following salary and perquisites from his employer during the previous year 2006-07 :

Basic pay	Rs. 66,000
Profit bonus	18,000
Commission on sales @ 4% of turnover of	18,50,000
Advance Salary of April to July 2007.	22,000
Employer's contribution towards recognised provident fund	18,000
Interest credited in provident fund a/c @ 18%	10,000
A rent - free furnished house in Patna (rent of unfurnished house paid by emp.)	84,000
Rent of furniture	18,000
Free services of a gardener (Salary)	4,000
Free services of cook (salary)	36,000
Free services of watchman (salary)	120
Free ration	3,000

During the previous year, he earns taxable income of Rs. 11,900 from the business. Determine the total income and tax liability of Mr. Purshottam for the assessment year 2007-08, assuming that he makes the following payments and investments :

(a) Own contribution towards recognised provident fund Rs. 20,000.

(b) Deposit in 10 year account under the Post Office Savings Bank (CTD) Rules 6,000. (Including advance deposit of Rs. 1,000).

(c) Deposit in public provident fund Rs. 35,000.

Ans: 1,94,040; 14,084. [66,000+18,000+74,000+22,000+1,200+4,722+23,700+18,000+ 4,000+2,400+120+3,000=2,37,142+11,900=2,49,042–55,000=1,94,002]

Problem 4.03-P7 (Difficult)

Shri Rajagopal is a senior executive of a Company in Mumbai. The following information is available about his income during the previous year ended 31.3.2007 :

(i) Monthly salary 40,000

(ii) Commission 1,25,000

(iii) House Rent Allowance for the full year. 1,80,000
Actual rent paid by him for the year. (Accommodation taken in Mumbai) 2,00,000

(iv) The terms and conditions of his employment were modified during the year partly to his disadvantage and for that the employer paid him a compensation of Rs. 2,50,000.

(v) He has been provided with a motor car for his personal use. All expenses of Rs. 50,000 including driver's salary, maintenance and petrol charges were borne by the employer.

(vii) He earned interest on fixed deposits with Canara Bank and State Bank of India which was Rs. 14,500 in the aggregate.

(viii) He contributed Rs. 40,000 to the Recognised Provident Fund; paid Rs. 26,000 as annual premium on a Life Insurance Policy taken on his life where the sum assured was Rs. 2 lakhs.

Compute the total income of Shri Rajagopal for Assessment Year 2007-2008 and calculate the tax on the total income.

Ans: 8,31,500; 2,03,439. [4,80,000+1,25,000+28,000+2,50,000+0=8,83,000+14,500=8,97,500–66,000=8,31,500]

Problem 4.03-P8 [Hons 1992]

Mr. K.P. Saxena is a public relations officer with a company. He furnishes the following particulars of his income / investment during the previous year, 2006-07.

(1) He draws salary @ Rs. 7,000 p.m. and dearness allowance @ Rs. 2,400 p.m. Dearness allowance, amounting to Rs. 400 p.m., forms part of the pay for superannuation benefits. He is provided with rent - free furnished accommodation. The rent paid by the company is Rs. 3,000 p.m. The company has also provided him the furniture and household appliances (original cost Rs. 32,000) but written down value is Rs. 24,000.

He has been paid Rs. 8,000 on account of arrears of bonus for 2005-06 and salary in lieu of leave of Rs. 4,000 for 2006-07. He has been provided chauffer driven car of 1.8 litres engine capacity for personal and official duties and the expenses of its maintenance are met by the company.

(2) He has paid Rs. 5,000 as life insurance premium on the life of his married son (sum assured Rs. 1,00,000. He has purchased National Savings Certificates VIII issue for Rs. 6,000 on 15-12-2006. He has purchased units of PNB mutual fund notified under section 10(23D), on 25-8-2006 for Rs. 10,000.

Compute his total income and tax liability for the assessment year 2007-08.

Ans: 1,20,920; 2,607. [84,000+28,800+13,920+3,200+8,000+4,000+0=1,41,920–21,000=1,20,920]

Problem 4.03-P9 [Hons 1991]

Mr. Joginder Pal is employed with a transport firm. He is member of an unrecognized provident fund. He has been drawing salary @ Rs. 8,000 p.m. since 01-01-2006. Dearness allowance, forming part of pay for superannuation benefits, is paid @ 10% of his salary.

He gets house rent allowance @ Rs. 1,200 per month. He pays rent of Rs. 2,000 p.m. He contributes @ 10% of his salary to the unrecognized provident fund and the employer contributes @ 20%. The employer also paid his club bills amounting to Rs. 9,000. Besides, he is paid Rs. 1,600 p.m. as out of station allowance.

He retires on 31-12-2006 after 20 years and 9 months of service. He gets Rs. 1,56,000 accumulated balance from the fund. It consists of Rs. 30,000 as his contribution and Rs. 22,000 interest thereon. The employer's contribution is Rs. 60,000 and interest thereon is Rs. 44,000. He also gets gratuity of Rs. 80,000.

After retirement, he gets pension @ Rs. 3,600 p.m. On 1st March, 2007 he surrenders one-half pension for a consolidated amount of Rs. 1,20,000.

He has made the following payment / investments during the previous year 2006-07 :

(i) Life Insurance Premium amounting to Rs. 4,000 on the policy taken on the life of his married son (sum assured Rs. 1,00,000).

(ii) Public provident fund deposit Rs. 10,000.

(iii) Refund of Rs. 22,000 to the life insurance corporation of India on account of loan taken for the purchase of a flat, allotted in March, 2006.

(iv) Purchases of National Savings Certificates, VIII issue amounting to Rs. 6,000.

(v) Contribution of Rs. 10,000 under the Jeevan Dhara Scheme of Life Insurance Corporation of India. Eligible for deduction under Section 80C.

From the above information you are required to compute his income under the head salary and tax liability for the assessment year 2007-08.

Ans: 2,66,320; 28,829. [96,000+9,600+960+0+9,000+5,760+60,000+44,000+0+9,000+40,000=2,74,320+22,000=2,96,320–30,000=2,66,320]

Typical

Problem 4.03-P10 (Typical)

Mr. Harsh Rathore is the Principal of Bajaj College, Mumbai, who retires on 31-3-2007. He is in the grade of Rs. 15,000-2,000-31,000 since 1st January 2006. He gets 60% of basic pay as dearness allowance and 8% of the basic pay as city compensatory allowance. He has been provided with a furnished accommodation by the college owned by it. Furniture costing Rs. 25,000 has also been provided by the college. He has been given a car of 16 H.P. rating, on 17-12-2006 which is used by him for office and personal purpose. He has been provided with the facility of a servant who is paid by the college Rs. 450 p.m.

He contributes 15% of his pay and dearness allowance to the recognised provident fund towards which the college contributes an equal amount. Interest amounting to Rs. 2,500 at 12.5% has been credited on the balance standing to the credit of his provident fund account.

Assuming that the salary becomes due on the first of the next month, determine the Income from salaries, taxable income and tax liability for the assessment year 2007-08.

Ans: 3,58,240; 58,621. [2,01,000+1,20,600+16,080+53,152+0+5,400+9,648+600=4,06,480–48,240=3,58,240]

Problem 4.03-P11 (Typical)

Mr. Jinesh is the manager in the Story and Poem Ltd., Kandla (population as per 2001 census 6,00,000). He gets basic pay @ Rs. 12,000 p.m., dearness allowance @ Rs. 1,000 p.m. and entertainment allowance @ Rs. 500 per month. He had been provided with a rent free house by the company. He was also provided by the company, with facility of free use of furniture costing Rs. 9,000 and refrigerator costing Rs. 6,000. The company has provided him 16 h.p. car along with driver. The expenses relating to use of car is borne by the company. The car is used partly for office purpose and partly for personal purpose. The bills of Rs. 2,000 relating to the education of his children were reimbursed by the company. The company has provided the amenity of free lunch and free refreshment during office hours. The estimated value of which is Rs. 1,500 and Rs. 100 per month respectively *(assume 25 days in a month)*. The payment is made by the employer directly to the restaurant. He and the company both contribute 14 per cent of basic pay and half the dearness allowance towards Recognised Provident fund. During the financial year 2006-07 interest credited to his provident fund account @ 12.5% amount to Rs. 12,500. Compute the taxable income from salaries and tax liability of Mr. Jinesh for the Assessment Year 2007-08, assuming that he has paid Rs. 2,000 tax on employment on 1-4-2007.

Ans: 1,62,200; 7,589. [1,44,000+12,000+6,000+13,200+0+2,000+0+3,000+3,000= 1,83,200–21,000=1,62,200]

Problem 4.03-P12 (Typical)

Miss Gunjan is the designer in the Sophisticated Ltd., Delhi. She furnishes following particulars of her income :

1. Net salary Rs. 80,000 after deduction of tax at source Rs. 4,000, contribution to recognised provident fund Rs. 9,000, Rs. 2,000 for life insurance premium and rent of bungalow @ 5% of basic salary.
   Commission on sales Rs. 40,000.
2. She resides in the bungalow of the company.
3. Employer's contribution to RPF is Rs. 7,000 and the interest credited to the PF @ 13% amounted to Rs. 16,250.
4. Her employer paid in March 2007 for her medical treatment in Germany Rs. 80,000, Rs. 15,000 for travelling in this connection and Rs. 25,000 for stay there.
5. The company paid income-tax penalty of Rs. 1,200.
6. She contributes 25% of sum assured as life insurance premium. Sum assured Rs. 80,000.

Determine the taxable income and tax liability for the assessment year 2007-08.

Ans: 1,34,580; 3,527 [1,00,000+40,000+16,000+0+4,375+1,200=1,61,580–27,000= 1,34,580]

Problem 4.03-P13 (Typical)

Mr. Taxcrazy was appointed as the branch manager of a company at Delhi on 1-1-2005 in the pay scale of 7,000-500-12,000. He also receives 10% of his pay as dearness allowance, Rs. 1,500 p.m. as medical allowance and Rs. 3,000 p.m. as conveyance allowance.

The company has given him a rent free residential house since 1-10-2006. The company has incurred following expenses in respect of this house from 1-10-2006 to 31-3-2007 :

Repairs	2,000
Electricity bills	350
Water bills	200
Telephone bills	800

On 1-10-2006 his conveyance allowance was stopped and he was given a motor car of 1.6 litre cubic rating for both official and personal use. All the expenses of running and maintenance of the car including salary of driver is paid by the company.

Company gifted him an item of Rs. 7,000 on 1-11-2006 and sold its products of Rs. 10,000 in Rs. 6,000 only.

He as well as company contribute 14.5% of his salary to a recognised provident fund. Interest credited during the previous year to his provident fund account @ 12.5% p.a. was Rs. 1,250.

Compute his income from salary and tax liability for the AY 2007-08 assuming that he has not spent any amount of conveyance allowance for official duties.

Ans: 1,34,850; 3,335. [91,500+18,000+9,150+18,000+8,325+350+200+0+0+2,288+300=1,48,113–13,268=1,34,845]

Problem 4.03-P14 (Difficult)

Mr. Vivek Dubey aged 65 years was an Assistant Engineer in Hewellet Packard, Delhi. He got Rs. 10,000 per month as basic pay, Rs. 2,000 per month as dearness allowance (under the terms of employment) and Rs. 1,250 per month as house rent allowance. He resides in his own house. He got Rs. 20,000 as travelling allowance but he spent only Rs. 14,000 on travelling. He also got Rs. 799 per month as transport allowance for commutation between office and residence.

He retired on 1st January 2007 and got Rs. 2,00,000 as gratuity and Rs. 2,50,000 as accumulated balance in his recognised fund. His own contribution and that of the factory to this fund was equal. He also received Rs. 1,44,000 being the amount of salary including dearness allowance for 12 months earned leave to his credit at the time of retirement.

He was allowed to get pension of Rs. 5,000 per month three-fourths of which was commuted for Rs. 1,50,000. He commenced service of this factory on 1st April 1975. Employment tax payable to State Government was Rs. 2,000 but he paid only Rs. 1,000 during the previous year against the due amount.

Calculate his income from salaries for the assessment year 2007-08.

Ans: 2,55,330; 14,891. [90,000+18,000+11,250+6,000+0+20,000+24,000+87,083=2,56,333–1,000=2,55,333]

Problem 4.03-P15 [CS D99]

Q.4b : X, the General Manager of Y Ltd., retired on December 31, 2006 after 30 years of service. The particulars of his income are as follows :

(i) Salary Rs. 8,000 per month from January 1, 2006. House rent allowance Rs. 3,000 per month from January 1, 2006.

(ii) Medical expenses reimbursed by employer : Rs. 21,000 for the period from April 1, 2006 which included Rs. 5,000 paid to a Government hospital.

(iii) The employer provides him a car (cubic capacity of engine exceeds 1.6 litres) for official and personal use. The expenses of running and maintenance of car and salary of a driver for official use was borne by the employer.

(iv) X contributes 22 per cent (12 per cent regular and 10% additional voluntary contribution) to a recognized provident fund and the company matches his regular contribution of 12 per cent.

(v) X has invested Rs. 20,000 in ULIP scheme of UTI and Rs. 10,000 in the public provident fund. He paid Rs. 9,000 towards life insurance premium on policy for a sum assured of Rs. 40,000.

(vi) He lives in a rented house in Delhi and pays Rs. 4,000 per month as rent.

(vii) X received Rs. 1,50,000 as gratuity. He is not covered by the Payment of Gratuity Act, 1972.

(viii) He received Rs. 1,60,000 for encashment of leave, being 16 months leave not availed of.

Compute X's income and his tax obligation for the assessment year 2007-08.

Ans: 1,29,160; 2,974. [72,000+1,000+0+30,000+80,000=1,83,000–53,840=1,29,160]

STRATEGY MAKER

It is the most important chapter and always attached with salary. Rebate u/s 88 to 88D has been deleted. Rebate u/s 88 shifted to 80C and rebate u/ss 88B, 88C and 88D shifted to slab rate. Types of problems asked are difficult. What to expect : Everything

Yes ! You have completed one whole cycle of income tax

What you saw in chapter 3 and chapter 4 was lots 'n' lots of rules. All that rules must be memorised. I am again repeating a golden rule of Income tax. If you memorise the provisions of income tax, there is no question which cannot be solved. Practice of question shall make you the master of that question and not the master of income tax, therefore memorise the rules.

Keep running

Why a building is called building when it is already built?

INCOME FROM HOUSE PROPERTY

TOPIC 5.00 INTRODUCTION

Generally income from house property is charged through rent. The property may be let out for residence or for commercial purpose. Further the property may be self occupied for residence or may be self occupied for business. Also the property may be fully vacant *i.e.* no one leaves in that building. All such cases have to be seen in light of sections 22 to 27.

House property includes flats, shops, factory, sheds and farmhouses whether situated in India or outside India.

TOPIC 5.01 *SECTION 22.* WHICH INCOME IS CHARGEABLE UNDER THE HEAD 'INCOME FROM HOUSE PROPERTY'? (CHARGEABILITY)

If all the following conditions are satisfied then income is chargeable under the head 'Income from House Property' :

a. The property should consist of any *building* or land appurtenant thereto.

   (Building means four walls having a roof whose construction is completed.The appurtenant land may be in the form of courtyard or compound forming part of the building. But such land is to be distinguished from an open plot of land, which is not charged under this head but under the head "Income from Other Sources" or under head "Profit from business" as the case may be.)

b. The assessee should be the owner of the property.

   (Suppose A let out the building to B and B let out it to C in this case rent earned by A shall be charged under the head House Property and rent earned by B shall be charged under the head Income from Other Sources.)

c. The property should not be used by the owner for the purpose of his *own* business or profession.

   (If the property is used by the owner for his own business or profession then such property is treated under the head Business or profession. Where the building is let out to its employees the income is charged under the head Business.)

If *all* the above three conditions are satisfied then only income is charged under the head "Income from House Property".

TOPIC 5.02 DISCUSS THE DIFFERENT TYPES OF PROPERTIES AND ITS TAXABILITY

Type of property	*Head*	*Gross Annual Value*
Let out for residence or let out for business.	House Property	Expected rent or actual rent whichever is higher less loss on account of vacancy
Building self occupied for residence.	House Property	nil
Building treated as deemed to be let out property. (DLOP)	House Property	Expected rent
Building vacant for whole year.	House Property	nil
Building self occupied for business.	Business	not applicable

Problems 5.02-P1

1. The property which is self occupied for business or profession is charged under the head income from house property. (True or false)
2. What about other properties *i.e.* the property which is self occupied for residence or property which is let out for residence or business or the property which is vacant.
3. Under which head income from independent plot of land is taxable.
4. What if such land is attached or is a part of building.
5. A ROR is liable to pay tax in India for all property whether situated in India or outside India. (True or False)
6. A RNOR and NR is liable to pay tax in India for all property whether situated in India or outside India. (True or False)
7. When a property is treated as deemed to be let out property and its meaning ?
8. When a property is treated as vacant property and its meaning ?

Solutions

1. False, such income is charged under the head business.
2. All such properties are charged under the head Income from House Property.
3. Under the head income from other sources if not charged under the head Profit from business, since there doesn't exist a building.
4. Then under the head income from house property.
5. True.
6. False, only on that property which is situated in India.
7. Where the property is not actually let out then also it is treated as deemed to be let out property. A property is treated as DLOP when assessee occupies more than one house for his self residence then one house selected by him is treated as SOP for residence and the remaining property is treated as deemed to be let out property.

8. Vacant property means a property in which no one lives. Even the owner does not live in that property. Property may remain vacant due to many following factors. Suitable tenant is not available, flood has damaged the house therefore could not be let out, etc.

TOPIC 5.03 COMPUTATION OF INCOME FROM HOUSE PROPERTY (assumed figures)

	Let out / DLOP	*SOP for residence*
Gross Annual Value *(GAV)*	5,100	nil
Less : Municipal tax paid by the owner during the relevant PY	100	nil
Net Annual Value *(NAV)* u/s 23	5,000	nil
Less : Deduction u/s 24		
(a) Standard Deduction *(30% of NAV)*	(1,500)	nil
(b) Interest on borrowed capital allowed as deduction on accrual basis	(2,500)	(25,000)
Income from House Property	1,000	(25,000)
Add : Arrears of rent if not taxed earlier u/s 25B	10,000	50,000
Less : Standard Deduction u/s 25B *(30% of arrears of rent)*	(3,000)	(15,000)
Income from House Property	8,000	10,000
Add : Unrealised rent of earlier years for which deduction has been claimed or allowed u/s 25A and 25AA *(Standard deduction not available)*	5,000	4,000
Income from House Property	13,000	14,000

Note

- In case of property which is self occupied for residence no deduction is allowed except interest on borrowed capital which is a maximum of Rs. 30,000. However a maximum of Rs. 1,50,000 if certain conditions are satisfied is allowed as deduction. *(discussed later)*
- Where the house remains vacant for whole year, then its gross annual value is taken as nil and also all deductions are allowed.

Problems 5.03-P1

1. What is the meaning of municipal tax ?
2. What is the basis of levying municipal tax ?
3. When municipal tax is not allowed as deduction ?
4. Are taxes levied on property by the State Govt. deductible ?
5. Can deduction be claimed for arrears of municipal tax or advance payment of municipal tax ?
6. When standard deduction u/s 24(a) is not available ?
7. When can NAV be nil or negative ?
8. Is deduction like repairs of house property, land revenue, ground rent, etc. available ?

Solutions

1. Municipal tax is the tax levied on property by the Municipal Authorities. Like water tax, sewage tax, fire tax or education cess. All these taxes known as municipal tax, since levied by the municipal authority.

2. Municipal valuation. E.g. MT 10%. MV 1,00,000; FR 1,50,000. MT levied shall be 10% of Rs. 1,00,000. Rs. 10,000.
3. When Municipal tax is paid by the tenant.
4. No.
5. Yes, only condition to be fulfilled is that municipal tax is paid by the owner during the relevant PY. Suppose you are computing income from house property for the PY 2003-04, to claim deduction municipal tax should be paid during the PY 2006-07. Otherwise deduction is not allowed.
6. When NAV is nil or in negative.
7. When municipal tax is equal to or more than GAV.
8. No, the only deductions available are those specified under section 24. So even if the question provides for repairs etc. it has to be ignored. All these deductions are now clubbed in Standard Deduction.

Illustration 5.03-P2

Compute Income from House Property for the AY 2007-08.

	Case 1	*Case 2*	*Case 3*
Gross Annual Value	40,000	60,000	25,000
Municipal tax paid by owner on			
• 31-5-2006	5,000	nil	30,000
• 1-4-2007	35,000	5,000	nil
Municipal tax paid by tenant on 11-8-2006	1,000	2,000	500
Interest on borrowed capital due for PY 2006-07 *(not yet paid)*	600	500	800

Ans: (1) 23,900; (2) 41,500; (3) (5,800).

Solution : Case 1

Gross Annual Value		40,000
Less : MT paid by the owner in the PY 2006-07		5,000
Net Annual Value		35,000
Less : Deduction u/s 24		
(a) Standard Deduction *(30% of NAV)*	10,500	
(b) Interest on borrowed capital *(on accrual basis)*	600	11,100
Income from House Property		23,900

Problem 5.03-P3 (Simple)

1. GAV Rs. 1,50,000; MT due for PY 2003-04 Rs. 14,000; MT due for PY 2004-05 Rs. 6,000; MT due for PY 2005-06 Rs. 1,000; MT due for PY 2006-07 Rs. 8,000; MT of PY 2007-08 Rs. 11,000. The payment of all MT being Rs. 40,000 is paid on 7-3-2007. Find out Income from House Property for the AY 2007-08.
2. X lets out a property on annual rent of Rs. 90,000 (Which is also the fair rent). During the previous year 2006-07, the following expenses are paid by X. Municipal taxes for 2006-07 - Rs. 30,000; municipal taxes for earlier years - Rs. 70,000; repairs - Rs. 6,000; interest on capital borrowed for construction - Rs. 25,000. Calculate income from the house property. [CS J02]

3. Y owns a house property, which is let out for Rs. 7,500 per month. The fair rent of the property is Rs. 1,00,000. Municipal taxes paid during the year for each half year is Rs. 4,200. The tenant has spent Rs. 12,000 towards repairs of the property during the year. Compute the income from house property for the assessment year 2007-08. [CS J03]

Ans: 77,000; (35,000); 64,120.

TOPIC 5.04 MEANING OF ANNUAL VALUE

Annual value represents earning capacity of the building. It is the value which building would fetch if the property is let out. To determine the annual value it is not necessary that building is actually let out, even if the building is not let out, expected rent of the building shall be treated as annual value. This is the only head in the Income Tax Act, where the notional income is charged to tax. This notional income is actually a loss for the assessee. *E.g.* Expected rent Rs. 80,000 and actual rent Rs. 50,000. What is taxable shall be Rs. 80,000. In this case Rs. 30,000 is notional income which is actually a loss for the assessee.

TOPIC 5.05 *SECTION 23(1)*. COMPUTATION OF INCOME FROM HOUSE PROPERTY IF PROPERTY IS LET OUT.

(A) STEPS TO COMPUTE GROSS ANNUAL VALUE

Step a : Section 23(1)(a). Compute expected rent of the property (ER)

Step b : Section 23(1)(b). Compute actual rent of the property (AR)

Step c : Section 23(1)(c). Compute loss on account of vacancy

Gross Annual value of let out property is 'a' or 'b' whichever is higher less 'c'.

(B) SECTION 23(1)(a). HOW TO DETERMINE 'EXPECTED RENT' OF THE BUILDING

Expected rent is the sum for which the property might reasonably be expected to let from year to year. Expected rent is the value which the property might fetch, if the property is let out. Expected rent depends upon following three factors :

1. *Municipal Valuation (MV) of the property* : For collection of municipal tax *(MT)*, the local authority makes a periodical survey of all buildings in its jurisdiction. Such valuation may be taken as strong evidence representing the earning capacity of the building.
2. *Fair Rent of the property (FR)* : Also known as market rent. Rent fetched by similar property in the similar locality. Where however Fair Rent is not given, then actual rent shall be treated as fair rent.
3. *Standard Rent (SR) of the property under the Rent Control Act* : It is the rent fixed by the State Government. For *example* Bombay Rent Control Act defines the SR as the rent that the tenant paid in 1940 or for building built after 1940, the rent paid when the property was first let out.

How to determine 'expected rent' of the property

As per Supreme Court judgement neither MV nor FR can exceed SR. Therefore expected rent of the building is MV or FR whichever is higher but limited to SR.

E.g. 1 : MV = 500; FR = 600; SR = 450. Therefore expected rent is 500 or 600 whichever is higher *i.e.* 600 but limited to 450. Therefore Expected Rent = 450.

E.g. 2 : MV = 800; FR = 900; SR = 1,000. Therefore expected rent is 800 or 900 whichever is higher *i.e.* 900 but limited to 1,000. Therefore Expected Rent = 900.

E.g. 3 : MV = 800; FR = 900; SR = NA, therefore expected rent is 800 or 900 whichever is higher *i.e.* 900.

(C) SECTION 23(1)(b). COMPUTATION OF 'ACTUAL RENT'

Meaning of actual rent : Actual rent in respect of building is the rent actually fetched by the owner where the property is let out.

Computation of Actual rent : Actual rent is computed for the period during which the property is *let out* (+) for the period during which the property remains *vacant* (–) unrealised rent of the current PY *(not of past years).* Period for which property is self occupied for residence is ignored.

(D) SECTION 23(1)(c). COMPUTATION OF 'LOSS ON ACCOUNT OF VACANCY'

Vacancy is computed only if the property is let out or where the property could not be let out inspite of the best effort of the owner. If the property is let out for 10 months for Rs. 5,000 per month. In this case loss on account of vacancy shall be Rs. 10,000 for two months.

Problem 5.05-P1

Compute actual rent and GAV from the following cases if expected rent is (A) Rs. 10,000 (B) 1,10,000.

Case 1	*Case 2*	*Case 3*	*Case 4*
let out for 12 months for Rs. 4,000 p.m.	let out for 10 months for Rs. 4,000 p.m. 2 months vacant. 1 month unrealised rent	let out for 10 months for Rs. 4,000 p.m. 2 months SOP for residence	let out for 10 months for Rs. 4,000 p.m. 1 month vacant. 1 month SOP for residence. Rs. 2,000 unrealised rent

Case 5	*Case 6*	*Case 7*
let out for first 4 months for Rs. 8,000 p.m and for next 6 months for Rs. 9,000 p.m. 2 months vacant. Rs. 6,000 unrealised rent	let out for first 9 months for Rs. 5,000 p.m. and for next 2 months for Rs. 4,000 p.m. 1 month SOP for residence. Rs. 5,000 unrealised rent	let out for first 3 months for Rs. 12,000 p.m. and for next 5 months for Rs. 11,000 p.m. 2 months SOP for residence. 2 months vacant. Rs. 13,000 unrealised rent

Ans: (A) (1) 48,000; (2) 44,000; (3) 40,000; (4) 42,000; (5) 98,000; (6) 48,000; (7) 1,02,000.

Ans: (B)(1)1,10,000; (2) 1,02,000; (3) 1,10,000; (4) 1,06,000; (5) 92,000; (6) 1,10,000; (7) 86,000

Hint: Annual rent concept has been done away with. Loss on account of vacancy at higher value is computed to take maximum benefit.

Solution

(A) *Computation of gross annual value*

	Case 1	*Case 2*	*Case 3*	*Case 4*	*Case 5*	*Case 6*	*Case 7*
a. Expected rent (ER)	10,000	10,000	10,000	10,000	10,000	10,000	10,000
b. Actual rent (AR)	48,000	44,000	40,000	42,000	98,000	48,000	1,02,000
c. Loss on account of vacancy	Nil	8,000	nil	4,000	18,000	nil	24,000
GAV (*a* or *b* whichever is higher less *c*)	48,000	36,000	40,000	38,000	80,000	48,000	78,000

(B) *Computation of gross annual value*

	Case 1	*Case 2*	*Case 3*	*Case 4*	*Case 5*	*Case 6*	*Case 7*
a. Expected rent (ER)	1,10,000	1,10,000	1,10,000	1,10,000	1,10,000	1,10,000	1,10,000
b. Actual rent (AR)	48,000	44,000	40,000	42,000	98,000	48,000	1,02,000
c. Loss on account of vacancy	Nil	8,000	nil	4,000	18,000	nil	24,000
GAV (*a* or *b* whichever is higher less *c*)	1,10,000	1,02,000	1,10,000	1,06,000	92,000	1,10,000	86,000

Problems 5.05-P2

1. Why expected rent is sometimes substituted for actual rent ?
2. What if the property could not be let out inspite of the best effort and the property remains vacant for whole year ?
3. What do you mean by unrealised rent or bad debt ?
4. What are the conditions to be satisfied to claim deduction of unrealised rent?
5. Deduction of unrealised rent can be claimed for earlier PY's. (True or False)
6. Unrealised rent of current year is subtracted from expected rent. (True or False)
7. Loss on account of vacancy is first added to actual rent and then always subtracted *i.e.* ER or AR whichever is higher. (True or False)

Solutions

1. It can be explained through an example. For *e.g.* the assessee might let out the property to a close relative which is less than ER. In such case AR does not reflect the true earning capacity of the building. To mitigate such situation ER is substituted for AR.
2. It might also happen in a case that inspite of all genuine effort the property could not be let out, in such case, ER of the building is reduced to zero and therefore its gross annual value is taken as zero.
3. It is the rent which the owner could not realise from the tenant.
4. Rule 4 : Following conditions should be satisfied to claim deduction of unrealised rent :

   (a) The tenancy is bona fide.

(b) The defaulting tenant has vacated the property or steps have been taken to compel him to vacate the property.

(c) The defaulting tenant is not in occupation of any other property of the assessee.

(d) The assessee has taken all reasonable steps to institute legal proceedings for the recovery of the unpaid rent or has satisfied the assessing officer that legal proceedings would be useless.

5. False. Deduction of unrealised rent can be claimed only for the current previous year.
6. False. Unrealised rent shall always be subtracted from actual rent and never from expected rent.
7. True.

Illustration & Problem 5.05-P3 (Simple)

Compute gross annual value from the following information:

	Case 1	*Case 2*	*Case 3*	*Case 4*	*Case 5*	*Case 6*
Municipal valuation p.a.	51	70	80	91	60	55
Fair Rent p.a.	46	65	75	96	72	45
Standard Rent p.a.	NA	63	99	99	52	44
Rent for 12 months	56	72	95	65	50	98
Unrealised rent *(UR)*	4	nil	5	6	nil	32

Ans: 52; 72; 90; 96; 52; 66.

Solution

	Case 1	*Case 2*	*Case 3*
a. Expected rent	51	63	80
b. Actual rent	52	72	90
GAV *(a or b whichever is higher)*	52	72	90

Illustration & Problem 5.05-P4 (Difficult)

K purchases the property on 11-9-2005. Find out the GAV for the AY 2007-08.

	Case 1	*Case 2*	*Case 3*	*Case 4*	*Case 5*	*Case 6*
Municipal valuation	100	100	185	97	36	22
Fair Rent	140	140	140	96	40	33
Standard Rent	160	160	200	NA	35	55
Actual Rent in month	15.33	14.5	20	8.25	2	NA
Unrealised rent in Rs.	20	50	50	20	nil	nil
Let out period *(in months)*	9	10	11	10	11	nil
Vacancy period *(in months)*	3	2	1	2	1	12

Ans: 118; 111; 170; 80.50; 33; Nil.

Solution

	Case 1	*Case 2*	*Case 3*
a. Expected rent	140	140	185
b. Actual rent	164	124	190
c. Loss on account of vacancy	15.33 × 3 = 46	14.5 × 2 = 29	20 × 1 = 20
GAV (*a or b whichever is higher less c*)	118	111	170

Illustration & Problem 5.05-P5 (Difficult)

(A) K purchases the property on 11-11-2005. Find out the gross annual value for the assessment year 2007-08.

	Case 1	*Case 2*	*Case 3*	*Case 4*	*Case 5*	*Case 6*
Municipal valuation	700	NA	380	200	120	900
Fair Rent	400	540	380	250	134	850
Standard Rent	800	460	390	60	NA	NA
Actual Rent in month	40	60	32	90	60	NA
Unrealised rent in Rs.	–	5	10	nil	20	nil
Let out period *(in months)*	12	11	1	0.50	8	nil
SOP for residence *(in months)*	nil	1	11	11.50	4	12

(B) What would be your answer if the property remains vacant instead of self occupied for residence.

Ans (A) : 700; 655; 380; 60; 460; Nil; (B) 700; 655; 28; 45; 460; Nil.

Solution

	Case 1	*Case 2*
a. Expected rent	700	460
b. Actual rent	(40 × 12) = 480	(60 × 11) – 5 = 655
GAV (*a or b whichever is higher less c*)	700	655

Illustration & Problem 5.05-P6 (Difficult)

K, purchases the property on 11-9-2005. Find out the GAV for the AY 2007-08.

	Case 1	*Case 2*	*Case 3*	*Case 4*	*Case 5*	*Case 6*
Municipal valuation	980	980	450	450	800	900
Fair Rent	850	850	600	600	134	850
Actual Rent in month	98	40	60	80	60	NA
Let out period *(in months)*	9	7	1	2	223 days	nil
SOP for residence *(in months)*	1	2	10	3	8 days	6
Vacancy period *(in months)*	2	3	1	7	135 days	6

Ans: 882; 860; 540; 160; 530; Nil.

Solution

	Case 1	*Case 2*	*Case 3*
a. Expected rent (ER)	980	980	600
b. Actual rent (AR)	1,078	400	120
c. Loss on account of vacancy	196	120	60
GAV (*a or b whichever is higher less c*)	882	860	540

Illustration 5.05-P7 (Typical)

Mr. Taxcrazy purchased a house on 1-9-2004 and was let out from 1-1-2005 at a rent of Rs. 4,000 p.m. On 1-9-2006 the tenant vacated the house and it remained vacant for five months. From 1-2-2007 it was again let out at a rent of Rs. 5,000 p.m. During the PY he paid Rs. 2,000 as municipal tax. You are required to compute Income from House Property for the AY 2007-08 on the following assumption :

Case 1 : Expected rent is Rs. 50,000

Case 2 : Expected rent is Rs. 1,00,000.

Ans: (1) 19,600; (2) 51,100.

Solution : Case 1

Computation of Income from House Property

a. Expected rent	50,000
b. Actual Rent (5 × 4,000 × 5 × 5,000 + 2 × 5,000)	55,000
c. Loss on account of vacancy (5 × 5,000)	25,000
Gross Annual Value (*a or b whichever is higher less c*)	30,000
Less : Municipal tax	2,000
Net annual value	28,000
Less : Standard deduction (30% of NAV)	8,400
Income from House Property	19,600

Problem 5.05-P8 (Typical)

(A) Mr. Taxcrazy purchased a house on 1-4-2006 and was let out from 1-4-2006 at a rent of Rs. 2,000 p.m. On 1-10-2006 the tenant vacated the house and it remained vacant for three months. From 1-1-2007 it was again let out at a rent of Rs. 3,000 p.m. During the PY he paid Rs. 5,000 as municipal tax and interest on borrowed capital Rs. 6,000. You are required to compute Income from House Property for the AY 2007-08 on the following assumption :

Case 1 : Standard Rent Rs. 24,000; Fair rent Rs. 18,000

Case 2 : Standard Rent Rs. 36,000; Fair rent Rs. 40,000

(B) What if the house is self occupied for residence instead of remaining vacant.

Ans (A) : (1) 5,200; (2) 9,400; (B) 5,200; 15,700.

Problem 5.05-P9 [Pass 2001]

'X' owns a house property consisting of three units of equal size. The property is let out on a monthly rent of Rs. 4,000 p.m per unit. Rent realised is Rs. 1,36,000 Fair rent of the house is Rs. 1,50,000. During the year one of the units remains vacant for two months. Find out the GAV.

Ans: 1,42,000.

Problem 5.05-P10 [Pass 2000]

Mr. X owns a house in Delhi since 2003. He let out the house on a monthly rent of Rs. 4,000. His tenant vacates the house on January 1, 2007. After that he uses the house for his own residential purpose. The municipal value of the house is Rs. 42,000 and its fair rental value is Rs. 48,000. During the PY 2006-07, Mr. X paid Rs. 5,000 as house tax, out of which Rs. 3,000 was collected from the tenant. Compute Income from house property for the AY 2007-08.

Solution

Computation of income from House Property for assessment year 2007-08

a. Expected Rent	48,000
b. Actual Rent	36,000
c. Loss on account of vacancy	Nil
GAV (a & b whichever is higher less c)	48,000
Less : Municipal tax	2,000
NAV	46,000
Less : Standard Deduction	13,800
Income from House Property	32,200

Problem 5.05-P11 [CS D01]

From the following information, find out the income from the house property which is let out for 9 months and self-occupied as residence for 3 months :

Rent received for 9 months (per month)	Rs. 3,000
Annual municipal valuation	Rs. 40,000
Fair rent	42,000
Municipal taxes - 10% of municipal valuation (only 80% was paid)	
Interest on borrowed capital	Rs. 20,000

Annual Charges and ground rent were also paid Rs. 15,000.

Ans: 7,160

Problem 5.05-P12 [CA M97]

Ram owned a house property at Madras which was occupied by him for the purpose of his residence. He was transferred to Bombay in June 2006 and therefore he let out the property with effect from July 1, 2006 on a monthly rent of Rs. 3,000. The corporation tax payable in respect of the property was Rs. 6,000 of which 50 per cent was paid by him before March 31, 2007. Interest on money borrowed for the construction of the property amounted to Rs. 20,000. Compute the income from house property for the assessment year 2007-08. assumming that municipal valuation is Rs. 28,000 and fair rent is Rs. 31,000 Standard rent is Rs. 30,000.

Ans: 3,100.

Problem 5.05-P13 [Pass 2004]

Compute taxable income from house property from the following particulars :

Fair market rent	80,000
Actual Rent	72,000
Municipal valuation	50,000
Standard Rent	60,000
Municipal Taxes	20%
Interest paid	18,000

Ans: 25,400.

Problem 5.05-P14 (Difficult)

Compute Income from House Property for the AY 2007-08.

	House 1 Let out for residence	*House 2 Let out for Business*	*House 3 SOP for business*
Fair Rent	1,50,000	2,00,000	60,000
Actual Rent	12,000 p.m.	20,000 p.m.	NA
Vacancy	NA	1 month	NA
Self occupied for residence	2 months	NA	NA
Municipal tax paid by owner on 1-1-2006	6,000	4,000	2,000
Interest on borrowed Capital	36,000	40,000	45,000

Ans: 1,83,000.

Problem 5.05-P15 (Difficult)

On the basis of following information compute Mr. Deepal's "Income from House Property" for the assessment year 2007-08.

	Property A	*Property B*	*Property C*
Municipal value (Rs.)	2,48,980	1,80,000	3,00,000
Fair Rent (Rs.)	2,64,000	2,40,00	3,00,000
Standard Rent (Rs.) (under Rent Control Act)	3,00,000	1,60,000	2,50,000
Let out at monthly rent of (Rs.)	23,000	14,000	25,000
Months during which property remained vacant during 2006-07	2	3	—
Annual Municipal tax fixed (Rs.)	24,000	18,000	30,000
Tax paid by tenant	—	4,500	5,000
Outstanding municipal tax as on 31.3.2007 (Rs.)	2,000	4,500	7,500
Collection Charges and Miscellaneous Expenses (Rs.)	72,000	48,000	84,000

Ans: 4,25,250.

(E) *COMPUTATION OF EXPECTED RENT AND ACTUAL RENT WHERE THE ASSESSEE BECOMES OWNER DURING THE RELEVANT PY TO COMPUTE GROSS ANNUAL VALUE

Where the assessee purchases the property during the PY 2006-76 or construction is completed during the PY 2006-07, then ownership is calculated from the date when building comes into existence.

E.g. Mr. X purchases the property on 1-4-2006 and let it out for Rs. 2,000 p.m. It means he is owner for 12 months for the PY 2006-07, therefore, expected rent and actual rent shall be computed for 12 months. But where however he purchases the property on 1-1-2007 then expected rent and actual rent shall be computed for only 3 months for the PY 2006-07.

Illustration & Problems 5.05-P16 (Typical)

(A) K, purchases the property on 1-6-2006 and is let out on the same day. Find out the GAV for the AY 2007-08.

	Case 1	*Case 2*	*Case 3*	*Case 4*
Municipal valuation in annum	3,600	1,780	1,100	2,100
Fair rent in annum	3,900	3,500	1,250	2,000
Standard rent in annum	4,200	3,980	NA	NA
Rent in month	350	420	100	210
Unrealised rent in Rs.	805	800	nil	210
Vacancy period *(in month)*	1	15 days	6	8

(B) Solve if the property remains self occupied for residence instead of remaining vacant.

Ans (A) : 2,900; 3,190; 441.67; 210; (B) 3,250; 3,190; 1,041.67; 1,750.

Solution

Computation of Gross Annual Value

Since the property is acquired on 1-6-2006, expected rent and actual rent shall be computed from 1-6-2006 to 31-3-2007 *i.e* for 10 months. ER & AR is to be converted in value of 10 months.

Expected rent of 12 months (*MV or FR whichever is higher limited to SR*)	3,900
a. Expected rent for 10 months	3,250
b. Actual rent for 10 months (350 × 10 – 805)	2,695
c. Loss on account of vacancy *(350 × 1)*	350
Gross Annual Value (*a or b whichever is higher less c*)	2,900

Problem 5.05-P17

(A) Mr. Taxcrazy purchased a house on 1-5-2006 and was let out on same day at a rent of Rs. 5,000 p.m. On 1-11-2006 the tenant vacated the house and it remained vacant for two months. From 1-1-2006 it was again let out at a rent of Rs. 7,000 p.m. During the PY he paid Rs. 1,000 as municipal tax and interest on borrowed capital Rs. 12,000. You are required to compute Income from House Property for the AY 2007-08 on the following assumption :

Case 1 : Standard rent Rs. 60,000; Fair rent Rs. 72,000

Case 2 : Municipal valuation Rs. 50,000; Fair rent Rs. 72,000.

(B) Solve if the property self occupied for residence instead of remaining vacant.

Ans (A) : 23,000; 23,700; (B) 25,800; 33,500.

(F) * TAX TREATMENT OF ADVANCE RENT

As you know actual rent is computed on due basis, therefore, treatment of advance rent shall be in the year in which it falls due and not in the year of receipt.

Problem 5.05-P18 (Typical)

Actual rent Rs. 8,000 p.m. X gets 8 months advance rent of Rs. 64,000 in the PY 2006-07. Expected rent of the property Rs. 75,000. Compute gross annual value for the AY 2007-08.

Ans: 96,000.

TOPIC 5.06 *SECTION 23(2)*. COMPUTATION OF INCOME FROM HOUSE PROPERTY IF PROPERTY IS 'SELF OCCUPIED FOR RESIDENCE'

(A) MEANING

Where the owner occupies the property for his own residence then such property is known as self occupied property for residence. Even if the property is occupied by his family members then also it is treated as self occupied property for residence. But where the house is occupied by other relatives or friends then such house shall not be treated as self occupied for residence.

(B) CONDITIONS FOR TREATMENT OF PROPERTY AS SELF OCCUPIED PROPERTY FOR RESIDENCE

1. *23(2)(a). SOP for residence* : Where one property is in the occupation of the owner for the purposes of his own residence for whole year then its GAV is taken as nil; or
2. *23(2)(b). Deemed SOP for residence* : Where the property cannot actually be occupied by the owner by reason of the fact that owing to his employment, business or profession carried on at any other place, he has to reside at that other place in a building not belonging to him. In such a case its GAV is taken as nil.

(C) DEDUCTION ALLOWED IF THE PROPERTY IS SELF OCCUPIED FOR RESIDENCE

No deduction on account of municipal tax or standard deduction is available except interest on borrowed capital which is maximum of Rs. 30,000. However if all the following conditions are satisfied then maximum of Rs. 1,50,000 interest is allowed as deduction.

1. The loan is borrowed for the purpose of *purchase or construction* of residential house property.
2. The loan is borrowed *on or after* 1-4-1999.
3. The residential property is purchased or construction is completed *within* 3 years of the end of the financial year in which loan is borrowed.

E.g. Suppose the date of borrowing is 15-6-2003, therefore it is borrowed in the FY 2003-04, end of the FY 2003-04 is 31-3-2004, add 3 years to it. It means the construction of the property should be completed by 31-3-2007. Let us now check each FY.

FY 2002-03	31-3-2006
FY 2003-04	31-3-2007
FY 2004-05	31-3-2008
FY 2005-06	31-3-2009

It means if any of the above three conditions are not satisfied maximum interest allowed is Rs. 30,000. E.g.

1. The loan is borrowed for the purpose of *repais, renovation* of residential house property.
2. The loan is borrowed *before* 1-4-1999.
3. The residential property is purchased or construction is completed *after* 3 years of the end of the financial year in which loan is borrowed.

Note

- Do note that maximum limit of interest applicable only to SOP for residence and not for let out and deemed to be let out property.

Problem 5.06-P1

1. When interest on borrowed capital is always limited to Rs. 30,000 in case where the house is occupied for self residence?
2. Is limit of interest on borrowed capital applicable to all types of properties?

Solution

1. Where the loan is borrowed for the purpose of repairs etc. *i.e.* not for purchase or construction of house then interest on borrowed capital is always to a maximum of Rs. 30,000 irrespective of when the loan is borrowed or construction is completed.
2. No. Refer the table below :

	Municipal tax	*Stan. Ded.*	*Interest*
a. Let out property	allowed	allowed	no limit
b. Deemed to be let out property	allowed	allowed	no limit
c. Vacant property for whole year	allowed	not allowed	no limit
d. Self occupied property for residence	Not allowed	Not allowed	limit it

Illustration 5.06-P2

	Loan 1	*Loan 2*
Purpose of loan	Construction	Repairs
Date of borrowing	1-6-2002	1-6-2002
Date of purchase	9-1-2005	NA
Situation 1 : Interest on borrowed capital	nil	40,000
Situation 2 : Interest on borrowed capital	1,80,000	nil
Situation 3 : Interest on borrowed capital	70,000	35,000
Situation 4 : Interest on borrowed capital	1,55,000	45,000

Solution

	Interest from Loan 1 limited to 1,50,000	*Interest from Loan 2 limited to 30,000*	*Total interest limited to 1,50,000*
Situation 1	nil	30,000	30,000
Situation 2	1,50,000	nil	1,50,000
Situation 3	70,000	30,000	1,00,000
Situation 4	1,50,000	30,000	1,50,000

- The aggregate deduction on account of interest cannot exceed Rs. 1,50,000 during the previous year.

Problem 5.06-P3 (Difficult)

Compute Income from house property from the following information :

	House 1	*House 2*	*House 3*
Expected rent	1,20,000	1,30,000	1,60,000
Actual Rent	15,000 p.m.	N.A.	N.A.
Self occupied property for residence	10 month	12 month	N.A.
Vacancy	N.A.	N.A.	12 month
Municipal tax paid	6,000	8,000	10,000
Interest on borrowed capital for repairs	60,000	70,000	11,000

Ans: (31,200)

Problem 5.06-P4 (Difficult)

Compute Income from house property from the following information:

	House 1	*House 2*	*House 3*	*House 4*
Expected rent	2,00,000	1,00,000	4,00,000	6,00,000
Actual Rent	16,000 p.m.	N.A.	12,000 p.m.	N.A.
Self occupied property for residence	1 month	N.A.	3 month	12 month
Vacancy	2 month	12 month	1 month	N.A.
Municipal tax paid	10,000	10,000	5,000	5,000
Interest on borrowed capital for repairs	6,000	31,000	32,000	1,55,000
Repairs	600	600	800	500

Ans: 2,69,700.

TOPIC 5.07 *SECTION 23(4)*. COMPUTATION IF HOUSE PROPERTY IS TREATED AS 'DEEMED TO BE LET OUT PROPERTY' (DLOP)

Where the assessee owns more than one property for his self residence for whole year and he derives no other benefit from such property then one house property according to his choice is treated as SOP for residence and the remaining property is treated as deemed to be let out property whose GAV is taken as Expected rent.

Generally the property whose GAV is maximum is taken as SOP for residence. However choice should be such that tax liability comes out to be minimum.

Problem 5.07-P1 (Difficult)

Compute Income from house property from the following information :

	House 1 SOP for residence	*House 2 SOP for residence*	*House 3 SOP for residence*
Expected rent	4,00,000	6,00,000	7,00,000
Municipal tax paid	6,000	7,000	15,000
Interest on borrowed capital for repairs	25,000	31,000	36,000

Ans: 6,04,900.

Problem 5.07-P2 (Difficult)

Compute Income from house property from the following information :

	House 1 SOP for residence	*House 2 SOP for residence*	*House 3 SOP for residence*	*House 4 Let out for residence*
Municipal valuation	1,00,000	2,00,000	60,000	95,000
Fair rent	1,50,000	3,00,000	N.A.	60,000
Standard rent	N.A.	1,90,000	70,000	40,000
Actual rent	N.A.	N.A.	N.A.	2,000 p.m.
Municipal tax paid	10%	15%	5,000	12%
Interest on borrowed capital	50,000	35,000	80,000	15,000

Ans: 18,480.

Problem 5.07-P3 [CS D00]

X owns two houses which he occupied for his residence. He submits the following particulars in respect of these houses for the financial year 2006-07 :

	House I	*House II*
Municipal valuation	12,000	24,000
Fair rent	15,000	27,000
Standard rent under Rent Control Act	9,000	20,400
Municipal tax paid	1,800	2,400
Amount spent on repairs	1,200	3,000
Interest payable on loan taken for building the houses	3,000	36,000

X also has dividends from Indian company amounting to Rs. 65,000 during the previous year. X requests you to compute his total income in a manner which minimizes his tax incidence.

Ans: (27,960)

Problem 5.07-P4

A is the owner of two houses E and H in Bombay and occupies them for the purposes of his own residence. The particulars in respect thereof are as under :

	E	H
1. Fair Rent	60,000	76,000
2. Municipal Valuation	50,000	60,000
3. House tax & Water tax paid	5,000	6,000
4. Cost of repairs	16,000	8,000
5. Fire Insurance	2,000	3,000
6. Ground Rent	1,000	2,000
7. Unrealised rent of PY 1998-99	500	Nil
8. Vacancy period	1 month	2 months

He has also to pay interest @ 18%, on the borrowed funds of Rs. 84,000 used in the construction of both the units. He has income of Rs. 24,000 from interest on securities. Compute the total income of A for Assessment Year 2007-2008.

Ans: 47,380.

Problem 5.07-P5 (Typical)

	SOP for residence House 1	*SOP for residence House 2*	*Let out for business House 3*
Date of borrowing	4-5-1999	31-3-1999	8-8-1997
Date of purchase	5-8-2002	31-3-2000	9-4-2000
Municipal valuation	1,00,000	80,000	90,000
Fair rent	2,00,000	60,000	80,000
Actual rent	–	–	12,000 p.m.
Municipal tax paid	1,000	2,000	3,000 by tenant
Interest on borrowed	1,35,000	2,000	40,000

Compute Income from House Property for the AY 2007-08 on the assumption that House 3 is self occupied for residence one month.

Ans: (30,000).

Problem 5.07-P6 (Difficult)

Mr. X owns four residential house property. Compute Total Income for the AY 2007-08 assuming that Profit from Business before allowing deductions is Rs. 3,51,000.

	House 1 SOP for residence	*House 2 SOP for residence*	*House 3 Let out for business*	*House 4 SOP for business*
Date of Purchase	1-6-2000	1-5-2000	1-8-1989	13-4-1992
GAV	60,000	70,000	90,000	1,00,000
Municipal Tax paid by owner	2,000	1,000	5,000 (by tenant)	4,000
Repairs	7,000	10,000	2,500	4,000
Interest on borrowed capital for purchase of house	36,000	2,000	1,10,000	30,000
Annual capital charge	–	1,000	–	6,000

Ans: (44,400) + 3,13,000 = 2,68,600.

Problem 5.07-P7 (Typical)

	Case 1		*Case 2*	
	House 1 SOP for residence	*House 2 SOP for residence*	*House 1 SOP for residence*	*House 2 SOP for residence*
Municipal valuation	40,000	70,000	N.A.	1,60,000
Fair rent	50,000	60,000	75,000	55,000
Standard rent	60,000	55,000	80,000	1,70,000
MT paid	10%	15%	5,000	12%
Interest on borrowed capital.	5,000	1,35,000	80,000	15,000

Compute Income from House Property for the AY 2007-08.

Ans: (47,800); (46,000).

Solution : Case 1

Let us assume both the property be DLOP

	House 1	*House 2*
Gross Annual Value	50,000	55,000
Less : Municipal tax paid [10% of MV]	(4,000)	(7,000)
Net Annual Value	46,000	48,000
Less: Standard Deduction u/s 24b [30% of NAV]	(13,800)	(14,400)
Less: Interest on borrowed capital	(5,000)	(1,35,000)
Income from House Property	27,200	(1,01,400)

Let us assume both the property be SOP-Residence

	House 1	*House 2*
Gross Annual Value	Nil	Nil
Less: Interest on borrowed capital [limited to Rs. 30,000]	(5,000)	(30,000)
Income from House Property	(5,000)	(30,000)

	House 1	*House 2*	*Total*
Option 1	SOP-R	DLOP	
	(5,000)	(1,01,400)	(1,06,400)
Option 2	DLOP	SOP-R	
	27,200	(30,000)	(2,800)

Option 1 is better since loss allowed to be set off and carry forward is more than option 2.

Problem 5.07-P8 (Typical)

Mr. X owns four residential house properties which are self occupied for residence. Compute minimum Total Income for the AY 2007-08.

	House 1	*House 2*	*House 3*	*House 4*
Date of borrowing	1-6-1998	1-5-1999	1-8-1988	13-4-1991
Date of Purchase	1-6-2001	1-5-1999	1-8-1988	13-4-1991
GAV	4,00,000	4,00,000	60,000	70,000
Interest on borrowed capital	1,80,000	2,00,000	22,000	nil

Ans: 19,000.

DEDUCTIONS UNDER SECTION 24

Introduction

No deduction other than the following two deductions are allowed from Income from House Property. However, where the property is occupied for his own business or profession then deduction like repairs, insurance, land revenue, ground rent which is incurred for business purpose can be claimed as deduction. However annual charge which is a personal charge cannot be claimed as deduction from profit from business.

TOPIC 5.08 *SECTION 24(a)*. STANDARD DEDUCTION

This is a statutory deduction and is allowed irrespective whether any expenditure in respect of building has been incurred or not. The deduction allowed is 30% of NAV. Where municipal tax is more than GAV, NAV becomes nil or negative and therefore, standard deduction of 30% of NAV is not available.

TOPIC 5.09 *SECTION 24(b)*. INTEREST ON BORROWED CAPITAL

(A) CONDITIONS

The deduction on account of interest on borrowed capital is allowed if

1. The loan is borrowed for the purpose of **P**urchase, **C**onstruction, **R**epair, **R**enewal, **R**econstruction, **R**enovation, **R**epayment of existing loan (**PCR⁵**). However where loan is borrowed for purpose other than those specified above then interest is not allowed as deduction. Like where the loan is borrowed for the purpose of payment of municipal tax then interest is not allowed as deduction;
   a. Deduction of interest is available only where there exists a relationship of borrower and lender.
   b. Interest on delayed payment or interest on unpaid interest is not deductible.
   c. Penal interest is not allowed as deduction.
2. Interest should accrue during the relevant previous year. Interest accrues if the loan is outstanding during the previous year. Interest is allowed as deduction on accrual basis and not on actual payment basis. *E.g.* Interest accrues Rs. 15,000 but he actually pays Rs. 20,000 including advance payment of Rs. 5,000. In such case deduction shall be allowed only for Rs. 15,000;
3. The building should be in existence during the relevant previous year. The building comes into existence in the previous year when construction of building is completed or when the building is purchased. If building is not in existence, interest on borrowed capital is not allowed as deduction. *E.g.* Suppose the date of construction of building is 5-5-2006. The previous year the building comes into existence shall be the year 2006-07 therefore deduction shall be allowed from the previous year 2006-07. Similarly it can be determined for other dates.

(B) INTEREST ON BORROWED CAPITAL IS DIVIDED INTO TWO CATEGORIES

1. *Pre-construction period interest.* The period other than post construction period is pre-construction period. Its computation is done as given below :

Ascertainment of pre-construction period

Date of Borrowing to	
31st March immediately prior to the date building comes into existence	Date of repayment of loan
whichever date is earlier	

The deduction of pre-construction period is allowed in 5 equal instalments from the previous year in which building comes into existence.

2. *Post-construction period interest.* The post construction period always starts from the previous year in which building comes into existence. Where the loan is repaid before the building comes into existence post construction period does not exist.

Illustration 5.09-P1 (Difficult)

Mr. Taxcrazy borrowed Rs. 1,00,000 @ 12% p.a. on 1-6-2002 for construction of the house. The loan is re-paid on 31-3-2009. The construction of house was completed on 5-9-2004. Compute interest on borrowed capital deductible u/s 24(b) of the Income Tax Act for the AY 2007-08.

Solution

Computation of pre-construction period interest

Date of borrowing 1-6-2002

Date of completion of construction (31-3-2004) 5-9-2004

Date of repayment of loan 31-3-2009

Comparing the two dates, date of purchase of property *i.e.* 5-9-2004 and date of repayment of loan *i.e.* 31-3-2009, the earlier date is 31-3-2004, therefore pre-construction period is from 1-6-2002 to 31-3-2004 which comes to 1 year 10 months. Interest for 1 year 10 months shall be Rs. 22,000. Deduction is allowed in 5 equal instalment which is equal to 22,000 ÷ 5 = Rs. 4,400.

Computation of post-construction period interest

Since the building comes into existence on 5-9-2004 therefore post-construction period starts from the PY 2004-05 *i.e.* from 1-4-2004 to till the date loan is repaid.

Allowability deduction of interest

Deduction of interest is allowed from the previous year in which the building comes into existence. In this case building came into existance on 5-9-2004 therefore deduction of interest shall be allowed from the previous year 2004-05.

	2004-05	2005-06	2006-07	2007-08	2008-09
Pre-construction period interest	4,400	4,400	4,400	4,400	4,400
Post-construction period interest	12,000	12,000	12,000	12,000	12,000
Total interest allowed as deduction	16,400	16,400	16,400	16,400	16,400

Note

- Though we have shown computation of 5 years, you are required to compute only for the PY 2006-07.

Illustration 5.09-P2 (Difficult)

Mr. Taxcrazy borrowed Rs. 1,00,000 @ 12% p.a. on 1-6-2003 for construction of the house. The construction of house was completed on 7-8-2005. The loan is re-paid on 5-1-2005. Compute interest on borrowed capital deductible u/s 24(b) of the Income Tax Act for the AY 2007-08.

Solution

Computation of pre-construction period interest

Date of borrowing 1-6-2003

Date of completion of construction (31-3-2005) 7-8-2005

Date of repayment of loan 5-1-2005

Pre-construction period interest

The earlier date is 5-1-2005, therefore pre-construction period is from 1-6-2003 to 5-1-2005 which comes to 1 year 214 days. Interest for 1 year 214 days shall be Rs. 19,133. *(1 year = 360 days)*. Deduction is allowed in 5 equal instalments which is equal to 19,133 ÷ 5 = Rs. 3,827.

Computation of post-construction period interest

Since the building comes into existence on 7-8-2005 therefore post-construction period start from the PY 2005-06 *i.e.* from 1-4-2005 to till the date loan is repaid. Since the loan is repaid before the building came into existence post construction period does not exist.

Allowability deduction of interest

Deduction of interest is allowed from the previous year in which the building comes into existance. In this case building came into existence on 7-8-2005 therefore deduction of interest shall be allowed from the previous year 2005-06.

	2005-06	2006-07	2007-08	2008-09	2009-10
Pre-construction period interest	3,827	3,827	3,827	3,827	3,827
Post - construction period interest	Nil	Nil	Nil	Nil	Nil
Total interest allowed as deduction	3,827	3,827	3,827	3,827	3,827

Illustration 5.09-P3 (Difficult)

Mr. Taxcrazy borrowed Rs. 1,00,000 @ 12% p.a. on 16-7-1997 for purchase of the house. He purchases the house on 31-3-2002. The loan is re paid on 17-7-2005. Compute interest on borrowed capital deductible u/s 24(b) of the Income Tax Act for the AY 2007-08.

Solution

Date of borrowing	16-7-1997
Date of purchase of property	31-3-2001 (31-3-2002)
Date of repayment of loan	17-7-2005

Pre-construction period interest

The earlier date is 31-3-2001, therefore pre-construction period is from 16-7-1997 to 31-3-2001 which comes to 3 years 255 days. Interest for 3 years 255 days shall be Rs. 44,500. *(1 year = 360 days)*. Deduction is allowed in 5 equal instalments which is equal to 44,500 ÷ 5 = Rs. 8,900.

Allowability deduction of interest

Deduction of interest is allowed from the previous year in which the building comes into existence. In this case building came into existence on 31-3-2002 therefore deduction of interest shall be allowed from the previous year 2001-02.

	2001-02	2002-03	2003-04	2004-05	2005-06	2006-07
Pre-construction period interest	8,900	8,900	8,900	8,900	8,900	Nil
Post - construction period interest	12,000	12,000	12,000	12,000	12,000	3,533
Total interest allowed as deduction	20,900	20,900	20,900	20,900	20,900	3,533

Problem 5.09-P4 (Difficult)

Mr. Taxcrazy borrowed Rs. 1,00,000 @ 12% p.a. for purchase of the house. Compute interest on borrowed capital deductible u/s 24(b) of the Income Tax Act as per the AY 2007-08.

	Case 1	*Case 2*	*Case 3*	*Case 4*	*Case 5*
Date of borrowing	1-10-1998	1-11-2004	1-7-2002	1-11-2000	1-6-2006
Date of purchase	1-11-2001	31-3-2007	1-1-2006	1-7-2002	31-3-20076
Date of repayment of loan	not paid	1-10-2006	1-5-2003	1-2-2007	1-3-2007
	Case 6	*Case 7*	*Case 8*	*Case 9*	*Case 10*
Date of borrowing	1-9-1999	1-10-1997	1-11-1999	15-7-2002	15-3-2000
Date of purchase	1-1-2005	31-3-2000	1-6-2004	31-3-2005	31-3-2005
Date of repayment of loan	1-5-2001	1-6-2006	1-10-2003	31-3-2005	31-3-2000

Ans:

	Case 1	*Case 2*	*Case 3*	*Case 4*	*Case 5*
Pre-interest	Nil	3,400	2,000	3,400	Nil
Post-interest	12,000	6,000	Nil	10,000	9,000
Total interest	12,000	9,400	2,000	13,400	9,000
	Case 6	*Case 7*	*Case 8*	*Case 9*	*Case 10*
Pre-interest	4,000	Nil	9,400	4,107	107
Post-interest	Nil	2,000	Nil	Nil	Nil
Total interest	4,000	2,000	9,400	4,107	107

Problem 5.09-P5 [Pass 1999]

Mr. 'X' is the owner of a house kept for self-residence. The particulars of the house are:

Standard rent	55,000
Municipal valuation	60,000
Fair rent	58,000

'X' borrowed Rs 20,000 @ 18% p.a. for construction of the house (date of borrowing 1-6-2003 date of repayment of loan 31-5-2006).

Compute the Income from house property for the AY 2007-08.

Ans: (600)

Problem 5.09-P6 [Pass 1998]

Mr. X took a loan of Rs 2,00,000 @15% interest per annum from L.I.C on 1-4-2001, for the purpose of the construction of his house. The house was completed on 20-3-2006.

Compute Income from House property for the AY 2007-08 if (i) Let out and (ii) self occupied property for residence.

Ans: (39,600); (30,000)

Problem 5.09-P7 [Pass 2001]

"Y' took a loan of Rs. 10,00,000 @ 18% p.a. on 1-5-2006 and acquired a new flat on the same day. Compute for the AY 2007-08 the amount of interest deductible in computing the income of house property if the flat is :

(i) let out; and

(ii) self-occupied.

Ans: 1,65,000; 1,50,000.

(C) *SECTION 25. INTEREST ON BORROWED CAPITAL

Section 25 Interest payable outside India : Notwithstanding anything contained in section 24, any interest chargeable under this Act which is payable outside India, on which tax has not been paid or deducted and in respect of which there is no person in India who may be treated as an agent under section 163 shall not be deducted in computing the income chargeable under the head "Income from house property".

Problem 5.09-P8 (Typical)

Compute Income from House Property for the AY 2007-08.

	House 1 Let out for business	*House 2 Let out for resid.*	*House 3 SOP for residence*	*House 4 SOP for business*
Fair Rent	70,000	1,00,000	6,00,000	1,00,000
Municipal Valuation	80,000	2,00,000	7,00,000	NA
Actual Rent	8,000 p.m.	5,000 p.m.	NA	NA
Vacancy (in period)	1 month	Nil	NA	NA
Unrealised Rent in Rs.	1,000	Nil	NA	NA
Municipal tax paid by tenant	3,000	2,000	Nil	Nil
Repairs	2,000	6,000	15,000	10,000
Interest on borrowed Capital	45,000	20,000	70,000	38,000

Ans: 1,05,900.

TOPIC 5.10 COMPUTATION OF INCOME FROM HOUSE PROPERTY WHERE PART OF THE PROPERTY IS PARTLY IS LET OUT AND REMAINING PART IS SOP-R OR VACANT OR BOTH

Illustration 5.10-P1 (Typical)

K, purchases the property on 15-2-2002, since then it is let out for residential purpose. Find out Income from House Property for the AY 2007-08.

10% SOP for resid.	Let out for 10 months at Rs. 1,800 p.m. 2 months self occupied for residence	Municipal valuation Fair Rent Interest on borrowed capital	25,000 20,000 20,000

Solution

Unit 1 (10% SOP-R)

Net annual value		Nil
Less : Deduction u/s 24		
• Standard deduction	Nil	
• Interest on borrowed capital *(10% SOP)*	2,000	(2,000)
Income from Unit 1		(2,000)

Unit 2 (90% let out property)

Expected rent *(90% of 25,000)*		22,500
Actual Rent *(1,800 × 10)*		18,000
Net annual value		22,500
Less : Deduction u/s 24		
• Standard deduction	6,750	
• Interest on borrowed capital *(90% of 20,000)*	18,000	24,750
Income from Unit 2		(2,250)

Computation of Income from House Property

Income from Unit 1	(2,000)
Income from Unit 2	(2,250)
Income from House Property	(4,250)

Problem 5.10-P2 [CS D96]

R owns a house. The municipal value of the house is Rs. 80,000. He paid Rs. 80,000 as local taxes during the year. He uses this house for his residential purposes but lets out half of the house at Rs. 3,000 per month with effect from 1st January, 2007. Compute the annual value of the house.

Ans: nil; 31,000.

Problem 5.10-P3 [Hons 2004]

A owns a residential house property. It has two identical units - Unit I and Unit II. While unit I is self-occupied by A and his family members, Unit II is let out (rent being Rs. 7,000 per month, this unit remained vacant for one month during which it was self-occupied.) Municipal value of the property is Rs. 1,25,000. Standard rent is Rs. 1,35,000 and fair rent is Rs. 1,50,000.

Municipal tax is imposed @ 12% (on Municipal value) which is paid by A. Other expenses for the previous year 2006-07 being repairs Rs. 5,000, insurance Rs. 6,000.

A borrowed Rs. 8,00,000 on 1-7-2003 from L.I.C @ 12% p.a. to construct the property. Construction of the house was completed on June 30, 2005. The entire loan is still unpaid.

Compute the income of Mr. A for the assessment year 2007-08 on the assumption that income of A from other sources is Rs. 2,00,000.

Ans: 1,19,050.

Problem 5.10-P4 [Pass 1996]

For the AY 2007-08, compute Income from House Property on the basis of the following information:

• Municipal value of the house	40,000
• Municipal taxes paid	8,000

House was self-occupied for residential purposes. But half of the house was let out @ Rs. 2,000 p.m. from 1-10-2006.

A loan of Rs 40,000 was taken on April 1, 2001 @ 15% p.a. for the construction of this house. The house was completed on 31-5-2002 and only half the loan was refunded on 1-10-2006.

Ans: (100)

Problem 5.10-P5 (Typical)

Mr. Taxcrazy started the construction of a house on 1-4-2005 and it was completed on 31-5-2006. This house consists of three residential units. First unit covers 50% area of the whole house while each of the second and third unit covers 25% area of the whole house. A loan of Rs. 1,00,000 was taken on 1-10-2005 for the construction of this house, the interest is payable @ 10% p.a. on it. 50% portion of the house is used by Taxcrazy for his own residence since 1st June., 25% portion of the house was let out to Sameer from

1st August at a rent of Rs. 1,250 p.m. and the remaining 25% portion was also let out to Pooja from 1st October, at a rent of Rs. 1,250 p.m. Pooja vacated 25% portion on 31st December and Taxcrazy used this portion also for his own residence from 1st January, 2007. The municipal valuation and fair rent of the whole house is Rs. 48,000. Local taxes are paid @ 10% of the municipal valuation. The details of the expenditure of this house are as under :

1.	Municipal tax paid *(for 10 months)*	Rs. 4,000
2.	Interest on loan paid *(from 1-10-2005 to 31-3-2007)*	Rs. 15,000

Compute the Income from House Property for the AY 2007-08.

Ans: (1,900) Let out Rs. 3,600; SOP for residence Rs. (5,500).

Illustration 5.10-P6 (Typical)

K purchases the property on 18-3-2005 and let it out on the same day. His income from business without allowing any deduction is Rs. 50,000. Interest on borrowed capital Rs. 10,000; annual charge Rs. 1,000; Municipal taxes paid Rs. 3,000; Land revenue Rs. 500; Depreciation of the building 12,000. Find out Taxable Income for the AY 2007-08.

25% is SOP for residence 25% SOP for business	50% let out for Rs. 5,000 p.m. for 8 months 4 months vacant	Municipal valuation Fair rent Unrealised rent	51,000 50,000 1,000

Solution

Unit 1 (25% SOP-R)

NAV		Nil
Less : Deduction u/s 24		
• Standard deduction	Nil	
• Interest on borrowed capital *(25% of 10,000)*	2,500	(2,500)
Income from Unit 1		(2,500)

Unit 2 (50% let out property)

(a) Expected rent (50% of 51,000)		25,500
(b) Actual Rent (5,000 × 12 – 1,000)		59,000
(c) Loss on account of vacancy *(4 × 5,000)*		20,000
GAV (a or b whichever is higher less c)		39,000
Less : Municipal tax paid *(50% of 3,000)*		1,500
NAV		37,500
Less : Deduction u/s 24		
• Standard deduction	11,250	
• Interest on borrowed capital *(50% of 10,000)*	5,000	16,250
Income from Unit 2		21,250

Unit 3 (25% self occupied for business)

Since the house is occupied for his own business, the income or expenditure is chargeable under the head 'Profit from Business'

Profit from Business		50,000
Less : Admissible		
• Municipal tax paid *(25% of 3,000)*	750	
• Depreciation *(25% of 12,000)*	3,000	
• Land revenue *(25% of 500)*	125	
• Interest on borrowed capital *(25% of 10,000))*	2,500	6,375
Profit from Business		43,625

Computation of Total Income

Income from House Property :		
• Income from Unit 1	(2,500)	
• Income from Unit 2	21,250	18,750
Profit from Business		43,625
Gross Total Income		62,375
Less : Deduction u/s 80C to 80U		nil
Total Income		62,375

Problem 5.10-P7 [Hons 2004C]

Mr. Z is an owner of a big house, the construction of which was completed in April 2004. 50% portion of the house was let out for residential purpose at Rs. 4,000 p.m. 25% portion is used by Z for his own profession whereas remaining portion is used by him for his own residence. The following expenses were incurred in connection with this house :

Municipal Taxes	10,000
Repairs	4,000
Interest on loan taken to renovate the house	3,200
Fire insurance premium	1,200
Ground rent	3,000

Municipal value of the house is Rs. 80,000 Rented portion remained vacant for one month. Income from business is Rs. 1,10,000 without debiting municipal tax and other incidental expenditure including admissible depreciation of Rs. 1,000 on the portion used for business. Determine taxable income of Mr. Z for the assessment year 2007-08.

Ans: 1,28,550.

Problem 5.10-P8 (Typical)

Taxcrazy, purchases the vacant plot of land on 1-1-2006 and completes the construction of ground floor on 1-5-2006 and one month later construction of first floor was also completed. Both the floors were self occupied on the date of completion of construction.

On 15-9-2006 it starts construction of second floor whose constuction was completed on 31-10-2006. The second floor was let out to Miss Moss on a monthly rent of Rs. 11,000 from the date of completion of construction.

Its roof top was also let out to Bharti for installation of cellular tower on the same day on a monthly rent of Rs. 35,000 and a refundable security deposit of Rs. 10,00,000.

Fair rent of house ascertained was Rs. 6,00,000. You are required to compute Total Income for the assessment year 2007-08.

Ans: 3,50,000.

Problem 5.10-P9 (Difficult)

Mr. X owns a house in Delhi. During the previous year 2006-07, 3/4th portion of the house was self-occupied for full year and 1/4th portion was let out for residential purposes from 1-4-2006 to 31-12-2006 on a rent of Rs. 1,400 p.m. From 1-1-2007 this portion was also used for own residence. Municipal valuation of the house is Rs. 20,000. He incurred the following expenditure in respect of the house property.

Municipal taxes due Rs. 12,000; Repairs Rs. 4,000; Fire insurance premium Rs. 7,000; Land Revenue Rs. 8,000; Ground Rent Rs. 4,000 were paid during the year. A loan of Rs. 2,00,000 was taken on 1-4-2002 @ 9% p.a. for the construction of the house which was completed on 28-3-2003. Nothing was repaid on loan account so far.

Find out his income from house property for the assessment year 2007-08.

Ans: (9,180)

TOPIC 5.11 *SPLITTING OF COMPOSITE RENT TO COMPUTE GROSS ANNUAL VALUE

1. What is let out is, building therefore what is chargeable to tax only rent of a building. But where owner lets out the building along with other facilities and receives composite rent from the tenant, then charges received for the facilities shall be deducted from composite rent to compute original rent of the building.
2. Facilitie includes amenities like furniture and fixtures, electricity supply, provision of lifts, supply of water, watchman & ward facilities.

   However no adjustment shall be made for following payments made by the tenant. Municipal tax, Insurance premium, repairs expenses of the house, Interest on security deposit made by the tenant.
3. Income from facilities provided shall be charged under the head "Profit from business" or "Income from Other Sources" depending upon case to case.
4. However if such composite rent is not separable, the entire rental income is assessed under the head "Income from Other Sources" or "Profits from Business" as the case may be.

Problem 5.11-P1 (Typical)

Mr. Taxcrazy owns a house property in Kolkata which is let out to Amir Khan on a composite rent of Rs. 6,000 p.m. Municipal tax levied @ 5% of the municipal valuation which during the PY amounted to Rs. 5,000. Half of the municipal taxes are borne by the tenant while remaining amount of municipal taxes were outstanding at the end of the PY. However Mr. Taxcrazy paid Rs. 4,350 of the municipal taxes during the PY which were outstanding for the PY 2004-05. Fair rent of the house is Rs. 80,000. Standard rent is not applicable. The total rent realised by the Taxcrazy during the year is Rs. 60,000. Amir Khan vacated the house at the end of February.

Amir Khan is provided with following amenities :

	Charges paid by Amir	*Expenditure incurred by the Taxcrazy*
Water facility	Rs. 30 p.m.	Rs. 20 p.m.
Electricity facility	Rs. 300 p.m.	Rs. 450 p.m.
Lift facility	Rs. 20 p.m.	Rs. 10 p.m.

Mr. Taxcrazy also owns a residential plot of land in Delhi which is let out to a warehousing company at the rent of Rs. 16,000 p.m.

Compute total income for the AY 2007-08 on the assumption that Rule 4 conditions are satisfied.

Ans: 2,53,220. [1,00,000–5,650=94,350–4,350=90,000–27,000=63,000+3,500–5,280+1,92,000=2,53,220.]

COMPREHENSIVE PROBLEMS

Problem 5.11-P2 [Pass 2006]

Mr. X owns a house property construction of which was completed on 1st Dec., 2005. It has been let out from 1st June, 2006 for residential purpose. Its particular for the pervious year 2006-07 are given below :

	Rs.
Municipal valuation	85,000
Expected rent	80,000
Standard rent	85,000
Actual rent (p.m.)	6,000
Municipal taxes paid (including Rs. 2,000 paid by tenant)	12,000
Collection charges	5,000

Mr. X took the loan of Rs. 60,000 @ 12% p.a. for the construction of the house on 1st April, 2003. Loan is still unpaid. Calculate the income under the head 'income from house property' for the previous year 2006-07.

Solution

Computation of Income from House Property for the AY 2007-08

		Rs.
Municipal valuation		85,000
Expected rent assumd to be a fair rent		80,000
Standard rent		85,000
Expected rent		85,000
Actual rent		72,000
Gross annual value		85,000
Less : Municipal tax		10,000
Net annual value		75,000
Less : Standard deduction	22,500	
Less : Interest on loan [See note]	10,080	(32,580)
Income from house property		42,420

Note : Interest on borrowed Capital

Interest on pre period [1-4-2003 to 31-3-2005] [2 years] [12% of 60,000 × 2 = 14,400] [14,400 ÷ 5]	2,880
Interest on post period [1-4-2006 to 31-3-2007] [1 year] [12% of 60,000]	7,200
Interest	10,080

Problem 5.11-P3 [Pass 2006C]

X owns a house in Delhi. From the particulars given below, compute income from house property for the assessment year 2007-08.

	Rs.
Municipal value	2,20,000
Fair rent	2,60,000
Standard rent	2,45,000
Actual Rent (let out for residential purpose @ 24,000 p.m.)	2,88,000
Municipal taxes paid	22,000
Expenses on repair	10,000
Insurance premium	4,000

X has borrowed a sum of Rs. 5,00,000 (five lakh) @ 12% p.a. On 1-4-2003 and the construction of the house was completed on 1st March, 2006.

Ans: 1,02,200.

Problem 5.11-P4 [Hons 2005]

Mr. X owns a house at Delhi whose Municipal value is Rs. 1,20,000 and fair rent is Rs. 1,44,000 p.a. During the previous year 2006-07 the house was vacant for 3 months. For rest of the period it was letout for residential purposes @ Rs. 15,000 p.m. He makes the following expenditure in respect of the house property :

Municipal taxes	Rs. 18,000
Repairs	Rs. 12,000
Fire Insurance Premium	Rs. 10,000

A loan of Rs. 3,00,000 was taken on 1-4-2004 @ 12% p.a. for the construction of the house which was completed on 12-3-2006, 50% of the loan has been paid back on October 1, 2006.

Find out his taxable income from house property for the assessment year 2007-08.

Ans: 47,700.

Problem 5.11-P5

Shri Mukesh owns a house at Ajmer whose construction was completed on June 30, 2006. It was let out from August 1, 2006 on a monthly rent of Rs. 9,000.

The other particulars of the house are as follows :	Rs.
Municipal Valuation	1,20,000
Fair rent	1,00,000
Standard rent	1,30,000

Municipal taxes paid by tenant Rs. 10,000

Shri Mukesh took a loan of Rs. 1,00,000 on 1st October, 2003 from Dena Bank for the contruction of this house at an interest rate of 10% per annum. The loan is still unpaid.

The tenant vacated the house on 31st March, 2007. However, the rent for the month of March could not be recovered from the tenant. Compute the taxable income from house property of Shri Mukesh for the assessment year 2007-08.

What difference would it make, if the house is let at Rs. 12,000 per month instead of Rs. 9,000 per month.

Ans: 41,700; 43,800.

Problem 5.11-P6

Mr. Ganesh is owner of two residential houses. The construction of the first house started on 1st January, 1995 and was completed on 31st December, 1998. He has taken a loan of Rs. 2 lakhs on 1st July 1997 for the construction of this house. Interest @ 10% per annum is payable on it. Half of this loan was paid on 1st August, 2002. It has been let out for residential purposes at a monthly rent of Rs. 2,500. The tenant vacated the house on 31st January, 2007 and it remained vacant upto 31st March, 2007. The rent for December, 2006 and January, 2007 could not be realised from the tenant. The details of expenditure for this house are as under :

	Rs.
Fair rent of each house	25,100
Municipal Taxes (10% of Municipal Value)	2,750
Insurance Premium paid	2,000
Ground Rent (outstanding)	1,000
Property tax to State Govt. (outstanding)	1,500

Municipal taxes were not paid during the previous year 2005-06. Therefore municipal taxes for two years were paid during the previous year.

The second house is used by him for his own residence. The construction of this house started on 1st March, 2004 and was completed on 31st December, 2006. A loan of Rs. 60,000 was taken on 1st April, 2005 for the construction of this house, the itnerestest @ 12% per annum is payable on it. Neither the principal amount not the interest on it was paid upto 31st March, 2007. The municipal valuation of this house is Rs. 40,000. The details of expenditure paid for this house are as under :

	Rs.
Municipal tax (for 3 months)	1,000
Insurance Premium (for 1 year from January, 2007)	2,000

Find out taxable income from house Property of Shri Ganesh for the assessment year 2007-08.

Ans: 1,900; (8,640)

Problem 5.11-P7 [CA M 2000]

Q.1c : X commenced construction of a residential house intended exclusively for his residence, on November 1, 2000. He raised a loan of Rs. 5,00,000 at 16 per cent interest for the purpose of construction on November 1, 1998. Finding that there was an over-run in the cost of construction he raised a further loan of Rs. 8,00,000 at the same rate of interest on October 1, 2005. What is the interest allowable under section 24, assuming that the construction was completed on March 31, 2006 ?

Ans: 1,66,667 limited to Rs. 30,000; 1,28,000; overall limit Rs. 1,50,000.

TOPIC 5.12 **SECTION 25A*. RECOVERY OF UNREALISED RENT UPTO AY 2001-02

Where a deduction has been allowed in respect of unrealised rent during AY 2001-02 or any earlier AY and the assessee has subsequently realised any amount in respect of such rent, the amount so realised will be chargeable to tax under the head Income from House Property. He will not be eligible to claim any deduction u/ss 23 & 24. Moreover expenditure incurred for recovery of unrealised rent is not allowed as deduction.

TOPIC 5.13 *SECTION 25AA. RECOVERY OF UNREALISED RENT APPLICABLE FROM THE AY 2002-03

Where a deduction has been allowed in respect of unrealised rent during AY 2002-03 or any subsequent AY and, subsequently, unrealised rent is realised, the amount so realised will be chargeable to tax under the head Income from House Property whether or not the assessee is the owner of such property in that PY. He will not be eligible to claim any standard deduction.

Illustration and Problem 5.13-P1 (Difficult)

Compute the amount of unrealised rent chargeable to tax for the AY 2007-08.

	Case 1	*Case 2*	*Case 3*
Recovery of unrealised rent on 4-9-2006	5,000	5,000	5,000
Deduction claimed on a/c of unrealised rent	10,000	10,000	10,000
Deduction allowed by Assessing officer	10,000	2,000	8,000

Ans: 5,000; (3,000); 3,000

Solution

	Case 1	*Case 2*
Deduction claimed on a/c of unrealised rent	10,000	10,000
Less : Deduction allowed by Assessing officer	10,000	2,000
Already taxed	Nil	(8,000)
Add: Recovery of unrealised rent	5,000	5,000
Balance Taxable	5,000	(3,000)

Note:

- Since unrealised rent deduction cannot be claimed for earlier PY, Rs. 3,000 further deduction is not allowed.

Problem 5.13-P2 (Difficult)

	Case 1	*Case 2*	*Case 3*
Expected rent of PY 2001-02.	2,00,000	3,00,000	5,00,000
The property is let out for 12 months.			
Actual rent of 12 month.	2,10,000	3,10,000	4,00,000
Unrealised rent of PY 2001-02.	40,000	50,000	20,000
Recovery of unrealised rent in PY 2006-07.	35,000	40,000	15,000

Compute how much unrealised rent is taxable in the PY 2006-07.

Ans: 5,000; nil; nil.

Illustration & Problems 5.13-P3 (Difficult)

From the undernoted information find out Income from House Property for the AY 2007-08.

	Case 1	*Case 2*	*Case 3*	*Case 4*
Fair rent for PY 2005-06 & 2006-07	56,000	84,500	46,800	74,100
Actual rent for PY 2005-06 & 2006-07	60,000	72,000	78,000	76,000
Unrealised rent for the PY 2005-06	10,000	8,500	9,500	15,000
Recovery of unrealised rent in the PY 2006-07	10,000	8,500	5,400	14,000

Ans: (1) 46,000; (2) 59,150; (3) 60,000; (4) 54,100.

Solution : Case 1

Computation of Unrealised rent

	Case 1	*Case 2*
Recovery of unrealised rent	10,000	8,500
Already taxed		
Less : ER – AR (56,000 – 50,000)	6,000	
Less : ER – AR (84,500 – 63,500)		21,000
Recovery of unrealised rent taxable in the PY 2006-07	4,000	nil

Computation of Income from House Property for the AY 2007-08

	Case 1	*Case 2*
a. Expected rent for the PY 2006-07	56,000	84,500
b. Actual rent for the PY 2006-07	60,000	72,000
Gross Annual Value *(a or b whichever is higher)*	60,000	84,500
Less : Standard deduction u/s 24a	18,000	25,350
Income from House Property	42,000	59,150
Add : Recovery of unrealised rent computed above	4,000	nil
Income from House Property	46,000	59,150

TOPIC 5.14 **SECTION 25B. RECEIPT OF ARREARS OF RENT*

Arrears of rent if not taxed earlier on due basis, then it shall be taxed in the year of receipt if following conditions are satisfied :

1. The taxpayer is the owner of any property consisting of any building or land appurtenant thereto which has been let out to a tenant.
2. He has received any amount, by way of arrears of rent from such property, not charged to income tax for any PY. Rent is not charged in earlier year since sometimes rent is increased with retrospective effect.
3. The amount so received (after allowing 30% deduction) shall be deemed to be the income chargeable under the head Income from house Property.
4. It is taxable in the PY in which it is received whether or not the assessee is the owner of such property in that PY.

Note

- Moreover expenditure incurred for recovery of arrears of rent is not allowed as deduction.

Problem 5.14-P1 (Difficult)

	Case 1	*Case 2*	*Case 3*
Expected rent of PY 2001-02.	3,00,000	4,00,000	8,00,000
The property is let out for 12 months.			
Actual rent of 12 month.	2,80,000	3,60,000	6,00,000
Rent increased with retrospective effect by	6,000 p.m.	4,000 p.m.	11,000 p.m.
Arrears of rent received in PY 2006-07.	72,000	48,000	1,32,000

Compute how much arrears of rent is taxable in the PY 2006-07.

Ans: 36,400; 5,600; nil.

Problem 5.14-P2

Mr. Taxcrazy furnishes following particulars :

	PY 2005-06	*PY 2006-07*
Municipal Valuation	1,00,000	1,00,000
Fair Rent	1,80,000	1,80,000
Actual rent	12,000 p.m.	20,000 p.m.

The rent was increased with retrospective effect from 1-4-2005 by Rs. 8,000 p.m. During the PY 2006-07 he received Rs. 96,000 arrears of rent. You are required to compute Income from House Property for the AY 2007-08.

Solution

Computation of Income from House Property

a. Expected rent		1,80,000
b. Actual Rent		2,40,000
Gross Annual Value *(a or b whichever is higher)*		2,40,000
Less : Standard deduction u/s 24		72,000
Income from House Property		1,68,000
Add : Recovery of arrears of rent computed as above	60,000	
Less : Standard deduction u/s 25B [see note]	18,000	42,000
Income from House Property		2,10,000

Note: Computation of receipt of arrears of rent

Receipt of arrears of rent	96,000
Less : Rent already charged in PY 2005-06 (ER – AR) (1,80,000 – 1,44,000)	36,000
Receipt of arrears of rent which is chargeable to tax in PY 2006-07.	60,000

Problem 5.14-P3 (CS NEW D02) - M 3

Q.1b : Mrs. X owns a house property which is let out @ Rs. 10,000 per month. During the previous year ending March 31, 2007, she received — (i) arrears of rent of Rs. 30,000; and (ii) unrealised rent of Rs. 20,000. Compute her income chargeable to tax under the head 'Income from house property'.

Ans: 1,25,000.

Problem 5.14-P4

Mr. Taxcrazy received Rs. 60,000 during the PY 2006-07 as arrears of rent which was increased with retrospective effect. Out of this Rs. 20,000 relates to PY 2004-05 and Rs. 40,000 relates to the PY 2005-06. How this receipt will be taxable.

Ans: 42,000.

Problem 5.14-P5

1. Can there be any income under the head 'Income from House Property' if a person is not an owner of a house in the relevant PY though he was owning the house earlier ?

Solution

1. Yes, if an income falls under sections 25A, 25AA and 25B.

TOPIC 5.15 *SECTION 26. TAX TREATMENT OF PROPERTY OWNED BY CO-OWNERS

It states that where a property is owned by 2 or more persons, and respective shares are definite and ascertainable, then

1. Assessment of income from such property is not made as an association of person.
2. The respective share of the co-owners is included in their individual incomes as per Section 22 to Section 25.
3. Such co-owners are individually entitled to relief u/s 23(2) in respect of self occupied property for residence.

   Section 23(2) — Where property is treated as self occupied property for residence, then its GAV is taken as nil.

Problem 5.15-P1 (Typical)

Soha and Joha are two sisters, fashion designer, who have inherited four houses from their father. The first house is residential in which both the sisters are living in equal parts. Both the sisters took a loan from bank and got renovated their respective portions. On 1-4-2006 Soha took a loan of Rs. 60,000 @ 16% p.a. rate of interest and on 1-5-2006 Joha took a loan of Rs. 50,000 @ 15% p.a. rate of interest. The municipal valuation of the house is Rs. 1,20,000.

The second house has been let out to a bank at a rent of Rs. 15,000 p.m. Municipal tax of Rs. 10,000 has been paid in respect of this house.

The third house is in Delhi which is kept vacant by both the sisters for their self use, because every year they stay in Delhi for two or three months and live in this house only. The expected rent of this house is Rs. 2,50,000. Each sister holds half portion of this house.

Fourth house has two residential units. Each unit has been let out at Rs. 3,000 p.m. for residential purposes. Municipal tax of Rs. 4,000 has been paid for this house. Later one tenant started doing his business in this unit, and took another house in his neighbourhood for his residence, on rent.

Compute the income from house property of Soha and Joha for the AY 2007-08.

Ans: 1,15,700; 1,18,425.

TOPIC 5.16 **SECTION 27.* DEEMED OWNER

For the purposes of sections 22 to 26 :

(i) An individual who transfers House Property to his or her spouse provided :
   - such transfer is made without adequate consideration.
   - the transfer is not in connection with an agreement to live apart.

(ia) An individual who transfers House Property to a minor child, provided
   - the transfer is made without adequate consideration.
   - the minor child is not a married daughter.

(ii) Holder of an impartible estate. Such holder is deemed to be the individual owner of all the properties comprising in the estate.

(iii) A member of a Co-operative society, Company or other association of person provided :

- the building or part thereof is allotted or leased to such member; and
- the allotment or lease is under a house building scheme of such society, Company or AOP.

(iiia) A person who is allowed to take or retain possession of any building or part thereof in part performance of a contract referred to in Section 53A of the Transfer of Property Act, 1882.

(iiib) A person who acquires any right in or with respect to any building or part thereof by way of sale or exchange or lease provided :

- the sale or exchange or lease is for a term of atleast 12 years.
- the lease is not from month to month or for a period not exceeding 1 year.

E.g. Mr. X transfers a property on lease for a period of 10 years to Mr. Y. The lease can be renewed for a further period of 10 years. In this case the total term of lease will be 20 years. Thus Mr. Y shall be treated as deemed owner.

Problem 5.16-P1 (CA - N98) - M 9

Q.1e : Y furnishes the following particulars relating to his house properties and other incomes and expenditure for the year 2006-07 :

First House : This house is taken by him on lease for 10 years which is let to a tenant, for his residence, at a monthly rent of Rs. 2,400.

He has incurred the following expenses during this year :

Lease rent	1,000 per month
Salary of durban	200 per month
Interest on loan taken to pay for the acquisition of the lease	200 per month

Second House : This house was constructed by him in 1992, but was transferred to his wife in 1996 out of love and affection. He however continues to stay in this house with his wife till date. He has taken a loan for the construction of this house for which interest of Rs. 6,000 becomes due for the year, but had not been paid by him. He has paid repair expenses of Rs. 1,000 during the year.

Taxable income from business for this year amounts to Rs. 64,000.

Compute gross total income of Y for the assessment year 2007-08.

Ans: 70,000.

5.17 COMPREHENSIVE PROBLEMS

Simple and Difficult

Problem 5.17-P1 [CA M97] [Marks 6]

Ram owned a house property at Madras which was occupied by him for the purpose of his residence. He was transferred to Bombay in June 2006 and therefore he let out the property with effect from July 1, 2006 on a monthly rent of Rs. 3,000. The corporation tax payable in respect of the property was Rs. 6,000 of which 50 per cent was paid by him before March 31, 2007. Interest on money borrowed for the construction of the property amounted to Rs. 20,000. Compute the income from house property for the assessment year 2007-08. assume that municipal valuation is Rs. 28,000 and fair rent is Rs. 31,000 Standard rent is Rs. 30,000.

Ans: (1,100).

Problem 5.17-P2

Sri Ramaswamy Karunakaran owns a two storied bungalow at Nungambakkam High Road, Madras. During the financial year 2006-2007, he used it for his personal residence from 1-4-2006 to 30-11-2006, and thereafter let it out from 1-12-2006 to M/s. South Coast Aqua-Culture Ltd. for residential use of their Managing Director, at a monthly rent of Rs. 16,000.

Other relevant particulars of the property are given below :

(i) Annual value determined by Madras Municipal Corporation	1,25,000
(ii) Annual fair rent on the basis of comparable rent of an adjoining property, which is identical to the assessee's property	1,50,000
(iii) Standard rent on the basis of computation under the Rent Control Act	1,60,000
(iv) Municipal taxes assessed not paid	5,000
(v) Actual expenses on repairs/maintenance etc. during the year	10,000
(vi) Annual Insurance premium for fire Insurance	1,000
(vii) Collection charges	2,500
(viii) Interest paid to M/s. Housing Development Finance Corporation on loan raised in 2003 for construction of the house	15,000

Compute the total income of Sri Karunakaran for Assessment Year 2007-2008, assuming that he has no other house property and no other source of income.

Ans: 90,000.

Problem 5.17-P3 [Pass 2005]

Mohan owns a house (Municipal valuation Rs. 30,000) of the fair rent of Rs. 43,200 per annum. During the previous year, the house is let out for residential purposes w.e.f. 1st April 2006 to 30th June, 2006 at the rate of Rs. 4,000 per month and self occupied for residential purposes for the remaining part of the year. He incurred the following expenses is respect of this house :

Municipal taxes Rs. 6,000, Ground rent Rs. 5,000 and Fire insurance Premium Rs. 1,000. A loan of Rs. 50,000 was taken on 1st April, 2000 at the rate of 10% per annum for the construction of the house which was completed on 1st January, 2003. No part of the loan has been repaid so far. Compute his income from house property for the Assessment year 2007-08.

Ans: 19,040.

Problem 5.17-P4 [Pass 2002]

'X' owns a house (Municipal valuation Rs. 25,000) of the fair rent of Rs. 28,000 p.a. During the previous year, he used it for his own residence from 1.4.2006 to 30.11.2006 and let out for residential purposes w.e.f. 1.12.2006 @ Rs. 2,600 p.m. He incurred the following expenses in respect of this house :

Municipal tax Rs. 5,100; A loan of Rs. 30,000 was taken on 1-4-2003 @ 15% p.a. for the construction of this house which was completed on 31-5-2005. No part of loan has been repaid so far. Compute his Income from house property for the AY 2007-08.

Ans: 9,730.

Problem 5.17-P5 [Hons 1992]

Mr. X, is the owner of a commercial house property whose construction was completed on 31-08-2003 and it has been let out from 01-12-2004 and its particulars are asunder :

	Rs.
Municipal valuation	11,000 p.a.
Expected fair rent	12,000 p.a.
Standard rent (p.m.)	1,200
Actual monthly rent	1,200
Municipal taxes paid (including Rs. 500 paid by the tenant)	1,500
Fire insurance payable	80
Interest on loan taken for the construction of the house.	
The interest has been paid outside India to a non resident without deduction of tax at source, as the non-resident agreed to pay tax on such interest direct to the Government. Stamp duty and registration charges incurred in respect of the lease agreement of the house	200
Recovery of unrealised rent	8,000

Mr. X has long term capital gains of Rs. 1,33,920.

Compute his tax liability for the assessment year 2007-08.

Ans: 1,51,300; 10,465.

Problem 5.17-P6 [Hons 2005C]

Mr. X owns a house which was completed on 30th June 2002. Other particulars are as under :

Rent per month	Rs. 8,000
Fair rental value	Rs. 1,00,000
Municipal value	Rs. 90,000
Standard rent	Rs. 95,000
Local taxes levied	10%
Local taxes paid	Rs. 6,000
Insurance premium paid	2,500
Interest on money borrowed taken for the purpose of repair and renovation	Rs. 7,500

Mr. X mortgaged the house for Rs. 2,00,000 on 1st January, 2005 at 9% interest per annum. The money was spent on his daughter's marriage. During the year 2005-06 he had claimed a deduction of unrealised rent of Rs. 15,000 out of which Rs. 10,000 was allowed as deduction. During the previous year 2006-07, he recovered Rs. 10,000 from the defaulting tenant.

Compute the income from house property for the assessment year 2007-08.

Ans: 60,500.

Problem 5.17-P7

Mr. A owns a house property at Delhi. He had let out the same @ Rs. 5,000 p.m. from 1-4-2006 to 30-6-2006. It was vacant for the next three months and was again let out at a rent of Rs. 8,000 p.m. w.e.f. 1-10-2006. The Municipal (rateable) value for tax purposes is Rs. 30,000 and Fair Rent of the House is Rs. 28,000. Municipal taxes to the extent of Rs. 6,000 were borne by the tenant during this year. The property is subject to ground rent of Rs. 12,000 per annum and insurance premium per annum comes to Rs. 6,000 but these have not been paid for the last 3 years. He is also in receipt of Rs. 84,000, received through court decree from a former tenant of a property he had sold away five years ago. His claim for deducting unrealised rent had been allowed in full to the extent of Rs. 1,08,000 representing rent for 3 years. Compute his income from this property.

Ans: 1,28,100.

Problem 5.17-P8 [Hons 1991]

Shri Pankaj Bhatia is the owner of a house property whose construction was completed on 31-03-2003. It has been let out from 01-04-2004 for residential purpose @ Rs. 3,000 p.m.

Other particulars:

		Rs.
(i)	Municipal valuation	24,000 p.a.
(ii)	Ground rent	100
(iii)	Urban land tax levied	1,000
(iv)	Municipal tax payable	2,000
(v)	Insurance premium paid (Rs. 400 for theft and Rs. 50 for fire)	450
(vi)	Rent collection charges	900
(vii)	There is unrealised rent of one month. The house was got vacated from the defaulting tenant and let out to other tenant at the same rate.	

(viii) He borrowed Rs. 60,000 from his neighbour on 01-09-2005 @ 15% p.a. for the reconstruction of the house. He has also refunded Rs. 12,000 on 01-10-2006.

Compute his tax liability for the assessment year 2007-08. Presuming that he is non-resident and his income from business/profession is Rs. 1,45,010.

Ans: 1,60,010; 7,142.

Problem 5.17-P9 [Hons 2000]

Mrs. P is the owner of a house property. She borrowed Rs. 40,000 from Life Insurance Corporation of India on September 1, 2000 @ 15% p.a. for the construction of this house. The construction was completed on 31-3-2002. Since then the house is under her self-occupation. On June 1, 2006 the house has been let out @ Rs. 4,500 p.m. The tenant vacated the house on August 1, 2006. She occupied the house for self-occupancy. The tenant paid only Rs. 3,000 as rent for the month of July 2006. The house is again let out @ Rs. 5,500 p.m. from September 1, 2006 to February 28, 2007. The house remained vacant for the month of March 2007.

Other particulars of the house for the PY 2006-07 are given below:

1.	Municipal value	70,500
2.	Fair Rent	60,000
3.	Municipal taxes disputed	2,000

4.	Refund of first loan instalment to Life Insurance Corporation on 1st October 2006	12,000
5.	PPF contribution	8,000

You are requested to compute taxable Income & tax liability assuming that Income from Other Sources is Rs. 1,20,000 for the AY 2007-08.

Ans: 1,40,400; 551.

Problem 5.17-P10 [Hons 2005C]

Details of Income of Shri M for the Assessment year 2007-08 is given below:

Income from business and profession		Rs. 46,000
Income from house Property	House 1	House 2
	Rs.	Rs.
Fair Rent	75,000	85,000
Rent received (House 2 remained vacant for two months in previous year)	78,000	78,000
Municipal valuation	76,000	75,000
Municipal Taxes (Due)	13,000	14,000
Municipal Taxes paid	3,500	4,700
Insurance paid	2,000	3,000
Interest. on capital borrowed by mortgaging House 1 (Funds are used for construction of House 2)	14,000	

Determine the Taxable income of Shri M for the Assessment year 2007-08.

Ans: 52,150+37,310

Problem 5.17-P11 [Hons 2006]

For the assessment year 2007-08, X submits the following information :

Income from business		Rs. 44,220
Interest on debentures		Rs. 1,05,000
	House 1	House 2
Property income	Rs.	Rs.
Fair rent	12,900	39,700
Municipal valuation	13,000	40,000
Annual rent	48,000	54,000
Municipal taxes paid	1,700	4,000
Standard rent	12,500	60,000
Repairs	200	18,000
Land revenue	2,000	16,000
Insurance	500	1,500
Unrealised rent of 2005-06	3,000	2,000
Unrealised rent of 2006-07	1,000	35,000
Interest on capital borrowed for purchase of house property	1,000	14,000
Repayment of loan taken from a friend for the purpose of House 1	3,640	—

Vacant period (Number of months)	(1)	(3)
Loss on account of vacancy	4,000	13,500
Actual rent received or receivable	43,000	5,500
Nature of occupation	Let out residence	Let out for profession
Data of completion of construction	March 31 2001	May 15, 1973

Determine the taxable income and tax liability for the assessment year 2007-08. Also calculate the amount of unrealised rent which can be claimed as deduction in the assessment year 2007-08.

Ans: 1,78,880; 10,992.

Problem 5.17-P12 [Hons 1994]

X has occupied two houses for his residential purposes and House 2 is let out to Y for his residence, particulars of which are as follows :

	House 1	*House 2*	*House 3*
• Standard rent under the Rent Control Act	50,000	89,000	62,000
• Municipal valuation	45,000	90,000	43,000
• Fair rent	52,000	92,000	59,000
• Actual rent	—	94,000	—
• Unrealised rent of the PY 2006-07	—	6,000	—
• Unrealised rent of the PY 2001-02	2,000	1,000	500
• Vacancy period	1 month	1.5 month	4 month
• Municipal taxes paid in PY 2006-07	51,000*	2,000	3,000

**for subsequent 5 AY*

X borrows Rs. 3,00,000 @ 15% per annum for construction of House II (date of borrowing: June 1, 2001, date of repayment of loan May 10, 2006). Construction of all the houses is completed on May 1, 2005.

Determine the taxable income of X for the AY 2007-08 on the assumption that his

(i) Income from Other Sources is Rs. 1,70,505

(ii) He paid Rs. 74,000 towards life insurance premium on the policy taken on the life of his married son. He purchased equity shares of public infrastructure Co. for Rs. 35,000 on 31-3-2007.

Ans: 82,680.

Problem 5.17-P13 [Hons 2003; 2006C]

Mrs. A owns two houses. The details of two houses are follows :

	First House	*Second House*
Municipal valuation	3,10,000	2,10,000
Fair rent	3,40,000	2,20,000
Standard rent	2,90,000	2,30,000
Annual rent *(Monthly rent being Rs. 17,300 rent is Rs. 17,300 X 12)*	—	2,07,600
Unrealised rent	—	17,000

The first house is used for own residence while the second is let out. She paid Rs. 35,000 as interest on loan taken for the construction of the first house. The second house remained vacant for two months during the year 2006-07.

Expenses in respect of the second house for the said year were as follows :

Municipal taxes paid Rs. 15,000 Land revenue due but unpaid Rs. 5,000. Interest on loan for reconstruction of the house Rs. 40,000. Fire insurance premium paid Rs. 5,000. During the FY 2006-07 Mrs. A was employed in ABC Ltd. at a monthly salary of Rs. 26,000. The company paid Rs. 2,900 as professional tax on her behalf. Compute total income and tax liability of Mrs. A for the AY 2007-08. Assuming that she does not have any other income.

Ans: 3,61,280; 55,982.

Problem 5.17-P14

Mr. Y purchased a flat in Chennai on 1.4.2006 which he let out on a monthly rent of Rs. 3,500 for a period of seven months in the previous year. Expenses on the flat were :

(i) Municipal Taxes	Rs. 7,000
(ii) Rent Collection Charges	Rs. 310
(iii) Repairs	Rs. 510

Mr. Y owns another house property in Bangalore since financial year 1998-99 which remained self-occupied throughout the previous year. Following expenses were incurred by him on this property :

(i) Interest on Borrowed Capital	Rs. 12,000
(ii) Municipal Taxes	Rs. 1,500
(iii) Repairs	Rs. 1,300

Compute the total income of Mr. Y for the assessment year 2007-2008 if during the relevant previous year he incurred a business loss of Rs. 2,100 and his income from other sources was amounting to Rs. 25,600.

Ans: 23,750.

Problem 5.17-P15 [Hons 1995]

Mr. X owns a house at Delhi. During the PY 2006-07 3/4th portion of the house is self-occupied for full year and ¼th portion is let out for residential purposes from April 1, 2006 to December 31, 2006 on a rent of Rs. 7,000 p.m. From January 1, 2007 this portion was used for own residence. Municipal valuation of the house is Rs. 3,00,000; fair rent Rs. 3,50,000 and Standard rent Rs. 3,10,000. He incurs the following expenditure in respect of the house property:

Municipal Taxes Rs. 8,000; A loan of Rs. 12,00,000 was taken on April 1, 2004 @13% p.a. from Syndicate Bank for the construction of the house which was completed on March 31, 2006. X, repays loan of Rs. 1,20,000 on 31-3-2007 Profit from Business Rs. 3,00,000.

Find out his taxable income for the AY 2007-08.

Ans: 65,650; nil.

Problem 5.17-P16 [Hons 2006]

Mr. Y owns a big house in Delhi consisting of two equal units : Unit I is let out for residential purpose on monthly rent of Rs. 7,000. However this unit remained vacant for 3 months (i.e., from Jan. 1, 2007 to March 31, 2007) during the previous year when it was used by Mr. Y for his own residential purpose.

Unit II - 50% portion is used by him for the purpose of business or profession carried on by him, while the remaining 50% protion is used for his own residential purpose for full year. The details of the property are as follows :

Municipal Valuation	Rs. 1,20,000
Fair Rent	Rs. 1,30,000
Standard Rent	Rs. 1,40,000

Municipal taxes paid 10% of municipal valuation. He also paid municipal taxes for the next 3 years in advance during 2006-07.

He took a loan of Rs. 2,00,000 @ 15% interest p.a. for the construction of the house on 1-6-2003. The construction was completed on 31-12-2005. no amount has been paid off so far.

The unrealised rent for the earlier years amount to Rs. 40,000 but a deduction has been claimed so far only for Rs. 30,000. There is a recovery of Rs. 20,000 from the defaulting tenant.

Compute Income from House property for the Assessment year 2007-08.

Ans: 25,050.

Typical

Problem 5.17-P17 (Typical)

The construction of three identical houses of Taxcrazy were completed on 31st March, 2002. Two houses are let out for residential purposes on a rent of Rs. 6,000 each per month and third house is occupied by Taxcrazy himself. Other relevant details are given below :

Expected rent of three houses	1,44,000
Municipal taxes for all three houses	12,000

On 1-6-2006 Taxcrazy had borrowed Rs. 20,000 @ 16% p.a. to repair the let out properties. One of the let out houses remained vacant for a period of two months during the previous year. During the previous year he received Rs. 5,000 from an old tenant as an arrears of rent. This amount was allowed as deduction in past year as unrealised rent.

Compute the taxable income from house property of Taxcrazy for the year ended 31st March, 2007 assuming that he let out the self occupied house also for 3 months at a monthly rent of Rs. 2,000 p.m.

Ans: 1,19,934.

Problem 5.17-P18 (Typical)

Mr. Taxcrazy owns two houses at Jamnagar. Municipal value of these houses are Rs. 56,000 including Rs. 20,000 for municipal value of first house.

Fair rent of first house is Rs. 24,000 p.a. During the PY 2006-07 this house was used by him for his own residence from 1-4-2006 to 30-6-2006 and let out from 1-7-2006 @ Rs. 2,500 p.m. as he was transferred. Tenant vacated this house on 1-2-2007 and it remained vacant in search of tenant.

In respect of house property he paid municipal taxes Rs. 6,000. A loan of Rs. 30,000 was taken on 31-3-2001 @ 15% p.a. for the construction of house. On 1-4-2003 he took another loan of Rs. 30,000 @ 10% p.a. to repay this loan. This house was completed on 1-4-2004. During the PY Rs. 7,000 was paid as interest including interest of earlier years. Nothing was repaid on loan account so far.

He treats his second house also as self occupied because his friend resides thereat. Fair rent of this house is Rs. 4,000 p.m. He paid municipal taxes @ 10%. He obtained a loan of Rs. 50,000 @ 12% p.a. from his friend in USA who is non-resident Indian. During PY interest was paid to him without any tax deducted at source. Earlier this house was let out to a tenant. He claims bad debts of Rs. 8,000 because a long pending court case is not yet decided. He incurred Rs. 2,000 in this regard during previous year.

Find out his income from house property for the AY 2007-08.

Ans: 3,700 + 31,080 = 34,780.

Problem 5.17-P19 (Typical)

Mr. Taxcrazy is the owner of the two houses. The municipal valuation of the first house is Rs. 30,000. One half of this house has been let out at a rent of Rs. 3,000 p.m. and the other one half is occupied by him for his own residence. He took a loan of Rs. 1,00,000 on 1-1-1999 for the purpose of construction of this house @ 10% p.a. which is still unpaid. There was a delay in payment of instalments so he paid Rs. 2,000 as interest on delayed interest. The construction of this house was completed on 31-12-2002. Municipal taxes paid on this house during PY was Rs. 3,000.

The second house, whose municipal valuation is Rs. 24,000 p.a. was let out till 30-6-2006 at a rent of Rs. 2,000 p.m. This house remained vacant for six months then it was let out at a rent of Rs. 2,500 p.m. from 1-1-2007. Municipal taxes paid during the PY was Rs. 1,500. Rs. 10,000 was received in the PY as arrears of rent with retrospective effect. He incurred Rs. 1,000 for legal charges in this respect. Rs. 500 was recovered in the PY 2006-07 against a bad debt allowed in earlier years. This house was sold in PY 2004-05.

He has started construction of a bungalow for self residence on 1-7-2005. For this purpose he took a loan of Rs. 8,00,000. Construction was not completed upto 31-3-2007 and interest was due Rs. 40,000 on loan amount.

Calculate income from house property for the AY 2007-08.

Ans: 23,550.

Problem 5.17-P20 (PE II - N03) - M 12

Q.2(a)-or- : A and B construct their houses on a piece of land purchased by them at New Delhi. The built up area of each house is 1,000 sq. ft. (ground floor and an equal area in the first floor). A starts construction on April 1, 2005 and completed it on March 31, 2006. B starts the construction on April 1, 2005 and completes the same on June 30, 2006. A occupies the entire house on April 1, 2006. However, B occupies the ground floor on July 1, 2006 and lets out the first floor for a rent of Rs. 15,000 per month. The tenant vacates the house on December 31, 2006 and B occupies the entire house during the period January 1, 2007 to March 31, 2007.

The following is the other information :

Fair rental value of each unit (ground floor/first floor) (per annum)	1,00,000
Municipal value of each unit (ground floor/first floor (per annum)	72,000
Municipal taxes paid by	
- A	8,000
- B	8,000
Repair and maintenance charges paid by	
- A	28,000
- B	30,000

A has availed a housing loan of Rs. 20 lakh @ 12 per cent on April 1, 2005. B has availed a housing loan of Rs. 12 lakh @ 10 per cent on July 1, 2005. No repayment is made by either of them till March 31, 2007.

Compute income from house property for A and B for the assessment year 2007-08.

Ans: (1,20,000); (52,800); (69,000); (8,800)

Problem 5.17-P21 (CA - M01) - M 15

Q.1a : The particulars of income of Mrs. X aged 55 years for the financial year 2006-07 are given below :

Gross salary received from ABC Ltd. for the year	4,00,000
Rental income received from a commercial complex (Rs. 12,000 per month)	1,44,000
Arrears of rent received from the complex, which were not charged to tax in any earlier years	30,000
Interest paid on loan taken for the purchase of a house from a scheduled bank for use as own residence	1,20,000
Repayment of instalments of loan taken from the bank for the purchase of the above property	60,000
Deposits in public provident fund account	
(a) Out of an earlier loan taken from PPF a/c	20,000
(b) Out of current year's income	40,000
Investment made in units of a mutual fund approved by the Board under section 80C(2) (xvii)	40,000

Compute the total income of Mrs. X and tax payable theiron in respect of assessment year 2007-08.

Ans: 3,91,800; 65,320.

Problem 5.17-P22 (Difficult)

Mr. Narendra is owner of four houses the Municipal valuation of these houses are Rs. 12,500; Rs. 16,000; Rs. 12,000 and Rs. 30,000 respectively. The Municipality levies 10% tax on the Municipal value of these houses. In first house Narendra resides himself & in second house he runs his own business the profit of which during the previous year amounted to Rs. 1,00,000. The other two house have been let out at a monthly rent of Rs. 750 and Rs. 2,750 respectively.

The fourth house remained vacant from April to July, The unrealised rent of the past years in respect of the fourth house amounted to Rs. 32,000. The unrealised rent of Rs. 8,000 in respect of thirds house for past years were realised during the previous year. It was allowed to deduction. Rs. 800 were spent on its realisation.

During the previous year the municipal taxes of first and second house were not paid, while in respect of third house two years municipal taxes were paid by Shri Narendra. Half of the municipal taxes in respectively of fourth house were paid by the tenant while the remaining half were outstanding.

The construction of all the houses was started in June, 1999. the construction of first and second house was completed in December, 2000 while the construction of third and fourth house was completed on 30th June, 2002 and 31st December, 2003 respectively. For the construction of these houses a loan of Rs. 4,00,000 was taken from Life Insurance Corporation on 1st October, 1999 at an interest rate of 12% per annum which is still outstanding. The amount of loan was utilised equally for all the houses.

Compute the taxable income from House Property of Mr. Narendra for the assessment year 2007-08.

Ans: (20,280)

Problem 5.17-P23 (ICWA - D02) - M 7

X is a cost accountant in ABC Ltd., Mumbai and gets Rs. 18,000 p.m. as salary. He owns a house which is let out to the employer company on a annual rent of Rs. 63,000 which in turn provided the same to X as rent free accommodation. Municipal tax paid for the house is Rs. 14,000.

Determine the net income of X for the AY 2007-08.

Ans: 2,82,700. [2,16,000+32,400=2,48,400+34,300=2,82,700]

Problem 5.17-P24

Mr. 'P' is employed with ABC Company Ltd. at a salary of Rs. 2,500 per month. He is the owner of House property whose construction was completed on 31st May, 2005. It has been let out from 1st July, 2006 for residential purpose @ Rs. 1,500 per month to a tenant who vacated it on 31st August, 2006. From 1st Oct. 2006 the house has been let out to ABC Company Ltd. at the same rent and the company has allotted the house to Mr. 'P', 'free of rent'. Other particulars in respect of the house for financial year 2006-2007 are as follows :

Municipal valuation	12,000
Fair Rent	13,000
Municipal tax disputed by the owner	2,000
Ground Rent outstanding	100
Insurance premium paid	450
Collection charges	900

He borrowed Rs. 30,000 from LIC 1st Sept., 2003 @ 15% per annum for construction of the house. He has refunded Rs. 12,000 on 1st Oct., 2006.

Compute the income of Mr. 'P' from House property and his gross total income for the Assessment Year 2007-2008.

Ans: 34,785.

STRATEGY MAKER

Points : Overall points 7; Practical - 7; Theory - 5.

Strategy : This chapter needs a holistic view, therefore start all over again and by noting very small points of each topic, start memorising those jottings. Few now you shall know it. Again solve only typical problems. See your energy level rising. You are now confident and can attempt any question.

Type of problem : Difficult.

wow! Completed second head of income

It is just remarkable that you have reached at this important juncture.

Keep it up. And my best wishes are with you.

Keep Running

Do you know which asset appreciates on its regular use.
No it is not land. It's your mind.

DEPRECIATION

TOPIC 6.00 INTRODUCTION

As per section 32(1) depreciation is computed for the current year which is charged on business assets. Current depreciation is subtracted from net profit to arrive at profit from business. As per Income-tax Act it is mandatory to claim depreciation.

TOPIC 6.01 ON FOLLOWING TANGIBLE AND INTANGIBLE ASSETS DEPRECIATION IS ALLOWED

There are four classes of assets on which depreciation is allowed. They are :

1. *Building* : It means superstructure only and does not include site. However it includes roads, bridges, wells, tubewells, etc.

   General rate of depreciation is 10%

   Special rates : Residential building used by employees - 5%; Building used as hotel - 10%; Building acquired on or after 1-9-2002 and put to use for the purpose of providing infrastructure facilities u/s 80IA(4)(i) - 100%; Temporary erection - 100%

2. *Any furniture or fittings including electrical fittings* **:** Furniture is not defined in the Act. It means article of convenience or decoration used to furnish a house, apartment, place of business or of accommodation.

   General rate of depreciation is 10%. No Special rates. (upto AY 2005-06 15%)

3. *Plant & Machinery* **:** *Section 43(3)* - "Plant" includes ships, vehicles, books, scientific apparatus and surgical equipment used for the purposes of the business or profession. It does not include tea bushes or livestock or buildings or furniture and fittings.

   General rate of depreciation is 15%. (upto AY 2005-06 25%)

   Special rates : Motor cars - 15% (upto AY 2005-06 20%); Computers including computer software and books (not annual publication) owned by professional - 60%; Books (annual publication) owned by assessee carrying on a profession or owned by an assessee carrying on business in running lending libraries - 100%; Pollution equipments - 100%; Ships - 20%; Aeroplanes or aeroengines - 40%.

4. *Intangible assets* : Know-how, patents, copyrights, trade marks, licences, franchises or any other business or commercial rights of similar nature, being intangible assets *acquired after 31-3-1999.*

   Know-how means any industrial information or technique likely to assist in the manufacture or processing of goods or in the working of a mine, oil-well or other sources of mineral deposits (including searching for discovery or testing of deposits for the winning of access thereto.

   Depreciation is not allowed on goodwill of the business or profession.

   General rate of depreciation is 25%. No Special rates.

TOPIC 6.02 *SECTION 2(11).* MEANING OF BLOCK OF ASSETS (BOA)

Depreciation is available on Block of Asset and not on individual assets. The term 'block of assets' means a group of assets falling within a class of assets in respect of which same percentage of depreciation is prescribed.

Illustration and Problems 6.02-P1 (Simple)

Find out the Block of Assets for the AY 2007-08.

Rates of Depreciation

	Amount	Case 1	Case 2	Case 3	Case 4
• Plant A	20,000	40%	15%	5%	40%
• Plant B	15,000	20%	15%	100%	50%
• Building A	25,000	10%	20%	100%	5%
• Building B	40,000	10%	20%	100%	5%
• Building C	1,00,000	20%	20%	100%	10%
• Trade Mark	3,50,000	25%	25%	25%	25%
• Copyright 1	1,50,000	25%	25%	25%	25%
• Copyright 2	50,000	25%	25%	25%	25%

Ans: 6 Block; 4 Block; 5 Block; 6 Block

Solution : Case 1

1st block : Plant A Rs. 20,000, Rate of depreciation 40%

2nd block : Plant B Rs. 15,000, Rate of depreciation 20%

3rd block : Building A & B Rs. 65,000, Rate of depreciation 10%

4th block : Building C Rs. 1,00,000, Rate of depreciation 20%

5th block : Trade Mark Rs. 3,50,000, Rate of depreciation 25%

6th block : Copyright Rs. 2,00,000, Rate of depreciation 25%

TOPIC 6.03 *SECTION 32.* WHEN DEPRECIATION IS ALLOWED

Depreciation shall be allowed on such tangible and intangible assets if :

1. Such asset is 'owned' wholly or partly by the assessee; and
2. Such asset is 'put to use' in the relevant PY for the purpose of business or profession in the case of any block of assets.

   To claim depreciation it is not only necessary to purchase the asset but a further condition is necessary that asset should be 'put to use' in the relevant PY *(actual use not necessary)* in the relevant PY *i.e.* depreciation is charged from the day when asset is put to use and not from the day of its acquisition.

E.g. Suppose the assessee purchases the asset on 5-5-2005 and it is put to use on 8-9-2006. It is eligible for depreciation in the PY 2006-07, since the asset is put to use on 8-9-2006, which falls in the PY 2006-07. But however if the asset is put to use on 15-4-2007, it is also eligible for depreciation but not in the PY 2006-07, but in the PY 2007-08.

Once the asset is 'put to use' depreciation is allowed whether the use of the asset is active or passive. 'Passive use' means asset remains idle due to lock-outs or strike. In passive use depreciation is available.

Problem 6.03-P1

1. Depreciation is allowed on individual assets. (True or False)
2. Depreciation can be claimed if the asset is used for personal purpose. (True or False)
3. If there are two joint owners of any asset then each of them shall get deduction of depreciation in respect of his own share in the property. (True or False)
4. Is it mandatory to claim depreciation.

Solution

1. False. Depreciation is not allowed on individual assets but on a group of assets known as block of assets.
2. False. Depreciation can be claimed if the asset is used for business or profession.
3. True.
4. Yes.

TOPIC 6.04 *SECTION 43(6)*. COMPUTATION OF WRITTEN DOWN VALUE (*assumed figures*)

Opening W.D.V. of BoA as on 1-4-2006			20,000
Add :			
• Purchase of an asset; or • The asset put to use	whichever later date falls in the PY 2006-07	10,000	
Less : Sale of assets during the PY 2006-07 [see note]		(2,000)	8,000
Closing W.D.V. of BoA as on 31-3-2007 (*This cannot be negative*)			28,000
Less : Depreciation for the PY 2006-07 *(10% of 28,000)*			2,800
W.D.V. of BoA as on 1-4-2007 *(Also called depreciated value)*			25,200

Note: Where any building, machinery, plant or furniture is sold, discarded, demolished or destroyed in the previous year, the amount by which the moneys payable in respect of such building, machinery, plant or furniture, together with the amount of scrap value, shall be deducted from the opeing W.D.V.

Moneys payable in respect of any building, machinery, plant or furniture includes—

(a) any insurance, salvage or compensation moneys payable in respect thereof;

(b) where the building, machinery, plant or furniture is sold, the price for which it is sold,

Sold includes a transfer by way of exchange or a compulsory acquisition under any law for the time being in force.

TOPIC 6.05 MANNER OF COMPUTATION OF DEPRECIATION

(A) INTRODUCTION

1. Depreciation is computed as per the written down value *(W.D.V.)* method at the rate of depreciation specified for each block of assets.
2. Depreciation is computed at the rate prescribed, on the written down value existing on the last day of the relevant PY. Therefore to compute depreciation, the rate of depreciation is multiplied by closing W.D.V. of block of assets on the last day of the PY. *(Depreciation = Rate of depreciation × W.D.V. as on 31-3-2007)*
3. There are 3 kinds of rates of depreciation.

   Full rate : It is rate of depreciation specified for whole year.

   Half rate : It means half of full rate. Suppose full rate of depreciation is 15%, half rate shall be 50% of full rate *i.e.* 50% of 15% = 7.5%.

   Nil rate : No depreciation is allowed.

   Do remember depreciation is allowed not on day-to-day basis but either depreciation is allowed for whole year or half year.

(B) WHEN HALF RATE OF DEPRECIATION IS APPLICABLE

When the asset is purchased and put to use in the same previous year for less than 180 days then half rate of depreciation is applicable. If both the above conditions are not satisfied then depreciation is charged at the full rate.

E.g. : Suppose the assessee purchases a plant on 5-8-2006 and it is put to use on 8-11-2006. As it can be seen that the plant is purchased and put to use in the same PY for less than 180 days therefore half rate of depreciation is applicable. Now suppose the plant is put to use on 11-9-2006 in this case although plant is purchased and put to use in the same PY however it is used for more than 180 days, therefore full rate of depreciation is applicable. In another case plant is purchased on 5-8-2005 and it is put to use on 18-11-2006. In this case although plant is used for less than 180 days however it is not purchased and put to use in the same previous year.

(C) WHEN NIL RATE OF DEPRECIATION IS APPLICABLE

No depreciation is allowed if on the last day of the PY following position exists :

	Block of assets	*Closing W.D.V. on 31-3-2007*
Case 1	is Empty	is more than zero
Case 2	is not empty	Zero

In Case 1, it says that BoA is empty *i.e.* all assets of the blocks are sold for less than the opening W.D.V. That's the reason why closing W.D.V. being positive. Now depreciation means wear & tear of the asset, if the BoA does not exist there is no wear & tear and therefore no depreciation even if closing W.D.V. is positive.

In Case 2, it says that BoA exists but closing W.D.V. is zero. Since Depreciation = x% of closing W.D.V. Closing W.D.V. = 0, therefore depreciation is zero.

Note: Where depreciation of a block is nil capital gain arises u/s 50. Refer topic below.

TOPIC 6.06 *SECTION 50.* SALE OF DEPRECIABLE ASSETS

(A) CONDITIONS WHEN S.T.C.G. ON DEPRECIABLE ASSETS ARISES

Short term capital gain on depreciable asset can arise only when on the last day of the PY either :

1. The Block of Assets is empty; or
2. The W.D.V. of BoA is Zero.

Note : If on the last day of the PY either W.D.V. is zero or block of assets is empty, then opening W.D.V. is taken as zero.

(B) RULES FOR COMPUTATION OF STCG ON SALE OF DEPRECIABLE ASSETS

1. Depreciable assets are always deemed as Short Term Capital Assets;
2. Gains are always deemed to be Short Term Capital Gain (STCG);
3. Gain is always computed for Block of Assets and not for individual assets;
4. Indexation is not allowed on depreciable assets.

(C) COMPUTATION OF STCG (ASSUMED FIGURES)

Sale consideration		2,00,000
Less :		
• W.D.V. of BoA as on 1-4-2006	50,000	
• Cost of assets acquired during the PY 2006-07	15,000	
• Expenses on transfer	5,000	70,000
STCG		1,30,000
Less : Exemption u/ss 54D, 54G & 54GA		30,000
STCG		1,00,000

Illustration and Problems 6.06-P1 (Simple)

Compute depreciation for the AY 2007-08.

	Case 1	*Case 2*	*Case 3*	*Case 4*
Rate of Depreciation	10%	15%	100%	40%
W.D.V. as on 1-4-2006				
• Plant A	5,000	25,000	60,000	1,00,000
• Plant B	15,000	50,000	Nil	20,000
Purchase of assets on 15-05-2006				
• Plant C	70,000	Nil	10,000	95,000
Sale of assets on 1-12-2006				
• Plant A	20,000	15,000	20,000	50,000
• Plant B	Not sold	75,000	Not sold	70,000
• Plant C	Not sold	Not sold	Not sold	5,000

Ans: (1) 7,000; (2) Nil; (3) 50,000; (4) Nil, since on the last day of the PY BOA is empty.

Solution

Computation of depreciation

	Case 1	*Case 2*	*Case 3*	*Case 4*
Rate of Depreciation	10%	15%	100%	40%
Opening W.D.V. as on 1-4-2006	20,000	75,000	60,000	1,20,000
Add: Purchases	70,000	Nil	10,000	95,000
Less: Sale of assets	(20,000)	(90,000)	(20,000)	(1,25,000)
Closing W.D.V. as on 31-3-2007	70,000	(15,000)	50,000	90,000
Less: Depreciation	(7,000)	nil	50,000	nil
Opening W.D.V. as on 1-4-2007	63,000	nil	nil	nil

Note: No STCG shall arise in case 1 and case 2 since depreciation is not nil.

Computation of STCG for the AY 2007-08

	Case 2	*Case 4*
Sale Consideration	90,000	1,25,000
Less:		
• W.D.V. of BoA as on 1-4-2006	(75,000)	(1,20,000)
• Cost of assets acquired during the PY 2006-07	(nil)	(95,000)
• Expenses on transfer	(nil)	(nil)
STCG	15,000	(90,000)

Problem 6.06-P2 [1. CA M95] [2. CS D02]

1. From the following figures, you are required to ascertain the depreciation admissible and other liabilities, if any, in respect of the previous year relevant to the AY 2007-08:

	Plant & Machinery	*Building*
Written down value at the beginning of the year	2,50,000	10,00,000
Additions during the year	3,00,000	NIL
Sales during the year	6,00,000	2,00,000

2. From the following figures, ascertain the depreciation admissible for the AY 2007-08 :

	Plant & Machinery	*Building*
Written down value at the beginning of the year	5,00,000	20,00,000
Additions during the year	6,00,000	Nil
Sale during the year	12,00,000	4,00,000

Ans: (1) STCG 50,000; Dep 80,000. (2) STCG 1,00,000; Dep 1,60,000.

COMPREHENSIVE PROBLEMS

Illustrations 6.06-P3 (Difficult)

Compute depreciation for the AY 2007-08 from the following information. Rate of depreciation 10%.

	Case 1	Case 2	Case 3	Case 4
Opening W.D.V. on 1-4-2006	2,00,000	3,00,000	6,00,000	5,00,000
Purchases made during the year				
• Plant A (elegible for half rate of depreciation)	1,00,000	50,000	2,00,000	40,000
• Plant B	50,000	70,000	90,000	20,000
Sale of the asset during the year	(1,40,000)	(2,00,000)	(7,90,000)	(5,30,000)

Solution

	Case 1	Case 2	Case 3	Case 4
Opening W.D.V. on 1-4-2006	2,00,000	3,00,000	6,00,000	5,00,000
Add : Purchases				
• Plant A (Half rate)	1,00,000	50,000	2,00,000	40,000
• Plant B	50,000	70,000	90,000	20,000
Less: Sale of the asset	(1,40,000)	(2,00,000)	(7,90,000)	(5,30,000)
Closing W.D.V. on 31-3-2007	2,10,000	2,20,000	1,00,000	30,000
Less: Depreciation for the PY 2006-07				
• Half	(5,000)	(2,500)	(5,000)	(1,500)
• Full	(11,000)	(17,000)	Nil	Nil
Opening W.D.V. on 1-4-2007	1,94,000	2,00,500	95,000	28,500

Illustration and Problems 6.06-P4 (Typical)

Compute depreciation allowance for the AY 2007-08 and AY 2008-09. Rate of depreciation 15%.

	Case 1	Case 2	Case 3	Case 4
W.D.V. on 1-4-2006	1,05,000	5,000	40,000	15,000

Purchase of asset

Particulars	*Amount*	*Date of Purchase*	*Date when asset is put to use*
Plant A	20,000	1-5-2005	2-04-2006
Plant B	5,500	1-1-2007	6-10-2007
Plant C	25,000	2-6-2007	5-12-2007
Plant D	50,000	1-7-2006	6-10-2006
Plant E	15,000	8-8-2006	5-03-2007

Sale of asset

Particulars	*Date of Sale*	*Amount*
Plant X	1-6-2005	1,000
Plant Y	1-12-2006	40,000
Plant Z	2-4-2007	90,000

Ans: Dep: (1) 17,625; 10,519; (2) 3,750; nil; (3) 7,875; 1,322; (4) 4,500; nil. STCG : (1) nil; (2) 13,250; (3) nil; (4) 4,000.

Problem 6.06-P5 [CA N00]

From the following data, calculate the depreciation admissible to an individual carrying on business, for assessment year 2007-08.

Factory building (w.d.v.)	5,00,000
Plant and machinery (w.d.v.)	8,00,000
• Additions	
- June 30, 2006	1,00,000
- December 31, 2006	1,00,000
• Sales on December 1, 2006	6,00,00
Computer - Addition on January 1, 2007	1,00,000
Furniture and fixtures (w.d.v)	1,00,000
Motor car (w.d.v.)	60,000

Ans: 1,39,500.

Problem 6.06-P6 [Hons 2004]

Z Ltd. furnishes you the following information : Block I : Plant and Machinery (consisting of 3 plants), rate of depreciation 15%. W.D.V. on April 1, 2006 : Rs. 2,50,000.

Block II : Buildings (two buildings), rate of depreciation 10% W.D.V on April 1, 2006 Rs. 6,00,000.

Acquired on June 2, 2006 , 2 plants for Rs. 2,00,000.

Sold on November 30, 2006 all the five plants for Rs. 5,00,000.

Acquired on December 15, 2006 , two plants for Rs. 1,50,000.

Admissible rate of depreciation in relation to all acquired plants is 15%.

Compute the amount of admissible depreciation claim of Z Ltd. for the AY 2007-08.

Ans: 7,500+60,000=67,500.

Problem 6.06-P7

1. Mr. Mohan is owner of two buildings which are used by him for his own business. The written down value of these buildings is Rs. 5,00,000 on 1st April 2006 and the rate of depreciation allowable on this block of assets is 10%. He purchased a third building on 1st December, 2006 for Rs. 2,50,000 and sold one of the two old buildings on 1st March, 2007 for Rs. 8,50,000. Transfer expenses amounted to Rs. 20,000.
   (a) Compute the deduction for depreciation allowable to Shri Mohan and the amount of capital gain taxable for the assessment year 2007-08.
   (b) What would have been the difference, had the building been sold for Rs. 4,00,000.
2. X Ltd. is a Company having financial year as previous year. It has 3 items of plant and machinery. The aggregate W.D.V. of the items at the beginning of the Financial Year 2005-2006 is Rs. 5,52,500. During the previous year, item No. 1 was sold for Rs. 2,00,000 and new item No. 4 falling in the same block was acquired during the year for Rs. 2,50,000. Determine depreciation for Assessment Year 2006-2007 and W.D.V. for Assessment Year 2007-2008.

Ans: (1) (a) Dep nil; STCG 30.000; (b) Dep 22,500; STCG nil; (2) 90,375; 5,12,125.

Problem 6.06-P8 [CA M99]

K industries owned six machines which were in use in its business in March, 2006. Depreciation on these machines was available as "plant". The written down value of these machines at the end of previous year relevant to assessment year 2006-07 was Rs. 6,50,000.

A new plant was bought for Rs. 6,50,000 on November 30, 2006. Three of the old machines were sold on June 10, 2006 for Rs. 9,00,000.

Required :

a. Compute the claim to depreciation for assessment year 2007-08 and

b. Capital gains liable to tax for the same assessment year.

c. If K industries had sold the three machines in June, 2006 for Rs. 14,00,000, will there be any difference in your working ? Explain.

Ans: 22,688; no capital gain; 1,97,500.

Problem 6.06-P9 (ICWA - D02)

Compute the depreciation allowable to an assessee for the AY 2007-08 on the basis of the following particulars :

1.	W.D.V. of Machinery on 1-4-2006	3,20,000
2.	Machinery purchased and installed on 1-12-2006	1,00,000
3.	Machinery purchased on 31-12-2005, not installed by 31-3-2007	1,50,000
4.	Sales proceeds of machinery purchased on 1-4-2003 for 1,00,000	1,50,000
5.	Machinery destroyed on 1-3-2007 by fire which was installed on 1-4-2005. Cost Rs. 50,000. Insurance claim received on 31-3-2007	30,000

Ans: 28,500.

Problem 6.06-P10 (ICWA - D95)

On April 1, 2006 X Ltd. owns the following assets. Rate of depreciation 15%.

Assets	Actual Cost	Depreciated value on April 1, 2006
Plant A	8,00,000	5,15,600
Plant B	4,10,000	2,05,400
Plant C	6,00,000	3,10,000
Plant D	2,18,000	1,85,300
Total	20,28,000	12,16,300

The aforesaid assets are covered by insurance against loss by fire. Plant A is purely damaged on June 2, 2006 by fire and X Ltd. receives Rs. 6,40,000 as compensation in respect of loss. It, however, spends Rs. 1,60,000 and restores the plant to working condition. The assessing officer wants to tax Rs. 4,80,000 (i.e. Rs. 6,40,000-Rs. 1,60,000) either as revenue receipt under section 28 or as capital receipt under section 45. Alternatively he wants to reduce the written down value of block of assets by Rs. 4,80,000 for determining depreciation for the previous year 2006-07.

Calculate the depreciation allowance and the written down value, value for the previous year 2006-07 relevant to assessment year 2007-08.

Ans: 1,10,445; 6,25,855.

Problem 6.06-P11 [Hons 1995]

From the following information work out the amount of depreciation admissible to Mr. Ram for the AY 2007-08. Total actual cost of machinery on March 31, 2006 is Rs. 9,00,000. Total amount of depreciation claimed upto March 31, 2006 Rs. 2,40,000. New machinery purchased on August 1, 2006 Rs. 3,00,000. Machinery purchased on January 1, 2003 at a cost of Rs. 1,00,000 *(accumulated depreciation Rs. 51,000)* was sold on March 15, 2007 for Rs. 80,000. The rate of depreciation on Machinery is 15%.

Ans: 1,32,000.

Problem 6.06-P12 (Typical)

Written down value of a building on 1-4-2004 was Rs. 60,000 on which 5% depreciation was allowed. On October 21, 2005 the company acquired another building of the same block for Rs. 2,40,000. On 1-6-2006 the company acquired a machine for Rs. 1,00,000 which was put to use for the purpose of business. During the year due to prolonged load shedding and lock-outs the asset was used for 100 days only for production purpose. Rate of depreciation 15%. Find out the allowable depreciation under the head business and profession for the AY 2007-08.

Ans: 14,407.50 + 15,000 = 29,407.50.

Problem 6.06-P13 (Typical)

X purchased a machine for business on 1-1-2007 for Rs. 6,40,000. The cost of installation was Rs. 60,000. The machine was destroyed by fire on 1-6-2007. An amount of Rs. 4,00,000 was received from insurance company. The company realised Rs. 5,000 from the sale of scrap. Eligible rate of depreciation 15%. Find out the amount of depreciation for the AY 2007-08 and AY 2008-09. Also compute capital gain if any. No other asset exists in this block.

Ans: 52,500; nil; (2,42,500).

Problem 6.06-P14 (Difficult)

Find out the admissible depreciation and income under the head capital gain for the AY 2007-08.

Depreciated value of the block of assets *(consisting of plants A, B and C)* on April 1, 2006	14,80,000
Addition of plant D made on September 1, 2006 *(it is put to use on September 6, 2006)*	1,60,000
Cost of plant E purchased on December 24, 2006.	3,10,000
Sale proceeds of plant A *(sold on March 3, 2007)* which was originally purchased on April 1, 1993 for Rs. 1,20,000	20,30,000
Expenses on transfer	1,000

Ans: Nil; 79,000.

Problem 6.06-P15 [Hons 2002]

From the following data calculate the depreciation admissible to an individual carrying on business, for the AY 2007-08 :

(i) Factory Building w.d.v. on 1-4-2006 (Rate 10%)	10,00,000
(ii) Plant and Machinery (Rate 15%) :	
• Written down value on 1-4-2006	8,00,000
• Additions on 30-6-2006	1,00,000
• Additions on 31-12-2006	1,00,000
• Sale of old plant on 1-12-2006	6,00,000
(iii) Motor car (Rate 15%) :	
• Written down value on 1-4-2006	1,20,000
• Sale of car on 30-9-2006	1,50,000

Ans: 1,87,500; 30,000.

Problem 6.06-P16 [CA N03]

Y Industries furnishes you the following information :

Block I : Plant and machinery (consisting of 10 looms) rate of depreciation : 15%, WDV on April 1, 2006 : Rs. 5,00,000.

Block II : Buildings (consisting of 3 buildings), rate of depreciation : 10% WDV on April 1, 2006 : Rs. 12,50,000.

Acquired on July 5, 2006 5 looms for Rs. 4,00,000.

Sold on December 7, 2006 15 looms for Rs. 10,00,000.

Acquired on January 10, 2007 2 looms for Rs. 3,00,000.

Compute depreciation claim for the assessment year 2007-08.

Ans: 1,40,000.

Problem 6.06-P17 [Hons 1993]

Depreciated value of the block of assets (consisting of plants A, B and C) on 01-04-2006 was Rs. 14,80,000. An addition of plant D was made on 01-09-2006 for Rs. 1,60,000 and it was put to use on 08-09-2006. Another plant E was purchased on 24-12-2006 and it was put to use on the same date for Rs. 3,10,000. Sale proceeds of plant A (sold on March 3rd, 2007) are Rs. 16,30,000 which was originally purchased on April 1st, 2000 for Rs. 1,20,000.

Assuming that the rate of depreciation is 15%, find out the admissible depreciation and income under the head capital gains for the assessment 2007-08.

Ans: 24,750.

Problem 6.06-P18 (Simple)

1. Mr. Taxcrazy acquired a patent right of a product for Rs. 2,50,000 during the financial year 2005-06. He acquired another patent right for Rs. 4,00,000 on 1-12-2006. Find out the allowable depreciation under the head business for the AY 2007-08.
2. An assessee acquired a patent on 10th November for Rs. 2,80,000 during previous year 2006-07. How much amount will be deducted for the same same while calculating income from business and profession?

Ans: 96,875; 70,000.

TOPIC 6.07 *SECTION 38(2). ASSET USED PARTLY FOR BUSINESS

Where the asset is partly used for personal purpose and partly for business purpose then depreciation is restricted to a fair proportionate part thereof which the Assessing Officer may determine, having regard to the user of such building, machinery, plant or furniture for the purposes of the business or profession.

Illustration 6.07-P1 (Difficult)

Mr. Taxcrazy purchases two computers on 1-7-2005 for Rs. 1,00,000 for business purpose. The computers are also used for personal purpose to the extent of 20% of its total use. Compute depreciation allowed for the AY 2006-07 and AY 2007-08.

Solution

Opening W.D.V. on 1-4-2005	Nil
Add : Purchase	1,00,000
Closing W.D.V. on 31-3-2006	1,00,000
Less : Depreciation 80% of 60% of 1,00,000	48,000
Opening W.D.V. on 1-4-2006	52,000
Less : Depreciation 80% of 60% of 52,000	24,960
Opening W.D.V. on 31-3-2007	27,040

TOPIC 6.08 *SECTION 43(1). ACTUAL COST

(A) STATUTORY MEANING

In sections 28 to 41 and in this section, unless the context otherwise requires. "Actual cost" means the actual cost of the assets to the assessee, reduced by that portion of the cost thereof, if any, as has been met directly or indirectly by any other person or authority.

(B) INCLUSIONS IN ACTUAL COST

The accepted accountancy rule for determining the cost of fixed assets is to include all expenditure

a. directly relatable to acquisition of the asset
b. Expenses necessary to bring the asset to site, install it and make it fit to use, and
c. Expenses incurred to facilitate the use of asset.
d. As per explanation 8 to section 43(1) interest pertaining to the period till the asset is put to use shall be treated as part of the actual cost of the asset. However interest relatable to any period after the asset is put to use cannot be included in actual cost. It can be claimed as deduction u/s 36(1)(iii). This clause shall apply even if the business is an existing one.
e. Travelling expenditure for acquiring depreciable asset is a part of actual cost.

Note:

Section 32 Explanation 1 : Any capital expenditure incurred by the assessee for the purposes of the business or profession in a building not owned by him then, such capital expenditure incurred shall be treated as deemed building for which the assessee (tenant) can claim depreciation.

TOPIC 6.09 *DEPRECIATION ON IMPORTED CAR

To claim depreciation on imported motor car, the car should be acquired after 31-3-2001 otherwise depreciation is not available.

TOPIC 6.10 *DEPRECIATION WHEN ASSET IS ACQUIRED ON HIRE PURCHASE

When an asset is acquired on Hire Purchase basis, then depreciation is charged on cash down payment value.

E.g. A plant was purchased by X Ltd. on hire purchase basis on 4-9-2006. X Ltd. was required to pay 20 monthly instalments of Rs. 2,000 each. The cash down value of the machine was Rs. 35,000. In this case depreciation shall be available on Rs. 35,000 and not on Rs. 40,000 (20 × 2,000).

TOPIC 6.11 **SECTION 32(1)(iia)*. ADDITIONAL DEPRECIATION ALLOWED UNDER THE INCOME TAX ACT

(A) ADDITIONAL DEPRECIATION, WHAT AND TO WHOM ?

Additional depreciation is over and above the normal depreciation.Additional depreciation is available to all assessees engaged in the business of manufacture or production of any article or thing.

(B) ADDITIONAL DEPRECIATION, CONDITIONS ?

1. Additional depreciation @ 20% shall be allowed on
2. any *new* machinery or plant, other than following assets,
   (a) any machinery or plant which, before its installation by the assessee, was used either within or outside India by any other person; or
   (b) any machinery or plant installed in any office premises or any residential accommodation, including accommodation in the nature of a guest house; or
   (c) any office appliances or road transport vehicles; or
   (d) any machinery or plant, the whole of the actual cost of which is allowed as a deduction *(whether by way of depreciation or otherwise)* in computing the income chargeable under the head "Profits and gains of business or profession" of any one previous year:
   (e) Ships and aircraft
   (f) Building and furniture
3. which has been acquired and installed after 31-3-2005.

(C) OTHER POINTS

1. Rate of additional depreciation is 20%. However if the asset is acquired and put to use in the same year for less than 180 days then rate of additional depreciation shall be 10%.
2. Additional depreciation is computed on individual assets and not on block of assets.
3. Additional depreciation is allowed even if the block of assets has nil or negative value.
4. Additional deprecition is not available if the new plant is sold in the year of acquisition.
5. Additional deprecition is available only for one year and not thereafter.

Problem 6.11-P1 (Difficult)

Nokia Ltd. is engaged in the business of manufacture of moblie phone since 2004. Compute normal depreciation and additional depreciation for the AY 2007-08. (Rate of depreciation 15%)

	Case 1	*Case 2*	*Case 3*
Written down value of plant on 1-4-2006	6,00,000	3,00,000	6,00,000
Purchases	2,00,000	6,00,000	1,50,000
Sale	7,00,000	10,00,000	50,000

Solution

	Case 1	*Case 2*	*Case 3*
Written down value of plant on 1-4-2006	6,00,000	3,00,000	6,00,000
Purchases	2,00,000	6,00,000	1,50,000
Sale	(7,00,000)	(10,00,000)	(50,000)
Written down value of plant on 31-3-2007	1,00,000	(1,00,000)	7,00,000
Less: Depreciation			
Additional depreciation	(30,000)	(90,000)	(22,500)
Normal depreciation	(15,000)	(nil)	(1,05,000)
Written down value of plant on 1-4-2007	55,000	nil	5,72,500

Problem 6.11-P2 (Difficult)

Motorola Ltd. is engaged in the business of manufacture of moblie phone since 2000. During the previous year following assets are acquired and put to use. Compute normal depreciation and additional depreciation for the AY 2007-08 Written down value of plant on 1-4-2006 is Rs. 16,00,000. (Rate of depreciation 15%)

Assets	*Date of Acquisition*	*Cost of Acquisition*	*Rate of Depreciation*
Furniture	11-8-2006	50,000	10%
Machine P	15-8-2006	4,00,000	15%
Machine Q	19-3-2007	2,50,000	100%
Machinery used in office	27-12-2006	80,000	15%
Air conditioner used in factory	18-12-2006	90,000	15%
Machine R (2nd hand)	21-12-2006	30,000	15%
Machine S	31-1-2007	5,00,000	15%

Ans: Normal Dep. Rs. 4,82,500; Additional Dep. Rs. 1,39,000

Problem 6.11-P3 (Difficult)

Dabur Ltd., engaged in the manufacture of health products, furnishes following details to compute normal and additional depreciation allowed for the 2007-08.

Written down value of the block of the assets on 1-4-2006 Rs. 2,00,000 (60%); Rs. 1,00,000 (15%); Rs. 1,50,000 (40%)

Assets	*Date of Acquisition*	*Cost of Acquisition*	*Rate of Depreciation*
Computers installed in factory	12-5-2006	4,50,000	60%
Plant A	17-5-2006	8,30,000	15%
Plant B	15-1-2007	6,86,000	40%
Plant C	15-9-2006	4,56,000	15%
Plant D	15-6-2006	3,50,000	15%
Plant E	18-3-2007	1,50,000	15%

Plant D was sold for Rs. 16,00,000 on 31-3-2007. Some of the old plants eligible for depreciation @ 40% were sold for Rs. 8,70,000

Ans: Normal Dep. Rs. 4,21,650; Additional Dep. Rs. 4,30,800; STCG Rs. 34,000

Problem 6.11-P4 [CS D05]

An industrial undertaking which commenced the manufacturing activity with effect from 1st September, 2006 has acquired the following assets during the previous year 2006-07:

Assets	*Date of Acquisition*	*Date when put to use*	*Cost of Acquisition*
Factory buildings	4-4-2006	1-9-2006	50,00,000
Plant and machinery:			
Air pollution control equipment	4-5-2006	1-9-2006	4,00,000
Machinery-A	5-5-2006	1-9-2006	2,00,000
Machinery-B	7-6-2006	1-9-2006	5,00,000
Machinery-C	30-8-2006	1-9-2006	10,00,000
Machinery-D	1-9-2006	31-10-2006	4,00,000
Machinery-E	1-1-2007	28-2-2007	3,00,000
Machinery-F (second hand)	11-1-2007	13-1-2007	2,00,000
Motor car	1-2-2007	1-2-2007	5,00,000
Air-conditioner (installed in the Office)	1-2-2007	2-2-2007	1,00,000

Compute the depreciation allowable for the assessment year 2007-08 and the written down value as on 1st April, 2007.

Ans: [5,00,000; 4,50,000] [4,00,000; nil] [3,67,500; 4,10,000; 24,22,500]

Problem 6.11-P5 (CA FINAL - N03)

The written down value of plant and machinery on April 1, 2003 of X Ltd. engaged in manufacturing of PVC granules is Rs. 10 crore. The company purchased additional plant and machinery of Rs. 8 crore on April 18, 2003 inclusive of a second - hand machine imported from China of Rs. 2 crore to increase its installed capacity of production from 1000 tonne per annum to 1500 tonne per annum. The production from new machine was taken with effect from December 1, 2003. Workout by giving reasons the amount of allowable depreciation.

Ans: 395 Lakhs

6.12 COMPREHENSIVE PROBLEMS

Problem 6.12-P1 [ICWA - D97] [Difficult]

The following data is available in respect of 4 assessees. A, B, C and D:

	A	B	C	D
Depreciated value of block on 1-4-2006	1,70,000	90,000	1,50,000	1,70,000
Add: Cost of plant purchased during April to September 2006	2,00,000	2,00,000	2,00,000	80,000
Less: Sale proceeds of plant sold during April to September 2006	(50,000)	(1,90,000)	(3,90,000)	(20,000)
Add: Cost of plant B purchased during Oct 5, 2006 to March 2007	2,00,000	2,00,000	2,00,000	2,00,000
Less: Sale proceeds of plant sold during October 2006 to March 2007	(50,000)	(2,10,000)	Nil	(4,37,000)
WDV of the block as on 31-3-2007	4,70,000	90,000	1,60,000	Nil

Calculate:

(a) Depreciation for the PY 2006-07

(b) WDV of the block of assets as on 1-4-2007

(c) STCG if any

Ans: (A) 55,500; 4,14,500; NIL (B) 6,750; 83,250; nil (C) 12,000; 1,48,000; nil (D) nil; nil; 7,000.

Problem 6.12-P2 [Difficult]

X owns the following assets as on April 1, 2007 (rate of depreciation 15%)

Assets	*W.D.V. on 1-4-2006*	*Date of acquisition*
Plant A	5,00,000	April 1, 1995
Plant B	3,00,000	May 10, 1994
Plant C	4,00,000	March 13, 1995

During the Previous Year 2006-2007 the following plants/assets were purchased/sold by X

Assets	*Rate of depreciation*	*Date of Purchase/sale*	*Selling price*	*Cost*
Plant D	15%	1-4-2006	-	3,00,000
Plant E	15%	1-1-2007	-	1,00,000
Plant F	40%	15-12-2006	-	2,00,000
Plant A	15%	15-3-2007	10,00,000	-
Building A	10%	15-3-2007	-	15,00,000
Plant C	15%	10-5-2006	8,00,000	-

Determine the amount of depreciation and capital gain/loss for Assessment year 2007-2008. Expenditure on sale of plants A & C is Rs. 10,000 each.

Ans: Dep 1,15,000; STCG 1,80,000

Problem 6.12-P3 [Typical]

DEF Limited owns following fixed assets as on 1-4-2005 :

Assets	*Actual cost*	*Written Down Value as on 31-3-2005*	*Rate of depreciation*
Building :			
A	20,00,000	12,50,000	10%
B	5,00,000	1,25,000	10%
C	2,00,000	40,000	5%
Plant and Machinery :			
L	70,000	35,100	15%
M	1,10,000	78,000	15%
N	20,000	7,000	40%
P	40,000	31,000	40%

Acquisition during 1-4-2005 to 31-3-2006 are :

Assets	*Cost (Rs.)*	*Date of acquisition*	*Date of putting into use*	*Rate of depreciation*
Building :				
D	8,00,000	30-5-2005	3-6-2005	10%
E	3,00,000	10-6-2005	7-3-2006	5%
Plant and Machinery :				
Q	5,00,000	2-8-2005	7-12-2005	15%
R	2,10,000	10-3-2006	1-12-2006	15%
T	90,000	9-5-2006	1-11-2006	40%

There were following sales too :

Assets	*Date of sale*	*Net sale consideration received (Rs.)*
Building A	10-5-2005	14,00,000
Plant and Machinery :		
M	15-5-2005	1,20,000
P	19-12-2005	1,15,000
N	9-12-2006	32,000

Compute amounts of admissible depreciation for Assessment Years 2006-07 and 2007-08.

Ans: Bldg 10% : 63,750; 57,375. Bldg 5% : 24,400; 15,680. Plant 15% : 35,710; 97,564. Plant 40% : nil; 11,600.

Problem 6.12-P4 [Typical]

X is carrying on two businesses. Compute the depreciation and capital gain for the AY 2007-08.

1. *Relating to steel rolling mill at Kanpur*

   (a) Opening W.D.V. on 1-4-2006 of factory building Rs. 6,20,000. This building, constructed 5 years back, was sold for Rs. 10,28,000.

(b) Machinery (entitled to depreciation at 15%) Opening W.D.V. on 1-4-2006 — Rs. 3,20,000.

(c) Car (entitled to depreciation at 15%) Opening W.D.V. on 1-4-2006 — Rs. 80,000.

2. *Relating to fertilizer unit at Cuttak*

   (a) Factory building (purchased in March 2005) Opening W.D.V. on 1-4-2006 — Rs. 2,80,000

   (b) Machinery (depreciation rate 15%) purchased in June 2006 — Rs. 4,40,000.

   (c) Car purchased on 16-12-2006 for Rs. 5,40,000.

3. All machines of Kanpur and Cuttack were sold in March 2007 for Rs. 5,10,000. New Machineries were purchased for Rs. 10 lakhs in March 2007 which were installed on April 2007.

Ans: 52,500; STCG (1,22,000).

STRATEGY MAKER

Points in 1 to 10	Overall Points 8; Practical 9; Theory 4.
Type of problem	Difficult. It is although an easy chapter.
What to expect (DU)	Practical questions are always there. Its questions are sometimes attached to Profit from Business questions. Do revise all the illustrations.
CA (PE II)	Everything.

Good, you are doing very fine

Completed a part of business and capital gain chapter. We are starting a next chapter. Capital Gain. It needs a high level of concentration.

Keep Running

Are capital receipts taxable? Yes on transfer of capital asset

CAPITAL GAIN

TOPIC 7.01 *SECTION 45(1)*. WHICH INCOME IS CHARGEABLE UNDER THE HEAD 'CAPITAL GAIN' (CHARGEABILITY)

Any profit or gain arising from the *transfer* of a *Capital Asset* is chargeable in the previous year in which transfer took place. *i.e.* the date of accrual of capital gain is the date when the transfer takes place. In other words "Year of transfer = Year of chargeability"

E.g. Suppose Mr. X 'transfer' *(essential condition)* a 'capital asset' *(essential condition)* on 11-6-2006, then gain arising shall be chargeable in the PY 2006-07 *i.e.* AY 2007-08.

TOPIC 7.02 *SECTION 2(14)*. MEANING OF CAPITAL ASSET

PART A DEFINITION : EVERY ASSET IS A CAPITAL ASSET WHETHER USED FOR BUSINESS PURPOSE OR PERSONAL PURPOSE

Capital asset means property of *any* kind (*movable / immovable / tangible / intangible*) held by an assessee, whether or not connected with his business but excluding the following assets.

PART B DEFINITION : EXCLUSIONS

1. *Business Asset* : Any stock in trade, consumable stores or raw materials, held for the purpose of business or profession.
2. *Movable asset used for domestic purpose* : Personal effects of the assessee held for his personal use or for the use of any member of his family dependent upon him *i.e.* those household goods which satisfies following conditions :
   (a) It should be a movable property, and
   (b) Should be held for his personal use.

However jewellery (ornaments made of gold, silver, platinum or any other precious metal or stone or any item made up of these) are not treated as personal effect and hence treated as capital asset.

(i) *Meaning of Jewellery

"Jewellery" includes :

(*a*) ornaments made of gold, silver, platinum or any other precious metal or any alloy containing one or more of such precious metals, whether or not containing any precious or semi-precious stone, and whether or not worked or sewn into any wearing apparel, or

(*b*) precious or semi-precious stones, whether or not set in any furniture, utensil or other article or worked or sewn into any wearing apparel.

3. *Rural agricultural land* : Agricultural land in India provided it is not situated in :

   (a) Any area within the jurisdiction of Municipality / Cantonment board having a population of 10,000 or more according to the last preceding census; or

   (b) In any area notified by the Central Govt. *(Govt. may notify a distance of not exceeding 8 k.m., from the local limits of municipality)*

It means rural agricultural land situated in India is not treated as capital asset.

Following agricultural land is treated as capital asset :

1. Agricultural land situated in Urban Area.

2. Agricultural land situated within the limits referred to above.

3. Agricultural land situated outside India is treated as capital asset.

4. *Gold Bonds* : Following Gold Bonds are not treated as capital asset :

   - Gold Deposit Bonds issued under the Gold Deposit Scheme, 1999.

   - 6½% Gold Bonds 1977 or 7% Gold Bonds 1980 or National Defence Gold Bonds 1980 issued by the Central Government. *(Not in existence since redeemed)*

5. Special Bearer Bonds 1991. *(Not in existence since redeemed)*

Note

- It should be noted that transfer of an asset which is not a "Capital Asset" does not give rise to capital gain.

Problems 7.02-P1

1. Every asset is a capital asset except certain exclusions. (True or False)
2. What are those exclusions ?
3. In which PY capital gain is charged to tax ?
4. Every land situated in rural area is not a capital asset. (True or False)
5. Name five intangible assets which are capital assets ?
6. Write name of two assets which are not capital assets ?

Solution

1. True.
2. Business asset, personal asset, agricultural land situated in India in rural area, gold bonds and special bearer bond.
3. In the PY in which transfer takes place.
4. False. Only agricultural land situated in rural area is not a capital asset.
5. Goodwill of a business, Right to subscribe for shares, trade mark, brand name, tenancy rights.
6. Rural agricultural land situated in India and Gold Bonds.

Problem 7.02-P2 (Simple)

State whether following are assets as per section 2(14) of the Income Tax Act and the year of chargeability :

1. Car for personal purpose sold at a gain of Rs. 12,000 on 15-6-2005.
2. Car for business purpose sold at a gain of Rs. 30,000 on 20-1-2007.
3. Car held by Maruti Udyog Ltd. sold at a gain of Rs. 2,000 on 1-4-2000.
4. Land situated in rural area sold at a gain of Rs. 55,000 on 9-3-2005.
5. Agricultural land situated in India in rural area sold at a gain of Rs. 2,000.
6. Gold held for personal use sold at a gain of Rs. 80,000 on 3-12-2011.
7. Shares held as investment sold at a gain of Rs. 400 on 26-8-2004.
8. Shares held as stock in trade.
9. M.F. Husain paintings purchased for personal use for Rs. 10,000 and sold for Rs. 1 Crore.

Ans: No; Yes (AY 2007-08); No; Yes (AY 2005-06); No; Yes (AY 2012-13); Yes (AY 2005-06); No; No.

TOPIC 7.03 KINDS OF CAPITAL ASSETS

(A) SECTION 2(42A). SHORT TERM CAPITAL ASSET (STCA)

It means any capital asset held by an assessee for not more than 36 months (i.e. *36 months or less than 36 months)*, immediately prior to the date of transfer.

However in the following cases of 'financial asset' an asset held for not more than 12 months *(i.e. 12 months or less than 12 months)* is treated as STCA.

Meaning of financial asset : It includes—

1. Equity shares or preference shares of a Company whether *listed or not*; or
2. Units of UTI or units of mutual funds specified u/s 10 (23D) whether *quoted or not*.
3. Government Securities.
4. Debentures or bonds *listed* in a recognised Stock Exchange of India.
5. Zero coupon bonds. Zero coupon bond means a bond issued by any infrastructure capital company or fund or any public company on or after 1-6-2005 in respect of which no payment or benefit is received before maturity or redemption fund. The Central Govt. notifes in the Official Gazette.

As seen in the previous chapter, the depreciable assets are always treated as short term capital asset irrespective of it's holding period.

For computing the period of holding of a capital asset, the date on which asset is sold is to be excluded.

The gain arising on transfer of a STCA is called Short Term Capital Gain (STCG). Similarly the loss arising on transfer of a STCA is called Short Term Capital Loss (STCL).

(B) SECTION 2(29A). LONG TERM CAPITAL ASSET (LTCA)

Any capital asset other than STCA is regarded as a LTCA *i.e.* an asset held for more than 36 months / 12 months as the case may be is treated as LTCA.

The gain arising on transfer of a LTCA is called Long Term Capital Gain (LTCG). Similarly the loss arising on transfer of a LTCA is called Long Term Capital Loss (LTCL).

Problem 7.03-P1 (Simple)

Find whether following assets are STCA or LTCA :

S.No.	*Type of capital assets*	*Date of acquisition*	*Date of sale*
1.	House Property	1-10-2002	2-10-2006
2.	Machinery on which depreciation claimed	1-1-1993	1-1-2007
3.	Equity shares held in Reliance Ltd.	5-4-2006	31-3-2007
4.	Listed debentures	6-11-2005	4-12-2006
5.	Unlisted debentures	1-1-2004	2-1-2007
6.	Debentures listed in NewYork Stock exchange	1-1-2005	2-1-2007
7.	Shares held in co-operative society	11-5-2005	5-1-2007

Ans: LTCA; STCA; STCA; LTCA; LTCA; STCA; STCA.

Problems 7.03-P2

1. What is the holding period of financial asset to constitute LTCA ?
2. Name the assets which remain under the possession of assessee for more than 3 years, still the gain arising from their transfer is treated as short term capital gain ?
3. Discuss the holding period of assets ?
4. What is the objective of differentiating short term capital gain and long term capital gain?

Solutions

1. It is more than 1 year except for unlisted debentures where it is more than 3 years.
2. Depreciable asset.
3. Holding period of

	STCA	LTCA
(a) Financial assets	1 year or less	more than 1 year
(b) Other capital assets	3 years or less	more than 3 years
(c) Depreciable assets	always STCA	always STCA

4.

(a) Rate of tax	Individual / HUF etc.	Firm / Company	Foreign Company
Short term capital gain	slab rate	30%	40%
STCG (STT paid)	10%	10%	10%
Long term capital gain	20%	20%	20%

(b) Also loss arising from sale of long term capital asset can set off only against long term capital gain. However loss arising from short term capital asset can be set off from both the long term and short term capital gain.

TOPIC 7.04 *SECTION 2(47).* WHAT IS TRANSFER?

General meaning of transfer : It is word of the widest import and includes every means by which the property may be passed from one person to another for consideration.

Transfer as per Income Tax Act.

Memory technique : **E SRCC (Asset) or E**

Exchange Sale Relinquishment Conversion Compulsory acquisition or Extinguishment of any rights therein.

- An *exchange* of capital asset takes place when the title in one property is passed in consideration of the title in another property.
- A *sale* takes place when title in the property is transferred for a price.
- *Relinquishment* of a capital asset arises when the owner surrenders his rights in property in favour of another person.
- *Conversion* of capital asset into stock in trade.
- *Compulsory acquisition* of an asset under any law is treated as transfer by the Government of India.
- *Extinguishment* covers every possible transaction which results in destruction, annihilation, extinction, termination, cessation or cancellation of all or any bundle of rights in a capital asset. For example termination of a lease or / and of a mortgagee's interest in a property.

Note

- The capital gain arises only on "transfer" of a capital asset *i.e.* where there is no 'transfer' there is no capital gain.

Problem 7.04-P1 (CS-J00) - M 6

Q.2b : X owns 1,000 partly paid-up shares in a company. These shares have been forfeited by the company for non-payment of call money. X wants to claim Rs. 8,000 (*i.e.*, amount paid at the time of application and allotment) as short-term capital loss. Is the claim of X tenable ?

Hint : Yes. Forfeiture of shares amounts to transfer u/s 2(47). Transfer in relation to capital asset includes extinguishment of any rights therein. In the above question since X's rights in the shares has extinguished, therefore X is entitled to claim short term capital loss of Rs. 8,000.

TOPIC 7.05 *SECTION 48.* COMPUTATION OF CAPITAL GAIN

(A) SECTION 2(42B). SHORT TERM CAPITAL GAIN (STCG) (ASSUMED FIGURES)

Sale Consideration (Full value of consideration)		50,000
Less :		
• Cost of Acquisition *(COA)*	20,000	
• Cost of Improvement *(COI)*	5,000	
• Expenses on transfer	2,000	(27,000)
STCG		23,000
Less : Exemption u/s 54B, 54D, 54G & 54GA *(cannot exceed STCG)*		3,000
STCG		20,000

(B) SECTION 2(29B). LONG TERM CAPITAL GAIN (LTCG) (ASSUMED FIGURES)

Sale Consideration (Full value of consideration)		100,000
Less :		
• Indexed Cost of Acquisition *(COA)*	50,000	
• Indexed Cost of Improvement *(COI)*	6,000	
• Expenses on transfer	9,000	(65,000)
LTCG		35,000
Less : Exemption u/s 54, 54B, 54D, 54EC, 54ED, 54F, 54G & 54GA *(cannot exceed LTCG)*		30,000
LTCG		5,000

TOPIC 7.06 INDEXATION

(A) CONCEPT

Indexation of cost of acquisition and indexation of cost of improvement is allowed only on transfer of long term capital asset. *(Not short term capital asset)*

But what is indexation? Suppose you buy an asset in the year 81-82 for Rs. 100 and now you sell the same asset for Rs. 797 in the year 2006-07. What is your actual gain? Is it Rs. 697? No, why so? As you know the purchasing power of the money decreases every year. Therefore if you want to buy the same asset in the year 2006-07 at what cost you could buy. Certainly not at Rs. 100 but at higher value. It means you have to inflate the value of Rs. 100 to the value in the year of sale. Let that value be Rs. 497. Now your actual gain shall be Rs. 797–497 = Rs.300.

A cost inflation indexation table is given below which offsets the decreasing value of money. Understand using the table through examples shown below.

(B) COST INFLATION INDEX (CII) OF EACH PY

1981-82 **100**	1988-89 **161**	1995-96 **281**	2002-03 **447**
1982-83 **109**	1989-90 **172**	1996-97 **305**	2003-04 **463**
1983-84 **116**	1990-91 **182**	1997-98 **331**	2004-05 **480**
1984-85 **125**	1991-92 **199**	1998-99 **351**	2005-06 **497**
1985-86 **133**	1992-93 **223**	1999-00 **389**	2006-07 **519**
1986-87 **140**	1993-94 **244**	2000-01 **406**	
1987-88 **150**	1994-95 **259**	2001-02 **426**	

(C) FORMULA FOR INDEXATION

1. Indexation is available only on long term capital asset.
2. Indexation of cost of acquisition is done only between transferers.

$$\frac{\text{Index value of sale year}}{\text{Index value of acquisition year}} \times \text{Cost of acquisition.}$$

3. Indexation of cost of improvement is done in respective year of improvement.

$$\frac{\text{Index value of sale year}}{\text{Index value of improvement year}} \times \text{Cost of improvement.}$$

(D) RULES FOR INDEXATION

1. *Proviso 3 to section 48.* Indexation is not available in case of long term capital asset being bonds or debentures. *(However indexation is available on Govt. Securities)*
2. *Proviso 1 to section 48.* Indexation is not available in case of transfer of foreign exchange assets held by a Non-Resident assessee.

TOPIC 7.07 STEPS TO COMPUTE CAPITAL GAIN

1. First identify the year of chargeability.
2. Identify whether it is long term capital asset or short term capital asset.
3. If it is a long term capital asset then convert cost of acquisition to indexed cost of acquisition and cost of improvement to indexed cost of improvement.

Do remember rules of indexation.

Illustration 7.07-P1 (Simple)

Abbreviations used : Cost of acquisition (COA); Sale consideration (SC); Cost of improvement (COI)

Compute capital gain chargeable to tax for the AY 2007-08.

sells lands to

X-->Y

COA as on 1-1-1991 Rs. 1,05,000 SC as on 1-6-2006 Rs. 5,50,000

Solution

Computation of Capital Gain for the AY 2007-08

Sale consideration	5,50,000
Less : Indexed cost of acquisition	
$\frac{\text{Year of sale } (2005\text{-}06)}{\text{Year of acquisition } (89\text{-}90)} \times \text{COA} = \frac{519}{182} \times 1,05,000 =$	2,99,422
LTCG	2,50,577

Illustration 7.07-P2 (Simple)

Compute capital gain chargeable to tax for the AY 2007-08

sells RHP to

X-->Y

COA as on 1-11-1985 Rs. 52,000 SC as on 1-2-2007 Rs. 11,00,000

COI as on 1-5-1993 Rs. 95,100

COI as on 1-1-2007 Rs. 2,02,000

Solution

Computation of Capital Gain for the AY 2007-08

Sale consideration		11,00,000
Less : Indexed cost of acquisition		
$\frac{\text{Year of sale } (2005\text{-}06)}{\text{Year of acquisition } (84\text{-}85)} \times \text{COA} = \frac{519}{133} \times 52,000 =$	2,02,917	

Less : Indexed cost of improvement

$\dfrac{\text{Year of sale}(2005\text{-}06)}{\text{Year of improvement}(92\text{-}93)} \times \text{COI} = \dfrac{519}{244} \times 95{,}100 =$ 2,02,282

Less : Indexed cost of improvement

$\dfrac{\text{Year of sale}(2005\text{-}06)}{\text{Year of improvement}(2005\text{-}06)} \times \text{COI} = \dfrac{519}{519} \times 2{,}02{,}000 =$ 2,02,000 6,07,200

LTCG 4,92,800

Problems 7.07-P3 (Simple)

In the following cases find out the amount of capital gain for the AY 2007-08.

(a) Mr. B sold a sewing machine (used by his wife) for Rs. 96,000 on 15-2-2007. It was purchased on 12-4-1985 for Rs. 20,000.

(b) One diamond necklace costing Rs. 50,000 purchased in June 2006 sold for Rs. 68,000 in March 2007.

(c) He sold his personal Maruti Car purchased in 1990 for Rs. 1,80,000 at Rs. 18,000.

(d) He sold 1,000 shares of TQM Ltd for Rs. 2,50,000 in December 2006 which was purchased in June 2005 for Rs. 1,00,000.

Ans: Nil; STCG 18,000; Nil; 1,45,573.

TOPIC 7.08 FULL VALUE OF CONSIDERATION

(A) GENERAL MEANING

Full value of consideration means amount received or receivable on transfer of asset. It does not mean market value. Where the consideration is received in instalment in different years, the entire value of consideration is taken into account in computing capital gain. Capital gain arises on accrual basis.

(B) SECTION 50C. FULL VALUE OF CONSIDERATION IN CASE OF SALE OF IMMOVEABLE PROPERTY

Where the consideration received or accruing as a result of the transfer by an assessee of land or building or both, is less than the value adopted or assessed by any authority of a State Government (hereafter in this section referred to as the "stamp valuation authority") for the purpose of payment of stamp duty in respect of such transfer, the value so adopted or assessed shall, for the purposes of section 48, be deemed to be the full value of the consideration received or accruing as a result of such transfer.

In other words higher of sale consideration or value adopted by the Stamp Valuation Authority of is treated as full value of consideration.

Problem 7.08-P1

X sold his Residential house property on 15-12-2006 for Rs. 9,00,000. It was acquired by him on 7-7-1995 for Rs. 80,000. The State stamp valuation authority fixed the value of the property at the time of transfer at Rs. 15,00,000. Compute capital gain in the hands of X.

Ans: 13,52,242.

TOPIC 7.09 *SECTION 55(2).* WHAT IS COST OF ACQUISITION?

Meaning of cost of acquisition (COA) : Purchase Price + Registration Charges + Brokerage paid + interest on loan taken for purchasing the capital asset provided it is capitalised and deduction is not taken in respect of such expenses under any other provisions of the Act + Other expenses incurred for acquisition and installation of the asset *i.e.* COA = purchase price + expenses on acquisition.

As per fifth proviso to section 48. Securities transaction tax paid either on transfer of asset or acquisition of assets is neither treated as expenses on transfer nor expenses on acquisition of the asset.

What is cost of acquisition if the asset is acquired before 1-4-1981: It is higher of Cost of acquisition or Fair Market Value *(FMV)* as on 1-4-1981.

Illustration and Problems 7.09-P1 (Simple)

Compute cost of acquisition in following cases.

	Case 1	*Case 2*	*Case 3*	*Case 4*
Date of purchase	19-05-1976	16-5-1947	24-2-1972	3-5-1982
Purchase price	2,00,000	60,000	50,000	40,000
Brokerage paid	1%	10%	5%	12%
FMV as on 1-4-1981	2,01,000	70,000	52,000	48,500

Ans: (1) 2,02,000; (2) 70,000; (3) 52,500; (4) 44,800.

Solution

Case 1 Purchase price + Brokerage paid = 2,02,000 or FMV as on 1-4-1981 whichever is higher. Therefore Rs. 2,02,000 is the cost of acquisition.

Case 2 Purchase price + Brokerage paid = 66,000 or FMV as on 1-4-1981 whichever is higher. Therefore Rs. 70,000 is the cost of acquisition.

TOPIC 7.10 *SECTION 55(1)(b).* COST OF IMPROVEMENT *(COI)*

It means any *capital* expenditure incurred for making any additions or alterations to the capital assets by the assessee or by the previous owner.

Note

- Cost of improvement undertaken before 1-4-1981 is to be ignored otherwise it should be considered accordingly.

TOPIC 7.11 EXPENSES ON TRANSFER

It includes any expenditure incurred wholly and exclusively for the purpose of transfer of capital assets. It means expenditure incurred which is necessary to effect transfer. E.g. brokerage, stamp duty, registration fees, legal expenses, advertisement expenses or litigation expenses incurred for claiming enhancement of compensation.

Expenses on transfer are different from expenses on acquisition. Acquisition expenses are added to actual cost of the asset whereas transfer expenses are deducted from sale consideration.

Illustration 7.11-P1 (Difficult)

Compute capital gain chargeable to tax for the AY 2007-08.

sells property to

X-->Y

COA as on 1-1-1981 Rs. 4,00,000 — SC as on 1-2-2007 Rs. 25,00,000

FMV as on 1-4-1981 Rs. 3,00,000 — Expenses on transfer 0.15%

Expenses on acquisition of property 1%

COI as on 31-3-1981 Rs. 5,000

COI as on 12-6-2000 Rs. 18,000

Solution

Computation of Capital Gain for the AY 2007-08

Sale consideration		2,500,000
Less : Indexed cost of acquisition		
$\frac{\text{Year of sale}(2005-06)}{\text{Year of acquisition}(81-82)} \times \text{COA} = \frac{519}{100} \times 4,04,000 =$	20,96,760	
Less : Indexed cost of improvement		
$\frac{\text{Year of sale}(2005-06)}{\text{Year of improvement}(2000-01)} \times \text{COI} = \frac{519}{406} \times 18,000 =$	23,010	
Less : Expenses on transfer (0.15% of 25,00,000) =	3,750	21,23,520
LTCG		3,76,480

Note

- Cost of improvement undertaken before 1-4-1981 therefore ignored.

Problem 7.11-P2 (Difficult)

J purchased a house property on 1-9-1979 for Rs. 2,10,000. Fair Market Value of the house property on 1-4-1981 was Rs. 1,70,000. He incurred the following expenses :

Construction of a room on the ground floor during 1980-81 Rs. 10,000

Renewals / constructions on 1-6-2004 Rs. 3,92,000

The property was sold on 31-3-2007 for Rs. 12,65,000. Compute Capital Gain.

Ans: (2,48,750)

Problems 7.11-P3 [Pass 2006]

Mr. X purchases a house property for Rs. 80,000 on July 31, 1970. Brokerage paid on acquisition Rs. 8,000. The following expenses are incurred by him for making addition to the house property :

(i) Cost of construction of first floor in 1975 - 76	1,00,000
(ii) Cost of construction of the second floor in 1984 - 85	2,40,000

Fair market value of the property on April 1, 1981 is Rs. 4,00,000. The house property is sold by X on August 20, 2006 for Rs. 30,00,000 (expenses incurred on transfer : Rs. 10,000). Find out the capital gain chargeable to tax in the previous year 2006-07.

Ans: (82,480)

Problem 7.11-P4 [Pass 2006C]

Mr. Arora provides the following informations for his residential house. Compute capital gain for the assessment year 2007-08 :

(i) House was purchased on 30th June, 1970 for	86,000
(ii) Cost of construction of first floor in 1975-76	1,10,000
(iii) Fair market value as on 1-4-1981	4,00,000
(iv) Cost of construction of second floor in 1985-86	2,32,000
(v) Cost of construction of third floor in 1991 - 92	3,44,000
(vi) Sold the house on 30th June, 2006 for	42,50,000
(vii) Expenses incurred on transfer	10,000

Ans: 3,61,511.

Problems 7.11-P5 (Simple)

In the following cases find out the amount of capital gain for the AY 2007-08.

a. Mr. X who owns a house property worth Rs. 2,48,000 on 1-4-2006, sold the same for Rs. 8,00,000. The fair market value of the property was Rs. 2,21,000 on 1-4-1981 which was acquired on 31-3-1981 for Rs. 2,20,000. He incurred Rs. 15,000 for construction of a room in the house in 1992-93.

b. One house in Delhi purchased in 1977 for Rs. 78,000, sold in January 2007 for Rs. 9,00,000. Expenses regarding the sale were borne by him of Rs. 25,000. In 1980 he spent Rs. 40,000 and in 1996-97 Rs. 43,000 for constructing the first and second floor of the house. FMV as on 1-4-1981 was Rs. 87,000.

c. 'X' sold equity shares of a company on 31-7-2006, which he had purchased in 1979 for Rs 50,000; their Fair Market Price on 1-4-1981 was Rs 70,000. Gross sale proceeds were Rs 3,24,700 and expenses on transfer were Rs 10,000. STT paid on transfer 0.01%.

d. Shri Raghav purchased 20,000 square yards of land in 1973 at Rs. 29 per square yard and sold it in January, 2007 at Rs. 125 per square yard. The fair market value of the said land as on 1-4-1981 was Rs. 29.27 per square yard. Brokerage paid on acquisition 1% per square yard.

Ans: (3,81,900); 3,50,300; (38,600); (5,40,302)

Problems 7.11-P6 (Difficult)

Mr. X sold his properties during previous year 2006-07 as under :

(i) Household TV and refrigerator costing Rs. 96,000 purchased in 2003, sold in Feb. 2007 for Rs. 1,00,000.

(ii) A car sold on 1-12-2006 for Rs. 1,80,000 which was purchased by him in Jan., 2005 for Rs. 2,80,000 and it written down value on 1-4-2006 was Rs. 1,52,000. The car is used for business purposes.

(iii) Agricultural land was sold for Rs. 9,00,000 on 1-2-2007 and its purchase price in 1983-84 was Rs. 1,00,000. He purchased new land for his own cultivation for Rs. 2,50,000 in June, 2007.

(iv) Gold ornaments acquired in July, 2003 for Rs. 2,00,000 were sold for Rs. 2,40,000 in June, 2006.

(v) Let out residential house in Agra was inherited by hi m in 1965. Sale price on 30-11-2006, Rs. 12,00,000. Fair market value on 1-4-1981 Rs. 2,00,000. Cost of improvement made during 1990 - 91 Rs. 40,000. Expenses on transfer Rs. 60,000.

Compute his total capital gains for the assessment year 2007-08.

Ans: nil; 28,000; nil; 15,810; (12,066)

Problems 7.11-P7 (Typical)

During the financial year 2006-2007, Seth Nirmal Kumar Moolchand Binani, resident of Cuffe Parade, Bombay sold following movable and immovable properties owned by him:

(i) A land plot measuring 1974 sq. metres situated at Katra Gulabrai, Chandni Chowk, Delhi, was purchased by Shri Binani on 30-6-1995 for Rs. 14,00,000 inclusive of purchase expenses on stamp duty, brokerage and transfer charges. This was sold by Shri Binani on 31-12-2006 to M/s. Real Calibre Property Developers (P) Ltd., Greater Kailash-II, New Delhi for Rs. 30,00,000. The expenditure on stamp duty and transfer charges was borne by the purchaser but Sri Binani had to pay Rs. 1,00,000 towards his share of brokerage and for advertisement etc.

(ii) In December, 2001, Sri Binani had purchased equity shares of 11 Indian companies through a firm of stock-brokers for Rs. 7,96,000 which included Rs. 96,000 incurred on transfer charges, stamp duty and brokerage. He got these shares registered in the books of the respective companies in January, 2006. All these shares were sold by Sri Binani on 5-3-2007 for Rs. 9,00,000 through the same stock-brokers. He had to pay a further brokerage of Rs. 18,000 at the time of sale of these shares. It also paid Rs. 1,200 as securities transaction tax.

(iii) Sri Binani had purchased certain diamond jewellery from M/s. Star-studded Ornaments, Bombay on 7-3-2004 at an aggregate cost of Rs. 1,80,000. This jewellery was sold by him on 10-2-2007 for Rs. 3,00,000 in a single lot.

Calculate the income of Sri Binani taxable under the head 'Capital gains' during Assessment Year 2007-2008.

Ans: 3,46,460.

TOPIC 7.12 *SECTION 47.* WHAT IS "NOT TRANSFER"

1. Transfer of assets under a gift or will or an irrevocable trust.

   Where any shares, debentures or warrants are allotted by a company to its employees under the ESOP in accordance with the guidelines issued by the Central Govt. on this behalf then such transactions shall be treated as transfer.

2. Any conversions of bonds/debentures, debentures stock/deposit certificate, of a company into shares or debentures of that company.

Note

- Since the above said transactions are not treated as transfer, hence, no capital gain arises.

TOPIC 7.13 COMPUTATION OF CAPITAL GAIN IF THE ASSET ACQUIRED THROUGH GIFT ETC. IS SUBSEQUENTLY TRANSFERRED

(A) SECTION 49(1). DEEMED COST OF ACQUISITION

Cost of acquisition is cost to the previous owner. *E.g.* X gifts the asset to Y and Y gifts to Z and Z subsequently sells to D. Here neither Y nor Z has acquired the asset by paying the price therefore cost of acquisition to Z shall be price paid by X.

(B) PERIOD OF HOLDING

To determine whether the asset is LTCA / STCA, period of holding is taken from the date when the previous owner acquires the asset.

Thus, *in the above example holding period shall be computed from the date X acquires the asset till the date of sale* i.e. *till the date when D acquires the asset.*

(C) INDEXATION OF COST OF ACQUISITION

Indexation of cost of acquisition is done only between transferers i.e. in the above example indexation of COA shall be done from D to Z since D and Z are transferer. However COA shall be cost to X who is the previous owner.

(D) INDEXATION OF COST OF IMPROVEMENT

Indexation of cost of improvement is done in respective year of improvement i.e. in the above example suppose improvement is undertaken by all assessees X, Y and Z. Then indexation of COI undertaken by X shall be done from D to X, similarly for Y, D to Y and for Z, D to Z.

Illustration 7.13-P1 (Typical)

Compute Capital Gain chargeable to tax for AY 2007-08.

Indexation

gifts land to — sells land to

T--->Mr. D---------------------------------> Mr. M

T	Mr. D	Mr. M
COA as on 1-7-1989	FMV as on 1-6-2004	SC as on 1-1-2007
Rs. 15,000	Rs. 65,000	Rs. 9,15,000
COI as on 1-4-1997	COI as on 1-4-2006	
Rs. 25,000	Rs. 55,000	

Period of holding & COA

How to Solve

1. Transactions between T & D is not treated as transfer and hence no capital gain. *(As per section 47, gift is not treated as transfer)*
2. Since indexation of COA is done between the transferers, indexation of COA shall be done from M to D.
3. Since D has not acquired the land by paying a price, COA is cost to the previous owner who is T. COA = Rs. 15,000.
4. Period of holding is taken from 1-7-1989 to 1-1-2007, therefore land is treated as LTCA.
5. Indexation of improvement done by T shall be from M to T and Indexation of improvement done by D shall be from M to D.

Solution

Computation of Capital Gain for the AY 2007-08

Sale consideration		9,15,000
Less :		
• *Indexed cost of acquisition*		
$\frac{\text{Year of Sale}(2005-06)}{\text{Year of acquisation }(2004-05)} \times \text{COA} = \frac{519}{480} \times 15{,}000 =$	16,219	
• *Indexed cost of improvement done by T*		
$\frac{\text{Year of sale}(2005\text{-}06)}{\text{Year of improvement}(97\text{-}98)} \times \text{COI} = \frac{519}{331} \times 25{,}000 =$	39,199	
• *Indexed cost of improvement done by D*		
$\frac{\text{Year of sale}(2006\text{-}07)}{\text{Year of improvement}(2006\text{-}07)} \times \text{COI} = \frac{519}{519} \times 55{,}000 =$	55,000	1,10,418
LTCG		8,04,582

Problem 7.13-P2 (Typical)

Compute capital gain chargeable to tax for the AY 2007-08.

Taxcrazy --- gifts land to --->	Mr. D --- sells land to --->	Mr. M
COA as on 1-1-1978 Rs. 35,000	FMV as on 1-8-2003 Rs. 6,00,000	SC as on 1-6-2006 Rs. 16,75,000
FMV as on 1-4-1981 Rs. 42,000	Cost of construction of first floor on 1-12-2005 Rs. 5,00,000	Advertising expenses by Mr. D Rs. 6,000
Stamp duty Rs. 9,000		
Cost of construction of house on 1-2-1991 Rs. 1,22,000		

Ans: 7,49,644

Problem 7.13-P3 (CS-J99) - M 10

Q.4b : X purchases a house property for Rs. 26,000 on May 10, 1963. He gets the first floor of the house constructed in 1968-69 by spending Rs. 40,000. He dies on September 12, 1987. The property is transferred to Mrs. X by his will, Mrs. X spends Rs. 80,000 and Rs. 26,700 during 1988-89 and 1989-90 respectively for renewals / reconstruction of the property. Mrs. X sells the house property for Rs. 41,50,000 on March 15, 2007 (brokerage paid by Mrs. X is Rs. 41,500). The fair market value of the house on April 1, 1981 is Rs. 4,60,000. Compute income under the head income from capital gains.

Ans: 21,78,446.

Problem 7.13-P4 [Hons 2005C]

Find out the amount of capital gain chargeable to tax for the Assessment Year 2007-08.

G purchases a house property on 10-5-1964	36,000
He spent on construction of the first floor of the house in 1968-69	80,000
He died on 12-9-1986. The property is transferred to Mrs. G by his will	
Mrs. G spent during 1995-96 for renewals/reconstruction of the house	40,000
Mrs. G sold the house property on 15-3-2007	15,50,000
Brokerage paid on sale	14,500
The fair market value of the house on 1-4-1981	1,10,000

Ans: 10,53,885.

Problem 7.13-P5

1. When cost of acquisition is equal to indexed cost of acquisition?
2. In case of long term capital assets, 'indexed cost of acquisition' is deductible from sale proceeds to find out the amount of long term capital gain. Is there any provision in the Income Tax Act, 1961 under which 'cost of acquisition' (not indexed cost of acquisition) is deductible even in the case of long term capital asset ?

Solution

1. It will be equal in the cases where capital asset is acquired by the assessee after April 1981 by gift, will etc., in a particular year and transferred in the same year.
2. Transfer of long term capital asset being debentures or bonds in which indexation is not allowed.

TOPIC 7.14 *SECTION 51.* FORFEITURE OF ADVANCE MONEY

The money forfeited by the *transferer* shall be deducted from the cost of acquisition or FMV as on 1-4-1981 whichever is higher.

Note

- Where however advance money is forfeited before 1-4-1981, even then it should be deducted either from COA or FMV as on 1-4-1981 as the case may be.

Illustration 7.14-P1 (Simple)

Compute capital gain chargeable to tax for the AY 2007-08.

sells Industrial land to

Taxcrazy -->Mr. D

COA as on 1-1-1997 Rs. 50,000 | SC as on 1-2-2007 Rs. 3,80,000

Amount forfeited Rs. 30,000

Solution

Computation of Capital Gain for the AY 2007-08

Sale Consideration	3,80,000
Less : Indexed cost of acquisition (519 ÷ 305 × 20,000)	34,033
LTCG	3,45,967

Note

- Rs. 20,000 shall be deducted from COA, since Taxcrazy is transferrer. COA = COA – amount forfeited = 50,000 – 30,000 = 20,000.

Illustration 7.14-P2 (Difficult)

Compute capital gain chargeable to tax for the AY 2007-08.

sells Industrial land to

Taxcrazy --->Mr. D

COA as on 1-1-1972 Rs. 40,000 SC as on 1-1-2007 Rs. 4,00,000
FMV as on 1-4-1981 Rs. 60,000
Amount forfeited Rs. 10,000

Solution

Computation of Capital Gain for the AY 2007-08

Sale Consideration	4,00,000
Less : Indexed cost of acquisition (519 ÷ 100 × 50,000)	2,59,500
LTCG	1,40,500

Note

- COA = COA or FMV as on 1-4-1981 whichever is higher – amount forfeited = 60,000 – 10,000 = 50,000.

Illustration 7.14-P3 (Typical)

(A) Compute capital gain chargeable to tax for the AY 2007-08.

gifts gold to sells gold to

Ms. Taxcrazy---------------------------------->Ms. D-->M

COA as on 1-1-1986	FMV as on 1-1-1995	SC as on 1-5-2006
Rs. 70,000	Rs. 90,000	Rs. 5,00,000
Amt. forfeited Rs. 10,000	Amt. forfeited Rs. 40,000	

(B) What if amount forfeited by D is Rs. 75,000.

Ans : 4,39,893; 5,00,000.

Solution

Sale Consideration	5,00,000
Less : Indexed cost of acquisition (519 ÷ 259 × 30,000)	60,116
LTCG	4,39,884

Note

- Since transferer is Ms D, therefore, amount forfeited by Ms. D shall be deducted. COA = COA – amount forfeited by the transferrer = 70,000 – 40,000 = 30,000.
- Rs. 10,000 forfeited by Ms. Taxcrazy is not taxable since capital receipt.

Problem 7.14-P4 (Difficult)

X received a house in May 2005 by way of gift from Y who had purchased the same in April 1980 for Rs. 12,00,000. The cost of improvements incurred by Y were Rs. 2,55,000 in March 1980 and Rs. 3,40,000 in November 1992. The fair market value of the house as on April 1, 1981 was Rs. 9,14,000. Before this house was gifted to X, Y had received an advance of Rs. 3,00,000 in March 2005 towards sale of this house from Z but the sale did not materialise and the advance was forfeited by Y. The house was sold by X in March 2007 for Rs. 48,00,000. Ascertain the capital gains chargeable to tax for the AY 2007-08.

Ans: 27,55,581.

Problem 7.14-P5 [Hons 2001]

Mr. Y purchased a house property in 1975 for Rs. 3,50,000. He renovated the floor of the house in 1980 at a cost of Rs. 50,000. In November 2000 he got the roof of the house repaired at a cost of Rs. 90,000.

In December 2001, he gifted the house to his son, Z. Before the house was gifted, Mr. Y got an advance of Rs. 50,000 for the sale of house on 1st April, 1981 for Rs. 12,00,000. However, the sale could not materialise and the amount of advance was forfeited. The fair market value of the house on 1st April 1981 was 12,00,000. Mr. Z sold the house in March 2007 for Rs. 22,00,000 and paid stamp duty, Rs. 50,000

You are required to compute capital gain for the AY 2007-08.

Ans: 6,89,810.

Problem 7.14-P6 [Hons 2000]

Mr. T purchased a house in 1978 for Rs, 10,00,000. He renovated the floor of the house in 1980 at a cost of Rs. 2,00,000. In November, 1995 he got the roof of the house changed at a cost of Rs. 3,00,000

He gifted this house to his son, G, in May 2004. Before this house was gifted, Mr. T got an advance of Rs. 2,00,000 on April 1, 1981 from Mr. M for the sale of the house for Rs. 20,00,000. However the sale could not materialise and the amount of advance was forfeited.

Mr. G sold this house in March 2007 for Rs. 45,00,000. Ascertain the capital gain chargeable to tax in the AY 2007-08.

Ans: 17,83,407.

TOPIC 7.15 *SECTION 50.* COMPUTATION OF CAPITAL GAIN IN CASE OF DEPRECIABLE ASSETS

This topic already discussed in chapter 6.

Problem 7.15-P1 [Typical]

Mr. R sold his factory and his residential house situated inside the compound. Compute the capital gains arising to him. The land measuring 5000 sq. yds. was purchased in Sept. 1988 for Rs. 5 lakhs. Out of this 500 sq. yds were carved out in one corner for his residence. The factory building was constructed by December, 1990. He incurred an expenditure of Rs. 7.5 lakhs upto 31-3-1990 and Rs. 22.5 lakhs further upto the end. He installed Plant and Machinery worth Rs. 90 lakhs by 30-6-1990. He had availed of Rs. 45 lakhs depreciation on the Plant & Machinery and Rs. 15 lakhs depreciation on the factory building. The sale consideration realised by him was Rs. 1.25 crores for the factory land and building and Rs. 17.5 lakhs for the Plant & Machinery.

The residential house was constructed over the same period of time incurring a cost of Rs. 2.5 lakhs upto 31-3-1990 and a further cost of Rs. 5 lakhs till the end. The consideration fixed for the house and the land appurtenant thereto was Rs. 15 lakhs.

The sale was registered in April 2006.

Ans: 1,05,50,000+(27,50,000)+(8,41,365) = 69,58,635.

Foundation created. Revise, memorise and make small notes and then run.

Keep running

TOPIC 7.16 COMPUTATION OF CAPITAL GAIN IN CASE OF TRANSFER OF SHARES OR DEBENTURES AND ITS COST OF ACQUISITION

Particulars	Cost of Acquisition
CoA of original share	Price paid for its acquisition
CoA of bonus shares	Nil. *(take FMV as on 1-4-1981, if bonus are allotted before 1-4-1981.*
CoA of right share for original allottee	Price paid for its acquisition to the company.
CoA of right share entitlement	Nil
CoA of right share for renouncee	Price paid for its acquisition to the company + price paid to the renouncer

Illustration 7.16-P1 (Difficult)

X purchased 500 equity shares of Rs. 10 each for Rs. 40 per share in 1980-81 and incurred an expenditure of Rs. 400 on brokerage. In May 1980 he received 400 bonus shares. Fair Market value of shares on 1-4-1981 was Rs. 35 per share. Again in May 2004 he received 100 bonus shares.

The company made a right issue in the ratio of 1 : 1 on July 15, 2005 at a premium of Rs. 40 per share. He acquired 800 shares and renounced 200 right to subscribe for shares in favour of Y at a price of Rs. 10 per right share entitlement.

(A) Compute cost of acquisition of different shares in the hands of X and Y.

(B) Compute capital gain if all shares are sold by X on 13-7-2006 for Rs. 80 per share.

(C) Compute capital gain on sale of right share entitlement for the AY 2006-07.

(D) Compute capital gain if all shares are sold by Y on 15-4-2006 for Rs. 20 per share.

Ans: (A) refer soln below; (B) LTCG (98,536); STCG 24,000; (C) 2,000; (D) STCG (8,000).

Solution

Computation of COA of shares for X

	Total cost	cost per share
COA of Original shares	500 × 40 + 400 = 20,400	20,400 / 500 = 40.80
COA of bonus shares allotted before 1-4-1981	400 × 35 = 14,000	35
COA of bonus shares allotted after 31-3-1981	nil	nil
COA of right shares *(Original shares at the time of right issue = 500 + 400 + 100 = 1,000)*. Out of 1,000 shares he subscribed only 800 shares and 200 shares renounced in favour of Y	800 × 50 = 40,000	50

Computation of COA of shares for Y

COA of 200 right shares purchased from X @ Rs. 10 per share	Price paid to the company Rs. 50 + price paid to X Rs. 10 50 + 10 = 60 per share

Problem 7.16-P2 (Difficult)

	Date of purchase	*Cost of acquisition*	*Sale Consd. in PY 2006-07*
1,000 original shares	1-5-1970	Rs. 50/share	Rs. 335/share
200 original shares	1-5-1979	Rs. 80/share	Rs. 450/share
500 bonus shares	1-5-1978	—	Rs. 360/share
300 bonus shares	1-5-1986	—	Rs. 50/share

You are required to compute Capital Gain for the AY 2007-08 on the assumption that fair market value as on 1-4-1981 was Rs. 70 per share. Brokerage paid on acquisition of original shares 1%.

Ans: (8,820)

Problem 7.16-P3 (CS-J01) - M 3

Q.1d : X purchases 1,200 equity shares in Y Ltd. at the rate of Rs. 15 per share (brokerage 1 per cent) on December 11, 1974. He has got 300 bonus shares (by virtue of his holding of 1,200 shares) on January 21, 1980. Fair market value of shares of Y Ltd., is Rs. 30. On March 7, 2007, X transfers all the 1,500 shares at the rate of Rs. 84 per share (brokerage 1.5 per cent). Compute the capital gain for the assessment year 2007-08.

Ans: (1,09,440)

Problem 7.16-P4 [CS J02]

X purchased 500 equity shares of Rs. 10 each for Rs. 40 per share in 2002-03 and incurred an expenditure of Rs. 400 on brokerage. In May 2004 he received 100 bonus shares. In September 2005, he got 100 rights shares for Rs. 20 each. He sold 100 bonus shares in November, 2006 @ Rs. 90 per share and 100 rights shares @ Rs. 80 per share in December 2006. Find out the capital gains for the assessment year 2007-08.

Ans: 14,911.

Illustration 7.16-P5 (Typical)

(A) Analyse the following information and compute capital gain chargeable to tax for the AY 2007-08.

X holds

- X holds 1,100 equity shares purchased on 1-8-1991 @ Rs. 15 per share.
- The company on 1-4-1995 allots bonus shares of one shares for 5 held.
- The company on 1-5-2002 declares right issue for 2 shares for 1 held @ Rs. 35 per share which was allotted on 1-6-2002.
- X renounces 1700 right shares in favour of Y @ Rs. 3 per share on 3-5-2002 and subscribes for the remaining shares.

X sells

- 100 original shares @ Rs. 60 per share on 1-9-1991.
- 700 original shares @ Rs. 50 per share on 11-7-2006 .

- Whole of the right shares @ Rs. 48 per share on 21-8-2006.
- Whole of the bonus shares for Rs. 5,000 on 1-3-2007.

Y sells

- Whole of right shares for Rs. 40,000 on 1-3-2003.

(B) Also solved for Mr. X for AY 92-93, 2003-04 and for Mr. Y for the AY 2003-04.

Ans: (A) refer soln below; (B) STCG 4,500; 5,100; STCG (24,600).

Solution

Computation of Capital Gain for the AY 2007-08 of X

	Original shares	*Right shares*	*Bonus shares*
Sale Consideration	35,000	33,600	5,000
Less : Indexed COA	27,384	28,446	nil
LTCG	7,616	5,154	5,000
Total LTCG			17,769

Note

- Indexed COA = 700 × 15 × 519 ÷ 199= 27,384; 35 × 700 × 519 ÷ 447 = 28,446
- On the date of allotment of bonus shares he held 1,000 original shares, therefore, bonus share entitlement = 1,000/5 = 200 bonus shares.
- On the date of issue of right shares he held 1,000 original shares + 200 bonus shares = 1200 shares, therefore, right share entitlement = 1200 × 2 = 2400 right shares. He renounces 1700 shares in favour of Y, therefore he is left with 700 right shares.

Problem 7.16-P6 [Typical]

During the Financial Year 2006-2007, 'R', an individual, has sold the following assets :

(i) 1000 shares of XYZ Ltd. for a consideration of Rs. 700 per share; and

(ii) self-occupied residential house property for Rs. 9,00,000 :

'R' had purchased 500 shares of XYZ Ltd. in December, 1980 @ Rs. 100 per share. The quoted price of these shares at BSE on 1-4-1981 was Rs. 170 per share. The balance represented 500 bonus shares issued to 'R' in December, 1996. The residential house was purchased by 'R' in September, 1993 for a sum of Rs. 3,00,000. Thereafter, he incurred a further expenditure of Rs. 1,50,000 in January, 1995 by way of improvements.

Compute the capital gains chargeable to tax in R's hand for the Assessment Year 2007-08.

Ans: (91,150) + 3,50,000 – 38,694 = 2,20,156.

Problem 7.16-P7 (Difficult)

Compute Capital Gain for the assessment year 2007-08.

	Unlisted debentures	*Listed Debentures*
Sale consideration	Rs. 4 lakhs on 31-3 2007	Rs. 5 lakhs on 7-5-2006
Cost of acquisition	Rs. 3 lakhs on 1-1-2006	Rs. 2 lakhs on 1-3-2004

Ans: STCG 1,00,000; LTCG 3,00,000.

Problem 7.16-P8 [1. CA N95] [2. CA M 2000]

1. P holds 500 shares of ABC Ltd., which were allotted to him on April 22, 1992 @ Rs. 30 per share. On July 22, 2006 ABC Ltd. made right issue to the existing shareholders at the rate of one share for every five shares held @ Rs. 20 per share. P instead of exercising his right to obtain right shares, has exercised his right of renouncement by renouncing the said right entitled in favour of Q @ Rs. 13 per right share entitlement on August 4, 2006. Determine the nature and amount of capital gain, if any, taxable in the hands of P. What will be the cost of acquisition of shares purchased by Q ?
2. Y is a shareholder of X & Co. Ltd., holding 1,000 shares of the face value of Rs. 10 each, allotted at the time of the company's incorporation in May, 1990. The company made a right issue in the ratio of 1 : 1 on July 15, 2006 at a premium of Rs. 40 per share. Instead of taking up the right, he renounced it in favour of Z at a price of Rs. 10 per share. What is the capital gain chargeable in the hands of Y ? What will be the cost of the shares in the hands of Z ?

Ans: (1) STCG on sale of right share entitlement Rs.1,300. Cost of acqusition of 100 shares in the hands of Q Rs. 3,300. (2) STCG on sale of right share entitlement Rs.10,000. Cost of acqusition of shares in the hands of Z Rs. 60 per share.

TOPIC 7.17 COMPUTATION OF CAPITAL GAIN IN CASE OF SALE OF CONVERTED SECURITIES

(A) SECTION 47(x). CONVERSION OF SECURITIES NOT A TRANSFER

Conversion of bonds or debentures, debentures stock or deposit certificate into shares or debentures of that company are not treated as transfer and hence no capital gain.

But if such converted shares or debentures are transferred subsequently then there arises capital gain which is computed by following rules as shown under :

(B) SECTION 49(2A). COST OF ACQUISITION OF CONVERTED SECURITIES

Cost of acquisition of converted securities is cost of shares or debentures which has been appropriated towards the converted securities.

Q.1 : Mr. X purchases 200 FCD for Rs. 70 each. 100% value of FCD is converted into equity shares. Determine the cost of acquisition of equity share.

A.1 : It is not given how much FCD is getting converted to equity share. Therefore it is assumed that 1 FCD = 1 equity share. Cost of acquisition = 14,000 ÷ 200 = Rs. 70 per share.

Suppose in the same question it is given 100% value of FCD is converted into 500 equity shares, then cost of acquisition = 14,000 ÷ 500 = Rs. 28 per share.

Q.2 : Mr. X purchases 200 PCD for Rs. 70 each. 60% value of PCD is converted into equity shares. Determine the cost of acquisition of equity share and cost of debentures.

A.2 : It is not given how much PCD is getting converted into equity share. Therefore it is assumed that 1 PCD = 1 equity share. Cost of acquisition of share = 60% of 14,000 ÷ 200 = Rs. 42 per share. Cost of acquisition of debenture = 40% of 14,000 ÷ 200 = Rs. 28 per debenture.

Suppose in the same question it is given 60% value of PCD is converted into 500 equity shares and 40% of value of PCD to 150 debentures, then cost of acquisition of share =

60% of 14,000 ÷ 500 = Rs. 16.80 per share. Cost of acquisition of debenture = 40% of 14,000 ÷ 150 = Rs. 37.33 per debenture.

Let us check it. 200 × 70 = 14,000 = (500 × 16.80) + (150 × 37.33) = 14,000.

(C) PERIOD OF HOLDING

To determine whether the asset is LTCA / STCA period of holding is taken *from the date of allotment of converted securities.*

(D) RULES OF INDEXATION

Indexation is **done** from the date of sale of shares or debentures to date of conversion of shares.

Illustration 7.17-P1 (Typical)

(A) S, gets converted 1,000 PCD of Rs. 200 each to 500 Debentures of Rs. 150 each and to 1,000 equity shares of Rs. 10 each. Conversion ratio of value being 60% to debentures and 40% to equity shares. Subsequently she sells all her securities to K.

COA — Indexation and Period of holding

converts — sells

PCD------------------------------->Debentures & equity shares--------------------------->Ms K

COA as on 18-2-1992	FMV as on 1-1-2005	SC as on 12-6-2006
Rs. 200 each	Rs. 1,80,000	Rs. 3,40,000

Compute capital gain chargeable to tax for AY 2007-08 on the assumption that all shares are sold for Rs. 2,00,000; debentures *(listed at National Stock exchange)* are sold at Rs. 1,40,000.

(B) Solve if the date of conversion is 1-7-2005.

Ans: (A) LTCG 1,33,500; (B) STCG 1,40,000

How to Solve

1. Conversion of PCD to debentures and equity shares is not treated as transfer and hence no capital gain.
2. COA of debenture = 60% of 2,00,000 ÷ 500 = Rs. 240 per debentures and COA of equity shares = 40% of 2,00,000 1,000 = Rs. 80 per share.
3. Indexation of COA shall be from 2006-07 to 2004-05 since indexation is done from date of sale to date of conversion of shares.
4. Period of holding is from 1-1-2005 to 12-6-2006 *i.e.* LTCA.

Solution

	Debentures	*Shares*
Sale consideration	1,40,000	2,00,000
Less : COA of debentures Rs. 240 × 500 *(indexation not allowed)* and indexed COA of Equity shares (519 ÷ 480 × 80,000)	1,20,000	86,500
LTCG	20,000	1,13,500

Problem 7.17-P2 (Typical)

Mr. X purchased 1,000 PCD @ Rs. 60 each on 1-6-1995. On 6-4-2006 Mr. X exercises his option to convert 70% of value of PCD into equity shares. On 1-3-2007, he sells 600 shares for Rs. 90 per share and 200 debentures for Rs. 50 per debenture. Compute capital gain chargeable to tax for the AY 2007-08.

Ans: STCG : 28,800; LTCG : 6,400.

Problem 7.17-P3 (Typical)

Mr. TRAI was allotted 200 FCD for Rs. 70/FCD. As per terms of allotment dated 7-5-1998, 70% of value of each FCD shall be converted to 2 equity shares on 8-1-2002 and remaining value of each FCD to 3 equity shares on 7-9-2005. As per the terms of allotment Mr. TRAI exercised its option on respective dates. On 8-7-2006 he sold 90% of number of equity shares for Rs. 55/share. Compute capital gain chargeable to tax as per AY 2007-08 by applying FIFO method.

Ans: LTCG : 10,061; STCG : 24,000.

Problem 7.17-P4 (CA - M97) - M 4

Q.3a : A is the holder of 1,000 debentures of A Ltd. having a face value of Rs. 1,000 each. The company has offered an option to the debenture holders either to redeem the debentures at Rs. 1,200 each or to convert the debentures into equity shares of equivalent value. The market value of the shares on the date of exercising the option is Rs. 1,200 per share (face value Rs. 1,000). What will be the tax consequence of the two options in the hands of the debenture holder A ?

Ans: Redemption of debentures shall give rise to capital gain however conversion of debentures to shares is not treated as transfer therefore no capital gain.

Problem 7.17-P5 (CA - M98) - M6

Q.1c : In April, 1999, Y subscribed to the first issue of equity capital of a public limited company (face value of each share was Rs. 100) to the extent of Rs. 25,000. In 2005, the company converted the face value of its shares from Rs. 100 to Rs. 10 each. Half of the holdings of the shares held by Y was sold by him in October, 2006 for Rs. 50,000. Y had to pay a brokerage of 2 per cent on sale.

What is the nature of gains realized and compute the same ?

Ans: 32,323

TOPIC 7.18 COMPUTATION OF CAPITAL GAIN IN CASE OF 'SELF GENERATED ASSETS' AND ITS COST OF ACQUISITION

'Self-generated assets' means the asset created and developed on its own without purchasing from outside agency.

Supreme Court has held that such self-generated assets which do not cost anything to the assessee in terms of money cannot be subjected to capital gain. It means that those capital assets whose COA & COI cannot be determined cannot be subjected to capital gain.

However Income Tax Act since then was amended and as per *Section 55(2)(a)(i)* following self-generated assets shall be subjected to capital gain whose COA is deemed to be nil.

	COA	COI
1. Brand name and Trademark associated with the business. (not of a profession)	Nil	Actual
2. Tenancy rights, route permits and loom hours	Nil	Actual
3. Goodwill of a business *(not of a profession)*	Nil	Nil
4. Right to manufacture, produce or process any article or thing, for a consideration *(e.g. Patent)*	Nil	Nil

Other points

1. Where the above asset is purchased from outside agency cost of acquisition is price paid to outside agency.
2. For computing cost of acquisition of the abovesaid assets FMV as on 1-4-1981 is not applicable whether the asset is self-generated or purchased from outside agency.
3. Asset such as goodwill of a profession, if transferred, is not subjected to capital gain since COA cannot be determined.

Problem 7.18-P1 (Difficult)

1. Mr. Ram Gopal Verma registered a trademark 'The Factory' in the year 1960 whose FMV as on 1-4-1981 is Rs. 50 Lakhs. Determine the cost of acquisition of the trademark.
2. Suppose the trademark 'The Factory' is purchased by Miss K.K. for Rs. 30 lakhs on 4-5-1979. Determine the cost of acquisition of the trademark for Miss KK if FMV as on 1-4-1981 is Rs. 50 Lakhs.

Ans: Nil; Rs. 30 lakhs since FMV is not applicable.

Problem 7.18-P2 (Difficult)

Compute capital gain chargeable to tax for the AY 2007-08 from the following information:

	Cost of Acquisition (Estimated or actual)	*Sale Consideration*
1. Brand name of a business (self-generated)	60,000	4,00,000
2. Trade-mark of a business (purchased from Nestle)	2,00,000	6,50,000
3. Patent (self-generated)	10,50,000	8,00,000
4. Goodwill of a profession		
– self-generated	8,00,000	90,000
– acquired from Ferguson	70,000	1,91,000

Ans: 4,00,000; 4,50,000; 8,00,000; nil; 1,21,000.

Problem 7.18-P3 (Difficult)

Mr. Rajeev Goel was in practice as a company secretary who had built up valuable goodwill by personal efforts. He sold his practice to Mr. Prabhat Nanda who paid Rs. 20 lakhs for goodwill. Is Mr. Rajeev Goel liable to any capital gain tax?

Ans: No.

Problem 7.18-P4 [Pass 2005C]

Mr. B individual transfers the following assets during 2006-07 :

	Sale of Acquisition	*Cost of Proceeds* Rs.	*Year Acquisition* Rs.
Jewellery	7,50,000	1,25,000	1984-85
Shares	5,50,000	50,000	1980-81
Goodwill (Self generated)	2,50,000	---	---
Tenancy Right (Self generated)	4,75,000	---	---

Compute capital gains. The fair market value of shares as on 1-4-1981 was Rs. 1,10,000.

Ans: 9,35,100.

Problem 7.18-P5 (Typical)

Compute capital gain chargeable to tax for the AY 2007-08 from following information :

	Unlisted bonds	*Godown*	*Car used for business purpose Rate of dep. 15%*	*Bonus shares*	*Tenancy rights purchased*
Date of acquisition	5-6-2003	7-9-1980	8-9-2003	1-3-1978	8-9-1980
Date of sale	4-6-2006	31-3-2007	31-3-2007	5-7-2006	6-1-2007
Cost of acquisition	60,000	23,000	3,50,000	NA	2,500
W.D.V. on 31-3-2006	NA	NA	1,00,000	NA	NA
F.M.V. on 1-4-1981	NA	15,000	NA	2,000	3,000
Sale consideration	25,000	1,92,000	30,000	80,000	65,000

Ans: 1,04,275

Problems 7.18-P6

1. Even if conditions of section 45 are satisfied then also gain is not chargeable to tax. When?
2. List two situations in which fair market value as on 1-4-1981 is treated as cost of acquisition?
3. List a situation in which fair market value as on 1-4-1981 is not applicable?
4. Is conversion of preference shares to equity shares is treated as transfer?

Solutions

1. As per Supreme Court judgement in case of those assets whose cost of acquisition cannot be determined and cannot be subjected to capital gain. But with the amendment of Income Tax Act, cost of acquisition of self-generated assets is deemed to be nil. But income tax act has not provided that COA of goodwill of a profession shall be nil. Therefore transfer of goodwill of a profession is not subjected to capital gain.
2. Where the bonus shares are allotted before 1-4-1981 and where cost of acquisition is less than fair market value as on 1-4-1981.

3. In case of following assets whether the assets are purchased or self generated fair market value as on 1-4-1981 is not applicable. (1) Brand name and Trademarks associated with the business. (not of a profession). (2) Tenancy rights, route permits and loom hours. (3) Goodwill of a business (not of a profession). (4) Right to manufacture, produce or process any article or thing, for a consideration (*e.g.* Patent).
4. Yes. In this case fair market value on the date of allotment of equity shares is treated as sale consideration and cost of acquisition is the price at which preference shares are acquired.

The question on sale of securities is fashionable in professional exam. Graduate courses are still waiting this phenomenon to happen and do you know tough mind wins and wait you are becoming one of them.

Keep running

DEEMED TRANSFER

TOPIC 7.19 **SECTION 45(1A).* INSURANCE CLAIM RECEIVED ON DESTRUCTION OF ASSET

(A) CONDITION

Where any person receives at any time during any previous year any money or other assets under an insurance from an insurer on account of damage to, or destruction of, any capital asset, as a result of—

(i) flood, typhoon, hurricane, cyclone, earthquake or other convulsion of nature; or

(ii) riot or civil disturbance; or

(iii) accidental fire or explosion; or

(iv) action by an enemy or action taken in combating an enemy (whether with or without a declaration of war),

then, any profits or gains arising from receipt of such money or other assets shall be chargeable to income-tax under the head Capital gains.

(B) COMPUTATION

Sale consideration	:	The amount of insurance claim received.
Year of transfer	:	In the year of destruction of the capital asset.
Year of chargeability	:	In the year when insurance claim is received either in full or part.
Indexation	:	Indexation shall be done from the date of destruction of assets to date of acquisition of assets.

Problem 7.19-P1 (Simple)

X owns a house at Kutch (Gujarat) which was purchased by him on 1-8-1976 for Rs. 1,80,000. The said property was destroyed by earthquake on 26-1-2006 and he received Rs. 20,00,000 from the insurance company on 15-6-2006. The market value of this property on 1-4-1981 was Rs. 3,00,000. Calculate amount of capital gain and state when it will be taxed.

Ans: AY 2007-08 : 5,09,000.

Problem 7.19-P2 [PE II N 06]

Mr. A, is an individual carrying on business. His stock an machinery were damaged and destroyed in a fire accident.

The value of stock lost (totally damaged) was Rs. 6,50,000. Certain portion of the machinery could be salvaged. The opening WDV of the block as on 1-4-2006 was Rs. 10,80,000.

During the process of safeguarding machinery and in the fire fighting operations. Mr. A lost his gold chain and diamond ring, which he had purchased in April, 2003 for Rs. 1,20,000. The market value of these two items as on the date of fire accident was Rs. 1,80,000.

Mr. A received the following amounts from the insurance company :

(i) Towards loss of stock	Rs. 4,80,000
(ii) Towards damage of Machinery	Rs. 6,00,000
(iii) Towards gold chain and diamond ring	Rs. 1,80,000

You are requested to briefly comment on the tax treatment of the above three items under the provisions of the Income - tax Act, 1961.

Ans: Business Loss (1,70,000); STCG (4,80,000); LTCG 45,486.

TOPIC 7.20 **SECTION 45(2)*. WHERE CAPITAL ASSET IS CONVERTED INTO STOCK-IN-TRADE

Where the owner converts its capital asset into, or treats it as a stock-in-trade of a business carried on by him, then in such case gain arising shall be chargeable to income-tax as his income of the previous year in which such stock-in-trade is sold or otherwise transferred by him.

Sale consideration	:	Fair Market Value (FMV) of the asset as on the date of conversion.
Year of transfer	:	On the date of conversion of investment into stock-in-trade.
Year of chargeability	:	The capital gain will be chargeable to tax in the PY when whole or part of the stock is sold *i.e.* taxability of capital gain is postponed to a later date when whole or part of the stock is sold.
Indexation	:	Indexation is done from the year of transfer (conversion) to the date of acquisition of the asset.

Note

- This provision became applicable from the AY 1985-86.

Illustration 7.20-P1 (Simple)

Mr. Taxcrazy converts its securities *(which he has held as investments)* into stock-in-trade as per information given below :

conversion of investment into

Investment---> Stock in trade

CoA as on 1-1-1980 Rs. 90,000 FMV as on 15-7-2004 Rs. 5,00,000

FMV as on 1-4-1981 Rs. 1,00,000

He sells whole of the stock in the PY 2006-07 for Rs. 7,00,000. Compute his Capital Gain & Profit from Business for the AY 2005-06 and AY 2007-08.

Solution

Computation of Capital Gain for the AY 2007-08

Sale Consideration	5,00,000
Less : Indexed COA (480 ÷ 100 × 1,00,000)	4,80,000
LTCG	20,000

Note : Indexation is done from 2004-05 to 81-82 and Rs. 37,000 is chargeable in the AY 2007-08 since 100% of the stock in trade is sold in the PY 2006-07. No capital gain arises in the PY 2004-05 (AY 2005-06).

Profit from business for the AY 2007-08

Sale Price	7,00,000
Less : FMV as on the date of conversion	5,00,000
Profit from business	2,00,000

Problem 7.20-P2

M/s D.L.F. Ltd. converts its 10,000 shares of Russel Ltd. into stock in trade on 11-4-2003 on which date fair market value of these shares at Rs. 27,50,000. The shares were acquired by the Company on 31-5-1970 for a sum of Rs. 5,000 and fair market value of these on 1-4-1981 was at Rs. 6,75,000. The shares were actually sold by the Company on 2-11-2006 for Rs. 30,00,000. Determine the Capital gains and business income of the Company taxable for the A.Y. 2007-08.

Ans: Business Income 2,50,000; Capital Gain (3,75,250).

Problem 7.20-P3 (Difficult)

(A) X invested Rs. 30,500 in That's That Ltd. to acquire 100 shares on 3-5-1999. Subsequently on 1-4-2003, he started a business of securities where value of these shares were treated as stock in trade of the business. The market value of these shares on the date of conversion was Rs. 70,000. These shares were sold on 20-1-2007 for a sum of Rs. 80,000. Compute the capital gain and business income if brokerage on acquisition of shares is 4%. STT paid Rs. 250.

(B) Compute capital gain if date of conversion of securities is 11-12-1999.

Ans: (A) 32,246; 10,000; (B) STCG 38,280.

Problem 7.20-P4 [CS J00]

X converts his capital asset (acquired on June 10, 1967 for Rs. 70,000, fair market value on April 1, 1981 : Rs. 1,80,000) into stock - in - trade on March 10, 2001 (fair market value : Rs. 4,80,000) and, subsequently, sells the stock - in - trade so converted for Rs. 7,30,000 on June 10, 2004. Determine the amount of assessable profit:

Ans: (2,50,800)

Problem 7.20-P5 [CS D05]

Pritish, who owns 9 acres of land near Chennai since July, 1985 purchased for Rs. 12 lakh, commenced real estate business from April, 1999 and introduced this land as his capital. Fair market value of the land on the date of commencement of the business was Rs. 65 lakh. However, the value of such land has been recorded at Rs. 80 lakh in the books of business. The entire land after development and conversion into housing plots was sold for Rs. 135 lakh between September, 2006 and February, 2007. Expenses incurred for project development were Rs. 37 lakh. Advise him as to the taxability of income and under what heads and in which assessment years.

Ans: Business Income 33,00,000; LTCG 29,90,226.

TOPIC 7.21 **SECTION 45(3).* TRANSFER OF CAPITAL ASSET BY AN INDIVIDUAL OR A PARTNER TO A FIRM / AOP / BOI

In this case an individual transfers a capital asset to a firm or other association of persons or body of individuals in which he is or becomes a partner or member, by way of capital contribution or otherwise.

Sale consideration : The amount recorded in the books of account of the firm, association or body of individuals.

Illustration 7.21-P1 (Simple)

X and Y are two partners of a firm, AC & Co. On January 1, 2007, B joins the firm and brings shares in a company as his capital contribution. Fair Market value of these shares on

January 1, 2007 is Rs. 2,86,000, whereas amount credited in B's account in the firm is Rs. 3,00,000. Assuming cost of acquisition in 1994-95 of these shares was Rs. 5,000, find out the amount of chargeable capital gain for the AY 2007-08.

Solution

Computation of Capital Gain as per AY 2007-08

Sale consideration	3,00,000
Less: Indexed COA (519 ÷ 259 × 5,000)	10,019
LTCG	2,89,981

Problem 7.21-P2 [CS J95]

X and Y are two partners of a firm, AC & Co. On 1st January, 2007, B joins the firm and brings shares in a company as his capital contribution. Fair market value of there shares on 1st January, 2007 is Rs. 1,46,000, whereas amount credited in B's account in the firm is Rs. 1,70,000. Assuming that cost of acquisition in 1997-98 of these shares was Rs. 48,000, find out the amount of chargeable capital gain for the assessment year 2007-08.

Ans: 94,737.

Problem 7.21-P3 (Simple)

Mr. Taxcrazy acquired a residential house property situated in village by way of will from his father on 11-9-2003. Fair market value on September 11, 2003 is Rs. 9,00,000. His father had acquired the house in the PY 1992-93 for Rs. 6,00,000. On 31-3-2007, Mr. Taxcrazy became a partner in the firm Give Take & Co. and introduced this property as his capital contribution to the firm. Fair Market value of this property on March 31, 2007 is Rs. 15,00,000, whereas amount credited in Taxcrazy's account in the firm is Rs. 10,00,000. Compute the capital gain chargeable to tax for the AY 2007-08.

Ans: 3,27,430

TOPIC 7.22 * *SECTION 45(4)*. DISTRIBUTION OF CAPITAL ASSET BY FIRM / AOP / BOI TO ITS PARTNERS ON ITS DISSOLUTION OR OTHERWISE

Sale consideration : Fair Market Value of the asset on the date of transfer.

Illustration 7.22-P1 (Difficult)

Pen and Sword are two partners of a firm. The firm is dissolved on April 8, 2006 and the following distributions are made. No other asset is held by firm apart from the following :

	Factory Building	*Bonus shares*	*Goodwill of a business*	*Land in a village*
Date of acquisition	15-9-1972	4-5-2003	NA	9-9-2001
Cost of acquisition	16,50,000	nil	nil	3,20,000
FMV on 8-4-2006	2,60,000	20,000	6,90,000	5,00,000
W.D.V. on 1-4-2006	1,00,000	NA	NA	NA
FMV on 1-4-1981	18,00,000	NA	2,00,000	NA
Agreed value as per dissolution deed	5,40,000	35,000	6,60,000	5,60,000

Factory building and bonus shares are transferred to Pen and whereas Goodwill of a business and land is transferred to Sword. Compute the capital gain chargeable to tax in the hands of firm for the AY 2007-08.

Ans: STCG 1,60,000; LTCG 8,20,141

TOPIC 7.23 **SECTION 45(5). COMPUTATION OF CAPITAL GAIN ON COMPULSORY ACQUISITION OF CAPITAL ASSET BY THE GOVERNMENT

(A) TAXABILITY OF COMPENSATION AWARDED IN THE FIRST INSTANCE

Where the capital gain arises from the transfer by way of compulsory acquisition under any law, the consideration for which was determined or approved by the Central Government or the Reserve Bank of India.

Sale consideration : The amount of initial compensation awarded in the first instance.

Year of transfer : On the date of compulsory acquisition.

Year of chargeability : Whole of compensation awarded is chargeable to tax in the PY in which such compensation which is awarded in the first instance (full or part) is first received *(not the year in which transfer takes place) i.e.* charge on capital gain is postponed to a later date when whole or part of the compensation is received.

Indexation : Indexation is done from the date of compulsory acquisition of the asset to the date of acquisition of the asset by the assessee.

Illustration 7.23-P1 (Difficult)

Compulsory acquisition of building by

Mr. Taxcrazy -->Govt.

COA as on 1-1-1991	Compensation awarded as on
Rs. 1,50,000	15-7-1998 Rs. 7,20,000

Mr. Taxcrazy receives Rs. 15,000 compensation out of Rs. 7,20,000 in the PY 2006-07 and remaining Rs. 7,05,000 on 16-3-2009. Compute Capital Gain chargeable to tax for the AY 99-2000, AY 2007-08 & 2009-10.

Solution

Computation of Capital Gain as per AY 2007-08

Sale consideration	7,20,000
Less : Indexed COA (351 ÷ 182 × 1,50,000)	2,89,286
LTCG	4,30,714

Note

- Indexation is done from 97-98 to 89-90. There is nil capital gain for the AY 97-98. Chargeability of capital gain is postponed to AY 2007-08 when first compensation is received.
- Rs 7,05,000 has already been charged in AY 2007-08. Hence no double taxation in the year of receipt.

(B) TAXABILITY OF ENHANCED COMPENSATION

Compensation or the consideration for such transfer can be enhanced by any court, Tribunal or other authority, the capital gain shall be dealt with in the following manner :

Sale consideration : The amount of enhanced compensation received.

Year of taxability : Only the amount which is received out of the enhanced compensation is taxable in the year of receipt. The taxability is on receipt by receipt basis.

Deduction : No deduction by way of cost of aacquisition and improvement is further allowed. However deduction is allowed on recovery of enhanced compensation like filing of suit, litigation expenses etc.

Illustration 7.23-P2 (Difficult)

In the preceding illustration Mr. Taxcrazy not satisfied with the award filed a suit of recovery. The Court enhanced the amount of compensation by Rs. 4,00,000. The Govt. paid 70% compensation on 5-8-2010 and remaining 30% on 6-9-2012. The cost of litigation incurred is Rs. 54,000.

Solution

Computation of Capital Gain for the AY 2011-12

Enhanced compensation	2,80,000
Less :	
• Cost of acquisition	Nil
• Litigation expenses	54,000
LTCG	2,26,000

Computation of Capital Gain for the AY 2013-14

Enhanced compensation	1,20,000
Less : Cost of acquisition	Nil
LTCG	1,20,000

Problem 7.23-P3 (Typical)

The State Govt. compulsorily acquired a land on April 5, 2002. The land was owned by Mr. Taxcrazy who acquired it by way of gift from his grandmother on 11-9-1988. His grandmother had acquired the land in the PY 1980-81 for — Rs. 20,000. Brokerage paid on acquisition Rs. 3,000.

Market value of the land on different dates are as follows : on 1-4-1981 — Rs. 30,000; on 11-9-1988 — Rs. 3,00,000; on 5-4-2002 — Rs. 9,00,000.

Mr. Taxcrazy incurred Rs. 2,00,000 in making certain capital improvement to the land during the PY 2001-02.

A compensation of Rs. 4,50,000 awarded to Taxcrazy which he received on July 15, 2006.

Taxcrazy files an appeal against the State Govt. in respect of the amount of compensation. The High Court enhances the compensation by Rs. 1,10,000 on March 2, 2009 which Taxcrazy receives on September 12, 2009. Taxcrazy incurs Rs. 32,000 as legal expenses in this connection.

Compute the capital gain arising in this case.

Ans: AY 2007-08 : 1,49,337; AY 2010-11 : 78,000.

(C) *. REDUCTION OF COMPENSATION AWARDED

Where in the assessment for any year, the capital gain arising from the transfer of a capital asset is computed by taking the enhanced compensation and subsequently such compensation is reduced by any court, Tribunal or other authority, then capital gain which has been assessed in the earlier year shall be recomputed by taking the reduced compensation.

Problems 7.23-P4

1 As per section 45(1), capital gain is chargeable to tax in the year when transfer is effected. Is there any exception to this rule? or When is capital gain not taxable in the year in which capital asset is transferred, but in some other year ?

2. List two situations in which fair market value is treated as full value of consideration ?

3. Explain chargeability section 45?

Solutions

1. Yes. Section 45(1A), 45(2) and 45(5).
2. Section 45(2) and section 45(4).
3. Section 45 has 6 sub-sections. They are (1), (1A), (2), (3), (4), (5). Discuss all the sub-sections.

Before you rush to next topics do revise and memorise all the preceding topics of capital gain. It will create the whole picture of capital gain in your mind and then you shall feel more confident.

Keep running

TOPIC 7.24 *FIRST PROVISO TO SECTION 48.* COMPUTATION OF CAPITAL GAIN IN THE CASE OF TRANSFER OF SHARES / DEBENTURES HELD BY NON-RESIDENTS

(A) CONDITIONS

1. Appilcable to Non- Resident (Indian citizen or a foreign citizen).
2. Such Non- Resident should acquire shares, debentures or bonds in an Indian Company (public or private both) by utilising foreign currency.
3. Such capital asset should be transferred during the year resulting in capital gain, STCG or LTCG.
4. Benefit of indexation not available. However assessee is allowed conversion of Indian currency into foreign currency.

(B) MANNER OF COMPUTATION OF CAPITAL GAIN

1. The sale consideration and expenses on transfer which is given in Rupee shall be converted into foreign currency at the average of buying & selling rate on the date of transfer of securities.

   Sale consideration – Expenses on transfer = Net Sale Consideration (NSC)

$$\frac{\text{Re (Net Sale Consideration)}}{\text{average of buying \& selling rate on the date of transfer}} = \$\text{NSC}$$

2. The cost of acquisition which is given in the rupee shall be converted into foreign currency at the average of buying & selling rate on the date of acquisition of securities.

$$\frac{\text{Re (Cost of acquisition)}}{\text{average of buying \& selling rate on the date of acquisition}} = \$\text{COA}$$

3. \$ LTCG = \$ NSC – \$ COA
4. \$ LTCG shall be reconverted into Re. LTCG at the buying rate on date of transfer. Re LTCG = \$ LTCG × buying rate on date of transfer.

Note

- Rate of tax on LTCG is levied @ 10% flat + surcharge as applicable + Education cess

Illustration 7.24-P1 (Difficult)

Mr. Taxcrazy, a Non-Resident provides following information for computation of capital gain for the AY 2007-08.

Sale consideration *(Date of sale 21-6-2006)*	Rs. 9,00,000
Cost of acquisition *(Date of acquisition 15-4-2002)*	Rs. 4,20,000
Average of buying and selling rate on the date of sale	Rs. 45
Average of buying and selling rate on the date of acquisition	Rs. 42
Buying rate on the date of sale	Rs. 46

Solution

Computation of Capital Gain for the AY 2007-08

Sale consideration *(9,00,000 ÷ 45)*	\$ 20,000
Cost of acquisition *(4,20,000 ÷ 42)*	\$ 10,000

LTCG	$ 10,000
LTCG in Rs. *(10,000 × 46)*	Rs. 4,60,000

Problem 7.24-P2

1. Section 48 Proviso 1 is applicable to all type of assets.

Solution

1. False. It is applicable only to shares and debentures acquired in foreign currency.

Problem 7.24-P3

A is a non-resident individual. He had purchased shares in an Indian Company in 1996 for U.S. $ 1,00,000, when the rate of exchange (assuming) was one US $ = Rs. 25. He sold the shares in April, 2006 for Rs. 30,00,000, when the rate of exchange (assuming) was U.S. $ 1 = Rs. 35. Determine the capital gains tax of A in respect of Assessment Year 2007-2008.

Ans: 9,00,000.

Problem 7.24-P4 (Typical)

Taxcrazy, a non-resident, remits US $ 1,90,000 to India on September 16, 1993 for purchasing Gold and shares of an Indian company. Details of all the assets held by him in India and outside India are given below :

	Property in USA	*Gold in India*	*Unlisted bonds in a Foreign Co.*	*Shares in an Indian Co.*
Date of acquisition	5-8-1850	18-9-1994	5-11-2003	5-11-2003
Cost of acquisition	$ 2,000	Rs. 16,000	Rs. 5,000	Rs. 6,85,000
Date of sale	15-3-2007	25-10-2006	25-10-2006	15-3-2007
Sale consideration	$ 99,00,000	Rs. 65,000	Rs. 4,100	Rs. 16,03,000
Expenses on transfer	$ 4,000	Rs. 5,000	Rs. 100	Rs. 3,000

You are required to compute capital gain chargeable to tax for the AY 2007-08 on the assumption that telegraphic transfer buying and selling rate of US dollars adopted by the State Bank of India is as follows:

	Buying (1$ = Rs.)	*Selling (1$ = Rs.)*
September 16, 1993	28	30
September 18, 1994	26	30
November 5, 2003	38	40
October 25, 2006	50	54
March 15, 2007	44	48

Ans: LTCG 7,85,552

Problem 7.24-P5 (Typical)

What if in the above question the investment is made in unlisted bonds of an Indian Company instead of foreign company?

Ans: STCG (2,564).

TOPIC 7.25 * *SECTION 115F.* SALE OF SPECIFIED ASSETS AND PURCHASE OF SPECIFIED ASSETS

1. *Applicability* : Applicable to assessee who is Non-resident Indian (either Indian citizen or a person of Indian origin) at the time of transfer who is not covered u/s 115AC or 115AD.
2. *Type of assets* : The asset which is transferred should be LTCA being specified securities acquired in foreign currency.
3. *Time limit* : Time limit to purchase new securities (Zero date --> 6 months) *i.e.* he should purchase specified securities in foreign exchange within 6 months from the zero date. 'Date of sale of original asset shall be treated as ZERO DATE'

What are specified assets

1. Shares of an Indian Company.
2. Deposits with an Indian public Co.
3. Central Govt. securities.
4. Debentures or bonds of an Indian public Co.

Amount of exemption : Proportionate exemption is available

$$\frac{\text{LTCG}}{\text{Net Sale Consideration}} \times \text{Amount invested in specified assets}$$

Consequences if new asset is transferred or converted into money within 3 years of purchase.

• Amount of capital gain exempted earlier shall be treated as LTCG in the year of transfer.

Illustration 7.25-P1 (Typical)

From illustration 7.24-P1 : X, an Indian citizen, Non-resident Indian in India for the AY 2007-08, purchases the following assets :

	Date of investment	*Amount*
1. Shares in a DQ (P) Ltd.	22-12-2006	15,000
2. Debentures of a DQ (P) Ltd.	24-6-2006	10,000
3. Bonds of RR Ltd.	25-6-2006	4,000
4. State Govt. securities	30-7-2006	18,000
5. Central Govt. securities	8-8-2006	20,000

Solution

LTCG	4,60,000
Less : Exemption u/s 115F *(51.111% of 24,000)*	12,267
LTCG	4,47,733

Note

- Percentage = LTCG ÷ NSC = 4,60,000 ÷ 9,00,000 = 51.111%
- Supra 1 - Exemption u/s 115F not available since investment is made after 6 months from the date of sale.
- Supra 2, 3 - Exemption u/s 115F not available since investment of debentures in private limited company and State Govt. securities is not applicable.

Problem 7.25-P2 [Hons 1996]

R, a non-resident Indian, remits US $ 40,000 to India on September 16, 2006. The amount is partly utilised on October 3, 2006 for purchasing 10,000 shares in A (Pvt.) Ltd., an Indian company at the rate of Rs. 30 per share. These shares are sold for Rs. 45 per share on January 30, 2007. He deposits Rs. 40,000 with an Indian public company on July 1, 2007 *(due date of filing return of income: July 31, 2007).*

You are required to compute capital gain chargeable to tax for the AY 2007-08 on the assumption that telegraphic transfer buying and selling rate of US dollars adopted by the State Bank of India is as follows:

	Buying (1$) *Rs.*	*Selling (1$)* *Rs.*
September 16, 2006	42	44
October 3, 2006	43	45
January 30, 2007	46	50

Ans: 1,17,614; 1,07,159.

EXEMPTIONS FROM CAPITAL GAIN

Section 54 to 54GA. Invest in certain assets within time limit and claim exemptions

TOPIC 7.26 *SECTION 54.* TRANSFER OF RESIDENTIAL HOUSE PROPERTY & PURCHASE OR CONSTRUCTION OF RESIDENTIAL HOUSE PROPERTY

(A) CONDITIONS FOR CLAIMING EXEMPTION

a. *Who can claim exemption* : Only individual or HUF can claim exemption under section 54.

b. *Which asset should be transferred* : The asset which is transferred should be Long Term Capital Asset being a residential house property. (It includes buildings or land appurtenant thereto which is chargeable under the head 'Income from House Property'.) Transfer of long term residential house shall give rise to long term capital gain from which exemption can be claimed on purchase or construction of new residential house within time limit.

c. *When new residential house property should be purchased or constructed* : New residential house property should be purchased or constructed within time allowed before or after the "Zero Date". Zero Date is the date of sale of original residential house property. Let us see the time limit.

   A new house should be *purchased* within 1 year *before* the 'zero date'.

   A new house should be *purchased* within 2 years *from* the 'zero date'.

   A new house should be *constructed* within 3 years *from* the 'zero date'.

   In short (1 year <--zero date --> 2 years purchase or 3 years construction)

   E.g. The date of sale of original residential house 6-10-2006. Find out the date by which he should purchase or construct a new residential house to claim exemption u/s 54.

   Zero date

   (P) 7-10-2005 <---------6-10-2006 ------------------>5-10-2008 (P)

   ------------------>5-10-2009 (C)

   It means to claim exemption a new house can be purchased on or after 7-10-2005 or by 5-10-2008 however construction of new house should be constructed on or after 6-10-2006 but by 5-10-2009.

d. *Deposit scheme u/s Section 54(2)* : Where the amount is not so utilised for purchase or construction of new residential house before the due date of furnishing of return, it shall be deposited by him on or before the due date of furnishing of return in the deposit account as per Capital Gain Account Scheme, 1988. Such deposited amount is deemed to be cost of acquisition of new asset on which exemption u/s 54 be claimed. *(Due date of furnishing of return for the AY 2007-08 is either 31-7-2007 or 31-10-2007 as the case may be)*

Note

- If the assessee plans to purchase / construct a new house after the due date of furnishing of return then he should deposit the amount in a Scheduled Bank on or before the due date of furnishing of return and such deposited amount should be utilised on or before 5-10-2008 or 5-10-2009 as the case may be for purchase or construction of new residential house property.

- To claim exemption under section 54 the assessee can purchase or construct as many residential houses.
- Self-financing scheme is also applicable.

Memory Technique : 'Zero date' is seen only when house is purchased or constructed and due date of furnishing of return is seen only when amount is deposited in a Scheduled Bank.

(B) COMPUTATION OF AMOUNT OF EXEMPTION

Amount invested in new residential house within zero date +	--
Amount deposited in Scheduled Bank on or before the due date of furnishing of return	--
Total exempted amount limited to LTCG	--

(C) CONSEQUENCES OF NON-UTILISATION OF DEPOSITED AMOUNT WITHIN ZERO DATE [CONSEQUENCES 1]

The deposited amount should be utilised either to purchase or construct a new residential house property within zero date, otherwise exemption claimed on the basis of amount deposited shall stand withdrawn or taken back.

Withdrawal of exemption shall be treated as LTCG which shall be chargeable after the expiry of 3 years from the zero date. Its computation is shown below.

Computation of LTCG (assumed figures)

Amount of capital gain exempted earlier from the deposited amount	3,000
Less : Amount utilised to purchase or construct a new RHP within 2 / 3 years from the 'zero date'	1,000
LTCG *(chargeable in the PY when period of 3 years expires from the* 'zero date'*)*	2,000

Note

- The remaining unutilised amount can be withdrawn at any time after the expiry of 3 years from the 'zero date'.

(D) CONSEQUENCES IF NEW RESIDENTIAL HOUSE IS TRANSFERRED WITHIN 3 YEARS FROM THE DATE OF ITS ACQUISITION [CONSEQUENCES 2]

When a new residential house is sold within 3 years of its acquisition, then there arises two types of gains :

1. STCG arises on sale of new house, since house is sold within 3 years of its acquisition.
2. A penalty gain meaning thereby the amount of capital gain exempted earlier for the new house shall stand withdrawn. We call it penalty gain since withdrawal of LTCG exemption is converted into STCG. See below how.

Computation of STCG (assumed figures)

The amount of capital gain exempted earlier	2,000
The amount of capital gain arising on transfer of new RHP *(sale consideration - cost of acquisition - cost of improvement - expenses on transfer) +*	5,000
STCG (chargeable to tax in the year of transfer of RHP)	7,000

(E) *OTHER POINTS

1. *Section 54H. Zero date in case where property is compulsorily acquired* : Zero date shall be the date when part or full initial compensation is received. In case of enhanced compensation the date of receipt of enhanced compensation shall be the zero date.
2. *Taxability of unutilised amount on the death of the owner of the property :* The unutilised deposit amount under the Capital Gains Account Scheme, 1988 in the case of an individual who dies before the expiry of the stipulated period cannot be taxed in the hands of the deceased. This amount is not taxable in the hands of legal heirs also as the unutilised portion of the deposit does not partake the character of income in their hands but is only a part of the estate devolving upon them.

Illustration 7.26-P1 (Difficult)

sells RHP to

Mr. Taxcrazy --> Mr. D

COA as on 1-1-2001 Rs. 1,75,000 SC as on 1-2-2007 Rs. 9,50,000

Compute capital gain for the AY 2007-08 on the assumption that due date of furnishing of return is 31-7-2007 from the following information :

	Date of purchase or deposited	*Amount invested or deposited*
• House 1	1-3-2006	50,000
• House 2	29-7-2007	30,000
• House at Raipur	1-2-2006	1,40,000
• Deposits	30-7-2007	2,00,000
• Deposits	1-8-2007	2,50,000

Solution

To claim exemption u/s 54, he should invest in new RHP within zero date which is 2-2-2006 ---> 1 -2-2007 ---> 31-1-2009 (P) or 31-1-2010 (C).

Computation of Capital Gain for AY 2007-08

Sale consideration		9,50,000
Less : Indexed COA (519 ÷ 406 × 1,75,000)		2,23,707
LTCG		7,26,293
Less : exemption u/s 54		
• House 1	50,000	
• House 2	30,000	
• Deposits	2,00,000	2,80,000
LTCG		4,46,293

Note

- Exemption of Rs. 1,40,000 is not available since house at Raipur is not purchased within 1 year before the zero date.
- Deposits made on 1-8-2007 is not available since deposit is made after the due date of furnishing of return.

Illustration 7.26-P2 (Typical)

(A) Continuing from the preceding illustration Mr. Taxcrazy acquires following houses from the deposited amount. Compute capital gain for AY 2010-11.

	Date of purchase/construction	*Amount Invested*
• House 3	2-2-2009 (purchase)	73,000
• House 4	16-1-2010 (construction)	75,000
• House 5	11-6-2008 (construction)	52,000

(B) What if House 4 & 5 is purchased instead of construction.

Ans: 73,000; 1,48,000.

Solution

Computation of Capital Gain for AY 2009-10

Amount of capital gain exempted earlier *(deposited amount)*		2,00,000
Less : Amount utilised within 2 / 3 years from the zero date.		
• House 4	75,000	
• House 5	52,000	1,27,000
LTCG		73,000

Note

- Since House 3 is purchased after 2 years from the zero date. Therefore exemption u/s 54 is not available.

Illustration 7.26-P3 (Typical)

Continuing from both the preceding illustrations Mr. Taxcrazy sells the following house properties. Compute capital gain chargeable to tax for AY 2008-09 & 2011-12.

	Date of sale	*Sale consideration*
• House 1	27-02-2008	2,00,000
• House 5	10-06-2010	20,000

Solution

Computation of Capital Gain

	AY 2008-09 *House 1*	*AY 2011-12* *House 5*
Amount of capital gain exempted earlier out of deposited amount	50,000	52,000
Sale Consideration – Cost of acquisition new house	1,50,000	(32,000)
STCG	2,00,000	20,000

Problem 7.26-P4

1. When can exemption be withdrawn or taken back?
2. Which capital gain arises when the deposited amount is not utilised?
3. Which capital gain arises when the new RHP is transferred within 3 years of its purchase or construction?

4. Which date is seen when new RHP is purchased or constructed?
5. Which date is seen when the amount is deposited in a Scheduled bank under the Capital Gain Account Scheme, 1988?
6. X Ltd. sells a house property on July 1, 2006 for consideration of Rs. 90 lakhs. The long terms capital gain generated on the transaction is Rs. 40,00,000. The company can claim exemption under section 54 by purchasing another residential house property.
7. Is it always beneficial to claim exemption u/s 54?
8. Can exemption u/s 54 be claimed if new house is purchased or constructed after the due date of furnishing of return but without depositing in a Scheduled Bank?

Ans:

1. When deposited amount is not fully utilised or when the new house is transferred within 3 years of it's purchase or construction.
2. LTCG.
3. STCG.
4. Zero date.
5. Due date of furnishing of return.
6. No.
7. No. When house is sold and purchase in same PY it is not beneficial to claim exemption (Refer illustration 7.25-P4-5)
8. No. (Refer Problem 7.25-P7)

Problem 7.26-P5

1.	Zero Date [Date of sale of original house property]	1-1-2007
	LTCG	8,00,000
	Deposits before due date of filing of return	5,00,000
	House purchased on 31-12-2008	4,00,000
2.	Zero Date [Date of sale of original house property]	1-1-2007
	LTCG	11,00,000
	Deposits before due date of filing of return	9,00,000
	House constructed on 1-1-2010	8,00,000
3.	Zero Date [Date of sale of original house property]	1-1-2007
	LTCG	15,00,000
	House purchased on 31-12-2006	16,00,000
	Sold the new house on 29-12-2009	18,00,000
4.	Zero Date [Date of sale of original house property]	1-1-2007
	LTCG	20,00,000
	House 1 purchased on 1-1-2007	12,00,000
	Deposits before due date of filing of return	9,00,000
	House 1 purchased on 1-1-2008	3,00,000
	House 2 constructed on 1-1-2009	2,00,000

5. Zero Date [Date of sale of original house property] 1-1-2007

   LTCG 21,00,000

   House purchased on 1-4-2006 25,00,000

   Sold the new house on 31-03-2007 28,00,000

Ans: (1) 3,00,000; 1,00,000 (2) 2,00,000; 9,00,000 (3) nil; 17,000,000 (4) nil; 3,00,000. (5) LTCG nil; STCG 3,00,000.

Problem 7.26-P6 [Hons 2006C]

Find out the amount of exemption and capital gain chargeable to tax for the Assessment year 2007-08.

Mrs. Q purchases a house property in Jaipur on 19-11-1988 Rs. 3,00,000

The fair market value of the house on 01-04-1981 Rs. 2,80,000

Mrs. Q sells house property on 21-12-2006 Rs. 15,40,000

She purchases a new residential house property in Delhi for the residence of her married daughter on 20-04-2006.

Ans: 5,72,919; nil.

Problem 7.26-P7 [Typical]

A and B were co-owners (having ½ share each) of a residential bungalow in a posh locality in Delhi. They sold the said bungalow on 5th May, 2006 for a consideration of Rs. 1,40,50,000. They incurred brokerage and other incidental expenses of Rs. 2,50,000/- on sale of the said property. The bungalow was purchased by them jointly in August, 1993 for Rs. 30,00,000 inclusive of purchase expenses on stamp duty, brokerage and transfer charges.

Out of his share of sale proceeds, 'A' purchased a residential flat for Rs. 24,00,000/- on 10th December, 2006 and also incurred expenses of Rs. 1,50,000/- on brokerage and stamp duty.

'B' on the other hand, gave an amount of Rs. 5,00,000 to his sister out of his share of sale proceeds. He also invested Rs. 30,00,000/- on construction of a residential house of himself. He completed the construction of the house in May, 2007.

Compute the long term capital gains liable to tax in the hands of 'A' as well as in the hands of 'B'.

Ans: 11,59,426; 7,09,426.

Problem 7.26-P8 (Typical)

X provides the following data regarding his transaction for the sale of residential house for the AY 2007-08 :

House purchased in 1987-88 2,50,000

House remodelled in 1995-96 20,000

House property sold in October 16, 2006 14,50,995

New house property purchased at Meerut in September 2006 3,58,500

He also deposits Rs. 3,60,000 in deposit account for availing exemption u/s 54. He purchases another RHP at Dadri on 19-10-2008 for Rs. 3,40,000 by withdrawing from the deposit account. Amount left in the deposit account was withdrawn on 25-10-2009. X had contracted to sell this property in June 1993, for Rs. 6,00,000 and had received an advance of Rs. 5,000 towards sale. The intending purchaser did not pay the balancing amount and the advance was forfeited by X. Compute the amount capital gain to be included in the total income.

Ans: AY 2007-08 nil; AY 2010-11 1,84,367.

Problem 7.26-P9 (Difficult)

Mr. X furnishes the following particulars for the PY ending 31-3-2007 and request you to compute the taxable capital gain :

He had a residential house, inherited from father in 1995, the fair market value of which on 1-4-1981 is Rs. 5,00,000. In the year 1997-98, further construction and improvements costed Rs. 6,00,000. On 10-5-2006, the house was sold for Rs. 50,00,000. Expenditure in connection with transfer is Rs. 50,000. On 20-12-2006 he purchased a residential house for Rs. 15,00,000.

Ans: 15,85,727.

Illustration 7.26-P10 (Typical)

Taxcrazy, an owner of 2 houses, sells a residential house property in Chennai for Rs. 15,00,000 on July 23, 2006. This house was inherited by him on August 16, 1991. This house was acquired for Rs. 60,000 on 4-5-1985 by the previous owner. On May 19, 2006, he purchased a flat in Delhi for Rs. 6,10,000 for the purpose of the residence of his son-in-law. On March 1, 2007, Taxcrazy sells the flat in Delhi for Rs. 10,20,000.

1. Compute the capital gains arising on the two transactions.
2. Is Taxcrazy eligible for exemption u/s 54 in respect of the second sale ?

Solution

Computation of LTCG for the AY 2007-08

	Option 1 Exemption is claimed	*Option 2 Exemption is not claimed*
Sale Consideration	15,00,000	15,00,000
Less : Indexed cost of acquisition (519 ÷ 199 × 60,000)	1,56,482	1,56,482
LTCG	13,43,518	13,43,518
Less : Exemption u/s 54	6,10,000	nil
LTCG	7,33,518	13,43,518

Computation of STCG for the AY 2007-08

Capital gain exempted previously	6,10,000	nil
Capital gain arising on sale of new RHP (10,20,000 – 6,10,000)	4,10,000	4,10,000
STCG	10,20,000	4,10,000

- As you know rate of tax on LTCG is 20% whereas on STCG is 30%. *(Surcharge as applicable in both the cases)*. To save tax it is better STCG is minimum and STCG is minimum only when exemption is not claimed.

Problem 7.26-P11 [Hons 2002]

X sells his residential house in Delhi for Rs. 10,90,000 on 23-5-2006. This house was purchased by him on 1-4-1992 for Rs. 2,90,000. On 30th June 2006, he purchased a flat in Mumbai for Rs. 8,70,000 for the purpose of the residence of his son-in-law. On 1-3-2007, he sells the Mumbai flat for Rs. 12,10,000. Compute the capital gain arising on the two transactions. Is X eligible for exemption under section 54?

Ans: LTCG 4,15,067; STCG 3,40,000. Though X is eligible to claim exemption, it is better not to claim exemption u/s 54.

Problem 7.26-P12 (Typical)

X owned a residential house at Bikaner, the original cost of which was Rs. 50,000. It was acquired on September 1, 1993. He sold the house on March 1, 2003 for Rs. 6,00,000 and constructed another house on January 30, 2006 at Bhiwani for Rs. 4,50,000. The house at Bhiwani was sold by him for Rs. 3,00,000 on December 30, 2008. Discuss the impact of these transactions with regard to assessment to capital gains.

Option 1: If Rs. 4,00,000 is deposited in capital gain deposit account scheme on 15-7-2003.

Option 2: If no such deposit is made.

Ans: Option 1 : AY 2003-04 1,08,402; AY 2006-07 nil; AY 2007-08 2,50,000.
Option 2 : AY 2003-04 5,08,402; AY 2006-07 NA; AY 2009-10 (1,50,000).

Problem 7.26-P13 (Typical)

(A) Mr. Remo furnishes following information for your consideration :

	COA	*Sale consid.*	*FMV*
RHP in urban area *(gifted to a firm)*	60,000 as on 6-1-1970	—	10,00,000 as on 1-5-2006
RHP in rural area *(sold to Mr. LP)*	2,68,000 as on 5-8-2001	88,000 as on 18-9-2006	—
RHP in industrial area *(acquired from X Ltd)*	18,910 as on 7-6-2003	9,00,000 on 19-9-2006	—
RHP in suburb *(acquired from a HUF)*	2,08,000 as on 17-5-2000	19,00,000 on 18-10-2006	—

To get exemption u/s 54 Remo purchases a residential house at Chandigarh on 20-10-2005 for Rs. 2,00,000 for his family. Besides on 19-10-2006 a house at Raipur was constructed at a cost of Rs. 6,90,000. He also deposits Rs. 12,00,000 on 31-7-2007 in the nationalised bank. The deposited amount is utilised by him for construction of a house on 17-10-2009 for Rs. 9,00,000. Compute capital gain chargeable to tax for the AY 2007-08 and AY 2010-11.

(B) What if House is constructed on 19-10-2009.

Ans: (A) 1,84,404 (B) 12,00,000.

Problem 7.26-P14 [Hons 2004C]

A acquires a residential house by way of will from his father on 15-6-1995. The father, in turn, inherited that house from his father in 1985-86. The grand father of A had acquired house in 1978 for Rs. 3 lakh. The market prices of this house on 1-4-1981 was Rs. 5 lakh. The above house was acquired by Government by issue of notification on 16-4-2002 and the compensation was fixed at Rs. 15 lakh which he received on 26-2-2006.

A purchased a new residential house on 25-04-2007 for Rs. 4 lakhs. A was not satisfied with the compensation and as such filed a suit in the court. The court vide its judgement on 29-1-2007 enhanced the compensation by Rs. 2 lakhs, which was received on 4-4-2007. Out of which he deposited Rs. 1,50,000 in capital gain scheme for purpose of residential house on 16-4-2007.

Compute the capital gains for various assessment years assuming the last data of filing return of income in his case is 31st July every year.

Ans: 7,04,626; 50,000. Exemption of Rs. 4,00,000 is not available since it is assumed that he has not deposited the same.

Practice Questions

Problem 7.26-P15 [Pass 2004C]

N sold a residential house on 25-12-2006 for Rs. 15,00,000. He had purchased this house on 19-11-1988 for Rs. 1,25,000 and spent Rs. 84,000 on its improvement of the house during the year 1990-91. He purchased a new house on 19-11-2006 for Rs. 8,00,000. This house was also sold by him on 1-1-2008 for Rs. 12,50,000. He purchased another house on 26-1-2008 for Rs. 10,50,000. Compute capital gains for the assessment year 2007-08 and 2008-09.

Ans: 57,511; 12,50,000.

Problem 7.26-P16 [Pass 2001]

From the following information of an assessee compute the chargeable capital gains :

Cost of acquisition of residential house in 1981-82	2,00,000
Cost of construction of first floor in 1992-93	3,00,000
Sale consideration of the house on 1-1-2006	28,00,000
Purchased another residential house on 1-10-2005	6,44,000
Deposited in Capital Gains A/c Scheme in July 2007	4,00,000

Ans: 19,794.

Problem 7.26-P17 [Pass 1998]

Mr. X provides the following information for his residential house and house hold furniture:

1. House purchased on 30-6-1990 Rs. 3,75,000
2. Household furniture purchased on 30-6-2000 Rs 50,000
3. Sold the house for Rs 15,00,000 and the furniture for Rs. 40,000 on 30-11-2006.
4. Purchased a new residential house on 15-9-2006 for Rs 4,00,000.

Calculate the taxable capital gain for the AY 2007-08.

Ans: 30,632.

Problem 7.26-P18 [Hons 1995]

Mr. Mahesh provides the following data regarding his transaction for sale of his residential house for AY 2007-08. Compute the amount of capital gain to be included in the total income for the AY 2007-08 and AY 2009-10.

• House purchased in 1990-91	7,80,000
• Sold in November 2006	35,00,000
• Purchased another house in September 2006	7,00,000
• Deposited in the Capital Gains Account Scheme in January 2007	8,00,000

The deposited amount was utilised to construct another house at Kanpur for Rs. 60,000 on 1-12-2008.

Ans: NIL; 5,15,714.

Problem 7.26-P19 [1. Pass 2005] [2. Pass 2003]

1. Mr. X owns a house, used for his residence. He purchased it on 30th November, 1981 for Rs. 2,00,000. Its fair market value of 1st April, 1981 was Rs. 3,00,000. He spent Rs. 50,000 on its improvement on 10-9-2006 and sold it on 30th December, 2006 for Rs. 20,00,000. He purchase another house on 25th February, 2007 for Rs. 4,00,000. Compute amount of exemption and taxable capital gain for the Assessment year 2007-08.
2. Mr. X owned a house, used for his residence. He purchased it on 15-7-1979 for Rs. 56,000. Its fair market value on 1st April, 1981 was Rs. 70,000. He spent Rs. 5,000 on its improvement on 10-9-2006 and sold it on 30-11-2006 for Rs. 6,00,000. He purchased another house on 25-2-2007 for Rs. 2,00,000. Compute taxable capital gain.

Ans: (1) 3,93,000; nil (2) 31,700.

TOPIC 7.27 *SECTION 54B.* CAPITAL GAIN ARISING FROM TRANSFER OF LAND USED FOR AGRICULTURAL PURPOSE

(A) CONDITIONS FOR CLAIMING EXEMPTION

(a) *Who can claim exemption* : Only individual can claim exemption u/s 54B.

(b) *Which asset should be transferred* : The asset which is transferred should be an agricultural land not situated in rural area.

Such asset can be either LTCA / STCA.

The agricultural land was used by the individual or his parents for agricultural purpose for a period of atleast 2 years immediately preceding the date of its transfer.

(c) *When new residential agricultural land should be purchased* : New agricultural land should be purchased within 2 years from the 'Zero Date'. Date of sale of original agricultural land is treated as 'ZERO DATE'.

E.g. Suppose zero date is 7-8-2006. A new agricultural land should be purchased by 6-8-2008. *(Zero date --->2 years).*

(d) Deposit scheme u/s Section 54(2) is applicable. Refer section 54 for detail. Topic 7.25d.

(B) COMPUTATION OF AMOUNT OF EXEMPTION (ASSUMED FIGURES)

Amount invested in new land *(within 2 years from the zero date)* +	6,000
Amount deposited in Scheduled Bank on or before the due date of furnishing of return	7,000
Total exempted amount *(limited to LTCG / STCG)*	13,000

Note

- The assessee can purchase more than one agricultural land to claim exemption u/s 54B.

(C) CONSEQUENCES OF NON-UTILISATION OF DEPOSITED AMOUNT WITHIN THE TIME LIMIT OF THE ZERO DATE [CONSEQUENCES 1]

Amount of capital gain exempted earlier out of deposited amount	7,000
Less: Amount utilised to purchase new agricultural land within 2 years years from the zero date	2,000
LTCG / STCG[1] *(Chargeable to tax in the PY when period of 2 years expires from the zero date)*	5,000

Note

- [1] Depends upon original capital asset transferred.
- The remaining unutilised amount can be withdrawn at any time after the expiry of 2 years from the zero date.

(D) CONSEQUENCES IF NEW LAND IS TRANSFERRED WITHIN *3 YEARS* AFTER THE DATE OF ACQUISITION OF NEW LAND [CONSEQUENCES 2]

• The amount of capital gain exempted earlier +	2,000
• The amount of capital gain arising on transfer of new land	8,500
STCG *(chargeable to tax in the year of transfer)*	10,500

Note

- Where land transferred is situated in rural area then this condition is not applicable.

Illustration 7.27-P1 (Simple)

sells agricultural land to

Mr. Taxcrazy ---> Mr. Dotcomguy

COA as on 1-1-1993 Rs. 1,09,000 SC as on 1-6-2006 Rs. 7,65,000

The land was used by his parents for agricultural purpose since the date of purchase. For claiming exemption u/s 54B Mr. Taxcrazy purchases new agricultural lands and deposits in the Scheduled Bank under the Capital Gain Account Scheme, 1988. Compute capital gain for the AY 2007-08 on the assumption that due date of furnishing of return for the AY 2007-08 is 31-10-2007.

	Date of purchase/deposited	*Amount Invested/deposited*
• AL 1 in rural area	30-07-2007	25,000
• AL 2 in urban area	2-08-2006	20,000
• AL in Surat	30-05-2006	1,30,000
• Deposits 1	30-09-2007	4,00,000
• Deposits 2	1-11-2007	3,55,000

Solution

Time limit (1-6-2006 ----->31-5-2008)

Computation of Capital Gain for AY 2007-08

Sale Consideration		7,65,000
Less : Indexed COA (519 ÷ 223 × 1,09,000)		2,53,682
LTCG		5,11,318
Less : exemption u/s 54B		
• AL 1	25,000	
• AL 2	20,000	
• Deposits 1	4,00,000	4,45,000
LTCG		66,318

Note

- Exemption on agricultural land in Surat not available since purchased before the zero date.
- Deposits made on 1-11-2007 is not available since deposit is made after the due date of furnishing of return.

Illustration 7.27-P2 (Difficult)

Continuing from the preceding illustration Mr. Taxcrazy acquires following agricultural land from the deposited amount.

	Date of purchase	*Amount Invested*
• AL 4 in urban area	2-6-2008	4,18,000
• AL 5 in urban area	2-12-2007	3,25,000
• AL 6 in rural area	11-6-2006	12,000

Compute Capital Gain chargeable to tax for the AY 2009-10.

Solution

Computation of Capital Gain for AY 2009-10

Amount of capital gain exempted earlier *(deposited amount)*	4,00,000
Less : Amount utilised within 2 years from the zero date -- AL 5 in urban area	3,25,000
LTCG	75,000

Note

- Since original land transferred was LTCA, therefore, LTCG arises.
- Exemption on AL 4 & AL 6 is not available since purchased after 2 years from the zero date.

Illustration 7.27-P3 (Difficult)

Continuing from both the preceding illustrations Mr. Taxcrazy sells the following agricultural land :

	Date of sale	*Sale consideration*
• AL 1	30-03-2010	1,80,000
• AL in Surat	13-05-2008	60,000
• AL 5	2-09-2009	4,50,000

Compute Capital Gain chargeable to tax for different AY's

Ans: nil; (70,000); 4,50,000.

Solution

Computation of Capital Gain

	AY 2010-11 AL 1	*AY 2009-10 AL in Surat*
Sale Consideration — COA of new agricultural land	Nil	(70,000)
Add : Amount of capital gain exempted earlier	Nil	Nil
STCG	Nil	(70,000)

Note : No capital gain arises since rural agricultural land is not a capital asset.

Problem 7.27-P4 [Pass 2004]

Compute taxable capital gain of Mr. X from the following particulars :

Gross sales proceeds of urban agricultural land on 10-11-2006 Rs. 16,00,000.

Paid 2% brokerage on sale.

This land was purchased by Mr. X in previous year 1988-89 for Rs. 2,50,000.

He purchased another urban agricultural land on 15-2-2007 for Rs. 4,00,000.

Ans: 3,62,099.

Problem 7.27-P5 (Difficult)

(A) Compute Capital gain for assessment year 2007-08.

sells agricultural land to

Mr. Joshi---> Mr. Prakash

COA as on 1-8-2004 Rs. 2,81,000 SC as on 1-7-2006 Rs. 8,05,000

This land was used by him for agricultural purpose since the date of purchase. For claiming exemption u/s 54B, Taxcrazy purchases new agricultural land in Noida on 29-6-2007 for Rs. 5,25,000.

(B) What is the amount of exemption if agricultural land is purchased on 1-1-2004.

Ans : 5,24,000; nil.

Solution

Computation of Capital Gain for AY 2007-08

Sale consideration	8,05,000
Less : Cost of acquisition	2,81,000
STCG	5,24,000
Less : exemption u/s 54B	Nil
STCG	5,24,000

Note : Since the agricultural land used by him is only for 1 year 11 months *i.e.* from 1-8-2004 to 1-7-2005 hence, exemption u/s 54B is not available.

Problem 7.27-P6 [CS D94]

During the previous year 2006-07, a Hindu Undivided Family (HUF), sells the following assets :

Assets	*Date of Sale*	*Sale proceeds*	*Date of purchase*	*Cost of acquisition*
Rural agricultural land	15-6-2006	2,00,000	01-3-1995	20,000
Urban agricultural land	1-11-2006	6,00,000	10-5-1996	58,000

AB (HUF) purchases agricultural land on 1st December, 2006 for Rs. 2,00,000.

Determine the taxable income for the assessment year 2007-08 on the assumption that income from business is Rs. 3,45,000.

Ans: 8,46,305.

(E) * (Section 54H)

Section 54H. Zero date in case where property is compulsorily acquired : Zero date shall be the date when part or full initial compensation is received. In case of enhanced compensation the date of receipt of enhanced compensation shall be the zero date.

(F) * [SECTION 10(37)]

Any capital gain, STCG or LTCG, arising to an individual or HUF from transfer of agricultural land (which is used for atleast 2 years for agricultural purpose by him or his parents) by way of compulsory acquisition by Govt. xshall be exempt if initial compensation is received on or after 1-4-2004 and enhanced compensation thereafter.

Problem 7.27-P7 (Simple)

(A) The Central Govt. compulsorily acquired an agricultural land situated in Delhi on April 5, 1999. The land was owned by X Ltd. which it acquired for Rs. 5,00,000 on 15-9-1986. A compensation of Rs. 25,00,000 was awarded to X Ltd. which he received on March 21, 2007. Out of the compensation amount, it purchases a new agricultural land in Nagpur on 31-7-2007 for Rs. 14,50,550. Compute the capital gain arising in this case.

(B) What if taxpayer is X, an individual.

Ans: AY 2007-08 11,80,451; nil.

Problem 7.27-P8 [CA M06]

X is in possession of agricultural land situated within urban limits, which is used for agricultural purposes during the preceding 3 years by his father. On 4-4-2006 this land is compulsorily acquired by the Government of India on a compensation fixed and paid by it for Rs. 10 lakhs. Advise X as to the tax consequences, assuming that the entire amount is invested in purchase of shares.

Ans: Entire sale consideration is exempt from tax u/s 10(37). No exemption in case of purchase of shares.

TOPIC 7.28 *SECTION 54EC.* TRANSFER OF ANY LTCA AND PURCHASE OF 2 SPECIFIED ASSETS

1. *Meaning of Specified Assets* : Following are the specified assets which should have a minimum lock-in period of 3 years from the date of issue.
   (a) National Highways Authority of India issued on or after 1-4-2000.
   (b) Rural Electrification Corporation Ltd. issued on or after 1-4-2001.

2. *Conditions*

   (a) *Applicability* : All assessees whether individual, HUF, Company etc. can claim exemption u/s 54EC.

   (b) *Type of assets* : The asset which is transferred should be a LTCA. The asset should be transferred on or after 1-4-2000.

   (c) *When is exemption available* : Exemption is available when the assessee purchases 5 specified assets within 6 month from the zero date. Date of sale of original LTCA is treated as 'ZERO DATE'. i.e. (zero date --->6 months). *E.g.* Suppose zero date is 16-8-2006. The specified asset should be purchased by 15-2-2007.

3. *Amount of exemption* : Amount invested in specified asset within zero date.

4. *Consequences if specified asset is transferred or converted into money or any loan/ advance is taken on the security of specified asset within 3 years of purchase*

   Amount of capital gain exempted earlier shall be treated as LTCG in the year of such transaction.

5. *Double benefit not available* : Deduction u/s 80C is not available if exemption is claimed under this section.

Difference between 80C and 54EC [Hints]

Deduction u/s 80C	Exemption u/s 54EC
Available only to Ind/ HUF	Available to all assessees
Investment only in relevant PY	Investment in 6 month from the zeo date
Available only from normal income	Exemption available only from LTCG
Deduction is a maximum of Rs. 1,00,000.	No limit. However limited to LTCG
It shall save tax of 10% to 30%	It shall save tax of 20%

Illustration 7.28-P1 (Typical)

Mr. X sells following assets. Compute his capital gain for the AY 2007-08.

Particulars	*Date of Acquis.*	*Cost of Acquis.*	*Date of Sale*	*Sale Consid.*
RHP 1	2005-06	1,00,000	2006-07	1,25,000
Urban AL	2005-06	80,000	2006-07	70,000
RHP 2	1998-99	4,00,000	1-6-2006	7,60,000
Gold	1993-94	6,00,000	1-3-2007	10,00,000
Units of UTI	2001-02	1,50,000	20-8-2006	4,90,000
Govt. Securities	2003-04	2,80,000	25-9-2006	3,70,000

He purchases following assets to claim exemptions

	Date of Purchase	*Amount*
Equity shares of National Highway Authority of India	26-3-2007	90,000
Bonds of Rural Electrification Corporation Ltd	19-8-2006	25,000
Debentures of National Highway Authority of India	12-12-2006	3,20,000
Equity shares of LG (P) Ltd	14-12-2006	20,000
Agricultural land in rural area	31-7-2007	25,000

Solution

Computation of STCG for the AY 2007-08

	RHP 1	*Urban AL*
Sale consideration	1,25,000	70,000
Less : Cost of acquisition	1,00,000	80,000
STCG	25,000	(10,000)

Computation of LTCG for the AY 2007-08

	RHP 2	*Gold*	*UTI*	*Govt. Securities*
Sale consideration	7,60,000	10,00,000	4,90,000	3,70,000
Less : Indexed cost of acquisition	5,91,453	12,76,230	1,82,746	3,13,866
LTCG	1,68,547	(2,76,230)	3,07,254	56,134
Less: Exemptions u/s 54EC				
• NHAI	nil	NA	nil	nil
• RECL	25,000	NA	nil	nil
• NABARD	nil	NA	3,07,254	12,746
LTCG	1,43,547	(2,76,230)	nil	43,388
Total LTCG				89,295

Problem 7.28-P2 [CS D97]

X sells a flat in commercial complex on 10th March, 2007 for Rs. 4,96,000 (indexed cost of acquisition : Rs. 1,60.000). On 17th March, 2007 he purchases the following :

(i) Bonds of National Highway Authority of India Rs. 1,24,000

(ii) Commercial flat Rs. 5,00,000

Find out the amount of capital gain chargeable to tax for the assessment year 2007-08.

Ans: 2,12,000.

Problem 7.28-P3 [Hons 2006]

Mr. D sells agricultural land situated in Haryana for Rs. 30,00,000 on 15-6-2006, which was purchased by him in August 1986 for Rs. 5,10,000. On 5-4-2007, he purchased agricultural land in rural area for Rs. 4,00,000 and deposited Rs. 5,00,000 in Capital Gains Account in State Bank of India in order to get exemption u/s 54B. He purchased NABARD Bonds notified u/s 54EC for Rs. 50,000 on 15-10-2006.

He purchased another agricultural land on 30th April, 2008 for Rs. 4,50,000 by withdrawing from the Deposit Account in State Bank of India. The balance of amount left in Capital Gains Deposit A/c is withdrawn in October, 2008.

Compute the taxable part of Capital Gains for the assessment year 2007-08 and 2009-10.

Ans: 1,59,357; 50,000.

Problem 7.28-P4 (Difficult)

X sells his only residential house on 24-8-2006 for Rs. 31,30,000 and incurred an expenditure of Rs. 20,000 in connection with the transfer. Cost of acquisition of the house in the year

1975 was Rs. 2,10,000 and on 1-4-1981 the fair market value was Rs. 5,00,000. On 10-1-2006 he invests Rs. 5,00,000 in the NHAI. On 16-1-2007 he purchased a residential flat for Rs. 2,40,000 and deposit Rs. 1,50,000 in the Capital Gain deposit scheme. Calculate the exemption available.

Ans: 8,90,000 limited to 6,25,000.

Problem 7.28-P5 (Typical)

Compute the capital gain chargeable to tax for the AY 2007-08.

	Bonds of NHAI	*Shares in NABARD*
Date of sale	17-5-2003	1-4-2006
Sale consideration	3,00,000	4,00,000
Date of acquisition	5-6-1997	17-9-2003
Cost of acquisition	2,82,000	1,90,000

For claiming exemption u/s 54EC Taxcrazy purchases Bonds in RECL for Rs. 3,00,000 on 18-6-2003. On 17-5-2006 due to financial commitments he pledges the bonds of RECL in Syndicate Bank for borrowing Rs. 2,00,000.

Ans: 2,05,019.

TOPIC 7.29 *SECTION 54F.* SALE OF ANY LTCA (OTHER THAN RESIDENTIAL HOUSE PROPERTY) AND PURCHASE/CONSTRUCTION OF RESIDENTIAL HOUSE PROPERTY

(A) CONDITIONS FOR CLAIMING EXEMPTION

(a) *Who can claim exemption* : Only individual or HUF can claim exemption under section 54F.

(b) *Which asset should be transferred* : The asset which is transferred should be Long Term Capital Assets other than residential house property. *E.g.* Sells gold purchases residential house or sells commercial house and or construct residential house property.

(c) *When new residential house property should be purchased or constructed.* It is same as that of section 54. (1 year <--zero date -->2 years purchase or 3 years construction) For detail refer topic 7.25c.

(d) *Deposit scheme u/s Section 54(2)* is applicable. For detail refer topic 7.25d.

(B) COMPUTATION OF AMOUNT OF EXEMPTION

Proportionate exemption is available which is calculated as given below :

$$\frac{\text{LTCG}}{\text{Net Sale Consideration}} \times \text{Amount invested in a new RHP or amount deposited}$$

(Net Sale Consideration = Sale Consideration - Expenses on Transfer)

(C) CONSEQUENCES OF NON-UTILISATION OF DEPOSITED AMOUNT WITHIN THE TIME LIMIT OF THE ZERO DATE [CONSEQUENCES 1]

Amount of proportionate capital gain exempted earlier	--
Less : Proportionate amount utilised within zero date	--
LTCG (chargeable to tax in the PY when period of 3 years expires from the zero date)	--

Note

- In other words it can be said that proportionate unutilised amount is treated as LTCG.
- The remaining unutilised amount can be withdrawn at any time after the expiry of 3 years from the zero date.

(D) CONSEQUENCES IF NEW RHP IS TRANSFERRED WITHIN 3 YEARS FROM THE DATE OF ACQUISITION OF NEW RHP [CONSEQUENCES 2]

1. Amount of proportionate capital gain exempted earlier shall be treated as LTCG in the year of transfer; and
2. Amount of capital gain arising on transfer of new residential house property is treated as STCG in the year of transfer.

Illustration 7.29-P1 (Difficult)

sells gold to

Mr. Taxcrazy---> Mr. Somu

COA as on 1-1-1996 Rs. 50,000 SC as on 15-2-2007 Rs. 7,66,000

For claiming exemption u/s 54F Mr. Taxcrazy deposits Rs. 5,00,000 on 1-7-2007 under Capital Gain Account Scheme, 1988 to purchase a new residential house property. Expenses on transfer was Rs. 2,000. Compute capital gain for AY 2007-08 on the assumption that due date of filing of return is 31-7-2007.

Solution

Computation of Capital Gain for AY 2007-08

Sale Consideration	7,66,000
Less : Expenses on transfer	2,000
Net sale consideration *(NSC)*	7,64,000
Less : Indexed COA (519 ÷ 281 × 50,000)	92,349
LTCG	6,71,651
Percentage (LTCG ÷ NSC)	87.912%
Less : Proportionate exemption u/s 54F of the deposited amount (87.912% of 5,00,000)	4,39,562
LTCG	2,32,089

Illustration 7.29-P2

In the above illustration Mr. Taxcrazy purchases a new residential house property on 14-07-2008 for Rs. 2,00,000 out of the deposited amount. Compute capital gain chargeable to tax.

Solution

Computation of Capital Gain for the AY 2010-11

Amount of proportionate capital gain exempted earlier	4,39,562
Less : Proportionate amount utilised within 2 years from the zero date (87.912% of 2,00,000)	1,75,825
LTCG	2,63,737

Note

- The remaining amount of Rs. 3,00,000 can be withdrawn after 14-2-2010.

Illustration 7.29-P3

In the above illustration Mr. Taxcrazy sells new residential house property on 13-06-2011 for Rs. 7,00,000.

Solution

Computation of Capital Gain for the AY 2012-13

1. Since new residential house property is sold within 3 years of its purchase therefore amount of capital gain exempted earlier i.e. Rs. 1,75,825 shall be treated as LTCG.
2. STCG = Sale Consideration – COA = 7,00,000 – 2,00,000 = 5,00,000

Problem 7.29-P4 (Simple)

Shri Arvind sold some shares on 1-9-2006 for Rs. 6,00,000. He had purchased these shares on 15th May, 1986 for Rs. 1,54,000. He purchased a residential house on 1st December, 2006 for Rs. 1,50,000. He did not own any other residential house. Assume that the shares have been sold outside a recognised stock exchange. Compute his taxable capital gain for the assessment year 2007-08.

Ans: 21,825.

Problem 7.29-P5 [CA M01]

X sold Govt. securities for Rs. 5,00,000 on October 1, 2006, which had been acquired by him in October 1987 for Rs. 50,000. He wants to utilize the said amount of sale consideration for purchase or construction of a new residential house. He already owns one residential house at the time of sale of the securities i.e., on October 1, 2006. He has deposited Rs. 4,00,000 under the Capital Gains Deposit Account Scheme with a specified bank on April 30, 2007. Ascertain the capital gain taxable in X's hands for assessment year 2007-08 and advice him as to what further action he has to take to avail of the exemption.

Ans: 65,400; He should purchase or construct new RHP out of deposited amount within specified time limit otherwise exemption of Rs. 26,160 allowed earlier shall be taxable in AY 2010-11.

Problem 7.29-P6 (Difficult)

sells rural industrial land to

Mr. Vaskar---> Mr. Tapas

COA as on 11-11-1991 Rs. 1,25,000 SC as on 15-7-2006 Rs. 9,20,000

For claiming exemption u/s 54F Mr. Vaskar deposits in scheduled bank on 15-6-2007 Rs. 8,00,000 for purchase of residential house property. Expenses on transfer was Rs. 15,000 Compute capital gain for the AY 2007-08, due date of furnishing of return being 31-7-2007.

Ans: 67,176

Problem 7.29-P7 (Typical)

X owns a residential house which is self-occupied and also a house plot. He sells the house on January 31, 2007 and the house plot on February 15, 2007 for Rs. 8,00,000 and

Rs. 5,00,000, respectively. The house was purchased on January 15, 1998 for Rs. 4,00,000 and the plot on March 31, 1998 for Rs. 2,00,000. X has purchased a new residential house on April 25, 2006 for Rs. 5,00,000. Compute the income chargeable under the head "capital gains" for the AY 2007-08.

Ans: 64,425

Problem 7.29-P8 [CS J03] [Typical]

On April 25, 2006, X sold an urban agricultural land for Rs. 37,50,000 which he had been using for agricultural purposes for several years. He acquired that land in 1979 for Rs. 2,50,000. The market value of such land as on April 1, 1981 was Rs. 5,00,000. He purchased rural agricultural land for Rs. 8,00,000 on June 23, 2006 which was sold for Rs. 12,50,000 on January 18, 2006. A sum of Rs. 12,50,000 was also invested by him in purchase of residential property on July 25, 2006. He did not own any house property before this date. The new house property was sold on March 28, 2007 for Rs. 15,00,000. Compute the capital gains taxable for the assessment year 2007-08.

Ans: LTCG 3,55,000; STCG 2,50,000.

Problem 7.29-P9 [Hons 1991]

Mr. X owns several assets but does not own any residential house. He sells the following assets and requests you to compute his capital gains income for the AY 2007-08.

1. Shares (non-listed) purchased in April 1998 for Rs. 1,20,000 sold on 15-12-2006 for Rs. 98,000.
2. On 01-04-1981, he had agreed to sell the jewellery to Mr. Y for Rs. 2,15,000 which was purchased in 1976 for Rs. 1,50,000. However, the sale could not be effected as Mr. Y backed out. He now sold the jewellery on 15-08-2006 for Rs. 15,20,000 and incurred Rs. 20,000 incidental selling expenses on account of brokerage and commission.
3. Debentures (non-listed) purchased in September 2005 for Rs. 50,000 sold on 31-12-2006 for Rs. 80,000.
4. In December 2006, he also purchased a small residential house for Rs. 1,50,000.
5. On 20-01-2007, he invested Rs. 2,00,000 in the bonds issued by National Highway Authority of India which are redeemable after 3 years.

Ans: 1,88,813.

Problem 7.29-P10 [Hons 1994]

X was the owner of the following assets:

	Year of Purchase	Cost (Rs.)	Fair market value as on 1-4-81
Gold	1976-77	5,70,000	6,91,000
Shares in 'A' (Pvt.) Ltd.	1972-73	2,73,000	1,82,000
Shares in Reliance Industries Ltd. (Listed)	1990-91	25,00,000	10,00,000

X died on 16-8-2003 and as per his will these assets get transferred to his son B. B now sells these assets on 10-6-2006 for a total consideration of Rs. 21,00,000 (gold Rs. 19,00,000 and shares of A Ltd. Rs. 2,00,000) and shares of Reliance industries Ltd. for Rs. 80,00,000.

For claiming exemption under capital gain he invests in following assets :

Date of Investment		Amount
• Bonds of National Highway Authority of India	1-1-2007	5,00,000
• Purchases a residential house property	1-3-2006	7,00,000
• Central Govt. securities	12-8-2007	4,00,000

Find out the amount of capital gains chargeable to tax for the AY 2007-08.

Ans: LTCG 6,04,774.

Problem 7.29-P11

Mr. Sachin sold the following long term capital assets on 15th February, 2007 :

	Gold (Rs.)	Unlisted Shares (Rs.)	Land (Rs.)
Sale consideration	5,40,000	2,70,000	8,60,000
Indexed Cost of Acquisition	2,03,000	1,62,400	4,06,000
Transfer expenses	40,000	20,000	60,000

Mr. Sachin owned one residential house property on 15th February, 2007, being the date of transfer of aforesaid assets. He has invested in the following assets after 31st March, 2007 but upto 31st July, 2007 being the last date of furnishing the return of income for the assessment year 2007-08 :

1. Bonds of National Highways Authority of India redeemable after 5 years Rs. 3,40,000.
2. Bonds of Rural Electrification Corporation Ltd redeemable after 6 years Rs. 2,20,000.
3. Residential house property Rs. 1,40,000.

Calculate the income taxable under the head "Capital gains" after giving maximum permissible exemption under different sections of the Income Tax Act.

Ans: 1,35,440.

Problem 7.29-P12 [CA N04]

Mr. 'X' furnishes the following data for the previous year ending 31-3-2007 :

(a) Preference shares of AB Ltd., 10,000 in number were sold on 31-5-2006, at Rs. 350, for cash share.

(b) The above shares of 10,000, were acquired by 'X' in the following manner:
   (i) Recieved as gift from his father on June 1, 1980, the market price on April 1, 1981 Rs. 50 per share. (5,000 shares)
   (ii) Bonus shares received from AB Ltd. on 21-7-1985 (2,000 shares).
   (iii) Purchased on 1-2-1994 at the price of Rs. 125 per share (3,000 shares).

(c) Purchased one residential house at Rs. 25,00,000, on 1-9-2007 from the sale proceeds of shares.

(d) 'X' is already owning a residential house, even before the purchase of above house.

You are required to compute the taxable capital gain. He has no other source of income chargeable to tax.

Ans: 2,40,340.

Problem 7.29-P13

Mr. Satish sold equity shares of Indian Companies on 1-9-2006 for Rs. 7,60,000. The cost of transfer was Rs. 10,000. Mr. Satish had purchased these shares during 1985-86 for Rs. 1,74,000. Mr. Satish purchased residential house on 1-12-2006 for Rs. 3,75,000.

Assuming that Mr. Satish owns a residential house (other than new asset) on 1-9-2006, calculate his taxable income from Capital Gains for the Assessment Year 2007-08, if :

(a) The shares are sold outside a recognised stock exchange,

(b) The shares are sold through a recognised stock exchange.

Ans: 35,504; nil.

Problem 7.29-P14

On 1-8-1976 Mr. Man Mohan purchased 400 shares of XYZ Co. Ltd. @ Rs. 95 per shares. On 31-12-1980 the XYZ Co. Ltd issued bonus shares. Mr. Man Mohan was allotted 600 bonus shares. The fair market Value of the shares on 1-4-1981 was Rs. 90 per shares. On 3-9-2006. Mr. Man Mohan sold all the 1,000 shares @ Rs. 800 per sharesand paid brokerage etc. @ 2% on sale consideration. Out of the sale consideration he invested Rs. 3,00,000 in the construction of a residential house which was completed before 30-6-2007.

Compute the taxable amount of capital gain of Mr. Man mohan for the assessment year 2007-08 assuming that he does not own any other residential house. The shares are sold outside a recognised stock exchange.

Ans: 1,61,062.

(E) * WHEN EXEMPTION U/S 54F IS NOT AVAILABLE

If on the date of transfer of the original asset the assessee owns 2 or more than 2 residential house properties, the exemption u/s 54F is not available. It means to claim exemption u/s 54F the assessee should not own more than one residential house property on the date of transfer of original asset.

Problem 7.29-P15 (Typical)

(A) Mr. Taxcrazy who owns a house at Tata and Meerut furnishes the following information for your perusal :

	Gold	*Precious stones*
Date of sale	7-6-2006	11-2-2007
Sale consideration	3,00,000	6,00,000
Date of acquisition	1995-96	7-4-1997
Cost of acquisition	80,000	60,000

On 2-7-2007 Mr. Taxcrazy constructs a residential house at Chandigarh for Rs. 7,60,000. Compute the capital gain chargeable to tax for the AY 2007-08.

(B) Solve if house at Tata is sold on 6-6-2006.

Ans: 6,58,163; 71,046.

Problem 7.29-P16 [CS J02]

X sells diamonds on June 30, 2006 for Rs. 2,53,000. He incurs Rs. 3,000 as expenses on the transfer of such diamonds. The diamonds were purchased by him on June 10, 1990 for

Rs. 80,000. Can he claim exemption under section 54F by purchasing a residential house for Rs. 1,00,000-

(i) assuming X does not own any residential house on the date of selling diamonds ?

(ii) assuming X owns two residential house on the date of selling diamonds ?

Ans: Yes; Rs. 13,121; No.

(F) * CONSEQUENCES IF ANY OTHER HOUSE *(OTHER THAN THE NEW RESIDENTIAL HOUSE)* IS PURCHASED / CONSTRUCTED WITHIN 2 / 3 YEARS FROM THE ZERO DATE

In such case the amount of proportionate capital gain exempted earlier shall be treated as LTCG which shall be chargeable to tax in the year of purchase / construction of new house. It means if more than one residential house property is purchased or constructed within the zero date exemption is not available in case of first house. If exemption is claimed in respect of the first house it shall be withdrawn and shall be taxed in the year of purchase of second residential house.

Problem 7.29.P17 (Typical)

Mr. Taxcrazy furnishes the following information:

	Gold	*RHP at Kaveri*
Date of sale	15-4-2003	31-3-2009
Sale consideration	8,00,000	3,24,406
Date of acquisition (or construction of RHP)	1-1-2000	17-4-2006
Cost of acquisition	5,23,000	1,90,000

For claiming exemption u/s 54F Taxcrazy purchases a residential house at Godavari for Rs. 1,20,000 on 18-6-2004 and for claiming exemption u/s 54EC he purchases bonds of RECL for Rs. 20,000 on 17-8-2003. Compute the capital gain chargeable to tax for the AY 2004-05 and AY 2007-08.

Ans: 1,30,883; 22,626.

Problem 7.29-P18 [Typical]

On entering into partnership with Aditi and Anindita with effect from 1-5-2006, Amrita brought the following assets as her capital contribution.

Assets contributed	Land	Jewellery	Shares
Amount credited to capital account	26 lakhs	10 lakhs	24 lakhs
Fair market value on date of transfer	29.80 lakhs	11.20 lakhs	23.52 lakhs
Date of acquisition	1952	30-4-2001	12-12-2005
Cost of acquisition	46,000	8.45 lakhs	26.70 lakhs
Fair market value as on 1-1-1981	4 lakhs		

As on 1-5-2006 Amrita owns a residential house. During 2006-07 she paid advance of Rs. 5 lakhs towards booking of another residential flat, construction of which is likely to be completed by 30-9-2008. Although the cost of flat booked is estimated at Rs. 18 lakhs,

Amrita deposited a further amount of Rs. 15 lakhs in capital Gains Accounts Scheme, 1988 on 13-5-2006. If for financial year 2006-07 Amrita has total income of Rs. 4,80,600 under other heads except capital gains what would be her tax liability for Assessment Year 2007-08 ?

What precautions should be taken by her so as to ensure that any tax advantage gained in regard to Assessment Year 2007-08 is not lost subsequently ?

Ans: 6,11,090; 1,22,684. (1) The construction of house should be completed by 30-6-2009 otherwise exemption of Rs. 5,46,040 shall be withdrawn. (2) No other house (other than new house which is being constructed) should be purchased or constructed by 30-6-2009 otherwise exemption of Rs. 5,46,040 shall be withdrawn.

(G) * SECTION 54H

Section 54H. Zero date in case where property is compulsorily acquired : Zero date shall be the date when part or full initial compensation is received. In case of enhanced compensation the date of receipt of enhanced compensation shall be the zero date.

Problems 7.29-P19

1. A person is chargeable to tax under the head "Capital gain" only if he has transferred a capital asset during the previous year. Is there any provision under the Income-tax Act, 1961 as to when a person is chargeable to tax under the head "Capital gain" if he purchases a capital asset? Give an example of such provision, if any?
2. Is there any provision under the Income-tax Act, 1961 as to when a person neither transfer a capital asset nor purchases a capital asset but still there arises a gain which is chargeable to tax under the head "Capital gain"?
3. How do you differentiate between section 54 and section 54F?

Solution

1. Section 54F (Refer Topic 7.29F)
2. Yes, Section 54EC When the assessee pledges the asset. (Refer Topic 7.28-4.)

3. *Section 54*. Sale of RHP and purchase/ construction of RHP.	*Section 54F*. Sale of LTCA *(other than RHP)* and purchase/construction of RHP.
On the date of sale *i.e.* on the zero date you may have more than 2 RHP, then also you get exemption.	On the date of sale *i.e.* on the zero date you should not own 2 or more than 2 RHP.
To claim exemption an assessee may purchase/construct as many RHP.	To claim exemption an assessee is allowed to purchase/construct only 1 RHP, otherwise exemption is withdrawn.
When a new RHP is sold within 3 years from the zero date only STCG arises.	When a new RHP is sold within 3 years from the zero date both LTCG and STCG arises.

Section 54 is the stepping stone for understanding exemptions. Keep on revising and memorising it until and unless you are able to capture the full picture. After this, remaining exemption shall automatically fall in line. All the best.

Keep Running

OTHER EXEMPTIONS AVAILABLE TO ALL ASSESSEES

TOPIC 7.30 *SECTION 54D. CAPITAL GAIN ON COMPULSORY ACQUISITION OF LAND & BUILDING FORMING PART OF INDUSTRIAL UNDERTAKING)

(A) CONDITIONS FOR CLAIMING EXEMPTION

(a) *Applicability* : All assessees whether individual, HUF, Company or any other person can claim exemption u/s 54D.

(b) *Type of assets* : The asset which is transferred should be a land or building forming part of an industrial undertaking. Such asset can be either LTCA / STCA / Depreciable asset. The industrial undertaking was used by the assessee for industrial purpose for a period of atleast 2 years immediately preceding the date of its transfer.

(c) *When is exemption available* : Exemption is available if a new land or building is acquired or constructed within 3 year from the zero date. Date of receipt of compensation, is treated as 'ZERO DATE'. i.e. Zero date -->3 years.
Newly acquired land or building is used for the purpose of shifting or re-establishing the said undertaking or setting up another industrial undertaking.

(d) Deposit scheme u/s Section 54(2) is applicable. Refer section 54 for detail. Topic 7.25d.

(B) COMPUTATION OF AMOUNT OF EXEMPTION (ASSUMED FIGURES)

Amount invested in such new asset within zero date +	6,000
Amount deposited in Scheduled Bank on or before the due date of furnishing of return	7,000
Total exempted amount *(limited to LTCG / STCG)*	13,000

(C) CONSEQUENCES OF NON-UTILISATION OF DEPOSITED AMOUNT WITHIN THE TIME LIMIT OF THE ZERO DATE [CONSEQUENCES 1]

Amount of capital gain exempted earlier out of deposited amount	7,000
Less: Amount invested in new assets within 3 years from the zero date	2,000
LTCG / STCG[1] *(Chargeable to tax in the PY when period of 3 years expires from the zero date)*	5,000

Note

- [1] Depends upon original capital asset transferred.
- The remaining unutilised amount can be withdrawn at any time after the expiry of 3 years from the zero date.

(D) CONSEQUENCES IF SUCH ASSET IS TRANSFERRED WITHIN *3 YEARS* AFTER THE DATE OF ACQUISITION OF NEW ASSET [CONSEQUENCES 2]

• The amount of capital gain exempted earlier +	2,000
• The amount of capital gain arising on transfer of such new asset	8,500
STCG *(chargeable to tax in the year of transfer)*	6,500

Problem 7.30.P1 (Typical)

X Ltd., located within the corporation limits, decided in December, 2005 to shift its industrial undertaking to non - urban area. The company sold some of the assets and acquired new assets in the process of shifting. The relevant details are as follows :

Particulars	*Land*	*Building*	*P & M*	*Furniture*
Sale proceeds (sale effected in March 2007)	8	18	16	3
Indexed cost of acquisition	4	10	12	2
Cost of acquisition in terms of section 50	–	4	5	2
Cost of new assets purchased in July, 2006 for the purpose of business in the new place	4	7	17	2

Compute the capital gains of X Ltd. for the assessment year 2007-08.

Ans: STCG 2,00,000.

TOPIC 7.31 *SECTION 54G CAPITAL GAIN ARISING ON TRANSFER OF ASSETS IN CASE OF SHIFTING OF INDUSTRIAL UNDERTAKING FROM NOTIFIED URBAN AREA TO AREA OTHER THAN URBAN AREA)

(A) CONDITIONS FOR CLAIMING EXEMPTION

(a) *Who can claim exemption* : All assessees whether individual, HUF, Company or any other person can claim exemption u/s 54G.

(b) *Which asset should be transferred* : The asset which is transferred should be a Plant, machinery, Land or Building or any right in land or building used for the purpose of industrial undertaking situated in urban area. Such asset can be either LTCA/ STCA/ Depreciable asset.

Urban area means any such area within the limits of a municipal corporation or municipality as the Central Government may, having regard to the population, concentration of industries, need for proper planning of the area and other relevant factors, by general or special order, declare to be an urban area for the purposes of this section.

(c) *When such new assets should be purchased* or constructd :

Such new assets should be purchased or constructed within time allowed i.e. 1 year before or 3 year after the "Zero Date". Zero Date is the date of sale of original assets.

E.g. Suppose zero date is 7-8-2006. New assets should be purchased by 8-8-2005 and by 7-8-2009 *(1 year <--------Zero date --->3years).*

Other Points

(i) purchased machinery or plant for the purpose of business of the industrial undertaking in the area to which the said undertaking is shifted.

(ii) acquired building or land or constructed building for the purposes of his business in the said area.

(iii) shifted the original asset and transferred the establishment to said area.

(iv) incurred expenses on such other purpose as may be specified in a scheme framed by the Central Govt. for the purpose of this section.

(d) Deposit scheme u/s Section 54(2) is applicable. Refer section 54 for detail. Topic 7.25d.

(B) COMPUTATION OF AMOUNT OF EXEMPTION (ASSUMED FIGURES)

Amount invested in such new asset within zero date +	6,000
Amount deposited in Scheduled Bank on or before the due date of furnishing of return	7,000
Total exempted amount *(limited to LTCG / STCG)*	13,000

(C) CONSEQUENCES OF NON-UTILISATION OF DEPOSITED AMOUNT WITHIN THE TIME LIMIT OF THE ZERO DATE [CONSEQUENCES 1]

Amount of capital gain exempted earlier out of deposited amount	7,000
Less: Amount invested in new assets within 3 years from the zero date	2,000
LTCG / STCG[1] *(Chargeable to tax in the PY when period of 3 years expires from the zero date)*	5,000

Note

- [1] Depends upon original capital asset transferred.
- The remaining unutilised amount can be withdrawn at any time after the expiry of 3 years from the zero date.

(D) CONSEQUENCES IF SUCH ASSET IS TRANSFERRED WITHIN *3 YEARS* AFTER THE DATE OF ACQUISITION OF NEW ASSET [CONSEQUENCES 2]

• The amount of capital gain exempted earlier +	2,000
• The amount of capital gain arising on transfer of such new asset	8,500
STCG *(chargeable to tax in the year of transfer)*	6,500

TOPIC 7.32 ***SECTION 54GA.* CAPITAL GAIN ARISING ON TRANSFER OF ASSETS IN CASE OF SHIFTING OF INDUSTRIAL UNDERTAKING FROM URBAN AREA TO SPECIAL ECONOMIC ZONE

(A) CONDITIONS FOR CLAIMING EXEMPTION

(a) *Who can claim exemption* : All assessees whether individual, HUF, Company etc. can claim exemption u/s 54GA.

(b) *Which asset should be transferred* : The asset which is transferred should be a Plant, machinery, Land or Building or any right in land or building used for the purpose of industrial undertaking situated in urban area. Such asset can be either LTCA / STCA / Depreciable asset.

(c) *When such new assets should be purchased* or constructd :

Such new assets should be purchased or constructed within time allowed i.e. 1 year before or 3 year after the "Zero Date". Zero Date is the date of sale of original assets.

E.g. Suppose zero date is 7-8-2006. New assets should be purchased by 8-8-2005 and by 7-8-2009 *(1 year <--------Zero date --->3years).*

Other Points

(i) purchased machinery or plant for the purpose of business of the industrial undertaking in the SEZ to which the said undertaking is shifted.

(ii) acquired building or land or constructed building for the purposes of his business in the SEZ.

(iii) shifted the original asset and transferred the establishment to SEZ.

(iv) incurred expenses on such other purpose as may be specified in a scheme framed by the Central Govt. for the purpose of this section.

(d) Deposit scheme u/s Section 54(2) is applicable. Refer section 54 for detail. Topic 7.25d.

(B) COMPUTATION OF AMOUNT OF EXEMPTION (ASSUMED FIGURES)

Amount invested in such new asset within zero date +	6,000
Amount deposited in Scheduled Bank on or before the due date of furnishing of return	7,000
Total exempted amount *(limited to LTCG / STCG)*	13,000

(C) CONSEQUENCES OF NON-UTILISATION OF DEPOSITED AMOUNT WITHIN THE TIME LIMIT OF THE ZERO DATE [CONSEQUENCES 1]

Amount of capital gain exempted earlier out of deposited amount	7,000
Less: Amount invested in new assets within 3 years from the zero date	2,000
LTCG / STCG[1] *(Chargeable to tax in the PY when period of 3 years expires from the zero date)*	5,000

Note

- [1]Depends upon original capital asset transferred.
- The remaining unutilised amount can be withdrawn at any time after the expiry of 3 years from the zero date.

(D) CONSEQUENCES IF SUCH ASSET IS TRANSFERRED WITHIN *3 YEARS* AFTER THE DATE OF ACQUISITION OF NEW ASSET [CONSEQUENCES 2]

• The amount of capital gain exempted earlier +	2,000
• The amount of capital gain arising on transfer of such new asset	8,500
STCG *(chargeable to tax in the year of transfer)*	6,500

RATE OF TAX ON CAPITAL GAIN

TOPIC 7.33 APPLICABILITY OF SECURITIES TRANSACTION TAX (STT)

Securities transaction tax (STT) is applicable if the following conditions are satisfied :

1. The asset which is transferred is

   (a) an equity share in a company; or

   (b) unit of an equity oriented fund. "Equity oriented fund" means a fund

Where the investible funds are invested by way of equity shares in domestic companies to the extent of more than 65% of the total proceeds of such fund; and which has been set up under a scheme of a Mutual Fund specified under section 10(23D).

Provided that the percentage of equity shareholding of the fund shall be computed with reference to the annual average of the monthly averages of the opening and closing figures.

2. The sale of said securities *i.e.* equity shares in a company or units of an equity oriented mutual fund is entered into in a recognised stock exchange; or

   Sale of unit of an equity oriented fund to the Mutual Fund itself.

3. The transaction of sale is entered into on or after 1-10-2004.
4. Such transaction is chargeable to securities transaction tax.

Note

- Do note that said securities can be acquired in any mode whether by way of conversion, allotment, amalgamation, inheritance etc. or at any date. What is relevant is that the transaction is entered in stock exchange and date of transfer should be on or after 1-10-2004.
- The rate of tax is applicable to all types of assessees including Non-residents and FII's.

1. STT is not applicable on sale of preference shares, debt oriented mutual fund, all unlisted securities, all non financial assets, land, building, gold etc.
2. STT is not applicable in case of buy back of shares, open offer for sale, sale of right share entitlement, delisted shares or negotiated deals etc., since all such transaction falls outside stock exchange.
3. The said securities are transferred before 1-10-2004.

TOPIC 7.34 *SECTION 111A.* TAX ON SHORT TERM CAPITAL GAIN

1. Short term capital gain shall be taxed @ 10% if securities transaction tax is applicable.
2. STCG shall be taxed at normal rates, if STT is not applicable

TOPIC 7.35 *SECTION 112.* TAX ON LONG TERM CAPITAL GAIN

(A) FOLLOWING LTCG IS FULLY EXEMPT FROM TAX, HENCE NO TAX

Where securities transaction tax is applicable, such long term capital gain is fully exempt from tax under section 10(38).

(B) TAX ON LONG TERM CAPITAL GAIN ARISING ON TRANSFER OF LISTED FINANCIAL ASSET, NOT COVERED UNDER SECTION 10

Meaning of 'Listed financial assets'

1. Listed shares, bonds or debentures.
2. Units of UTI or mutual fund.
3. Government securities.
4. Rights or interest in such securities.

Tax on LTCG is 10% without indexation or 20% with indexation whichever is lower. Surcharge and education cess as applicable.

(C) TAX ON LONG TERM CAPITAL GAIN ARISING ON TRANSFER OF OTHER ASSETS, NOT COVERED ABOVE

Tax on long term capital gain arising on transfer of other assets not covered above is chargeable @ 20% flat.

Problem 7.35-P1

1. Rate of tax on LTCG arising on sale of listed bonds or debentures is always 10%. (True or False)
2. Tax on LTCG arising on sale of listed bonus shares is always 10%. (T or F)
3. Tax on LTCG arising on sale of self-generated trademark is always 10%. (T or F)
4. In stock market either the income from transfer of shares is tax free or is taxable @ 10%. Do you agree.
5. What about transactions entered into other than stock market?

Solution

1. True, since indexation of bonds or debentures are not allowed.
2. True, since COA of bonus shares is nil if allotted on or after 1-4-1981.
3. False tax shall be levied @ 20%, since trademark is not a financial asset.
4. Yes. LTCG arising on sale of equity shares or units of equity oriented fund through stock market is fully exempt from tax. However STCG arising on transfer of equity shares or units of equity oriented fund through stock market is subject @ 10%. However Gain arising on transfer of debentures or bonds or units of debt oriented fund is subjected to either 10% or 20% or normal rates as the case may be.
5. LTCG is subject to either 10% or 20% as a case may be and STCG at normal rates.

Problem 7.35-P2

Compute tax on following categories of incomes for the AY 2007-08 on the assumption that the assessee is an individual :

1. LTCG arising on sale of residential house property	60,000
2. LTCG arising on sale of unlisted bonds	80,000
3. LTCG arising on sale of listed bonus shares (STT paid)	1,00,000
4. LTCG arising on sale of unlisted bonus shares	12,50,000
5. STCG arising on sale of listed bonus shares (STT paid)	70,000
6. STCG arising on sale of unlisted bonus shares	11,00,000
7. LTCG arising on sale goodwill of a business	1,10,000

Ans: (1) 12,240; (2) 16,320; (3) nil; (4) 2,80,500; (5) 7,140; (6) 3,14,160; (7) 22,440.

Illustration 7.35-P3

Compute tax on LTCG for the AY 2007-08 from the following information :

sells Govt. Securities to

X---> Y

COA in the PY 2004-05 Rs. 22,000 SC in the PY 2006-07 Rs. 4,00,000

Solution

Computation of Capital Gain for the AY 2007-08

	Option 1 (without indexation)	*Option 2 (With Indexation)*
Sale consideration	4,00,000	4,00,000
Less :		
• Cost of acquisition	22,000	
• Indexed cost of acquisition (519 ÷ 480 × 22,000)		23,788
LTCG	3,78,000	3,76,213
Tax on LTCG	37,800	75,243

Since Tax on LTCG is lower in case of option 1, therefore, Rs. 37,800 + education cess @ 2% = Rs. 38,556 is the answer.

Problem 7.35-P4

Compute Tax on LTCG for the AY 2007-08 assuming his STCG is Rs. 2,00,000.

sells Govt. securities

X--> Y

COA in the PY 91-92 Rs. 1,18,000 SC in the PY 2006-07 Rs. 3,45,000

Ans: 7,599.

Illustration 7.35-P5

Compute total income and tax liability for the assessment year 2007-08 if the assessee is (i) firm or domestic company; (ii) foreign company and (iii) individual or HUF.

Income from House Property	2,20,000
Short Term Capital Gain	
- on sale of unlisted equity shares on 30-9-2006	60,000
- on sale of listed equity shares on 30-11-2006	20,000
- on sale of land	1,50,000
Long Term Capital Gain	
- on sale of listed equity shares on 30-11-2006 at NSE	1,10,000
- on sale of listed bonds on 30-7-2006	80,000
- on sale of gold	4,00,000
Income from units of UTI	1,000
Dividend from Indian Company	65,000
Deduction u/s 80G	20,000

Solution

Computation of total income for AY 2007-08

Income from House Property	2,00,000
Short Term Capital Gain	
- on sale of unlisted equity shares on 30-9-2006	60,000
- on sale of listed equity shares on 30-11-2006 (STT paid)	20,000

- on sale of land	1,50,000
Long Term Capital Gain	
- on sale of listed equity shares on 30-11-2006 (STT paid) [exempt u/s 10(38)]	nil
- on sale of listed bonds on 30-7-2006	80,000
- on sale of gold	4,00,000
Income from units of UTI [exempt u/s 10(35)]	nil
Dividend from Indian Company [exempt u/s 10(34)]	nil
Gross Total Income	9,30,000
Less : Deduction u/s 80G	20,000
Total Income	9,10,000

Computation of tax liability for AY 2007-08

	Firm or D. Co.	*Foreign. Co.*	*Ind/HUF*
Incomes subject to special rates			
Short Term Capital Gain on sale of listed equity shares on 30-11-2006 (STT paid) on Rs. 20,000 @ 10%	2,000	2,000	2,000
Long Term Capital Gain on sale of listed bonds on 30-7-2006 on Rs. 80,000 @ 10%	8,000	8,000	8,000
Long Term Capital Gain on sale of gold on Rs. 4,00,000 @ 20%	80,000	80,000	80,000
Incomes subject to Normal rates			
Normal income on Rs. 4,10,000	1,23,000	1,64,000	73,000
Tax liability	2,13,000	2,54,000	1,63,000
Add : Surcharge	21,300	6,350	–
Tax payable	2,34,300	2,60,350	1,63,000
Add : Education cess @ 2%	4,686	5,207	3,260
Tax Payable	2,38,986	2,65,557	1,66,260

Problem 7.35-P6 [CS J05]

Abhay purchased 1,000 listed equity shares of Rs. 10 each at Rs. 100 per share from a broker on 4th May, 1996. He paid Rs. 3,000 as brokerage. On 15th March, 2006, he was given bonus shares by the company on the basis of one share for every two shares held. On the same date, he was also given a right to acquire 1,000 rights shares @ Rs. 90 per share. He acquired 50% of the rights shares offered and sold the balance 50% of the rights shares for the sum of Rs. 67,500 on 7th April, 2006. The rights shares were allotted to him on 30th April, 2006.

All the shares held by him were sold on 24th September, 2006 @ Rs. 280 per share through a recognised stock exchange.

(i) Computed capital gain and tax for the assessment year 2007-08 assuming his income from other sources is Rs. 1,40,000.

Ans: (i) LTCG(STT PAID) 1,04,731 exempt from tax 10(38); STCG STT PAID 1,40,000+95,000=2,35,0000. STCG 67,500= Total Income = Rs. 4,42,500. Tax Rs. 40,800.

Problems 7.35-P7

Compute tax payable by Mr. Taxcrazy for the AY 2007-08.

	Case 1 *ROR*	*Case 2* *NR in India*	*Case 3* *RNOR*
Income from Salary	1,00,000	20,000	1,40,000
STCG on sale of right share entitlement	20,000	6,000	10,000
LTCG on sale of self generated Trade Mark	38,000	11,000	1,000
LTCG on sale of unlisted bonus shares	2,000	3,000	500
LTCG on sale of listed bonus shares (STT paid)	6,000	13,000	4,500
LTCG on sale of listed bonds	14,000	1,25,000	7,500
PPF contribution	5,000	6,000	8,000

Ans: (1) 11,118; (2) 15,606; (3) 5,355.

Problem 7.35-P8 [Hons 1996]

X Ltd. has transferred listed bonds (being LTCA) for Rs. 8,50,000 during the PY 2006-07. Cost of acquisition of bonds in the year 1999 Rs. 8,00,000. On the date of transfer, it does not own a residential house property. It purchases a residential house property for Rs. 17,00,000 on June 30, 2006. Compute the capital gain & tax liability chargeable to tax.

Ans: 50,000; 5,610.

TOPIC 7.36 BASIC EXEMPTION ALSO ALLOWED FROM SPECIAL INCOMES IF CERTAIN CONDITIONS ARE SATISFIED

1. *Basic exemption in case of*
   (a) Resident woman : Rs. 1,35,000
   (b) Resident senior citizen : Rs. 1,85,000
   (c) In case of other resident individual or HUF : Rs. 1,00,000
2. *Special incomes are* : Short term capital gain (STT paid) and Long term capital gain.
3. *Condition* :
   (a) The assessee is resident individual or HUF.
   (b) The rule is basic exemption is allowed from special income only when normal income is less than basic exemption. Do remember basic exemption is not available from casual income.
4. *Computation* : First allow basic exemption from normal income and then whatever left from special income. Again do remember basic exemption is not available from casual income.

Illustration 7.36-P1

Compute tax liability of individual for the AY 2007-08 from the following information if such individual is (a) resident woman (b) resident senior citizen (c) resident HUF (d) Non-resident individual.

	Case 1	*Case 2*
Income from House Property	10,000	(3,00,000)
LTCG on sale of residential house property	1,00,000	4,00,000
STCG on sale of units of equity oriented fund (STT paid)	2,00,000	15,00,000
STCG on sale of diamonds	20,000	5,000

Casual income	40,000	6,000
Gross Total income	3,70,000	16,11,000
Deduction u/s 80G	10,000	5,000
Total Income	3,60,000	16,06,000

Let us suppose basic exemption is Rs. 1,00,000

	LTCG	*STCG (STT paid)*	*Casual Income*	*Normal Income*	*Total*
Income	1,00,000	2,00,000	40,000	20,000	3,60,000
Less : Basic exemption	80,000	—	—	20,000	1,00,000
Income	20,000	2,00,000	40,000	Nil	2,50,000
Tax	4,000	20,000	12,000	Nil	36,000
Add : Education cess @ 2%					720
Tax on the above income					36,720

Solution : Case 1

	Resident HUF	*Resident woman*	*Resident senior citizen*	*Non-Resident Individual*
LTCG	1,00,000	1,00,000	1,00,000	1,00,000
7STCG (STT paid)	2,00,000	2,00,000	2,00,000	2,00,000
Casual Income	40,000	40,000	40,000	40,000
Normal Income	20,000	20,000	20,000	20,000

Computation of tax liablitiy

Tax on LTCG	4,000	nil	nil	20,000
Tax on STCG (STT paid)	20,000	18,500	13,500	20,000
Tax on casual income	12,000	12,000	12,000	12,000
Tax on normal income	nil	nil	nil	nil
Total tax	36,000	30,500	25,500	52,000
Add : Education cess @ 2%	720	610	510	1,040
Tax after education cess	36,720	31,110	26,010	53,040

Solution : Case 2

	Resident HUF	*Resident woman*	*Resident senior citizen*	*Non-Resident Individual*
LTCG	1,00,000	1,00,000	1,00,000	1,00,000
STCG (STT paid)	15,00,000	15,00,000	15,00,000	15,00,000
Casual Income	6,000	6,000	6,000	6,000
Normal Income	nil	nil	nil	nil

Computation of tax liablitiy

Tax on LTCG	nil	nil	nil	20,000
Tax on STCG (STT paid)	1,50,000	1,46,500	1,41,500	1,50,000
Tax on casual income	1,800	1,800	1,800	1,800
Tax on normal income	nil	nil	nil	nil
Total tax	1,51,800	1,48,300	1,43,500	1,71,800
Add : Surcharge @ 10%	15,180	14,830	14,350	17,180
Tax & surcharge	1,66,980	1,63,130	1,57,850	1,88,980
Add : Education cess @ 2%	3,340	3,263	3,153	3,780
Tax after education cess	1,70,320	1,66,393	1,60,783	1,92,760

Note : Loss from house property is set off from LTCG to compute mimimum tax. No loss is allowed to be set off from casual income.

Illustration 7.36-P2

Compute tax liability of resident individual for the AY 2007-08 from the following information if such individual is (a) resident woman (b) resident senior citizen (c) resident HUF (d) Non-resident individual.

	Case 1	*Case 2*	*Case 3*	*Case 4*
Income from House Property	60,000	(1,20,000)	4,00,000	10,000
LTCG on sale of land	1,54,000	nil	15,000	40,000
STCG on sale of equity shares (STT paid)	8,42,000	2,56,000	1,25,000	4,45,100
STCG on sale of listed bonds	20,000	50,000	10,000	41,420
Casual income	1,54,200	1,000	55,410	98,701
PPF contribution	80,000	50,000	1,00,000	5,000

Ans: (1) 1,58,494; 1,50,640; 1,42,898; 1,80,934 (2) 3,978; 408; 306; 14,178 (3) 76,625; 73,055; 64,385; 76,625 (4) 74,218; 70,647; 65,547; 83,762.

Problem 7.36-P3 (CA N02) - M 6

Q.1c : Mrs. Z, a resident, attains the age of 65 years on December 23, 2006. She had following income for the previous year ending March 31, 2007 :

Short term capital gain on sale of shares covered u/s 111A.	26,000
Long term capital gain on sale of land	1,76,000

Compute the tax liability of Mrs. Z for the assessment year 2007-08.

Ans: 1,734.

Problem 7.36-P4 [CS D96]

On transfer of gold, X has generated a long - term capital gain of Rs. 2,24,000 for the assessment year 2007-08. (His other income being Rs. 39,000). Can be reduce his tax bill by depositing Rs. 50,000 in public provident fund ?

Ans: Yes to the extent of Rs. 39,000 only. Tax 25,296.

Problem 7.36-P5 [Hons 2004]

Mr. X - a senior citizen sold a residential building at Ajmer for Rs. 20,00,000 on October 1, 2006. This building was acquired by his father on 1-1-79 for Rs. 1,00,000. On the death on his father on July 5, 1979, he inherited this building. Fair market value of this property on 1-4-1981 was Rs. 1,40,000. He paid brokerage @ 1% to the real estate agent at the time of sale of the building. He purchased a residential building at Bangalore on March 7, 2006 for Rs. 8,00,000 and deposited Rs. 3,00,000 on April 20, 2007 in NHAI capital gains bonds.

His other incomes are Rs. 50,000. He deposited Rs. 10,000 in P.P.F.

Compute taxable income and tax liability of Mr. X for the assessment year 2007-08.

Ans: 8,27,770; 1,29,697.

Problem 7.36-P6 [Hons 1997]

X, an owner of two houses, sells a residential house in Mumbai for Rs. 10,90,000 on May 1, 2006. This house was purchased by him on April 1, 1995 for Rs. 3,10,000. On 30-5-2006 he purchased a flat in Delhi for Rs. 4,28,000 for the purpose of residence of his son-in-law.

During the PY his only other income was from house property amounting to Rs. 30,000. He contributed Rs. 40,000 to equity linked saving scheme of UTI and deposited Rs. 10,000 in 15 year account under the P.O Savings Bank (CTD) Rules 1959.

Compute total income and tax liability for the AY 2007-08.

Ans: 89,440; nil.

Problem 7.36-P7 (Typical)

(A) Compute total income of Mrs. Taxcrazy from the following information for AY 2007-08.

	Agricultural land in TATA (LTCA)	*Agricultural land in Delhi (STCA)*	*Agricultural land in rural area (STCA)*
Date of sale	28-5-2006	1-3-2007	31-3-2007
Sale consideration	15,00,000	10,00,000	2,00,000
Indexed cost of acquisition	4,00,000	Not applicable	Not applicable
Cost of acquisition	45,000	2,00,000	50,000

All land was used by her for agricultural purpose for the last 5 years immediately preceding the date of transfer. For claiming exemption u/s 54B Mrs. Taxcrazy purchases new agricultural land in rural area on 31-7-2007 for Rs. 13,00,000. Compute the tax liability for the AY 2007-08 on the assumption she also invests Rs. 1,05,000 in ICICI infrastructure bonds out of the sale proceeds of agricultural land situated in rural area.

Ans: 74,460.

Problem 7.36-P8

1. Loss arising on sale of LTCA can be set off only against LTCG. (True or False)
2. Loss arising on sale of STCA can be set off against both the profits LTCG and STCG. (True or False)
3. Highlights the features of LTCG and STT paid.

Solution

1. True this is as per section 74 which we shall discussed it later.
2. True this is as per section 74 which we shall discussed it later.
3. Deduction u/s 80C to 80U is not available.

   Rate of tax is levied is either @ 20% or 10% as the case may be.

7.37 COMPREHENSIVE PROBLEMS

Simple and Difficult

Problem 7.37-P1 [Hons 1993]

During the previous year 2006-07, Mrs. R sells the following capital assets :

Land : It was acquired in 1978 for Rs. 18,50,000 and its fair market value as on 01-04-1981 is Rs. 22,00,000 and it was sold for Rs. 91,87,000.

Gold : It was acquired in 1980 for Rs. 2,40,000 and its fair market value was Rs. 2,00,000 and it was sold for Rs. 10,58,000.

Listed Debentures : It was acquired in 1976 for Rs. 75,000 and its fair market value as on 01-04-1981 was Rs. 40,000 and it was sold for Rs. 1,57,000.

Assuming that her business income is Rs. 1,46,000, determine her net income and tax liability for the assessment year 2007-08. She has completed the age of 65 years on 01-01-2007 and she is non-dent.

Ans: 1,46,000; 4,692.

Problem 7.37-P2

Compute the taxable income under the head 'Capital Gains' arising from the following transactions in respect of various assets during the PY ended on March 31, 2007 :

(i) Mr. T sold his agricultural land on 6-8-2006 for Rs. 11,50,000 and paid Rs. 12,000 for brokerage and other expenses. This land was purchased by him in 1990-91 for Rs. 2,80,000 and since then it was being used for agricultural purposes by his parents. He purchased an urban agricultural land for Rs. 1,80,000 on 18-11-2006 and has deposited Rs. 60,000 under the Capital Gains Account Scheme on 26-5-2007.

(ii) Mr. Om sold certain ornaments in July 2006 for Rs. 4,50,000 and paid Rs. 15,000 for brokerage. These ornaments were purchased by him for the use of his wife in 1970-71 for Rs. 24,000. The fair market value of these ornaments on 1-4-1981 was Rs. 65,000. He purchased a house for his own residence for Rs. 2,50,000 in September 2007. He did not own any house on the date of the sale of ornaments.

(iii) Mr. Uddesh sold a plot of land on 15-12-2006 for Rs. 21,00,000 and incurred an expenditure of Rs. 50,000 on its transfer. He got this plot in 1990-91 from his father in gift. His father acquired it in 1988-89 for Rs. 6,00,000.

   He made the following investments on 6-3-2007 from the proceeds of the above plot :

   (a) Bonds issued by the National Highway Authority of India redeemable after 3 years for Rs. 5,000.

   (b) Bonds issued by the Rural Electrical Corporation Limited redeemable after 3 years for Rs. 5,000.

Ans: 53,116; 74,660; 2,29,535

Problem 7.37-P3

Compute the taxable income under the head 'Capital Gains' for the AY 2007-08.

(i) Mr. Meedhansh Agrawal sold a residential house for Rs. 4,95,000 on May 18, 2006. He purchased this house during 1996-97 for Rs. 1,80,000. He purchased another residential house on December 2005 for Rs. 1,20,000 which he sold in January, 2007 for Rs. 1,80,000.

What difference would it make if Mr. Meedhansh does not sell the house purchased in December 2005.

(ii) Mr. Manas sold some ornaments on 10-9-2006 for Rs. 2,80,000 which he received as gift from his uncle on 15-12-1998. His uncle purchased these ornaments on 18-5-1992 for Rs. 1,50,000 and the fair market value of these ornament on the date of gift was Rs. 1,65,000. He purchased on 8-3-2007 a residential house for Rs. 1,40,000.

(iii) Mr. Manendra purchased a plot of agricultural land in September 2003 for Rs. 1,80,000. He was using this plot for agricultural purposes but in July 2006 he sold this plot for Rs. 2,50,000 and purchased a residential house for Rs. 2,80,000. In March 2007 he sold this residential house also for Rs. 3,50,000. The agricultural plot lies in the local limits of Nagpur Municipal Corporation.

(iv) Mr. Mukund sold a Honda car in December 2006 for Rs. 1,80,000. It was purchased by him in June 1997 for Rs. 1,40,000 and it was being used by him and his family members for their personal work.

Ans: (i) 1,62,544; 60,000; (ii) 29,103; (iii) 1,40,000; (iv) nil

Problem 7.37-P4

Compute the taxable income under the head 'Capital Gains' arising from the following transactions in respect of various assets during the PY ended on March 31, 2007.

(i) Mr. Dvaipayan sold jewellery on 5-6-2006 for a consideration of Rs. 81,000. Rs. 1,000 were paid for brokerage. The jewellery was purchased by him on 1-6-1994 for Rs. 18,200. Out of the net consideration received only Rs. 50,000 were invested on 15-11-2006 in purchasing a residential house. The assessee already owns one residential house.

(ii) Mr. Malay had 500 shares of Rs. 100 each of the Mandar Ltd. which he had purchased in April 1988 for Rs. 50,000. He commenced the business of dealing in shares on 1-5-2004 and treated these shares as stock in trade of this business. The fair market value of these shares on that date was Rs. 160 per share. He sold these shares on 1-11-2006 at Rs. 175 each.

(iii) Mr. Sankarshan had purchased a second hand car for Rs. 75,000 on 28-2-1993 for the purpose of his business. He sold the car on 15-1-2007 for Rs. 37,000. It was the only asset with him in this block, the written down value of which was Rs. 44,000.

(iv) Mr. Malhar had purchased 1,000 equity shares of Rs. 100 each of IWS Ltd. on 23-7-1995 for Rs. 90,000. The company issued him 500 bonus shares in December 2006. He sold 1,000 shares on 12-2-2007 including all the bonus shares for Rs. 200 each.

Ans: 16,324; (69,068); (7,000); 1,33,772.

Problem 7.37-P5

Mrs. X owned two motor cars which were mainly used for business purposes. The written down value on April 1, 2006 of the block of assets comprising of only these two cars, both of which were purchased in May 1999, was Rs. 1,81,000. These two cars were sold in June, 2006 for Rs. 1,50,000. In February 2007, she sold 1,300 shares in X Ltd., an Indian company, for Rs. 2,00,000. She had purchased the same during March 1998, for Rs. 3,10,000. A house plot purchased by her in March, 1995 for Rs. 3,00,000 was sold by her for Rs. 4,35,000 on January 18, 2007.

Compute the amount of net capital gains chargeable to tax in respect of the above transactions for the assessment year 2007-08.

Ans: (31,000); (2,86,073); (1,66,158)

Problem 7.37-P6

During the financial year 2006-07, Mr. V sold the following shares :

	ABC Ltd.	*DEF Ltd.*	*Shares of GHI Ltd.*
Sale consideration	5,00,000	4,00,000	6,89,000
Cost of acquisition	26,000	1,10,000	20,000
Date of acquisition	10-5-1984	6-6-1985	6-4-1986
Whether listed in Stock Exchange	Yes	Yes	No

V's income under other Heads aggregate to Rs. 7,86,000. He paid Rs. 50,000 towards Life Insurance premium of his wife.

You are to compute exemption u/s 10(38), total income and tax liability in regard to Assessment Year 2007-08.

Ans: 13,50,857; 3,29,612.

Typical

Problem 7.37-P7 [Hons 1998]

'X' sells a commercial house on December 15, 2006 for Rs. 17,00,000 *(cost of acquisition on 23rd April 1981 Rs. 1,20,000)*.

For claiming exemption under sections of capital gain he invested in following assets.

	Particular of assets	*Date of purchase*	*Amount*
1.	Residential House property	14-3-2007	2,00,000
2.	Agricultural Land	31-3-2007	1,50,000
3.	Shares of NHAI (Redeemable on 4-1-2010)	5-1-2007	2,76,206
4.	Bonds of NHAI (Redeemable on 4-1-2011)	14-7-2007	53,354
5.	Bonds of Rural Electrification Corporation Ltd. *Redeemable on 1-5-2009*	1-3-2005	70,000

He does not own any other house. He also incurred a short term capital loss amounting to Rs. 30,000 during the PY 2006-07. During the PY his only other income was from business amounting to Rs. 50,000. He donated Rs. 12,000 in Prime Minister's National Relief Fund and deposited Rs. 20,000 in Public Provident Fund.

Compute the total income and tax liability of 'X' for the AY 2007-08.

Ans: 6,62,270; 1,14,703.

Problem 7.37-P8 [CA M06]

Mr. A who transfers land and building on 2-1-2007, furnishes the following information :

(i) Net consideration received Rs. 10 lakhs.

(ii) Value adopted by stamp valuation authority, which was not contested by Mr. A Rs. 12 lakhs.

(iii) Value ascertained by Valuation officer on reference by the Assessing Officer Rs. 13 lakhs.

(iv) This land was distributed to Mr. A on the partial partition of his HUF on 1-4-1981. Fair market value of the land as on 1-4-1981 was Rs. 1,10,000.

(v) A residential building was constructed on the above land by Mr. A at a cost of Rs. 3,20,000 (construction completed on 1-12-2003) during the Financial year 2003-04.

(vi) Short-term capital loss incurred on sale of shares during the Financial year 2003-04 Rs. 2,05,000.

Compute amount of gain annd also Mr. A seeks your advice as to the amount to be invested in NHAI bonds so as to be exempt from clutches of capital gain tax.

Ans: 65,396; nil.

Problem 7.37-P9 [PE II N06]

Mr. Malik owns a factory building on which he had been claiming depreciation for past few years. It is the only asset in the block. The factory building and land appurtenant there to were sold during the year. The following details are available :

Building completed in September, 2002 for	---	10,00,000
Land appurtenant thereto purchased in April, 2001 for	---	12,00,000
Advance received from a prospective buyer for land in May 2002 forfeited in favour of Assessee, as negotiations failed	---	50,000
WDV of the building block as on 01-04-2006	---	8,74,800
Sales value of Factory building in November, 2006	---	8,00,000
Sale value of Appurtenant land	---	16,00,000

The Assessee is ready to invest in long - term specified Assets under Section 54EC, within specified time.

Compute the amount of taxable capital gain for the assessment year 2007-08 and the amount to be invested under Section 54EC for availing the maximum exemption.

Ans: 1,24,200; 1,98,944.

Problem 7.37-P10 [Hons 1992]

Z Ltd., an Indian company, furnishes following particulars of its income / assets / investments for the previous year 2006-07 :

• Business profits before depreciation	2,00,000
• W.D.V. of plant and machinery used in business on 01-04-2006	20,00,000
(i) Machinery purchased in July 2006 and put to use on the same date	4,00,000
(ii) Machinery sold in Nov. 2006	6,00,000
• Sale of shares (non-listed) in Sept. 2006 (Purchased in April 2001 for Rs. 60,000)	65,000

- Sale of land in Dec. 2006 — 13,00,000
  (Purchased in April 1995 for Rs. 5,00,000)
- Invested in bonds of National Highways Authority of India under section 54EC in March 2007 — 2,00,000

Compute the total income of the company for the assessment year 2007-08 and also the w.d.v. of plant and machinery as on 31-03-2007 after depreciation for the previous year 2006-07 after depreciation for the previous year 2006-07.

Ans: 62,090; 15,30,000.

Problem 7.37-P11 (ICWAI-D98) - M 6

Manohar acquired a plot of land on June 30, 1984 for Rs. 1,10,000. The funds invested were borrowed at the rate of 9% per annum (The amount was repaid by Manohar on March 31, 1988). Manohar sells the plot of land on June 30, 2006 for Rs. 5,00,000. What will be the amount of Capital Gains for the assessment year 2007-08? Can Manohar claim deduction of ground rent paid by him? (Ignore the cost inflation index for working out the problem.)

Ans: (8,418)

STRATEGY MAKER

Points in 1 to 10	Overall Points 7; Practical 8; Theory 6.
Type of problem	Difficult. Most of the students find it difficult to digest this chapter. Its logic goes beyond known boundary. I can understand. But I know your determination and hardwork shall conquer this CAPITAL GAIN. In the year 2003 this chapter was very strangely asked. The question was 'Define first proviso of section 48'? Yes! from now on unimportant sections are also required to be memorised. The toughness of paper setter and the hardwork of students. Who wins? YOU!
What to expect (DU)	Revise all the illustrations from this book without fail. One may leave special cases of computing capital gain (Deemed transfer).
CA (PE II)	Everything. [Nov 2006 attempt total marks 30]

The Ant Philosophy

Ants never quit. That's a good philosophy. If they're headed somewhere and you try to stop them, they'll look for another way. They'll climb over, they'll climb under, they'll climb around. They keep looking for another way. And that's the only way to succeed.

Keep running, Keep trying, never never quit and NEVER SAY DIE.

Let me allow to say that you have completed the most difficult step of income tax. It means what is coming next is very very easy as compared to Capital Gain. But do not stop working very hard.

Keep running

fully exempted income with a rider

8

AGRICULTURAL INCOME

TOPIC 8.00 *SECTION 10(1).* AGRICULTURAL INCOME FULLY EXEMPT FROM TAX

1. *Section 10(1).* Agricultural income as defined under section 2(1A) is fully exempt from tax but with a rider. Since agricultural income is exempt from tax it doesn't form part of total income.
2. However if certain conditions are satisfied, then agricultural income is included in total income, only for computing tax liability.
3. The agricultural income has been made exempted since Constitution of India gives exclusive powers to the State Legislature to make laws with respect to taxes on agricultural income.

TOPIC 8.01 *SECTION 2(1A).* MEANING OF AGRICULTURAL INCOME

(a) Any rent or revenue derived *(directly)* from land situated in India used for agricultural purpose.

The abovesaid income is computed under the head '*Income from Other Sources*' and all expenses as specified under section 57 shall be allowed as deduction.

(b) Any income derived from such land by :

(i) agriculture (e.g. *tilling of land, sowing of seed, watering the land, planting and manuring etc.)*; or

(ii) the performance by a cultivator or receiver of rent-in-kind of any process ordinarily employed by a cultivator to render the produce fit to be taken to market (e.g. *weeding, pruning, cutting, harvesting and rendering the produce fit for market)*; or

(iii) the sale by a cultivator or receiver of rent-in-kind of the produce raised or received by him, in respect of which no process has been performed other than a prescribed process.

The abovesaid income shall be computed under the head '*Profit from business*' and all adjustments as specified under section 28 to 44D shall be made.

(c) • Any income derived from any building, which is situated on or is in the immediate vicinity of the land.

• Such building by reason of his connection with the land, is used as a dwelling house, or as a store-house, or other out-building.

• Such land is either assessed to land revenue in India or is subject to a local rate assessed. However where the land is not so assessed to land revenue or subject to a local rate, then it should be situated outside the urban area.

However where income is derived from such building by letting it out for residential purpose or for the purpose of any business or profession, then such income shall not be agricultural income.

The abovesaid income shall be computed under the head *'Income from House Property'* and all deductions as specified under section 24 shall be allowed.

Problem 8.01-P1

1. Income received from letting of a land situated in India, which is used for agricultural operations is treated as agricultural income. (Yes or No)
2. Income from trees and plants grown by nature on the land is treated as agricultural income. (Yes or No)
3. Income from letting of tractors for agricultural operations is treated as agricultural income. (Yes or No)
4. Income from Tea Garden in Dhaka is treated as agricultural income. (Yes or No)
5. Income from growing and selling of paddy in Kerala is treated as agricultural income. (Yes or No)
6. Income arising from sale of forest trees, wild grass, bamboos and seeds, fruits and flowers which grow on land spontaneously without the aid of human skill and labour, is treated as agricultural income. (Yes or No)
7. A cultivator sells the produce at his own shop at a higher price, the whole of income is treated as agricultural income. (Yes or No)
8. Where the cultivator sells such product which he has purchased from other person the income derived shall be treated as agricultural income. (Yes or No)
9. Income from fisheries is treated as agricultural income. (Yes or No)
10. Agricultural income as defined in section 2(1A) is included in gross total income. (Yes or No)
11. Mr. X is a manager of an agricultural farm and received a salary of Rs. 90,000 which he claims to be agricultural income and therefore exempt from tax. Is claim of X tenable.
12. Income from supplying of water for irrigation is an agricultural income. (True or False)
13. If a firm carries out agricultural activities then any interest or salary received by its partners shall be treated as agricultural income in the hands of partners. (True or False)
14. Income from growing of flowers and creepers is treated as agricultural income. (True or False)
15. Dividend / interest received from a company engaged in agricultural activity. (True or False)
16. Income from dairy farming, poultry farming, stone quarries is not treated as an agricultural income. (True or False)

Ans:

1. Yes. This is as per section 2(1A)(a).
2. No, since no agricultural operations performed by the cultivator.

3. No.
4. No, since land is situated outside India.
5. Yes since agricultural operation is performed by the cultivator and land is situated in India.
6. No, since no agricultural operations have been performed by the cultivator.
7. Yes, since cultivator is selling his own produce.
8. No, since no agricultural operations have been performed by the cultivator.
9. No, since fish is not the produced of land.
10. No.
11. No.
12. False.
13. True.
14. True.
15. False.
16. False.

TOPIC 8.02 *INCOME WHICH IS PARTIALLY AGRICULTURAL AND PARTIALLY FROM BUSINESS

Income from following composite business is disintegrated into agricultural income and non-agricultural income. Maximum part is agricultural income and remaining part is non-agricultural income.

	Agricultural Income	*Non-Agricultural Income*
Rule 7A. Manufacture of rubber	65%	35%
Rule 7B(1). Sale of coffee grown and cured by seller	75%	25%
Rule 7B(1A). Sale of coffee grown, cured, roasted and grounded by seller in India with or without mixing chicory or other flavouring ingredients	60%	40%
Rule 8. Growing and manufacturing tea in India	60%	40%

Problem 8.02-P1

1. 100% of income from growing and selling tea in India is treated as agricultural income. (True or False)
2. 100% of income from manufacturing and selling tea in India is treated as Non-agricultural income. (True or False)

Solution

1. True, since disintegration is done only if an assessee is engaged in growing and manufacturing tea in India. But in this case the assessee is growing and selling tea and not manufacturing the tea.
2. True, since the assessee is not growing tea.

Problem 8.02-P2 (PE II - N04) - M 5

Q.1b : Mr. R had estates in Rubber, Tea and Coffee. He derives income from them. He has also a nursery wherein he grows plants and sells. For the previous year ending 31-3-2007, he furnishes the following particulars of his sources of income from estates and sale of

Plants. You are requested to compute the agricultural income and taxable income for the assessment year 2007-08:

(i) Manufacture of Rubber	5,00,000
(ii) Manufacture of Coffee grown and cured	3,50,000
(iii) Manufacture of Tea	7,00,000
(iv) Sale of Plants from Nursery	1,00,000

Ans: 11,07,500; 5,42,500.

TOPIC 8.03 SCHEME OF PARTIAL INTEGRATION OF AGRICULTURAL INCOME WITH NON-AGRICULTURAL INCOME

The scheme of partial integration of agricultural income with non-agricultural income is done only for computing tax liability and agricultural income never forms part of total income.

If all the following conditions are satisfied agricultural income is added to total income to compute tax liability. It is also called as partial integration of agricultural income ith Non-agricultural income.

1. The assessee is an Individual or HUF or BOI, or AOP or artificial juridical person. (The integration is not applicable to firm and company)
2. Non-agricultural income i.e total income exceeds basic exemption limit of slab rate. Basic exemption is for
   a. Resident woman : Rs. 1,35,000
   b. Resident senior citizen : Rs. 1,85,000
   c. In case of other individual or HUF : Rs. 1,00,000
3. Agricultural Income exceeds Rs. 5,000.

If all the above 3 conditions are satisfied then tax liability is computed as under by applying slab rates:

Computation of Tax Liability (assumed figures)

Tax on (Non-agricultural income + Agricultural income) at slab rate (let us call it Tax 1)	8,000
Tax on *(Agricultural income + basic exemption limit)* at slab rate (let us call it Tax 2)	5,000
Tax (Tax 1 minus Tax 2)	3,000

Illustration and Problems 8.03-P1 (Difficult)

(A) Compute tax liability in the following cases for the AY 2007-08.

	Case 1	*Case 2*	*Case 3*	*Case 4*	*Case 5*
Status (resident)	HUF	Woman	Woman (66 years)	Woman (65 years)	Individual (65 years)
Business Income	6,80,000	9,00,000	11,10,000	6,00,000	2,60,000
Agricultural Income	25,00,000	80,000	65,000	5,000	6,00,000
Investment in NSC VIII issue out of agricultural income	80,000	1,00,000	10,000	70,000	80,000

(B) Solve if the assessee is a company.

Ans: (A) 1,53,000; 1,99,920; 3,07,989; 98,940; nil (B) 2,28,888; 3,02,940; 3,73,626; 2,01,960; 87,516

Solution

Computation of total income

	Case 1	*Case 2*
Gross Total Income	6,80,000	9,00,000
Less : Deduction u/s 80C	80,000	1,00,000
Total Income	6,00,000	8,00,000

Computation of tax liability

	Case 1	*Case 2*
Tax 1 (Tax on 31,00,000 at slab rate) (Rs. 6 lakhs + Rs. 25 lakhs)	8,80,000	2,14,000
Tax 2 (Tax on 26,00,000 at slab rate) (Rs. 25 lakhs + Rs. 1 lakhs)	7,30,000	18,000
Tax (Tax 1 - Tax 2)	1,50,000	1,96,000
Add : Education cess @ 2%	3,000	3,920
Tax payable	1,53,000	1,99,920

Problem 8.03-P2

1. Agricultural income is fully exempt from tax but with a rider. Explain.

Solution

1. Refer illustration 8.03-P1 Case 1. Compute tax liability on Non-agricultural income it shall come to Rs. 1,32,600. Whereas, if agricultural income is integrated with Non- agricultural income tax liability comes to Rs. 1,53,000. It means the assessee is paying Rs. 20,400 by way of tax liability on agricultural income even though it is exempt.

Illustration and Problems 8.03-P3 (Typical)

Compute tax liability of Mrs. Taxcrazy for the AY 2007-08:

	Case 1	*Case 2*
Income from Salary.	2,00,000	1,15,000
Rent from building used for agricultural purpose.	60,000	1,00,000
Receipt from sale of crops (own produce).	1,00,000	20,000
Expenses incurred on purchase of seeds and sale of crops.	85,000	60,000
Salary from a firm in which he is a partner engaged in agricultural activity.	93,000	3,20,000
STCG on sale of rural agricultural land situated in India.	25,00,000	40,00,000
LTCG on sale of an industrial rural land.	60,000	85,000
LTCG on sale of listed bonds.	70,000	nil
Winning from lotteries.	35,000	20,000
Deductions u/s 80C.	70,000	10,000

Ans: (1) 2,95,000; 28,560. (2) 2,10,000; 14,280.

Solution : Case 1

	Non-Agricultural Income	*Agricultural Income*
Income from Salary	**2,00,000**	—
Income from House Property	—	42,000

Profit from Business :		
• Income from sale of crops	—	15,000
• Salary from a firm engaged in agricultural activity	—	93,000
LTCG on sale of land	60,000	—
LTCG on sale of listed equity bonus shares	70,000	—
Winning from lotteries	35,000	—
Total	3,65,000	1,50,000

Computation of Total Income

Gross Total Income	3,65,000
Less : Deductions u/s 80C	70,000
Total Income	2,95,000

Computation of Tax Liability

Tax on LTCG @ 20% on Rs. 60,000	12,000
Tax on LTCG @ 10% on of 70,000	7,000
Tax on Winning from lotteries @ 30% of 35,000	10,500
Tax on Normal income +AI on Rs. 2,80,000 at slab rate (2,95,000 + 1,50,000 – 1,65,000)	34,000
Tax liability (Tax 1)	63,500
Tax on Rs. 2,85,000 at slab rate (1,50,000 + 1,35,000) (Tax 2)	35,500
Tax 1 minus Tax 2	28,000
Add : Education cess @ 2%	560
Tax payable	28,560

Problem 8.03-P4

1. Calculate tax liability of Mr. Sharma for the assessment year 2007-08 :

   Total taxable income including LTCG of Rs. 17,000. 1,70,000

   Agricultural Income 20,000

2. Compute the tax liability of a person if his total taxable income is Rs. 2,00,000 and he deposited Rs. 50,000 in the PPF and purchased NSC of Rs. 30,000. Agricultural income Rs. 5,000.

Ans: 11,220; 2,040.

Problem 8.03-P5 [CA M06]

The total income of Mrs. Z computed for the assessment year 2007-08 is Rs. 2,00,000 which includes the following :

Long-term capital gains	30,000
Winning from lotteries	20,000
Short-term capital gains covered by Sec. 111A	10,000

Agricultural income earned by her was Rs. 50,000. Compute the tax payable by Mrs. Z.

Ans: 14,280.

Problem 8.03-P6 [CS J05]

For the assessment year 2007-08, Ms. Puja (date of birth 19th September, 1940) furnishes the following information :

Gross agricultural income	2,21,000
Expenditure on earning agricultural income	1,000
Non - agricultural income	3,50,000

Determine the tax liability of Ms. Puja for the assessment year 2007-08 on the assumption that she contributes Rs. 60,000 towards public provident fund and pays insurance premium of Rs. 20,000 on her life insurance policy (sum assured : Rs. 1,50,000).

Ans: 26,010.

8.04 COMPREHENSIVE PROBLEMS

Problem 8.04-P1

From the following particulars, compute the income - tax liability of Mrs. Gautam for the assessment year 2007-08 :

(i) Income from house property (computed)	10,000
(ii) Income from business & Profession	2,65,000
(iii) Long term capital gain (computed)	20,000
(iv) Short term capital gain	30,000
(v) Winnings from Rajasthan State Lottery	60,000
(vi) Winnings from Horse races	10,000
(vii) Net Agricultural Income	25,000
(viii) Deposited in the mutual fund of the Unit trust of India	15,000
(ix) Repayment of the amount borrowed from the National Housing Bank for the purchase of residential house property	6,000

Ans: 66,504.

Problem 8.04-P2 [Hons 1995]

The taxable incomes of an individual, computed as per provisions of the Income Tax Act for the PY ended on March 31, 2007 are as under:

1. Income from Business	1,60,000
2. Income from House property: (Loss from self-occupied house on account of interest on loan taken for construction of house)	(70,000)
3. STCG	8,000
4. LTCG	1,50,000
5. Winning from horse race	2,60,000
6. Agricultural Income	1,55,000

During the year he purchased National Savings Certificates *(VIII Issue)* for Rs. 1,10,000. Find out his tax liability for the AY 2007-08.

Ans: 89,760.

Problem 8.04-P3 (CA - M98) - M 9

Q.1b : From the following information, compute total income for the AY 2007-08 :

Income from business — letting cycles on hire	40,000
Lease rent received from lands given to tenants for agricultural operations	48,000
Sale of agricultural produce (landlord's share)	30,000
Sale proceeds of agricultural lands situated in a village	1,20,000
Fixed deposit interest received from companies on deposits made of sale proceeds of land	18,000
Dividends (received in April, 2006) from an Indian company having rubber plantations	6,000
Salary received as a partner from a firm manufacturing tea	36,000
Payments of Government tax on agricultural lands	6,000
Expenses on power, irrigation cess and farm labour	10,000
Purchase of seeds	1,000
Tractor hire charges *(for agricultural operations)*	2,500

Compute total income and agricultural income.

Ans: 94,000; 58,500.

STRATEGY MAKER

Points in 1 to 10	Overall points 5; Practical points 3; Theory points 6.
Type of problem	Simple. Practical questions are attached with salary problem. Separate practical questions are generally not asked.
What to expect (DU)	Partial integration. Do revise all illustrations.
CA (PE II)	Everything.

"I think, therefore I am" *Rene Descartes*

Keep Running

Earn, Save and claim deductions

DEDUCTIONS ALLOWED FROM GROSS TOTAL INCOME

Introduction

At this stage you already know computation of gross total income and total income which has already been discussed in Chapter 1. If you do not remember do refer it again before proceeding further.

Broadly section 80C to 80U is divided into 4 parts as shown below :

A.	Section 80A to 80B	General
B.	Section 80C to 80GGC	Deductions in respect of certain payments
C.	Section 80LA	Deductions in respect of certain incomes
D.	Section 80U	Other deductions

TOPIC 9.00 GENERAL CONDITIONS APPLICABLE TO ALL SECTIONS

1. *Section 80A.* Deductions u/s **80C to** '' shall not exceed Gross Total Income.
2. The deductions u/s 80C to **80U is not allowed** from special incomes *i.e.*, LTCG and STCG (STT paid) and Casual **income.**

E.g. Suppose Income from Salary is Rs. 5,000 and LTCG, STCG (STT paid) and Casual Income is Rs. 95,000. Now the deduction u/s 80C to 80U cannot exceed Rs. 5,000.

Special point (Section 80AB. Deductions to be made with reference to the income included in the gross total income)

Where any deduction is required to be made or allowed under any section included in this Chapter under the heading "*C. Deductions in respect of certain incomes*" in respect of any income of the nature specified in that section which is included in the gross total income of the assessee, then, notwithstanding anything contained in that section, for the purpose of computing the deduction under that section, the amount of income of that nature as computed in accordance with the provisions of this Act (before making any deduction under this Chapter) shall alone be deemed to be the amount of income of that nature which is derived or received by the assessee and which is included in his gross total income.

DEDUCTIONS RELATING TO SPECIFIED POLICIES

TOPIC 9.01 *SECTION 80C* : DEDUCTION AVAILABLE FROM SPECIFIED INVESTMENT OR SPECIFIED EXPENDITURES

Already discussed in detail in chpater 4.

TOPIC 9.02 *SECTION 80CCC.* CONTRIBUTION TO PENSION FUNDS OF LIC OR APPROVED PVT. INSURERS

1. *Who can claim deduction* : Any individual can claim deduction. Such individual may be Resident in India or NR in India. He may be an Indian citizen or a foreign citizen.
2. *Name of the scheme* : Where the deposit is made in any
   (a) Pension plan of Life Insurance Corporation (LIC) also known as annuity scheme; or
   (b) Pension Plan of any other Private Insurer as approved by Controller of Insurance.

   for receiving pension from the fund set up by the said corporation.
3. *Amount of deduction allowed* : Contribution made or Rs. 1,00,000 whichever is lower is allowed as deduction. However overall deduction u/s 80C + 80CCC + 80CCD cannot exceed Rs. 1,00,000.

Note

- The payment or deposit should be made out of income chargeable to tax.
- Surrender value received is taxable in the year of receipt in the hands of the assessee or nominee.

Problems 9.02-P1

1. Deduction u/s 80CCC is available to HUF. (True or False)
2. Deduction u/s 80CCC is available only to resident Individual. (True or False)
3. Mr. X borrowed Rs. 1,10,000 and contributed Rs. 60,000 towards PPF and Rs. 50,000 towards pension plan of HDFC. How much deduction is allowed u/s 80C and 80CCC.

Solutions

1. False. Deduction u/s 80CCC is available only to Individual.
2. False. Sec*tion 80CCC is* available *to both Resident and Non Resident.*
3. Rs. 60,000 deduction is allowed u/s 80C and no deduction is allowed u/s 80CCC.

Problem 9.02-P2

X, Non-resident individual, furnishes following information. Compute deduction allowed u/s 80C & 80CCC for the AY 2007-08.

	Case 1	*Case 2*	*Case 3*	*Case 4*
PPF contribution	8,000	5,000	54,000	1,10,000
Amount deposited under an annuity plan of LIC	98,000	82,000	26,000	25,000

Ans: 1,00,000; 87,000; 1,00,000; 80,000; 1,00,000.

TOPIC 9.03 ******SECTION 80CCD.* DEDUCTION IN RESPECT OF CONTRIBUTION TO PENSION SCHEME OF CENTRAL GOVERNMENT

Already discussed in detail in chapter 4.

TOPIC 9.04 *SECTION 80D.* CONTRIBUTION TOWARDS HEALTH INSURANCE PREMIUM

1. *Who can claim deduction* : An individual or HUF who contributes towards health insurance premium can claim deduction.

   Such individual should take health insurance on the health of his family members. (Family means self, spouse, dependent children or dependent parents)

   In case of HUF who takes insurance on the health of any member of its family.

   The residential status of an Individual or HUF may be ROR or RNOR or NR in India whether Indian citizen or foreign citizen.

2. *Name of the scheme* : Where the health insurance premium is paid in any
   - (a) Mediclaim of General Insurance Corporation (GIC) which is approved by Central Govt.; or
   - (b) Health Insurance Plan of any other Private Insurer which is approved by the Insurance Regulatory & Development Authority.

3. *Amount of deduction allowed* : Deduction allowed is
   - (a) Upto Rs. 10,000 paid during the relevant PY;
   - (b) Upto Rs. 15,000 if Mediclaim Insurance premium is paid to effect an insurance of *resident* senior citizen in relation to the assessee. (*Where the payment is made in respect of Non-Resident senior citizen deduction is limited to Rs. 10,000)*

Note

- Overall deduction cannot exceed Rs. 15,000.
- No deduction is allowed if health insurance premium is paid in cash *i.e.* to claim deduction payment should be made through draft or cheque (bearer, crossed or account payee).
- The payment or deposit should be made out of income chargeable to tax.

Problems 9.04-P1

1. The company can claim deduction u/s 80D for taking health insurance for employees. (True or False)
2. Can an employee claim deduction for the payment of health insurance premium made by the company in his behalf?
3. Mr. X takes health insurance of his Non-Resident father aged 66 years. Maximum deduction available is Rs. 15,000 since his father is a senior citizen. (True or False)
4. How is family u/s 80D different from family as stated in provisions for medical facilities?

Solution

1. False, since deduction u/s 80D is applicable only to Individual or HUF.
2. No, since section 80D says the payment should be made out of income chargeable to tax and mediclaim insurance premium paid by employer is exempt in the hands of employee.

3. False. To claim deduction of Rs. 15,000 two conditions have to be satisfied. First he should be senior citizen and secondly his residential status should be Resident in India.
4. Section 80D : Family means self, spouse, *dependent children* or dependent parents. Medical facilities : Family means self, spouse, *dependent or not dependent children* or dependent parents. Difference is italicised.

Problem 9.04-P2

(A) X, resident individual, furnishes following information. Compute deduction allowed u/s 80D for the AY 2007-08.

	Case 1	*Case 2*	*Case 3*	*Case 4*
Amount deposited in the scheme of Mediclaim of GIC				
• for X	8,000	1,000	6,000	3,000
• for son of Mr. X not dependent on him	2,000	3,000	9,000	15,000
• for mother of X not dependent on him	5,000	8,000	1,000	3,000
• for daughter dependent on him	3,000	2,000	9,000	2,500
• for grandfather dependent on him	2,000	4,000	1,500	13,000
• for father of X *(66 years)* who is resident in India and dependent on X	2,000	16,000	4,000	4,000

(B) Compute deduction u/s 80D if the age of X's father is 64 years?

(C) Compute deduction u/s 80D if Mediclaim insurance premium of GIC is paid out of agricultural income?

(D) Compute deduction u/s 80D if Mediclaim insurance premium payment is made in cash?

Ans: (A) 12,000; 15,000; 14,000; 9,500; (B) 10,000; 10,000; 10,000; 9,500; (C) Agricultural income is exempt from tax and since the payment should be made out of income chargeable to tax therefore deduction u/s 80D is not available; (D) deduction u/s 80D is not available.

Hint: Section 80D is applicable to mother only when she is dependent on the assessee. Section 80D is not applicable to grandfather whether he is dependent or not dependent.

Problem 9.04-P3

Basic Salary Rs. 6,00,000. LIP paid by employer on behalf of employee Rs. 7,000. Mediclaim insurance premium paid by employer on behalf of employee Rs. 6,000. Other Income Rs. 3,00,000. PPF contribution Rs. 90,000. Compute total income.

Ans: 8,10,000.

DEDUCTIONS RELATING TO DISABLED PERSON AND SPECIFIED DISEASE

TOPIC 9.05 *SECTION 80DD.* DEDUCTION IN RESPECT OF MAINTENANCE INCLUDING MEDICAL TREATMENT OF A DEPENDANT WHO IS A PERSON WITH DISABILITY

1. *Who can claim deduction* : A Resident Individual / Resident HUF who maintains disabled dependent person. The individual may be an Indian citizen or a foreign citizen. Resident means ROR or RNOR. Where the residential status of such individual or HUF is Non Resident in India then deduction u/s 80DD is not allowed.

2. *Meaning of disabled dependent* : A disabled dependent means a person who
   (a) in the case of an individual, the spouse, children, parents, brothers and sisters of the individual or any of them;
   (b) in the case of a Hindu undivided family, a member of the Hindu undivided family, dependant wholly or mainly on such individual or Hindu undivided family for his support and maintenance,
   (c) is not dependent on any person other than such Individual or HUF for his support or maintenance; and
   (d) is suffering from permanent physical disability certified by a Medical Authority.
3. *Amount of deduction allowed* : Deduction allowed is
   (a) Rs. 50,000 fixed deduction is allowed irrespective of expenditure incurred.
   (b) Rs. 75,000 fixed in case of person with severe disability.

Note

- The assessee should have incurred some expenditure for the medical treatment including nursing, training and rehabilitation of a disabled dependent, otherwise deduction is not available.
- The assessee can claim deduction if any amount is deposited under an approved scheme of LIC or UTI or any other insurer during the PY for the benefit of such disabled dependent.
- If the disabled dependant predeceases the assessee, an amount withdrawn shall be deemed to be the income of the assessee of the previous year in which such amount is withdrawn.
- Double benefit of Section 80DD and 80U is not available.

(i) Special point (Meaning of disability etc.)

Meaning of disability : (i) blindness; (ii) low vision; (iii) leprosy-cured; (iv) hearing impairment; (v) locomotor disability; (vi) mental retardation; (vii) mental illness.

Person with disability : It means a person suffering from not less than 40% of any disability as certified by a medical authority.

Person with severe disability : It means a person with 80% or more of one or more disabilities.

TOPIC 9.06 *SECTION 80DDB.* MEDICAL TREATMENT ETC. OF SPECIFIED DISEASE OF SELF OR HIS DEPENDENTS

1. *Who can claim deduction* : A Resident Individual / Resident HUF.

   Such individual incurs expenditure on medical treatment of himself or his dependent family members who are suffering from specified disease. Where the taxpayer is a HUF then the expenditure should be incurred on the members of HUF.

   The individual may be an Indian citizen or a foreign citizen. Resident means ROR or RNOR. Where the residential status of such individual or HUF is Non-Resident in India then deduction u/s 80DDB is not allowed.

   Dependent family members have the same meaning as specified in section 80DD.
2. *Amount of deduction* : Deduction allowed is
   (a) Rs. 40,000 *or* the actual expenditure incurred for specified disease whichever is less is allowed as deduction.
   (b) *In case of resident senior citizen :* Rs. 60,000 *or* the actual expenditure incurred for specified disease whichever is less is allowed as deduction.

Note

- Insurance claim of received shall be reduced from the amount of deduction allowed.

(i) Special point (Meaning of Specified disease)

(i) Neurological diseases : (a) Dementia (b) Dystonia Musculorum Deformans (c) Motor Neuron Disease (d) Ataxia (e) Chorea (f) Hemiballismus (g) Aphasia (h) Parkinson's Disease. *(These diseases shall be treated as chronic and protracted, if the disability has been certified to be 40% and above.)* (ii) Cancer (iii) Full Blown Acquired Immuno-Deficiency Syndrome (AIDS) (iv) Chronic Renal failure (v) Hemophilia (vi) Thalassaemia.

Illustration and Problems 9.06-P1

(A) X, resident individual furnishes following information. Compute deductions allowed for the AY 2007-08.

1. He incurs an expenditure of Rs. 2,000 p.m. for maintenance of disabled son aged 9 years.
2. He incurs an expenditure of Rs. 50,000 in respect of his Non-Resident father aged 67 years who is suffering from a notified disease.

(B) What is the amount of deduction u/s 80DDB if his father is resident in India for the PY 2006-07 and receives insurance compensation of Rs. 35,000.

Ans: 90,000; 15,000.

Solution

• Section 80DD	50,000
• Section 80DDB	40,000
Total	90,000

Note

- Deduction u/s 80DDB available is Rs. 60,000 only when person is a *resident* senior citizen.

Problems 9.06-P2 [CA N 02]

Discuss the allowability of the following :

(i) X has to pay to a hospital for treatment of a dependent (being a person with disability) Rs. 42,000 and spent nothing for life insurance or for maintenance of the dependent.

(ii) X has incurred for treatment Rs. Nil in the previous year and deposited Rs. 25,000 which LIC for maintenance of (being a person with severe disability) dependents.

(iii) X has incurred Rs. 20,000 for treatment and Rs.. 35,000 was deposited with LIC for maintenance of dependent (being a person with disability)

Ans: 50,000; 75,000; 50,000.

TOPIC 9.07 *SECTION 80U.* DEDUCTION AVAILABLE TO SUCH INDIVIDUAL WHO IS HIMSELF A DISABLED

1. *Who can claim deduction* : A resident individual who is completely blind or suffers from permanent physical disability certified by a Medical Authority.
2. *Amount of deduction* : Deduction allowed is

   (a) Rs. 50,000 fixed deduction is allowed irrespective of expenditure incurred.

(b) Rs. 75,000 fixed in case of person with severe disability.

Note

- Double benefit of Section 80DD and 80U is not available.

Problem 9.07-P1 (Typical)

Mr. X and Mrs. X , a resident, both are suffering from low vision (60% disability). Mrs. X is dependent on Mr. X and is suffering from cancer. Expenditure incurred for treatment of cancer is Rs. 40,000 in the PY 2006-07. Income from salary of Mr. X is Rs. 2,10,000. Compute his total income for the AY 2007-08.

Ans: 1,20,000

Problems 9.07-P2 (Difficult)

Mr. Taxcrazy, furnishes following information, you are required to compute total income for the AY 2007-08 if he is (a) Non-resident in India (b) Resident in India.

Basic Salary for services rendered in India	60,000
Rent from building situated in Kovlam, India	30,000
Rent from building situated in Bali, Indonesia	1,00,000
Interest from company deposits from TELCO	13,000
Dividend from Indian company, received outside India	6,000
Interest from loan of Central Govt. (Loan is used outside India)	17,000
Dividend from foreign company, received in India	12,000
Contribution towards mediclaim insurance premium of GIC on the health of his resident mother	11,000
PPF contribution	15,000

His father a resident in India dependent on Mr. Taxcrazy suffers from notified disease. Mr. Taxcrazy spends Rs. 15,000 p.a. on his treatment.

Ans: 98,000; 1,53,000. [60,000+21,000+13,000+0+17,000+12,000=1,23,000–15,000–10,000=98,000]; [60,000+91,000+0+42,000=1,93,000–15,000–15,000–10,000=1,53,000]

OTHER DEDUCTIONS

TOPIC 9.08 *SECTION 80L* DEDUCTIONS FROM ELIGIBLE INCOME

Omitted from the AY 2007-08.

TOPIC 9.09 *SECTION 80G* DONATIONS

Who can claim deduction : The deduction u/s 80G is available to all assessees who make donation in 'specified fund'. The deduction allowed is either 100% of donation made or 50% of donation made. However donation made in kind is not eligible for deduction.

Meaning of specified fund : Specified fund is divided in two parts. Part A and Part B.

Part A : Where no maximum permissible limit is specified to the fund for making the donation. It means any amount donated irrespective of the gross total income is eligible for deduction.

Name of the fund	*Deduction allowed*
1. *National* Defence Fund	100%
2. The Army *Central* Welfare Fund of the Indian Naval Benevolent Fund or the Air Force Central Welfare Fund	100%
3. *National* Sports Fund set up by the Central Government	100%
4. *National* Cultural Fund set up by the Central Government	100%
5. *National* Foundation for Communal Harmony	100%
6. *National* State Blood Transfusion Council	100%
7. *National* Illness Assistance Fund	100%
8. Zila Saksharta Samiti	100%
9. Prime Minister's *National* Relief Fund	100%
10. *National* Eminent University/Educational Institution approved by the prescribed authority	100%
11. Fund of Technology Development and Application set up by the *Central* Government	100%
12. *National* Trust for Welfare of Persons with Autism, Cerebral Palsy, Mental Retardation and Multiple Disabilities	100%
13. Prime Minister's Drought Relief Fund	50%
14. Jawaharlal Nehru Memorial Fund	50%
15. National Children Fund	50%
16. Indira Gandhi Memorial Trust	50%
17. Rajiv Gandhi Foundation	50%

Memory technique : The fund where the word national / central is used, the deduction allowed generally is 100%. Only five funds from 13 to 17 have 50% others have 100%.

Part B : Where maximum permissible limit is specified to the fund. It means amount of donation *(not deduction)* cannot exceed the maximum permissible limit. Maximum permissible limit is 10% of Adjusted Gross Total Income (GTI).

Computation of Adjusted GTI : It includes all incomes except special incomes which are LTCG and STCG (STT paid), exempted incomes and after allowing all deductions u/s 80C to 80U except section 80G.

It means amount of donation cannot exceed the above said limit however it may be lower than that which is amount of donation made.

Name of the fund	*Deduction allowed*
1. Donation to Govt. / approved Local Authority, Institution, to be utilised	
• for promoting family planning	100%
• for charitable purpose other than promoting family planning	50%
2. Any notified temple, mosque, gurudwara, church or other place (for renovation or repair)	50%
3. Donation made by a *company* to the Indian Olympic association or to an institute notified u/s 10(23G) for the development of infrastructure for sports in India or for sponsorship of sports or games in India	100%

Illustration and Problems 9.09-P1 (Difficult)

Compute deduction allowed u/s 80G for the AY 2007-08.

	Case 1	*Case 2*	*Case 3*	*Case 4*
Business income	75,000	1,40,000	1,59,000	89,000
LTCG	20,000	80,000	nil	1,000
STCG (STT paid)	5,000	20,000	4,000	19,000
Dividend from Indian Company	12,000	8,900	62,000	52,000
Donation to Govt. for promotion of family planning	8,000	10,000	8,000	Nil
Donation to Govt. for charitable purpose	Nil	6,000	14,000	8,000
PPF contribution	5,000	20,000	4,000	19,000

Ans: 7,000; 11,000; 11,750; 3,500.

Solution

Computation of Total Income

	Case 1	*Case 2*
Business income	75,000	1,40,000
LTCG	20,000	80,000
STCG (STT paid)	5,000	20,000
Gross Total Income	1,00,000	2,40,000
Less : Deduction u/s 80C	5,000	20,000
Less : Deduction u/s 80G	7,000	11,000
Total Income	88,000	2,09,000

Computation of adjusted GTI

	Case 1	*Case 2*
Gross Total Income	1,00,000	2,40,000
Less : Special Incomes	25,000	1,00,000
Less : Deduction u/s 80C	5,000	20,000
Adjusted GTI	70,000	1,20,000
10% of adjusted GTI	7,000	12,000
Donation to Govt. for Family planning	7,000	10,000
Balance donation to Govt. for charitable purpose	nil	2,000

Note

- **To get the maximum deduction apportion the amount first to family planning, then the balance amount to charity.**
- **Dividend from Indian Company is exempt u/s 10(36), therefore do not form part of taxable income.**

Illustration and Problems 9.09-P2 (Typical)

Compute total income for the AY 2007-08.

	Case 1	*Case 2*	*Case 3*	*Case 4*
STCG	53,000	1,58,000	53,000	5,000
STCG (STT paid)	3,000	3,60,000	45,000	20,000
LTCG	27,000	40,000	5,000	10,000
LTCG (STT paid)	80,000	9,00,000	70,000	11,111
Interest from Cent. Govt. Securities	16,000	66,000	Nil	10,000
Winning from Games	6,000	3,00,000	50,000	1,18,000
Contribution to Mediclaim of GIC	3,000	3,000	nil	nil
Donation to National Defence Fund	2,000	1,00,000	10,000	nil
Donation to Govt. for family planning	3,000	30,000	10,000	nil
Donation to Govt. for charitable purpose	2,000	50,000	10,000	16,000
PPF contribution	15,000	15,000	nil	10,000

Ans: 81,000; 7,65,700; 1,32,850; 1,48,000.

Solution

Computation of Total Income

	Case 1	*Case 2*
Capital Gain		
• STCG	53,000	1,58,000
• STCG (STT paid)	3,000	3,60,000
• LTCG	27,000	40,000
Income from Other Sources		
• Interest from Central Govt. Securities	16,000	66,000
• Winning from Games	6,000	3,00,000
Gross Total Income	1,05,000	9,24,000
Less:		
• Deduction u/s 80C	15,000	15,000
• Deduction u/s 80D	3,000	3,000
• Deduction u/s 80G		
-National Defence Fund *(100%)*	2,000	1,00,000
-Govt. for Family planning *(100% of 3,000, 30,000)*	3,000	30,000
-Govt. for Charitable purpose *(50% of 2,000, 20600)*	1,000	10,300
Total Income	81,000	7,65,700

Computation of adjusted GTI

	Case 1	*Case 2*
Gross Total Income	1,05,000	9,24,000
Less :		
• LTCG + STCG (STT paid)	30,000	4,00,000
• Deduction u/s 80C to 80U except 80G	18,000	18,000
Adjusted GTI	57,000	5,06,000
10% of adjusted GTI	5,700	50,600
Donation to Govt. for Family planning	3,000	30,000
Balance donation to Govt. for charitable purpose	2,000	50,000

Problem 9.09-P3

Following are the particulars of income etc. of Sudarshan for the previous year ending on 31st March, 2007 :

(i) Income from house property (Taxable)	5,000
(ii) Long term capital gain (Computed)	80,000
(iii) Winning from Lottery (Gross)	45,000
(iv) Dividend from Unit Trust of India	10,000
(v) Donation to National foundation for communal harmony	10,000
(vi) Donation to approved educational institutions	15,000
(vii) Purchased N.S.C. (VIIIth issue)	5,000

Compute the total income and tax payable by Shri Sudarshan for the AY 2007-08.

Ans: 1,25,000; 13,770.

Problem 9.09-P4

The Particulars of income of Shri Gupta for the Previous year 2006-07 are as under :

(a) Business Income	1,20,000
(b) Income from House Property	23,000
(c) Short-term Capital Gains	15,000
(d) Long-term Capital Gains (computed)	50,000
(e) Interest received on Govt. Securities	8,000
(f) Dividend from Unit Trust of India	5,000
(g) Interest from Bank Deposits	13,000
(h) Dividend from Indian Companies	7,000

He has made the following payments out of the above mentioned incomes during the previous year :

(i) Life Insurance Premium - For himself and children (sum assured Rs. 1,00,000)	28,000
(ii) Deposited in Public Provident Fund	35,000
(iii) Medical insurance premiuim on health of his wife by cheque	5,000
(iv) Donations to approved institutions	15,000

Compute the amount of tax payable by Shri M.L. Gupta for the Assessment year 2007-08.

Ans: 1,55,450; 6,212. [1,20,000+23,000+15,000+50,000+21,000=2,29,000–63,000–5,000–5,550=1,55,450]

TOPIC 9.10 *SECTION 80GG* DEDUCTION IN RESPECT OF RENT PAID

CONDITIONS

1. He lives in a rented accommodation proided by employer or otherwise.
2. He is not in receipt of HRA.
3. He, spouse, minor child or the HUF of which he is a member must not own any RHP at the place where he works or if he owns then he should not claim any concession in respect of SOP for residence u/s 23(2).

AMOUNT OF DEDUCTION

Maximum Formula Formula	• Rs. 2,000 p.m. • 25% of adjusted GTI • Rent Paid – 10% of adjusted GTI	Least is deductible

Adjusted GTI (for the purpose of 80GG) is GTI – special income – all deductions u/s 80C to 80U except 80GG.

Problem 9.10-P1 [CA N96]

Calculate the deduction allowable under section 80GG to an assessee having the following income for the assessment year 2007-08 :

Business income	55,000
Interest from bank	5,000
PPF contribution	5,000

Rent paid by him for a house occupied by him for the purpose of his residence Rs. 1,250 per month.

Ans: 9,500; 45,500.

Problem 9.10-P2

Compute his total income from the following information:

Business Income	5,00,000
Other Income	1,00,000
PPF contribution	1,00,000
Contribution towards pension plan of LIC	10,000
Rent paid	80,000

Ans: 4,76,000. [5,00,000+1,00,000=6,00,000–1,00,000–24,000=4,76,000]

Problem 9.10-P3

Compute his total income from the following information:

Basic Salary	5,00,000
He is provided with accommodation by employer at Delhi @ Rs. 70,000	
Other Income	20,000
PPF contribution	1,05,000

Ans: 4,01,000. [5,00,000+5,000+20,000=5,25,000–1,00,000–24,000=4,01,000]

Problem 9.10-P4 [CA M00]

X is a retired Government Officer aged 65 years, who derived the following income in respect of financial year 2006-07. He resides in Cochin :

Pension	2,80,000
Interest from bank deposits	67,000
Total income	3,47,000

He has paid Rs. 18,000 as premium to effect an insurance on his health and his dependant parents (age 65 years). He pays a rent of Rs. 3,000 per month in respect of furnished accommodation. Compute total income and what is his eligibility for deduction under section 80GG ? What are the conditions to be satisfied by him to qualify for the deduction?

Ans: 3,29,200. [2,80,000+67,000=3,47,000–15,000–2,800=3,29,200]

Problem 9.10-P5

Neeta, an employee of G & Co. draws a salary of Rs. 10,000 p.m. She occupies for residence a house at Delhi for which she pays a monthly rent of Rs. 1,900. Neeta has no house of her own nor is she a member of a family which has any house. She has been given three different options. Compute total income in each case.

(a) The rent is paid by G & Co. directly to the landlord, G & Co being recorded as tenants. Neeta pays rent to his employer of Rs. 12,000.;

(b) Neeta pays the rent herself and gets a house rent allowance of Rs. 1,700 per month from the employer.

(c) Neeta pays the rent herself but receives nothing from the employer.

Ans: 1,15,800; 1,29,600; 1,09,200.

Problem 9.10-P6

Shri Sohan who is 70 years old has submitted the following particualrs of his income for the previous year 2006-07 :

(i) Income from Profession as musician Rs. 2,52,000.
(ii) Interest on Govt. Securities Rs. 20,000.
(iii) Accrued interest on National Savings certificates purchased during past years Rs. 17,000.

During the previous year he has made the following payments :

(i) National Savings Certificates VIII Issue purchased for Rs. 10,000.
(ii) Life Insurance Premium paid on a Joint life policy taken on his life and the life of his wife R.s 6,000.
(iii) Deposited in Public Provident Fund Account Rs. 10,000.
(iv) Health Insurance Premium of his Children Rs. 11,000 paid by cheque.

Rent @ Rs. 2,500 per month was paid for the house taken on rent for his own residence.

Compute his total income and tax payable by him for the assessment year 2007-08.

Ans: 2,29,600; 21,338. [2,52,000+20,000+17,000=2,89,000–43,000–10,000–6,400= 2,29,600]

Problem 9.10-P7 (Typical)

Mr. Taxcrazy, Resident in India and a Foreign Citizen, a physically disabled, works in a NPLH Ltd. *(manufacturer of disabled equipment),* Goa draws following salary for the year ended March 31, 2007:

Basic Salary	45,000
Transport Allowance	24,000

(100% is used for commutation between residence and office)

He is provided with accommodation five k.m. away from his office @ Rs. 2,500. Population as per 2001 census is 35 lakhs.

He purchases a brand new wheelchair of Rs. 3,500 from the company for Rs. 2,000.

The gas bill amounting to Rs. 500 is paid by Company. The bill is in the name of Company.

He is also provided with car facility for his family members. Expenditure incurred by the company is Rs. 16,540.

On sale of unlisted shares of NPLH Ltd. he earned an income of Rs. 25,000. (holding *period of shares 24 months)*

Interest from NSC VIII issue Rs. 1,000 *(reinvested)*.

(A) Compute his total income and tax payable for the AY 2007-08 if he is Resident in India.

(B) What if he is a Non-Resident in India.

Ans: (A) 28,580; Nil; (B) 79,770; 5,100. [45,000+4,800+4,970+0+0+0=54,770+25,000+1,000=80,770–1,000–1,193–50,000=28,578] [45,000+4,800+4,970+0+0+0=54,770+25,000+ 1,000=80,770–1,000=79,770]

TOPIC 9.11 *SECTION 80E.* DEDUCTION ON ACCOUNT OF PAYMENT OF INTEREST IN RESPECT OF LOAN TAKEN FOR HIGHER EDUCATION

Higher education : It means full-time studies for any graduate or postgraduate course in engineering, medicine, management or for postgraduate course in applied sciences or pure sciences, including mathematics and statistics;

Who can claim deduction : Allowable to an individual *who* has taken loan from any Financial Institution or Banking company or any approved charitable institution for the purpose of pursuing his own higher education.

Amount of deduction : Any amount paid by the assessee in the PY by way of payment of interest. From the AY 2007-08 deduction by way of repayment of loan is not allowed as deduction.

Note

- The amount is paid out of income chargeable to tax.
- The deduction shall be allowed from the year the assessee starts payment of interest and subsequent 7 assessment year.

Problem 9.11-P1 (CS J03) - M 3

Q.1e : Gross total income of A for previous year 2006-07 is Rs. 1,50,000. He had taken a loan of Rs. 4,00,000 in 2003-04 from a bank for pursuing the MBA course from Indian Institute of Management (IIM), Bangalore. During the previous year 2006-07, he repaid the first instalment of loan of Rs. 1,30,000 including interest thereon Rs. 55,000. Compute his total income for the AY 2007-08.

Ans: 95,000.

TOPIC 9.12 *SECTION 80GGA.* DEDUCTION AGAINST DONATION FOR SCIENTIFIC RESEARCH/RURAL DEVELOPMENT

1. *Who can claim deduction* : Any assessee not having business income but making donation to specified institution or fund.
2. *Name of the institution to which contribution has to be made* :
   (a) To approved University, college, or other institution to be used for scientific research or social science or statistical research.
   (b) To an association or institution approved for the purpose of section 35CCA for undertaking rural development programme or training of persons for implementing programmes of rural development.
   (c) Contribution to public sector company or a local authority for carrying out any eligible project or scheme.
   (d) Contribution to National Urban Poverty Eradication Fund.
   (e) Contribution to National Fund for Rural Development.
3. *Amount of deduction* : Amount donated is allowed as deduction.

TOPIC 9.13 *SECTION 80GGB & 80GGC.* CONTRIBUTION MADE TO POLITICAL PARTIES

80GGB : It is applicable to Indian Company who gives contribution to any political party, 100% of contribution is allowed as deduction.

80GGC : In computing the total income of an assessee, being any person, except local authority and every artificial juridical person wholly or partly funded by the Government, there shall be deducted any amount of contribution made by him, in the previous year, to a political party.

TOPIC 9.14 *SECTION 80JJA.* PROFITS FROM BIODEGRADABLE WASTES

1. *Who can claim deduction* : All assessees.
2. *Nature of Income* : Engaged in the business of collecting and processing or treating of biodegradable wastes for generating power or producing bio-fertilizer, bio-pesticides or other biological agents or for producing bio-gas, making pellets or briquettes for fuel or organic manure.
3. *Amount of Deduction* : 100% of profits of such business for the initial 5 consecutive AYs from the PY when the business commences.

Problem 9.14-P1 [Hons 2001]

Miss Anjani, a resident assessee, furnishes the following particulars of her income and its application for the PY 2006-07.

1.	Income from production and sale of bio-gas, made by collecting and treating degradable waste	6,30,000	
	Less: Deposit made in PPF in the name of her minor son, M	30,000	6,00,000
2.	Income from house Property		1,20,000
	Less: Medical expenditure, incurred for the treatment of her husband, a senior citizen, suffering from specified disease prescribed under Rule 11DD		65,000
			55,000
3.	Long term capital gain from the sale of A(Pvt.) Ltd. bonus shares, issued in July 1999		1,42,000
4.	Gross dividends from co-operative societies		1,38,000

You are requested to compute Miss Anajani's total income and determine her tax liability for the AY 2007-08.

Ans: 3,10,000; 34,170.

TOPIC 9.15 **SECTION 80JJAA.* DEDUCTION IN RESPECT OF EMPLOYMENT OF NEW REGULAR WORKMEN

1. *Who can claim deduction* : An Indian company.
2. *Nature of Income* : Engaged in the manufacture or production of an article or thing and employing atleast 100 regular workmen.
3. *Amount of Deduction :*

   First AY : 30% of the additional wages paid to the new regular workmen employed in the previous year.

Next 2 AY : Available only if there is increase of 10% or more of regular workmen on the last day of the PY.

Note

- This deduction is over and above salary or wages which is allowed as business expenses.

4. *Conditions* : Following conditions should be satisfied
   (a) The industrial undertaking is not formed by splitting up or reconstruction of any existing undertaking or amalgamation with another industrial undertaking.
   (b) A report of a Chartered Accountant.

TOPIC 9.16 *SECTIONS 80QQB.* DEDUCTION IN RESPECT OF ROYALTY INCOME, ETC., OF AUTHORS OF CERTAIN BOOKS OTHER THAN TEXT-BOOKS.

1. *Who can claim deduction* **:** A resident individual who is an author including a joint author who earns royalty income from the copyright of books.

   Meaning of Book : Book being a work of literary, artistic or scientific nature, or of royalty or copyright fees (whether receivable in lump sum or otherwise) in respect of such book. However books shall not include brochures, commentaries, diaries, guides, journals, magazines, newspapers, pamphlets, text-books for schools, tracts and other publications of similar nature, by whatever name called.

   Royalty income is earned by (a) assigning all rights in a book. In this case author receives lump sum consideration (b) assigning publishing and distribution rights but retaining copyright. In this case author receives lumpsum consideration plus royalty on yearly basis.

2. *Computation of royalty* : It is given that where the author receives royalty on yearly basis *(not a lump sum consideration in lieu of all rights)* in such case royalty cannot exceed 15% of the value of such books sold during the previous year.

   E.g. Where the royalty received @ 18% is Rs. 28,800. In this case excess of 15% shall be ignored *i.e.* 3%. Let us first find out the sales value of book by way of following formula. 18% of x = 28,800, therefore x = 1,60,000. In this case deduction allowed is limited to 15% of sales value of book which is 15% of 1,60,000 = 24,000.

   All such expenses which are attributable for earning the royalty income are subtracted from royalty income.

3. *Amount of deduction* : An amount equal to the royalty income as computed above *(which may be brought in India)* or Rs. 3,00,000 whichever is less is allowed as deduction.

4. *Conditions*
   (a) Where the income is earned from any source outside India, then the deduction shall be limited to so much of the income which is brought into India in convertible foreign exchange within a period of 6 months from the end of the previous year in which such income is earned or within such further period as the competent authority may allow in this behalf.
   (b) The assessee shall furnish a certificate in the prescribed form, duly signed by the prescribed authority, along with the return of income setting forth such particulars as may be prescribed.

Illustration 9.16-P1 (Difficult)

	Case 1	*Case 2*	*Case 3*	*Case 4*
Sales value of book in India	5,00,000	2,00,000	3,00,000	Not given
Sales value of book in USA	9,00,000	40,000	6,50,000	NA
Amount of royalty remitted to India	90,000	3,600	84,000	NA
Rate of royalty	20%	12%	14%	25%
Amount of royalty on yearly basis	2,80,000	Compute it	Compute it	7,00,000
Amount of royalty on lump sum basis	NA	3,00,000	50,000	80,000
Expenditure incurred on earning royalty	14,000	16,000	8,000	2,30,000

Solution

Royalty not exceeding 15% of sales value of book in India +	75,000	24,000	42,000	4,20,000
Amount of royalty remitted to India +	90,000	3,600	84,000	NA
Lump sum royalty	—	3,00,000	50,000	80,000
Gross Royalty	1,65,000	3,27,600	1,76,000	5,00,000
Less : Expenditure incurred on earning royalty	14,000	16,000	8,000	2,30,000
Net Royalty	1,51,000	3,11,600	1,68,000	2,70,000
Deduction allowed limited to Rs. 3 Lakhs	1,51,000	3,00,000	1,68,000	2,70,000

Problem 9.16-P2 (CA M99) - M 5

Q.1d: A, an individual, has written a book in English which has been approved by the State Government of Maharashtra and prescribed as a text-book in colleges in that State. The publisher of the book has paid to A Rs. 2,50,000 as lump sum consideration for transfer of author's interest in the copyrights of the book to the publisher. The amount was paid to A in October, 2006. For the assessment year 2007-08, A claims a deduction under section 80QQB. Will he succeed? Discuss.

Ans: No.

TOPIC 9.17 *SECTIONS 80RRB.* DEDUCTION IN RESPECT OF ROYALTY ON PATENTS

1. *Who can claim deduction :* Where in the case of an assessee, being an individual, who is resident in India (may be ROR or RNOR) and
   (a) a patentee *(Patentee means the person, including a co-patentee, being the true and first inventor of the invention, whose name is entered on the patent register as the patentee under the Patents Act, 1970)*
   (b) is in receipt of any income by way of royalty in respect of a patent registered on or after the 1-4-2003 under the Patents Act, 1970.
2. *Nature of income (Meaning of Income by way of Royalty) :* Royalty in respect of a patent means consideration for
   (*i*) the transfer of all or any rights (including the granting of a licence) in respect of a patent; or
   (*ii*) the imparting of any information concerning the working of, or the use of, a patent; or
   (*iii*) the use of any patent; or
   (*iv*) the rendering of any services in connection with the activities referred to in sub-clauses (*i*) to (*iii*).

Note

- Royalty income excludes any consideration chargeable under the head "Capital gains" or consideration for sale of product manufactured with the use of patented process or of the patented article for commercial use.

3. *Amount of deduction* : An amount equal to the royalty income *(which may be brought in India)* or Rs. 3,00,000 whichever is less.
4. *Conditions* : Same as that of section 80QQB.

Problems 9.17-P1

1. Name the deductions allowed only to individual.
2. Name the deductions allowed only to resident.
3. Name the deductions which are allowed on fixed basis.
4. Name the deductions which are allowed to all assessees.
5. Name the deductions allowed to individual and HUF both.
6. Name the deductions allowed only to Indian Company.

Solutions

1. 80CCC; 80CCD; 80GG; 80E; 80QQB; 80RRB and 80U.
2. 80DD; 80DDB; 80QQB; 80RRB and 80U.
3. 80DD and 80U.
4. 80G; 80GGA and 80JJA. Deduction u/s 80GGB and 80GGC can be claimed by all assessees except local authority and artificial juridical person.
5. 80C; 80D; 80DD and 80DDB
6. 80JJAA & 80GGB.

TOPIC 9.18 REBATE UNDER SECTION 88E : AVAILABLE TO SHARE-BROKERS ON STT PAID

Where the total income of an assessee in a previous year includes any income, chargeable under the head "Profits and gains of business or profession", arising from taxable securities transactions, he shall be entitled to a rebate, from the amount of income-tax on such income arising from such transactions, to the extent of minimum of the following two amounts :

(1) Securities transaction tax paid by such assessee (broker who deals in sale and purchases of securities)

(2) Average of income tax × business income from such taxable securities transactions.

Average of income tax = Total tax after all rebate except 88E ÷ total income × 100

Available on all taxes : Normal and special rates.

Illustration and Problems 9.18-P1

Compute tax payable for AY 2007-08 from the following information for all assessees.

	Case 1	*Case 2*	*Case 3*
Income arising from sale and purchase of equity shares	2,00,000	1,30,000	8,90,000
Other Income	1,00,000	90,000	4,00,000
Securities transaction tax paid	30,000	10,000	45,125
Donation to PM Natioanl Relief fund	10,000	500	1,00,000

Ans: (1) 10,604; 7,914; 11,712; 63,954 (2) 6,405; 2,870; 9,078; 62,664 (3) 2,89,897; 2,80,360; 2,93,824; 3,49,924

Solution : Case 1

	Woman 29 yrs	*Woman 66 yrs*	*HUF*	*Firm/D.Co*
Tax on Total Income on Rs. 2,90,000	33,500	25,000	37,000	87,000
Less : Rebates u/s 88E *(Note 1)*	23,103	17,241	25,517	30,000
Tax payable	10,397	7,759	11,483	57,000
Add : Surcharge	N.A.	N.A.	N.A.	5,700
Tax payable	10,397	7,759	11,483	62,700
Add : Education cess @ 2%	208	155	230	1,254
Tax Payable	10,604	7,914	11,712	63,954

Note 1 : Rebate u/s 88E

	33,500	25,000	37,000	87,000
	2,90,000	2,90,000	2,90,000	2,90,000
1. Average rate of tax	11.522%	8.621%	12.759%	30%
2. Income from sale and purchase of shares	2,00,000	2,00,000	2,00,000	2,00,000
3. Compute (1 × 2)	23,103	17,241	25,517	60,000
4. STT paid	30,000	30,000	30,000	30,000
5. 3 or 4 whichever is lower is rebate u/s 88E	23,103	17,241	25,517	30,000

Problem 9.18-P2 (PE II-M05) - M 6

Q.1c, M 6 : Total income of Mrs. Priti, aged 64, a resident of Mumbai for the financial year 2006-07 is Rs. 1,60,000. It includes an income of Rs. 22,000 from the business of dealing in shares on which she has paid securities transaction tax of Rs. 1,500. She has also deposited Rs. 15,000 in he P.P.F. account with the State Bank of India. Compute her tax liability for the AY 2007-08.

Ans: 865

9.19. COMPREHENSIVE PROBLEMS

Tax liability question

Problem 9.19-P1 [Hons 2005C]

Mrs. N received the following amounts during the financial year 2006-07

Gross Salary	5,50,000
Family Pension (Rs. 6,000 per month × 12)	72,000
Income of a minor daughter suffering from disability	15,000
Deposited in PPF Account	50,000

Calculate tax liability of Mrs. N for the assessment year 2007-08.

Ans: 1,07,002.

Problem 9.19-P2 [Hons 1999]

The gross total income of a permanently disabled resident individual aged 67 years for the AY 2007-08 consists of the following.

1.	Income from Other Sources	Rs. 60,000
2.	LTCG on sale of house property	Rs. 1,90,000
3.	Cost incurred for construction of house property	Rs. 35,000

Find out his tax liability for the AY 2007-08.

Ans: 1,020

Problem 9.19-P3 [Hons 1998]

Compute his taxable income and tax liability for AY 2007-08 from the following information. Income of Mrs. T who has attained the age of 65 years during the PY 2006-07, shows his income of Rs. 2,10,000 after claiming deduction u/s 80DD in respect of dependent disabled sister. During the PY 2006-07 she also contributes Rs. 6,000 to PPF A/c. You are required to compute her corrected total income and tax liability for the AY 2007-08 if she is (a) Resident in India (b) Non Resident in India.

Ans: 3,876; 14,484.

Problem 9.19-P4 [Hons 1996]

Mrs. X (date of birth: July 15, 1937) is a person of Indian origin having British passport. Income of Mrs. X chargeable to tax in India for the AY 2007-08 is Rs. 2,60,000 (which includes LTCG on sale of gold of Rs. 1,50,000 and LTCG STT paid Rs. 5,000 and STCG STT paid Rs. 9,000). She contributes Rs. 1,000 in PPF and Rs. 16,000 towards medical insurance premium on 1-1-2007. Her husband who is resident in India is suffering from cancer. Medical expenditure incurred for treatment of cancer Rs. 48,000. Compute tax liability for the AY 2007-08 if she is (a) resident (b) non-resident.

Ans: 18,666; 31,518.

Total Income and Tax liability questions

Problem 9.19-P5 [Hons 2006]

X, an Indian citizen gives the following particulars of his income and expenditure for the previous year 2006-07 :

	Rs.
Business income	1,10,000
Long-term capital gain	2,00,000
Short term capital gain on sale of shares taxable	10,000
Other short-term capital gains	5,000
Donation of Prime Minister's National Relief Fund	11,000
Donation to government of India for family planning	3,000
Donation to an approved institution	9,000
Payment of medical Insurance. Premium on his own wife	5,000

Determine the net income and tax liability of X for the assessment year 2007-08.

Ans: 40,188.

Problem 9.19-P6 [Hons 2006C]

Find out the tax liability of Shri X for the Assesment year 2007-08 :

Long-term capital gain on sale of shares on which Securities Transaction Tax has been paid	1,00,000
Short-term capital gain on sale of shares on which Securities Transaction Tax has been paid	20,000
Long-term capital gain on Gold	15,000
Short-term capital gain on other Assets	12,000
Income from Business	1,28,000
Deposit in PPF	10,000
Contribution for LIC premium of his dependent mother	5,000
Spent on dependent mother's cancer treatment	40,000

Ans: 3,060.

Problem 9.19-P7 (PE II - N02) - M 6

Q.2a : For the assessment year 2007-08, the gross total income of X was Rs. 3,36,240 which includes long term capital gains of Rs. 45,000 and short term capital gains of Rs. 1,08,000 from sale of house property. The gross total income also includes interest income from banks of Rs. 80,000. X has invested in PPF Rs. 60,000 and also paid a medical insurance premium Rs. 11,000. X also contributed Rs. 25,000 to public charitable trust eligible for deduction under section 80G. X invested in Equity Linked Saving Scheme of Rs. 12,000. Compute the total income and tax thereon of X, who is 70 years old as on March 31, 2007.

Ans: 2,42,830; 11,797. [45,000+1,08,000+80,000+1,03,240=3,36,240–72,000–10,412–11,000=2,42,828]

Problem 9.19-P8 (Typical)

Srininvas had the following incomes during the financial year 2006-07 :

(i) Profits from business Rs. 35,000.

(ii) Interest received from Shruti Rs. 1,800 who is an Engineer in Maharashtra Government.

(iii) Interest received on Fixed Deposit with the firm M/s Mohan Lal Sohan Lal Rs. 3,000.

(iv) Interest received on Bank of Baroda Saving Bank Account Rs. 3,060.

(v) Interest received on Fixed Deposits Account for 2 years in Allahabad Bank Rs. 1,800.

(vi) Interest received on Delhi Government Securities Rs. 11,010 in January, 2007.

(vii) Dividend received from the units of UTI Rs. 4,000.

(viii) Monthly rent received from residential house property Rs. 6,000. Municipal taxes in respect of this house are paid @ 15% p.a. Rs. 12,000.

(ix) He received Rs. 1,20,000 from the sale of gold ornaments which he had purchased in 1997-98 for Rs. 41,340. Within 6 months from the sale of these ornaments he purchased a residential house for Rs. 40,000.

(x) He also works on a part time basis in a foreign company from where he draws a total emolument of Rs. 67,333.

(xi) During the previous year he donated Rs. 12,000 to an approved educational institution of National eminence and gave Rs. 16,000 to government for the promotion of family planning programme. He also invests Rs. 10,000 in ULIP of UTI.

Compute the total income and tax liability of Srinivas for the Assessment year 2007-08.

Ans: 1,68,520; 10,741. [35,000+1,800+3,000+3,060+900+11,010+0+47,600+36,787+67,333= 2,06,490–10,000–27,970=1,68,520]

STRATEGY MAKER

Points in 1 to 10	Overall Points 7; Practical 7; Theory 6.
Type of problem	Difficult. "Ab bahot ho gaya. I cannot go further". This is the kind of reaction you might be experiencing when you finish this chapter. Do not worry. Let me tell you this is the beginning of income tax. Relax for 3 hours. But how? Start all over from first Chapter. Just revise it in 3 hours. You will feel not only confident but shall have a sense of pride that you know income tax. Your hard work is the best weapon. Generally practical questions that are asked are attached with salary. Sometimes separate practical questions are also asked.
What to expect (DU)	Everything.
CA (PE II)	Everything.

For your mind

" Climb High; Climb far.
Your goal the sky; Your aim the star"
- inscribed at William College

Keep Running

Left over income

INCOME FROM OTHER SOURCES

TOPIC 10.01 *SECTION 56.* CHARGEABILITY

56(1). Income which is not chargeable to tax under any of the first four heads is chargeable under the head 'Income from Other Sources' and also such income should not be exempt from tax.

56(2). It lays down the indicative list of incomes which are charged under the head 'Income from Other Sources'.

Do remember if any of the incomes which does not fall under section 56(2) may fall under section 56(1) and such income shall be taxed under the head 'Other Sources'.

TOPIC 10.02 *SECTION 57(iii).* DEDUCTIONS ALLOWED

Any expenditure (not being in the nature of capital expenditure) laid out or expended wholly and exclusively for the purpose of making or earning such income is allowed as deduction.

As per section 58 personal expenses are not allowed as deduction.

TOPIC 10.03 ENUMERATE THE INCOMES CHARGEABLE UNDER THE HEAD 'INCOME FROM OTHER SOURCES'

(A) FOLLOWING INCOMES SINCE NOT CHARGEABLE UNDER THE HEAD 'SALARY' THEREFORE CHARGEABLE UNDER THE HEAD 'INCOME FROM OTHER SOURCES'

1. *Director's sitting fees, commission etc.* : Fees for attending the Board Meeting is always charged under the head Income from Other Sources. However other remuneration or commission may be charged under the head Income from Salary if directors are employed as the employee of the Company. However if the Directors are not appointed as the employee then any remuneration received by them shall be charged under the head Income from Other Sources. Deduction u/s 57(iii) is allowed.

   Deduction u/s 57(iii) is allowed : Any revenue expenditure incurred for the purpose of earning such income is allowed as deduction.

2. *Examinership remuneration* : The remuneration for checking the answer sheet is charged under the head Income from Other Sources. Deduction u/s 57(iii) is allowed.

3. *Remuneration received by Members of Parliament* : The remuneration is charged under the head Income from Other Sources since MPs or MLAs are not the servant of the Government. Deduction u/s 57(iii) is allowed.
4. *Family pension* : Family pension means a regular monthly amount payable by the employer to a person belonging to the family of an employee in the event of his death. It is chargeable in the hands of legal heirs of the deceased.

   Section 57(iia). A standard deduction of 1/3 of pension or Rs. 15,000 whichever is less is allowed.

(B) FOLLOWING INCOMES SINCE NOT CHARGEABLE UNDER THE HEAD 'HOUSE PROPERTY' THEREFORE CHARGEABLE UNDER THE HEAD 'INCOME FROM OTHER SOURCES'.

1. *Income from Subletting* : It is charged under the head Income from Other Sources since the assessee who has further let out the building is not the owner of the building. Deduction of rent paid to the owner is allowed as deduction. Deduction u/s 57(iii) is allowed.
2. *Rent from a vacant piece of plot of land* : It is charged under the head Income from Other Sources since there doesn't exist a building. Deduction u/s 57(iii) is allowed.

(C) FOLLOWING INCOMES SINCE NOT CHARGEABLE UNDER THE HEAD 'BUSINESS' THEREFORE CHARGEABLE UNDER THE HEAD 'INCOME FROM OTHER SOURCES'.

1. *Interest on Bank deposits* : It is charged under the head Income from Other Sources if account is held as investment. Deduction u/s 57(iii) is allowed.
2. *Interest on Deposit with companies* : It is charged under the head Income from Other Sources if account is held as investment. Deduction u/s 57(iii) is allowed.
3. *Insurance commission* : It is charged under the head Income from Other Sources. Deduction u/s 57(iii) is allowed.
4. *Agricultural income from agricultural land situated outside India* : It is charged under the head Income from Other Sources. However if there is an agricultural income from a land situated in India then such income is exempt under section 10(1). Deduction u/s 57(iii) is allowed.
5. *Royalty income* : It is charged under the head Income from Other Sources. It is also for eligible for 80QQB or 80RRB deductions if certain conditions are satisfied. Deduction u/s 57(iii) is allowed.
6. *Interest on delayed refund of income tax* : It is charged under the head Income from Other Sources. However refund of tax is not taxable since it is not an income. Deduction u/s 57(iii) is allowed.
7. *Section 56(2). Profit from activity of owning and maintaining race horses* : This income is chargeable under the 'Income from Other Sources'.

   Deduction allowed : Any allowances or expenses incurred in connection with activity of owning and maintaining race horses is allowed as deduction.

(D) OTHER INCOMES CHARGEABLE UNDER THE HEAD 'INCOME FROM OTHER SOURCES'

(a) 56(2)(ii). Income from letting out of plant & machinery, furniture :

Income from machinery, plant or furniture belonging to the assessee and let on hire, if not charged under the head business, is chargeable to income-tax under the head "Income from Other Sources".

(b) 56(2)(iii). Income from composite letting of plant & machinery, furniture with building

Where an assessee lets on hire machinery, plant or furniture belonging to him and also buildings, and the letting of the buildings is inseparable from the letting of the said machinery, plant or furniture, the income from such letting, is chargeable to income-tax under the head "Income from Other Sources".

Problem 10.03-P1

M/s. L.L. Ltd. constructed a cinema theatre at the cost of Rs. 75 lakh. The cost of land, building, machinery and furniture was Rs. 5 lakh, Rs. 40 lakh, Rs. 20 lakh and Rs. 10 lakh respectively. Due to financial problems, the company could not run the theatre. Therefore it was given on a composite lease to M/s. R.S. Ltd. at an annual lease rent of Rs. 20 lakh.

Discuss the taxability of the lease rent with reference to various heads of income. If M/s. L.L. Ltd. had paid interest of Rs. 5 lakh on borrowed capital, compute its income under the appropriate head of income.

Ans: Rs. 7,00,000 is taxable under the head other sources.

(c) Section 56(2)(ib). Casual Income

1. *Definition of casual income :*

   Meaning of lottery It includes winnings from prizes awarded to any person by draw of lots or by chance or in any other manner whatsoever, under any scheme or arrangement by whatever name called.

   Meaning of "card game" and other game of any sort. It includes any game show, an entertainment programme on television or electronic mode, in which people compete to win prizes or any other similar game. We shall call this type of income to be casual income & rate of tax to be casual rate.

2. *58(4).* No deduction (in respect of expenses incurred to earn such casual income) shall be allowed in connection with income from lotteries, crossword puzzles, races, card games, gambling etc.

3. No deduction u/s 80C to 80U is allowed from casual income. However rebate u/s 88E is allowed from tax on casual income.

4. *115BB.* Rate of tax levied is @ 30% flat rate + surcharge and cess as applicable.

(d) Section 10(10D). Amount received under Life Insurance Policy

Any sum received under a life insurance policy, including the sum allocated by way of bonus on such policy is taxable under the head 'Other Sources' if—

(a) any sum is received under section 80DD(3); or

(b) any sum received under a Keyman insurance policy; or

   It means a life insurance policy taken by a person on the life of another person who is or was the employee of the first-mentioned person or is or was connected in any manner whatsoever with the business of the first-mentioned person.

(c) any sum received under an insurance policy issued on or after the 1-4-2003 in respect of which the premium payable for any of the years during the term of the policy exceeds 20% of the actual capital sum assured.

However where any sum is received on the death of a person it is fully exempt from tax u/s 10(10D).

(e) 56(2)(v). Gifts

1. Where any sum of money
2. exceeding Rs. 50,000 in aggregate
3. is received without consideration
4. by an individual or a Hindu undivided family
5. from any person or persons
6. on or after 1-4-2006,

The whole of such sum shall be chargeable to Income-tax under the head "Income from Other Sources". If any of the above 6 conditions are not satisfied then such sum is not taxable since treated as capital receipt.

Note:

1. Where gift is received in kind of any value is not taxable. *E.g.* Mr. X receives jewellery worth Rs. 2 crore from his friend.
2. Where the sum of money exceeds Rs. 50,000 in aggregate from person(s) in a previous year it is taxable. Mr. X receives Rs. 15,000 each from his 5 friends. Whole of Rs. 75,000 is taxable. However if the amount received is Rs. 10,000 each from his 5 friends it is not taxable.

However, this clause shall not apply to following transactions.

(a) Gifts received from any relative on any occasion not taxable. *E.g.* Gift received on birthday from a relative not taxable however gift received from a friend is taxable; or

(b) Gifts received from any person on the occasion of the marriage of the individual. *E.g.* gift received on marriage from a relative or a friend not taxable; or

(c) Gifts received under a will or by way of inheritance; or

(d) Gifts received in contemplation of death of the payer.

(e) Money received from local authority.

(f) Money received from any fund, foundation, university, other educational insitiution, hospital, medical insitiution, any trust or insitiution referred to in section 10(23C).

(g) Money received from a charitable institute regesitered u/s 12AA.

Meaning of "relative" (i) spouse of the individual, (ii) brother or sister of the individual, (iii) brother or sister of the spouse of the individual, (iv) brother or sister of either of the parents of the individual, (v) any lineal ascendant or descendant of the individual, (vi) any lineal ascendant or descendant of the spouse of the individual, and (vii) spouse of a person referred to in items (ii) to (vi) mentioned above.

TOPIC 10.04 COMPUTATION OF INCOME FROM OTHER SOURCES

Income specified above is chargeable under the head 'Other Sources'	8,000
Less : Deductions u/s 57 if applicable	2,000
Income from Other Sources	6,000

Problem 10.04-P1

Mr. X attends a Board Meeting at Delhi for which he receives a fees of Rs. 10,000. He incurs a travelling expenditure of Rs. 2,000 for attending the Board meeting.

Mr. X also gets interest on Central Govt. Securities of Rs. 16,000. Collection charges being Rs. 100. Compute Income from Other Sources.

Solution

Computation of Income from Other Sources

Board Sitting fees (10,000 – 2,000)	8,000
Interest from Central Govt. Securities (16,000 – 100)	15,900
Income from Other Sources	23,900

Problem 10.04-P2

Mr. Taxcrazy furnishes the following particulars of his income for the PY ending 31st March, 2007 :

1.	Interest on securities *(held as investment)* – collection charges Rs. 200.	5,000
2.	Dividend from a foreign company – collection charges Rs. 9,000.	21,000
3.	Dividend from an Indian company – collection charges Rs. 100	2,000
4.	Family pension	6,000 p.m.
5.	Lottery income *(Cost of lottery ticket Rs. 3,000)*	7,000
6.	Refund of income tax including interest of Rs. 200	1,200
7.	Board sitting fees at Mahe *(Rs. 2,000 incurred for travelling to Mahe)*	10,000
8.	Gift received from a friend on the occasion of his first wedding anniversary	51,000

Find out the Gross Total income for the AY 2007-08.

Ans: 1,40,000. [4,800+12,000+0+57,000+7,000+200+8,000+51,000=1,40,000]

Problem 10.04-P3 (PE II - M05) - M 6

Mr. Y submits the following information pertaining to the year ended 31st March, 2007 :

(i) On 30-11-2005, when he attained the age of 60, his friends in India gave a flat at Surat as a gift, each contributing a sum of Rs. 20,000 in cash. The cost of the flat purchased using the various gifts was Rs. 3.4 lakhs.

(ii) His close friend abroad sent him a cash gift of Rs. 75,000 through his relative, for the above occasion.

(iii) Mr. Y sold the above flat on 31-1-2007 for Rs. 3.6 lakhs. The Registrar's valuation for stamp duty purposes was Rs. 3.7 lakhs. Neither Mr. Y nor the buyer questioned the value fixed by the Registrar.

(iv) He has purchased some equity shares in X Pvt. Ltd. on 5-2-2006 for Rs. 3.5 lakhs. These shares were sold on 15-3-2007 for Rs. 2.8 lakhs.

You are requested to calculate the total income of Mr. Y for the assessment year 2007-08.

Ans: 1,05,000; Long term loss can be set off only with long term capital gain.

TOPIC 10.05 *SECTION 145*. BASIS OF CHARGEABILITY

Income under this head is recognised either on mercantile basis or on cash basis depending upon the method of accounting regularly followed by the assessee.

1. Where the assessee follows Mercantile System of accounting the income would be taxable in the year when income accrues or is earned irrespective of year of receipt.

2. Where the assessee follows cash system of accounting the income would be chargeable to tax in the year of receipt irrespective of the year when it is earned.

The same method is equally applied for claiming deduction on account of expenditure. However dividend is chargeable as per the method specified under section 8. (Discussed later)

TOPIC 10.06 *SECTION 56(2)(id)*. INTEREST ON SECURITIES

(A) UNDER WHICH HEAD INTEREST ON SECURITIES IS TAXABLE

1. Where securities are held as *stock in trade* interest is chargeable under the head 'Profit from Business'. Deduction allowed u/s 28 to 44D.
2. Where securities are held as *investment* interest is chargeable under the head 'Income from Other Sources'. Deduction allowed u/s 56 to 59.

(B) COMPUTATION OF INTEREST

1. Interest is computed on due basis but is chargeable to tax as per the method of accounting followed by the assessee.
2. Interest on securities falls due on the date specified by the issuing authority. These dates are either quarterly, half yearly or yearly. It means that the amount of interest to be charged to tax does not depend upon the holding period of securities. It depends that, on the date when interest falls due, whose name appears in the register of security holders kept with the company.
3. Whole of interest which falls due on the due date is chargeable to tax, to that person, even if the securities are held by him for a day.
4. Whole of such interest which falls due to an assessee is chargeable to tax in a particular PY as per the method of accounting followed by the assessee.

Illustration 10.06-P1

(A) Mr. Taxcrazy on 11-12-2005 purchases 7% unlisted debentures of Timken Ltd. for Rs. 90,000 par value Rs. 1,00,000. On 25-12-2006 he sells 50% of his debentures for Rs. 51,000. Due date of interest Jan. 1 every year. He received his interest income on 31-3-2007. Compute interest income chargeable to tax for the AY 2006-07 and 2007-08 if (a) He maintains account on mercantile basis. (b) He maintains account on cash basis.

(B) Also compute capital gain.

Ans (A) : (a) 7,000; 3,500; (b) 10,500; (B) 6,000.

Solution : Case 1

Due date	*Outstanding amt.*	*Interest*	*Chargeability*
1-1-2006	1,00,000	7,000	AY 2006-07
1-1-2007	50,000	3,500	AY 2007-08

(C) *SECTION 57(i)*. ALLOWABILITY OF DEDUCTION FROM INTEREST

Following deductions are allowed from interest income :

1. *Expenses for earning interest :* Any expenditure incurred in earning interest income is allowed as deduction. Suppose Mr. X borrows Rs. 1,00,000 @ 8% p.a. and invest it in

11% p.a. debentures of KIL Ltd. Interest income shall be 11% of 1,00,000 - 8% of 1,00,000 = Rs. 3,000.

2. *Collection charges :* Sometimes Banks, to encash the cheque, collects some charges known as collection charges. Collection charges depends upon the amount of cheque. Suppose Mr. X receives a cheque of Rs. 11,000 and bank collects collection charges @ 0.05%. In such case collection charges shall be 0.50% of 11,000 = Rs. 55.

Problem 10.06-P2

Compute the amount of interest taxable under the head Other Sources for the AY 2007-08.

1. Mr. Taxcrazy borrows Rs. 40,000 @ 5% p.a. on 1-9-2006 which he invests in 9% p.a. debentures. Due date of interest first January every year. Amount of TDS Rs. 100. Collection charges 1%.
2. Mr. Taxcrazy borrows Rs. 2,00,000 @ 6% p.a. on 1-7-2006 which he invests in 7% p.a. debentures. On 1-11-2006, he sells Rs. 40,000 debentures. Due date of interest first December every year. Amount of TDS Rs. 400. Collection charges 1%.
3. Mr. Taxcrazy borrows Rs. 80,000 @ 6% p.a. on 1-5-2006 which he invests in 7% p.a. debentures. On 1-8-2006, he sells Rs. 50,000 debentures. Due date of interest first January and first July every year. Amount of TDS Rs. 300. Collection charges 1%.

Ans: (1) 3,600–1,167–35=2,398 (2) 11,200–9,000–108=2,092 (3) 3,850–4,400–36 = –586.

(D) *SECTION 10(15)*. INTEREST ON THE FOLLOWING SECURITIES ARE EXEMPT FROM TAX

1. Interest on investment in
   (a) Post Office Cash Certificates.
   (b) Post Office National Savings Certificates. (12 years / 7 years)
   (c) Post Office Saving Bank Accounts.
   (d) Post Office Cumulative Time Deposit (CTD) scheme.
   (e) Schemes of Fixed Deposits governed by the Post Office (Fixed Deposits) Rules 1968.
2. Interest exemptions available to NRI's or Non-Resident
   (a) Non Resident (Non-Repatriable) Rupee Deposit Scheme.
   (b) NRI Bonds — 1998 issued by State Bank of India.
   (c) NRI Bonds (second series) issued by State Bank of India.
3. Interest exemptions available on securities issued by notified companies.
4. Interest on Bonds issued by local authority and notified by the Central Government.
5. Interest on Govt. securities :
   (a) Interest on 7% Capital Investment Bonds for individual / HUF.
   (b) Interest on 9% or 10% Relief Bonds in case of Individual / HUF.
   (c) Interest on Gold Deposit Bonds issued under Gold Deposit Scheme, 1999.

Illustration 10.06-P3 (Typical)

X had the following investments during the year 2006-07 :

	Amount invested	*Gross interest*	*TDS*
9% Relief bonds	50,000	4,500	NA
8% Securities of MP Govt.	20,000	1,600	NA
11% less-tax listed debentures of Surf Ltd.	1,00,000	5,500	10.2%
12% less-tax non listed debentures of Areil Ltd.	10,000	1,200	20.4%

Interest in all cases is payable on January 1 every year. On December 1, 2006 X sells Rs. 50,000 11% debentures of Surf Ltd.

On 1-8-2006 he borrows Rs. 2,00,000 at 3% p.a. and invest in 5% listed debentures of Classic Ltd. (Due date of interest January 1 and July 1 every year)

He pays 1% commission to bank for collecting interest on securities.

Business Income Rs. 10,50,000. Investment in NSC VIII issue Rs. Rs. 80,000. Interest accrued in NSC Rs. 21,000.

Determine the total income of X for the AY 2007-08 on the assumption that he maintains account on mercantile basis and none of the interest is received in the FY 2006-07. *(Apply TDS provisions wherever applicable)*

Solution

1. 8% securities of MP Govt.	1,600.00	
Less : 1% collection charges (1% of 1,600)	16.00	1,584
2. 11% less-tax listed debentures of Surf Ltd.		
(11% of 1,00,000 / 2)	5,500.00	
Less : 1% collection charges i.e. 1% (5,500 – 561)	49.39	5,450.61
3. 12% less-tax non listed debentures of Areil Ltd.	1,200.00	
Less : 1% collection charges i.e. 1% (1,200 – 244.80)	9.55	1,190.45
4. 5% listed debentures of Classic Ltd.		
(5% of 2,00,000 / 2)	5,000.00	
Less : 1% collection charges i.e. *1% (5,000 – 510)*	(44.90)	
Less : Interest on loan borrowed @ 3%.		
3% of 2,00,000 × 8 / 12	(4,000.00)	955.10
Income from Other Sources		9,180.15
Business Income		10,50,000.00
Gross Total Income		10,59,180.15
Less : Deduction u/s 80C		1,00,000.00
Total Income (rounded off)		9,59,180.15

Problem 10.06-P4 (CA - M92) - M 5

Q.3a : X, who maintains books of accounts on mercantile basis borrowed Rs. 22,000 at 6 per cent annum on August 1, 2006 and invested it in 7 per cent tax-free securities of the Central Government purchased at Rs. 110 (par value Rs. 100), due date of interest, January 1 and July 1 every year. On August 31, 2006, he borrowed Rs. 30,000 at 6 per cent per annum for investing in 10 per cent listed debentures of C Ltd. (date of payment of interest April 15 every year). Interest on borrowings for the period ending March 31, 2007 is, however, paid by X on April 15, 2007. He pays 2 per cent commission to his bank on net amount of interest realised. Compute his income chargeable under the head "Income from other sources".

Ans: (1,244).

Problem 10.06-P5 (CA - M91) - M 5

Q.3d : K, an individual, holds 8 per cent Government of India Loan, 2007 of the face value of Rs. 2,50,000. Interest on this holding is paid on May 1 and November 1 every year. He spends Rs. 1,000 every year by way of bank charges and commission for realising the interest. For the assessment year 2007-08, indicate what will be the amount of interest that would be brought to tax under the income-tax and under what head ?

Ans: 19,000.

Problem 10.06-P6 (CS-J98) - M 10

Q.4b : An assessee who maintains books of account on mercantile basis borrowed Rs. 33,000 at 7 per cent per annum on August 1, 2006 and invested it in 8 per cent tax-free securities of the Central Government purchased at Rs. 110 (face value Rs. 100), due date of interest is January 1 and 1 July 1 every year. On August 31, 2006, he borrowed Rs. 40,000 at 7 per cent per annum for investing it in 11 per cent listed debentures of C Ltd. (date of payment of interest April 15 every year). Interest on borrowing for the period ending March 31, 2007 is, however, paid by the assessee on April 25, 2007. Compute his income chargeable under the head income from other sources.

Ans: (1,973).

Problem 10.06-P7 (Typical)

X had the following investments during the year 2006-07:

(i) Rs. 15,000 10% Govt. paper.

(ii) Rs. 40,000 10% debentures of Cloth Mill Company.

(iii) Rs. 7,500 10% debentures of Jaipur Spinning Mills.

(iv) Rs. 20,000 15% Preference Shares of an Indian company.

Interest on above investment is payable on 1st June and 1st Dec. every year.

On 1st September, 2006 he bought Rs. 20,000 8% U.P. Govt. loan at Rs. 20,600 the interest on which is payable on 30th June and 31st December. For this purpose he took a loan from his Bankers of Rs. 12,000 @ 8% p.a. The Bank also charged 2% commission on realisation of interest and dividend and 1% commission on purchase of securities. Debentures of Cloth Mills Co. are listed at Bombay Stock Exchange while debentures of Jaipur Spinning Mills are not listed at any Stock Exchange.

Find out the taxable income from other sources assuming that interest and dividend in each case is paid by account payee cheque only.

Ans: 6,352. [1,470+3,920+738+784=6,912–560=6,352]

TOPIC 10.07 *SECTION 56(2)(i)*. TAXABILITY OF DIVIDEND

(A) UNDER WHICH HEAD DIVIDEND TAXABLE

Dividend income is always taxable under the head 'Income from Other Sources' whether shares are held as stock in trade or as an investment.

For the purpose of set off of losses dividend income shall be treated as income treated under the head 'Profit from business'.

57(i). Deduction shall be allowed in connection with earning such income like interest and collection charges.

(B) BASIS OF CHARGE

Section 8(a). Final Dividend : It is chargeable to tax on the date of declaration of dividend in the Annual General Meeting.

Section 8(b). Interim Dividend : It is chargeable to tax in the year of receipt.

(C) DIVIDEND INCOME FROM THE FOLLOWING SOURCES ARE EXEMPT FROM TAX

1. *Section 10(34)*. Dividend from Indian Company is exempt in the hands of shareholders. However Dividend from foreign company is fully taxable.
2. *Section 10(35)*. Income received in respect of the units of a Mutual Fund specified under section 10(*23D*) or units of UTI is exempt from tax.

TOPIC 10.08 GROSSING UP OF INCOME

(A) CONCEPT

1. Under the TDS scheme, the person, who is making the payments under the specified sources, is required to deduct tax at source at the prescribed rate. The person who deducts tax is known as tax deducter.
2. The tax deducted at source is regarded as income of the assessee and it is included in his gross total income.
3. If the income given in the question is net of TDS (it means tax has been deducted at source), it has to be grossed up.
4. Grossing up of tax depends upon the rate of TDS. TDS table is given on next page.
5. Grossing up of income is done through following formula :

$$\text{Gross income} = \frac{\text{Amount (net of TDS)}}{100 - \text{Rate of TDS}} \times 100$$

(B) RATE OF DEDUCTION OF TAX AT SOURCE TO BE DEDUCTED DURING THE FINANCIAL YEAR 2006-07

(i) 193. Interest on securities

	Rate of TDS
1. Payee is resident non-corporate assessee	
(a) Listed securities	10% + surcharge + Ed. cess
(b) Unlisted securities	20% + surcharge + Ed. cess
2. Payee is a domestic company	20% + surcharge + Ed. cess

In the following cases interest is not subjected to TDS, therefore grossing up of income is not applicable.

(a) Securities of Central Govt. and State Govt. not subjected to TDS.

(b) Interest on listed debentures payable to an individual by an account payee cheque and the aggregate amount of interest during the previous year do not exceed Rs. 2,500 then such interest payment is not subjected to TDS.

(ii) 194A. Interest other than interest on securities

1.	Payee is resident non-corporate assessee	10% + surcharge + Ed. cess
2.	Payee is a domestic company	20% + surcharge + Ed. cess

No tax shall be deducted at source if during the financial year, interest payable by the payer to payee does not exceed Rs. 5,000.

(iii) 194B. Winning from lotteries, crossword puzzles, card games and any other game

Rate of TDS is 30% + surcharge + Ed. cess if the payment exceeds Rs. 5,000 for all types of assessee.

(iv) 194BB. Winning from horse race

Rate of TDS is 30% + surcharge + Ed. cess if the payment exceeds Rs. 2,500 for all types of assessee.

(v) 194I. Payment of rent

1.	Payee is resident ind or HUF	15% + surcharge + Ed. cess
2.	Any other case	20% + surcharge + Ed. cess

No tax shall be deducted at source if during the financial year, rent payable by the payer to payee does not exceed Rs. 1,20,000.

(vi) Surcharge and education cess is levied in the following cases

	Ind / HUF	*Firm / Company*
Surcharge	10% if payment exceeds Rs. 10,00,000	10% at all levels of payment
Education cess	2% at all levels of payment	2% at all levels of payment

Illustration 10.08-P1

(A) Mr. Taxcrazy receives interest on listed debentures of Rs. 8,980 (net of TDS). Find out the gross interest which is included in his income.

Solution : Rate of TDS shall be 10% + 2% cess = 10.20%. Surcharge is not applicable since the payment does not exceed Rs. 10,00,000. Applying formula:

It is a simple formula whereby we assume gross interest to be x. Therefore tax deducted is 10.20% of x. The amount which is received shall be x – 10.20% of x = 8,980, solving x = Rs. 10,000.

$$\frac{8,980}{100-10.20} \times 100 = 10,000.$$

Problem 10.08-P2

Compute the gross amount chargeable to tax from the following information if the recipient is an (i) Individual (ii) Firm (iii) Company.

1. Received interest of Rs. 9,000 is from unlisted debentures.
2. Received interest on unlisted debentures Rs. 11,00,000.

3. Received interest of Rs. 2,500 from listed debentures.
4. Received as first prize from Lotto lottery Rs. 90,000.
5. Received Rs. 9,00,000 as rent for letting out a building to a company.
6. Received Rs. 4,000 as interest on fixed deposit from Canara Bank.

Ans: Ind : 11,307; 14,18,257; 2,500; 1,29,683; 10,82,121; 4,000; Firm : 11,604; 14,18,257; 2,816; 1,35,665; 11,60,392; 4,000; Company : 11,604; 14,18,257; 3,223; 1,35,665; 11,60,392; 4,000.

(C) TYPES OF SECURITIES

1. Tax free Govt. securities : Interest on tax free Govt. securities are fully exempt from tax u/s 10(15) and therefore interest on such securities are not subjected to TDS provision. Such interest since exempted do not form part of total income.
2. Less tax (taxable) Govt. securities : W.e.f. 31-5-1997 Govt. securities are not subjected to TDS provision therefore grossing up is not done.
3. Tax free Non Govt. securities : Tax free Non Govt. securities are not tax free therefore such interest is required to be grossed up.
4. Less tax (taxable) Non Govt. securities : On these securities tax is deducted at source therefore grossing of interest is done.

10.09 COMPREHENSIVE PROBLEMS

Simple and Difficult

Problem 10.09-P1 [CA N00]

From the following particulars, you are required to work out the tax payable by Mrs. X, aged 70 years, in respect of the assessment year 2007-08 :

Family pension gross	75,000
Income from house property (net)	1,24,000
Income from other source	
• Interest on bank deposits	15,000
• Income from horse racing	20,000
Capital gains on transfer of land - long term	15,000
Agricultural income	25,000
Total income	2,74,000

Ans: 2,34,000; 12,036.

Problem 10.09-P2 [CA N01]

Y, a writer and a professional, furnishes the following particulars for the previous year ended March 31, 2007 :

Royalty on school books	1,42,000
Expenditure on book	8,000
Income from profession	2,30,000
Deposited in public provident fund and ULIP on March 15, 2007	80,000

You are required to compute taxable income and tax payable for assessment year 2007-08.

Ans: 2,84,000; 35,904.

Typical

Problem 10.09-P3

Mr. P. Chidambram is the retired professor of the Department of Law in Delhi University. He is also a Member of Parliament. The particulars of his income for the FY 2006-07 are as follows:

1. Salary received as a Member of Parliament Rs. 8,000 p.m.
2. Income from articles published in the Business Today Rs. 15,000.
3. Remuneration received for the lectures delivered in Faculty of Law Rs. 26,500.
4. Remuneration received for working as an examiner of various universities Rs. 12,000.
5. He is author of many text-books. He received royalty of Rs. 8,00,000 in the PY. He claims the following deductions out of his income :
   (a) Salary of a clerk Rs. 60,000.
   (b) Books purchased for revising the books Rs. 20,000.
   (c) Telephone expenses in connection with the printing and sale of book Rs. 10,000.
6. He has fixed deposits of Rs. 5,00,000 in ICICI Bank. He earned Rs. 14,000 (gross) on 1-5-2006 as interest on such deposits.
7. He earned Rs. 2,000 in March 2007 from Playwin lottery. He had spent Rs. 200 during the PY on the purchase of lotteries ticket.
8. He got an income of Rs. 9,800 from agricultural land in Japan and Rs. 3,500 from another agricultural land in Tamilnadu.
9. His other incomes are :
   (a) Interest received from bonds of the Government of Germany Rs. 6,000 (gross).
   (b) Winning from chess game Rs. 2,400.
   (c) Winning from card games and betting Rs. 1,900.
   (d) Received interest on Relief bonds for a nominal value of Rs. 1,00,000 @ 9% p.a.
   (e) Interest from Public Provident Fund Rs. 5,000.
   (f) Interest on Post Office (CTD) Scheme Rs. 1,520.
10. He purchased a plot of land on 1-7-2006 for constructing a house for himself. On account of remaining busy he could not get the house constructed. Hence on 1-1-2007 he let out this land on a monthly rent of Rs. 6,000 p.m.
11. Dividend from Foreign Company declared on 1-3-2007 received on 1-4-2007 Rs. 6,000.
12. On 1-3-2007 he donates Rs. 30,000 to Govt. for charitable purpose.
13. He paid Rs. 14,000 as medical insurance premium to GIC on health of his Non-Resident Father aged 66 years. It also included Rs. 2,000 as contribution to pension plan of LIC.

Comute his total income for the AY 2007-08.

Ans: 8,92,600. [96,000+15,000+26,500+12,000+7,10,000+14,000+2,000+9,800+6,000+2,400+1,900+18,000+6,000=9,19,600–2,000–10,000–15,000=8,92,600]

Problem 10.09-P4

Sona furnishes the following information for computation of taxable income :

1. He is a director of a company. From there he received salary Rs. 45,000, entertainment allowance Rs. 15,000 and fee Rs. 2,500. He spent on entertainment in respect of the

work of the company Rs. 6,000. Both the company and the director contributes Rs. 5,500 each to recognised provident fund.

2. He worked as invigilator for 45 days in annual examination conducted by the ICAI in May 2006 and November 2006 and received Rs. 2,000 as his remuneration for the same in December 2006.
3. Received a scooter worth Rs. 36,000 (net) and Rs. 6,000 (net) in cash in March 2007 in respect of winning from lottery.
4. He earned interest on Fixed deposit on 1-5-2006 from State Bank of India Rs. 10,000 and from M/s Kissu Ltd. Rs. 6,000.
5. He maintains horses for horse race. During the PY he earned Rs. 48,900 from his business. The income was calculated before deduction of Rs. 19,000 for expenses which were related to this business.
6. He occasionally bets in Horse Race and Camel Race also. During the PY he lost Rs. 13,000 in it.
7. Nestle Swiss Ltd. (a foreign company) proposed an Interim dividend of Rs. 3,000 on February 2006. Dividend warrants posted in April 2006 and payment received in May 2006.
8. Interest from Listed Debenture of Reliable Industries Ltd. Rs. 10,800 (Net).
9. Amount received in respect of a winning in a quiz contest organised by Zee Rs. 1,40,000. (net)
10. Lump sum withdrawal from Public Provident Fund on maturity Rs. 2,00,000.

Ans: 3,76,275. [56,500+100+2,000+60,519+16,000+29,900+3,000+12,027+2,01,729= 3,81,775–5,500=3,76,275]

Problem 10.09-P5

Compute total income and tax liability of Mr. Taxcrazy, resident in India, from the following :

1. He is employed as a Manager (Agricultural production) in a Bio Technology Ltd on a monthly salary of Rs. 20,000. The company is listed in National Stock Exchange Ltd.
2. On a fixed deposit of Rs. 2,00,000 with Bio Technology Ltd (listed) he earned an interest of Rs. 16,110 (Net of TDS) during the previous year.
3. He has let out his farm house on an annual fees of Rs. 3,000. The farm house is located in Portugal. Municipal value of farm house as per Portugal law is Rs. 40,000.
4. Long term capital gain Rs. 1,50,000.
5. Interest accrued in NSC VIII issue which is reinvested Rs. 15,000.
6. Donation to Prime Minister drought relief fund Rs. 8,000.
7. Income from agricultural land situated in Balrampur Rs. 96,000.
8. Agricultural loss brought forward from AY 2005-06 in respect of his land situated in Balrampur — Rs. 30,000.

Ans: 4,31,940; 77,706. [2,40,000+28,000+1,50,000+17,940+15,000=4,50,940–15,000–4,000=4,31,940]

Problem 10.09-P6 [CS J04]

From the following particulars, compute the gross total income of Radha :

(i) She is employe on a part time basis in a fashion designing firm on a monthly salary of Rs. 5,000.

(ii) She has a house property situated in Delhi which has been let out at a rent of Rs. 3,000 p.m.

(iii) She holds the following shares and securities :

- 1,000 Equity shares in X Ltd. of Rs. 10 each, bought @ Rs. 40 per share.
- Rs. 20,000, 8% ICICI Bonds.
- 1,000, 12% Preference shares of Rs. 100 each in Rosa Ltd. a foreign company. Dividend received on 25th March, 2007.
- X Ltd. an Indian company declared 18% equity dividend on 25th March, 2005, but the cheque was received subsequent to 31st March, 2007. Other interest and dividends were, however, duly received.

(iv) She had set up a factory with building, plant, machinery, furniture, etc. However, she decided to give it on hire at a composite rent of Rs. 12,000 p.m.

During the year, she spent Rs. 15,000 for repairs and Rs. 5,000 for insurance of the factory. The depreciation allowable is Rs. 50,000. She had borrowed Rs. 5,00,000 interest thereon. The amount was spent for marriage of her brother.

Ans: 1,72,800. [60,000+25,200+1,600+12,000+74,000=1,72,800]

Problem 10.09-P7

Shri Mani Ram Verma submits details of his income for the previous year ending on 31st March, 2007. You are required to find income from Other Sorces :

(i) Century Mills Limited (a listed company) issued 12% debentures (face value of Rs. 100) at a discount of Rs. 5 on 1-09-2006. Mr. Mani Ram paid Rs. 71,250 for acquiring these debentures. Interest on these debentures is payable on 31st July and 31st January.

(ii) On 1st June, 2006 he hired a house at a rent of Rs. 3,000 per month and sub let the half portion of this house on the same day to another person at a rent of Rs. 2,500 per month.

(iii) He is an authorised Agent for the distribution of Rajasthan Government lottery tickets. For this work he got a commission of Rs. 810 during the previous year.

(iv) Received from Horse Race Rs. 10,410 (net).

(v) Interest on public deposits from a company Rs. 17,800 (Gross).

(vi) Dividend from a Co-operative society of Rs. 1,000.

(vii) Income from agricultural land Rs. 10,000.

(viii) Interest received on listed debentures of Dipa Ltd. Rs. 5,388 (net) Shri Verma claims following expenses :

(ix) Bank commission was charged @ 2% on the amount of dividend and interest realised. He incurred expenses for lottery tickets Rs. 2,000 and expenses in winning horse races Rs. 1,000.

Ans: 54,646. [4,500+10,000+810+15,000+17,444+1,000+5,892=54,646]

Each of us will one day be judged by our standard of life, not by our standard of living; by our measure of giving, not by our measure of wealth; by our simple goodness, not by seeming greatness. *(William Arthur Ward)*

A true commitment is a heartfelt promise to *yourself* from which you will not back down. *(David McNally)*

Keep Running

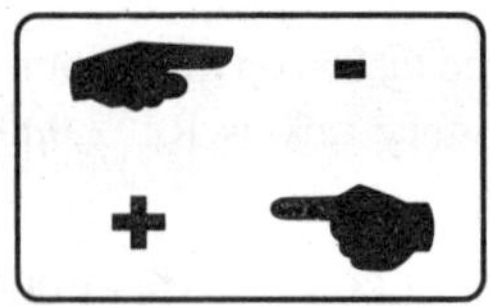

Past, present and future losses - profits

11

SET OFF AND CARRY FORWARD OF LOSSES

TOPIC 11.00 INTRODUCTION

How do you compute Gross Total Income? By adding all five heads of income and making two adjustments. First is clubbing of income and the second is setting off the losses. Clubbing of income is discussed in chapter 14. Let us first discuss set off of losses.

There are certain rules for setting off of the losses which are discussed below.

(A) SETTING OFF THE CURRENT YEAR LOSSES

1. *Section 70.* Set off of loss from one source against income from another source under the same head of income. It talks about losses which can be set off under same heads of income. Also known as Inter source adjustment or Intrahead adjustment.

   E.g. Suppose Income from first house is Rs. 8,000 and loss from second house is Rs. 5,000. In this case loss of Rs. 5,000 shall be set off with Rs. 8,000. Income from House Property shall be Rs. 3,000.

2. *Section 71.* Set off of loss from one head against income from another. It talks about losses which can be set off with different heads of income. Also known as Interhead adjustment.

   E.g. Suppose Income house property is Rs. 8,000 loss and Income from Salary is Rs. 15,000. In this case loss of Rs. 8,000 shall be set off against an income of Rs. 15,000. Gross Total Income shall be Rs. 7,000.

(B) SETTING OFF THE PAST YEAR LOSSES

Carry forward and adjustment of brought forward losses. *(It means adjustment of brought forward loss with the current year income.)*

E.g. Suppose Loss from house property is Rs. 8,000 and Income from Salary is Rs. 2,000. In this case loss of Rs. 8,000 shall be set off against an income of Rs. 2,000. Gross Total Income shall be nil. The remaining house property loss of Rs. 6,000 shall be carried forward to next year.

(C) BASIC RULES FOR SETTING OF OFF THE LOSSES

1. First apply section 70 and then section 71 and lastly adjust brought forward losses to arrive at the Gross Total Income.

2. It is mandatory to set off the losses.
3. No loss can be set off against income which is exempt from tax.

TOPIC 11.01 RULES TO SET OFF OF LOSSES & CARRY FORWARD & SET OFF OF LOSSES

As you know there are 5 heads of income but for set off of losses we are creating 7 heads. *(This is done only to simplify this chapter)*. As you know loss cannot arise under the head Income from Salary. Therefore we are left with 4 heads which are further divided into separate heads. *(refer the table below)*

		Whether loss can be set off within same head S - 70	Whether loss can be set off with different heads S - 71	Whether loss can be carried forward
1st Head. (House Property)	Loss from House Property	Yes	Yes	Yes for 8 AY (S – 71B)
2nd Head. (Business)	Business loss	Yes	Yes (Note 1)	Yes for 8 AY (S – 72)
3rd Head. (Business)	Speculation business loss	Yes	No	Yes for 4 AY (S – 73)
	Note 1 : However as per section 71(2A) loss arising under the head 'business' is not allowed to be set off with Income from Salary			
4th head. (Capital Gain)	Loss under the head capital gain. Short term capital loss (STCL) and long term capital loss (LTCL)	Yes (Note 2)	No	Yes for 8 AY (S - 74)
	Note 2 : LTCL can be set off only against LTCG but never against STCG. However STCL can be set off both from STCG and LTCG.			
5th Head. (Other Sources)	Loss from activity of owning and maintaining race horses	Yes	No	Yes for 4 AY (S - 74A)
6th Head. (Other Sources)	Loss from winnings from races, lotteries, crossword puzzles, etc. (Note 3)	No	No	No
	Note 3 : Also no loss can be set off against the profit from winnings from races, lotteries, crossword puzzles, etc.			
7th Head. (Other Sources)	Other losses	Yes	Yes	No

Illustration 11.01-P1

Compute gross total income and amount of loss allowed to be carried forward to next year.

	Case 1	*Case 2*	*Case 3*	*Case 4*
Income from Salary	20,000	20,000	20,000	20,000
Income from House property	(8,000)	7,000	10,000	9,000
Profit from business	(1,000)	(4,000)	(16,000)	(13,000)

Ans: (1) 12,000; 1,000; (2) 23,000; Nil; (3) 20,000; 6,000; (4) 20,000; 4,000.

Hint : As per section 71(2A) loss from business cannot be set off with income from salary, however house property loss can be set off with income from salary. In this case gross total income is Rs. 12,000 and Rs. 1,000 shall be carried forward to next year.

Illustration 11.01-P2

Compute gross total income and amount of loss allowed to be carried forward to next year.

	Case 1	*Case 2*	*Case 3*	*Case 4*
Income from Salary	20,000	20,000	20,000	20,000
Profit from business	(10,000)	40,000	(15,000)	(30,000)
Profit from speculation business	40,000	(10,000)	(16,000)	5,000

Ans: (1) 50,000; nil (2) 60,000; 10,000; (3) 20,000; 31,000; (4) 20,000; 25,000.

Problem 11.01-P3

Compute gross total income and amount of loss allowed to be carried forward to next year.

	Case 1	*Case 2*	*Case 3*	*Case 4*
STCG	(10,000)	40,000	15,000	(2,000)
LTCG on sale of land	40,000	(10,000)	(6,000)	800
LTCG on sale of shares (STT paid)	90,000	(50,000)	(12,000)	95,601
Income from House Property	nil	5,000	(2,000)	500

Ans: (1) 30,000; nil (2) 45,000; 10,000; (3) 13,000; 6,000; (4) 500; 1,200.

Problem 11.01-P4

Compute gross total income and amount of loss allowed to be carried forward to next year.

	Case 1	*Case 2*	*Case 3*
Profit from activity of owning and maintaining race horses	(10,000)	15,000	(10,000)
Profit from activity of owning and maintaining race camel	40,000	(10,000)	(8,000)

Ans: (1) 40,000; 10,000; (2) 5,000; nil. (3) nil; 18,000

Problem 11.01-P5

Compute gross total income and amount of loss allowed to be carried forward to next year.

	Case 1	*Case 2*	*Case 3*	*Case 4*
Profit from business	(10,000)	40,000	15,000	(2,000)
Winning from horse race	40,000	(10,000)	(6,000)	(80,000)
Winning from camel race	4,000	1,000	(600)	50,000
Profit from activity of owning and maintaining race horses	nil	nil	(1,000)	8,000

Ans: (1) 44,000; 10,000; (2) 41,000; nil; (3) 15,000; 1,000; (4) 56,000; nil.

Problem 11.01-P6

Compute gross total income and amount of loss allowed to be carried forward to next year.

	Case 1	*Case 2*	*Case 3*
Profit from business	(10,000)	40,000	(15,000)
LTCG on sale of land	40,000	(10,000)	(6,000)

Ans: (1) 30,000; nil (2) 40,000; 10,000 (3) nil; 21,000

Problem 11.01-P7

Compute gross total income and amount of loss allowed to be carried forward to next year.

	Case 1	*Case 2*	*Case 3*
Profit from business	(10,000)	40,000	15,000
Agricultural income from a land situated in Punjab	40,000	(10,000)	(6,000)
Agricultural income from a land situated in Karnataka	(30,000)	4,000	1,000

Ans : (1) nil; 10,000; (2) 40,000; nil; (3) 15,000; nil.

Illustration 11.01-P8 (Difficult)

Compute Total Income from the following information for the AY 2007-08.

Particulars	*Source I*	*Source II*	*Source III*
1. Income from Salary	30,000	45,000	51,000
2. Income from House Property	20,000	(10,000)	(30,000)
3. Speculation Business	25,000	(55,000)	25,000
4. Non-speculation Business	40,000	(20,000)	(30,000)
5. STCG on shares (STT paid)	1,000	(2,300)	(4,900)
6. LTCG on sale of land	500	18,000	(100)
7. Profit from activity of owning & maintaining race horses	(5,800)	1,400	1,600
8. Winning from Lotteries	(10,000)	2,000	5,000
9. Interest on debentures	6,000	(1,500)	(7,000)

Solution

First apply section 70 and then section 71 and lastly adjust b.f. losses.

Particulars	*Section 70*	*Section 71*	*C.f. of loss*
1. Income from Salary	30,000 + 45,000 + 51,000	1,26,000	–
2. Income from House Property	20,000 – 10,000 – 30,000	(20,000)	–
3. Speculation Business	25,000 – 55,000 – 25,000	–	(5,000)
4. Non-speculation Business	40,000 – 20,000 – 30,000	(10,000)	–
5. STCG (STT paid)	1,000 – 2,300 – 4,900 = – 6,200	–	–
6. LTCG on sale of land	500 + 18,000 – 100 = 18,400	–	–
Capital Gain (LTCG – STCG)	18,400 – 6,200	12,200	–
7. Profit from activity of owning & maintaining race horses	– 5,800 + 1,400 + 1,600	–	(2,800)
8. Winning from Lotteries	2,000 + 5,000	7,000	–
9. Interest on debentures	6,000 – 1,500 – 7,000	(2,500)	–
Gross Total Income		1,12,700	

Problem 11.01-P9

1. Which are the losses not allowed to be carried forward?
2. For how many years losses can be carried forward?
3. Which are the losses allowed to be set off with different head?
4. In case of interhead adjustment which loss should be given the first priority?
5. Examine the statement 'Loss cannot arise from casual income'.
6. Which are the losses allowed to be carried forward?

Solution

1. There are only two such losses. Casual losses and other losses.
2. Where the losses are allowed to be carried forward it can be carried forward for a maximum period of 8 years except in case of specualtive losses and losses from activity of owning and maintaining horse races where the loss is allowed to be carried forward for 4 assessment years.
3. There are only three such losses. Loss from house property, Non speculation business loss and other losses.
4. Obviously the loss which is not allowed to be carried forward which is 'other losses' under the head Income from Other Sources.

5. Expenditure for earning casual income is not allowed as deduction, Deduction u/s 80C to 80U is not allowed, Casual loss is not allowed to be set off from casual income, No other loss can be set off against the casual income. Therefore 'Loss cannot arise from casual income'.
6. Loss from House Property; Business loss; Capital loss and Loss from activity of owning and maintaining race horses.

CARRY FORWARD & SET OFF OF LOSSES OF PAST YEARS

TOPIC 11.02 *SECTION 71B.* CARRY FORWARD AND ADJUSTMENT OF BROUGHT FORWARD LOSS FROM HOUSE PROPERTY

1. Carry forward of loss from house property is applicable from the AY 99-2000. It means losses of PY 98-99 and later can be adjusted with current year income. Any house property loss of PY 97-98 or earlier years cannot be adjusted and therefore has to be ignored.
2. Brought forward house property loss can be set off only against profit of house property.
3. The loss is allowed to be carried forward to 8 AY.
4. Section 80 is not applicable meaning thereby a loss can be carry forward even if return of loss is not filed in time.

Illustration 11.02-P1 (Typical)

(A) Compute GTI and carry forward of loss from house property for the AY 2007-08 assuming that return of loss for the AY 2004-05 was not filed in time.

	Case 1	*Case 2*	*Case 3*	*Case 4*
Income from Salary	1,000	20,000	10,000	21,000
Income from House Property				
• House 1	3,000	6,000	2,000	(10,000)
• House 2	(1,000)	(8,000)	(13,000)	4,000
• Brought forward loss of AY 98-99	(100)	(6,000)	–	–
• Brought forward loss of AY 2004-05	(500)	(1,000)	–	(18,000)

(B) What if in Case 1 if brought forward house property loss of AY 2004-05 is Rs. 3,500.

Ans (A) : (1) 2,500; nil; (2) 18,000; 1,000; (3) nil; 1,000; (4) 15,000; 18,000 (B) 1,000; 1,500.

Solution : Case 1

Income from Salary		1,000
Income from House Property *(3,000 – 1,000)*	2,000	
Less : Brought forward loss from house property	500	1,500
Gross Total Income		2,500

Solution : Case 2

Income from Salary		20,000
Income from House Property	6,000	
Less : Current year loss from house property	(8,000)	(2,000)
Gross Total Income		18,000

Note

- Since brought forward loss of house property can be adjusted only against income from house property, therefore loss of Rs. 1,000 shall be carried forward to next AY.

TOPIC 11.03 *SECTION 72.* CARRY FORWARD AND ADJUSTMENT OF BROUGHT FORWARD BUSINESS LOSSES

1. Brought forward business loss (non-speculation) can be adjusted against both business profit and speculation profit. However in case where shares are held as stock in trade dividend from such shares shall be treated under the head 'Business'.
2. The business in respect of which a loss is incurred need not be continued.
3. Loss can be set off only by that assessee who has incurred the loss. But it has few exceptions as under :
   (a) 72A. Accumulated business loss of amalgamating company can be carried forward and set off by amalgamated company
   (b) 72A. Accumulated business loss of demerged company can be carried forward and set off by resulting company.
   (c) 72A. Conversion of proprietorship concern into a company.
   (d) 72A. Conversion of firm into a company.
   (e) Losses of business acquired on inheritance u/s 78(2).
4. The loss can be carried forward for 8 AY. Exception to this are in:
   (a) Section 33B
   (b) Section 41
5. *Section 80.* The return of loss should be filed in time otherwise right to carry forward of loss is lost.

TOPIC 11.04 *SECTION 73.* CARRY FORWARD AND ADJUSTMENT OF BROUGHT FORWARD SPECULATION BUSINESS LOSS

1. Brought forward speculation loss can be set off only against speculation profit.
2. The business in respect of which a loss is incurred need not be continued.
3. Loss can be set off only by that assessee who has incurred the loss.
4. The loss can be carried forward for 4 AY.
5. *Section 80.* The return of loss should be filed in time otherwise right to carry forward of losses will be lost.

TOPIC 11.05 *SECTION 74.* CARRY FORWARD AND ADJUSTMENT OF BROUGHT FORWARD LOSS UNDER THE HEAD CAPITAL GAIN

1. Brought forward LTCL can be set off only against LTCG but never against STCG. However brought forward STCL can be set off both from STCG and LTCG.
2. The loss can be carried forward for 8 AY.
3. *Section 80.* The return of loss should be filed in time otherwise right to carry forward of losses will be lost.

TOPIC 11.06 *SECTION 74A.* CARRY FORWARD AND ADJUSTMENT OF BROUGHT FORWARD LOSSES IN OWNING AND MAINTAINING HORSE RACES

1. Brought forward losses from owning and maintenance of horse races are allowed to be set off only against income of such business.
2. The business in respect of which a loss is incurred should be continued.
3. Loss can be set off only by that assessee who has incurred the loss.
4. The loss can be carried forward for 4 AY.
5. *Section 80.* The return of loss should be filed in time otherwise right to carry forward of losses will be lost.

   "*Horse race*" means a horse race upon which wagering or betting may be lawfully made.

TOPIC 11.07 *SECTION 32(2).* CARRY FORWARD AND SET OFF OF UNABSORBED DEPRECIATION

(A) MEANING OF UNABSORBED DEPRECIATION

1. It should be distinguished from current depreciation which is dealt in section 32(1). Whereas unabsorbed depreciation is dealt under section 32(2). It is also known as brought forward depreciation.
2. The unabsorbed depreciation simply means depreciation which is not absorbed by the profit of the business.
3. Do remember there can be no loss under the head profit from business because of depreciation.

Illustration 11.07-P1 (Simple)

	Case 1	*Case 2*	*Case 3*	*Case 4*
Profit from business	40,000	40,000	nil	(10,000)
Current Depreciation	(10,000)	(60,000)	(2,000)	(15,000)
Profit from business	30,000	nil	nil	(10,000)
Unabsorbed Depreciation	nil	(20,000)	(2,000)	(15,000)

(B) RULES FOR TREATMENT OF UNABSORBED DEPRECIATION

1. The unabsorbed depreciation can be set off with any head's of income except casual income and salary income. But it shall be first set off with Business Income.
2. The business in respect of which there is unabsorbed depreciation need not be continued.
3. Loss can be set off only by the assessee who has incurred the loss with certain exception as specified in section 72.
4. The unabsorbed depreciation can be carried forward for indefinite period.
5. The return of loss even if not filed in time, unabsorbed depreciation is allowed to be carried forward.

(C) ORDER OF PRIORITY TO SET OFF LOSSES

1. *Section 35, 36(1)(ix).* Current scientific research capital expenditure and family planning promotion capital expenditure.

2. *Section 32(1)*. Current depreciation.
3. *Section 72*. Brought forward business losses.
4. *Section 36(1)(ix)*. Unabsorbed family planning promotion capital expenditure.
5. *Section 32(2)*. Unabsorbed depreciation.
6. *Section 35(4)*. Unabsorbed scientific research capital expenditure.

Problem 11.07-P2 (Difficult)

Dr. Mohan Singh has presented the following particulars in respect of his income for last four years :

Assessment year	*Profit or loss before depreciation*	*Depreciation for the year*
2004-05	(3,50,000)	1,90,000
2005-06	4,50,000	2,04,000
2006-07	6,80,000	1,60,000
2007-08	7,24,000	3,69,000

Calculate his gross total income for different assessment years.

Ans: Nil; Nil; 2,26,000; 3,55,000.

Problem 11.07-P3 (Typical)

From the following particulars compute the assessable income for each of the following previous years of Mr. Steve Irwin a Crocodile Hunter:

2003-04	Income from house property	15,000
	Loss in paper industry	15,000
	Loss in electronic business	7,500
	Depreciation on assets used in paper industry	6,000
2004-05	Income from house property	(5,000)
	Profit from paper industry	13,000
	Depreciation for the year	3,000
2005-06	Income from house property	15,000
	Profit from paper industry	8,000
	Loss in electronic business *(Discontinued at the end of the year)*	22,500
	Depreciation for the year	1,500
2006-07	Profit from paper industry	15,000
	Depreciation for the year	1,500
	Loss from diamond business	4,500

Ans: nil; nil; nil; nil; Rs. 500 unabsorbed depreciation shall be carried forward to next AY 2008-09.

Problem 11.07-P4

Indicate the order in which the following amounts have to be set-off from the current years' (AY 2007-08) income of Rs. 25 lakhs, which includes Rs. 5 lakhs as income from 'Other sources' :

(i) Brought forward business loss : Rs. 1.5 lacs for AY 2004-05; Rs. 2.5 lacs for AY 2005-06 and Rs. 8 lacs for AY 2006-07, all assessed figures.

(ii) Unabsorbed depreciation for the same three years at Rs. 5 lakhs, Rs. 4 lakhs and Rs. 3.75 lakhs respectively.

(iii) Current depreciation Rs. 2 lakhs has to be allowed.

(iv) Rs. 7 lakhs representing speculation loss for AY 2005-06.

Ans: Business Income (25–2–1.5–2.5–8–5–4–2=nil). Other Sources (5–1.75=3.25). Total Income =3.25 Lakhs. Carryforward 7 lakhs

Problem 11.07-P5 [Hons 1999]

X submitted the following particulars of his income / assets for the PY 2006-07:

1.	Business profits before depreciation	90,000
2.	Sale of Govt. securities in September 2006 (Securities were purchased for Rs. 81,000 in April 2000)	1,09,000
3.	Sale of land (purchased in 1996-97 for Rs. 5,40,000) in December 2006	11,46,000
4.	Written down value of plant and machinery on 1-4-2006 (Depreciation @ 15%)	20,00,000
5.	Machinery purchased in November 2006	4,00,000
6.	One plant sold in December 2006	6,00,000

Compute the total income of X for the AY 2007-08 and written down value of the plant and machinery as on 1-4-2007.

Ans: TI 2,32,570; W.D.V. 15,60,000; 32(2) 1,50,000.

11.08 COMPREHENSIVE PROBLEMS

Set Off Questions

Problem 11.08-P1 (PE II - M03) - M 15

Compute the tax liability of X for the assessment year 2007-08 from the following particulars:

Net house property income as computed under the head "Income from house property"	2,70,000
Income from business before adjusting the following	90,000
(a) Carried forward business loss	70,000
(b) Current depreciation	30,000
(c) Carried forward unabsorbed depreciation	1,40,000
Short term capital gains - jewellery	1,60,000
Long term capital loss - land	40,000
Long term capital loss - listed shares (STT paid)	30,000
Long term capital gain - Debentures	2,00,000
Dividend on shares of an Indian company held as stock-in-trade	10,000
Dividend from a company carrying on agricultural operation	12,000
Income from growing and manufacturing coffee (cured and roasted)	1,00,000

During the previous year 2006-07, the assessee has donated Rs. 35,000 to an approved local authority for the promotion of family planning and purchased NSC VIII issue for Rs. 1,00,000.

Ans: 3,58,000; 53,448.

Problem 11.08-P2 (CA - M02) - M 8

Q.3a **:** From the following particulars of X for the previous year ending March 31, 2007, compute the income under each head, and the taxable income with reasons and also explain the provisions of carry forward of such loss, that could not be absorbed :

• Income from business (proprietary concerns) :	
(a) Net adjusted profit from textile trade	20,000
(b) Net adjusted loss from automotive trade	(30,000)
(c) Loss in shares traded (shares were never taken delivery)	(40,000)
• Negative income from house property	(25,000)
• Capital gains :	
(a) Short-term loss	(20,000)
(b) Long-term gain from sale of gold	30,000

Ans: Nil; 25,000; 40,000.

Problem 11.08-P3 (CA - M99) - M 14

Q.3 : X submits the following information for the financial year ending March 31, 2006. Compute the gross total income and ascertain the amount of losses that can be carried forward.

He has two houses :	
(a) House I - After all statutory deduction net annual value	36,000
(b) House II - Current year loss	10,000
(c) Brought forward loss of assessment year 1997-98 of House II representing unadjusted interest on borrowed capital	30,000
He has three proprietary businesses:	
(a) Textile business :	
(i) Discontinued from October 31, 2006 - current year loss	25,000
(ii) Brought forward business loss of the year 2002-03	80,000
(b) Chemical business :	
(i) Discontinued from March 1, 2006 - hence no profit/loss	NIL
(ii) Bad Debts allowed in earlier year recovered during this year	30,000
(iii) Carried forward business loss for the assessment year 2005-06	20,000
(c) Leather business : Profit for the current year	70,000
Short-term capital gains	20,000
Long-term capital loss from sale of land	15,000

Ans: 46,000.

Problem 11.08-P4 (CA - N96) - M 6

Q.1b **:** From the following figures, you are required to compute the total income of X for assessment year 2007-08:

Income from property	(–)10,000
Capital gains :	
Short-term	1,05,000
Long-term from sale of commercial house	(–) 75,000
Other sources	10,000

The assessee has unabsorbed depreciation of Rs. 25,000 brought forward from 1998-99, when the business was closed and all the assets disposed of. He has also paid interest on money borrowed for construction of property, relating to previous years relevant to assessment years 1997-98 and 1998-99 which have not been set off in the earlier years, of Rs. 5,000 each.

Ans: 80,000.

Problem 11.08-P5 (Typical)

Mr. X submits the following particulars :

1.	Income from House Property (computed)	8,000
2.	Profit from personal business	30,000
3.	Short term capital gain	18,000
4.	Long term capital gain on sale of building	17,000
5.	Long term capital gain on sale of unlisted bonus shares	14,000
6.	Long term capital gain on sale of listed bonus shares (STT paid)	(99,000)
7.	Dividend on shares from a Foreign company (held as stock in trade)	10,000
8.	Speculation profits	8,000
9.	Brought forward from preceding assessment year :	
	(a) Business loss	40,000
	(b) Loss of speculation	15,000
	(c) Unrealised rent of PY 2003-04	10,000
	(d) Long term capital loss of AY 2000-01	13,000
	(e) Long term capital loss of AY 1998-99	7,000

Compute his gross total income for the AY 2007-08.

Ans: 44,000.

Problem 11.08-P6 (ICWA-NEW - J03) - M 5

Q.3 : The following particulars are available about X for the previous year ending March 31, 2007 :

Profits of business A carried on in India		80,000
Loss of business B carried on in India		(–) 30,000
Profits of business C carried on in the UK and controlled from India, the profit having been received in the UK		52,000
Loss of business D carried on in the UK, the business being controlled from Mumbai		(–) 46,000
Income from property in India		32,000
Income from properties in the UK, 25% of which is receivable in India		1,92,000
Royalty received in the UK for use of chemical formula in :		
a. India	60,000	
b. U.K.	30,000	90,000
Gain on sale of land in India		50,000

Determine the total income of X for the assessment year 2007-08 assuming that his status is (a) resident and ordinarily resident in India; (b) resident and not ordinarily resident in India; (c) non-resident in India.

Ans: 4,20,000; 2,46,000; 2,40,000.

Problem 11.08-P7

The following particulars of the income of Mr. 'X' for the financial year 2006-07 are available :

A. Income from House property :	28,000
B. Income from Profits & Gains from business	
(i) Profits from 'X' business	40,000
(ii) Loss from 'Y' business	(–) 50,000
(iii) Profits from speculation in silver	40,000
(iv) Loss from speculation in gold	(–) 10,000
C. Capital gains :	
(i) Long-term Capital gains	30,000
(ii) Short-term Capital loss	(–) 10,000
D. Income from other sources :	
(i) Loss in Card games	(–) 1,000
(ii) Loss incurred in Mumbai from the activity of owning and maintaining horses	(–) 40,000
(iii) Profit earned in Mumbai from the activity of owning and maintaining horses	(+) 40,000
(iv) Dividend from Indian Companies (Gross)	10,000

The following losses have been carried forward by Mr. 'X' :

(a) Loss under the head Long-term Capital Gains from the Assessment Year 2001-02.	18,000
(b) Loss from speculation in silver from the assessment year 99-2000. Speculation business was discontinued in the Assessment year 2001-02.	25,000
(c) Loss from 'X' business from the Assessment Year 99-2000.	15,000

Compute the gross total income of Mr. 'X' for the Assessment Year 2007-2008.

Ans: 30,000.

Problem 11.08-P8

Shri Ramrattan has shown the following incomes and losses in his income-tax return for Assessment Year 2007-2008 :

(i) Income from house property	24,300
(ii) Business income from a proprietory concern	3,24,700
(iii) Speculation Business Loss	74,600
(iv) Other sources	1,25,700

Out of the above he has claimed adjustment of the following items :

(a)	Current year's depreciation	73,500
(b)	Brought forward business loss (Non-speculation) from AY 2004-05	1,75,000
(c)	Brought forward business loss (Speculation business) from AY 2003-04	34,500
(d)	Loss under the head Income from house property relatable to AY 2001-02	9,500
(e)	Unabsorbed depreciation for Assessment Years 2002-03 and 2001-02	2,75,500

He is eligible under Chapter VIA for a deduction of Rs. 12,000 from the Gross Total Income.

Compute the total income of Shri Ramrattan for Assessment Year 2007-08.

Ans: nil.

Problem 11.08-P9 (Typical)

M/s. D.L. Pvt. Ltd. filed its return of income for assessment year 2007-08 on 15-12-2007. From the information given below, compute its income/loss and indicate the period upto which loss, if any, can be carried forward :

1.	Business loss	(1,00,000)
2.	Income from speculation business	30,000
3.	Depreciation of current year	20,000
4.	Short-term capital loss	(50,000)
5.	Long-term capital gain	50,000
6.	Income from Other Sources	30,000
7.	Business loss brought forward from A.Y. 2003-04	(30,000)
8.	Unabsorbed depreciation of A.Ys. 2003-05 and 2004-05	(40,000)
9.	Long-term capital loss brought forward from A.Y. 2005-06	(10,000)

Ans: Total Income Nil; Business loss of Rs. 40,000 of the AY 2007-08 shall not be carried forward since return of income not filed in time. However unabsorbed depreciation of Rs. 20,000 shall be carried forward. Other losses which can be carried forward are Business Loss 30,000; Unabsorbed depreciation of A.Ys. 2003-04; 2004-05 and 2007-08. Long-term capital loss brought forward from A.Y. 2005-06 Rs. (10,000).

Problem 11.08-P10

M/s. XYZ Ltd. filed its return of income for assessment year 2007-08 on 30-10-2007. From the following information, please compute the income and indicate the losses and allowances to be carried forward—

(A) Current year's particulars—	(Rs.)
(i) Business income (before depreciation of Rs. 7,50,000)	25,00,000
(ii) Loss from speculation business	2,00,000
(iii) Income from other sources	3,00,000
(iv) Long-term capital gains	2,25,000
(v) Short-term capital loss	1,50,000
(vi) Income from house property	50,000

(B) Losses & allowances of earlier years—

(i) Unabsorbed business losses of —	
A.Y. 97-98	2,00,000
A.Y. 2000-01	1,00,000
(ii) Long-term capital loss of A.Y. 96-97	1,75,000
(iii) Loss from house property in A.Y. 2004-05	25,000
(iv) Unabsorbed depreciation brought forward from A.Y. 97-98	5,00,000

Ans: Total Income Rs. 15,50,000. C.f. speculation loss Rs. 2,00,000.

Problem 11.08-P11

The following are the details of the income of Shri Y for A.Y. 2007-08. Determine total income and carry forward loss, if any

(a) Taxable salary — Rs. 5,20,000

(b) Loss from House Property 'A' — Rs. 60,000.

(c) Income from House Property 'B' — Rs. 40,000.

(d) Brought forward Business loss for A.Y. 2003-04 — Rs. 1,00,000.

(e) Current year Business income — Rs. 80,000.

(f) Bank interest — Rs. 20,000.

Ans: 5,20,000.

Tax Liability Questions

Problem 11.08-P12

Mr. Mehta submits the following particulars for the F.Y. 2006-07, compute the total income and tax payable for Assessment Year 2007-08 including unabsorbed loss and depreciation to be carried forward.

(i) Business loss before depreciation	3,80,000
(ii) Current depreciation as per I.T. Act	98,000
(iii) Income from other sources	45,000
(iv) Long-term capital gains (on sale of house)	76,000

Mr. Mehta has paid L.I.P. of Rs. 10,000 during the year and purchased NSC VIII issue of Rs. 15,000.

Ans: 56,916. [2,82,000+45,000+76,000=4,03,000-25,000=3,78,000] [15,200+40,600=55,800+1,116=56,916]

Problem 11.08-P13

From the following particulars of Shri Aalok, Compute the Gross Total Income for the assessment year 2007-08 :

		Rs.
1.	Salary received	36,000
2.	Short term Capital Gain	40,000
3.	Long term Capital loss	50,000
4.	Interest on debentures of company	20,000
5.	Profits from maintaining horses for horse races in Mumbai	30,000
6.	Loss from maintaining horses for horse races in Delhi	20,000
7.	Profits of business before depreciation	30,000

8.	Loss from house property let - out	1,00,000
9.	Current year's depreciation	10,000
10.	Loss from business set up in free trade zone [income is exempt u/s 10A]	20,000
11.	Donation to National Children fund	2,000

Ans: Total Income Rs. 30,000. Tax Rs. 9,180.

Problem 11.08-P14 (Typical)

Compute the minimum tax liability of Mr. Taxcrazy, a resident in India, for the AY 2007-08.

Income from House Property	4,00,000
LTCG on sale of gold	4,50,000
Income from Lottery	6,15,000
Business Loss	(80,000)
Deduction under section 80G	3,90,000
Provident fund contribution	20,000

Ans: 2,43,720.

Problem 11.08-P15 [Hons 1996]

X furnishes the following statement of account for the AY 2007-08

• Business loss	(1,20,000)
• Short-term capital gains	5,00,000
• Short-term capital gains STT paid	3,50,000
• Long-term capital gains	1,75,000
• PPF contribution	1,10,000

Compute his minimum tax liability for the AY 2007-08.

Ans: 1,06,080; 1,18,320.

STRATEGY MAKER

Ranking in 1 to 10	Overall rank - 6; Practical - 8; Theory - 8
Type of problem	Difficult
What to expect (DU)	Everything. Till last exam no separate questions have been asked. Generally questions are attached to business problems.
CA (PE II)	Everything

Quote for success

The man who succeeds has a programme. He fixes his course and adheres to it. He lays his plans and executes them. He goes straight to his goal. He knows where he wants to go and he knows that he's going to get there. He loves what he's doing and loves the journey that is taking him to the object of his desires. He is bubbling over with enthusiasm and he is filled with zeal. This is the man or woman who succeeds.

Keep Running

Revenue receipt - Revenue expenditure = profit

12

PROFITS AND GAINS FROM BUSINESS OR PROFESSION

TOPIC 12.00 *SECTION 28.* CHARGEABILITY

(A) *SECTION 28(i).* BUSINESS SHOULD BE IN EXISTENCE

The profit of any business which was carried on by the assessee at any time during the relevant PY shall be chargeable to income tax under the head "Profits & Gains of Business or Profession".

(i) Analysing it, we get following three essential points

1. There should be a 'business'. Business is defined u/s 2(13) of the Income Tax Act, 1961.
2. The business should be carried on by the 'assessee'. It means whosoever carries on the business shall be treated as an assessee, he may or may not be the owner of the business.
3. The business should be 'carried on during the PY'. It means the business should be carried on by the assessee during the PY. Even if a business is carried on for a day the whole of the profit shall be chargeable to tax under the head business.

(ii) What about the transaction undertaken before the commencement of the business?

Any income arising before the commencement of business is treated as capital receipt and therefore not chargeable to tax. This is so because business is not being carried on by the assessee during the relevant PY.

Similarly any expenditure incurred before the commencement of business is treated as capital expenditure and therefore not deductible. This is so because business is not being carried on by the assessee during the relevant PY.

(iii) What about the transaction undertaken after the closure of the business?

Any income arising after the closure of the business is not chargeable to tax, since business is not carried on by the assessee during the relevant PY.

Similarly any expenditure incurred after the closure of the business is not deductible, since business is not carried on by the assessee during the relevant PY.

Any exception? Yes it is provided in section 41. It says income specified u/s 41, is chargeable to tax under the head Profit from Business, even if the business has been closed down. *E.g.* Recovery of bad debt after closure of business is chargeable to tax under the business.

(B) OTHER INCOME TAXABLE UNDER THE HEAD BUSINESS

1. Any compensation received by any person who is managing the whole or substantially the whole of the affairs of an Indian company, at or in connection with the termination of his management or the modification of the terms and conditions relating thereto.
2. Income derived by a trade, professional or similar association from specific services performed for its members.
3. Export incentives.
   1. Profits on sale of a licence granted under the Imports (Control) Order, 1955, made under the Imports and Exports (Control) Act, 1947;
   2. Cash assistance (by whatever name called) received or receivable by any person against exports under any scheme of the Government of India;
   3. Any duty of customs or excise repaid or repayable as drawback to any person against exports under the Customs and Central Excise Duties Drawback Rules, 1971.
4. The value of any benefit or perquisite, whether convertible into money or not, arising from business or the exercise of a profession. E.g. (a) Tax liability of A paid by B was held to be chargeable u/s 28(iv) where A is rendering consultancy service to B. (b) Tips given to a taxi driver in the ordinary course of his business are profits and gains of employment.
5. Any interest, salary, bonus, commission or remuneration, by whatever name called, due to, or received by, a partner of a firm from such firm.
6. Any sum, whether received or receivable in cash or kind, (a) under an agreement for not carrying out any activity in relation to any business; or (b) not sharing any know-how, patent, copyright, trademark, licence, franchise or any other business or commercial right of similar nature or information or technique likely to assist in the manufacture or processing of goods or provision for services.
7. Any sum received under a Keyman insurance policy including the sum allocated by way of bonus on such policy.
8. Income from speculative transaction.

(C) IN WHICH PY BUSINESS INCOME IS RECOGNISED TO TAX?

The business income is recognised to tax as per the method of accounting followed by the assessee.

Section 145. Method of Accounting : The assessee can choose either mercantile system of accounting or cash system of accounting to prepare P & L A/c. If there is any change in the method of accounting the assessee should notify the same in the Balance Sheet.

1. *Mercantile System :* If the assessee accounts are kept on the mercantile basis, the income would be taxable when it accrues or is earned irrespective of receipt. Even if certain amount of income earned is not likely to be realised, it should nevertheless be included in the accounts.

As per the Companies Act, 1956, companies are required to maintain their accounts only on mercantile system.

2. *Cash System* : On the other hand, if the accounts are maintained on the cash basis income would be chargeable in that accounting year in which it is received even if the source of income has ceased to exist. It depends upon the method of accounting followed by the assessee.

   E.g. 1 Mr. X makes a credit sale of Rs. 6,00,000 on 1-3-2007 to Mr. Y. The amount of Rs. 6,00,000 is received on 2-4-2007. Now the question is in which PY sale shall be recognised.

   If the assessee follows mercantile system, Rs. 6,00,000 shall be taxable in the PY 2006-07. However if the assessee follows cash system the income shall be taxable in the PY 2006-07.

   (You must remember accounting method is important only for two heads of income i.e. *'Business' and 'Other sources'.)*

TOPIC 12.01 AMOUNTS EXPRESSLY ALLOWED AS DEDUCTIONS UNDER *SECTION 30 TO 37*

(A) SECTION 30. RENT, RATES, TAXES, REPAIRS & INSURANCE OF BUILDINGS USED FOR THE PURPOSE OF THE BUSINESS

(a) Rent of the premises is allowed as deduction. However notional rent paid by proprietor is not allowed as deduction. But rent paid by firm to its partner for using his premises is allowed as deduction.

(b) Current repairs if the assessee bears the cost of repairs are allowed as deduction. However capital repairs incurred by the assessee are never allowed as deduction whether premises is occupied as a tenant or as a owner. Instead the capital repairs incurred shall be deemed to be a building and depreciation shall be claimed.

(c) Any sum on account of land revenue, local taxes or municipal taxes subject to section 43B. As per section 43B deduction shall be allowed only if such sum is actually paid on or before the due date of furnishing of return; and

(d) Insurance charges against the risk of damage or destruction of building is allowed as deduction.

As per section 38 if the building is not used exclusively for the purpose of business or profession then the deduction shall be restricted to a fair proportion of above expenditure which the assessing officer may determine.

(B) SECTION 31. REPAIRS & INSURANCE OF PLANT, MACHINERY & FURNITURE

(a) Amount paid on account of current repairs to the plant, machinery and furniture is allowed as deduction. However capital repairs incurred by the assessee are never allowed as deduction whether plant is leased or is purchased. Instead the capital repairs incurred shall be deemed to be an asset eligible for depreciation.

(b) Premium paid for insurance against the risk of damage or destruction of plant, machinery or furniture is allowed as deduction.

As per section 38(2) if the plant is not used exclusively for the purpose of business or profession then the deduction shall be restricted to a fair proportion of above expenditure which the assessing officer may determine.

(C) SECTION 32. DEPRECIATION

Already discussed in chapter 6. Depreciation

(D) SECTION 36(1)(i). INSURANCE OF STOCKS

The amount of insurance premium paid in respect of insurance against risk of damage or destruction of *stocks or stores* used for the purpose of the business is allowed as deduction.

(E) SECTION 36(1)(ib). INSURANCE PREMIUM ON HEALTH OF EMPLOYEES

It is allowed as deduction if following conditions are satisfied :

(a) The premium is paid by cheque (bearer or crossed) by the employer; and

(b) Premium is paid under a scheme framed in this behalf by the General Insurance Corporation of India and approved by the Central Government or any other insurer and approved by IRDA.

(F) SECTION 36(1)(ii). BONUS OR COMMISSION PAID TO EMPLOYEES

The deduction of bonus or commission paid to employees is allowed as deduction but is subject to Section 43B. As per section 43B deduction shall be allowed only if such sum is actually paid on or before the due date of furnishing of return.

(G) SECTION 36(1)(iii). INTEREST PAID ON MONEY BORROWED FOR THE PURPOSE OF BUSINESS OR PROFESSION

(i) Conditions

As per Supreme Court judgement

1. The sum of money should be borrowed from another assessee. The loan may be borrowed from any Bank, financial institution, Govt., public, friends or relatives. Loan may be in the form of debentures or deposits etc. Interest on capital or loan to proprietor is not allowed as deduction since the loan is not borrowed from another person. However interest paid by firm to its partners on their capital contribution is allowed as deduction subject to section 4b.
2. Such borrowed money should be used for the purpose of business or profession. But where the amount of loan is used for personal purpose it is not allowed as deduction. *E.g.* the loan is borrowed for the payment of income tax not allowed as deduction. However loan is borrowed for payment of dividend or sales tax is allowed as deduction.
3. The interest has accrued during the relevant previous year. However where the interest falls under section 43B *i.e* where interest is payable to banks or financial institutions, then to claim deduction such interest should actually be paid on or before the due date of furnishing of return.

(ii) Proviso 1 to 36(1)(iii). Interest on borrowing for acquiring new assets

1. Interest accrued before the commencement of business is not allowed as deduction but has to be capitalised and added to the actual cost of the fixed asset acquired out of borrowed capital.
2. Interest accrued after the commencement of business but before the asset is put to use is not allowed as deduction but has to be capitalised and added to the actual cost of the fixed asset acquired out of borrowed capital.
3. Interest accrued after the asset is put to use is allowed as deduction under section 36(1)(iii).

(iii) Other points

1. Where interest is paid outside India without deduction of tax at source is not allowed as deduction.
2. Income tax department cannot question the need for borrowing and the rate of interest.
3. Interest other than interest on borrowing is allowed as deduction under section 37 and not under this clause. *E.g.* Interest on late payment of sales tax etc.

(H) SECTION 36(1)(iv). EMPLOYER'S CONTRIBUTION TOWARDS RECOGNISED PROVIDENT FUND OR AN APPROVED SUPERANNUATION FUND

Employer's contribution paid towards recognised provident fund or an approved superannuation fund is allowed as deduction subject to Section 43B.

However as per section 40A(9) contribution towards any Non-Statutory fund or unapproved fund is not allowed as deduction. Where contribution is made towards any fund or for welfare of employees in any form without specific requirement of law then such contribution is not allowed as deduction.

(I) SECTION 36(1)(v). EMPLOYER'S CONTRIBUTION PAID TOWARDS AN APPROVED GRATUITY FUND

Employer's contribution towards an approved gratuity fund created by the employer exclusively for the benefit of his employees under an irrevocable trust is allowed as deduction subject to section 43B.

As per section 40A(7) contribution towards unapproved gratuity fund is not allowed as deduction.

However where employee retires during the year gratuity payable to such employees during the year is allowed as deduction if no deduction was claimed earlier. Where part of gratuity is payable next year for which provision is made, deduction can be claimed in current year.

(J) SECTION 36(1)(va). EMPLOYEE'S CONTRIBUTION TOWARDS STAFF WELFARE SCHEME

Any sum received by the assessee from his employees as contributions

1. to any provident fund or
2. superannuation fund or
3. any fund set up under the provisions of the Employees' State Insurance Act, or
4. any other fund for the welfare of such employees

is treated as income as per section 2(24) in the hands of assessee unless such employee's contribution is credited in employee's account on or before the 'due date' specified under the provisions of any law or terms of contract of service or otherwise.

However employer's contribution (not employee's contribution) towards such fund is allowed as deduction subject to section 43B *i.e.* such contribution is paid on or before the due date of furnishing return.

(K) SECTION 36(1)(vii). BAD DEBTS

(i) Conditions

If following conditions are satisfied amount of debt is allowed as deduction. As per section 36(2) conditions are :

1. Such debt or part thereof has been taken into account in computing the income of the assessee of the previous year in which the amount of such debt or part thereof is written off or of an earlier previous year,

or

2. Represents money lent in the ordinary course of the business of banking or money-lending which is carried on by the assessee.

and

3. It has been written off as irrecoverable in the account of the assessee for the previous year

   E.g. credit sale made of Rs. 1,00,000 not realised. Rs. 1,00,000 shall be allowed as deduction since sale is treated as income. Advances made for purchase of stocks. Advance forfeited not allowed as deduction since advance money not a part of income. However such loss can be claimed under section 28.

(ii) Notes

1. Bad debt can be claimed as deduction by the successor of the business. *E.g.* Conversion of firm into a company. However where business is discontinued bad debt is not allowed as deduction. Such bad debt cannot be deducted even from profits of a separate existing business.
2. However provision for bad debt is not allowed as deduction.
3. Do note that a deduction on account of bad debt is based upon a mere estimate.

(iii) Recovery of bad debt

Where a deduction has been allowed in respect of a bad debt or part of debt under section 36(1)(vii), then, if the amount subsequently recovered on any such debt is greater than the difference between the debt and the amount so allowed, the excess shall be deemed to be profits and gains of business or profession, and chargeable to income-tax as the income of the previous year in which it is recovered, whether the business or profession in respect of which the deduction has been allowed is in existence in that year or not.

Illustration and Problem 12.01-P1 (Simple)

Compute the amount of bad debt chargeable to tax for the AY 2007-08.

	Case 1	*Case 2*	*Case 3*
Amount of debt	10,000	10,000	10,000
Bad debt written off as irrecoverable	10,000	2,000	8,000
Recovery of Bad Debt	5,000	5,000	1,000

Solution

	Case 1	*Case 2*	*Case 3*
Amount of debt	10,000	10,000	10,000
Less : Bad debt written off as irrecoverable	10,000	2,000	8,000
Already taxed	Nil	(8,000)	(2,000)
Add : Recovery of Bad Debt	5,000	5,000	1,000
Balance Taxable/deductible	5,000	(3,000)	(1,000)

(L) SECTION 36(1)(ix). FAMILY PLANNING EXPENDITURE INCURRED BY COMPANY

Deduction in respect of *revenue* expenditure for promoting family planning amongst its employees is allowed as deduction and in case of *capital* expenditure 1/5th of expenditure incurred is allowed as deduction in 5 equal instalments.

Note : In case of assessee *(other than company)* deduction on account of family planning revenue expenditure can be claimed under section 37 and capital expenditure is disallowed as deduction though the assessee can claim depreciation.

Treatment of unabsorbed family planning capital expenditure is same as that of section 32(2)—Unabsorbed depreciation.

(M) SECTION 36(1)(xiii). BCTT

Any amount of banking cash transaction tax (BCTT) paid by the assessee during the previous year on the taxable banking transactions entered into by him.

TOPIC 12.02 *SECTION 37.* GENERAL DEDUCTION

(A) CONDITIONS

This is a residuary section. Hence this section covers only those items of business expenditure which are not covered under sections 30 to 36. The deduction u/s 37 is allowed if expenditure satisfies all the three conditions mentioned below :

1. Expenditure is incurred wholly and exclusively for the purpose of the business. The word 'wholly' refers to the quantum of expenditure and the word 'exclusively' refers to the motive, object or purpose of the expenditure. The expression 'for the purpose of the business' is essentially wider than the expression 'for the purpose of earning profits'.
2. Such expenditure is not in the nature of personal expenditure.
3. Such expenditure is not of capital in nature *i.e.* expenses should be of revenue in nature. The word "capital" connotes permanency and "capital expenditure" is, therefore, closely akin to the concept of securing something, tangible or intangible property, or corporeal or incorporeal right, so that they could be of a lasting or enduring benefit to the enterprise in issue. Revenue expenditure, on the other hand, is operational in its perspective and solely intended for the furtherance of the enterprise.
4. It should not have been incurred for any purpose which is an offence or is prohibited by any law.

Following expenditures were held to be incurred wholly and exclusively for the purpose of the business.

a. Official or Administrative expenses.

b. Audit or legal fees.

c. Advertising expenses, travelling or conveyance expenses.

d. Entertainment expenses.

e. Interest paid for overdraft facility.

f. Remuneration payable to employees or other expenses incurred for the benefit of employees.

g. Diwali expenses.

h. Interest paid on payment of dividend is allowed as deduction. *(However interest on payment of Income tax or other personal liability is not allowed as deduction.)*

Following expenditures were held to be personal expenses.

a. Drawings by the owner for personal use.

b. Interest on own capital in case of proprietorship concern.

c. Remuneration paid to owner of the business in case of proprietorship concern.

d. Donations u/s 80G or any other similar donations not connected with business of the assessee. *(However business donation is allowed as deduction)*

Revenue expenditure vs capital expenditure

a. Purchase of capital assets used for the purpose of business. *(However depreciation can be claimed u/s 32)*

b. Annual listing fee paid to any recognised stock exchange *(However initial listing fee is not allowed as deduction since treated as capital expenditure).*

c. Expenditure on raising loans for the purpose of business is allowed as deduction, since treated as revenue expenditure. However expenditure on raising equity shares or preference shares is not allowed as deduction, since treated as capital expenditure. As per Supreme Court judgement expenditure incurred on raising bonus shares is allowed as deduction;

d. Expenses on registration of Trade Marks;

Others (not allowed as deduction)

a. Any provision or reserve made for contingencies, anticipated loss, dividend, sales tax, custom duty, excise, gratuity, bonus etc. *(However actual payment of sales tax, excise duty or custom duty is allowed as deduction subject to section 43B)*

b. Notional expenses i.e. rent paid for own building etc.

(B) PENALTY PAID FOR ANY BREACH OF LAW

For the removal of doubts, it is hereby declared that any expenditure incurred by an assessee for any purpose which is an offence or which is prohibited by law shall not be deemed to have been incurred for the purpose of business or profession and no deduction or allowance shall be made in respect of such expenditure.

The Court had ruled in the Hazi case that no deduction can be allowed for a penalty incurred for contravention of any specific statutory provision. Such penalty cannot be said to be a commercial loss falling on the assessee as a trader. Therefore following expenditures are disallowed as deduction :

1. Expenses incurred in defending the assessee in any proceedings for breach of any law relating to sales tax, income tax etc. *(However penalty or damages paid for breach of contract is allowed as deduction.)*

2. Penalty paid for non payment of sale tax, excise, custom etc. within prescribed time. *(However damage or penalty paid for infringement of law is not allowed as deduction).*

(C) SECTION 37(2B).

Expenditure on advertising in any souvenirs, brochure etc. of a political party shall not be allowed as deduction. However an assessee can claim deduction u/s 80GGB or 80GGC for donation made to political party.

TOPIC 12.03 IS BUSINESS LOSS DEDUCTIBLE ?

Yes, even though there is no specific provision of deduction provided in the Act. As you know income include loss, therefore, loss arising due to business shall be dealt in section

28 itself. Examples are :

a. Loss on account of robbery, theft, embezzlement etc.;
b. Loss on account of valuation of Stock-in-Trade;
c. Loss on account of fluctuation in currency rates.

TOPIC 12.04 ADJUSTMENT OF VALUATION OF STOCK

Stock is valued at cost or market price whichever is lower. However where the business is being dissolved the stocks are valued at market price.

Any over valuation of opening stock or under valuation of closing stock shall decrease the net profit, therefore the amount of difference shall be added back to net profit.	Any over valuation of closing stock or under valuation of opening stock shall increase the net profit, therefore the amount of difference shall be subtracted from net profit.

TOPIC 12.05 *SECTION 40a.* AMOUNTS EXPRESSLY DISALLOWED AS DEDUCTION

1. *Section 40(a)(ib).* Any sum paid on account of securities transaction tax (STT) on purchase or sale of equity shares, derivatives or units of equity oriented fund on or after 1-10-2004. It means STT paid is not allowed as deduction as business expenditure however rebate u/s 88E is available.
2. *Section 40(a)(ic).* Any sum paid on account of fringe benefit tax.
3. *Section 40(a)(ii) & (iia).* Income tax, income tax penalty and wealth tax or any provision made thereof.
4. *Section 40(a)(v).* Any income tax payment borne by the employer, on behalf of employee in respect of non- monetary perquisites, which is exempt in the hands of employee under section 10(10CC).

Problem 12.05-P1

How will you deal with the following in computing the total income of the company ?

1. Fees paid to an architect for valuation of the office building and factory building for contesting excessive municipal tax levied : Rs. 12,500;
2. Compensation paid to a director on termination of service : Rs. 1,30,000;
3. Expenses paid to management consultant for preparation of budgeting formats : Rs. 34,000;
4. Payment of Rs. 15,000 in advance as a non refundable deposit for getting a new telephone connection;
5. Expenditure incurred for repairing a property taken on lease for business : Rs. 4,000;
6. Expenses incurred for registration of the trade marks of a product : Rs. 11,150;
7. Anticipated loss on forward contract for purchase of raw material as a result of a fall in market price : Rs. 1,20,780;
8. Expenditure incurred initially on installation of the fluorescent tube light : Rs. 800;
9. Cost of lunch given at a 5-Star hotel where four representatives of suppliers were treated to lunch along with the purchase manager and secretary of the Company : Rs. 3,800;
10. Purchased a new plant costing Rs. 3,00,000 on deferred payment (interest payable for the period subsequent to the installation amounting to Rs. 1,00,000 has been capitalised along with the cost);

11. Spent Rs. 20,000 for digging a bore well, which, however, did not yield any water;
12. Paid interest of Rs. 30,000 for a shortfall in advance tax paid for the financial year 2003-04.
13. Supplied spare parts to customers (free of charge) under a warranty clause (cost is Rs. 1,20,000, normal selling price Rs. 1,80,000);
14. Spent Rs. 1,70,000 towards training an employee in Germany (air fare Rs. 1,00,000 and daily allowance at Rs. 2,000 per day for 35 days);
15. Purchased a building for Rs. 5,00,000, to be used exclusively as a family planning centre for the employees;
16. Donated Rs. 1,00,000 to the Prime Minister's National Relief Fund.

Ans: Discuss with your friends.

TOPIC 12.06 HOW TO COMPUTE "PROFIT FROM BUSINESS OR PROFESSION"?

(A) COMPUTATION OF PROFIT FROM BUSINESS OR PROFESSION (ASSUMED FIGURES)

Net Profit as per P & L A/c		8,000
(+) Inadmissibles *(Capital expenditure or personal expenditure debited to P & L A/c)*	12,000	
(+) Additions *(Business receipts not recorded in P & L A/c)*	3,000	
(–) Admissibles *(Revenue expenditure of business in nature not recorded in P & L A/c)*	(2,000)	
(–) Subtraction *(Other than business income credited to P & L A/c)*	(4,000)	9,000
Profits from business or profession		17,000

(B) HOW TO PREPARE PROFIT AND LOSS ACCOUNT AS PER INCOME TAX RULE?

<table>
<tr>
<td>
RULE OF ADMISSIBLE

All revenue expenditures which are business in nature should be allowed as deduction and therefore as a rule should be debited to P/L A/c.

But if they are not debited (i.e. not claimed as deduction) then such expenses should be subtracted from net profit.

RULE OF INADMISSIBLE

Similarly no capital expenditure are allowed as deduction and therefore as a rule should not be debited to P/L A/c.

But if they are debited (i.e. claimed as deduction) then such expenses should be added back to net profit.
</td>
<td>
RULE OF ADDITION

All revenue receipts which are business in nature are income, and therefore as a rule should be credited to P/L A/c.

RULE OF SUBTRACTION

Similarly incomes which are not chargeable under the head 'Business' and therefore as a rule should not be credited to P/L A/c

but if credited then subtract such profit from Net profit to compute Profit from Business.
</td>
</tr>
</table>

Illustration 12.06-P1 (Difficult)

Mr. Sudeep who runs a Gas Agency furnishes the following P & L A/c *(maintained as per mercantile system)* for the PY ending 31-3-2007:

Dr. Particulars	*Amount*	*Particulars*	*Amount Cr.*
1. Office expenses	1,95,000	Gross Profit	2,05,000
2. Purchase of Building	50,000	**6.** Rent from House Property	4,000
3. Purchases a computer for personal use	18,000	**7.** Dividend from an Indian Company	20,000
4. Provision for bad debts	2,000	**8.** Other receipts	55,000
5. Household expenses	20,000	**9.** Interest on bank deposits	10,000
Net profit	35,000	**10.** Profit from sale of land	26,000
Total	3,25,000	Total	3,20,000

Additional informations :

11. Audit fees of Rs. 2,000 not debited to P/L A/c.

12. He also purchases printer worth Rs. 36,000 for the purpose of business. This amount is not debited to P/L A/c. *(the rate of depreciation 15%)*

13. He has received an interest from company deposits of Rs. 500 which is not credited to P/L A/c.

14. On 1-6-2006, he made a sale worth Rs. 30,000 not recorded in P & L A/c.

15. On 31-3-2007 he contributed Rs. 10,000 in pension plan of LIC.

Hints for Computation

1. Office expenses are allowed as deduction *(since it is revenue expenditure and is incurred for the purpose of business)* and are debited to P/L A/c, therefore no further adjustment.

2. Purchase of building is not allowed as deduction since capital expenditure. However depreciation @ 10% be claimed.

3. Personal expenses are not allowed as deduction.

4. Provisions are not allowed as deduction.

5. Household expenses not allowed as deduction since personal expenditure.

6. Rent from House property is chargeable under the head Income from House Property therefore should be subtracted from net profit.

7. Dividend from Indian company is chargeable under the head Income from Other Sources but exempt u/s 10(34).

8. Other receipts are deemed to be business receipts.

9. Interest from bank deposit is chargeable under the head income from other sources.

10. Profit from sale of land is chargeable under the head of capital gain.

11. Audit fees is allowed as deduction.

12. Purchase of printer is a capital expenditure though depreciation is allowed.

13. Interest from company deposit is chargeable under the head income from other sources.

14. Since sale is revenue receipt therefore should be added to P & L A/c.

Computation of profit from business

Net profit		35,000
Add : Inadmissibles		
(+) Purchase of building	50,000	
(+) Purchase of computer for personal use	18,000	
(+) Provision for bad debts	2,000	
(+) Household expenses	20,000	
Add : Additions		
(+) Sale not recorded in P & L A/c	30,000	1,20,000
Less : Admissibles		
(–) Audit fees	(2,000)	
(–) Depreciation u/s 32(1) *(10% of 50,000 + 15% of 36,000)*	(10,400)	
Less : Subtraction		
(–) Rent from House Property	(4,000)	
(–) Dividend from Indian Company	(20,000)	
(–) Interest from Bank deposits	(10,000)	
(–) Profit from sale of land	(26,000)	(72,400)
Profit from Business		82,600

Computation of Total Income

Income from House Property *(4,000 - 1,200)*	2,800
Profit from Business	82,600
Capital Gain	26,000
Income from Other Sources	10,500
Gross Total Income	1,21,900
Less : Deduction u/s 80CCC	10,000
Total Income	1,11,900

Problem 12.06-P2 [CS D01]

X is a company secretary and has prepared the following income and expenditure account for the year ended March 31, 2007 :

	Rs.		Rs.
Office expenses	10,000	Professional fee	70,500
Employees salary	5,000	Gift from father - in - law	5,050
Magazines	600	Dividend	8,000
Personal expenses	17,000	Profit on sale of investment	6,450
Donation to National Defence fund	500	Consultancy fee	50,000
Interest	600		
Income-tax	13,300		
Car expenses	2,000		
Net surplus	91,000		
	1,40,000		1,40,000

You are required to compute his professional income and total income for the assessment year 2007-08 considering the following points :

(i) The car is used equally for official and personal purposes.

(ii) Rs. 1,000 for domestic servant's salary is included in employees salary.

(iii) X is owner of a building. Its written down value is Rs. 80,000 on April 1, 2006. The building is used for office purpose. Besides this, furniture having written down value of Rs. 25,000 as on April 1, 2006 is also used for profession.

Ans: 93,800; 99,750. [91,000+1,000+1,000+17,000+500+13,300–5,050–8,000–6,450–8,000–2,500=93,800]; [93,800+6,450–500]

Problem 12.06-P3 (Difficult)

M/s. ABC (P) Ltd., a trading company, filed its return on 31-12-2007 for the Assessment Year 2007-2008. The Trading and Profit & Loss Accounts filed by it are as under :

	Rs.		*Rs.*
To Opening Stock	15,75,000	By Sales	1,08,44,000
To Purchases	97,42,600	By Closing Stock	8,56,000
To Gross Profit	3,82,400		
	1,17,00,000		1,17,00,000
To Salaries	96,000	By Gross Profit b/d	3,82,400
To Rent	58,500	By Net loss	1,02,615
To Interest	12,400		
To Advertisement	5,000		
To Travelling Expenses	18,725		
To Bad debts	49,500		
To Sales Tax	1,08,440		
To Depreciation	1,12,250		
To Miscellaneous Expenses	24,200		
	4,85,015		4,85,015

Examination of the case revealed the following :

(1) There was a survey in the premises on 14-2-2008 which revealed that the Closing Stock as on 31-3-2006 was Rs. 20,75,000 and the closing stock as on 31-3-2007 was Rs. 12,50,000, as per inventories found.

(2) The Manager admitted that during the year purchases to the extent of Rs. 10 lakhs were not recorded in the books and also sales to the extent of Rs. 15 lakhs were kept out.

(3) Rent shown at Rs. 58,500 included expenditure on current repairs at Rs. 22,500.

(4) Bad debts were claimed after setting off Rs. 15,000 received out of amount written off in the earlier years.

(5) Miscellaneous expenses included Rs. 18,000 on account of entertainment.

(6) Depreciation includes Rs. 80,000 on account of a second hand Toyota Car of Japanese make purchased during the year.

Compute the business income for this year.

Ans: Business Income [–1,02,615+3,94,000–5,00,000–10,00,000+15,00,000 =2,91,385]

Problem 12.06-P4 (Difficult)

The profit and loss account of Shri X for the year ended 31st March 2007 is as under :

Dr. Particulars	*Amount*	*Particulars*	*Amount Cr.*
Salary to employee	20,000	Gross profit	60,000
Rent	10,000	Sundry incomes	6,000
New year expenses of his family	600	Commission	8,000
Interest on loan	2,000	Interest on listed securities	800
Sundry Expenses	3,000	Bad debts recovered	100
Donation in Mandir	800	Rent received from house property	2,400
Bad Debts	1,800		
Provision for bad debts	1,500		
Interest on capital	1,600		
Advertisement expenses	2,400		
Advance payment of income-tax	2,100		
Postage and stamps	500		
Loss by theft	1,000		
Dinner expenses	1,800		
Gift and Present to Mrs. X	625		
Audit fees	300		
Net profit	27,275		
Total	77,300	Total	77,300

Compute income from Business and Profession and total income of Mr. X for the Assessment Year 2007-08 keeping in view the following information :

(i) The amount of salary includes an amount of Rs. 2,400 paid to X's son as salary. X's son looks after his business and assists him in the management of business.

(ii) The amount of rent includes an amount Rs. 1,800 being rent of office premisses, the premises belong to Mr. X.

(iii) The amount of interest on loan includes an amount of Rs. 1,300 being interest on loan taken from wife of X. She gave this loan from her stridhan. The amount of loan taken from wife was utilised for the payment of arrears of income tax.

(iv) Rs. 500 spent on the guest of X's son and Rs. 200 spent on the marriage of sister of X's wife were included in sundry expenses.

(v) The expenses of dinner are in connection with a party given to friend of X's brother.

(vi) The amount of donations are in respect of the donation given to approved social welfare fund.

(vii) Loss by theft occurred as embezzlement by the employees.

(viii) Municipal Taxes of house property amounting to Rs. 300 included in sundry expenses.

Ans: 37,200; 39,070. [27,275+1,800+600+1,300+500+200+800+1,500+1,600+2,100+1,800+625+300–800–2,400=37,200+1,470+800]

Problem 12.06-P5 (Difficult)

Dr. Mahesh Chand is a medical practitioner. Compute his professional income and taxable income, on the basis of the following income-expenditure statement for the AY 2007-2008.

Expenditure		*Income*	
Salary	48,000	Professional fees	6,50,000
Conveyance	24,000	Interest from Bank	50,000
Stationery	9,000	Interest from others	25,000
Periodicals and Journals	7,000	Interest on securities	45,000
Health Insurance premium of employees	33,000		
Tea & snacks in office	12,000		
Telephone expenses	25,000		
Motor Car expenses	30,000		
Electricity	21,000		
Donation to unapproved fund	6,000		
Office repairs	30,000		
Depreciation on motor car	23,000		
Net Profit	5,35,000		
Total	7,70,000	Total	7,70,000

Other information available is as under :

(i) Salary paid by him includes Rs. 24,000 paid to a boy who helps him in the clinic and also at home. (Assessing officer disallowed 1/3rd of expenses incurred.)

(ii) Car is used for business purpose. Depreciation on car is claimed in expense account as per Income-tax Rules.

(iii) Out of Rs. 33,000 Health Insurance premium, Rs. 5,000 is paid in cash. He has also paid health insurance on health of his family members Rs. 12,000.

Other Incomes are:

(i) He received salary of Rs. 1,80,000 from a Private Ltd. Company running a Nursing Home of which he is the managing director.

(ii) The company by its resolution had further paid Rs. 50,000 for his visit abroad with his wife to attend a medical conference.

Ans: 4,34,000; 7,24,000. [5,35,000+6,000+8,000+5,000–50,000–25,000–45,000=4,34,000] [4,34,000+1,80,000+50,000+25,000+45,000–10,000]

Problem 12.06-P6 (Difficult)

Dr. Ratan is a registered medical practitioner. He has prepared the following Income and Expenditure Account:

Expenses	*Rs.*	*Income*	*Rs.*
Household exps.	20,000	Consultation fees	10,000
Car purchased	30,000	Visiting fees	20,000
Travelling exps. (Personal)	4,000	Gain on race (Gross)	10,000

Donation	1,000	Sale of ancestral House	34,000
Income Tax	2,000	Profit on Sale of Securities	6,000
Salaries	8,000	Dividend on Shares	5,000
Gift to Daughter	7,000	Interest on Saving Bank of Post Office	600
Establishment exps.	1,000	Gift from Father in law	2,000
Medical Books	1,200	Interest on fixed Deposit	1,300
L.I.C. Premium	2,000	Bad debts recovered (Not allowed in earlier years)	2,000
Surgical Equipments	4,000		
Wealth Tax	1,000		
Interest on Capital	1,000		
Surplus	8,700		
	90,900		90,900

Rate of depreciation on Car and Surgical equipments is 15%. Compute his income from profession for the assessment year 2007-08.

Ans: [Professional income =8,700+20,000+30,000+1,000+2,000+7,000+4,000+1,200+ 2,000+1,000+1,000+4,000–600-2,000–2,000–34,000–10,000–6,000–1,300–5,000–4,500– 600–720=15,180]. Total income=15,180+10,000+4,000+6,000+1,300–2,000=34,480]

Problem 12.06-P7 (Typical)

Mr. Prem Sagar, CEO, furnishes P & L A/c of Travelling and Adventure Equipment Ltd. for the PY ending 31-3-2007 which maintains account on mercantile basis.

Dr. Particulars	*Amount*	*Particulars*	*Amount Cr.*
Opening stock	2,70,000	Sales	52,00,000
Purchases	42,80,000	Closing stock	54,000
Purchase of audio visual equipment	20,000	Other receipts	3,00,000
Advertising of a product in a soya citizens political party.	1,100	LTCG on sale of Trade Mark	2,29,125
Expenses incurred in respect of premises taken on rent - Current repairs Rs. 2,000 - Capital repairs Rs. 12,000 - Insurance of premises Rs. 3,000 - Municipal tax Rs. 5,000	22,000	Recovery of bad debt *(earlier Rs. 6,000 allowed as deduction out of Rs. 30,000)*	25,000
Interest A/c - Interest on overdraft Rs. 3,000 - Interest on loan to pay dividend Rs. 6,000 - Interest on loan to pay advance tax Rs. 15,000 - Interest on debentures Rs. 8,000 - Interest on company deposits Rs. 1,000	33,000		

Contribution towards RPF	13,000		
Contribution towards unapproved gratuity fund	6,500		
Provision for doubtful debts	8,000		
Health insurance premium	10,000		
Expenses to raise debentures	11,000		
BCTT	200		
Transfer to Debenture Redemption Reserve account	45,000		
Fringe benefit tax	620		
Net profit	10,87,705		
Total	58,08,125	Total	58,08,125

Additional Information :

1. Municipal tax which falls due on 31-3-2006 is paid on 1-4-2007.
2. Health insurance premium taken on health of employees. Out of Rs. 10,000, Rs. 7,000 is paid in cash.
3. Audio visual equipment is used for promotion of family planning amongst employees. Expenses incurred for promoting family planning is Rs. 3,500 p.a. not debited to P & L A/c.
4. The company enters into a contract with Mr. Bellow for supply of travel equipment. However due to strike of workers, the company was unable to supply and has to pay damages of Rs. 50,000 on February 28, 2007. This amount is not debited to P/L A/c.
5. The company imported goods worth Rs. 50,000 from China. The company paid custom duty of Rs. 15,000 and Rs. 2,000 as penalty for not complying the provisions of Customs Act. The total amount i.e. Rs. 67,000 is not debited to P/L A/c.
6. The company's stocks has been valued at 10% below the cost price.
7. Trademark was self-generated and was sold for Rs. 3,29,125. The company estimated its cost to be of Rs. 1,00,000.
8. As per lease agreement of premises 70% of capital repairs shall be borne by the owner and remaining 30% by the tenant.
9. The company donated Rs. 20,825 to National Defence Fund on 31-3-2007 and Rs. 30,000 to Zila Saksharta Samiti on 1-4-2007. Both the amounts are not debited to P/L A/c.

You are required to compute its total income and tax liability for the AY 2007-08.

Ans: 11,11,240; 3,37,115. [BI=10,87,705+6,000+16,000+1,100+12,000+15,000+6,500+8,000+7,000+45,000+620–30,000–360–3,500–50,000–65,000–2,29,125–24,000=8,02,940] [TI=8,02,940+3,29,125–20,825=11,11,240]

Problem 12.06-P7 [CA N05] [M 7]

Q.1(b) : Following is the Profit & Loss account of Mr. A, a dealer in shares and securities for the year ended on 31st March, 2007 :

	Rs.		*Rs.*
To Trading Expenses	62,60,000	By Sales	72,54,000
To Administrative Expenses	1,05,000	By Interest on FD with bank	16,500
To Financial Expenses	48,265	By Dividend from Indian Co.	64,360
To Demat and Delivery charges	4,350	By Interest on I.T. Refund (A.Y. 2006-07)	230
To STT paid	5,500		
To Net Profit before depreciation	9,11,975		
	73,35,090		73,35,090

Compute total income, the rebate available under Section 88E and tax liability.

Ans: 8,53,115; 5,500; 2,04,445. [9,11,975–16,500-64,360–230+5,500=8,36,385+16,500 +230] [2,05,396–5,500+4,009]

Problem 12.06-P9 (Typical)

The profit and loss account of Jhunjhunwala, a share broker in BSE & NSE and sub broker of NYSE, for the year ended 31st March, 2007 submits the P & L A/c as under. You are required to compute profit from business, total income and tax liability for the AY 2007-08.

Dr. Particulars	*Amount*	*Particulars*	*Amount Cr.*
Trading expenses	5,00,000	Brokerage received	8,70,000
STT paid	25,000	Speculation profits	3,00,000
Annual fees paid to SEBI	15,000	Interest on refund of income tax	2,000
Computer expenses	90,000	Interest on debentures	80,000
Fees paid for acquiring the sub broker rights in NYSE	8,00,000	Recovery of service tax (earlier allowed as deduction)	500
Donation to political party	1,000	Dividend from foreign company	1,65,580
Collection charges for interest on debentures	200	Dividend from Indian Co.	30,000
Fees paid for appearance before ITAT and CESAT	1,11,000	Net loss	94,120
Total	15,42,200	Total	15,42,200

Following expenses were not debited to P & L A/c :

(1) Life insurance premium paid for securing his own life Rs. 6,000.

(2) One time fees paid for acquisition of brokership rights to BSE and NSE Rs. 10,00,000 each on 4-5-2005 and 12-12-2006.

(3) Medical expenses incurred for specified disease on his father—Rs. 3,000.

(4) Interest on loan to purchase shares of Indian and foreign companies Rs. 15,000 and Rs. 4,000 respectively.

(5) Penalty paid to stock exchange for non compliance of stock exchange laws. Rs. 16,400.

Additional information : Business Income from transaction incurred in relation to STT paid Rs. 30,000.

Ans: 5,400; 1,58,980; 5,624. [BI= –94,120+25,000+8,00,000+1,000–2,000–1,65,580–16,400–30,000–5,12,500=5,400] [TI=5,400+1,61,580+2,000–6,000–3,000–1,000] [Tax=6,796–1,282+110=5,624]

TOPIC 12.07 *SECTION 35.* EXPENDITURE ON SCIENTIFIC RESEARCH

(A) INTRODUCTION

Section 43(4). Scientific Research means any activity for the extension of knowledge in the fields of natural or applied sciences including agriculture, animal husbandry, fisheries. Deduction in respect of scientific research is allowed to encourage development of indigenous technology and self-reliance in industry.

Deduction is allowed both in respect of revenue and capital expenditure. Following table explains the kind of expenditure allowed as deduction.

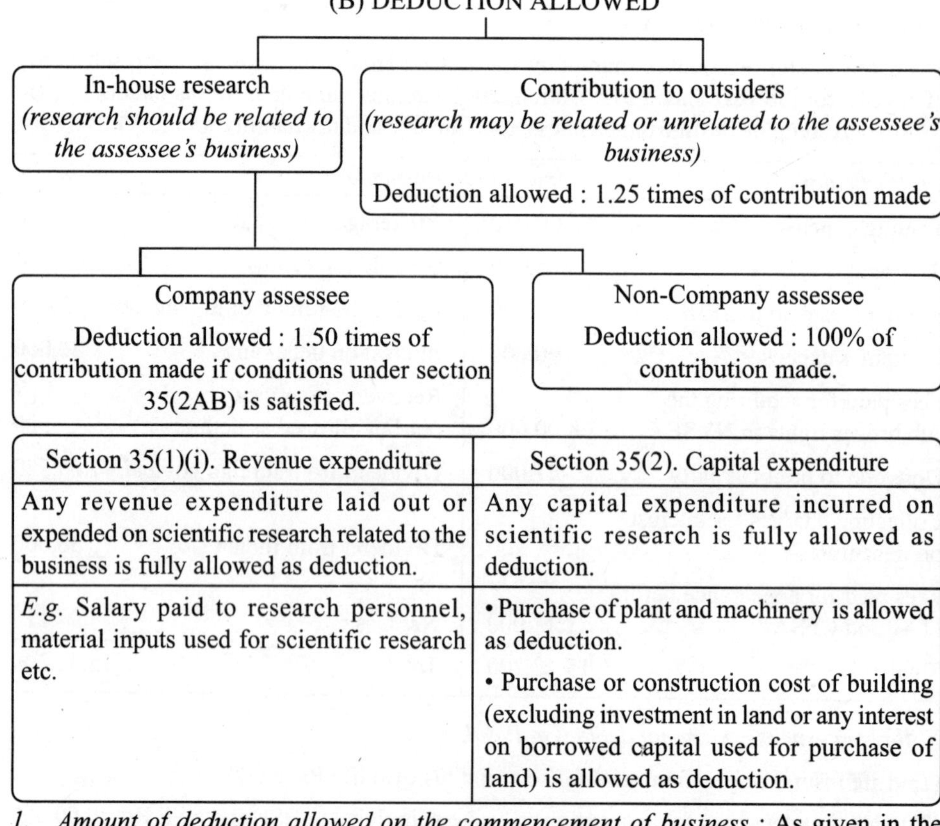

Section 35(1)(i). Revenue expenditure	Section 35(2). Capital expenditure
Any revenue expenditure laid out or expended on scientific research related to the business is fully allowed as deduction.	Any capital expenditure incurred on scientific research is fully allowed as deduction.
E.g. Salary paid to research personnel, material inputs used for scientific research etc.	• Purchase of plant and machinery is allowed as deduction. • Purchase or construction cost of building (excluding investment in land or any interest on borrowed capital used for purchase of land) is allowed as deduction.

1. *Amount of deduction allowed on the commencement of business* : As given in the above figure.

2. *Amount of deduction allowed before the commencement of business :* Where any revenue expenditure or capital expenditure is incurred before the commencement of business, the aggregate of such expenditure incurred within 3 years immediately preceding the commencement of business is allowed in the PY in which business is commenced.

Note

- Double benefit of section 32 and section 35 not allowed.
- If an assessee incurs any capital expenditure on scientific research related to his business, then deduction is available even if the relevant asset is not put to use for research and development during the previous year.
- Value of perquisite paid before the commencement of business is not allowed as deduction.
- However, the deduction relating to revenue expenditure is limited to the extent it is certified by the prescribed authority.

(C) SECTION 35(2AB). EXPENDITURE ON IN-HOUSE RESEARCH & DEVELOPMENT EXPENSES FOR CORPORATE ASSESSEES

Conditions

1. The taxpayer is a Company.
2. It is engaged in the business of bio-technology or in the business of manufacture or production of any drugs, pharmaceuticals, electronic equipment, computer, telecommunication equipment, chemicals or any other article or thing notified by the Board. (Manufacture of helicopter or aircraft or computer software or automobiles and automobile components)
3. The expenditure may be of capital and revenue in nature (excluding cost of land and building). Only expenses incurred after commencement of business is eligible.
4. Expenditure is incurred upto March 31, 2007.
5. The taxpayer has entered into an agreement with the prescribed authority for co-operation in such research and development and for audit of accounts maintained for that facility. Such R & D facility is approved by the prescribed authority.

(D) CONTRIBUTION MADE TO OUTSIDERS

Amount of deduction allowed shall be a sum equal to one and one- fourth times the sum so paid. For claiming deductions conditions are:

(a) Section 35(1)(ii)/(iii)

1. Any contribution made to approved scientific research association which has the object of undertaking scientific research.
2. To a approved university, colleges or other institution for the use of scientific research or for the use of social science or statistical research.
3. The research may be related or unrelated to the business.

Approval is given by Central Govt. The deduction is allowed even if after the date of making the contributions, the approval granted to these institution has been withdrawn.

(b) Section 35(2AA)

Conditions

1. The payment is made to (i) National Laboratory, University, Indian Insitute of Technology or (ii) specifed person as approved by prescribed authority.
2. The above payment is made under a specific direction that the said sum shall be used for scientific research undertaken under a programme approved in this behalf by the prescribed authority.

Note: National Laboratory" means a scientific laboratory functioning at the national level under the aegis of the Indian Council of Agricultural Research, the Indian Council of Medical Research, the Council of Scientific and Industrial Research, the Defence Research and Development Organisation, the Department of Electronics, the Department of Bio-Technology or the Department of Atomic Energy and which is approved as a National Laboratory by the prescribed authority in such manner as may be prescribed.

TOPIC 12.08 *SECTION 35D.* AMORTISATION OF CERTAIN PRELIMINARY EXPENSES

(A) 35D(1). WHO CAN CLAIM DEDUCTION?

1. An Indian company or a resident non-corporate resident assessee can claim deduction. Do remember a foreign company is not eligible for deduction under section 35D even if resident.
2. Assessee should have incurred preliminary expenses.
3. Preliminary expenses is incurred either before or after commencement of business.
4. Where the assessee is a person other than a company or a co-operative society, the assessee shall get his accounts audited by a Chartered Accountant for the year or years in which the preliminary expenditure is incurred. The assessee furnishes, along with his return of income for the first year in which the deduction under this section is claimed, the report of such audit in the form 3B duly signed and verified by such chartered accountant and setting forth such particulars as may be prescribed.

(B) 35D(2). MEANING OF PRELIMINARY EXPENSES

Following expenses relate to all assessees :

1 In order to be eligible such work should be carried out by the assessee himself or by a concern approved by the Board.
   (a) Preparation of feasibility report and project report.
   (b) Conducting market survey or any other survey necessary for the business.
   (c) Engineering services relating to the business.
2. Legal charges for drafting any agreement between the assessee and any other person for any purpose relating to the setting up or conduct of the business of the assessee.

Following expenses in addition to the above relate only to corporate assessee :

1. Legal charges for drafting and printing of Memorandum of Association (MOA) and Articles of Association (AOA) .
2. Registration fees of a company paid to Registrar of Companies.

3. Expenditure incurred on issue of shares or debentures like underwriting commission, brokerage and charges for drafting, printing and advertising for prospectus.
4. Such other items of expenditure (not being expenditure eligible for any allowance or deduction under any other provision of this Act) as may be prescribed.

(C) PRELIMINARY EXPENSES, ELIGIBILITY

1. *New Business*: The above expenses are incurred for setting up an industrial undertaking or a business before the commencement of business.
2. *Existing Undertaking* : The above expenses are incurred in connection with extension of an industrial undertaking or in connection with setting up a new industrial unit. *E.g.* preliminary expenses incurred for setting up of a new retail chain are not eligible for deduction u/s 35D.

(D) AMOUNT OF DEDUCTION

Deduction is allowed in 5 equal instalments over a period of 5 years beginning with the previous year in which the business commences or the previous year in which the extension of the industrial undertaking is completed or the new industrial unit commences production or operation.

(E) 35D(3). PRELIMINARY EXPENSES, COMPUTATION

(i) In case of non corporate assessee

Aggregate amount of eligible expenditure or 5% of the cost of project whichever is lower. *E.g.* Eligible expenditure Rs. 15,000; Cost of project Rs. 2,00,000; 5% of cost of project Rs. 10,000; Deduction allowed u/s 35D shall be Rs. 2,000 in 5 equal instalments from the PY when business commences.

(ii) In case of corporate assessee

Aggregate amount of eligible expenditure shall be limited to 5% of the cost of project or 5% of capital employed whichever is higher.

E.g. Eligible expenditure Rs. 9,000; Cost of project Rs. 80,000; Capital employed Rs. 1,00,000. 5% of cost of project Rs. 4,000; 5% of capital employed Rs. 5,000. Deduction allowed u/s 35D shall be Rs. 5,000 in 5 equal instalment from the PY when business commences.

(a) Meaning of Cost of project

In case of new business : It is the actual cost of the fixed assets, being land, buildings, leaseholds, plant, machinery, furniture, fittings and railway sidings (including expenditure on development of land and buildings), which are shown in the books of the assessee as on the last day of the previous year in which the business of the assessee commences.

In the case of existing business : It is the actual cost of the fixed assets, as specified above on the last day of the previous year in which the extension of the industrial undertaking is completed or the new industrial unit commences production or operation, in so far as such fixed assets have been acquired or developed in connection with the extension of the industrial undertaking or the setting up of the new industrial unit of the assessee.

(b) Meaning of capital employed

In a case of new business : The aggregate of the issued share capital, debentures and long-term borrowings as on the last day of the previous year in which the business of the company commences.

In the case of existing business : The aggregate of the issued share capital, debentures and long-term borrowings as on the last day of the previous year in which the extension of the industrial undertaking is completed, or, as the case may be, the new industrial unit commences production or operation, in so far as such capital, debentures and long-term borrowings have been issued or obtained in connection with the extension of the industrial undertaking or the setting up of the new industrial unit of the company.

(c) Meaning of long-term borrowings

1. Any moneys borrowed by the company from the Government or the Industrial Finance Corporation of India or the Industrial Credit and Investment Corporation of India or any other financial institution which is eligible for deduction under section 36(1)(viii) or any banking institution (not being a financial institution referred to above), or
2. Any moneys borrowed or debt incurred by it in a foreign country in respect of the purchase outside India of capital plant and machinery, where the terms under which such moneys are borrowed or the debt is incurred provide for the repayment thereof during a period of not less than seven years.

(F) 35D(5), (5A). EFFECT OF AMALGAMATION OR DEMERGER

1. Where the assessee, being an Indian company, is entitled to the deduction is transferred to another Indian company,
2. before the expiry of the 5-year period,
3. in a scheme of amalgamation or demerger,
4. the provisions of this section shall apply to the amalgamated company or the resultant company as they would have applied to the amalgamating company or demerged company if the amalgamation or demerger had not taken place.

Problem 12.08-P1 (CA - M00) - M 6

Q.1b : X Ltd. is an existing Indian company which sets up a new industrial unit. It incurs the following expenditure in connection with the new unit :

Preparation of project report	4,00,000
Market survey	5,00,000
Legal and other charges for issue of additional capital required for the new unit	2,00,000
Total	11,00,000

The following further data is given :

Cost of project	30,00,000
Capital employed in the new unit	40,00,000

What is the deduction admissible to the company under section 35D for assessment year 2007-08 ?

Ans: 40,000.

Problem 12.08-P2 (Typical)

Dr. Kush Saha carries on a business of research and marketing of Bio Medicines. He furnishes following P & L A/c for the PY ending 31-03-2007 :

Dr. Particulars	Amount	Particulars	Amount Cr.
Salary		Sales	49,90,000
- to research personnel	10,00,000	Research activities receipt	5,10,000
- to other staff	3,00,000		
Purchase of inputs			
- for research	7,00,000		
- for other purpose	2,00,000		
Marketing, conveyance and advertising expenses	12,00,000		
Purchase of furniture	50,000		
Net profit	20,50,000		
Total	55,00,000	Total	55,00,000

Additional Information :

1. The date of commencement of business 1-4-2006.
2. Dr. Kush invested in following assets :
   - Acquired land for Rs. 1,00,000 for research activities on 16-7-2002.
   - Acquired building for Rs. 3,00,000 both for research and business activities on 31-3-2003.
   - Acquired Plant and Machinery for Rs. 7,00,000 for research activities on 8-5-2003.
3. Following expenditure were also incurred for research activities in its respective PY :

	Salary	*Perquisites*	*Raw materials & inputs*
- PY 2002-03	30,000	5,000	11,000
- PY 2003-04	70,000	15,000	45,000
- PY 2004-05	2,00,000	60,000	1,30,000
- PY 2005-06	4,00,000	1,00,000	3,00,000

4. On 4-3-2007, he made contribution of Rs. 65,000 to National Laboratory for research in irrigation in drip technology. The research is not related to the business.
5. 70% of building is used for research activities and remaining 30% for business activities.
6. Depreciation on assets are not debited to P & L A/c. Rate of depreciation of Building - 10%; Plant - 15%; Furniture - 10%.
7. Balance sheet shows preliminary expenses outstanding as on 31-3-2006 is Rs. 1,00,000.

You are required to compute its profit from business and tax liability for the AY 2007-08.

Ans: 1,27,970; 2,853. [20,50,000+50,000–5,000–20,776–7,00,000–11,45,000–81,250–20,000]

TOPIC 12.09 *SECTION 35DDA*. AMORTISATION OF EXPENDITURE INCURRED UNDER VOLUNTARY RETIREMENT SCHEME

(A) SECTION 35DDA(1). APPLICABILITY

Where an assessee incurs any expenditure in any previous year by way of payment of any sum to an employee at the time of his voluntary retirement, in accordance with any scheme or schemes of voluntary retirement, 1/5th of the amount so paid shall be deducted in computing the profits and gains of the business for that previous year, and the balance shall be deducted in equal instalments for each of the 4 immediately succeeding previous years.

Problem 12.09-P1 (Typical)

Shri Narendra's Trading and Profit and Loss Account for the year ended on 31st March, 2007 is as under :

Opening Stock	40,000	Sales	5,40,000
Purchases	2,05,000	Closing Stock	60,000
Wages	95,000		
Royalty	26,000		
Factory expenses	45,000		
Gross profit c/d	1,89,000		
	6,00,000		6,00,000
Compensation	50,000	Gross Profit b/d	1,89,000
Rent, rates and taxes	3,000	Commission	8,000
Sundry expenses	5,300	Interest from customers	2,000
Salaries and Bonus	9,500	Dividends	5,000
Contribution to R.P.F.	2,100	Contribution by employees towards R.P.F. a/c	2,100
Legal expenses	1,800	Profit on sale of building	16,500
Provision for depreciation	1,500		
Travelling expenses	4,000		
Repairs	5,800		
Entertainment exp.	14,400		
Rural development expenses	300		
Advertisement expenses	4,900		
Banking cash transaction tax	50		
Miscellaneous expenses	3,450		
Net Profit	1,16,500		
	2,22,600		2,22,600

Additional Information :

(i) The value of opening and closing stock is at 20% below cost price. The market price was higher than the cost price.

(ii) A sum of Rs. 1,500 paid on the accident of an employee is included in the factory expenses.

(iii) Rs. 500 of the legal expenses relate to sales tax appeal and the rest to a suit filed for recovering an outstanding sum from a debtor.

(iv) Allowable depreciation is Rs. 1,800.

(v) Amount of sales includes a sum of Rs. 6,200 representing the value of goods withdrawn by Shri Narendra for his personal use. These goods were purchased at a cost of Rs. 3,400.

(vi) Advertisement expenses include Rs. 3,000 for advertisement in the souvenir published by a political party.

(vii) Sundry expenses include Rs. 2,000 of a payment made for conservation of natural resources.

(viii) Sundry expenses include Rs. 1,000 and contribution to recognised provident fund are unpaid.

(ix) Compensation was paid to an employee on his retirement under the voluntary retirement scheme of the business.

Determine his taxable profits of business.

Ans: Business income 1,44,300. [1,16,500+1,500+300+3,000+2,100+2,100+40,000+ 2,000+15,000–10,000–5,000–16,500–1,800]

RESTRICTIONS ON DEDUCTIONS (SECTION 40 to 43B)

TOPIC 12.10 *SECTION 40(a).* PAYMENT MADE WITHOUT DEDUCTION TAX AT SOURCE

Some of the clauses of this sections we have already discussed in preceding pages of this chapter. Now let us see the remaining clauses.

(A) SECTION 40(a)(i). PAYMENT MADE BY WAY OF INTEREST, ROYALTY, TECHNICAL FEES TO A NON-RESIDENT WITHOUT DEDUCTING TAX AT SOURCE

Any interest, royalty, fees for technical services or other sum chargeable under this Act, which is payable

(A) outside India (to a resident or Non-resident); or

(B) in India to a non resident or to a foreign company,

on which tax is deductible at source and on which tax has not been deducted or, after deduction, has not been paid before the expiry of the time prescribed under section 200(1), then above said payment is not allowed as deduction.

Note

- However where in respect of any such sum, tax has been deducted in any subsequent year or, has been deducted in the previous year but paid in any subsequent year after the expiry of the time prescribed under section 200(1), such sum shall be allowed as a deduction in computing the income of the previous year in which such tax has been paid.
- Tax should be deposited within 7 days from the last day of month in which tax was deducted. Where tax is deducted in the month of March then tax should be deposited by 31st May.

(B) SECTION 40(a)(ia). PAYMENT MADE BY WAY OF INTEREST, COMMISSION ETC., TO A RESIDENT WITHOUT DEDUCTING TAX AT SOURCE

Any interest, commission or brokerage, rent, fees for professional services or fees for technical services, royalty or amounts payable to a contractor or sub-contractor, being resident, for carrying out any work (including supply of labour for carrying out any work), on which tax is deductible at source and such tax has not been deducted or, after deduction, has not been paid during the previous year, or in the subsequent year before the expiry of the time prescribed under section 200(1).

Note

- However where in respect of any such sum, tax has been deducted in any subsequent year or, has been deducted in the previous year but paid in any subsequent year after the expiry of the time prescribed under section 200(1), such sum shall be allowed as a deduction in computing the income of the previous year in which such tax has been paid.
- Tax should be deposited within 7 days from the last day of month in which tax was deducted. Where tax is deducted in the month of March then tax should be deposited by 31st May.

(C) SECTION 40(a)(iii) PAYMENT MADE BY WAY OF SALARY

Any payment which is chargeable under the head "Salaries", if it is payable

(A) outside India to a resident or non resident; or

(B) in India to a non-resident,

and if the tax has not been paid thereon nor deducted therefrom, then deduction shall never be allowed.

TOPIC 12.11 *SECTION 40A(2)*. PAYMENT MADE TO RELATIVES ALLOWED AS DEDUCTION SUBJECT TO CERTAIN CONDITIONS

Where any payment is made to the relative of any person or person having substantial interest, and the Assessing Officer is of the opinion that such expenditure is excessive or unreasonable having regard to the fair market value of the goods or services for which the payment is made, so much of the expenditure as is so considered by him to be excessive or unreasonable, shall not be allowed as a deduction.

MEANING OF RELATED PERSON

Where assessee is	*Followings are treated as related person*
1. An individual	a. An individual who is relative of the assessee.
	b. An individual having a substantial interest in the business of the assessee.
2. A Company	a. Director of the company or ay relative of a director
	b. An individual having a substantial interest in the business of the assessee.
3. A firm	a. Partner of the firm or relative of a partner
	b. An individual having a substantial interest in the business of the assessee.
4. An AOP	a. Member of the AOP or relative of a member

	b. An individual having a substantial interest in the business of the assessee.
5. An HUF	a. Member of the family or relative of such person
	b. An individual having a substantial interest in the business of the assessee.

Substantial Interest means holding atleast 20% of voting power or share in a concern.

Problem 12.11-P1 [CS J97]

Profit and loss account of X, an individual, shows net loss of Rs. 6,000 for the year ending 31st March, 2007. Particulars noted from accounts are as under :

(a) Salary to staff debited to the profit and loss account include entertainment allowance of Rs. 45,000 paid to employees.

(b) Entertainment expenditure debited to profit and loss account is Rs. 9,000.

(c) Cost of goods purchased includes goods of Rs. 3,80,000 purchased on 10th May, 2006 from B Ltd. in which X holds 70% equity capital (similar goods were purchased on 11th May, 2006 from market for Rs. 2,86,000).

Ans: 88,000.

TOPIC 12.12 *SECTION 40A(3)*. CASH EXPENDITURE

(A) PROVISIONS

Where the assessee incurs any expenditure in respect of which payment is made, of a sum exceeding Rs. 20,000 otherwise than by an account payee cheque or an account payee demand draft, then 20% of such expenditure shall not be allowed as a deduction.

(B) ANALYSIS

Section 40A(3) gets attracted if following three conditions are satisfied :

1. In case of any expenditure for which deduction is *claimed* and
2. where the payment is made otherwise than through account payee cheque or draft i.e. in *cash* or through *bearer* cheque or through crossed cheque or crossed demand draft
3. in excess of Rs. 20,000,

then 20% of such payment shall not be allowed as deduction.

Problem 12.12-P1 (Typical)

Following cash payments are found debited in P & L A/c. Determine the amount which shall be added back to net profit u/s 40A(3).

1.	Salary paid to staff	Rs. 54,000
2.	Purchase of raw materials	Rs. 14,000
3.	Purchase of machinery used for the purpose of scientific research	Rs. 1,21,000
4.	Purchase of building	Rs. 25,000
5.	Payment of Health Insurance Premium on health of employees	
	- in cash	22,000
	- through bearer cheque	28,000
	- through account payee cheque	70,000

6. Payment to relatives *(The assessing officer did not allow Rs. 28,000 as deduction since excess payment)* Rs. 52,000

Ans: 10,800; nil; 24,200; nil; 22,000 - section 36(1)(ib), 5,600; nil; 4,800.

(C) OTHER POINTS

The payment amount and the bill amount both should exceed Rs. 20,000, then only section 40A(3) gets attracted. It means :

1. Where one bill consists of amount exceeding Rs. 20,000 and payment is made in part and no part exceeds Rs. 20,000, then section 40A(3) does not get attracted.

   E.g. 1 : Bill No. 340 Rs. 80,000. Rs. 20,000 is paid 4 times Section 40A(3) does not get attracted.

   E.g. 2 : Bill No. 850 Rs. 36,000. Rs. 8,000 is paid by account payee cheque and Rs. 28,000 in cash. Rs. 5,600 is not allowed as deduction.

   E.g. 3 : Bill No. 30 Rs. 64,000. Rs. 14,000 is paid by account payee cheque and Rs. 50,000 in cash. In this case 20% of Rs. 50,000. Rs. 10,000 is not allowed as deduction under section 40A(3).

2. Where two bills are paid at a time exceeding Rs. 20,000, then also section 40A(3) does not get attracted. But if any part payment exceeds Rs. 20,000, then section 40A(3) gets attracted.

   E.g. 1 : Bill No. 112 Rs. 15,000 and Bill No. 154 Rs. 17,000. Rs. 32,000 payment is made in cash. Section 40A(3) does not get attracted.

   E.g. 2 : Bill No. 112 Rs. 25,000 and Bill No. 154 Rs. 20,000. Rs. 45,000 payment is made in cash. Rs. 5,000 is disallowed as deduction.

(D) RULE 6DD. EXCEPTIONS IN CASE OF FOLLOWING CASH PAYMENTS SECTION 40A(3) IS NOT APPLICABLE

1. Payment made to Financial Institutions or Banks.
2. Payment of Sales tax, custom, excise, income tax, etc.
3. Where the payment is made in a village or town, which on the date of such payment is not served by any bank, to any person who ordinarily resides, or is carrying on any business, profession or vocation, in any such village or town.
4. Where the payment was required to be made on a day on which the all banks were closed either on account of holiday or strike.
5. Where the payment is made for the purchase of (i) agricultural or forest produce; or (ii) the produce of animal husbandry (including hides and skins) or dairy or poultry farming; or (iii) fish or fish products; or (iv) the products of horticulture or apiculture, to the cultivator, grower or producer of such articles, produce or products.
6. Payment made by a book adjustment.
7. Where the payment is made for the purchase of the products manufactured or processed without the aid of power in a cottage industry, to the producer of such products.
8. Where any payment by way of gratuity, retrenchment compensation or similar terminal benefit, is made to an employee of the assessee or the heirs of any such employee on or in connection with the retrenchment, resignation, discharge or death of such employee, if the income chargeable under the head "Salaries" of the employee in respect of the financial year in which such retirement, resignation, discharge or death took place or the immediately preceding financial year did not exceed Rs. 7,500.

9. Where the payment is made by an assessee by way of salary to his employee after deducting the income-tax from salary in accordance with the provisions of section 192 of the Act, and when such employee
   (A) is temporarily posted for a continuous period of fifteen days or more in a place other than his normal place of duty or on a ship; and
   (B) does not maintain any account in any bank at such place or ship;
10. Where the payment is made by any person to his agent who is required to make payment in cash for goods or services on behalf of such person.
11. Where the payment is made by an authorised dealer or a money changer against purchase of foreign currency or travellers cheques in the normal course of his business.

Problem 12.12-P2 [CS D02]

Determine the amount of disallowance under the head "Profit and gains of business or profession" :

(i) X Ltd. purchases raw materials on credit from Y who holds 20% equity share capital in X Ltd. The amount of bill is Rs. 42,000 (market value : Rs. 38,000). The bill is paid in cash on June 15, 2006.

(ii) A Ltd. purchases goods on credit from B Ltd. on April 10, 2006 for Rs. 12,000 and on April 16, 2006 for Rs. 15,000. Total payment of Rs. 27,000 is made by cash on May 1, 2006.

(iii) X Ltd., purchases goods on credit from Y Ltd. on September 9, 2006 for Rs. 32,000 which he pays by a bearer cheque on November 11, 2006.

Ans: 11,600; Nil; 6,400.

Problem 12.12-P3 [CA M01] [M 6]

Discuss the tax implications of the following transactions in the case of X, a doctor running a nursing home :

a.	Amount paid to a scientific research association approved by the Central Government and run by a drug manufacturing company	20,000
b.	Amounts received from the employees of the nursing home as contributions towards provident fund for the months of March 2005, paid to the P.F. Commissioner on April 25, 2005	25,000
c.	Payments made in cash towards purchases of medicines	50,000
d.	Repayment of loan taken from a bank for doing a Post - Graduate Course in medicine - Instalment	50,000
	Interest	10,000

Ans: 25,000 deduction allowed u/s 35; No deduction if PF paid after due date of PF regulation Act.; 10,000 disallowed; 10,000 allowed as deduction u/s 80E if paid from taxable income.

TOPIC 12.13 *SECTION 43B.* CERTAIN EXPENSES ALLOWED AS DEDUCTION ONLY ON ACTUAL PAYMENT

Where the assessee maintains account on mercantile basis, the assessee can claim deduction on accrual basis even if actual payment is not made. But under section 43B certain expenses like interest, bonus etc. are allowed as deduction only when actual payment is made.

(A) SECTION 43B IS APPLICABLE ONLY TO FOLLOWING KINDS OF PAYMENTS

1. *Indirect Tax payment :* Any sum payable by the assessee by way of tax, duty, cess or fee, by whatever name called, under any law *i.e.* Sales tax, Excise duty, custom duty etc., municipal tax, land revenue etc., or
2. *Interest payment* by way of following :
   (a) any sum payable by the assessee as interest on *any loan or borrowing* from
   a public financial institution (IDBI, ICICI, IFCI etc.) or
   a State financial corporation (UPSIDC, DFC, PICUP, HSFC etc.) or
   a State industrial investment corporation or
   (b) any sum payable by the assessee as interest on any *term loan or advance* from a scheduled bank (SBI, Canara Bank, PNB etc.).
3. *Certain payments made to employees*
   (a) Employer's contribution to any provident fund or superannuation fund or gratuity fund or any other fund for the welfare of employees, or
   (b) Bonus or commission payable to employees.
   (c) any sum payable by the assessee as an employer in lieu of any leave at the credit of his employee. *(Leave salary)*

(B) IN WHICH YEAR DEDUCTION IS ALLOWED?

If the payment is made on or before the relevant due date of furnishing of return, then deduction is allowed in the year of accrual.

If the payment is made after the relevant due date of furnishing of return, then deduction is allowed in the year of payment.

Problem 12.13-P1 (Difficult)

Debit side of the profit and loss account of X Ltd. shows the following expenses, which have been due but are outstanding as on March 31, 2007 :

1. Leave encashment expenses Rs. 65,000. First payment on June 1, 2007 Rs. 15,000. Second payment on Dec. 25, 2007 Rs. 50,000.
2. Excise duty payable Rs. 14,000. First payment on June 10, 2007 Rs. 3,000. Second payment on April 1, 2008 Rs. 11,000.
3. Sales tax payable Rs. 48,000. First payment on Oct. 5, 2007 Rs. 48,000.
4. Bonus payable to employees Rs. 87,000. First payment on May 2, 2007 Rs. 30,000. Second payment on October 30, 2007 Rs. 57,000.
5. Interest payable to LIC on loan Rs. 75,000. First payment on May 13, 2008 Rs. 50,000. Second payment on January 10, 2009 Rs. 25,000.
6. Municipal tax payable Rs. 5,000. Not yet paid.
7. Interest on loan taken from Z Ltd Rs. 5,00,000. Paid on 7-11-2007.

Due date of filing return of income is October 31, 2007.

Find out the previous years in which the aforesaid payment are deduction. The company maintains book of account on the basis of mercantile system of accounting.

Ans:

1. First payment PY 2006-07; Second payment PY 2007-08.
2. First payment PY 2006-07; Second payment PY 2008-09.

3. First payment PY 2006-07.
4. First payment PY 2006-07; Second payment PY 2007-08.
5. First payment PY 2007-08; Second payment PY 2008-09.
6. Deduction not allowed since not yet paid.
7. PY 2006-07 since 43B is not applicable to payment made to companies therefore deduction is allowed in the year of accrual of liability.

Problem 12.13-P2 [CS J03]

Debit side of the profit and loss account of X Ltd. Shows the following expenses, which have been due but are outstanding as on March 31, 2007:

Payment	*First payment*			*Second payment*	
	Outstanding on March 31, 2007	*Date of payment*	*Amount paid*	*Date of payment*	*Amount paid*
(1) Leave encasement expenses	65,000	June 1, 2007	15,000	Dec. 25, 2007	50,000
(2) Excise duty payable	14,000	June 10, 2007	3,000	Dec. 13, 2007	11,000
(3) Sales tax payable	48,000	Oct. 5, 2007	48,000	—	—
(4) Bonus payable to employees	87,000	May, 2, 2007	30,000	October 30, 2007	57,000
(5) Interest payable to LIC on loan	75,000	May, 13, 2007	50,000	January 10, 2008	25,000

Due date of filing return of income is October 31, 2007.

Find out the previous years in which the aforesaid payment are deduction. The company maintains book of account on the basis of mercantile system of accounting.

Ans: (1) 2006-07; 2007-08 (2) 2006-07; 2007-08 (3)2006-07 (4)2006-07; 2006-07 (5) 2006-07; 2007-08.

Problem 12.13-P3 [CS J96]

Net profit as per P & L A/c. of X is Rs. 6,86,000 for the year ending 31-3-2007. The following information is noted from accounts:

(a) Advertisements expenditure debited to P & L A/c include the following:
   (i) Rs. 16,000 being cost of advertisment which appeared in a newspaper owned by a political party.
   (ii) Rs. 11,400 being capital expenditure on advertisement.
   (iii) Rs. 7,000 paid to a concern in which X has substantial interest. (amount is excessive to the extent of Rs. 1,400.)

(b) Out of salary to employees of Rs. 8,70,000 debited to the profit and loss account :
   (i) Rs. 40,000 is employee's contribution to recognised provident fund, Rs. 37,500 of which is credited in the employee's account in the relevant fund before the 'due date';
   (ii) Rs. 46,000 is bonus which is paid on 13th November, 2007;

(iii) Rs. 36,000 is commission which is paid on 1st December, 2007;

(iv) Rs. 20,000 is incentive to workers which is paid on 10th December, 2007;

(v) Rs. 40,000 is paid outside India respect of which tax is not deducted at source;

(vi) Rs. 6,000 being capital expenditure for promoting family planning amongst employees; and

(vii) Rs. 40,000 being entertainment allowance given to employees.

Determine the net income ignore depreciation.

Ans: 8,44,100. [6,86,000+16,000+11,400+1,400+2,500+46,000+36,000+40,000+4,800]

Problem 12.13-P4 (Difficult)

M/s Blue Blood Ltd. a garment manufacturing Company has its Manufacturing and Trading account for Assessment year 2007-2008 as below :

Profit & Loss A/c

Salary and Sales Promotion	7,17,572	Gross Profit	24,57,534
Rent, Rates & Taxes	1,44,000		
Interest	97,557		
Depreciation	1,90,778		
Bonus	1,32,000		
Insurance	1,95,750		
Penalty under Income Tax Act for violation of S. 269SS	55,000		
Net Profit	9,24,877		
	24,57,534		24,57,534

The Company also provides following details :

(a) Written down value of the block of building on which depreciation has been claimed is Rs. 11,50,800 as on 31-3-2007. The rate of depreciation claimed is 10%.

(b) Company has paid Rs. 67,500 in cash at one go to an employee for sale promotion in addition to the salary for this additional responsibility.

(c) Company purchased raw material from M/s. Cottonex Ltd. on 30-9-2006 for Rs. 18,700 and on 28-2-2007 for Rs. 19,300. The total amount of Rs. 38,000 was paid in cash on 30-3-2007.

(d) The amount of bonus Rs. 1,32,000 is outstanding on 31-3-2007. Rs. 52,000 was paid on 30-10-2007and the whole of rest on 27-2-2008.

Compute the total taxable income of the assessee Company.

Ans: 11,49,075. [9,24,877+55,000+1,90,778–1,15,080+80,000+13,500]

Problem 12.13-P5 (Difficult)

M/s Deesons (P) Ltd., a manufacturing-cum-trading company, has filed its return of income for the Assessment Year 2007-2008. The manufacturing-cum-trading and Profit & Loss Accounts, as filled by it, are as under :

Dr.	*Rs.*	*Cr.*	*Rs.*
To Salaries	1,30,000	By Gross Profit b/d	17,86,000
To Rent	60,000		
To Interest	2,80,000		
To Depreciation :			
(a) Machinery	1,20,000		
(b) Furniture	80,000		
To Provision for bad debts	1,60,000		
To Income-tax	90,000		
To Entertainment	36,000		
To Advertisement	25,000		
To Net Profit	8,05,000		
	17,86,000		17,86,000

Examination of the case revealed the following :

(1) Written down value of Machinery and Furniture as on 31-3-2006 was Rs. 6,50,000 and Rs. 1,30,000 respectively as per income-tax records;

(2) Out of provision for bad debts, only Rs. 90,000 was written off as irrecoverable;

(3) Interest is payable on term loan obtained from a scheduled bank but it remained unpaid upto September, 2007.

(4) Expenditure on advertisement included Rs. 12,000 paid for advertisement in a souvenir published by a political party;

Compute the total income and the tax liability of the company for the AY 2007-08.

Ans: 13,46,500. [8,05,000+70,000+90,000+2,00,000–97,500–13,000+2,80,000+12,000]

Problem 12.13-P6 (Difficult)

Following is the Trading A/c and Profit and Loss A/c of M/s Bharat & Co. Pvt. Ltd., a domestic company, for the financial year 2006-2007 :

Profit and Loss Account

Salary	7,00,000	Gross Profit	35,00,000
Interest	3,50,000		
Rent, Rates & Taxes	1,75,000		
Entertainment	60,000		
Bad Debts written off	3,20,000		
General Exp.	2,80,000		
Provision for Income Tax	7,00,000		
Depreciation	1,50,000		
Net profit	7,65,000		
Total	35,00,000		35,00,000

Following further information is available :

(a) Donation of Rs. 50,000 paid to a political party is included in general Expenses.

(b) Rent, rates and taxes include Central Sales Tax of Rs. 35,000 which was paid on 30.6.2007 *i.e.,* after the close of the accounting year.

(c) Rent, rates and taxes also include a penalty of Rs. 10,000 levied for non-payment of Octroi Duty.

(d) Interest includes an amount of Rs. 25,000 paid to Income Tax Department.

(e) Depreciation as per Income Tax Rules works out to Rs. 1,85,000.

Compute the taxable income of the company for the AY 2007-2008.

Ans: 14,65,000. [7,65,000+7,00,000+50,000+10,000+25,000+1,50,000–1,85,000= 15,15,000–50,000]

Problem 12.13-P7 (Typical)

Compute the taxable income of Rupesh & Co., a public limited company on the basis of following Trading Account and Profit & Loss Account for the financial year 2006-2007:

Profit and Loss Account

Dr.	*Rs.*	*Cr.*	*Rs.*
Salary	1,00,000	Gross Profit	50,00,000
Rent	40,000		
Interest	1,00,000		
Provision for Income-tax	6,00,000		
Entertainment	40,000		
Donation	10,00,000		
Sales Tax	70,000		
Repairs	50,000		
Net Profit	30,00,000		
	50,00,000		50,00,000

Following further information is available :

(i) Sales tax paid this year includes Rs. 20,000 as liability towards sales made last year and Rs. 10,000 towards penalty for default in making payment in time.

(ii) Interest includes Rs. 30,000 paid to Income Tax Department.

(iii) Donation is made to a political party.

(iv) Purchases include cash payment of Rs. 50,000 for a single consignment from one party.

(v) The company floated new shares this year. Out of the application money received by it, the company forfeited Rs. 15,00,000 because some of the applicants did not subscribe to the share capital after allotment of shares to them.

Ans: 36,50,000. [30,00,000+600,000+10,00,000+30,000+10,000+10,000=46,50,000– 10,00,000]

Problem 12.13-P8 (Typical)

XYZ Ltd. is a manufacturing company. For financial year 2006-2007, the company earned a net profit of Rs. 5,00,000 after providing depreciation of Rs. 2 lakhs as per I.T. Rules, 1962. The following information is also supplied :

(a) Salary includes bonus paid amounting to Rs. 1,80,000. However, bonus payable under the Payment of Bonus Act, 1965 works out to Rs. 1,20,000. Payment made by the Company was in pursuance of settlement approved by the Labour Court.

(b) Interest debited includes Rs. 2,00,000 as interest paid on deposits received from the public.

(c) Interest on Government securities of Rs. 60,000 is credited to P&L A/c.

(d) The company paid Rs. 2,04,000 to its three whole time Directors as remuneration.

(e) The interest includes (i) Rs. 10,000 paid on instalments granted for Sales Tax payment (ii) Rs. 10,000 paid to non-resident outside India without deducting tax at source.

(f) The donation includes (i) Rs. One lakh to an approved Scientific Research Association (ii) Rs. 80,000 to a trust, Trust being run for the benefit of a particular community.

(g) Miscellaneous Expenses include Rs. 30,000 paid towards penalty for non-fulfilment of delivery conditions of a contract of sale for reasons beyond control.

(h) The credit side of P&L A/c includes an amount of Rs. 1,50,000 received from an Indian Company for supply of know how in the installation of Machinery. This contract was approved by the Central Government/CBDT.

Compute the total income of the company based on the above information for Assessment Year 2007-2008.

Ans: 5,65,000. [5,00,000–60,000+10,000–25,000+80,000=5,05,000+60,000]

Problem 12.13-P9 (Typical)

Mr. Sunil Sharma, a lawyer, who maintains his books of accounts on cash basis, furnishes following receipt and payment account for the PY 2006-07 :

Receipt	*Amount*	*Payment*	*Amount Cr.*
Balance b/d :	6,80,000	Purchase of car	8,00,000
Fees from clients		Salary to staff	3,20,000
- for 2006-07 Rs. 5,40,000 - for 2005-06 Rs. 1,50,000 - for 2004-05 Rs. 1,00,000	7,90,000	Employer's contribution to RPF	60,000
Loan from Sachin Tendulkar	2,00,000	LIP paid on own life	15,000
Interest on fixed deposits from Canara Bank *(net)*	23,500	Interest to Bank on overdraft facility	4,000
Fees for publishing articles	2,000		
Royalty from book *(company law)*	15,200	Balance c.f.	5,11,700
Total	17,10,700	Total	17,10,700

Additional Information :

1. A client extremely satisfied by Mr. Sunil Sharma's hardwork and superb performance in a court case, makes a gift of Rs. 7,000 in addition to his usual fees.
2. An approved charitable institution which obtained certain professional advice from Mr. Sunil Sharma pays Rs. 6,000 to him. Mr. Sunil Sharma was reluctant to accept this amount, deposited it back to the institution. This amount is not included in receipt and payment A/c.

3. Fees due but outstanding Rs. 3,50,000.
4. Car is purchased for personal purpose.
5. Rs. 4,000 contribution to RPF was paid on August 18, 2007.

You are required to compute profit from business, taxable income and tax liability for the AY 2007-08.

Ans: 4,23,000; 4,48,369; 86,201.

Problem 12.13-P10 (Typical)

Mr. Santosh, a dairy farmer, who also carries on a business of Greening World, by planting trees and selling them. He furnishes following P & L A/c for the PY ending 31-3-2007. Compute profit from business.

Dr. Particulars	*Amount*	*Particulars*	*Amount Cr.*
Purchases	6,80,000	Sales	12,11,900
- Raw materials : Bill No. 485 Rs. 25,000; Bill No. 550 Rs. 10,000; Bill No. 786 Rs. 3,00,000	3,35,000	Loan from a bank	1,50,000
- Furniture *(Stock in trade)*	35,000	Net loss	1,20,000
- Cloths for personal use	5,000		
- Saplings *(in cash)*	2,00,000		
- Milks from milkman	70,000		
Payments to :			
- Bank as interest *(in cash)*	30,000		
- Income tax penalty	2,000		
- Sales tax penalty	3,500		
- Staff as salary	58,900		
- Relatives as salary	56,000		
Income tax paid on perquisites on behalf of employee	6,500		
Total	14,81,900	Total	14,81,900

Additional Information :

1. The payment of Bill No. 485 & 550 is made is Rs. 27,000 in cash and balance Rs. 8,000 through account payee cheque. The payment of Bill No. 786 is made by pay order.
2. Rs. 1,00,000 is received in cash from a party.
3. Payment to relatives is unreasonable to the extent of Rs. 25,000 and Rs. 31,000 is paid in cash.

Ans: 2,16,800.

Problem 12.13-P11 (Typical)

Mr. X runs a proprietor business M/s Agency Centre which is a distributor. He has agencies of Britannia and Nestle for which he gets commission on sales at a fixed percentage. He presents the following particulars for the year ended March 31, 2007:

Commission receivable from Britannia Rs. 4,00,000.

Commission receivable from Nestle Rs. 6,00,000.

During the year 500 cartons of Maggi were purchased @ Rs. 5,00,000 of which 400 cartons were sold at Rs. 6,00,000. Shop expenses Rs. 2,65,000. On an examination following items included in shop expenses :

1. Expenses of Rs. 45,000 on the marriage of Mr. X's son.
2. Rs. 27,000 being cost of calendars and diaries.
3. Rs. 13,000 arc estimated for the repairs for residential house.
4. Penalty of a Rs. 23,000 imposed for bringing goods without paying octroi.
5. A cash advance of Rs. 25,000 in connection with purchase of scanner.

Compute his total income for under the head 'Profit from Business' and tax liability for the AY 2008-09.

Ans: 10,41,000; 2,94,301.

Problem 12.13-P12 (CA - M94) - M 6

Q.1 : X, a businessman, submits the following Profit and Loss Account for the year ending March 31, 2007 :

Salaries	75,000	Gross profit	4,50,000
Travelling expenses	25,800	Interest on Government bonds	8,500
Rent and rates	3,000	Discount received	1,500
Interest on capital	5,000		
Administrative charges	25,000		
Depreciation	25,000		
Income-tax	50,000		
Net Profit	51,200		
	2,60,000		2,60,000

The following additional information is furnished :

1. Salaries include payment of Rs. 16,000 to Mrs. X, who is acting as supervisor of the quality control department. She does not have any other income during this year. Till February 2006, she was employed in Sanvats Ltd. in a similar post for 10 years and was drawing a monthly salary of Rs. 1,500.
2. X had gone on a foreign tour in connection with the business. The journey was for 15 days in which he spent 3 days on visiting tourist spots. Total expenses incurred, which were within RBI norms also, in respect of this foreign tour were Rs. 20,000.
3. Administrative charges include expenses in respect of donation of Rs. 1,000 to the trade association for the purpose of an advertisement in the souvenir published by it.
4. Depreciation allowance as per the Income-tax Rules, 1962 is Rs. 45,000.
5. X raised a loan from LIC of India on the security of his life insurance policy and used the same for the payment of expenses relating to repairs of machinery. Interest of Rs. 2,500 in respect of this loan was paid out of his drawings.
6. Birthday gifts presented to his minor son includes cash of Rs. 20,000 which was deposited in a nationalized bank. Interest accrued up to March 31, 2007 was Rs. 2,500.
7. S, brother of X, is suffering from a permanent deafness. Since he could not earn money for his livelihood, X takes care of him in respect of all expenses being Rs. 8,000.

8. During the previous year, X has paid Rs. 10,000 by way of cheque towards medical insurance premia of himself, his wife and minor son.
9. From the above particulars, prepare a statement showing the total income of X for the assessment year 2007-08.

Ans: 3,700. [51,200+5,000+50,000+25,000–8,500+4,000–45,000–2,500+1,000=79,200+ 8,500+1,000=88,700–75,000–10,000=3,700]

COMPUTATION OF INCOME ON ESTIMATED BASIS

(A) INTRODUCTION

Till now we were computing income on actual basis but in following sections income shall be computed on estimated basis known as presumptive rate of taxation.

(B) GENERAL CONDITIONS APPLICABLE TO ALL SECTIONS 44AD, 44AE AND 44AF

1. The profit from business which is computed on estimated basis is all comprehensive *i.e.* all deductions and depreciations which should be allowed under sections 28 to 44D are deemed to be already allowed and no further adjustment is required to be made.
2. Deductions u/s 80C to 80U and rebate u/s 88E are available.
3. Taxpayer can adjust brought forward losses.
4. The written down value of any asset used for the purpose of the business shall be deemed to have been calculated as if the assessee had claimed and had been actually allowed the deduction in respect of the depreciation for each of the relevant assessment years.
5. Disallowance u/s 40, 40A and 43B has already been deemed to be adjusted.
6. Taxpayer need not comply with Sections 44AA or 44AB in claiming income on estimated basis. If however he claims a lower income he must maintain books and get them audited u/s 44AA & Section 44AB respectively.
7. A taxpayer may voluntarily claim a higher income.
8. Where however the business is carried on a partnership basis, section 40b deduction shall be allowed.

TOPIC 12.14 *SECTION 44AD.* TAXPAYER IS ENGAGED IN BUSINESS OF CIVIL CONSTRUCTION OR SUPPLY OF LABOUR FOR CIVIL CONSTRUCTION WORK

Conditions

1. Applicable to all assesses whether resident or non resident who is engaged in the business of civil construction or supply of labour for civil construction

   "Civil construction" includes—

   (a) the construction or repair of any building, bridge, dam or other structure or of any canal or road;

   (b) the execution of any works contract.
2. Whose gross receipts from such business do not exceed Rs.40 lakhs. It shall not include the value of material supplied by the client.

3. *Computation of deemed profit* : Income from such business is estimated at 8% of gross receipts paid or payable. Gross receipts do not include the material supplied by client. A taxpayer may voluntarily claim a higher income on the estimated basis.

Problem 12.14-P1 [Hons 2002]

Mrs. X is engaged in the business of civil construction (turnover of 2006-07 being Rs. 18,90,000). She wants to claim the following deductions:

Salary to employees Rs. 2,75,000; Depreciation Rs. 1,35,000 Cost of Materials used Rs. 12,95,000 Other expenses Rs. 1,72,500.

Determine the Total Income and tax liability of Mrs. X for the AY 2007-08 assuming that:

(i) She has not maintained accounts as required under Section 44AA.

(ii) Taxable income from other business is Rs. 95,000.

(iii) Long-term Capital Gain is Rs. 40,000.

(iv) She has paid Rs. 5,000 donation to Municipal Corporation of Delhi for promoting family planning.

(v) She also pays Rs. 13,000 as tuition fees for her son studying in Doon School Dehradun.

Ans: 2,68,200; 25,643.

TOPIC 12.15 *SECTION 44AE.* TAXPAYER IS ENGAGED IN BUSINESS OF PLYING, LEASING OR HIRING TRUCKS

Conditions

1. Available to all assessees whether resident or non-resident.
2. Assessee is owning not more than 10 goods carriages at any time during the PY. Carriages may be taken on hire purchase / instalment and he shall be deemed to be the owner of such goods or carriage.
3. Computation of deemed profit
   (a) *In case of heavy vehicle* : Rs. 3,500 p.m. (or part of the month) per heavy vehicle during which goods carriage is *owned* by the assessee.
   (b) *Medium or light vehicle* : Rs. 3,150 p.m. (or part of the month) per medium or light vehicle during which goods carriage is *owned* by the assessee.

Problem 12.15-P1

Q.3a, M 6 : Mr. Sukhvinder Singh is engaged in the business of plying goods carriages. On 1st April, 2006 he owns 10 trucks (out of which 6 are heavy goods vehicles). On 2nd May, 2006, he sold one of the heavy goods vehicles and purchased a light goods vehicle on 6th May, 2006. This new vehicle could however be put to use only on 15th June, 2006. BCTT paid Rs. 500.

Compute the total income of Mr. Sukhvinder for the assessment year 2007-08.

Ans: 4,02,850.

Problem 12.15-P2 [Hons 2001]

Mr. G retired from Govt. Service in March 2006. He got Rs. 18 lakhs on account of retirement benefits. Out of the aforesaid sum, he purchased on 23rd April 2006 a few motor vehicles and got their delivery on that date. The particulars of the vehicles are given below :

	Cost of the Vehicle
1. Heavy good vehicles - 2	8,00,000
2. Medium good vehicles - 4	4,00,000
3. Light commercial vehicles - 3	3,00,000

He formed GM and Associates (a sole proprietorship concern), along with his son M as an employee on 1-6-2006 and started plying the vehicles from 4-6-2006.

On an average every vehicle remains off the road for about a week for repairs and maintenance. GM and Associates maintains no account and vouchers. However, it maintains a rough record of its receipts and outgoings which is given below.

(i) Receipts	4,40,000
Less: Expenses (excluding depreciation and salaries to M)	30,000
	4,10,000

You are required to compute the total income of GM and Associates from the business of goods carriage for the PY 2006-07 relevant to the AY 2007-08.

Assume rate of depreciation 40% and salary to M at Rs. 1,00,000 p.a.

Ans: 3,48,600.

TOPIC 12.16 *SECTION 44AF.* TAXPAYER IS ENGAGED IN RETAIL TRADE

Conditions

1. Available to all assessees whether resident or non-resident.
2. Turnover should not exceed Rs. 40 lakhs.
3. *Computation of deemed profit* : Income from such business is estimated at 5% of gross receipts paid or payable.

Problem 12.16-P1 (Typical)

Mr. Taxcrazy owns a "Margin Free" retail outlet in Kerala. He furnishes following particulars of his business. You are required to advise Mr. Taxcrazy whether he should follow actual income approach or estimated income approach.

	Case 1	*Case 2*	*Case 3*
Total sales accrued during PY 2005-06	25,00,000	30,00,000	36,00,000
(cash received in PY 2006-07)	4,00,000	2,00,000	5,00,000
Total sales accrued during PY 2006-07	30,00,000	41,00,000	40,00,000
(cash yet not received)	6,00,000	9,00,000	1,00,000
Purchases due and paid during PY 2006-07	27,00,000	30,00,000	35,00,000
Expenses due and paid during PY 2006-07	50,000	1,00,000	1,50,000

You are required to compute his profit from business if he

1. Maintains account on mercantile basis.
2. Keeps his books of account on cash basis.

Ans: (1) 1,50,000; 50,000 (2) 10,00,000; 1,70,000 (3) 2,00,000; 7,50,000.

Problem 12.16-P2 [CA M04]

A furnishes you the following information for the year ending March 31, 2007:

Income from playing of vehicles (computed as per books) (he owns 5 heavy goods vehicle throughout the year)	2,10,400
Income from retail trade of garments (computed as per books) (sales turnover Rs. 21,70,000)	75,000
He has brought forward depreciation relating to assessment year 2007-08	1,00,000
Deposit into his PPF account on January 6, 2007	1,00,000

Compute taxable income of A and his tax liability for the assessment year 2007-08 with reasons for your computation.

Ans: 85,400.

12.17 COMPREHENSIVE PROBLEMS

Simple & Difficult

Problem 12.17.P1 [Hons 2006]

Mrs. Gopinath carries on her own business. For the year ending 31-3-2007 her Trading and Profit and Loss A/c was as follows :

Trading & Profit & Loss A/c
(for the year ended 31-3-2007)

Opening Stock	20,000	Sales	1,89,000
Purchases	1,08,000	Closing stock	52,000
Salaries	6,000	Interest on debentures	2,000
Rent	11,000	Dividend from UTI	2,000
Bonus	3,000	Discount received	12,000
Printing and postage	4,000	Race winning (gross)	12,000
BCTT	1,000		
Miscellaneous expenses	4,000		
Advertisement expenses	22,000		
Drawings	12,000		
LIC premium	5,000		
Car expenses :			
Driver's salary	6,000		
Petrol and Repair	12,000		
Property tax	4,000		
Medical expenses of disabled son	3,000		
Cost of NSC (VIII issue)	3,000		
Net profit	45,000		
	2,69,000		2,69,000

Additional information provided by her is :

(a) Advertisement expenses included cost of 20 gift packets of Rs. 1,100 each presented to customers on occasion of Diwali.

(b) Assume taxes deduced at source on dividends and debentures are Nil.

(c) The car was used both for business and personal purposes. 2/3rd is for the business purposes.

(d) The property tax of Rs. 4,000 was in respect of her self-occupied house whose rental value is Rs. 18,000.

Compute gross total income and total income of Mrs. Gopinath for the assessment year 2007-08 showing the incomes under various heads.

Ans: 18,000.

Problem 12.17-P2 (Typical)

The trading and profit and loss account of M/s. ABC Pvt. Ltd., a domestic company, for the financial year 2006-2007 is as under :

Profit & Loss Account

Salaries	4,75,000	Gross Profit	29,64,200
Rent, rates & taxes	2,20,000		
Interest	3,25,500		
Bad debts written off	70,000		
Advertisement & publicity	75,000		
Entertainment	45,500		
Donation	25,000		
Income Tax	82,000		
General expenses	2,70,000		
Depreciation	2,60,000		
Net Profit	11,16,200		
	29,64,200		29,64,200

The following other information is available :

1. Rent, rates and taxes include an amount of Rs. 15,000 in respect of sales tax paid in Feb., 2008 and Rs. 35,000 penalty levied by the Excise Department.
2. Donation of Rs. 25,000 is to a political party.
3. Entertainment expenses include an amount of Rs. 7,000 in respect of tea to office staff.
4. A new machinery worth Rs. 3,50,000 has been purchased. The expenditure has been debited under the head "Manufacturing expenses". The machinery was purchased and installed in May, 2006.
5. Interest includes an amount of Rs. 50,000 paid to the bank for loan taken for purchase of new machinery. It includes an interest of Rs. 4,167 till the asset is put to use.
6. The company had the following block of assets as on 1.4.2006.
   (i) Building (Rate of depreciation—10%) W.D.V. Rs. 9,50,000
   (ii) Plant & machinery (Rate of depreciation—15%) W.D.V.Rs. 4,20,000

Determine the total income of the company for assessment year 2007-08.

Ans: 16,51,242. [11,16,200+25,000+82,000+2,60,000+15,000+35,000+3,50,000+4,167–95,000–1,16,125=16,76,242–25,000] Dep [15% of (4,20,000+3,54,167)]

Problem 12.17-P3 (Typical)

Dr. 'A' is a renowned medical practitioner. He furnishes his Receipts and Payments account for the Financial Year 2006-2007 as under:

Receipts		*Payments*	
To Balance brought forward	35,000		
To Consultation fees :	Rs.	By Clinic Rent :	Rs.
F.Y. 2006-2007	3,000	F.Y. 2006-2007	600
F.Y. 2007-2008	27,000	F.Y. 2007-2008	4,800
F.Y. 2008-2009	2,000	F.Y. 2008-2009	600
	32,000		6,000
To Visiting fees	30,000	By Water & Electricity	2,000
To Loan from Bank for profession	25,000	By Purchase of books for professional use	8,000
To Sale of medicines	73,000	By Household expenses	7,800
To Remuneration from articles published in professional journals	6,000	By Municipal taxes paid for House property	2,000
To Rent from House property	11,000	By Purchase of car	45,000
To Interest on Post Office National Savings Certificates.	7,000	By Fire insurance for the House property	200
To Gifts received from patients	5,000	By Purchase of surgical instruments	4,700
		By Advance Income tax	13,000
		By Salary to the Compounder	12,000
		By Entertainment expenses	6,000
		By Expenses on income-tax proceedings	15,000
		By LIC Premia	15,000
		By Gift to wife	5,000
		By Interest on loan	2,000
		By Loan Account payment of instalment	5,000
		By Car expenses	15,000
		By Donation to Congress party	500
		By Purchase of medicines	35,000
		By Balance carried forward	24,800
	2,24,000		2,24,000

Compute the income of Dr. 'A' from profession and also his gross total income for the Assessment Year 2007-2008 after taking into account the following additional information :

(a) 1/3rd of car expenses relate to personal use.

(b) Depreciation on motor car is allowed @ 15%.

(c) The construction of the House property was completed in February, 1998. It was let out for residence purposes.

(d) Expenses on Income-tax proceedings include a sum of Rs. 1,000 paid for preparation of the return of income.

(e) Dr. 'A' follows the cash system of accounting.

Ans: 38,795. [32,000+30,000+73,000+5,000–6,000–2,000–4,800–4,500–705–12,000–6,000–15,000–2,000–10,000–35,000=41,995+6,300+6,000=54,295–15,000–500=38,795]

Typical

Problem 12.17-P4 (Typical)

Compute the taxable income under different heads from the following Profit and Loss Account relating to a newly established industry of Shri Ram for the year ending 31st March 2007 :

	Rs.		*Rs.*
Interest	30,000	Gross Profit	47,55,000
Salaries	5,56,000	Rent of House Property	20,000
Payment of tax on perquisites of an employee	4,000	Profit on transfer of Duty Entitlement Pass Book Scheme	2,00,000
Depreciation	4,10,000	Profit from Business of dealing in equity shares	60,000
Preliminary exp.	1,00,000		
Advertisement	3,00,000		
Travelling exp.	1,00,000		
Entertainment exp.	24,000		
Securities Transaction Tax.	6,000		
Rural Development expenses	3,00,000		
Miscellaneous exp.	1,00,000		
Net profit	31,05,000		
	50,35,000		50,35,000

Additional Information

(i) The factory started production on 1st April, 2006.

(ii) Salaries include Rs. 35,000 paid to an employee outside India and Rs. 20,000 paid to another non - resident employee in India for services rendered in India, from which no tax has been deducted at source, nor the employees have paid any tax on it.

(iii) Travelling expenses include Rs. 60,000 for travelling outside India to promote sales outside India.

(iv) The actual cost offixed assets on 31st March, 2007 was Rs. 57,00,000 including actual cost of machinery Rs. 14,00,000.

(v) The whole of preliminary expenses have been written off this year though it was spent during 2004-05 and 2005-06.

(vi) The allowable depreciation is Rs. 3,70,000.

(vii) A sum of Rs. 1,30,000 was spent during the financial year 2005-06 on scientific research, the details of which are as follows not debited to P & L A/c. :

	Rs.
Machinery	40,000
Pay of Research Officers	60,000
Materials consumed for research	30,000

(viii) Interest includes Rs. 2,000 payable on loan taken to construct the let out house property.

(ix) Advertisement expenses include Rs. 80,000 for advertisement outside India. The advertisement expenses in India Rs. 2,20,000 include Rs. 60,000 paid for salary to the employees engaged in this work and Rs. 14,000 for an advertisement in a souvenir published by the Lokpal party.

(x) Miscellaneous expenses include Rs. 22,000 paid for setting up an unapproved Employees Welfare Trust and Rs. 13,000 as contribution to the Trust for the year which has been paid.

Ans: 34,13,000. [31,05,000+35,000+20,000+4,10,000–3,70,000+2,000+14,000+35,000+2,000+6,000+3,00,000+4,000–20,000–60,000–30,000–40,000=34,13,000]

Problem 12.17-P5 [Hons 2003]

Mr. A is an advocate in the Delhi High Court. He keeps his books on cash basis. His Receipt and Payment A/c for the FY 2006-07 is given below :

Balance brought forward	83,000	Rent paid	1,20,000
Consultancy fee	2,00,000	Office expenses	32,000
Remuneration from Univ as evaluator of LLB Exams	2,000	New car purchased on 1-05-2006	3,75,000
Salary from law faculty for working as a part time lecturer	45,000	Magazines and journals subscribed	10,000
Dividend from Housing Cooperative Society	4,000	Computer purchased on 1-4-2006	50,000
Dividend from U.T.I.	5,000	Legal books purchased	25,000
Interest from bank deposit	9,000	Car Expenses	40,000
Special Commission for providing consultancy	15,000	Electricity and Water charges paid	10,000
Sale proceeds of residential house	5,00,000	Donations to approved charitable institution *(allowed under sec 80G)*	15,000
Fringe benefit tax	6,000	Income Tax paid	20,000
Son's college fee paid	50,000		
Gift to daughter	20,000		
Interest from Gold deposit scheme, 1999	5,000	Life Insurance premium paid on own life	10,000
		Balance carried forward.	97,000
Total	8,74,000	Total	8,74,000

Additional information

(i) On 31-3-2007 legal fees outstanding amounted to Rs. 20,000.

(ii) Rent is payable @ Rs. 12,000 p.m.

(iii) Car is party used for official purpose only 70% of the expenditure is for office use only.

(iv) Legal books for Rs. 10,000 were purchased on 1-5-2006 and for Rs. 15,000 on 1-11-2006.

(v) The residential house was sold on 1-6-2006 while it was purchased on 1-1-1986 for Rs. 88,500.

(vi) Half of the house taken on rent is being used for residential purpose.

Compute the total income and tax liability of Mr. A for the AY 2007-08.

Ans: 1,90,750; (1,487)

Problem 12.17-P6 [CA M 96]

S is a chartered accountant in practice. He is a resident and ordinarily resident in India. His profit and loss account for the year ended March 31, 2007 reads as follows :

		Rs.			*Rs.*
Salaries to paid staff		4,25,000	Fees earned :		
Stipends to article clerks		10,500	Audit	5,10,400	
Incentives to articles clerks		5,000	Taxation services	5,40,000	
Rent		24,000	Consultancy Services	4,62,000	15,12,400
Printing and stationery		5,600	Dividend on share of Indian Co.		10,623
Contribution to recognized provident fund		30,000	Income from Unit Trust of India		5,600
Meeting, seminar and conference		45,000	Profit on sale of shares		15,620
Interest on loan		56,000	Honorarium received from various institutes for valuation of answer papers		6,230
Books and periodicals eligible for 100% depreciation		16,500	Rent received from residential flat let out (municipal valuation : Rs. 68,000, fair rent :		
Repairs, maintenance and petrol for car		17,500	Rs. .76,000, standard rent : Rs. 70,000		72,000
Depreciation :					
Car	7,500				
Computer	15,000				
Typewriter	4,500				
Furniture	2,500	29,500			
Traveling expenses		55,000			
Municipal tax paid in respect of house property		1,000			
Net profit		7,29,373			
		16,22,473			16,22,473

Other information :

1. Fees from consultancy services include Rs. 1,40,000 received in US dollar from one company in Singapore for rendering professional service there (assume that the entire convertible foreign exchange was received within permitted period).
2. Travelling expenses include Rs. 20,000 incurred in connection with his visit to Singapore for rendering service as indicated in (1) above.
3. Included in meeting, seminar and conference expenses, a sum of Rs. 18,000 incurred for entertaining various clients in hotels and clubs.
4. Incentives to articles clerks represent amount paid to two articles clerks for passing intermediate examination at first attempts.
5. One - fourth of use of car is attributable to personal purposes.
6. 50 per cent of loan was used for the purpose of construction of the house property and 50 per cent of loan was used for purchasing office computer.
7. R follows accrual basis of accounting year 2006-07 which was not provided for in that year due to oversight.
8. The written down values of various assets as on March 31, 2007 are as follows

Car (acquired on April 1, 2001)	81,920
Computer (acquired on December 15, 2006 at cost of Rs. 1,50,000)	Nil
Typewriter (acquired on April 1, 2004)	15,000
Furniture (acquired on April 1, 2006)	16,667

9. Salaries include Rs. 25,000 paid to a computer specialist in cash for assisting R in one professional assignment.
10. R paid life membership subscription of Rs. 500 to chartered accountants' benevolent fund recognized under section 80G. The amount was debited to his drawings account.
11. Shares sold were held for 8 months before sale.

You are required to compute the total income of S for assessment year 2007-08.

Ans: 6,44,340. [7,29,373+29,500+1,000–10,623–5,600–15,620–72,000+4,375–6,230+28,000+2,000–58,133+5,000=6,37,272+21,700+15,620=6,74,592–30,000–250=6,44,340]

Problem 12.17-P7 (PE II - M03) - M 6

Q.2(a)-or- : X, a retail trader of Cochin, gives the following trading and profit and loss account for the year ending March 31, 2007 :

Opening Stock	90,000	Sales	12,11,500
Purchases	10,04,000	Income from UTI	2,400
Gross profits	3,06,000	Other business receipts	6,100
		Closing Stock	1,80,000
	14,00,000		14,00,000
Salary	60,000	Gross Profit b/d	3,06,000
Rent and rates	36,000		
Interest on loan	15,000		
Depreciation	1,05,000		

Printing and stationery	23,200		
Postage and telegram	1,640		
Loss on sale of shares (short term)	8,100		
Other general expenses	7,060		
Net Profit	50,000		
	3,06,000		3,06,000

Additional information :

It was found, some stocks were omitted to be included in both the opening and closing stock, the values of which were—opening stock : Rs. 9,000; closing stock : Rs. 18,000.

Salary includes Rs. 10,000 paid to his brother, which is unreasonable to the extent of Rs. 2,000.

The whole amount of printing and stationery was paid in cash.

The depreciation provided in the profit and loss account Rs. 1,05,000 was based on the following information :

The written down value of plant and machinery is Rs. 4,20,000. A new plant falling under the same block of depreciation of 15 per cent was bought on July 1, 2006 for Rs. 70,000. Two old plants were sold on October 1, 2006 for Rs. 50,000.

Rent and rates include sales tax liability of Rs. 3,400 paid on April 7, 2007.

Other business receipts include Rs. 2,200 received as refund of sales tax relating to 2005-06.

Other general expenses include Rs. 2,000 paid as donation to a public charitable trust.

You are required to advise X whether he can offer his business income under section 44AF, *i.e.*, presumptive taxation.

Ans: 1,12,340; 59,580 [Normal provisions = 50,000+8,100-2,400+18,000-9,000+2,000+ 4,640+1,05,000-66,000+2,000=1,12,340-1,000=1,11,340] [44AF=60,575-1,000]

Problem 12.17-P8 (CS-NEW - J03) - M 15

Q.4a : From the following profit and loss account of X for the year ending March 31, 2007, Compute his gross total income for the assessment year 2007-08 :

	Rs.		*Rs.*
Opening Stock	4,00,000	Sales	40,00,000
Purchases	30,00,000	Closing stock	4,80,000
Salaries	8,00,000	Income from house property	80,000
Rent, Rates & Taxes	1,20,000	Dividend from an Indian Co.	9,000
Legal charges	40,000		
Miscellaneous expenses	20,000		
Provision for bad debts	30,000		
Provision for gratuity	20,000		
Provision for income-tax	40,000		
Salary to Mrs. X	36,000		
Depreciation	40,000		
Net profit	23,000		
Total	45,69,000		45,69,000

Purchases include Rs. 1,00,000 paid in cash to a cultivator for purchase of an agricultural produce. Purchases also include Rs. 10,000 paid by way of compensation to a supplier as the assessee was unable to take the delivery of goods due to lack of storage space and finances.

Opening stock was overvalued by 25 per cent and closing stock was undervalued by 25%.

Salary included Rs. 15,000 paid as customary bonus on the occasion of Diwali over and above the bonus payable under the Payment of Bonus Act, 1965.

Rent, rates and taxes include Rs. 10,000 on account of disputed sales tax demand, Rs. 3,000 on account of municipal taxes for property let-out. It also includes Rs. 5,000 as customs penalty paid during the year.

An amount of Rs. 20,000 from a customer was written off from the provision for bad debts.

An employee retires on March 28, 2006. Gratuity payable to him was Rs. 20,000. A provision was created for the same this year and it was paid on April 2, 2006.

Mrs. X is a law graduate and is actively working in the assessee's firm.

Ans: 3,15,900. [23,000+10,000+40,000–80,000-9,000+1,60,000+80,000+10,000+3,000+5,000+20,000=2,62,000+53,900=3,15,000]

STRATEGY MAKER

Points in 1 to 10	Overall Points 8; Practical 8; Theory 5.
Type of problem	Difficult. Asked 100 students 99 will tell you PGBP is the most difficult. Why so? Only reason, students tend to study everything in it at one go. They end up remembering "I can never understand PGBP". From examination point of view, whatever is given in this book is more than enough. For professional exam we have discussed remaining topics in Level 2.
What to expect (DU)	You are bound to get a question from it. Do not leave anything and do it with utmost perfection. But do not do more than this.
PE (II)	Everything from start to finish is absolutely important. You miss this chapter and you miss 35% marks.

A legendary story for you

There's a legend about a bird, the thornbird, which sings just once in its life, more sweetly than any other creature on the face of the earth. From the moment it leaves the nest it searches for a thorn tree, and does not rest until it has found one. Then, singing among the savage branches, it impales itself on the longest, sharpest spine, and dying, it rises above its own agony. One superlative song, existence the price. But the whole world listens for the best is only bought at the cost of the great pain... or so says the legend.

The next chapter Assessment of Firm is byproduct of Profit from Business. Let's Run.

Keep Running

Form of organisation

13

ASSESSMENT OF FIRM

TOPIC 13.00 INTRODUCTION

1. A partnership firm is treated as separate entity under the Income Tax Act.
2. It is assessed in respect of its own income and not in respect of the income of its partners.
3. The partners, on the other hand, are liable for their own income and not of the income of the firm in which they are partners.

TOPIC 13.01 *SECTION 184.* ASSESSMENT OF FIRM

(1) A firm shall be assessed as a firm for the purposes of this Act, if

  (i) the partnership is evidenced by an instrument; and

  (ii) the individual shares of the partners are specified in that instrument.

(2) A certified copy of the instrument of partnership shall accompany the return of income of the firm of the previous year relevant to the assessment year in respect of which assessment as a firm is first sought.

If the above conditions are satisfied then section 40b becomes applicable and interest on capital contributed by partners and remuneration allowed to partners are allowed as deduction.

If conditions of section 184 are not satisfied then remuneration allowed to partners and interest on capital shall not be allowed as deduction, though such firm shall be continued to be assessed as a firm and not as an Association of Persons.

TOPIC 13.02 COMPUTATION OF TOTAL INCOME OF FIRM AND ITS PARTNERS

Computation of profit from business in the hands of firm	*Computation of profit from business in the hands of partners*
Section 40b. Remuneration to working partner *(i.e. not a sleeping partner)* is allowed as deduction if authorised by partnership deed but subject to limit specified in section 40b. *Section 40b.* Interest on loan or capital contributed by partners is allowed as deduction if authorised by partnership deed but subject to a limit of 12% p.a. Interest on drawings by partners are treated as business income in the hands of firm. The firm is liable to pay tax on profit from business after allowing deduction of remuneration and interest allowed to partners. Rate of tax on firm is 30% on normal income + surcharge @ 10% + education cess @ 2%.	*Section 40b.* Remuneration which is allowed as deduction in the hands of firm shall be distributed amongst partners as per remuneration ratio as specified in partnership deed. Remuneration payable to partners shall be chargeable under the head 'Profits from Business'. Deduction is allowed u/ss 28 to 37 in earning remuneration. *Section 40b.* The interest which is allowed as deduction in the hands of firm is treated as income in the hands of partners and is chargeable under the head 'Profits from Business'. Deduction is allowed u/ss 28 to 37 in earning interest. *Section 10(2A).* Share of profit from the firm is exempt in the hands of partners, since the firm has already paid tax on its income. Rate of tax for partners is as per slab rate.

TOPIC 13.03 *SECTION 40b* COMPUTATION OF MAXIMUM REMUNERATION PAYABLE TO PARTNERS

Firm engaged in specified profession	*Other firm*	*Maximum remuneration payable to partners*
Book profit upto 1,00,000	Book profit upto 75,000	90% of book profit or Rs. 50,000 whichever is more
next 1,00,000	upto 75,000	60%
balance	balance	40%
or		
Remuneration allowed to working partners as per partnership deed *whichever is less is deductible*		

Specified profession : We have already defined under section 44AA - maintenance of accounts; refer topic 11.14A.

How to use the table : Suppose book profit is Rs. 2,50,000.

Professional firm		*Other firm*	
90% of first Rs. 1,00,000	90,000	90% of first Rs. 75,000	67,500
60% of next Rs. 1,00,000	60,000	60% of next Rs. 75,000	45,000
40% of balance Rs. 50,000	20,000	40% of balance Rs. 1,00,000	40,000
Maximum remuneration u/s 40b	1,70,000	Maximum remuneration u/s 40b	1,42,500

An alternative short cut method to compute remuneration

Professional firm		*Other than Professional firm*	
Upto 1,00,000	90% of BP or 50,000 whichever is more	Upto 75,000	90% of BP or 50,000 whichever is more
1 Lakh to 2 Lakhs	60% of BP + 30,000	75,001 to 1,50,000	60% of BP + 22,500
more than 2 Lakhs	40% of BP + 70,000	more than 1,50,000	40% of BP + 52,500

Remuneration = 40% of 2,50,000 + 70,000 = 1,70,000

Remuneration = 40% of 2,50,000 + 52,500 = 1,42,500

We shall follow short cut method.

Illustration and Problems 13.03-P1 (Difficult)

(A) The firm is engaged in the business of selling computers. Compute remuneration payable to partners u/s 40b which shall be allowed as deduction.

	Case 1	*Case 2*	*Case 3*	*Case 4*
Book Profit	1,80,000	2,90,000	(53,000)	50,000
Remun. as per partnership deed :				
A *(working partner)*	70,000	38,500	100,000	14,000
B *(working partner)*	52,000	20,000	60,000	15,000
C *(working partner)*	67,000	91,500	10,000	16,000
Total	1,89,000	1,50,000	1,70,000	45,000

(B) Solve Case 1 if A is a sleeping partner & Case 2 if C is a sleeping partner.

(C) Solve Case 1, 2, 3 & 4 assuming that it is a firm of company secretaries.

(D) Solve Case 3 assuming that remuneration allowed to all working partners is Rs. 40,000 only.

Ans: (A) 1,24,500; 1,50,000; 50,000; 45,000; (B) 1,19,000; 58,500; (C) 1,38,000; 1,50,000; 50,000; 45,000; (D) 40,000.

Solution

Computation of remuneration as per section 40b

Case 1 : Book profit=Rs. 1,80,000, therefore remuneration u/s 40b = 40% of 1,80,000 + 52,500 = 1,24,500 or 1,89,000 *(remuneration allowed to working partner)* whichever is less. Therefore 1,24,500 is deductible remuneration.

Case 2 : Book profit = Rs. 2,90,000, therefore remuneration u/s 40b = 40% of 2,90,000 + 52,500 = 1,68,500 or 1,50,000 *(remuneration allowed to working partner)* whichever is less. Therefore 1,50,000 is deductible remuneration.

TOPIC 13.04 COMPUTATION OF BOOK PROFIT IN VARIOUS CASES

(A) GENERAL COMPUTATION OF BOOK PROFIT

1. Book profit is computed for computation of remuneration.
2. Book profit is computed under the head 'Business' by making all adjustments under section 28 to 44D except remuneration allowed to partners.

Computation of Book Profit (Assumed figure)

Net profit as per P & L A/c after making all adjustments u/ss 28 to 44D except section 40b	1,00,000
Less : Interest allowed to partners under section 40b	25,000
Book profit	75,000

Maximum remuneration allowed to partners as per section 40b is Rs. 67,500

Illustration 13.04-P1 (Difficult)

(A) X, Y and Z are partners in Armani & Co. (Firm) sharing profit in ratio of 1 : 4 : 2 satisfying the requirement of section 184 furnishes following P & L A/c for the PY ending 31-3-2007 :

Particulars	*Amount*	*Particulars*	*Amount*
Purchases	31,00,000	Sales	31,73,000
Remuneration to partners :		Interest on drawings :	
X (working partner) - 25,000 Y (sleeping partner) - 5,000	30,000	X @ 5% - 400 Y @ 4% - 600	1,000
Interest to partners X @ 15% - 3,000 Y @ 10% - 1,000	4,000		
Net profit	40,000		
Total	31,74,000	Total	31,74,000

Additional Information :

1. Entertainment expenses of Rs. 4,300 not debited to P/L A/c.
2. Interest on capital allowed to Z (working partner) is @ 16% on capital contribution of Rs. 1,20,000 and remuneration allowed to him is Rs. 15,000. Both the amounts are not debited to P & L A/c.

Compute 1. Book Profit 2. Remuneration allowed as deduction under section 40b 3. Profit of Business of Firm 4. Tax Liability of Firm 5. Taxable income of partners (no other individual income) for the AY 2007-08.

(B) Compute profit from business of firm if the conditions of section 184 is not satisfied.

Solution

Computation of profit from business

Net profit		40,000
(+) Remuneration to partners		30,000
(+) Interest to partners treated separately		4,000
(-) Entertainment expenses		(4,300)
Profit after making all adjustment except section 40b		69,700
(-) Interest to partners allowed as deduction		
X @ 12% (12 ÷ 15 × 3,000)	2,400	
Y @ 10%	1,000	
Z @ 12%	14,400	17,800

(-) Remuneration allowed as deduction (Note 1)	40,000
Profit from Business	11,900
Tax @ 33.66% of 11,900	4,006

Note 1 : Computation of book profit and remuneration

Profit after making all adjustment u/s 28 to 44D except section 40b	69,700
Less : Interest to partners allowed as deduction	17,800
Book Profit	51,900

Remuneration allowed as deduction is 90% of 51,900 = Rs. 46,710 or Rs. 50,000 whichever is more but limited to Rs. 40,000. Maximum remuneration allowed as per partnership deed is Rs. 40,000.

Computation of income in the hands of partners

	X	*Y*	*Z*
Remuneration to partners	25,000	nil	15,000
Interest upto 12%	2,400	1,000	14,400
Profit from Business	27,400	1,000	29,400

(B) Where conditions of section 184 is not satisfied no deduction on account of interest and remuneration to partners is allowed. Therefore profit of business of firm is Rs. 69,700.

Problem 13.04-P2 (Difficult)

Profit of a partnership firm is Rs. 3,00,000 after charging interest on capital @ 20% of its total capital of Rs. 5,00,000. How much maximum remuneration can be paid by this firm to its partners, if it is a business firm ?

Ans: 1,88,500.

Problem 13.04-P3 [CA N96]

ABC is a partnership firm carrying on business in which A, B and C are partners sharing profits and losses equally. In respect of assessment year 2007-08 it furnishes the following particulars :

1. Loss as per profit and loss a/c after debiting remuneration and interest to partners — 2,50,000
2. Remuneration to partners :
   - A — 90,000
   - B — 60,000
   - C — 30,000
3. Interest paid on capital

	Capital	Interest
A	1,00,000	20,000
B	1,00,000	20,000
C	1,00,000	20,000

You are required to work out the income of the firm and of the partners A, B and C assuming that the partners have no other income.

Ans: (96,000); 37,000; 28,670; 20,330.

Problem 13.04-P4 [CA N 01]

X & Co., a partnership firm as such, furnishes the following profit and loss account for the previous year ending March 31, 2007 :

	Rs.		*Rs.*
Cost of goods	2,80,000	Sales	2,92,000
Other expenses	91,000	Net loss	1,72,000
Interest to partners	25,000		
Remuneration to partners	68,000		
	4,64,000		4,64,000

The other expenses debited include Rs. 13,600 not allowable under section 37(1). Interest to partners is excess by Rs. 7,100 (not statutory allowable).

You are required to compute for the assessment year 2007-08 the income of the firm.

Ans: (1,33,300)

Problem 13.04-P5 [DU 1994]

Profit and Loss account of ABC & Co. (a firm of company secretaries) for the year ending March 31, 2007 is as follows:

Dr	*Rs.*	*Cr*	*Rs.*
Expenses	82,000	Receipts from clients and audit fees	1,70,000
Depreciation	20,000	Bank Interest	15,000
Remuneration to partners	60,000	Net Loss	12,000
Interest to partners	35,000		
Total	1,97,000	Total	1,97,000

Other information:

1. The firm satisfies the condition of section 184.
2. Out of expenses of Rs. 82,000; Rs. 7,400 is not deductible by virtue of Sections 36 and 37.
3. Depreciation as per Section 32 is Rs. 19,500.
4. Interest to partners is fully deductible u/s 40(b).

Ans: 5,900; 1,986. [–12,000+60,000+35,000+500+7,400-15,000=75,900–35,000–50,000 = –9,100+15000=5,900]

Problem 13.04-P6 [DU 2006 NEW]

Profit and Loss of R Co. (a partnership firm) for the year ending 31-3-2007 is as follows :

	Rs.		*Rs.*
Cost of goods sold	10,00,000	Sales	15,00,000
Remuneration to partners	1,49,000	Rent of house property	60,000
Interest to partners @ 18% p.a.	60,000	Dividend from Indian Co.	1,70,000
Municipal taxes of house property	25,000		
Other expenses	2,36,000		
Net profit	2,60,000		
	17,30,000		17,30,000

Other Information:

(i) Out of the other expenses, Rs. 18,400 is not deductible under section 36, 37(1) and 43B.

(ii) On 15-1-2007, the firm pays an outstanding sales tax liability of Rs. 54,700 of the previous year 2005-06. As this amount pertains to the previous year 2005-06, it has not been debited to the aforesaid profit and loss account.

(iii) Fringe benefit tax of Rs. 2,000 is not debited to P & L A/c.

Calculate remuneration deductible under Section 40(b) and find out the net income of the firm.

Ans: 84,620. [2,60,000+1,49,000+60,000+25,000+18,400–1,70,000–54,700=2,27,700–40,000–1,27,580=60,120+24,500=84,620]

Problem 13.04-P7 (Difficult)

M/s LMN & Co. is a partnership firm consisting of L, M and N as partners. They share profit and Loss in the ratio of 40%, 40% and 20% respectively. The firm declared a net profit of Rs. 2,40,000 after debiting the following expenses in P&L A/c for financial year 2006-2007 :

	L	*M*	*N*
(i) Interest on capital @ 20% authorised in the partnership deed	10,000	6,000	Nil
(ii) Salary as per partnership deed	Nil	1,92,000	1,44,000
(iii) Commission on sales authorised in the partnership deed	Nil	36,000	32,000
(iv) Rent for office premises	24,000	Nil	Nil

The firm paid interest of Rs. 4,000 to Sales Tax Department for delayed payment of tax. But this amount is included in interest payment of Rs. 29,000 debited to P&L A/c. The firm paid demurrage of Rs. 5,000 for not lifting goods from Railways. The firm employed the son of Mr. 'L' at a salary of Rs. 5,000 p.m. The person is a fresh graduate and in open market he could get only Rs. 2,000 p.m. Compute the total income and tax of the firm/partners for Assessment Year 2007-2008.

Ans: 3,59,340; 1,20,954; 22,800; nil; 1,88,180; 12,889; 1,42,480; 3,566.

Problem 13.04-P8 [CS J94]

X and Y are two partners of XY Co. (a trading firm). The deed of partnership provides the following salary and interest to partners.

	X	*Y*
Salary	2,000 per month	4,000 per month
Interest	24% per annum	24% per annum

The profits and loss account of XY Co. for the year ending 31st March, 2007 is as follows :

	Rs.		*Rs.*
Office expenses	1,10,000	Gross profit	2,00,000
Salary to employees	70,000	Net loss	67,000
Salary to X	24,000		

Salary to Y	48,000	
Interest on capital to X @ 24%	6,000	
Interest on capital to Y @ 24%	9,000	
	2,67,000	2,67,000

Other information:

(i) Out of office expenses, Rs. 800 is not deductible by virtue of sections 30 to 37.

(ii) Personal income and investments of partners are as follows :

	X	*Y*
Dividend from UTI	60,000	3,000
Bank interest	10,000	2,000
Deposit in public provident fund	10,000	15,000
Mediclaim insurance premium	2,000	1,000

Find out the net income of the firm and partners for the AY 2007-08.

Ans: (44,200); 30,670; 43,333.

Problem 13.04-P9 (Typical)

X, Y and Z are partners in a firm sharing profit and losses in the ratio of 2:3:6. The firm's profit and loss account for the year ending on March 31, 2007 showed a net profit of Rs. 50,000 after debiting the following amounts :

1. Salary of Rs. 40,000 paid to X who is a sleeping partner.
2. Rs. 42,000 paid for purchase of patent right.
3. Rs. 1,600 for partnership deed expenses.
4. Fringe benefits tax paid Rs. 400.
5. Commission on sales paid to Y Rs. 70,000.
6. Interest on capital Rs. 4,000; Rs. 2,000 and Rs. 3,000 paid to X, Y and Z respectively.
7. Rs. 9,900 paid to Y on account of rent for the portion of the building owned by him which is used for firm's office.
8. BCTT paid Rs. 100.
9. Donation to approved institutions Rs. 20,000.

The net profit includes Rs. 10,000 being interest received from Govt. securities. The remuneration to partners and interest on capital are as per instrument of partnership.

Compute the total income of the firm and tax payable for the AY 2007-08.

Ans: 1,36,330; 45,889. [50,000+40,000+42,000+1,600+400+70,000+4,000+2,000+3,000+ 20,000–10,000–10,500=2,12,500–9,000–70,000=1,33,500+10,000=1,43,500–7,175=1,36,325]

Problem 13.04-P10 (Typical)

A partnership legal consultancy firm of Mr. X (Company Secretary), Miss Y (Chartered Accountant) and Mrs. Z (Lawyer aged 65 years) furnishes following receipts and payments account for the year ending March 31, 2007 :

Receipts	*Rs.*	*Payment*	*Rs.*
Balance b/d	3,54,000	Office expenses	1,04,000
Audit fees	65,000	Purchase of law books	11,000
Consultation fees	6,40,000	Computer	80,000
		Motor car expenses	30,000
Income tax refund	15,000	Professional association fee	5,000
Interest on Gold bonds	50,000	Legal fees	2,250
Interest on listed securities (net)	27,500	Entertainment expenses	30,250
Sale of listed bonus shares		Income tax	45,000
held for 2 years	40,000	Salary to Mr. X	2,80,000
Interest on Bank deposits	4,000	Salary to Miss Y	1,30,000
		Salary to Mrs. Z	3,00,000
		Interest to Mr. X @ 10%	60,000
		Interest to Miss Y @ 15%	20,000
		Interest to Mrs. Z @ 11%	12,000
		Donation to Delhi University	10,000
		Service tax not yet paid	80,000
		Balance c/d	57,500
Total	11,95,500	Total	11,95,500

Additional information : Following information are found not recorded in receipt and payment account :

1. Foreign consultancy fees of Rs. 9,00,000.
2. Long term capital loss on sale of land Rs. 25,000.
3. Short term capital gain on sale of office furniture Rs. 6,000.
4. Winning from State Lottery Rs. 5,000.
5. Brought forward depreciation of PY 19921-93 Rs. 2,86,500.

Compute total income and tax liability of firm for the AY 2007-08. Also compute tax liability of its partners for the AY 2007-08.

Ans: 5,65,980; 1,90,509; 24,077; nil; 5,220. [65,000+6,40,000+9,00,000-1,04,000–11,000–48,000–30,000–5,000–2,250–30,250=13,74,500–88,000–4,70,000=5,30,000+30,980 +4,000+6,000+5,000=5,75,980–10,000=5,65,980]

Problem 13.04-P11 (CA - M99) - M 6

The net profits of S Brothers, a partnership firm, consisting of three partners carrying on business for the accounting year ended March 31, 2007 was Rs. 5,20,000. The said net profits were after charging salary payable to all the partners amounting to Rs. 1,08,000, but before crediting interest to partners accounts on their fixed capitals amounting to Rs. 10 lakh totally. The partnership deed provided for payment of interest on fixed capitals amounting to Rs. 10,00,000 totally. The partnership deed provided for payment of interest on fixed capital at 22 per cent per annum. The deed does not, however, specify any salary entitlement to partners.

On this information, you are required to compute the total income of the firm if the firm satisfies the conditions of section 184 and when conditions of section 184 are not satisfied.

Ans: 4,00,000; 6,28,000.

Problem 13.04-P12 (ICWA-NEW - J03) - M 5

X, Y and Z are the three partners of a firm, sharing profits and losses as 2 : 3 : 5. It is constituted by a deed of partnership, but there has been a change in the profit - sharing ratio in the financial year 2006-07 from the earlier year. The firm did not submit a certified copy of the new deed of partnership. The profit and loss account of the firm for the year ending on March 31, 2007 shows the following :

	Rs.	*Rs.*
Opening stock	1,21,000	—
Sales	—	21,40,000
Purchases	15,70,000	—
Other business receipts	—	66,000
Other expenses	1,57,000	—
Closing stock	—	32,000
Remuneration to partners (X: Rs. 60,000 + Y : Rs. 80,000 + Z : Rs. 1,02,000)	2,42,000	—
Interest to partners @ 24% per annum (X : Rs. 30,000 + Y : Rs. 36,000 + Z: Rs. 42,000)	1,08,000	—
Net profit	40,000	
	22,38,000	22,38,000

Other income of partners :

	X Rs.	*Y* Rs.	*Z* Rs.
Interest on Government securities	34,000	7,000	42,000
Interest on company deposits	15,500	10,000	20,000
Contribution to PPF	10,000	20,000	16,000

Determine the tax liability of the firm as also of X, Y and Z for the AY 2007-08.

Ans: 1,31,274; Nil; Nil; Nil.

(B) *[COMPUTATION OF BOOK PROFIT WHERE BOTH THE ADJUSTMENT OF UNABSORBED DEPRECIATION UNDER SECTION 32(2) AND BUSINESS LOSS UNDER SECTION 72 ARE TO BE MADE]

As you know book profit is computed by allowing all deductions u/ss 28 to 44D except remuneration allowed to partners. The specifics are current depreciation u/s 32(1) and unabsorbed depreciation u/s 32(2). Both are required to be subtracted from net profit to compute book profit. What if brought forward business loss is also there which is specified under section 72?

Section 72 adjustment shall not be made since while computing book profit, it falls outside sections 28 to 44D. Secondly, it is known that allowance for unabsorbed depreciation is allowed only after set off of brought forward business loss.

To solve this problem, it is better that brought forward business loss is reduced notionally from the book profit, to see what amount of unabsorbed depreciation is available for set off.

Isn't it Simple? Ok, do not worry, refer example.

E.g. Compute book profit from following information : Book profit = Rs. 6,00,000; B.f. business loss = Rs. 4,60,000; Unabsorbed depreciation = Rs. 3,00,000.

Soln. 6,00,000 – 4,60,000 = 1,40,000. Rs. 3,00,000 shall be limited to Rs. 1,40,000 and book profit = 6,00,000 – 1,40,000 = 4,60,000.

Problem 13.04-P13 (Typical)

Net Profit before allowing following deductions 5,50,000

1. Remuneration allowed to partners as per partnership deed :

Partners	*Salary*	*Bonus*	*Perquisites*
-X (Working partner)	80,000	20,000	3,000
-Y (Sleeping partner)	50,000	Nil	2,000
-Z (Working partner)	70,000	30,000	3,500

2. Interest allowed to partners :

Partners	*Rate of interest*	*Capital contributed 2 as on 31-3-2007*
-X	8%	6,00,000
-Y	20%	2,00,000
-Z	15%	1,50,000

3. Cash purchases	1,20,000
4. Depreciation under section 32(1)	1,50,000
5. Depreciation under section 32(2)	20,000
6. Long term capital gain on sale of land	1,90,000
7. Brought forward business loss under section 72	2,00,000
8. LTCG on sale of listed equity shares on 5-3-2007.	5,00,000
9. STCG on sale of listed equity oriented fund on 15-5-2006.	10,000
10. Donation to Prime Minister Relief fund	40,000

Compute total income and tax liability of the firm for the AY 2007-08.

Ans: 1,80,000; 39,270. [5,50,000–1,20,000+24,000–1,50,000=3,04,000–90,000–1,32,500=81,500–81,500=0+10,000+1,90,000–20,000=1,80,000-0=1,80,000]

Problem 13.04-P14 (Typical)

Net profit after allowing following deductions 4,00,000

1. Office expenses 8,000
2. Interest on loan to Govt. of India accrued on 31-3-2007 but paid on 1-11-2007 50,000
3. Remuneration allowed to partners as per partnership deed :

Partners	*Salary*	*Bonus*	*Commission*
-X (Working partner)	1,80,000	4,000	10,000
-Y (Working partner)	2,50,000	2,000	5,000
-Mrs. Z (Sleeping partner)	—	—	1,05,000

4. Interest allowed to partners

Partners	*Rate of interest*	*Interest*
-X	8%	15,000
-Y	20%	16,000
-Z	15%	1,00,000

5. Donation to an unapproved charitable institution	2,50,000
6. Sales tax liability paid on 7-11-2007	6,000
7. Depreciation under section 32(1)	2,00,000

Other information :

1. Brought forward depreciation under section 32(2) 10,000
2. Brought forward business loss under section 72 3,50,000
3. Brought forward speculation loss under section 73 15,000

Compute book profit and total income of the firm if it satisfies the conditions of section 184.

Ans: 12,28,400; 4,27,400.

(C) COMPUTATION OF BOOK PROFIT WHERE PROFIT IS COMPUTED ON PRESUMPTIVE BASIS UNDER SECTIONS 44AD, 44AE AND 44AF

Estimated income is computed under the head Profit from Business. It means all deductions and depreciation which are allowed under sections 28 to 44D have been deemed to be already allowed, except deductions allowed under section 40b. Now to compute book profit only interest on capital contributed by partners shall be allowed as deduction.

Problem 13.04-P15 (Difficult)

Solve Illustration 12.04.P1 if the Armani and Co. satisfies the condition of section 44AF *i.e.* the company is into retail trade of garments.

Solution

Computation of profit from business

Estimated income *(5% of 31,73,000)*	1,58,650
(–) Interest @ 12% allowed to partners	17,800
Book Profit	1,40,850
Less : Remuneration u/s 40b	40,000
Profit from business	1,00,850

Problem 13.04-P16 (Difficult)

Bahamas, Bali & Co., a Firm, furnishes following figures. Compute Profit from business for the AY 2007-08.

	Retail trade covered u/s 44AF	*Civil construction covered u/s 44AD*
Turnover	18,00,000	25,00,000
Less : Purchases	9,80,000	19,00,000
Less : Other expenses	2,00,000	1,00,000
Balance	6,20,000	5,00,000
Less : Interest @ 15%	20,000	1,00,000
Less : Remuneration	1,00,000	1,20,000
Profit from Business	5,00,000	2,80,000

Ans: 7,400; 25,500.

Problem 13.04-P17 [Hons 2006C]

PQ & Associates, a partnership firm engaged in the business of civil construction, has a gross receipt	Rs. 38,00,000
The partnership deed provides for payment of salary to each opf the partners P & Q (per month / partner)	Rs. 8,000
The firm uses machinery for the purpose of its business and the WDV of the machinery as on 01-04-2006	Rs. 4,00,000
The machinery is eligible for depreciation	25%

Compute the profits of the firm if the firm opts for the scheme under Section 44AD.

Ans: 1,29,900.

Problem 13.04-P18 (CS-J00) - M 3

Q.1d : X and Co., a firm, is engaged in the business of civil construction (turnover of 2006-07 being Rs. 37,80,000). It wants to claim the following deductions :

Salary and interest to partner [as permitted by section 40(b)]	60,000
Salary to employees	4,90,000
Depreciation	2,70,000
Cost of materials used	25,90,000
Other expenses	3,45,000
Total	37,55,000
Net Profit (Rs. 37,80,000 minus Rs. 37,55,000)	25,000

Determine the net income of X and Co. for the assessment year 2007-08 assuming that (i) taxable income from other business is Rs. 4,90,000; (ii) long-term capital is Rs. 1,40,000; and (iii) the firm is eligible for a deduction of Rs. 15,000 under section 80G.

Ans: 8,57,400.

Problem 13.04-P19

A, B & Co., is a partnership firm of two partners, A & B with equal shares. The firm is engaged in the business for civil construction. The firm has been assessed as firm for the Assessment year 2007-2008. The profit and loss account of the firm for the year ending March 31, 2007 is as follows :

	Rs.		*Rs.*
(i) Opening stock of raw materials	33,000	(i) Receipt from business of civil construction	39,50,000
(ii) Depreciation	2,50,000	(ii) Rent from godowns	50,000
(iii) Salary to employees	1,30,000		
(iv) Purchase of raw materials	25,00,000	(iii) Interest on Government securities (Rs. 2,40,000 + TDS 60,000)	3,00,000
(v) Interest on loan for investment in securities	12,000	(iv) Closing stock of raw materials	1,40,000
(vi) Interest on loan for business purposes	50,000		
(vii) Other expenses	4,50,000		

(viii) Municipal taxes and insurance of godowns (Rs. 5,000 + Rs. 2,000)		7,000	
(ix) Salary to partners as per partnership deed			
A	1,50,000		
B	50,000	2,00,000	
(x) Profit		8,08,000	
		44,40,000	44,40,000

Additional information :

(i) Other expenses include a sum of Rs. 30,000 paid to under world to restrict the entry of rivals in the business.

(ii) On April 1, 2006 the firm owns following depreciable assets :

Block A W.D.V. Rs. 1,50,000 (rate of depreciation : 15%)

Block B W.D.V. Rs. 2,00,000 (rate of depreciation : 40%)

(iii) The firm gave donation of Rs. 1,50,000 to charitable institutions which is included in other expenses.

(iv) Purchase of raw material include cash purchases of Rs. 5,00,000 in excess of Rs. 20,000 of each item.

(v) The firm has carried forward business losses of Rs. 40,000 and Rs. 12,000 from Assessment Year 2005-2006 and Assessment Year 2006-2007 respectively.

Compute the total income of the firm and tax payable.

Ans: 3,84,370; 69,379.

13.05 COMPREHENSIVE PROBLEMS

Simple and Difficult

Problem 13.05-P1

M/s. Mohanlal & Sons, a partnership firm, is engaged in the business of manufacture and sale of chemicals. The firm has three partners, Shri Mohanlal and his two sons, Amit and Sumit, each having 1/3 share. Amit and Sumit are actively engaged in the business of the firm. Amit and Sumit have been paid a salary of Rs. 1,20,000 and Rs. 84,000 respectively as per the partnership deed. The salary is debited under the head 'Salary & Wages' in the P&L account. Shri Mohanlal, Amit and Sumit have been paid interest of Rs. 72,000, Rs. 36,000 and Rs. 24,000 respectively on their capital at 24%.

The manufacturing and profit & loss account of the firm for the year ending 31-3-2007 is as under :

Dr.			*Cr.*
Opening Stock		Sales	85,60,000
Raw material	3,55,000	Interest	5,36,500
Finished goods	9,12,500	Closing Stock :	
Purchases	54,67,500	Raw material	7,56,250
Manufacturing expenses	4,10,000	Finished goods	13,05,150

Godown rent	36,600	
Salary & Wages	4,42,000	
Interest	7,12,100	
Purchase of new machinery	14,92,000	
Miscellaneous expenses	2,35,700	
Depreciation	8,50,000	
Municipal taxes of godown	7,200	
Insurance of goods & godown	27,800	
Net Profit	2,09,500	
	1,11,57,900	1,11,57,900

Other available information is as under :

(i) The firm had the following block of assets as on 1.4.2006

Block A (entitled to 10% depreciation)	W.D.V. Rs. 3,70,000
Block B (entitled to 15% depreciation)	W.D.V. Rs. 5,50,000
Block C (entitled to 100% depreciation)	W.D.V. Nil

(ii) Salary & Wages include bonus of Rs. 35,000 paid in December, 2005. Prepare an assessment order of the firm for A.Y. 2007-2008. Compute its total income and also work out the tax payable by it.

Ans: 22,74,200; 7,65,496.

Problem 13.05-P2 [Hons 2006]

A and B are partners in a firm assessed as such they are equal partners. Compute the Book Profits and total income of the firm and partners for the assessment year 2007-08.

The following is the Profit and Loss A/c given :

To Sundry Expenses		80,000	By Sales		4,50,000
To Depreciation		20,000	By income from house property		10,000
To Donation to National Defence Fund		8,000	By Capital gains : LTCG	25,000	
			STCG	15,000	40,000
To Remuneration to partners :			By Winnings from lotteries		15,000
A	60,000				
B	40,000	1,00,000			
To Interest on Capital @ 15% p.a. :					
A	11,250				
B	18,750	30,000			
To office Salaries		75,000			
To Reserve for Bad debts		15,000			
To Entertainment Expenses		19,000			
To Sales Tax unpaid		30,000			

To Net Profit :			
A	69,000		
B	69,000	1,38,000	
		5,15,000	5,15,000

Additional Information is given below :

(1) Depreciation according to Sec. 32 is Rs. 25,000.

(2) Sundry Expenses includes an expense which is inadmissible worth Rs. 4,000.

(3) Sales tax for Rs. 10,000 paid on 31-7-2007 and Rs. 5,000 paid on 31-10-2007.

(4) Other incomes of partners :

(A) Rs. 90,000

(B) Rs. 86,000

Ans: 1,75,000; 1,59,000; 1,41,000. [1,38,000+4,000+8,000+1,00,000+30,000+15,000 +20,000–5,000–10,000–25,000–15,000–15,000=2,45,000–24,000–1,00,000= 1,21,000+7,000+25,000+15,000+15,000=1,83,000-8,000=1,75,000]

Problem 13.05-P3 [Hons 2006C]

A, B & C are partners of a firm enjoying profits and losses in the ratio of 2 : 2 : 1. From the following available particulars, compute the total income and tax payable of the three partners in the firm for the assessment year 2007-08 assuming the firm fulfils the conditions of Section 184 :

Profit and Loss Account
(for the year ending on 31st March, 2007)

		Rs.		*Rs.*
Sundry Trade Expenses		1,10,000	Gross Profit	3,00,000
Interest on Capital @ 15% p.a.			Interest on Securities	10,000
A	20,000			
B	17,500			
C	15,000	52,500		
Commission to C		36,000		
Rent to B		30,000		
Salary to B			72,000	
Net profit		9,500		
		3,10,000		3,10,000

Other informations are as follows :

(1) Sundry Trade Expenses included amount for personal expenses of partners :

B Rs. 3,000

C Rs. 2,000

(2) B and C are the working partners of the firm.

Ans: 36,700; 16,000; 99,200; 44,100. [9,500+5,000+52,500+1,08,000–10,000=1,65,000– 42,000–96,300=26,700+10,000=36,700]

Problem 13.05-P4 [Hons 1999]

From the following information, compute the tax payable by a Firm for the AY 2007-08 :

1.	LTCG on sale of share in a BSE on 1-1-2007	8,25,000
2.	Lottery winnings (gross)	50,000
3.	Income from house property	30,000

Ans: 26,928.

Problem 13.05-P5 [Hons 1998]

'A', 'B' and 'C' are partners sharing profits in the ratio 2:2:1 in a firm *(satisfies the conditions of section 184,)* whose particulars of income for the PY ending on March 31, 2007 are given below:

1.	Rent from house property	20,000
2.	Interest on listed securities (net)	18,804
3.	Income from legal profession	2,52,500
4.	Long term capital gain	30,000

Income from legal profession is before making the deduction for salary payable to 'A' 'B' and 'C' at Rs. 55,000 p.a. each as per firm's deed. 'A' also has income from TV program's on 'Legal Advice' amounting to Rs. 4,000, but other partners had no other income. 'A' deposited Rs. 2,000 in Public Provident Fund during the financial year.

Compute the total income and tax liability of the firm and 'A'.

Ans: 1,52,680; 45,650; 57,000.

Typical

Problem 13.05-P6 [Hons 1992]

A, B and C are partners in a firm sharing in the ratio 5 : 3 : 2. Given below is the profit and loss account of the firm for the previous year 2006-07.

Profit and Loss Account

Particulars	*Amount*	*Particulars*	*Amount*
To Purchases	5,00,000	By Sales	12,71,000
To Salaries and bonus	2,70,000	By discount	10,000
To Sales tax payable	30,000	By Interest (gross) from Indian comp.	60,000
To General expenses	1,00,000	By interest on drawings	10,000
To expenditure on technical know - how	36,000		
To Expenses on sales tax proceedings	15,000		
To Advertisements	50,000		
To interest on capitals	20,000		
To Rent of buildings owned by firm	30,000		
To Net profit	3,00,000		
	13,51,000		13,51,000

Additional information is given below :

1. Purchases include a cash purchase of Rs. 20,000 from a farmer who lives in a village which is not served by any bank.
2. Advertisements include presentation of 50 VIP bags in January 2007 costing Rs. 350 each.
3. Salaries and bonus includes the following payments to partners :
   - Salary - A = Rs. 25,000, B = Rs. 17,000, C = Rs. 10,000
   - Bonus - A = Rs. 14,000, C = Rs. 16,000
   - Commission - A = Rs. 8,000, B = Rs. 10,000, C = Rs. 5,000
4. Interest on capital drawings include -
   - Interest on capitals - A = Rs. 7,000, B = Rs. 8,000, C = Rs. 5,000
   - Interest on drawings - A = Rs. 5,000, B = Rs. 3,000, C = Rs. 2,000
5. The firm has carry forward business loss from the assessment year 2003-04 amounting to Rs. 1,00,000.
6. The w.d.v. of buildings on 01-04-2006 was Rs. 2,50,000.
7. Technical know - how was purchased and put to use on 01-07-2006.

Compute the total income of the firm, allocate it among the partners and show how you would treat the share of profit in the personal assessment of the partners. The firm has complied with all the conditions of section 184.

Ans: 2,62,000; 88,189.

Problem 13.05-P7 [Hons 2005]

A and B are partners in a Firm. The firm satifies the condition of section 184. They share profits and losses in the ratio of 60% and 40% respectively. The profit and loss account for the financial year 2006-07 is as under :

	Rs.		*Rs.*
Salaries & Wages	6,00,000	Gross Profit	14,50,000
Advertisement	1,00,000	Long term Capital gains (gold)	4,00,000
Depreciation on business assets	50,000	LTCG (STT paid)	90,000
Donation to an approved trust	70,000	Recovery of Debts	50,000
Interest paid	2,30,000		
General Expenses	3,50,000		
Net profit	3,90,000		
	19,90,000		19,90,000

Additional Informations :

(i) Salaries and interest on capital were allowed as per partnership deed.

(ii) Salaries and wages include the sum of Rs. 1,00,000 and Rs. 60,000 paid to A and B respectively.

(iii) Payment of Interest includes :

(a) Interest to A on a deposit made by his minor son 'X' amounting to Rs. 30,000 @ 15% on a deposit of Rs. 2,00,000.

(b) Interest to B amounting to Rs. 30,000 @ 12%.

(c) Interest of Rs. 20,000 paid on loan taken for the payment of firm's income tax liability.

(iv) The amount of depreciation allowable is Rs. 40,000.

(v) Y a minor son of B, has been admitted to the benefit of partnership in another firm. He has received salary and interest amounting to Rs. 40,000 and Rs. 15,000 from the firm out of which salary of Rs. 10,000 and interest of Rs. 5,000 has been desallowed to the firm.

(vi) Other income of partners : A Rs. 60,000; B Rs. 90,000.

(vii) A has purchased NSC VIII issue on 31-3-2005 for Rs. 40,000 and B has deposited Rs. 60,000 in PPF A/c during the year 2004-05.

Compute for the assessment year 2006-07;

(a) Total income of the firm;

(b) Tax liability of the firm;

(c) Total income of the partners.

Ans: (a) 4,41,300; (b) 98,765; (c) A. 1,61,310; B. 2,02,190. [3,90,000+70,000+10,000+1,60,000+20,000+30,000-90,000=1,90,000–30,000–1,16,500=43,500+4,00,000=4,43,500–2,175=4,41,330]

Problem 13.05-P8 [Hons 2005C]

X and Y are equal partners in a firm. The firm satifies the condition of section 184. From the following profit and loss account, compute the total income of the firm for the assessment year 2007-08.

Profit and Loss Account
for the year ending on 31st March 2007

		Rs.		*Rs.*
Interest on Capital @ 15%			Business Profits	1,30,000
X	9,000		Income from house property	10,100
Y	15,000	24,000		
Partners			Capital Gains	
X	60,000		Long Term (Gold)	20,000
Y	30,000	90,000	Short Term (Debentures)	10,000
	30,000		LTCG (STT paid)	80,000
Approved Charitable Donations		10,000		
Share of profit				
X	63,050			
Y	63,050	1,26,100		
		2,50,100		2,50,100

The remuneration and interest on capital are as per the partnership deed. Other information is given below :

(i) X paid interest to the firm on drawings for household expenses which is included in the business profits Rs. 2,000

(ii) Y paid interest on money borrowed to contribute to the capital in the firm Rs. 10,000

(iii) X purchased a Car in June, 2006 Rs. 1,80,000

(iv) Expenses on running and maintenance of the Car by X. Rs. 20,000

(v) X says that the car has been used for the firm and other personal purposes.

(vi) The use of the car for personal purposes may be taken as 50%. Proper amount is charged to Profit and Loss A/c.

Ans: 60,320. [1,26,100+24,000+90,000+10,000–10,100–1,10,000=1,30,000–19,200–88,980=21,820+10,100+30,000=61,920–1,596=60,320]

Problem 13.05-P9 [Hons 2004]

Profit and Loss account of A.B. & Co. a partnership to firm of A.B. and C of satisfying the conditions of section 184 for the year ending March 31, 2007 is as follows :

	Rs.		*Rs.*
Cost of goods sold	15,70,000	Sales	27,00,000
Remuneration to Partners :		Rent of the house property (half portion)	1,00,000
A	3,00,000	Interest on debentures	
B	2,00,000	(Gross)	1,20,000
C	1,00,000		
Interest to Partners :			
A	80,000		
B	50,000		
C	1,20,000		
Municipal tax of the house property (Entire property)	10,000		
Other expenses	4,00,000		
Net profit	90,000		
	29,20,000		29,20,000

Other information :

(i) On scrutiny, it was found that the firm purchases raw materials on credit from D-brother of partner A. The amount of bill is Rs. 42,000 (market value is Rs. 38,000). The bill is paid in cash on August 5, 2006.

(ii) On December 1, 2006, firm pays an outstanding custom duty liability of Rs. 80,000 of the previous year 2005-06. As this amount pertains to the previous year 2005-06, it has not been debited to the aforesaid profit and loss account.

(iii) C is not a working partner. Salary has been given as per the partnership deed.

(iv) Interest on capital to partners not deductible under Section 40(b) is Rs. 25,000.

(v) The firm owns a house, the ground floor is used for business purposes, the first floor is given on rent. The municipal taxes were due on 31-3-2007 and were paid on July 1, 2007.

(vi) The firm donated Rs. 10,000 to Prime Minister's National Relief Fund. This amount of Rs. 10,000 is included in other expenses duly debited to Profit and Loss A/c.

Find out the net income of the firm (and also the tax treatment of the payments to partners in their hands) for the assessment year 2007-08 assuming that three concerned partners are to share profit and losses equally.

Ans: Firm 3,92,460; Partners 2,17,484; 1,41,656; 95,000. [90,000+6,00,000+2,50,000+ 5,000+4,000+7,600+10,000–1,00,000–1,20,000–80,000=6,66,600–2,25,000– 2,29,140=2,12,460+70,000+1,20,000=4,02,460–10,000=3,92,460]

Problem 13.05-P10 [Hons 2004C]

X, Y and Co. is a partnership firm satisfying the conditions of section 184. It has two partners X and Y (1 : 2). The firm is engaged in the business of civil construction including repairs of dams and supply of labour as a firm for AY 2007-08. The profit and loss Account of this firm for the year ending 31-03-2007 is as follows :

Opening stock of raw material		21,700	Receipts from business of civil construction	58,70,700
Depreciation		2,39,430	Rent of godown	48,000
Salary to employees		1,30,000	Interest on Company deposit	2,60,000
Purchase of raw material		44,10,210	Closing stock of raw material	1,31,600
Interest on loan taken to make deposit in companies		13,800		
Interest on loan taken for business purpose		74,400		
Travelling, entertainment and advertisement exp.		57,800		
Other expenses		4,12,000		
Municipal tax (6,000) and Insurance of godown (1,200)		7,200		
Salary to partners as per deed :				
X	1,08,000			
Y	72,000	1,80,000		
Interest to partners as per deed :				
X	12,000			
Y	57,000	69,000		
Net profit		6,94,760		
		63,10,000		63,10,300

Additional information :

1. Out of other expense, debited to P & L A/c Rs. 20,000 is not deductible u/s 37(1).
2. Out of Travelling, advertisement and entertainment expenses. Rs. 25,000 is not deductible u/s 37(1).
3. On 1-4-2006, the firm owns the following depreciable assets :

- Plants A, B and C, depreciated value. Rs. 3,70,000, rate of depreciation 15%

- Plants D and E, depreciated value Rs. 1,98,000 rate of depreciation 40%.

  On 1-1-2007 the firm sells plants D for Rs. 9,10,000 and purchases Plant F (Rate of depreciation 15%) for Rs. 4,86,000.

4. The firm gives a donation of Rs. 1,70,000 to a notified charitable institution which is included in other expenses.
5. The firm wants to set-off the following losses brought forward from earlier years :

	AY 2005-06	AY 2006-07
Business loss	20,000	—
Capital loss (Short-term)	2,000	1,000

6. Income of partners X and Y is as follows :

	X	*Y*
Bank Interest	40,000	93,000
P.P.F. Contribution	10,000	20,000

Find out net income and tax liability of the firm and partners for the assessment year 2007-08.

Ans: Firm 16,48,100; 5,54,750; Partners Income 1,50,000; 2,02,000; Partners tax 5,100; 15,708. [6,94,760+13,800+7,200+1,80,000+69,000+45,000+1,70,000+1,47,480–48,000–2,60,000=10,19,240–69,000–1,80,000=7,70,240]

Problem 13.05-P11 [Hons 2003]

The following is the Profit and Loss A/c of Alpha & Co. a partnership firm of A, B & C which satisfies the condition of the section 184 who share profits and losses in ratio of 2 : 3 : 4 for the financial year 2006-07 :

Particulars		*Amount*	*Particulars*	*Amount*
Cost of goods sold		71,80,000	Sales	80,00,000
Interest on capital to @ 18%			Interest on public deposits with a Company	90,000
A	54,000			
B	18,000			
C	81,000	1,53,000		
Remuneration to partners			Rent of house building *(for 1/3 portion)*	75,000
A	1,20,000			
B	90,000			
C	60,000	2,70,000		
Municipal Taxes *(paid on Sept. 20, 2007)*		10,000		
Other business expenses		2,51,000		
Net profit		3,01,000		
Total		81,65,000	Total	81,65,000

Other relevant information :

(i) B is not a working partner.

(ii) The firm owns a Building. First floor of this building is let out on rental basis whereas the ground floor and second floors are used for own business purpose.

(iii) Out of other business expenses Rs. 10,000 is not deductible under various sections of the Income Tax Act.

(iv) On December 1, 2006 firm paid Rs. 5,000 being sales tax liability pertaining to the PY 2002-03 which has not been debited in P & L A/c.

Find out the net income and tax liability of the firm for the AY 2007-08.

Ans: 4,27,830; 1,44,008. [3,01,000+1,53,000+2,70,000+3,333+10,000–90,000–5,000–75,000=5,67,333–1,02,000–1,80,000=2,85,333+52,500=4,27,830]

Problem 13.05-P12 [Hons 2002]

X and Y are equal partners in a firm. It satisfies the condition of Section 184. From the following Profit and Loss Account, compute Book Profit and Total Income of the firm for the PY relevant to the AY 2007-08 :

Profit and Loss Account (year ending on 31-3-2007)

Particulars		*Amount*	*Particulars*	*Amount*
To Sundry Expenses		85,000	By Gross Profit	2,25,000
To Depreciation		15,000	By Income from House Property (computed)	10,100
To donation to an approved Institution		10,000	LTCG on sale of residential house property	20,000
To interest on capital @ 12% pa			LTCG (STT paid)	5,000
X	9,000		STCG (STT paid)	10,000
Y	15,000	24,000	STCG (on sale of gold)	10,000
To remuneration to partners :			By Income from other sources	5,000
X	60,000			
Y	30,000	90,000		
To Profit :				
X	30,550			
Y	30,550	61,100		
Total		2,85,100	Total	2,85,100

Additional Information:

(i) The remuneration and interest on capital were allowed as per partnership deed and satisfies the conditions of section 184.

(ii) Inadmissible expenses included in Sundry expenses were Rs. 5,000. Depreciation allowed as per Section 32 was Rs. 10,000.

(iii) X paid interest to the firm on drawings for personal purposes amounting to Rs. 2,000 which is included in income from other sources.

Ans: 73,800; 20,353. [61,100+10,000+24,000+90,000+5,000+5,000–10,100–25,000–20,000–3,000=1,37,000–24,000–90,000=23,000+10,100+20,000+0+10,000+10,000+3,000=76,100–2,304=73,800]

Problem 13.05-P13 [Hons 2001]

P, Q, R, & Associates sharing profit and losses equally, are exporting computer software outside India. The P & L A/c account for the PY 2006-07 is given below

To purchase	20,42,000	By total sales	34,00,000
To salaries	4,10,000	By sale of import licences	4,10,000
To interest to partners	1,08,000	By brokerage & commission	60,000
To salaries to partners	6,00,000	By profit from Japan branch	2,90,000
To depreciation on plant and machinery	2,00,000	By profit on sale of land held for the last 2 1/2 years	6,00,000
Purchase of trade marks	2,00,000		
To net profit	12,00,000		
Total	47,60,000	Total	47,60,000

You are further informed :

1. The partnership firm has satisfied all conditions of section 184.
2. Interest and salaries to partners have been paid as below :

		P	Q (sleeping partner)	R
a.	Interest	7,000	45,000	56,000
b.	Salaries	2,00,000	2,00,000	2,00,000

Payments authorised by partnership deed are given below:

a.	Interest	14% p.a.	18% p.a.	14% p.a.
b.	Salaries (p.m.)	Rs. 10,000	Rs. 10,000	Rs. 10,000

3. Written down value of the plant and machinery, as on 1-04-2006 is Rs. 20,00,000. Rate of depreciation is 15%.
4. Excise duty of Rs. 4,00,000 for the PY 2005-06 was paid on 31-12-2006 but not included in the above profit and loss account.
5. The firm has brought forward depreciation, long-term capital loss, short term capital loss amounting Rs. 2,36,000; Rs. 3,00,000 and Rs. 2,00,000 from the AY 2006-07 respectively.

You are required to compute the total income of the firm and determine its tax liability for the AY 2007-08.

Ans: 7,98,000; 2,68,607. [12,00,000+6,00,000+1,08,000+2,00,000–6,00,000–1,50,000–4,00,000=9,58,000–84,000–2,40,000=6,34,000+2,36,000=3,98,000+4,00,000=7,98,000]

Problem 13.05-P14 [Hons 2000]

A, B and C are equal partners in a firm doing business. B and C are looking after sales / purchases and other business matters. A is not associated with business affairs as he has contributed double the amount of capital, contributed by B and C.

The Profit and Loss Account of the firm for the PY 2006-07 is given below :

To Purchases	10,54,000	By Sale	22,00,000
To Business Expenses	6,00,000	By Stock	1,50,000
To Depreciation	50,000	By Interest on B's drawing	30,000
To Salaries to partners:		By Sundry receipts	20,000
A	1,20,000	By LTCG (on sale of gold)	1,00,000
B	60,000	By LTCG (STT paid)	50,000
C	1,80,000		
To Interest on Capitals:			
A - 14%	84,000		
B - 18%	27,000		
C - 16%	24,000		
To Sundry expenses	1,01,000		
To Net Profit	2,50,000		
Total	25,50,000	Total	25,50,000

You are further informed that:

1. Payment of salaries and interest to partners are duly authorised by partnership deed and it satisfies the conditions of section 184.
2. Purchases include cash purchases of Rs. 1,00,000
3. Excise duty of Rs. 1,07,000 for the PY 2005-06 was paid on 31-12-2006 but not included in the Profit and Loss Account
4. Recovery of bad debts during the year from a discontinued business, Rs. 1,00,000 but not included in the profit and loss account. Deduction was allowed in respect of bad debts.
5. (a) WDV of the machinery as on 1-4-2006 (depreciation 15%) 5,00,000

   (b) Machinery sold during the year, sale price 1,00,000

   (c) Machinery acquired during the year in December, cost of machine 4,00,000
6. Brought forward losses:

   (a) Business loss AY 2004-05 3,00,000

   (b) Depreciation AY 2005-06 2,00,000

You are required to compute and show:

1. Book profit of the firm;
2. Remuneration to partners, deductible as per income - tax law;
3. Total income of the firm; and
4. Carry forward of business loss and unabsorbed depreciation.
5. Total income of partners.

Ans: 3,60,000; 1,96,500; Nil; 37,500; 1,00,000 Partners 72,000; 77,625; 1,96,875. [BI: 2,50,000+3,60,000+1,35,000+20,000+1,00,000–40,000–1,07,000–1,50,000= 5,68,000–1,08,000–1,96,500=2,63,500]

Problem 13.05-P15 [Hons 1997]

The Profit and Loss Account of the Business run by A and B *(do not satisfies the conditions of section 184,)* sharing profit and loss in the ratio of 3:2 for the PY ending March 31, 2007 is as follows:

Dr	*Rs.*	*Cr*	*Rs.*
Cost of goods sold	5,65,000	Sales	9,50,000
Other expenses	1,00,000	Bank Interest	30,000
Remuneration to employees	1,70,000	LTCG on sale of gold	1,90,000
		STCG (STT paid)	20,000
Interest to Partners		Interest on drawings	
A	20,000	A	10,000
B	20,000	B	10,000
Remuneration to partners		LTCG on sale of equity share	
A	1,00,000	on NSE on 1-3-2007	40,000
B	2,00,000		
Sales tax outstanding	10,000		
Net profit	75,000		
Total	12,50,000	Total	12,50,000

Additional information:

1. Other expenses include the following:
   (a) Entertainment expenses Rs. 20,000
   (b) Employer's contribution to Provident Fund amounting to Rs. 10,000 was paid on 10-7-2007.
   (c) Rs. 30,000 paid in cash to a supplier who refused to accept payment by a cheque.
2. Outstanding sales tax was paid on September 14, 2007.
3. Other Income of partners: A: Rs 90,000; B: Rs 86,000.

You are required to compute total income and tax liability of firm for the AY 2007-08.

Ans: 3,91,000; 1,05,850. [75,000+3,00,000+40,000+10,000+6,000–30,000–2,30,000–20,000=1,51,000-0-0=1,51,000+1,90,000+30,000=3,91,000]

Problem 13.05-P16 [Hons 1996]

X and Y are two partners (1:2) of X Co., a firm engaged in manufacturing chemicals. The P/L A/c of the firm for the year ending 31-3-2007 is as follows

Dr	*Rs.*	*Cr*	*Rs.*
Cost of goods sold	13,00,000	Sales	23,00,000
Salary to staff	2,00,000	LTCG	40,000
Depreciation	80,000	Other business receipts	31,000
Remuneration to partners :			
X	2,00,000		
Y	1,60,000		

Interest on capital to partners @ 20%			
X	25,000		
Y	17,500		
Other expenses	3,70,000		
Net profit	10,000		
Total	23,71,000	Total	23,71,000

Other Information:

1. The firm completed all legal formalities to get the status of 'firm' under section 184.
2. The firm has given donation of Rs. 80,000 to a notified public charitable trust which is included in other expenses.
3. Salary and interest is paid to partners as per the partnership deed.
4. Depreciation allowable under section 32 is Rs. 78,000.
5. Income and investment of X and Y are as follows :

	X	*Y*
• Interest on company deposit	30,000	15,000
• Dividend from companies registered outside India	7,000	2,000
• Long-term capital gains	(2,000)	23,500
• Short-term capital gains	88,000	(6,000)
• Winnings from lottery (gross)	Nil	5,000
• Contribution towards Home Loan Account scheme of the National Housing Bank	55,000	35,000
• Payment made towards purchase of Residential House Property	25,000	40,000

Find out the net income and tax liability of the firm & partners for the AY 2007-08.

Ans: Firm 2,34,660; 74,499. Partners 1,84,500; 74,600; 12,138; 1,530. [10,000+3,60,000+42,500+2,000+80,000–40,000=4,54,500–25,500–2,24,100=2,04,900+40,000=2,44,900–10,245=2,34,660]

Problem 13.05-P17 [Hons 1995]

The profit and loss account of the a firm of M/s A and B *(which satisfies the conditions of section 184)*, sharing profit and loss in the ratio of 3:2, for the PY ending on March 31, 2007 is as follows:

Dr	*Rs.*	*Cr*	*Rs.*
Cost of goods sold	5,45,000	Sales	9,50,000
Remuneration to partners	3,00,000	Dividend from Indian Company	20,000
Remuneration to employees	1,70,000	LTCG	1,90,000
Interest to partners	15,000		
Other expenses	1,00,000		
Sales tax outstanding	10,000		
Net profit	20,000		
Total	11,60,000	Total	11,60,000

Additional information :

1. Employer's contribution towards Provident Fund amounting to Rs. 10,000 was paid by cheque on 10-7-2007.
2. Outstanding sales tax was paid on August 14, 2007.
3. The detailed particulars of remuneration and interest to A and B, working partners, are given below :

		Amount actually paid		*Amount authorised by partnership deed*	
		A	*B*	*A*	*B*
(a)	Salaries	70,000	80,000	60,000	1,00,000
(b)	Bonus	60,000	40,000	40,000	20,000
(c)	Commission	20,000	30,000	50,000	30,000
(d)	Interest	9,000	6,000	7,200	4,800

You are required to compute tax liability of the firm and it's partners for the AY 2007-08.

Ans: Firm 2,16,700; 51,623; Partners 55,350; 54,950. [20,000+3,00,000+15,000+10,000–20,000–1,90,000=1,35,000–12,000–96,300=26,700+1,90,000=2,16,700]

Problem 13.05-P18 (ICWA-NEW - D02) - M 10

X, Y and Z are partners of the trading firm XYZ & Co., sharing profits and losses as X : Y : Z :: 5 : 3 : 2, and interest, and other remuneration are paid to them as per deed of partnership. The Profit and Loss A/c of the firm for the year ended March 31, 2007 is as below:

		Rs.		*Rs.*
Remuneration to partners:			Gross profit	5,95,000
X	Rs. 50,000		Rent of house	70,000
Y	Rs. 30,000		Bank interest (fixed deposit)	16,000
Z	Rs. 20,000	1,00,000	Commission from agency	35,000
Interest on loan of Y @ 20% per annum		40,000	Sale proceeds of depreciable assets	80,000
Interest on Capital at 24% per annum			Gain on sale of shares purchased in 2001-02	30,000
X	Rs. 24,000		Dividend from Indian Company	12,000
Z	Rs. 72,000	96,000	Bad debts recovered	8,000
Sundry Expenses		85,000		
Bonus to Y		10,000		
Commission to Z		8,000		
Municipal tax for house (paid)		12,000		
Establishment charges		50,000		
Depreciation		25,000		
Provision for bad debts		4,000		
Donation to National Defence Fund		3,000		

Share of profit:				
X	Rs. 1,56,500			
Y	Rs. 93,900			
Z	Rs. 62,600	3,13,000		
		8,46,000		8,46,000

Other information:

(i) Municipal tax paid includes arrears of Rs. 2,000 for the preceding year.

(ii) Depreciation as per Income tax rules, Rs. 35,000.

(iii) On May 30, 2007, the firm paid sales tax of Rs. 15,000 relating to the 2002-2003.

(iv) Sundry expenses include Rs. 60,000 paid in cash to a supplier.

(v) The whole block of plant and machinery depreciated at 100 per cent was sold for 80,000 as shown in the Profit & Loss A/c.

Compute : (i) The books profit. (ii) Total income and tax of the firm for the assessment year 2007-08.

Ans: 4,08,000; 4,53,600; 1,49,316.

Problem 13.05-P19 (ICWA-NEW - D03) - M 10

The following information pertaining to X & Co., a partnership firm engaged in business consisting of three partners with equal profit sharing ratio, relating to the year ending March 31, 2007 is available :

	Rs.		*Rs.*
Interest to partners:		Gross profit	3,80,000
X	30,000	Profit on sale of residential house	50,000
Y	45,000	Income from speculation business	40,000
Z	54,000	Rental receipts	84,000
Remuneration to partners:			
X	60,000		
Y	84,000		
Z	96,000		
Other expenses (including depreciation)	95000		
Net profit	90,000		
	5,54,000		5,54,000

Additional Information:

1. X is a partner representing the Hindu undivided family of which he is the Karta. X and Y are working partners.
2. Interest has been provided to Y and Z at 18 per cent simple interest and to X at 12 per cent. Interest accrues uniformly throughout the year.

3. In the earlier assessment year for which the return was filed in time, there is unabsorbed depreciation of Rs. 34,500 and carried forward business loss of Rs. 70,000. These items have not been considered earlier.
4. The firm derives agricultural income of Rs. 1,20,000 from lands at Kolkata.
5. The residendial house purchased in May 2004 for Rs. 4,00,000 is sold in July 2006 for Rs. 4,50,000.

Compute the total income of the partnership firm for the assessment year 2007-08. Brief computation will suffice.

Ans: 1,03,000.

STRATEGY MAKER

Points in 1 to 10	Overall Points 10; Practical 10; Theory 4.
Type of problem	Difficult. This chapter is an extension of chapter Profit from Business.
What to expect (DU)/CS	You are bound to get a question from it and therefore do it with utmost perfection and try to score atleast 90%. Assessment of firm is most important.
CA	Not in your syllabus. But sometimes the questions have been asked.

For your mind

If you are successful, you will win false friends and true enemies.

Succeed anyway.

Every beginner is a winner.

The me I see... is the me I'll be.

"And when you have reached the mountain top,
then you shall begin to climb"

Keep Running

Your income is my income

14

CLUBBING OF INCOME

TOPIC 14.01 WHAT IS CLUBBING OF INCOME?

Clubbing means addition of income in the hands of transferrer who has transferred any asset or income to any specified person if certain conditions are satisfied.

TOPIC 14.02 *SECTION 60.* TRANSFER OF INCOME WITHOUT TRANSFERRING THE OWNERSHIP OF THE ASSETS

Where income is arising to any person without holding any asset then such income is clubbed in the hands of that person who holds the assets.

transfer of interest on Fixed Deposit of Rs. 1,00,000
Mr. X--->Mr. Y
but hold Fixed Deposit in his name

In this case income from fixed deposit *i.e.* Rs. 1 lakh shall be clubbed in the hands of Mr. X as he has transferred only interest on fixed deposit and not fixed deposit itself. Here ownership of the asset is not transferred to Mr. Y.

TOPIC 14.03 CLUBBING PROVISIONS RELATING TO INCOME OF SPOUSE

The word spouse means for male assessee his wife and for female assessee her husband.

(A) SECTION 64(1)(ii). REMUNERATION RECEIVED BY SPOUSE

In computing the total income of any individual, there shall be included all such income as arises directly or indirectly to the spouse of such individual by way of salary, commission, fees or any other form of remuneration whether in cash or in kind from a *concern* in which such individual has a *substantial interest.*

Note :

- A person is said to be having substantial interest in a concern if he along with his relatives holds at least 20% of equity shares *(in a company)* or has at least 20% share in profits of the concern *at any time* during the PY.
- *Section 2(41).* Relative in relation to an individual means the husband, wife, brother or sister or any lineal ascendant (mother, father, grandmother, grandfather) or descendant (son, daughter, grandson, granddaughter) of that individual.

In whose hands such remuneration is clubbed : Remuneration is included in the hands of that individual who has substantial interest.

But where both husband and wife have a substantial interest in the concern and both are in receipt of the remuneration from such concern, remuneration shall be included in the total income of husband or wife whose total income, excluding such remuneration, is greater.

Note

- Remuneration is clubbed even if the spouse is employed before marriage.

When remuneration is not allowed to be clubbed : In case where the spouse possesses technical or professional qualifications and the income is solely attributable to the application of his or her technical or professional knowledge and experience, then such income shall not be clubbed.

(B) SECTION 64(1)(iv). ASSET TRANSFERRED BY SPOUSE WITHOUT ADEQUATE CONSIDERATION

Where an asset *(other than House Property — treated u/s 27)* is transferred by individual to his or her spouse without adequate consideration then income arising from that asset shall be clubbed in the hands of transferrer.

(C) SECTION 64(1)(vii). ANY ASSET TRANSFERRED TO ANY PERSON FOR THE BENEFIT OF SPOUSE

Where an individual transfers any asset to any person or AOP for the benefits of his or her spouse, without adequate consideration, the income from such assets shall be clubbed in the hands of transferor to the extent the benefit goes to the spouse.

Note

- To attract clubbing provisions relating to spouse the relationship of husband and wife should subsist at the time of transfer of asset and at the time of accrual of such income from the asset. Thus income of the spouse derived before marriage cannot be clubbed.

(D) WHEN INCOME OF THE TRANSFERRED ASSET IS NOT ALLOWED TO BE CLUBBED

1. Asset is transferred for adequate consideration.
2. Marriage doesn't subsist at the time of transfer and at the time when income accrues; or
3. Assets are transferred in connection with an agreement to live apart.

TOPIC 14.04 CLUBBING PROVISION RELATING TO INCOME OF SON'S WIFE

A. *Section 64(1)(vi).Any asset transferred to son's wife* : Where an asset is transferred by an individual to son's wife without adequate consideration then income arising from that asset shall be clubbed in the hands of transferor.

B. *Section 64(1)(viii). Any asset transferred to any person for the benefit of son's wife :* Where an individual transfers any asset to any person or AOP, without adequate consideration, the income from such assets shall be clubbed in the hands of transferor to the extent the benefit goes to the son's wife.

When income is not allowed to be clubbed

1. Asset is transferred for adequate consideration.
2. Relationship of father-in-law or mother-in-law and daughter-in-law doesn't subsist at the time of transfer *and* at the time when income accrues.

UNDERSTANDING SECTION 64(1). SPOUSE AND SON'S WIFE

Income from asset transferred is to be clubbed

Q.1 : Mr. X transfers fixed deposit to her wife without adequate consideration. Interest on fixed deposit is Rs. 15,000. Whether Rs. 15,000 shall be clubbed in the hands of Mr. X? If yes, why?

A.1 : Yes. Rs. 15,000 shall be clubbed in the hands of Mr. X u/s 64(1)(iv), since income is arising from the asset transferred.

Income from income is not allowed to be clubbed

Q.2 : From Q. 1....Mrs. X purchases 7% debentures from interest on transferred fixed deposit. Her interest income from debentures is Rs. 5,000. Whether Rs. 5,000 shall be clubbed in the hands of Mr. X?. If no, why?

A.2 : No. Rs. 5,000 shall not be clubbed in the hands of Mr. X, since income is not arising from the asset transferred, but from the income of the asset transferred. Section 64(1)(iv) gets attracted only where income is arising from the asset transferred.

Income from change of identity of assets is to be clubbed

Q.3 : Mr. X gifts Rs. 10,00,000 to her wife on her birthday. From that cash she purchases 11% debentures. Her interest income from such debenture is Rs. 20,000. Whether Rs. 20,000 shall be clubbed in the hands of Mr. X? If yes, why?

A.3 : Yes. Rs. 20,000 shall be clubbed in the hands of Mr. X u/s 64(1)(iv), since income is arising from the asset transferred. Change in identity of asset does not make any difference.

Income from accretion of assets is not clubbed

Q.4 : Mr. X gifts 1,000 equity shares of ACC Ltd to her wife. The company declares a bonus of 200 shares and dividend @ Rs. 2 per share. Explain its tax treatment.

A.4 : Rs. 2,000 dividend from equity shares shall be clubbed in the hands of husband, since it is income from the transferred asset. Rs. 400 dividend from bonus shares shall not be clubbed, since it is an income from accretion of asset.

*AMOUNT INVESTED IN BUSINESS

For the purposes of section 64(1)(*iv*) and 64(1)(*vi*), where the assets transferred directly or indirectly by an individual to his spouse or son's wife (hereafter referred to as "the transferee") are invested by the transferee,

(*i*) in any business, (not being a partnership firm) that part of the income arising out of the business to the transferee in any PY, which bears the same proportion to the income of the transferee from the business as the value of the assets aforesaid as on the 1st day of the PY bears to the total investment in the business by the transferee as on the said day, shall be included in the total income of the individual in that previous year.

For example, X transfers Rs. 1,00,000 to his wife. Mrs. X invest Rs. 5,00,000 in a beauty parlour business and earned an income of Rs. 80,000. Hence

$$\frac{1,00,000}{5,00,000} \times 80,000 = 16,000 \text{ shall be included in the income of Mr. X.}$$

(*ii*) in the nature of contribution of capital as a partner in a firm, that part of the interest receivable by the transferee from the firm in any PY, which bears the same proportion to the interest receivable by the transferee from the firm as the value of investment aforesaid as on the 1st day of the PY bears to the total investment by way of capital contribution as a partner in the firm as on the said day, shall be included in the total income of the individual in that previous year.

Problem 14.04-P1 (PE II - N04) - M 5

Q.1c. : A Proprietor Business was started by Mrs. R in the year 2004. As on 1-4-2005 her capital in business was Rs. 3,00,000.

Her husband gifted Rs. 2,00,000, on 10-4-2005, which amount Mrs. R invested in her business on the same date. Mrs. R earned profits from her proprietory business for the financial years 2005-06, Rs. 1,50,000 and financial year 2006-07 Rs. 3,90,000. Compute the income, to be clubbed in the hands of R's husband for the assessment year 2006-07 with reasons.

Ans: 1,20,000 (profit invested); 1,56,000 (profit not invested)

TOPIC 14.05 *SECTION 64(IA)*. CLUBBING OF INCOME OF MINOR CHILD

In computing the total income of any *parent*, it shall include such income which accrues to his minor child and shall be clubbed in the hands of that parent whose total income *(excluding the income to be clubbed)* is greater.

If you read the sentence carefully it says that *all* income accruing to a minor child shall be clubbed. *i.e.* from whatever sources income is accruing it shall be clubbed. It is not only income arising from transferred asset but also income arising from other assets which minor child may have acquired shall also be clubbed. Income from income, income from accretion of assets shall also be clubbed.

Note

- Where the marriage of the parent does not subsist, the income of the minor child will be included in the hands of that parent who maintains the minor child in the relevant PY.
- Where any such income is once included in the total income of either parent, any such income arising in any succeeding year shall not be included in the total income of the other parent unless the AO is satisfied *(after giving that parent an opportunity of being heard)* that it is necessary to do so.

When income is not allowed to be clubbed

1. Minor child suffering from any disability specified u/s 80U.
2. Income accruing to a minor child where it involves manual work or application of his skill, talent or specialised knowledge and experience.

Note

- *Section 10(32)* provides exemption upto Rs. 1500 per child in the hands of the parent in whose hand income is clubbed.
- Income of a minor child is clubbed in respect of his income accruing till the date he attains majority.
- 2(15B). Minor child means legal child. He may be a adopted child or step child.

UNDERSTANDING SECTION 64(1A). MINOR CHILD

Q.1 : Master Bhavesh earns Rs. 5,000 p.m. from an asset transferred to him by his grandfather. Whether such income shall be clubbed? If yes, in whose hands such income shall be clubbed?

A.1 : Yes. Rs. 5,000 p.m. shall be clubbed in the hands of that parent whose income is greater. It does not matter who transfers the asset. The only requirement of section 64(1A) is that income should accrue to a minor child from whatever reasons or sources.

Q.2 : Master Janu earns Rs. 2,00,000 from child acting. Whether such income shall be clubbed?

A.2 : No. Income arising to a minor child from application of his own skill is not clubbed.

Q.3 : From Q. 2....Rs. 2,00,000 being income from acting is deposited in a bank which earns an interest of Rs. 5,000. Whether interest income shall be clubbed?

A.3 : Yes, since interest income accrues to a minor child and it is not earned by applying his own skill.

14.06 COMPREHENSIVE PROBLEMS

Problem 14.06-P1 (CA - M96) - M 8

Q.3c : A was holding 3,000 shares in W Ltd. purchased by him on August 8, 2004 at Rs. 60 per share. He gifted these shares to his girlfriend C on February 10, 2006. A married C on March 1, 2006. C was allotted bonus shares by the company at the rate of one share for every three shares held on September 10, 2006. C sold all the shares including the bonus shares on March 31, 2007 at Rs. 150 per share.

State in whose hands capital gains on sale of shares is taxable. Also compute the capital gains.

Ans: LTCG 2,63,625; STCG 1,50,000 taxed in the hands of C. However section 10(38) may become applicable.

Problem 14.06-P2 (CS-D02) - M 3

Q.1c : X and Mrs. X hold 20% and 30% equity shares in ABC Ltd. respectively. They are also employed in ABC Ltd. (Monthly salary being Rs. 20,000 and Rs. 30,000 respectively) without any technical/professional qualification.

Other incomes of X and Mrs. X are Rs. 70,000 and Rs. 1,00,000 respectively. Find out the net income of X and Mrs. X for the assessment year 2007-08.

Ans: 70,000; 7,00,000.

Problem 14.06-P3 (CS-J02) - M 5

Q.4a : X is a fashion designer having lucrative business. His wife is a model. X pays her monthly salary of Rs. 10,000. The Assessing Officer, while admitting that the salary is an admissible deduction in computing total income of X, has applied the provisions of section 64(1) and has clubbed the income (salary) of his wife in X's hands. Discuss the correctness of the action of the Assessing Officer.

Ans: Action of AO is not correct.

Problem 14.06-P4 (Difficult)

On 1-6-2002 X gifted some shares of a foreign company to small X (son of X) whose date of birth is 16-5-1999. The shares were purchased by him on 17-8-1988 for Rs. 20,000 the face value was Rs. 10,000. Small X received dividend of 10% on these shares in May 2006 and sold these shares on 1-7-2006 for Rs. 50,000 and deposited the sale proceeds in a company at 15% p.a. interest. Calculate the taxable income from above transactions and also indicate to whom will be taxed and how much.

Ans: 33,292 shall be clubbed in the hands of that parent whose income is greater.

Problem 14.06-P5 (CA - M90) - M 6

D is born on June 7, 1990. Her betrothal took place on March 5, 2006. On the said day she received cash gift of Rs. 25,000 each from her father, father's mother, father's father, mother, mother's mother and mother's father. All the six relatives made similar gifts on the days of marriage *i.e.* on April 1, 2006. The amount so received is deposited in a private Ltd. company in which her husband has substantial interest. For the year ended March 31, 2007 the company has paid her interest @ 14% *i.e.* Rs. 42,000. Discuss how this income will be assessed to Income Tax.

Ans: All income accruing to minor child shall be clubbed in the hands of that parent whose income is greater.

Problem 14.06-P6 (CS-D01) - M 5

Q.3c : X gifts Rs. 2 lakh to his wife on April 1, 2006 which she invests in a firm on interest @ 18% per annum, On January 1, 2007, Mrs. X withdraws the money and gifts it to their son's wife. She claims that the interest which has accrued to the daughter-in-law from January 1, 2007 to March 31, 2007 on the investment made by the daughter-in-law is not assessable in her hands but in the hands of X. Is this correct? What would be the position, if Mrs. X had gifted the money to their minor son, instead of the daughter-in-law ?

Ans : Discuss with your friends.

Problem 14.06-P7 [Hons 2004]

G transferred a house property to Miss D on 10-5-2005 without any consideration. On 1-7-2006. D married R-son of G. D received Rs. 1,00,000 as income from the gifted property. The assessing officer has clubbed the above income in the hands of G. Is the action of the assessing officer tenable under the law ?

Ans: No. since the relationship of father in law and daughter in law do not subsits both at the time of the transfer of the asset and at the time when income accrues.

Problem 14.06-P8 [Hons 1997]

Master Monu, who is minor son of Mr. X, submits the following particulars of his income for the PY ending March 31, 2007:

1. Computed income under the head, "Income from house property" Rs. 25,000. The house has been gifted to him by his maternal uncle.
2. Interest from debentures of an Indian Company Rs. 20,000. The debentures have been gifted to him by his mother.
3. Income from his acting in a film Rs. 1,00,000.

Who will be liable to pay tax on the above income? Would it make any difference in your answer if Master Monu was a disabled child?

Soultion

Clubbing of Income of Master Monu

1.	Income from House Property *(shall be clubbed)*	25,000
2.	Interest from debentures *(shall be clubbed)*	20,000
3.	Income from acting *(shall not be clubbed)*	1,00,000

Working notes

Note: These incomes (1 & 2) will be included in the total income of that parent whose total income is higher *(excluding the income to be clubbed).*

If Master Monu is a handicapped child none of the above said income shall be clubbed in the hand of parents.

Problem 14.06-P9 [CA N 98]

Y is a trader, particulars of his income and those of the members of his family are given below. These incomes relate to the previous year ending March 31, 2007 :

Income from Y's business	90,000
Salary derived from a educational institution by Mrs. Y	50,000
Interest on company deposits derived by Master Z (minor son). These deposits were made in the name of Z by his father's father about 6 years ago	12,000
Receipts from sale of paintings and drawings made by minor A (minor daughter of Mr. and Mrs. Y and a noted child artist)	60,000
Income by way of lottery earnings by Master B (minor son of Y)	6,000

Discuss whether the above will from part of the assessable income of any individual and also compute the assessable income of Y.

Ans: 1,05,000; 50,000; 60,000.

Problem 14.06-P10 [CA N99]

X is the Karta of a HUF, whose members derive income as given below :

Income from X's own business	50,000
Mrs. X a dermatologist draws salary	80,000
Minor son A (earning interest on fixed deposit with ABC Ltd., which were gifted to him by his grandfather)	15,000
Minor daughter B gave a dance performance and received remuneration	1,00,000
A got winnings from lottery (gross)	2,00,000

Explain how the above will be taxed.

Ans: 50,000; 2,93,500; nil; 1,00,000.

Problem 14.06-P11 (Typical)

Mr. Taxcrazy and his family members furnishe following particulars. You are required to compute total income of Mr. Taxcrazy and his family members.

1. *Self-Income*

a.	Income from Business	88,000
b.	Interest on company deposits	8,000
c.	Share of profit from firm (loss)	(10,000)

2. *Wife's income*

a.	Income from profession	1,20,000
b.	Dividend from a foreign company *(foreign company is a 100% subsidiary of an Indian company)*	3,100
c.	Rental income from commercial house property gifted by her father	36,000

d. Interest on debentures gifted by her husband — 18,000

e. Interest on bank deposits less expenses *(Fixed deposit is made in an Indian Bank in USA)* — (6,000)

3. *Major Son's income*

a. Salary including dearness allowance and perquisites from a foreign company for services rendered in India — 80,000

b. Income from TV Game show — 2,000

c. A self occupied residential house property gifted by his father in 2000 when he was 17 years old (Interest accrued during the year which was paid on 16-4-2007 to HDFC Bank of Rs. 38,000) — nil

4. *Minor Son's income who is a renowned painter*

a. Interest on Central Govt. deposits — 16,000

b. Income from painting — 45,000

c. Reward for essay writing competition — 20,000

5. *Minor daughter's income*

a. Dividend from an Indian Company *(shares gifted by her brother)* — 6,000

b. Rental income from house property situated in Australia *(House is gifted by her grandfather)* — 25,000

c. Interest on investment in her name invested by her father — 15,000

Ans: 1,14,000; 1,87,800; 52,000; 45,000; Nil.

Problem 14.06-P12 (Typical)

Determine the gross total income of X and his wife from the following particulars for the year ending March 31, 2007 :

1. X and his wife are partners in a firm carrying on paper business. Their respective shares of profits are Rs. 18,000 and Rs. 10,000. X received Rs. 24,000 as salary and Rs. 10,000 as interest from the firm while Mrs. X received Rs. 16,000 as interest.
2. Their 17-year-old son is a partner in another firm from which he received Rs. 15,000 as his share of profit in the firm.
3. A house property in the name of X was transferred to his wife on December 1, 2006, for adequate consideration. This property has been let at a rent of Rs. 3,000 p.m. Annual value of the house is 30,000.
4. Debentures of a company of Rs. 10,000 and Rs. 8,000 purchased 2 years ago are in the name of X and his wife respectively, on which interest is receivable @ 12% p.a. His wife had transferred Rs. 5,000 out of her income to X for the purchase of debentures.
5. X had transferred Rs. 80,000 to his wife in the year 1990 without any consideration. She earned Rs. 22,000 as interest during the earlier previous years. During the financial year 2006-07 she received interest @ 10% p.a. on Rs. 1,02,000.
6. X transferred Govt. securities to Mrs. X in 1996-97. He purchased these Govt. securities for Rs. 22,300. Mrs. X sold these Govt. securities for Rs. 1,00,000 during the previous year and purchased a residential house worth Rs. 60,000 and a commercial house worth Rs. 30,000. She received Rs. 2,600 as interest on these Govt. securities during the previous year.

Ans: 83,623; 28,160. [X:24,000+10,000+16,800+600+8,000+24,223=83,623] [**Mrs.X:** 16,000+8,400+1,560+2,200=28,160]

Problem 14.06-P13 [Hons 2002]

Find the tax liability of Mrs. Gupta (aged 60 years), a resident individual, for the AY 2007-08 from the following particulars of her incomes and spending for the previous year ending March 31, 2007:

Income from House property *(computed)*	1,30,000
Dividend from an Indian Company	15,000
Family pension *(gross)*	60,000
Interest on Central Govt. securities	16,000
Income of minor child *(against the amount deposited in the name of* Minor child*)*	18,000
Winnings from lotteries	5,000
Long-term capital gain	40,000
Payment for purchase osf National Savings Certificates (VIII issue)	71,000

Ans: 9,843.

STRATEGY MAKER

Points in 1 to 10	Overall Points 6; Practical 3; Theory 8.
Type of problem	Simple. Once you are able to understand this chapter it becomes the most interesting chapter. I have tried it to make it as simple as possible.
What to expect (DU)	I have put what is generally asked in your exams. Therefore memorise everything properly.
CA (PE II)	Everything.

Rest and Play even God took one day off !

Make it fun to understand income tax. Live your hobby. If you enjoy seeing a movie, do see it. Don't give up. When you are not enjoying your day or a moment you are not understanding income tax.

Keep Running

Creating equity among unequals

INCOME NOT FORMING PART OF TOTAL INCOME "EXEMPTED INCOME"

TOPIC 15.00 INTRODUCTION

Following incomes are exempt from tax under section 10 and hence are not included in the taxable income of an assessee. Exempted income is never a part of total income and therefore it is shown by way of note.

Exempted income refers to income excluded from the total income of the person for a particular year. Thus this is the income earned but not taxed.

FOLLOWING EXEMPTIONS HAVE ALREADY BEEN DISCUSSED IN THE PRECEDING CHAPTERS

1. *Section 10(1).* Agricultural income as defined u/s 2(1A) is exempt from tax.
2. *Section 10(2A).* Partner's share in the firm's income.
3. *Section 10(5).* Leave travel concessions.
4. *Section 10(7).* Payment of allowance or perquisites by Govt. of India.
5. *Section 10(10).* Gratuity.
6. *Section 10(10A).* Pension.
7. *Section 10(10AA).* Leave Salary.
8. *Section 10(10CC).* Tax on non-monetary perquisites paid by employer on behalf of employee.
9. *Section 10(10D).* Life insurance maturity proceeds.
10. *Section 10(11), (12).* Payment from provident fund.
11. *Section 10(13).* Payment from an approved superannuation fund.
12. *Section 10(13A).* House Rent Allowance.
13. *Section 10(14).* Special allowances.
14. *Section 10(15).* Interest on certain sources.

15. *Section 10(16)*. Educational Scholarship.
16. *Section 10(32)*. Income of minor child.
17. *Section 10(33)*. Capital gain on transfer of US 64.
18. *Section 10(34)*. Dividend from domestic company.
19. *Section 10(35)*. Income from mutual funds.
20. *Section 10(36)*. LTCG on transfer of listed equity shares.
21. *Section 10(37)*. Compulsory acquisition of agricultural land in specified urban area.
22. *Section 10(38)*. LTCG arising on transfer of STT paid securities.

OTHER EXEMPTIONS

TOPIC 15.01 *SECTION 10(2)*. RECEIPT FROM HUF

Subject to the provisions of section 64(2), any sum received by an individual as a member of a Hindu undivided family, where such sum has been paid out of the income of the family, or, in the case of any impartible estate, where such sum has been paid out of the income of the estate belonging to the family.

TOPIC 15.02 *SECTION 10(6)(ii)*. EXEMPTION TO OFFICIALS OF EMBASSY

The remuneration received by him as an official, by whatever name called, of an embassy, high commission, legation, commission, consulate or the trade representation of a foreign State, or as a member of the staff of any of these officials, for service in such capacity:

Provided that the remuneration received by him as trade commissioner or other official representative in India of the Government of a foreign State (not holding office as such in an honorary capacity), or as a member of the staff of any of those officials, shall be exempt only if the remuneration of the corresponding officials or, as the case may be, members of the staff, if any, of the Government resident for similar purposes in the country concerned enjoys a similar exemption in that country:

Provided further that such members of the staff are subjects of the country represented and are not engaged in any business or profession or employment in India otherwise than as members of such staff;

TOPIC 15.03 *SECTION 10(6)(vi)*. EXEMPTION TO EMPLOYEE OF FOREIGN ENTERPRISES

The remuneration received by him as an employee of a foreign enterprise for services rendered by him during his stay in India, provided the following conditions are fulfilled—

(a) the foreign enterprise is not engaged in any trade or business in India;

(b) his stay in India does not exceed in the aggregate a period of ninety days in such previous year; and

(c) such remuneration is not liable to be deducted from the income of the employer chargeable under this Act.

TOPIC 15.04 *SECTION 10(6)(viii)*. EXEMPTION TO EMPLOYEE OF FOREIGN SHIP

Any income chargeable under the head "Salaries" received by or due to any such individual being a non-resident as remuneration for services rendered in connection with his employment on a foreign ship where his total stay in India does not exceed in the aggregate a period of ninety days in the previous year.

TOPIC 15.05 *SECTION 10(6)(xi).* EXEMPTION TO EMPLOYEE OF THE GOVERNMENT OF A FOREIGN STATE

The remuneration received by him as an employee of the Government of a foreign State during his stay in India in connection with his training in any establishment or office of, or in any undertaking owned by,—

(i) the Government; or

(ii) any company in which the entire paid-up share capital is held by the Central Government, or any State Government or Governments, or partly by the Central Government and partly by one or more State Governments; or

(iii) any company which is a subsidiary of a company referred to in item (ii); or

(iv) any corporation established by or under a Central, State or Provincial Act; or

(v) any society registered under the Societies Registration Act, 1860, or under any other corresponding law for the time being in force and wholly financed by the Central Government, or any State Government or State Governments, or partly by the Central Government and partly by one or more State Governments;

TOPIC 15.06 *SECTION 10(8).* REMUNERATION RECEIVED BY INDIVIDUAL UNDER CO-OPERATIVE TECHNICAL ASSISTANCE PROGRAMMES AND PROJECTS

In the case of an individual who is assigned to duties in India in connection with any co-operative technical assistance programmes and projects in accordance with an agreement entered into by the Central Government and the Government of a foreign State (the terms whereof provide for the exemption given by this clause)

(a) the remuneration received by him directly or indirectly from the Government of that foreign State for such duties, and

(b) any other income of such individual which accrues or arises outside India, and is not deemed to accrue or arise in India, in respect of which such individual is required to pay any income or social security tax to the Government of that foreign State.

TOPIC 15.07 *SECTION 10(8A).* 10(8B).10(9). REMUNERATION RECEIVED BY NON RESIDENT CONSULTANTS, THEIR EMPLOYEES AND THEIR FAMILY MEMBERS

(A) SECTION 10(8A). EXEMPTION AVAILABLE TO CONSULTANT

In the case of a consultant

(a) any remuneration or fee received by him or it, directly or indirectly, out of the funds made available to an international organisation [hereafter referred to in this clause and clause (8B) as the agency] under a technical assistance grant agreement between the agency and the Government of a foreign State; and

(b) any other income which accrues or arises to him or it outside India, and is not deemed to accrue or arise in India, in respect of which such consultant is required to pay any income or social security tax to the Government of the country of his or its origin.

Explanation. In this clause, "consultant" means

(*i*) any individual, who is either not a citizen of India or, being a citizen of India, is not ordinarily resident in India; or

(*ii*) any other person, being a non-resident,

engaged by the agency for rendering technical services in India in connection with any technical assistance programme or project, provided the following conditions are fulfilled, namely :

(*1*) the technical assistance is in accordance with an agreement entered into by the Central Government and the agency ; and

(*2*) the agreement relating to the engagement of the consultant is approved by the prescribed authority for the purposes of this clause.

(B) SECTION 10(8B). EXEMPTION AVAILABLE TO EMPLOYEES OF CONSULTANT

In the case of an individual who is assigned to duties in India in connection with any technical assistance programme and project in accordance with an agreement entered into by the Central Government and the agency—

(*a*) the remuneration received by him, directly or indirectly, for such duties from any consultant referred to in clause (*8A*) ; and

(*b*) any other income of such individual which accrues or arises outside India, and is not deemed to accrue or arise in India, in respect of which such individual is required to pay any income or social security tax to the country of his origin, provided the following conditions are fulfilled, namely :

  (*i*) the individual is an employee of the consultant referred to in clause (*8A*) and is either not a citizen of India or, being a citizen of India, is not ordinarily resident in India ; and

  (*ii*) the contract of service of such individual is approved by the prescribed authority before the commencement of his service.

(C) SECTION 10(9). EXEMPTION AVAILABLE TO FAMILIES OF CONSULTANT

The income of any member of the family of any such individual as is referred to in section 10(*8*) or 10(*8A*) or, as the case may be, 10(*8B*) accompanying him to India, which accrues or arises outside India, and is not deemed to accrue or arise in India, in respect of which such member is required to pay any income or social security tax to the Government of that foreign State or, as the case may be, country of origin of such member.

TOPIC 15.08 *SECTION 10(10BC)*. COMPENSATION RECEIVED FOR DISASTER

Any amount received or receivable from the Central Government or a State Government or a local authority by an individual or his legal heir by way of compensation on account of any disaster, except the amount received or receivable to the extent such individual or his legal heir has been allowed a deduction under this Act on account of any loss or damage caused by such disaster.

Explanation.—For the purposes of this clause, the expression "disaster" shall have the meaning assigned to it under clause (d) of section 2 of the Disaster Management Act, 2005.

TOPIC 15.09 *SECTION 10(17)*. DAILY ALLOWANCE ETC., ALLOWED TO M.P.'s OR M.L.A's

Any income by way of

(i) daily allowance received by any person by reason of his membership of Parliament or of any State Legislature or of any Committee thereof.

(ii) any allowance received by any person by reason of his membership of Parliament under the Members of Parliament (Constituency Allowance) Rules, 1986.

(iii) all other allowances not exceeding Rs. 2,000 per month in the aggregate received by any person by reason of his membership of any State Legislature or of any Committee thereof, which the Central Government may, by notification in the Official Gazette, specify in this behalf.

TOPIC 15.10 *SECTION 10(17A)*. AWARD OR REWARD

Any payment made, whether in cash or in kind,

(i) in pursuance of any award instituted in the public interest by the Central Government or any State Government or instituted by any other body and approved by the Central Government in this behalf; or

(ii) as a reward by the Central Government or any State Government for such purposes as may be approved by the Central Government in this behalf in the public interest.

TOPIC 15.11 *SECTION 10(18)*. PENSION ALLOWED TO AWARDEE OF "PARAM VIR CHAKRA" OR "MAHA VIR CHAKRA" OR "VIR CHAKRA"

Any income by way of

(i) pension received by an individual who has been in the service of the Central Government or State Government and has been awarded "Param Vir Chakra" or "Maha Vir Chakra" or "Vir Chakra" or such other gallantry award as the Central Government may, by notification in the Official Gazette, specify in this behalf.

(ii) family pension received by any member of the family of an individual referred to in sub-clause (i).

TOPIC 15.12 *SECTION 10(19)*. FAMILY PENSION RECEIVED BY THE WIDOW OF ARMED FORCES

Family pension received by the widow or children or nominated heirs, as the case may be, of a member of the armed forces (including para-military forces) of the Union, where the death of such member has occurred in the course of operational duties, in such circumstances and subject to such conditions, as may be prescribed.

TOPIC 15.13 *SECTION 10(19A)*. ANNUAL VALUE OF ONE PALACE

The annual value of any one palace in the occupation of a Ruler, being a palace, the annual value whereof was exempt from income-tax before the commencement of the Constitution (Twenty-sixth Amendment) Act, 1971, by virtue of the provisions of the Merged States (Taxation Concessions) Order, 1949, or the Part B States (Taxation Concessions) Order, 1950, or, as the case may be, the Jammu and Kashmir (Taxation Concessions) Order, 1958:

Provided that for the assessment year commencing on the 1-4-1972, the annual value of every such palace in the occupation of such Ruler during the relevant previous year shall be exempt from income-tax.

STRATEGY MAKER

Points in 1 to 10	Overall Points 2; Practical 2; Theory 2.
Type of problem	Simple. You have been learning this chapter right from step 1. Any provision starting from section 10 is from this chapter. Therefore start noticing now.

The path of finding success is taking decisions that are from the heart and practical. The idea is to be yourself.

Keep Running

Practical Questions on Assessment of Individual

This chapter can be done only when you know all the provisions of Income Tax right from Chapter 1 to 15

16.01 COMPREHENSIVE PROBLEMS

Simple and Difficult

Problem 16.01-P1 (PE II - M03) - M 6

Q.1a : X, Finance Manager of K Ltd., Mumbai, furnishes the following particulars for the financial year 2006-07 :

Salary : Rs. 46,000 per month

Value of medical facility in a hospital maintained by the company : Rs. 7,000.

Rent free accommodation owned by the company.

Housing loan of Rs. 6,00,000 at the interest rate of 5% per annum (no repayment made during the year) (SBI lending rate 8.75%).

Gifts made by the company on the occasion of wedding anniversary of X : Rs. 4,750.

A wooden table and 4 chairs were provided to X at his residence (dining table). This was purchased on May 1, 2003 for Rs. 60,000 and sold to X on August 1, 2006 for Rs. 30,000.

Personal purchases through credit card provided by the company amounting to Rs. 10,000 was paid by the company. No part of the amount was recovered from X.

An ambassador car which was purchased by the company on July 16, 2003 for Rs. 2,50,000 was sold to the assessee on July 14, 2006 for Rs. 80,000.

Other income received by the assessee during the previous year 2006-07:

Interest on fixed deposits with a company	5,000
Income from specified mutual fund	3,000
Interest on bank deposits of a minor married daughter	3,000
Income from UTI received by his disabled minor son	1,200

Contribution to LIC towards premium under section 80CCC	10,000
Deposit in PPF account made during the year 2006-07	75,000
Bonds of ICICI (tax savings) eligible for deduction u/s 80C	25,000

Compute the total income of X and the tax thereon for the AY 2007-08.

Ans: 6,57,800; 1,50,287. [5,52,000+0+82,800+22,500+0+2,000+12,000+0+80,000= 7,51,300+5,000+0+1,500+0=7,57,800-90,000-10,000=6,57,800]

Problem 16.01-P2 (CA - N95) - M 25

X, a resident individual, retired from AB Co. Ltd. on February 1, 2007 after 20 years and 9 months of service. He joined PQ Co. Ltd. on the same day, *i.e.* February 1, 2007 and remained in service till March 31, 2007, when he furnished the following information :

Salary and allowance from April 1, 2006 to January 31, 2007 from AB Co. Ltd :

Basic salary	8,000 p.m.
Dearness allowance (part of salary for retirement benefits)	1,000 p.m.
Commission calculated @ 4% on turnover of Rs. 1,00,000 achieved by X	4,000
Gratuity received (not covered by the payment of Gratuity Act, 1972)	1,05,000
Salary and allowances from PQ Co. Ltd.	
Basic salary	6,000 p.m.
Entertainment allowance	800 p.m.
Fixed medical allowance	200 p.m.
House rent allowance	500 p.m.
Leave salary received	3,000

Other information:

X resides in his own house throughout the year, on which municipal tax of Rs. 5,000 has been paid during the year.

X is also the partner of XYZ Co., a partnership firm, assessed a firm as such and receives a share income of Rs. 11,140 from the firm during the previous year ended on March 31, 2007 (it does not include remuneration and interest). He incurs a loss of Rs. 4,820 from a speculation business carried on during the year.

X received Rs. 2,500 as interest on Post Office Saving Bank Account and Rs. 1,500 as dividend from a company incorporated in England. Interest on deposits in companies in the name of his minor son amounted to Rs. 4,000.

X paid a premium of Rs. 16,000 on the policy of Rs. 50,000 on life of his minor child. Contribution to an approved superannuation fund and the Jeevan Dhara Scheme of the LIC amounted to Rs. 7,500 and Rs. 4,500, respectively.

Compute X's total income for the assessment year 2007-08.

Ans: 1,05,000; 510. [Sal: 80,000+10,000+4,000+11,000+12,000+1,600+400+1,000+ 3,000=1,23,000] [TI: 1,23,000+0+0+4,000=1,27,000-22,000=1,05,000]

Problem 16.01-P3 [CA N01]

From the following particulars furnished by X for the previous year ending March 31, 2007, compute the taxable income for the assessment year 2007-08.

He owns a house property at a metro city. The fair rental value per annum in Rs. 27,000 and the municipal value is Rs. 24,000.

The house was let out from April 1, 2006 to August 31, 2006 @ Rs. 2,100 per month. From September 1, 2006, X occupies the house for his residence (self).

Expenditure incurred on property and paid : (a) municipal tax Rs. 4,000; (b) fire insurance Rs. 2,500; (c) land revenue Rs. 4,600; and (d) repairs Rs. 1,000.

Interest paid on borrowings for construction : (a) for the year Rs. 21,600 (b) proportionate preconstructs interest Rs. 12,960.

Income from firm (PFA/c) as partner : salary Rs. 25,000, interest on capital Rs. 20,000; and share income Rs. 35,000.

Ans: 26,540. [27,000-4,000=23,000–6,900–34,560=–18,460+25,000+20,000+0=26,540.]

Problem 16.01-P4 (CA - M02)

Q.1a : X submits the following information for the year ending March 31, 2007, for his proprietary business :

Net profit (as per profit and loss account)	1,12,500

The following expenditure was part of debits to the trading and profit and loss account :

• He used goods for his personal use. The value was credited to sales Rs. 25,000. The cost of which was Rs. 20,000	
• Rent of residence, Rs. 3,000 per month	36,000
• Payments in cash for purchase exceeding Rs. 20,000	4,00,000
• Sales tax in dispute provided	20,000
• Interest on term loan from State Bank of India, paid in the month of May 2007 70,000	

The following amounts were credited to profit and loss account :

• Agriculture income	50,000
• Income from Unit Trust of India (Monthly income plan)	30,000
• Winnings from lottery (gross) (tax deducted at source Rs. 30,000)	1,00,000

Compute the total income, assuming X has no residential house. Give reasons for the claim under each head of income.

Ans: 1,43,850. [1,12,500–5,000+36,000+80,000+20,000–50,000–30,000–1,00,000= 63,500+1,00,000=1,63,500-0-19,650=1,43,850]

Problem 16.01-P5 (CA - N02)

Q.1a : Compute the total income of X for the assessment year 2006-07 :

Net income from tyre business	30,000
Interest on Post office savings Bank Account	900
Share of profit from a partnership concern	22,000
Short term capital gain on land	24,000
Long term capital gain on house property	1,20,000
Share of income from HUF in which he is a member	8,200
Winning from camel race	10,000

Interest on bank deposits :	
- Deposit in his own name	4,000
- In the name of minor son	1,300
Expenditure incurred for the medical treatment of his disabled 67 years old brother (dependent of X, being a person with disability)	42,000
Payment of interest in respect of loan taken for part-time studies for graduate course in management	10,000
Donation to Prime Minister's National Relief Fund	20,000

Ans: 1,30,000. [30,000+24,000+1,20,000+10,000+4,000+0=1,88,000–50,000–0–20,000= 1,30,000] [Rs. 70,000 is limited to Rs. 58,000 since deduction u/s 80C to 80U is not available from special income and casual income]

Problem 16.01-P6 (ICWA-NEW - J03) - M 5

Q.2 : X, a reputed vocal musician, is also a part time employee in a company. He furnishes the following particulars of his income and expenditure for the year ending March 31, 2007.

Net salary received Rs. 30,000 after deduction of income-tax Rs. 6,000, contribution to recognized provident fund Rs. 5,400 and rent for quarters Rs. 4,600 at 10% of salary only.

Commission on sales at 3 per cent of turnover Rs. 8,00,000 as per the appointment letter.

Salary paid to a servant Rs. 1,200 per month who is used for both domestic and professional purposes. (Assume 70% of expenditure is utilised for professional purposes.)

Doctor's bills paid Rs. 2,000 for treatment of throat so as to improve his voice.

His gross professional receipts amounted of Rs. 50,000 for the year including Rs. 6,000 earned for performances in the USA. He claims exemption on Rs. 6,000.

Cost of two instruments Rs. 1,000 (Rs. 500 each).

He resides in his own house, the annual letting value of which as per municipal assessment is Rs. 2,400, and the fair rent is Rs. 500 per month. The municipal tax is Rs. 650.

A purse of Rs. 50,000 was presented to him at a function as a token of appreciation of the services rendered by him to the cause of music.

Life insurance premium paid Rs. 40,000 on a policy for Rs. 5,00,000.

Agricultural income Rs. 6,000. His minor son earned Rs. 10,000 from agricultural lands gifted by X to him in 2002.

How should the above items be dealt with under the Income-tax Act, 1961?

Ans: 1,23,770. [46,000+24,000+9,400=79,400] [50,000+50,000–10,080–0–150=89,770]

Problem 16.01-P7

Mrs. X (Resident in India and 66 years old) a low vision resident of Jaipur who is sole proprietor of a textile mill, showed a profit of Rs. 3,00,000 for the year ending on 31st March, 2007. The other details in respect of his income are given below :

(i) Rent of let — out house at Jaipur (Annual) Rs. 6,000. Local taxes paid in respect of this house Rs. 500.

(ii) Dividends from U.T.I. Rs. 18,000

(iii) Agriculture income Rs. 50,000.

(iv) She is also radio artist. She visited London and New York during the previous year and collected a net income of Rs. 40,000 which she has not brought into India.

(v) Life insurance premium paid Rs. 7,500 (Premium of Rs. 2,500 was paid on a policy of Rs. 20,000 taken on her own life and remaining premium was on a policy of Rs. 40,000 taken for her major married son).

(vi) Donation to Prime Minister's National Relief Fund Rs. 5,000.

Compute the tax liability of Mrs. X for the assessment Year 2007-08.

Ans: 2,81,350; 38,153. [3,00,000+3,850+40,000=3,43,850–5,000–50,000–7,500=2,81,350]

Problem 16.01-P8 [CA M97]

In respect of assessment year 2007-08, an author of text - books for school furnishes the following particulars and requests you to work out his tax liability :

Royalty from Printers Ltd. on publication of books		2,20,000
Capital gain (long-term)		60,000
Other sources :		
(a) Interest on bank deposits	Rs. 12,000	
(b) Dividend income (declared on April 16, 2006)	Rs. 3,000	
(c) Income from units of UTI	Rs. 5,000	20,000
Gross total income		20,00,000
Deductions :		
(i) Contributions towards :		
(a) LIC pension scheme		15,000
(b) LIC premium		10,000
(ii) Contribution to public provident fund		10,000
(iii) Investment in National Savings Certificates		50,000
(iv) Medical treatment of dependent relative (being a person with disability)		20,000

Ans: 1,57,000. [2,20,000+60,000+12,000=2,92,000-70,000-15,000-50,000=1,57,000]

Problem 16.01-P9

X, a senior citizen, has furnished the following particulars relating to his house properties :

	House I Self-occupied	*House II Let out*
Municipal valuation	60,000	1,20,000
Fair rent	90,000	1,50,000
Standard rent	75,000	90,000
Actual rent per month	—	9,000
Municipal taxes paid	6,000	12,000
Interest on capital borrowed	70,000	90,000

Loan for both houses were taken on April 1, 2000. Construction of both the house was completed within 2 years. House II was remained vacant for 4 months. Besides the above two houses, X has inherited during the year an old house from his grand father on

1-5-1982. Due to business commitments, he sold the house for a sum of Rs. 2 crore. However, the fair market value as on April 1, 1981 was Rs. 20 lakh. With the sale proceeds, X purchased a new house in March 2007 for a sum of Rs. 100 lakh and the balance was used in his business.

The other income particulars of X besides the above are as follows (AY 2007-08)

Business loss	2,00,000
Income from other sources (bank interest)	1,00,000
Investments made during the year public provident fund	70,000
ICICI Infrastructure Bond	30,000

Compute total income of X and his tax liability for the assessment year 2007-08.

Ans: 1,67,460. [–1,09,600+4,77,064–2,00,000+1,00,000=2,67,464–1,00,000=1,67,464]

Problem 16.01-P10 [CA M04]

M : Y retires as General Manager of XYZ co. Ltd. on Novemebr 30, 2006 after rendering service for 20 years and 10 months. He received Rs. 3,00,000 as gratuity from the employer. He is not covered by Gratuity Act, 1972. His salary particulars are given below :

Basic pay	Rs. 10,000 per month up to June 30, 2006.
Basic pay	Rs. 12,000 per month from July 01, 2006.
Dearness allowance eligible for, retirement benefits	50% of basic pay
Transport allowance	Rs. 1,500 per month

He resides in his own house. Interest on money borrowed for the self-ocupied house is Rs. 24,000 for the year ending March 31, 2007.

From a fixed deposit with a bank, he gets interest income of Rs. 18,000 for the year ending March 31, 2007. Compute taxable income of Y for the assessment year 2007-08.

Ans: 2,72,600. [90,000+45,000+5,600+1,38,000=2,78,600–24,000+18,000=2,72,600]

Problem 16.01-P11

Shri Dinesh Mehta has furnished the following particulars of income earned by him during the financial year :

(i) Net Commission income from 'arhat' business. Rs. 1,35,500

(ii) Dividend income from shares of India Companies. Rs. 15,500

(iii) On 15.12.2006, he sold govt securities for Rs. 1,20,000, which he had purchased on 11-12-1998 for Rs. 75,000.

(iv) He is the owner of a residential flat which he has let out on a monthly rent of Rs. 6,300. He has paid annual interest of Rs. 30,000 on loan borrowed from National Housing Bank for purchasing the aforesaid flat, besides loan repayment of Rs. 60,000. The municipal tax and the insurance premium paid for the said flat are Rs. 3,600 and Rs. 2,600 respectively.

Compute the taxable income and income tax liability of Shri Dinesh Mehta for the assessment year 2007-08.

Ans: 1,05,003. [20,400+1,35,000+9,103=1,65,003–60,000=1,05,003]

Problem 16.01-P12

Narain Agarwal, who is 75 years old, is deriving rental income of Rs. 15,000 per month from his residential flat in Delhi. The municipal tax and the insurance premium for the said flat are Rs. 4,500 and Rs. 3,500 respectively. He decided to sell the flat and therefore got it vacated on 31-12-2006. In February 2007, he sold the flat for Rs. 32,60,500. He paid brokerage of Rs. 65,000 for transfer of the flat. The flat had been purchased by him in August, 1989 for Rs. 2,85,000. In February, 1998 he had renovated the flat and spent an amount of Rs. 1,75,000 on the same.

Shri Agarwal also earned bank interest of Rs. 1,36,000 during the year 2006-07 on account of deposit of sale proceeds of the flat in the bank. The amount was deposited for purchase of new flat. He had also won a lottery of Rs. 6,500 in August, 2006.

Compute the taxable income of Shri Agarwal for AY 2007-08 and also his tax liability.

Ans: 2,33,850; 10,628. [91,350+0+1,36,000+6,500=2,33,850]

Problem 16.01-P13

Shri Radhe Lal has furnished following information to the Income Tax Department in respect of Financial Year 2006-2007. Please compute his total income and tax payable by him.

(i) Interest income from Savings Bank Account. 5,000

(ii) Dividend income from Units of Unit Trust of India. 20,000

(iii) Interest on Government securities. 25,000

(iv) On April 15, 2006, he sold listed shares for Rs. 1,50,000 which he had purchased on 1-6-2005 for Rs. 1,72,000.

(v) On Dec. 15, 2006 he sold his residential house for Rs. 5 lakhs. It was purchased by him on March 3, 1990 for Rs. 1 lakh. It had been in his own occupation. Out of the consideration received from sale of this house, he invested Rs. 2 lakhs on 15-1-2007 in purchase of a new house for himself and Rs. 1 lakh on marriage of his daughter. Half of the new house is used by him for his own residence and the remaining half is let out to a tenant for monthly rent of Rs. 4,000. He has also taken interest free deposit of Rs. 50,000 from the tenant.

Ans: 54,200; nil. [7,000+39,196–22,000+30,000=54,196]

Problem 16.01-P14

Shri Dinesh Mehta has furnished the following particulars of income earned by him during the financial year :

(i) Net Commission income from 'arhat' business. Rs. 1,35,000

(ii) Dividend income from shares of India Companies. Rs. 15,500

(iii) On 15-12-2006, he sold preference shares for Rs. 1,20,000, which he had purchased on 11-12-1998 for Rs. 75,000.

(iv) He is the owner of a residential flat which he has let out on a monthly rent of Rs. 6,300. He has paid annual interest of Rs. 30,000 on loan borrowed from National Housing Bank for purchasing the aforesaid flat, besides loan repayment of Rs. 60,000. The municipal tax and the insurance premium paid for the said flat are Rs. 3,600 and Rs. 2,600 respectively.

Compute the taxable income and income tax liability of Shri Dinesh Mehta for the assessment year 2007-2008.

Ans: 1,05,000; 1,020. [20,400+1,35,500+9,103=1,65,003–60,000=1,05,003]

Typical

Problem 16.01-P15 (Typical)

Mr. Neo, a resident in India, a computer programmer working in Matrix Ltd. furnishes following particulars of his salary for the year ended March 31, 2007. Compute his total income and tax liability for the AY 2007-08.

Basic Salary	16,000 p.m.
Project Allowance	3,000 p.m.

He has been provided with following facilities :

1. The Company allotted him 400 shares at Rs. 70 each whereas the market value per share on the date of allotment was Rs. 120. Allotment was not done under stock option plan.
2. He is a member of an unrecognized provident fund to which he contributes 15% of his salary and his employer also contributes an equal amount.
3. Reimbursement of medical bills Rs. 17,000 *(treatment was done in a Government hospital in India)*
4. He has also been provided by the company with facility of free use of water and light for which employer paid Rs. 1,300 during the previous year.
5. The employer provided him travel concession of Rs. 4,000 in September 2006. At Srinagar he stayed in the Holiday Home maintained by the company. The expenses of boarding and lodging amounting to Rs. 2,000 were borne by the company.
6. He was also sent to attend a trainee course at Ahmedabad for 15 days, the fee of Rs. 500 was paid by the company.

He furnishes other information in respect of his income and savings :

1. He also receives pension from Nepal Government in respect of his deceased wife Rs. 6,000 p.m. *(He received the pension in Nepal and deposited in an Indian bank there)*
2. He donated Rs. 5,000 to Zila Saksharta Samiti on 1-4-2006.
3. He also pays Rs. 1,200 in cash to GIC for insuring his own health.
4. Rs. 3,200 paid in cheque for insuring the health of X's minor dependent brother.
5. He has a disabled son *(with severe disability)*, dependent on him, for whom he incurs expenses for his medical treatment and rehabilitation. He also deposits a sum of Rs. 25,000 for the benefit of his son under a scheme framed by UTI for such a purpose.

He also purchases 500 equity shares of National Highway Authority of India for Rs. 1,20,000.

Ans: 1,06,300; 643. [1,92,000+36,000+0+0+0+1,300+0=2,29,300+57,000=2,86,300–5,000–0–75,000–1,00,000=1,06,300]

Problem 16.01-P16 (Typical)

Mr. X furnishes following information for your computation :

Basic Salary	12,000 p.m.
HRA	6,000 p.m.

Children education allowance to meet the hostel expenditure of three children	5,000 each
Re-imbursement of medical bills :	
- on health of Mr. X	7,000
- on health of his grandfather	3,000

On 1-4-2005 he takes loan of Rs. 10,00,000 @ 12% p.a. from his employer for construction of house at Mumbai. He repays Rs. 50,000 on 15th of every month starting from the month of March 2007.

On 1-1-2006 being the date of completing of construction of house, the employer presented him imported furniture worth Rs. 1,00,000. On 31-3-2007 he sold all his furniture for Rs. 1,05,000.

On 1-1-2007, Mr. X shifted in his own house with his family. Till 31-12-2006 he was paying 80% of HRA as rent.

Other income Rs. 1,85,000

Compute taxable income and tax liability for the AY 2007-08.

Ans: 1,83,250; 11,883 [1,44,000+39,600+5,400+3,000+0+0=1,92,000–1,43,750+1,85,000=2,33,250–50,000=1,83,250]

Problem 16.01-P17 (CA - N99) - M 15

Q.1 : Following details are furnished by X, an Indian citizen, for the year ending March 31, 2007 :

Salary (net of tax and X's contribution to provident fund)	48,000
X's contribution to provident fund	4,950
Employer's contribution to provident fund	4,950
Interest credited to provident fund (@ 6.75% per annum)	14,000
Leave travel allowance received	3,600
House rent allowance (rent paid on house in Hyderabad : Rs. 4,500)	4,500
Dividend from ACC Ltd., an Indian company	2,500
Dividend collection charge	200
Tax deduction at source on salary	1,500
Contribution to public provident fund	4,000
Contribution to National Laboratory approved under section 35	5,000
Amount received on maturity of a Keyman insurance policy	6,000

X acquired 2,000 shares of Rs. 5 lakh during 1984-85. Company allotted him equal value of bonus shares during 1990-91. Second bonus issue was made during March 2006, when received 1 bonus share for every 2 shares held by him. The entire shares held in the company have been sold by him through recognised stock exchange during November, 2006 @ Rs. 1,100 per share.

Determine the total income and tax liability of X for the assessment year 2007-08.

Ans: 22,55,000; 2,41,454. [54,450+0+0+0+4,500+6,000=64,950+22,00,000=22,64,950–4,950–5,000=22,55,000]

Problem 16.01-P18 (CS-D03) - M 10

Q.3a : Rajesh, a director at Young Pvt Ltd., Mumbai, carrying on transport business, has submitted the following particulars of his income for the assessment year 2007-08. Compute his total income and tax payable :

(i) Director's remuneration and perquisites :

Remuneration @ Rs. 11,000 p.m. : Rs. 1,32,000.

Free use of car of engine capacity of 1,500 cc provided by the company.

The company has provided rent-free accommodation (unfurnished) to Rajesh at Mumbai. It is ascertained that for his purpose the company has obtained a flat on lease from Prem Ltd. for which the company pays rent of Rs. 40,000 p.a. which is also the fair rental value.

Medical expenses met by the company on ordinary treatment to Rajesh and members of his family Rs. 4,500.

(ii) Rajesh was occupying a bungalow on rent at New Delhi since November, 1986. He agreed to transfer his tenancy right in the said bungalow in favour of Bala Ltd. for a sum of Rs. 2,00,000 payable as follows :

Rs. 50,000 in cash.

A flat valued at Rs. 1,50,000 (at cost) in the new building to be put up by Bala Ltd. to be allotted free of cost. The cash payment was made on 5th April, 2006 and the flat was allotted to him on 5th October 2006 which was kept for his own residence from that date.

Ans: 2,16,200; 15,157. [1,32,000+0+19,800+14,400=1,66,200+(2,00,000–1,50,000)= 2,16,200]

Problem 16.01-P19 (CS-J02) - M 15

Q.3b : X is in the service of A Ltd. since 1980. He dies on January 31, 2007. The following information is available :

Basic salary : Rs. 20,000 per month; dearness allowance : Rs. 6,000 per month (40 per cent of which is included for the purpose of determining retirement benefit); transport allowance: Rs. 3,800 per month (out of which only Rs. 600 are used for the journey between office and residence; the remaining amount is not spent); and entertainment allowance : Rs. 1,000 per month. He contributes 15 per cent of basic salary towards recognised provident fund and A Ltd., also makes a matching contribution. Interest is credited at the rate of 9 per cent.

After the death of X, his legal heirs (*i.e.*, Mrs. X and his minor children) get the following payments from A Ltd. :

1. Salary for the month of January 2007.
2. Family pension : Rs. 10,000 per month.
3. Encashment of leave standing to the credit of X on January 31, 2007 : Rs. 2,40,000 (as per service rules X is entitled for 45 days leave for each year of service).
4. Provident fund balance : Rs. 3,90,000.
5. Gratuity : Rs. 2,60,000 (X is not covered by the Payment of Gratuity Act, 1972, nor is there any agreement with employer to get gratuity).

X is a doctor. He runs a small clinic near his residence which is discontinued after the death of X. His income from the clinic for the period April 1, 2006 to January 31, 2007 is Rs. 49,000.

After the discontinuation of the clinic, Mrs. X recovers some of the outstanding bill issued by X (amount recovered during February 1, 2007 to March 31, 2007 : Rs. 76,000). Mrs. X does not have any other income. On March 30, 2007, Mrs. X withdraws Rs. 1,40,000 being the balance in account of X in National Saving Scheme, 1987.

Assuming that salary, allowances and pension become "due" on the last day of the month, find out :

(a) who will be chargeable to tax in respect of the aforesaid receipts ?

(b) net income and tax liability for the assessment year 2007-08.

Ans: (X) 3,22,120; 47,569; (Mrs. X) 2,06,330; 13,021. [2,00,000+60,000+30,000+10,000+3,120=3,03,120+49,000=3,52,120–30,000=3,22,120] [20,000–6,667=13,333+1,93,000=2,06,333]

Problem 16.01-P20 (CS-J03) - M 10

***Q.3a* : X furnishes the following information relevant for the assessment year 2007-08:**

General expenses	23,400	Gross profit	3,05,500
Bad debts	8,000	Commission	9,500
Provision for outstanding sales tax & Excise duty	10,000	Brokerage	12,000
Advance tax	11,000	Sundry receipts	2,500
Legal expenses (paid to a chartered accountant for preparation of income tax return)	4,000	Bad debts recovered (earlier allowed as deduction)	5,000
		Interest on debentures, (*i.e.*, net amount Rs. 11,250 + TDS Rs. 1,250)	12,500
Insurance	1,600	Interest on deposit with the company [(non - trade) net interest Rs. 5,850 + TDS Rs. 650]	6,500
Salary of staff	25,000		
Leave encashment to staff	5,000		
Salary to X	24,000		
Interest on overdraft	6,000		
Interest on loan to Mrs. X	32,000		
Interest on Capital of X	22,000		
Expenditure on account of Deepawali	8,000		
Depreciation	45,000		
Advertisement expenses	7,000		
Contribution to employees recognized provident fund	12,000		
Net profit	1,09,500		
	3,53,500		3,53,500

The amount of depreciation allowable is Rs. 50,500 as per the Income-tax Act, 1961.

Income of Rs. 25,000 received on January 20, 2007 on units of mutual fund specified under section 10(23D) is not recorded in profit and loss account.

Loan from Mrs. X was taken for payment of arrears of income-tax.

Salary to staff includes payment of Rs. 9,000 to a relative, which is unreasonable to the extent of Rs. 4,000.

Out of outstanding sales tax and excise duty, Rs. 2,000 is paid on July 25, 2007 and Rs. 5,000 is paid on October 13, 2007. The balance is not yet paid. Due date of filing return of income is July 31, 2007.

Interest on debenture is paid to X in December 2006.

General expenses include Rs. 5,000 incurred for payment of school fees of X's son.

X has taken an annuity plan of LIC for receiving pension, and paid premium of Rs. 10,400 on March 27, 2007.

Assuming that the insurance premium is paid by X on the life policy (sum assured Rs. 3,40,000) of his major son Rs. 70,000 on March 25, 2007 and he invests Rs. 20,000 in Industrial Development Bank of India (IDBI) infrastructure bonds on March 30, 2007, determine the taxable income and tax liability of X for the assessment year 2007-08.

Ans: 2,00,000; 20,500.

Problem 16.01-P21 (Typical)

Mr. Sukhvinder Singh was born on 1st July, 1934 in the Lahore city of undivided India. On partition he came to India in September, 1947 and since then he has been living in India as the citizen of India. He submits the following particulars of his income for the year ending 31st March 2007:

(a) He was employed at a monthly salary of Rs. 12,000 and he was member of an unrecognized P.F. to which he contributed 10% of this salary. The employer's contribution was 15%. He resigned from this service and was relieved on 1-7-2006. He got Rs. 2,50,000 from his P.F. which included Rs. 1,20,000 as employer's contribution and Rs. 30,000 as interest thereon. Balance Rs. 1,00,000 his own contribution and interest thereon was Rs. 80,000 and Rs. 20,000 respectively.

(b) He owned a house which was let out at Rs. 8,000 per month. The municipal valuation is Rs. 24,000 and municipal taxes are 10% p.a. of its municipal valuation. The municipal taxes are paid by tenant. The construction was started on 1-4-1995 and was completed on 31-3-1996. The construction cost, including the cost of land, was Rs. 79,600. On 31st March 2007 he sold this house for Rs. 3,80,000 and purchased bonds of National Highway Authority worth Rs. 1,15,000 on 10th May, 2007 redeemable after 3 years.

(c) He runs a flour mill also. The written down value of the two machines of this mill as on 1-4-2006 was Rs. 10,000. He sold out the two machines, one machine for Rs. 13,000 on 1st January, 2007. The written down value of the furniture was Rs. 2,000 as on 1-4-2006. The profits of his business before charging depreciation on machines and furniture were Rs. 47,900 for the previous year 2006-07.

(d) His wife transferred him 1,000 equity shares of Rs. 10 each of a foreign company in May 1988 without consideration. He got dividend on these shares several times and invested in the shares of company. The company allotted him bonus shares also, now he has 4,000 shares. The company declared a dividend of 20% on these shares in August, 2006 which was received by him in December, 2006.

(e) He received Rs. 11,940 (net) as winnings from the Rajasthan State Lottery in July, 2006 and Rs. 18,800 (net) as winning from M.P. State Lottery in January, 2007.

(f) During the previous year he made the following deposits and payments :

(i) Rs. 6,000 as donation to a corporation established by Central Govt. for welfare of the members of minority community.
(ii) Rs. 10,000 as donation to P.M. National Relief Fund, Rs. 6,000 to National Foundation for Communal Harmony.
(iii) Rs. 2,000 as donation for repair of Taj Mahal which is approved for deduction u/s 80G.
(iv) Deposited Rs. 5,000 in the scheme of Life Insurance Plan and deposited Rs. 40,000 in Home Loan Account Scheme of National Housing Bank.
(v) He contributed Rs. 14,000 to unit linked Insurance Plan.

Compute the total income and the tax payable by Sh. Sukhvinder Singh for the assessment year 2007-08.

Ans: 4,16,180; 64,317. [1,86,000+67,200+47,700+1,17,981+3,000+70,294=4,92,175–76,000=4,16,175]

Problem 16.01-P22 (PE II - N05) - M 16

Q.1(a) : Mr. Ashok owns a property consisting of two blocks of indentical size. The first block is used for business purposes. The other block has been let out from 1-4-2006 to his cousin for Rs. 10,000 p.m. The cost of construction of each block is Rs. 5 lakhs (fully met from bank loan), rate of interest on bank loan is 10% p.a. The construction was completed on 31-3-2006. During the year ended 31-3-2007, he had to pay a penal interest of Rs. 2,000 in respect of each block on account of delayed payments to the bank for the borrowings. The normal interest paid by him in respect of each block was Rs. 42,000. Principal repayment for each block was Rs. 23,000. An identical block in the same neighbourhood fetches a rent of Rs. 15,000 per month. Municipal tax paid in respect of each block was Rs. 12,000.

The income from business prior to adjustment towards depreciation on any asset is Rs. 2,20,000. He follows Mercantile system of accounting.

Depreciation on equipments used for business is Rs. 30,000.

On 23-3-2007, he sold shares of B Ltd., a listed share in BSE for Rs. 2,30,000. The share had been purchased 10 months back for Rs. 1,80,000. Security transaction tax paid may be taken as Rs. 220.

Brought forward business loss of a business discontinued on 12-1-2006 is Rs. 80,000. This loss has been determined in pursuance of a return of income filed in time and the current year is the seventh year.

The following payments were effected by him during the year :

(i) LIP of Rs. 20,000 on his life and Rs. 12,000 for his son aged 22, engaged as a software engineer and drawing salary of Rs. 25,000 p.m.
(ii) Mediclaim premium of Rs. 6,000 for himself and Rs. 5,000 for above son. The premiums were paid by cheque.

You are required to compute the total income for the assessment year 2007-08 and the tax payable. The various heads of income should be properly shown. Ignore the interest on bank loan for the period prior to 1-4-2006, as the bank had waived the same.

Ans: 1,24,600. [HP:1,80,000–12,000=1,68,000–50,400–42,000=75,600] [BI: 2,20,000–30,000–0–50,000–1,40,000–80,000=60,000] [CG: 2,30,000–1,80,000–50,000] [TI: 75,600+60,000+50,000=1,85,600–55,000–6,000=1,24,600]

Problem 16.01-P23 (PE II - N03) - M 15

Q.1a : X provides the following information for the year ending March 31, 2007 :

Sales (retail trade in garments) (no books of account maintained)	32,00,000
Rent from house property at Chennai (per month)	10,000
Vacant site lease rent	48,000

X purchases 20,000 shares of A Co. Ltd., unlisted who declares 1 : 1 bonus on January 1, 2004.

X sells 1,000 bonus shares in September 2006 for Rs. 1,20,000.

X gets Rs. 50,000 on February 12, 2007, being amount due from Y relating to electronic goods supplied by X's father, which was written off as bad debt by his father in assessment year 2005-06 and allowed as deduction. X's father dies in August 2005.

X has brought forward business loss relating to discontinued automobile business pertaining to assessment year 2005-06 : Rs. 2,00,000; brought forward depreciation relating to the same business : Rs. 1,50,000.

X contributes Rs. 15,000 to the Prime Minister's National Relief Fund Rs. 10,000 to Heritage Charitable Trust enjoying exemption under section 80G.

Compute total income of X for the assessment year 2007-08.

Ans: 91,400. [BI:1,60,000+50,000=2,10,000–2,00,000=10,000–10,000=0] [TI: 84,000+0+1,20,000+48,000=2,52,000–1,40,000(to be first set off with LTCG)=1,12,000–15,000–11,200=91,400]

Problem 16.01-P24 (CA - N89) - M 5

Q.1/29 : Arun retired from Government service on 30-9-2006 as Director of Medical Health and Services. He started practising as consulting physician from 1-10-2006. From 1-11-2006, he also undertook contractual appointment with Sarada Nursing Home as Superintendent. He furnishes the following particular of his income of the previous year ending 31-3-2007. Compute his total income for the Assessment Year 2007-08.

(a) Salary Particulars :		
As director of Medical services up to 30-9-06		30,000
Pension per month from October 2006 @ Rs. 1,500		9,000
Leave salary in respect of earned leave at his credit		13,500
Gratuity		1,10,000
Provident Fund		1,50,000
Commuted Pension		32,000
Sarada Nursing Home (1-11-2006 to 31-3-2007) (5 months)		25,000
(b) Consultancy Profession :		
Gross consultancy receipts (1-10-2006 to 31-3-2007)		50,000
Expenditure incurred		
Salary to the Staff	12,000	
Rent for premises belonging to his wife	6,000	
Pathological equipment purchased on 20-10-2006	20,000	
Petrol expenses for the car	5,000	43,000

Donation to Charitable hospital approved u/s 11 of Income Tax Act		3,000
(c) Further Information :		
Interest on Public Provident Fund Account	8,000	
On Fixed and Savings Bank Accounts with Bank	10,000	18,000
Dividends :		
On shares with companies	5,000	
On units with Unit Trust of India	4,000	9,000

The car was acquired on 15-9-2006 for Rs. 75,000. 15% of the use of the car is attributed to personal purposes.

He made the following investments :

Donation to school	25,000
10 Years Post Office Savings Bank (CTD) Rules, 1959	10,000
National Saving Certificate VIII issue	10,000

Ans: 77,750. [64,000+50,000–12,000–6,000–1,500–4,000–11,250+10,000=89,250–10,000–1,500=77,750]

Problem 16.01-P25 (CA - N87) - M 5

Q.1/33 : A, a musician and a play back singer, entrusts his accounts to you for preparation of a return of income for the Assessment Year 2007-08. From an analysis of the Bank accounts, you notice the following :

Concert receipts (local)	24,000
Receipts from film producers and companies	78,000
Royalty received from companies on records sold	10,000
Amount from Life Insurance Corporation on a maturity of a policy in the name of wife	26,000
Interest on Savings Bank accounts	16,500
Life Insurance Premium paid on a policy in wife's name (sum assured Rs. 1 lakh)	12,500
Life Insurance Premium on own life policy (sum assured Rs. 1.2 lakh)	10,000
Deposited in a Public Provident Fund account	30,000
Cost of train and air tickets for a party taken by A, on a concert tour of Kolkata, Shillong and Guwahati	14,000
Payments to accompanying artists for the above	8,000
Concert receipts on the tour of Eastern India region	65,000
Motor car expenses — car used to attend concerts recording sessions etc.	18,000
Rent paid (Half premises used for professional purposes)	30,000

A also trains disciples in his spare time and in the relevant year he collected from such disciples Rs. 12,000 in cash which were utilised to meet the household expenses. A has some agricultural land in his ancestral village and during the year, he received Rs. 10,000 by way of sale of paddy. His father had left him some government securities on which he collected interest (gross) of Rs. 12,000 in the year. Compute A's total income and its tax.

Ans: 1,10,000; 1,020. [24,000+78,000+10,000+65,000+12,000=18,900–14,000–8,000–18,000–15,000=1,34,000+16,500+12,000=1,62,500–52,500–4,000=1,10,000]

Problem 16.01-P26 [PE II N 06]

Mr. Rajesh is serving in a Public Limited Company as General Manager (Finance). His total emoluments for the year ended 31st March, 2007 are as follows :

Basic Salary	Rs. 5,40,000
HRA (Computed)	Rs. 1,80,000
Transport allowance	Rs. 12,400

Apart from the above, his employer has sold the following Assets to him on 1st January, 2007:

(i) Laptop computer for Rs. 20,000 (Acquired in September, 2005 for Rs. 1,20,000).

(ii) Car 1800 cc for Rs. 3,20,000 (purchased in April, 2004 for Rs. 8,50,000).

He also owns a residential house, let out for a monthly rent for Rs. 15,000. The fair rental value of the property for the let out period is Rs. 1,50,000. The house was self-occupied by him from 1st January, 2007 to 31st March, 2007. He has taken a loan of Rs. 20 lacs for the consumption of the property, and has repaid Rs. 1,05,000 (including interest Rs. 40,000) during the year.

Mr. Rajesh sold shares of different Indian companies on 14th April, 20065 :

Name	*Sale Value (per share)*	*Purchase price (per share)*	*Acquired on*	*No. of Shares*
A Ltd.	Rs. 150	Rs. 120	2nd May, 2004	200
B Ltd.	Rs. 82	Rs. 65	16th April, 2005	125

Sale proceeds were subject to brokerage of 0.1% and securities transaction tax of 0.075%. On the gross consideration. He received I.T. refund of Rs. 5,750 (including interest Rs. 750) relating to the Assesment Year 2005-06.

Compute the total income of Rs. Rajesh to the Assessment year 2007-08.

Ans: 10,24,670. [Sal: 5,40,000+1,80,000+2,800+40,000+2,24,000=9,86,800] [HP: 2,00,000–60,000–40,000=1,00,000] [CG: 10,250–8,125–10=2,115] [TI: 9,86,800+ 1,00,000+2,115+750=10,89,665–65,000=10,24,670]

Problem 16.01-P27 [Hons 1999]

X, a non-resident, is the owner of a big house in India. He has occupied half of it for his own business since its completion. The other half has been let out on a rent of Rs. 3,000 p.m. from 1-5-2006 . The house remained vacant for the month of April 2006. He furnishes the other particulars of the house for the PY ending March 31, 2007:

The Municipal value of the house is Rs. 78,000 and he has paid Rs. 7,200 as municipal taxes. Other expenses incurred for the house is:

1. Annual revenue charge Rs. 3,600
2. Fire insurance premium Rs. 1,800
3. Interest on loan taken for renovation of the house Rs. 15,000. Loan is borrowed from Sydney and interest is payable outside India. Tax of Rs. 1,530 has been deducted at source.
4. The house is subject to land revenue of Rs. 600 p.a. He paid it for the last year and current year during the year.

His taxable income from business is Rs. 2,10,000 (before adjusting any expenses related to portion used for business)

Compute his total income ignoring depreciation.

Ans: 2,12,580; 17,866. [HP:36,000–3,600=32,400–9,720–7,500=15,180] [BI: 2,10,000–3,600–0–900–7,500–600=1,97,400]

Problem 16.01-P28 [Hons 2002]

Dr. Paul, Principal Government College, Alwar, received salary of Rs. 20,000 p.m. and dearness allowance Rs. 5,000 p.m. He was provided with a chauffeur-driven Maruti Zen (less than 1600 cc) car for both official and personal use. All expenses were borne by the college. He retired from service on June 30, 2006 after 35 years of service, when along with his salary for June 2006, he received the following amounts :

Encashement of Leave Salary	Rs.1,95,000
Accumulated Balance of Provident Fund	Rs. 6,15,000
Gratuity	Rs. 3,00,000
The monthly pension of Dr. Paul was fixed at	Rs. 9,000

Salary / Pension was due and payable on 1st of next month.

After the retirement Dr. Paul was employed in a tutorial college for an honorarium of Rs. 10,000 p.m. w.e.f. July 1, 2006.

He got his 1/3 of pension commuted for Rs. 3,30,000 w.e.f. 1-1-2007

Dr. Paul owns a house at Alwar, one-half portion of it was used for self occupation and the remaining half was let out for Rs. 3,000 p.m. Municipal valuation being Rs. 78,000. Municipal Taxes paid were : Rs. 20,000, for the house during the year. He paid Rs. 36,000 *(Interest Rs. 18,000 and Principal Rs. 18,000)* to Bank as installments against a loan taken for the construction of house two years back. The let out portion remained vacant for two months during the previous year.

Other receipts of the year were :

(i) Medical reimbursement during April-June, 2006 were Rs. 5,000.

(ii) Interest from Gold deposit scheme, 2001 Rs. 15,000 in the name of his spouse against the money deposited by him.

(iii) Dividend from Cooperative society Rs. 3,000.

(iv) Maturity value of Life Insurance Policy Rs. 4,50,000 received on December 15, 2006 was put in fixed deposit with State Bank of India for 2 years on 1-1-2007 at 9% interest per annum. (At no part of the year premium exceeded 20% of the assured amount)

Dr. Paul's contribution to Statutory Provident Fund while in service was Rs. 16,000 and he paid a premium of Rs. 8,000 on an approved Mediclaim policy for himself during the year.

Compute Total Income and Tax Liability of Dr. Paul (Resident individual) for the previous year relevant to the AY 2007-08.

Ans: 2,25,230; 20,447. [Sal: 80,000+20.000+0+0+0+66,000=1,66,000+90,000=2,56,000] [HP: 33,000–10,000=23,000–6,900–9,000=7,100–9,000=–1,900] [TI:2,56,000–1,900+10,125+3,000=2,67,225–34,000–8,000=2,25,230]

Problem 16.01-P29 [Hons 1998]

The following is the receipts and payments account of a Medical Practitioner for the year ending March 31, 2007.

Receipts	*Rs.*	*Payment*	*Rs.*
Balance b/d	1,05,000	Office expenses	1,04,000
Visiting fees	65,000	Purchase of medical books	11,000
Consultation fees	65,000	Surgical equipment	80,000
Sale of medicines	25,000	Motor car expenses	30,000
Operation theatre rent	15,000	Medical association fee	7,200
Bank loan	2,00,000	Audit fees	2,250
Interest on securities (gross)	27,500	Entertainment expenses	30,250
Life insurance policy maturity proceeds	4,00,000	Medicines purchase	45,000
Rent from flat	52,500	Purchase of flat	2,80,000
LTCG	20,000	Bank interest on flat	30,000
		Balance c/d	3,55,300
Total	9,75,000	Total	9,75,000

Additional information:

1. A cash payment of Rs. 1,10,000 was given to him by a patient in appreciation of his medical services, but was not recorded in books.
2. A flat was purchased on 1-5-2006 and 25% of the plot was self-occupied for residence. Remaining portion of the flat was let out @ Rs. 5,000 p.m. The tenant vacated it on the last day of February 2007 and it remained vacant throughout the month of March. The municipal value of the flat is Rs. 80,000 p.a. Fair Rent Rs. 70,000 Standard rent Rs. 90,000 p.a. Municipal taxes assessed, though not paid Rs 4,200. The owner could not realise 15 days rent from the tenant.
3. One third of motor car expenses relate to his personal use, depreciation on car allowable under I.T. Act for professional use is Rs. 12,000.
4. The rate of depreciation on surgical equipment is 15%. The W.D.V. of equipment on 1-4-2006 is Rs. 50,000. He sold equipment for Rs. 30,000 during the year. New equipment was purchased on 1-11-2006.
5. The date of purchase of medical books 5-10-2007
6. In PY 2004-05 life insurance premium amount exceeded 20% of assured sum.

Compute total income & tax liability for AY 2007-08.

Ans: 4,04,310; 70,679. [BI:65,000+65,000+25,000+15,000+1,10,000–1,04,000–3,300–9,000–20,000–12,000–7,200–2,250–30,250–45,000=47,000.] [HP: 56,875–17,063–22,500=17,313–7,500=9,813] [TI: 9,813+47,000+20,000+27,500+4,00,000=5,04,313–1,00,000=4,04,310.]

Problem 16.01-P30 [CA N94]

X, a civil assistant surgeon, was in Government service till June 30, 2006. He joined as an adviser (part time) from October 1, 2006 in a charitable dispensary on an honorarium of Rs. 3,000 per month. He owns a house property. Ground floor is occupied by him for his residence, the annual value of which is Rs. 30,000. First floor was built by him and was let out from June 1, 2006 on a monthly rent of Rs. 2,500, after its completion on May 31, 2006. He is also a visiting surgeon to various hospitals. From the following further information, furnished for the year ending March 31, 2006, you are requested to (a) compute the total income for the assessment year 2007-08, and (b) Calculate the rebate of tax permissible.

Salary from Government service		24,000
House rent allowance		4,500
Gratuity received		1,30,000
Leave encashment		48,000
Provident fund		75,000
Commuted pension		30,000
Pension		18,000
Gross receipts from various hospitals as visiting surgeon		90,000
Car petrol for official purpose.		18,000
Books and periodicals for official purpose.		9,000
He owns a car purchased on June 1, 2004 used for visits to hospitals Written down value as on April 1, 2006		80,000
Life Insurance Maturity proceeds. (Premium paid for a year exceeded 20% of the assured amount)		25,000
Royalty received on the text books authored by him and recommended as text book for university		30,000
Municipal tax on house property		
Ground floor	Rs. 4,000	
First floor paid on April 15, 2007	Rs. 6,000	10,000
Donation to Prime Minister's National Relief Fund		10,000
Repayment to Housing Development Finance Corporation Ltd. (paid in June 2007 Principal Rs. 10,000 + interest Rs. 15,000 on loan taken for construction of first floor)		25,000
Deposit into public provident fund account		30,000

Ans: 1,62,100; 7,568. [64,500+2,500+1,54,600+55,000=2,12,100–40,000–10,000=1,62,100]

Problem 16.01-P31 [CA N97]

X retired from Government service in March, 2006 and got a sum of Rs. 20,00,000 lakh on account of retirement benefits. Out of the aforesaid sum, X purchased on April 26, 2006, two heavy goods vehicles for Rs. 2 lakh for the purpose of carrying on business of plying, hiring and leasing goods carriages. However X could actually start business of plying the aforesaid vehicles on July on July 4, 2006 only though X had got the delivery of the aforesaid vehicles on the date of purchase it self. X had been keeping a full record of all receipts and expenditure incurred in a diary in respect of the aforesaid business. However he did not maintain the regular books of account as also the vouchers in respect of the aforesaid business. As per X's diary his gross receipts during the financial year ending March 31, 2006 Rs. 1,77,600 and the sum total of the entire business expenditure (other than depreciation) is Rs. 52,100.

X had inherited a house from his father in the year 1994 with the condition that X shall pay a sum of Rs. 1,000 per month to his ailing grandfather throughout his life, irrespective of the fact whether the said house was fetching any rent or not. During financial year 2006-07, X was able to let out this house only for eight months at a monthly rent of Rs. 5,000. X has also furnished the following information in relation to this house :

- Municipal taxes paid by the tenant during financial year 2006-07, based on municipal valuation of Rs. 53,000 — 5,300
- Insurance premium to insure the house, paid by the tenant during financial year 2006-07 — 1,300
- Interest paid on loan taken for renovation of the house during financial year 2005-06 — 12,000
- Actual repair and renovation expenses incurred during financial year 2006-07 — 8,400
- Water taxes levied and paid to municipal corporation working under the State Government during financial year 2006-07 — 400

After inheriting the aforesaid house in the year 1994, X decided to sell his personal house which was being let out earlier. X finally sold his personal house on April 4, 1995. During assessment year 1995-96, X was able to get a deduction of Rs. 22,000 on account of unrealized rent in the assessment order under the head 'Income from house property' in respect of his personal house. On April 4, 2006, X was able to recover the unrealized rent of Rs. 22,000, but X had to pay a sum of Rs. 11,000 on account of litigation expenses with the old tenant (including advocate's fee) during financial year 2006-07.

During financial year 2006-07, X received Rs. 60,000 on account of pension from Government, X contributed the entire sum of Rs. 60,000 in his PPF account during financial year 2006-07. X's PPF account was also credited with Rs. 44,000 on account of interest during financial year 2006-07.

During financial year 2006-07, X also suffered long term capital loss on account of sale of shares on various dates, amounting to Rs. 44,000.

X requires you to compute his total income for assessment year 2007-08. X also requires you to give reasons in respect of each and every item above and further state the reliefs to which X is entitled to.

Ans: 3,48,800. [TI: 60,000+38,000+3,10,800=4,08,800–60,000=3,48,600] [HP: 40,000–12,000=16,000+22,000=38,000] [BI: 2×12×3,500+6×12×3,150=3,10,800]

Problem 16.01-P32 [CA M04]

Dr. X furnishes the following information :

Income and expenditure account for the year ending March 31, 2007 :

	Rs.		*Rs.*
Medicines consumed	2,42,000	Fee receipts	8,47,500
Staff salary	1,65,000	Rent	27,000
Hospital consumables	47,500	Dividend from Indian companies	9,000
Rent paid	60,000		
Administrative expenses	1,23,000		
Net income	2,46,000		
	8,83,500		8,83,500

Rent paid includes rent for his residential accommodation of Rs. 30,000 (paid by cheque).

Hospital equipments (eligible for depreciation @ 25 per cent)

Opening WDV on April 1, 2006 Rs. 5,00,000

Acquired (cost) on December 12, 2006 Rs. 2,00,000

Medicines consumed include medicines (cost) Rs. 10,000 used for Dr. X's family.

Rent received relates to a property situated at Mysore (gross annual value). The municipal tax of Rs. 2,000 paid in December, 2006 has been included in the administrative expenses.

He gets Rs. 5,000 per month as salary from Full Cure Hospital. This has not been included in the "fee receipts" credited to income and expenditure account.

He transfers a vacant site in July, 2006 for Rs. 5,00,000. It was inherited by him from his father in January, 1998. The site was acquired by his father in December 1990 for Rs. 1,50,000.

Compute Dr. X's taxable income for the assessment year 2007-08.

Ans: Employed outside Mysore 4,32,500; Employer in Mysore 4,44,300. [BI: 8,47,500–2,32,000–1,65,000–47,500–30,000–1,21,000–1,50,000=1,02,000] [CG: 5,00,000–2,35,196=2,64,804] [TI: 60,000+17,500+1,02,000+2,64,804+0=4,44,304–12,050=4,32,250.]

Problem 16.01-P33 [CA M06]

Mr. Ram who does not maintain books of accounts for the year ended 31-3-2007 requests you to compute his total income and the tax payable theorem for the assessment year 2007-08 from the following :

(i) Basic Salary 20,000 p.m.

CCA 1,000 p.m.

HRA 5,000 p.m.

(ii) Ram resides in Chennai paying a rent of Rs. 6,000 per month.

(iii) Ram is paid an Education allowance of Rs. 500 per month per child for all the three of his children. Actual expenses (tuition fees only) amounts to Rs. 15,000, Rs. 10,000 and Rs. 5,000 respectively.

(iv) Employer's contribution to Staff Group Insurance Scheme Rs. 5,440.

(v) He bought a heavy goods vehicle on 7-6-2006 and has been letting it on hire from the same date. He declares an income of Rs. 34,900 from the same.

(vi) Interest from Company deposits is Rs. 15,000 and bank interest is Rs. 5,000.

(vii) Interest is payable on bank loans available for buying the truck and making company deposits as follows :

Purpose	*Date of Loan*	*Amount*	*Interest Rate*
Truck purchase	1-4-2006	5 lakhs	10% p.a.
Company deposit	1-10-2006	1 lakh	9% p.a.

(viii) Loss carried forward arising from speculating in shares during the preceding previous year and eligible for set off is Rs. 1,00,000.

(ix) Ram has invested Rs. 12,000 is notified equity linked saving scheme of UTI, Rs. 53,000 in notified infrastructure sector bonds. Rs. 9,000 as Life Insurance premium on his own life (sum assured Rs. 40,000) and Rs. 15,000 towards Pension fund of LIC.

Ans: 2,30,100; 21,440. [Sal: 2,40,000+12,000+12,000+15,600+0=2,79,600] [TI: 2,79,600+35,000+15,500=3,30,100–12,000–52,000–8,000–25,000=2,30,100]

Problem 16.01-P34 [CA M06]

Thomas took voluntary retirement from State Bank of India on 1st March, 2006 under the Voluntary Retirement Scheme (VRS) and received a sum of Rs.25 lakh on account of VRS benefits. Later, he started a business of plying, hiring and leasing of goods carriages from 1st June, 2006 by acquiring 3 heavy goods vehicles for Rs. 12 lakh, 2 medium goods vehicles for Rs. 5 lakh and 3 light commercial vehicles for Rs.6 lakh. Although, he did not maintain regular books of account for his business, the diary maintained by him revealed gross receipts of Rs. 2,12,000 for the financial year ended 31st March, 2007 and he incurred an expenditure of Rs. 78,300 on the business towards salaries of drivers, repairs, fuel, *etc*. Depreciation on vehicles is not included in the said expenditure.

During the financial year 2006-07, he received a sum of Rs. 72,000 on account of pension from bank and he contributed a sum of Rs. 50,000 to his PPF account maintained with the said bank in the same year. His PPF account was credited with interest of Rs. 35,000 during the financial year 2006-07.

Further, he had two residential properties, one is selfoccupied and other is let-out. During the financial year 2006-07, Thomas was able to let-out his property only for 11 months on a monthly rent of Rs. 7,000. The total municipal taxes on the let-out property was Rs. 8,000, 50% of which was paid by the tenant and 50% by him during the financial year 2006-07. The interest on loan taken for renovation of the house paid by him during the year was Rs. 14,000. The insurance premium on the house and actual repairs and collection charges paid are Rs. 1,600 and Rs. 18,000 respectively and the entire expenditure is borne by him. During the financial year 2006-07, he was able to recover the unrealised rent of

Rs. 13,000 from old tenant who vacated the house during July, 2005 after spending litigation expenses of Rs. 5,000. During the financial year 2006-07, Thomas suffered long-term capital loss on account of sale of shares on various dates amounting to Rs. 31,500.

From the aforesaid information, you are required to compute the total income of Thomas for the assessment year 2007-08 giving reasons in respect of each and every item and indicate the relief/rebate/deduction which he is entitled to claim.

Ans: 3,34,600. [HP: 77,000–4,000=73,000–21,900–14,000=37,100+13,000=50,100] [BI: 3,500×3×10+3,150×2×10+3,150×3×10=2,62,500] [TI: 72,000+50,100+2,62,500= 3,84,600–50,000=3,34,600]

STRATEGY MAKER

Points in 1 to 10	Overall Points 10; Practical 10; Theory 1.
Type of problem	Typical.
What to expect (DU)	Everything.
CA (PE II)	Everything.

If hundreds of students all over India can score 100% in subject like income tax. Why not you? You can. You will. You must. Now Run since you are confident, determined, dedicated, devoted, exceptionally good, fantastic, hard working etc. Score 100% in Income Tax. My best wishes are with you. Mail me.

Keep running

Inform the Tax Department of your expenses and income timely

17

FILING OF RETURN BRIEF

TOPIC 17.01 MEANING OF RETURN OF INCOME

It is a statement of total income and tax liability filled in the prescribed form duly signed and filed with the Income Tax authority on or before the due date of furnishing of return. The Act stipulates an obligation on the assessee that he files regular return every assessment year to the department disclosing the income earned by him.

TOPIC 17.02 *SECTION 139.* WHO SHOULD FILE THE RETURN OF INCOME ?

Every person is required to file the return whose total income exceeds the maximum amount which is not chargeable to tax, even if tax payable is nil or refundable.

Therefore following persons are liable to file their return of income.

Person	*Gross Total Income before giving effect to section 10A, 10B & 10BA*
Individual, HUF, AOP, BOI and Artificial Juridical person	Exceeds Rs. 1,00,000 (for woman Rs. 1,35,000; for senior citizen Rs. 1,85,000)
3rd proviso — Firm or Company	Any income even if there is a loss.

TOPIC 17.03 *SECTION 139.* WHAT ARE THE DUE DATES OF FILING OF INCOME TAX RETURN ?

Return of the financial year or the previous year is required to be filed on the specified dates of the relevant assessment year.

1. Corporate assessee — *Section 139(1)* : October 31 of AY

Other than company — Section 139(1)

2. Where the accounts are being audited : October 31 of AY
3. A working partner of the firm whose accounts are required to be audited : October 31 of AY
4. One by six scheme : October 31 of AY

5. In case of any other assessee : July 31 of AY

Co-operative society — Section 139(4A)

1. Where it seeks exemption u/ss 11 & 12 : October 31 of AY
2. Any other case : July 31 of AY

Political party — Section 139(4B)

1. Where it seeks exemption u/s 13A : October 31 of AY
2. Any other case : July 31 of AY

For AY 2007-08 (relevant to PY 2006-07), last day of filing of return shall be either July 31, 2007 or October 31, 2007 as the case may be.

Illustration 17.03-P1

Find out whether following persons are required to file their return of income, if yes, find out its due date.

Assessee	*Turnover*	*Gross Total Income*	*Total Income*
Mr. A	30 lakhs	6 lakhs	1 Lakh
Mrs. P	58 lakhs	2 lakhs	1.35 Lakhs
Mrs X aged 66 years	41 lakhs	1,85,000	1.80 Lakhs
Z	40 lakhs	(10,000)	Nil
Firm 1	10 lakhs	1 lakh	5,000
Firm 2	52 lakhs	40,000	40,000
Firm 3	30 lakhs	Business Loss (60,000)	nil
T Ltd.	5 lakhs	80,000	15,000
S Ltd.	100 lakhs	Business Loss (60,000)	nil

Solution

Assessee	*Applicable section*	*Due date*
A	139(1)	31-7
P	139(1)	31-10
X	NA	Not necessary to file return of income
Z	139(1)	Not necessary to file return of income
Firm 1	139(1)	31-7
Firm 2	139(1)	31-10
Firm 3	3rd proviso to 139(1)	31-7
T Ltd.	139(1)	31-10
S Ltd.	3rd proviso to 139(1)	31-10

Problem 17.04-P2 (CS-J01) - M 3

Q.1c : X is a partner in a firm whose turnover for the previous year 2006-07 in Rs. 60 lakh. What is the due date for filing the return of income by X, if —

(i) X is a working partner and is entitled to remuneration from the firm?

(ii) X is only getting interest on capital from the firm? and

(iii) X is neither entitle to remuneration nor any interest on capital from the firm, and although he has other income, yet he does not have any business income ?

Ans: 31-10-2005; 31-07-2005; 31-07-2005.

STRATEGY MAKER

Points in 1 to 10	Overall Points 6; Practical 1; Theory 9.
Type of problem	Application oriented.
What to expect (DU)	Not in your syllabus.
CA (PE II)	It is one of the most important chapter. Do not leave anything and keep on discovering new questions.

You have not lived until you have done something for which you cannot be repaid.

Keep Running

ANNEXURE
(APPLICABLE FOR PE II NOV 2007 ATTEMPT)

(C) ACCOMMODATION PROVIDED TO PRIVATE EMPLOYEES OR SEMI GOVT. EMPLOYEES

	Cities having a population of more than 4 lakhs as per 2001 census	*Any other city (4 lakhs or less)*
Accommodation is owned by employer	20% of salary taxable	15% of salary is taxable
Accommodation is leased or rented	Amount of lease rent paid or payable or 20% of salary whichever is less is taxable	

Illustrations and Problems 3.20-P1 (Simple)

Compute value of accommodation from the following information :

	Case 1	*Case 2*	*Case 3*	*Case 4*
Accommodation is	owned	leased	rented	owned
City Population as per 2001 census	4 lakhs	3 lakhs	not available	130 lakhs
Lease rental	–	7,100	28,000	–
Accommodation's Salary	1,88,000	2,14,400	1,31,000	1,64,000

Ans: (1) 28,200; (2) 7,100; (3) 26,200; (4) 32,800

All answers are of value of accommodation. We have given some of the answers. Rest of the answers can be computed accordingly.

Problem 3.20-P4 *Ans*: 16,780; 25,396; 34,400

Problem 3.20-P5 *Ans*: 37,776.

Problem 3.20-P6 *Ans*: 14,000.

Problem 3.20-P7 *Ans*: 10,000.

Problem 3.20-P8 *Ans*: 37,450.

Problem 3.20-P9 *Ans*: 25,200.

Problem 3.20-P10 *Ans*: 64,420.

Problem 3.20-P11 *Ans*: 13,430.

Problem 3.20-P12 *Ans*: 51,288.

Problem 3.20-P13 *Ans*: 2,083.